OUR SOCiAL WORLD

CONDENSED

4e

SAGE

Los Angeles | London | New Delhi
Singapore | Washington DC | Boston

⊗SAGE | 50 YEARS

4e
CONDENSED

OUR SOCiAL WORLD

JEANNE H. BALLANTINE
Wright State University

KEITH A. ROBERTS
Hanover College

KATHLEEN ODELL KORGEN
William Paterson University

Los Angeles | London | New Delhi
Singapore | Washington DC | Boston

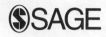

Los Angeles | London | New Delhi
Singapore | Washington DC | Boston

FOR INFORMATION:

SAGE Publications, Inc.
2455 Teller Road
Thousand Oaks, California 91320
E-mail: order@sagepub.com

SAGE Publications Ltd.
1 Oliver's Yard
55 City Road
London EC1Y 1SP
United Kingdom

SAGE Publications India Pvt. Ltd.
B 1/I 1 Mohan Cooperative Industrial Area
Mathura Road, New Delhi 110 044
India

SAGE Publications Asia-Pacific Pte. Ltd.
3 Church Street #10-04 Samsung Hub
Singapore 049483

Printed in Canada

Cataloging-in-publication data is available for this title from the Library of Congress.

ISBN 978-1-4833-6861-0

Acquisitions Editor: Jeff Lasser
Senior Development Editor: Nathan Davidson
eLearning Editor: Gabrielle Piccininni
Editorial Assistant: Alexandra Croell
Production Editor: Laura Barrett
Copy Editor: Melinda Masson
Typesetter: C&M Digitals (P) Ltd.
Proofreader: Scott Oney
Indexer: Rick Hurd
Cover & Interior Designer: Gail Buschman
Marketing Manager: Erica DeLuca

This book is printed on acid-free paper.

15 16 17 18 19 10 9 8 7 6 5 4 3 2 1

Brief Contents

Detailed Contents

PART II. Social Structure, Processes, and Control 51

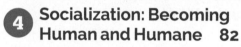

3 Society and Culture: Hardware and Software of Our Social World 52

4 Socialization: Becoming Human and Humane 82

Preface
To Our Student Readers

This book will transform how you view the world—and your place in it. You will gain a sociological perspective on the world that will change what you notice and how you make sense of your social world. Some of you will become sociology majors. All of you will find the subject matter of this course relevant to your personal and professional lives. You will learn how society works—and how you can influence it; develop interpersonal skills; and gain new information about social life in small groups and global social systems. As the broadest of the social sciences, sociology has a never-ending array of fascinating subjects to study.

Sociology and this book ask you to think outside the box. Why? The best way to become a more interesting person, to grow beyond the old familiar thoughts and behaviors, and to make life exciting is to explore new ways to view your social world. The world in which we live is intensely personal and individual in nature, with much of our social interaction occurring in intimate groups of friends and family. Our most intense emotions and most meaningful links to others are at this small-group "micro" level of social life.

However, these intimate micro-level links in our lives are influenced by larger social structures and global trends. The social world you face is influenced by changes and forces that are easy to miss. Like the wind, which can do damage even if the air is unseen, social structures are themselves so taken for granted that it is easy to miss seeing them. However, their effects can be readily identified. Sociology's new perspectives will help you to better understand your family, friends, work life, leisure time, and place in a diverse and changing world.

THE SOCIAL WORLD MODEL

A well-constructed course, like an effective essay, needs to be organized around a central question, one that leads to other subsidiary questions and intrigues the participants. For you to understand sociology as an integrated whole rather than a set of separate chapters in a book, we have organized this book around the *social world model*: a conceptual model that demonstrates the relationships between individuals (micro level); organizations, institutions, and subcultures (meso level); and national societies and global structures (macro level). At the beginning of each chapter, a visual diagram of the model will illustrate this idea as it relates to the topic of that chapter, including how issues related to the topic have implications at various levels of analysis in the social world, influencing and being affected by other parts of society. No aspect of society exists in a vacuum. On the other hand, this model does not assume that everyone always gets along or that relationships are always harmonious or supportive. Sometimes, different parts of the society are in competition for resources, and in conflict with one another.

This micro- to macro-level analysis is a central concept in the discipline of sociology. It will help you to develop a *sociological imagination*, an ability to see the complex links between various levels of the social system, from the micro level of close relationships to the macro level of globalization. Within a few months, you may not remember all the specific concepts or terms that have been introduced, but if the way you see the world has been transformed during this course, a key element of deep learning has been accomplished. Learning to see things from alternative perspectives is a precondition for critical thinking. This book will help you recognize connections between your personal experiences and problems and larger social forces of society. Thus, you will learn to take a new perspective on the social world in which you live.

A key element of that social world is diversity. We live in societies in which there are people who differ in a host of ways: ethnicity, socioeconomic status, religious background, political persuasion, gender, sexual orientation, and so forth. Diversity is a blessing in many ways to a society because the most productive and creative organizations and societies are those that are highly diverse. This is the case because people with different backgrounds solve problems in very different ways. When people with such divergences come together, the outcome of their problem solving can create new solutions to vexing problems. However, diversity often creates challenges as well. Misunderstanding and "us" versus "them" thinking can divide people. These issues will be explored throughout this book. We now live in a global village, and in this book, you will learn something about how people on the other side of the village live and view the world.

We hope you enjoy the book and get as enthralled with sociology as we are. It genuinely is a fascinating field of study.

Jeanne H. Ballantine

Jeanne H. Ballantine
Wright State University

Keith A. Roberts

Keith A. Roberts
Hanover College

Kathleen Odell Korgen

Kathleen Odell Korgen
William Paterson University

Your authors—teaching "outside the box."

Instructors
How to Make This Book Work for You

Special features woven throughout each chapter support the theme of the book. These will help students comprehend and apply the material and make the material more understandable and interesting. These features are also designed to facilitate deep learning, to help students move beyond rote memorization, and to increase their ability to analyze and evaluate information.

For students to understand both the comparative global theme and sociology as an integrated whole rather than as a set of separate chapters in a book, we have organized the chapters around the *social world model*: a conceptual model that demonstrates the relationships between individuals (micro level); organizations, institutions, and subcultures (meso level); and societies and global structures (macro levels of analysis). At the beginning of each chapter, a visual diagram of the model will illustrate this idea as it relates to the topic of that chapter, including how issues related to the topic have implications at various levels of analysis in the social world.

"THINK ABOUT IT"

So that students can become curious, active readers, we have posed questions at the outset of each chapter that we hope are relevant to everyday life, but that are also tied to the micro-meso-macro levels of analysis that serve as the theme of the book. The purpose is to transform students from passive readers who run their eyes across the words into curious active readers who read to answer a question and to be reflective. Active or deep reading is key to comprehension and retention of reading material (Roberts and Roberts 2008). Instructors can also use this feature to encourage students to think critically about the implications of what they have read. Instructors might want to ask students to write a paragraph about one of these questions before coming to class each day. These questions might also provide the basis for in-class discussions.

We encourage students to start each chapter by reading and thinking about these questions, looking at the topics in the chapter outlined just below the "Think About It" feature, and asking some questions of their own. This will mean that they are more likely to stay focused, remember the material long term, and be able to apply it to their own lives.

"WHAT'S COMING IN THIS CHAPTER"

Each chapter begins with a simple listing of the key topic headings. Research on deep reading shows that if students have an overview of what they read and begin to ask questions and become active as readers at the outset, they comprehend and retain more of the material. This feature is included in response to suggestions by reviewers of the text.

A GLOBAL PERSPECTIVE AND THE SOCIAL WORLD MODEL

This book incorporates a global perspective throughout. This is done so that students can see not only how others live different but rewarding lives, but also the connections between others' lives and their own. Students will need to think about and relate to the world globally in future roles as workers, travelers, and global citizens. Our analysis illustrates the interconnections of the world's societies and their political and economic systems, and demonstrates that what happens in one part of the world affects others.

This global approach attempts to instill interest, understanding, and respect for different groups of people and their lifestyles. Race, class, and gender are an integral part of understanding the diverse social world, and these features of social life have global implications. The comparative global theme is carried throughout the book in headings and written text, in examples, and in boxes and selection of photos. As students read this book, they should continually think about how the experiences in their private world are influenced by and may influence events at other levels: the community, organizations and institutions, the nation, and the world.

OPENING VIGNETTES

Chapters typically open with an illustration relevant to the chapter content that will grab the attention of students. For instance, in Chapter 2, "Examining the Social World," the case of Hector, a Brazilian teenager living in poverty in a *favela*, is used to illustrate research methods and theory throughout the chapter. Chapter 3, "Society and Culture," begins with scenarios of mealtime scenes and foods from around the world to illustrate the variations in human cultures. In Chapter 4, "Socialization," the case of Phoebe Prince, a 15-year-old immigrant from Ireland, who was so harassed and bullied by peers that she hung herself, begins the discussion. Chapter 7, "Stratification," begins with a discussion of the royal wedding of Prince William and Kate Middleton. These vignettes are meant to interest students in the upcoming subject matter by helping them relate to a personalized story. In several cases, the vignettes serve as illustrations throughout the chapters.

"THINKING SOCIOLOGICALLY" QUESTIONS

Following major topics throughout chapters, students will find thought-provoking questions that ask them to think critically and apply the material just read to some aspect of their lives or the social world. The purpose of this feature is to encourage students to apply the ideas and concepts in the text to their lives, to develop critical thinking skills, and to use the material for better recall. These questions can be the basis for in-class discussions and can be assigned as questions to start interesting conversations with friends and families to learn how the topics relate to their own lives. Note that some of these questions have a miniature icon—a small version of the chapter-opening model—signifying that these questions reinforce the theme of micro, meso, and macro levels of social influence.

"ENGAGING SOCIOLOGY"

Perhaps the most innovative feature in this book is called "Engaging Sociology"—and the double entendre is intentional. We want students to think of sociology as engaging and fun, and to engage with the material. These features—such as applying a population pyramid to the business world, taking a survey to understand why differences in social and cultural capital make first-generation students feel alienated on a college campus, and reading a map and learning to analyze the patterns—help students understand how interesting and useful sociology can be. There are 30 of these features in this edition.

KEY CONCEPTS, EXAMPLES, AND WRITING STYLE

Key terms that are defined and illustrated within the running narrative and that appear in the glossary appear in **bold** with an italicized definition following. Other terms that are defined but are of less significance are italicized. The text is rich in examples that bring sociological concepts to life for student readers. Each chapter has been student tested for readability. Both students and reviewers describe the writing style as reader friendly, often fascinating, and accessible, but not watered down.

SPECIAL FEATURES

Featured inserts provide even more in-depth illustrations of the usefulness of the sociological perspective to understand how sociology is relevant to a student's life. "Sociologists in Action" features appear in most chapters and examine profiles of people using sociological tools to make a positive impact on society. This helps students grasp what sociologists—and sociology students—can do with sociology. Nearly every chapter examines the issues of "technology and society" as they would be relevant to that chapter. We have especially sought out materials that have to do with the Internet and with communications technology.

SOCIAL POLICY AND BECOMING AN INVOLVED CITIZEN

Many chapters include discussion of some social policy issues and the relevance of sociological findings to current social debates. Furthermore, because students sometimes feel helpless and do not know what to do about social issues that concern them at the macro and meso levels, we have concluded every chapter with a few ideas about how they might become involved as active citizens, even as undergraduate students. Some suggestions in the "Contributing to Our Social World: What Can We Do?" sections may be assigned as extra credit, service learning, or term projects.

SUMMARY SECTIONS AND DISCUSSION QUESTIONS

Each chapter ends with review material: a "What Have We Learned?" feature that includes a "Key Points" bulleted summary of the chapter's core material. The summary is followed with probing discussion questions that ask students to go beyond memorization and apply the material in the chapter to their own lives. Research indicates that unless four discrete sections of the brain are stimulated, the learning will be not long term and deep but surface and short term (Zull 2002). These questions are carefully crafted to activate all four critical sections of the brain.

A LITTLE (TEACHING) HELP FROM OUR FRIENDS

Whether the instructor is new to teaching or an experienced professor, there are some valuable ideas in this text that can help invigorate and energize the classroom. As we have noted, substantial literature on teaching methodology tells us that student involvement is key to the learning process. In addition to the engaging sociology questions and exercises in the text, there are a number of teaching suggestions in the supplements and teaching aids for active learning in large or small classes.

INSTRUCTOR TEACHING SITE

http://edge.sagepub.com/ballantinecondensed4e

SAGE edge for Instructors supports your teaching by making it easy to integrate quality content and create a rich learning environment for students.

- **Test banks** provide a diverse range of prewritten options as well as the opportunity to edit any question and/or insert your own personalized questions to effectively assess students' progress and understanding.
- **Learning objectives** reinforce the most important material.
- **Sample course syllabi** for semester and quarter courses provide suggested models for structuring your courses.
- Editable, chapter-specific **PowerPoint® slides** offer complete flexibility for creating a multimedia presentation for your course.
- **Lecture notes** summarize key concepts by chapter to help you prepare for lectures and class discussions.
- **Class assignments** are specially designed to accompany each chapter for professors to use in and out of the classroom.
- **Recommended readings** for each chapter help students dive into information further.
- Chapter-specific **discussion questions** prompt students to engage with the material by reinforcing important content.
- **Teaching tips** provide suggestions and resources for using the social world model for traditional and online Introduction to Sociology courses.
- Carefully selected chapter-by-chapter **video and multimedia** content enhances classroom-based explorations of key topics.
- EXCLUSIVE! Access is granted to full-text **SAGE journal articles and readings** that have been carefully selected to support and expand on the concepts presented in each chapter.

STUDENT STUDY SITE

http://edge.sagepub.com/ballantinecondensed4e

SAGE edge for Students provides a personalized approach to help students accomplish their course-work goals in an easy-to-use learning environment.

- Mobile-friendly **eFlashcards** strengthen understanding of key terms and concepts.
- Mobile-friendly practice **quizzes** allow for independent assessment by students of their mastery of course material.
- **Web exercises** and meaningful web links facilitate student use of Internet resources, further exploration of topics, and responses to critical thinking questions.
- Chapter-specific **discussion questions** help launch classroom interaction by prompting students to engage with the material and by reinforcing important content.
- Carefully selected chapter-by-chapter **video and multimedia** content enhances classroom-based explorations of key topics.
- EXCLUSIVE! Access is granted to full-text **SAGE journal articles and readings** that have been carefully selected to support and expand on the concepts presented in each chapter.
- Unique **photo essay** assignments encourage students to observe and evaluate social issues in creative ways.

WHAT IS NEW IN THE FOURTH CONDENSED EDITION?

In this major revision we have reorganized several chapters and updated all data, added many new studies, and included new emphases in sociology. There are two types of boxed features in this book, "Engaging Sociology" and "Sociologists in Action," both of which actively involve readers in what sociologists do and what students can do with sociology. Most chapters have *extensive* updates: Chapter 9, for example, has new material with 83 new citations (and dozens of dated references were dropped). Considerable attention has also been given to clarifying and simplifying definitions throughout the book and determining what should be in the glossary. The core elements of the book—with the unifying theme and the social world model at the beginning of every chapter—have not changed.

Finally, although we have been told that the writing was extraordinarily readable, we have tried to simplify sentence structure in a number of places. In short, we have tried to respond to what we heard from all of you—both students and instructors (and yes, we *do* hear from students)—to keep this book engaging and accessible.

A Personal Note to the Instructor

What is truly distinctive about this book? This is a text that tries to break the mold of the typical textbook synthesis, the cross between an encyclopedia and a dictionary. *Our Social World: Condensed* is a unique course text that is *a coherent essay on the sociological imagination—understood globally*. We attempt to radically change the feel of the introductory book by emphasizing coherence, an integrating theme, and current knowledge about learning and teaching, but we also present much traditional organization and content. Instructors will not have to throw out the well-honed syllabus and begin from scratch, but they can refocus each unit so it stresses understanding of micro-level personal troubles within the macro-level public issues framework. Indeed, in this book, we make clear that the public issues must be understood at several levels of analysis, including global.

Here is a text that engages students. *They* say so! From class testing, we know that the writing style, the structure of chapters and sections, the "Thinking Sociologically" features, the wealth of examples, and other instructional aids help students stay focused, think about the material, and apply it to their lives. It neither bores them nor insults their intelligence. It focuses on deep learning rather than memorization. It develops sociological skills of analysis rather than emphasizing memorization of vocabulary. Key concepts and terms are introduced, but only in the service of a larger focus on the sociological imagination. The text is both personal and global. It speaks to sociology as a science as well as addressing public or applied aspects of sociology. It has a theme that provides integration of topics as it introduces the discipline. This text is an analytical essay, not a disconnected encyclopedia.

As one of our reviewers noted,

Unlike most textbooks I have read, the coverage in this one is very impressive. It challenges students with college-level reading. Too many textbooks give only passing treatment to most of the topics, writing in nugget-sized blocks. More than a single definition and a few sentences of support, the text forces students deep into the topics covered and challenges them to see interconnections.

Normally, the global perspective within textbooks, which seemed to grow in popularity in the mid- to late 1990s, was implemented by using brief and exotic examples to show differences between societies—a purely comparative approach rather than a globalization treatment. They gave, and still give, a token nod to diversity. This textbook, however, forces students to take a broader look at similarities and differences in social institutions around the world, and structures and processes operating in all cultures and societies in the world of which they are a part.

So our focus in this book is on deep learning, especially expansion of students' ability to role-take or "perspective-take." Deep learning goes beyond the content of concepts and terms and cultivates the habits of thinking that allow one to think critically. Being able to see things from the perspective of others is essential to doing sociology, but it is also indispensible to seeing weaknesses in various theories or recognizing blind spots in a point of view. Using the sociological imagination is one dimension of role-taking because it requires a step back from the typical micro-level understanding of life's events and fosters a new comprehension of how meso- and macro-level forces—and even global ones—can shape the individual's life. Enhancement of role-taking ability is at the core of this book because it is a *prerequisite* for deep learning in sociology, and it is the core competency needed to *do* sociology. One cannot do sociology unless one can see things from various positions on the social landscape.

This may sound daunting for some student audiences, but we have found that instructors at every kind of institution have had great success with this book because of the writing style and instructional tools used throughout. We have made some strategic decisions based on these principles of learning and teaching. We have focused much of the book on higher-order thinking skills rather than memorization and regurgitation. We want students to learn to think sociologically: to apply, analyze, synthesize, evaluate, and comprehend the interconnections of the world through a globally informed sociological imagination. However, we think it is also essential to do this with an understanding of how students learn.

Many introductory-level books offer several theories and then provide a critique of each theory. The idea is to teach critical thinking. We have purposefully refrained from extensive critique of theory (although some does occur) for several reasons. First, providing critique to beginning-level students does not really teach critical thinking. It trains them to memorize someone else's critique. Furthermore, it simply confuses many of them, leaving students with the feeling that sociology is really just contradictory ideas, and the discipline really does not have anything firm to offer. Teaching critical thinking needs to be done in stages, and it needs to take into account the building steps that occur before effective critique is possible. That is why we focus on the concept of deep learning. We are working toward building the foundations that are necessary for sophisticated critical thought at upper levels in the curriculum. Thus, we offer contrasting theories in this text, but rather than telling what is wrong with each one, we encourage students through "Thinking Sociologically" features to analyze the use of each and to focus on honing synthesis and comparison skills.

Finally, research tells us that learning becomes embedded in memory and becomes long lasting only if it is related to something that learners already know. If they memorize terms but have no unifying framework to which they can attach those ideas, the memory will not last until the end of the course, let alone until the next higher-level course. In this text, each chapter is tied to the social world model that is core to sociological thinking. At the end of a course using this book, we believe that students will be able to explain coherently what sociology is and construct an effective essay about what they have learned from the course as a whole. Learning to develop and defend a thesis, with supporting logic and evidence, is another component of deep learning. In short, this text provides instructors with the tools to teach sociology in a way that will make a long-term impact on students.

ORGANIZATION AND COVERAGE

Reminiscent of some packaged international tours, in which the travelers figure that "it is Day 7, so this must be Paris," many introductory courses seem to operate on the principle that it is Week 4, so this must be deviance week. Students do not sense any integration, and at the end of the course, they have trouble remembering specific topics. This book is different. A major goal of the book is to show the integration between topics in sociology and between parts of the social world. The idea is for students to grasp the concept of the interrelated world. A change in one part of the social world affects all others, sometimes in ways that are mutually supportive and sometimes in ways that create intense conflict.

Although the topics are familiar, the textbook is organized around levels of analysis, explained through the social world model. This perspective leads naturally to an integrated discussion in which all topics fit clearly into an overall view, a comparative approach, and discussions of diversity and inequality. It hangs together!

As seen in the Table of Contents, the book includes 14 chapters plus additional online materials, written to fit into a semester or quarter system. It allows instructors to use the chapters in order, or to alter the order, because each chapter is tied into others through the social world model. We strongly recommend that Chapter 1 be used early in the course because it introduces the integrating model and explains the theme. Also, if any Part IV chapters are used, the four-page section opener on "Institutions" may be useful to include as well. Otherwise, the book has been designed for flexible use. Instructors may want to supplement the core book with other materials, such as those suggested on the Instructor Teaching Site. Each chapter, for example, has an online exercise that helps students grasp the practical, public implications of sociology. While covering key topics in introductory sociology, the cost and size of a condensed book allows for flexibility. Indeed, for a colorful introductory-level text, the cost of this book is remarkably low—roughly half the cost of some other very popular introductory texts.

A UNIQUE PROGRAM SUPPORTING TEACHING OF SOCIOLOGY

There is one more way in which *Our Social World* has been unique among introductory sociology textbooks. In 2007, the original authors (Ballantine and Roberts) teamed with SAGE to start a new program to benefit the entire discipline. Using royalties from *Our Social World*, we helped establish a new award program called the SAGE Teaching Innovations & Professional Development Award, designed to prepare a new generation of scholars within the teaching movement in sociology. People in their early-career stages (graduate students, assistant professors, newer PhDs) can be reimbursed $600 each for expenses entailed while attending the daylong American Sociological Association (ASA) Section on Teaching and Learning's preconference

workshop. The workshop is the day before ASA meetings. In 2007, 13 young scholars—graduate students or untenured faculty members—received this award and benefited from an extraordinary workshop on learning and teaching. Since then, 23 other SAGE authors have supported this program from textbook royalties, and a total of 176 young scholars have been beneficiaries of more than $90,000 as of 2014. We are pleased to have had a hand in initiating and continuing to support this program.

We hope you find this book engaging. If you have questions or comments, please contact us.

Jeanne H. Ballantine

Jeanne H. Ballantine
Wright State University
jeanne.ballantine@gmail.com

Keith A. Roberts

Keith A. Roberts
Hanover College
robertsk@hanover.edu

Kathleen Odell Korgen

Kathleen Odell Korgen
William Paterson University
korgenk@wpunj.edu

Acknowledgments

Knowledge is improved through careful, systematic, and constructive criticism. The same is true of all writing. This book is of much greater quality because we had such outstanding critics and reviewers. We, therefore, wish to honor and recognize the outstanding scholars who served in this capacity. These scholars are listed on this page and the next.

We also had people who served in a variety of other capacities. Authors of short sections within the book include Kevin Bales, Mary Gatta, Susan Guarino-Ghezzi, Thomas Horejes, David Kirk, Elise Roberts, Brent Staples, Jay Weinstein, Nancy Diggs, Ellis Jones, Anna Misleh, Ossama Zyoud, and six students from William Paterson University: Donna Yang, Christian Agurto, Michelle Benavides, Brianne Glogowski, Deziree Martinez, and Michele Van Hook. The religion chapter has some new approaches to denominationalism and to church polity, and David Yamane drafted early versions of much of that.

All three of us are experienced authors, and we have worked with some excellent people at other publishing houses. However, the team at SAGE Publications is truly exceptional in support, thoroughness, and commitment to this project. Our planning meetings have been fun, intelligent, and provocative. Jeff Lasser has provided wonderful support as the SAGE sociology editor, and Nathan Davidson, the associate editor, has been a terrific photo researcher and supporter in other ways. Folks who have meant so much to the quality production of this book include Nick Pachelli, editorial assistant; Sheri Gilbert, permissions editor; Erica DeLuca, senior marketing manager; and Melinda Masson, our wonderful copy editor extraordinaire who has also been more like a research assistant. We have become friends and colleagues with the staff at SAGE Publications. They are all greatly appreciated.

Thanks to the following reviewers:

Sabrina Alimahomed
University of California, Riverside

Richard Ball
Ferris State University

Fred Beck
Illinois State University

David L. Briscoe
University of Arkansas at Little Rock

James A. Crone
Hanover College

Jamie M. Dolan
Carroll College (MT)

Obi N. I. Ebbe
The University of Tennessee at Chattanooga

Stephanie Funk
Hanover College

Lance Erickson
Brigham Young University

Loyd R. Ganey, Jr.
Western International University

Mary Grigsby
University of Missouri–Columbia

Chris Hausmann
University of Notre Dame

Todd A. Hechtman
Eastern Washington University

Keith Kerr
Blinn College

Elaine Leeder
Sonoma State University

Jason J. Leiker
Utah State University

Stephen Lilley
Sacred Heart University

David A. Lopez
California State University, Northridge

Akbar Madhi
Ohio Wesleyan University

Gerardo Marti
Davidson College

Laura McCloud
The Ohio State University

Meeta Mehrotra
Roanoke College

Melinda S. Miceli
University of Hartford

Leah A. Moore
University of Central Florida

Katy Pinto
California State University at Dominguez Hills

R. Marlene Powell
University of North Carolina at Pembroke

Suzanne Prescott
Central New Mexico Community College

Olga Rowe
Oregon State University

Paulina Ruf
Lenoir-Rhyne University

Sarah Samblanet
Kent State University

Martha L. Shockey-Eckles
Saint Louis University

Toni Sims
University of
    Louisiana–Lafayette

Terry L. Smith
Harding University

Frank S. Stanford
Blinn College

Tracy Steele
Wright State University

Rachel Stehle
Cuyahoga Community College

Amy Stone
Trinity University

John Stone
Boston University

Stephen Sweet
Ithaca College

Ruth Thompson-Miller
Texas A & M University

Tim Ulrich
Seattle Pacific University

Thomas L. Van Valey
Western Michigan University

Connie Veldink
Everett Community College

Chaim I. Waxman
Rutgers University

Debra Welkley
California State University
    at Sacramento

Debra Wetcher-Hendricks
Moravian College

Deborah J. White
Collin County Community College

Jake B. Wilson
University of California, Riverside

Laurie Winder
Western Washington University

Robert Wonser
College of the Canyons

Luis Zanartu
Sacramento City College

John Zipp
University of Akron

edge.sagepub.com/ballantinecondensed4e

SAGE edge for Students
provides a personalized approach
to help you accomplish your
coursework goals in an easy-
to-use learning environment.

PART I

Understanding Our Social World

The Scientific Study of Society

Can an individual make a difference? How does your family influence your chances of gaining a college degree and a high-paying job? If you were born into a poor family, what are your chances of becoming wealthy? How does your level of education impact your likelihood of marrying—and staying married? How does the wealth of your country affect your opportunities? How can sociology help you answer these questions and be an effective member of society?

Those are some of the questions you will be able to answer as you develop a deeper understanding of our social world. Sociology is valuable because it gives us new perspectives on our personal and professional lives and because sociological insights and skills can help all of us make the world a better place. Sociology can change your life—and help you change the world.

By the time you finish reading the first two chapters, you should have an initial understanding of what sociology is, what you can gain from studying sociology, the roots of the sociological perspective, and how sociologists carry out research. We invite you to view our social world through a sociological lens and learn how you can use sociology to make a difference in your life, your community, and the world.

Corbis/ Cameron Davidson

1 Sociology

A Unique Way to View the World

Sociology involves a transformation in the way one sees the world—learning to recognize the complex connections among our intimate personal lives, large organizations, and national and global systems.

MICRO

● ME (MY FAMILY AND CLOSE FRIENDS)

● LOCAL ORGANIZATIONS AND COMMUNITY
My school, place of worship, hangouts

MESO

● NATIONAL ORGANIZATIONS, INSTITUTIONS, AND ETHNIC SUBCULTURES
My political party, ethnic affiliation

MACRO

● SOCIETY
Type of national government and economic system

● GLOBAL COMMUNITY
United Nations, World Bank, Doctors Without Borders, multinational corporations

LEARNING OBJECTIVES

1.1 Explain the sociological perspective.

1.2 Describe the benefits of studying sociology.

1.3 Summarize the social world model.

This model illustrates a core idea carried throughout the book—how your own life is shaped by your family, community, society, and world, and how you influence them in return. Understanding this model can help you to better understand your social world and to make a positive impact on it.

THINK ABOUT IT

Micro: Small Groups and Local Community	How can sociology help me understand my own life and help me to be a more effective citizen in my community?
Meso: National Institutions; Complex Organizations; Ethnic Groups	How do sociologists help us understand and even improve our lives in work organizations and health care organizations?
Macro: National and Global Systems	How might national and global events affect my life?

The womb is apparently the setting for some great bodywork. It may win the prize for the strangest place to get a back massage, but according to a recent scientific article, by the fourth month of gestation, twin fetuses begin reaching for their "womb-mates," and by 18 weeks, they spend more time touching their siblings than themselves or the walls of the uterus (Weaver 2010). Fetuses that have single-womb occupancy tend to touch the walls of the uterus a good deal to make contact with the mother. Nearly 30% of the movements of twins is directed toward their companions. Movements such as stroking the back or the head are more sustained and more precise than movements toward themselves—touching their own mouths or other facial features. As one team of scholars put it, we are

© Keith A. Roberts

Within hours of their birth in October 2010, Jackson and Audrey became highly fussy if the nurses tried to put them in separate bassinets. At one point shortly after birth they were both put in a warmer, and Jackson cried until he found Audrey, proceeding to intertwine his arms and legs with hers. Twins, like all humans, are hardwired to be social and in relationships with others.

"wired to be social" (Castiello et al. 2010). In short, humans are innately social creatures.

The social world is not merely something that exists outside us. As the story of the twins illustrates, the social world is also something we carry inside. We are part of it, we reflect on it, and we are influenced by it, even when we are alone. The patterns of the social world engulf us in ways both subtle and obvious, with profound implications for how we create order and meaning in our lives. The point is that we need others—and that is where sociology enters.

Sometimes it takes a dramatic and shocking event for us to realize just how deeply embedded we are in our relationships in the social world that we take for granted. "It couldn't happen in the United States," read typical world newspaper accounts. Yet on September 11, 2001, shortly after 9 a.m., a commercial airliner crashed into New York City's World Trade Center, followed a short while later by another pummeling into the paired tower. This mighty symbol of financial wealth collapsed. After the dust settled and the rescue crews finished their gruesome work, nearly 3,000 people were dead and many others injured. The world as we knew it changed forever that day. This event taught U.S. citizens how integrally connected they are with the international community.

Such terrorist acts horrify people because they are unpredicted and unexpected in a normally predictable world. They violate the rules that support our connections to one another. They also bring attention to the discontent and disconnectedness that lie under the surface in many societies—discontent that can come to the surface and express itself in hateful violence. Such discontent and hostility are likely to continue until the root causes are addressed.

Terrorist acts represent a rejection of the modern civil society we know. The terrorists themselves see their acts as justifiable, as a way they can strike out against injustices and threats to their way of life. Few outside the terrorists' inner circle understand their thinking and behavior. When terrorist acts occur, we struggle to fit such events into our mental picture of a just, safe, comfortable, and predictable social world. The United States is a world power, yet its values such as consumerism, individualism, freedom of religion, and tolerance of other perspectives challenge and threaten the views of many people around the world. For many U.S. citizens, a sense of loyalty to the nation was deeply stirred by the events of 9/11. Patriotism abounded. The nation's people became more connected as a reaction to an act against the United States.

A similar sense of patriotism and connectedness arose immediately after the bombing at the Boston Marathon in 2013. First responders and marathon runners pierced with shrapnel were held up as heroes and symbols of U.S. pride and perseverance in the face of terrorist attacks. As Émile Durkheim, one of the founders of sociology, first pointed out, acts that break normal rules of behavior, as terrorism does, can unite the rule-following members of society (Durkheim [1895] 1982).

Most of the time, we live with social patterns that we take for granted as routine, ordinary, and expected. These social patterns are essential in social groups so we understand what is happening and know what to expect. Unlike our innate drives, social expectations come from those around us and guide (or constrain) our behaviors and thoughts. Without shared expectations among humans about proper patterns of behavior, life would be chaotic. Our social interactions require some basic rules, and these rules create routine and normalcy in everyday interaction. For the people in and around the World Trade Center on 9/11 and Boston on April 15, 2013, the social rules governing everyday life broke down.

This chapter examines the social ties that make up our social world, as well as sociology's focus on those connections. You will learn what sociology is, what sociologists do, how sociology can be used to improve

The terrorist bombing of the 2013 Boston Marathon inspired residents in the Boston area and marathon runners to stand strong in the face of terrorism. The 2014 Boston Marathon attracted even more participants and spectators.

your life and society, and how the social world model helps us understand how society works.

WHAT IS SOCIOLOGY?

<u>Sociology</u> *is the scientific study of social life, social change, and social causes and consequences of human behavior.* Sociologists examine how society both shapes and is shaped by individuals, small groups of people, organizations, national societies, and global social networks.

Unlike the discipline of psychology, which focuses on the attributes, motivations, and behaviors of individuals, sociology focuses on group patterns. Whereas a psychologist might try to explain behavior by examining the personality traits of individuals, a sociologist would examine the positions of different people within the group and how these positions influence what individuals do. Sociologists seek to analyze and explain why people interact with others and belong to groups, how groups work, why some groups have more power than other groups, how decisions are made, and how groups deal with conflict and change.

Sociologists also examine the causes of social problems, such as child abuse, crime, poverty, and war, and ways they can be addressed.

Two-person interactions—*dyads*—are the smallest units studied by sociologists. Examples of dyads include roommates discussing their classes, a professor and student going over an assignment, a husband and wife negotiating their budget, and two children playing. Next in size are small groups consisting of three or more interacting people who know each other—a family, a neighborhood or peer group, a classroom group, a work group, or a street gang. Then come increasingly larger groups—organizations such as sports or scouting clubs, neighborhood associations, and local religious congregations. Among the largest groups contained within nations are ethnic groups and national organizations or institutions, such as the auto industry, the Republican and Democratic national political parties, and national religious organizations like the Southern Baptists. Nations themselves are still larger and can sometimes involve hundreds of millions of people. In the past several decades, social scientists have also pointed to globalization, the process by which the entire world is becoming a single

© Keith A. Roberts

Here children experience ordered interaction in the competitive environment of a football game. What values, skills, attitudes, and assumptions about life and social interaction do you think these young boys are learning?

Social Rules and Disaster

interdependent entity. Of particular interest to sociologists is how these various groups are organized, how they function, why they can come into conflict, and how they influence one another.

● Thinking Sociologically

Identify several dyads, small groups, and large organizations to which you belong. Did you choose to belong, or were you born into membership in these groups? How does each group influence who you are and the decisions you make? How do you influence each of the groups?

Ideas Underlying Sociology

The idea that one action can cause something else is a core idea in all science. Sociologists also share several ideas that they take for granted about the social world. These ideas about humans and social life are supported by considerable evidence, and they are no longer matters of debate or controversy. They are considered to be true. These core assumptions help us see how sociologists approach the study of people in groups.

- People are social by nature.
- People live much of their lives belonging to social groups.
- Interaction between the individual and the group is a two-way process in which each influences the other.
- Recurrent social patterns, ordered behavior, shared expectations, and common understandings among people characterize groups.
- The processes of conflict and change are natural and inevitable features of groups and societies.

As you read this book, keep in mind these basic ideas that form the foundation of sociological analysis.

Sociological Findings and Commonsense Beliefs

Through research, sociologists have shown that many commonly held beliefs are not actually true, and some "commonsense" ideas have been discredited by sociological research. Here are three examples:

Belief: Most of the differences in the behaviors of women and men are based on "human nature"; men and women are plainly very different from each

other. Research shows that biological factors certainly play a part in the behaviors of men and women, but the culture (beliefs, values, rules, and way of life) that people learn as they grow up determines who does what and how biological tendencies are played out. A unique example illustrates this: In the nomadic Wodaabe tribe in Africa, women do most of the heavy work, while men adorn themselves with makeup, sip tea, and gossip (Cultural Survival 2010; Loftsdottir 2004). Each year the group holds a festival where men show their white teeth and the whites of their eyes to attract a marriage partner. Such dramatic variations in the behavior of men and women around the world are so great that it is impossible to attribute behavior solely to biology or human nature alone.

Belief: Racial groupings are based on biological differences among people. Actually, racial categorizations are socially constructed (created by members of society) and vary among societies and over time within societies. A person can be seen as one race in Brazil and another in the United States. Even within the United States, racial categories have changed many times. All one has to do is look at old U.S. Census records and see how racial categories change over time—even within the same nation!

Belief: Given the high divorce rates in the United States and Canada, most marriages do not last. The highest divorce rates in the United States are found

In the early 20th century, immigrants to the United States who were of Irish or Italian ancestry were not considered "white" in Virginia and some other states, and their children had to go to segregated schools for blacks. This woman would not have been considered "white" in Virginia in 1910.

©Oliver Strewe/Lonely Planet Images/Getty Images

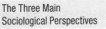 The Three Main Sociological Perspectives

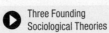 Three Founding Sociological Theories

among those below the average in education and living in poverty. Those who are middle class or higher tend to have stable marriages (Luscombe 2010; Pew Research Center 2010).

As these examples illustrate, the discipline of sociology provides a method to assess the accuracy of our commonsense assumptions about the social world. To improve the lives of individuals in our communities and in societies around the world, decision makers must have accurate information. Sociological research can be the basis for more rational and just social policies—policies that better meet the needs of all groups in the social world. The sociological imagination, discussed below, helps us gain an understanding of social problems.

The Sociological Imagination

Events in our social world affect our individual lives. If we are unemployed or lack funds for a college education, we may say this is a personal problem. Yet, broader social issues are often at the root of our situation. The sociological imagination holds that we can best understand our personal experiences and problems by examining their broader social context—by looking at the big picture.

Many individual problems (or private troubles) are rooted in social or public issues (what is happening in the social world outside one's personal control). Distinguished sociologist C. Wright Mills called the ability to understand this *complex interactive relationship between individual experiences and public issues* the **sociological imagination.** For Mills, many personal experiences can and should be interpreted in the context of large-scale forces in the wider society (Mills 1959).

Consider, for example, someone you know who has been laid off from a job. This personal trauma is a common situation during a recession. Unemployed persons often experience feelings of inadequacy or lack of self-worth because of the job loss. Their unemployment, though, may be due to larger social forces such as unsound banking practices, corporate downsizing, or a corporation taking operations to another country where labor costs are cheaper and where there are fewer environmental regulations on companies. People may blame themselves or each other for personal troubles such as unemployment or marital problems, believing that they did not try hard enough. Often, they do not see the connection between their private lives and larger economic and social forces

beyond their control. They fail to recognize the *public issues* that create *private troubles*.

If you are having trouble paying for college, that may feel like a very personal trouble. High tuition rates, though, relate to a dramatic decline in governmental support for public higher education and financial aid for students. The rising cost of a college education is a serious public issue that our society needs to address. Individuals, alone, cannot reduce the high price of college.

As you learn about sociology, you will begin to notice how social forces shape individual lives, and how this knowledge helps us understand aspects of everyday life we take for granted. In this book, we investigate how group life influences our behaviors and interactions and why some individuals follow the rules of society and others do not. You will learn to view the social world and your place in it from a sociological perspective as you develop your *sociological imagination.* Connecting events from the global and national levels to the personal and intimate level of our own lives is the core organizing theme of this book.

● Thinking Sociologically

How has divorce, poverty, or war caused personal troubles for someone you know? Give examples of why is it inadequate to explain these personal troubles by examining only the personal characteristics of those affected.

Questions Sociologists Ask—and Don't Ask

Perhaps you have had late-night discussions with your friends about the meaning of life, the existence of God, the ethical implications of stem cell research, or the morality of abortion. These are philosophical issues that sociologists, like other scientists, cannot answer through scientific research. What sociologists *do* ask are questions about people in social groups and organizations—questions that can be studied scientifically. Sociologists may research how people feel about the above issues (the percentage of people who approve of umbilical cord stem cell research, for example), but sociologists do not say what are right and wrong answers to such value-driven opinions. They are more interested in how people's beliefs influence their behavior. They focus on issues that can be studied objectively and scientifically—looking for causes or consequences.

 Applying the Sociological Imagination

Sociologists might ask, *who gets an abortion, why do they do so, and how does the society as a whole view abortion?* These are matters of fact that a social scientist can explore. However, sociologists avoid making ethical judgments about whether abortion is sometimes acceptable or always wrong.

Likewise, sociologists might ask, *what are the circumstances around individuals becoming drunk and acting drunk?* This question is often tied more to the particular social environment than to the availability of alcohol. Note that a person might become very intoxicated at a fraternity party but not at a family member's wedding reception where alcohol is served. The expectations for behavior vary in each setting. The researcher does not make judgments about whether use of alcohol is good or bad or right or wrong and avoids—as much as possible—opinions regarding responsibility or irresponsibility. The sociologist does, however, observe variations in the use of alcohol in different social situations and the resulting behaviors. The focus of sociology is on facts and what causes behaviors and their results.

Thinking Sociologically

Consider the information you have just read. What are some questions sociologists might ask about drinking and drunkenness? What are some questions sociologists would not ask about these topics, at least while in their roles as researchers?

The Social Sciences: A Comparison

Not so long ago, our views of people and social relationships were based on stereotypes, intuition, superstitions, supernatural explanations, and traditions passed on from one generation to the next. Natural scientists (e.g., chemists, astronomers, biologists, and oceanographers) first used the scientific method, a model later adopted by social scientists. Social scientists, including anthropologists, psychologists, economists, cultural geographers, historians, and political scientists, as well as sociologists, apply the scientific method to study social relationships, to correct misleading and harmful misconceptions about human behavior, and to guide policy decisions. Consider the following examples of specific studies various social scientists have conducted.

Some anthropological studies focus on garbage. They examine what people discard to understand what kind of lives they lead (Bond 2010). *Anthropology* is the study of humanity in its broadest context. It is closely related to sociology, and the two areas have common historical roots and sometimes overlapping methodologies and subject matter. However, anthropologists have four major subfields within anthropology: physical anthropology (which is related to biology), archaeology, linguistics, and cultural anthropology (sometimes called *ethnology*). This last field has the most in common with sociology. Cultural anthropologists study the culture, or way of life, of a society.

A psychologist may wire research subjects to a machine that measures their physiological reaction to a violent film clip, and then ask them questions about what they were feeling. *Psychology* is the study of individual behavior and mental processes (e.g., sensation, perception, memory, and thought processes). It differs from sociology in that it focuses on individuals rather than on groups, institutions, and societies.

Binge drinking, losing consciousness, vomiting, or engaging in sexual acts while drunk may be sources of storytelling at a college party but would be offensive at a wedding reception.

In this study by a psychologist, the researcher is using some equipment and a computer to measure how the eye and the brain work together to help create depth perception.

Although there are different branches of psychology, most psychologists are concerned with individual motivations, personality attributes, attitudes, perceptions, abnormal behavior, mental disorders, and the stages of normal human development.

A political scientist studies opinion poll results to predict who will win the next election, how various groups of people are likely to vote, or how elected officials will vote on proposed legislation. *Political science* is concerned with government systems and power—how they work, how they are organized, the forms of government, relations among governments, who holds power and how they obtain it, how power is used, and who is politically active. Political science overlaps with sociology, particularly in the study of political theory and the nature and uses of power.

Many economists study the banking system and market trends to try to predict trends in the global economy. *Economists* analyze economic conditions and explore how people organize, produce, and distribute material goods. They are interested in supply and demand, inflation and taxes, prices and manufacturing output, labor organization, employment levels, and comparisons between postindustrial, industrial, and nonindustrial nations.

What these social sciences—sociology, anthropology, psychology, political science, and economics—have in common is that they study aspects of human behavior and social life. Social sciences share many common topics, methods, concepts, research findings, and theories, but each has a different focus or perspective on the social world. Each of these social sciences relates to topics studied by sociologists, but sociologists focus on human interaction, groups, and social structure, providing the broadest overview of the social world.

Thinking Sociologically

Consider the issue of unemployment in the United States. What is one question that a person in each discipline—anthropologist, psychologist, political scientist, economist, and sociologist—might ask about this social issue?

WHY DOES SOCIOLOGY MATTER?

Sociology is important not only to understand our relationships with other people and because it can inform social policy decisions, but also because we can pursue a career in sociology or use skills developed through sociology in a wide range of career fields.

Why Study Sociology?

The sociological perspective helps us to be more effective as we carry out our roles as life partners, workers, friends, family members, and citizens. For example, an employee who has studied sociology may better understand how to work with groups and how the structure of the workplace affects individual behavior, how to approach problem solving, and how to collect and analyze data. Likewise, a schoolteacher trained in sociology may have a better understanding of classroom management, student motivation, the causes of poor student learning that have roots outside the school, and why students drop out.

A sociological perspective allows us to look beneath the surface of society and notice social patterns that others tend to overlook. When you view our social world with a sociological perspective, you

1. become more self-aware by understanding your social surroundings, which can lead to opportunities to improve your life;
2. have a more complete understanding of social situations by looking beyond individual explanations to include group analyses of behavior;

 Why Is Sociology Important?

3. understand and evaluate problems more clearly, viewing the world systematically and objectively rather than in strictly emotional or personal terms;

4. gain an understanding of the many diverse cultural perspectives and how cultural differences are related to behavioral patterns;

5. assess the impact of social policies;

6. understand the complexities of social life and how to study them scientifically;

7. gain useful skills in interpersonal relations, critical thinking, data collection and analysis, problem solving, and decision making; and

8. learn how to change your local environment and the larger society.

What Do Sociologists Do?

Graduates with a bachelor's degree in sociology who seek employment immediately after college are most likely to find their first jobs in social services, administrative assistantships, or some sort of management position. The first jobs of sociology majors are indicated in Figure 1.1. With graduate degrees—a master's or a doctoral degree—graduates usually become college teachers, researchers, clinicians, or consultants. Table 1.1 on page 12 provides some ideas of career paths for college graduates with a major in sociology.

Many sociologists work outside of academia, using their knowledge and research skills to address the needs of businesses, nonprofit organizations, and government. For example, they often work in human resources departments and as consultants for businesses. In government jobs, they provide data such as population projections for education and health care planning. In social service agencies, they help provide services to those in need, and in health agencies, they may be concerned with outreach to immigrant communities. Both sociologists who work in universities and those who work for business or government can use sociological tools to improve society. You will find examples of sociologists in the "Sociologists in Action" boxes throughout the book.

Thinking Sociologically

From what you have read so far, how might sociological tools (e.g., social interaction skills and knowledge of how groups work) be useful to you in your anticipated major and career or current job?

FIGURE 1.1 Occupational Categories for Sociology Graduates' First Jobs

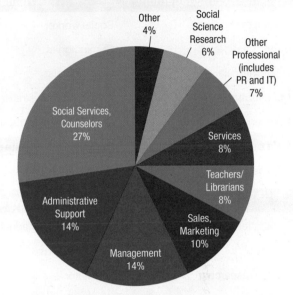

Source: Based on *21st Century Careers With an Undergraduate Degree in Sociology*, American Sociological Association 2009.

What Do Employers Want?

Ask employers what they want in a new hire, and the focus is likely to be on writing, speaking, and analytical skills—especially when the new employee will be faced with complex problems. Other desired skills in demand include the ability to cope with change, work effectively in diverse teams, and gather and interpret quantitative information. The left column in Table 1.2 indicates what employers want from college graduates; the right column indicates the skills and competencies that are part of most sociological training. Compare the two, noting the high levels of overlap.

We now have a general idea of what sociology is and what sociologists do. It should be apparent that sociology is a broad field of interest; sociologists study all aspects of human social behavior. The next section of this chapter shows how the parts of the social world that sociologists study relate to each other, and it outlines the model you will follow as you continue to learn about sociology.

Thinking Sociologically

Imagine that you are a mayor, legislator, police chief, or government official. You make decisions based on information gathered by social science research rather than on your own intuition or assumptions. What are some advantages to this decision-making method?

TABLE 1.1 What Can You Do With a Sociology Degree?

Business or Management	Human Services	Education
Market researcher	Social worker	Teacher
Sales manager	Criminologist	Academic research
Customer relations	Gerontologist	Administration
Manufacturing representative	Hospital administrator	School counselor
Banking or loan officer	Charities administrator	Policy analyst
Data processor	Community advocate or organizer	College professor
Attorney		Dean of student life

Research	Government	Public Relations
Population analyst	Policy advisor or administrator	Publisher
Surveyor	Labor relations	Mass communications
Market researcher	Legislator	Advertising
Economic analyst	Census worker	Writer or commentator
Public opinion pollster	International agency representative	Journalist
Interviewer	City planning officer	
Policy researcher	Prison administrator	
Telecommunications researcher	Law enforcement	
	FBI agent	
	Customs agent	

Source: American Sociological Association 2006.

Note: Surveys of college alumni with undergraduate majors in sociology indicate that this field of study prepares people for a broad range of occupations. Notice that some of these jobs require graduate or professional training. For further information, contact your department chair or the American Sociological Association in Washington, DC, for a copy of *21st Century Careers With an Undergraduate Degree in Sociology* (2009).

THE SOCIAL WORLD MODEL

Think about the different groups you depend on and interact with on a daily basis. You wake up to greet members of your family or your roommate. You go to a larger group—a class—that exists within an even larger organization—the college or university. Understanding sociology and the approach of this book requires a grasp of **levels of analysis**—that is, *social groups from the smallest to the largest*. It may be relatively easy to picture small groups, such as a family, a group of friends, a sports team, or a sorority or fraternity. It is more difficult to visualize large groups, such as corporations—Gap, Abercrombie & Fitch, Eddie Bauer, General Motors Company, or Starbucks—or organizations such as local or state governments. The largest groups include nations or international organizations, such as the sprawling networks of the United Nations or the World Trade Organization. Groups of various sizes shape our lives. Sociological analysis involves an understanding of these groups that exist at various levels of analysis and the connections among them.

The **social world model** helps us picture *the levels of analysis in our social surroundings as an interconnected series of small groups, organizations, institutions, and societies*. Sometimes these groups are connected by mutual support and cooperation. However,

TABLE 1.2 What Employers Want and What Sociology Majors Can Deliver

Employers Who Want Colleges to "Place More Emphasis" on Essential Learning Outcomes		Traits and Knowledge That Are Developed in Most Sociological Training
Knowledge of Human Culture	**% Seeking**	**Skills and Competencies**
1. Global issues	72	➢ Knowledge of global issues ➢ Sensitivity to diversity and differences in cultural values and traditions
2. The role of the United States in the world	60	➢ Sociological perspective on the United States and the world
3. Cultural values and traditions—U.S. and global	53	➢ Understanding diversity ➢ Working with others (ability to work toward a common goal)
Intellectual and Practical Skills	**% Seeking**	
4. Team work skills in diverse groups	76	➢ Effective leadership skills (ability to take charge and make decisions) ➢ Interpersonal skills (working with diverse coworkers)
5. Critical thinking and analytic reasoning	73	➢ Analysis and research skills ➢ Organizing thoughts and information ➢ Planning effectively (ability to design, plan, organize, and implement projects and to be self-motivated)
6. Written and oral communication	73	➢ Communication skills (listening, verbal and written communication) ➢ Working with peers ➢ Effective interaction in group situations
7. Information literacy	70	➢ Knowledge of how to find information one needs—online or in a library
8. Creativity and innovation	70	➢ Flexibility, adaptability, and multitasking (ability to set priorities, manage multiple tasks, adapt to changing situations, and handle pressure) ➢ Creative ways to deal with problems
9. Complex problem solving	64	➢ Ability to conceptualize and solve problems ➢ Ability to be creative (working toward meeting the organization's goals)
10. Quantitative reasoning	60	➢ Computer and technical literacy (basic understanding of computer hardware and software programs) ➢ Statistical analysis
Personal and Social Responsibility	**% Seeking**	
11. Intercultural competence (teamwork in diverse groups)	76	➢ Personal values (honesty, flexibility, work ethic, dependability, loyalty, positive attitude, professionalism, self-confidence, willingness to learn) ➢ Working with others ➢ Ability to work toward a common goal
12. Intercultural knowledge (global issues)	72	➢ Knowledge of global issues

Source: Based on American Sociological Association 2009; Hansen and Hansen 2003; WorldWideLearn 2007. See also Association of American Colleges and Universities and Hart Research Associates 2013.

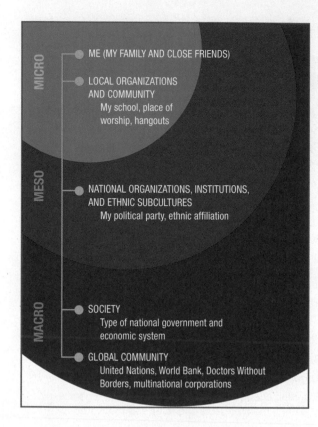

MICRO

● ME (MY FAMILY AND CLOSE FRIENDS)

● LOCAL ORGANIZATIONS
AND COMMUNITY
My school, place of
worship, hangouts

MESO

● NATIONAL ORGANIZATIONS, INSTITUTIONS,
AND ETHNIC SUBCULTURES
My political party, ethnic affiliation

MACRO

● SOCIETY
Type of national government and
economic system

● GLOBAL COMMUNITY
United Nations, World Bank, Doctors Without
Borders, multinational corporations

sometimes there are conflicts and power struggles over access to resources. What we are asking you to do here and throughout this book is to develop a sociological imagination—the basic lens used by sociologists. Picture the social world as connected levels of increasingly larger circles. To understand the units or parts of the social world model, look at the model shown above (and at the beginning of each chapter).

We use this social world model throughout the book to illustrate how each topic fits into the big picture—our social world. The social world includes both *social structures* and *social processes*.

Social Structures

Picture the human body, held together by bones and muscles. The units that make up that body include the brain, heart, lungs, and kidneys. In a similar manner, **social units** are *interconnected parts of the social world ranging from small groups to societies*. These social units include dyads, small groups like the members of a family, community organizations including schools and churches, large-scale organizations such as political parties or state and national governments, and global societies such as the United Nations.

All these social units connect to make up the **social structure**—*the stable patterns of interactions, statuses, roles, and organizations that provide stability for the society and bring order to individuals' lives*. Think about these parallels between the structure that holds together the human body and the structure that holds together societies and their units.

Sometimes, however, the units within the social structure are in conflict. For example, a religion that teaches that some forms of birth control are wrong may conflict with the health care system regarding how to provide care to women. This issue has been in the U.S. news as many religious organizations and religious business owners have fought against the requirements of the 2010 Affordable Care Act in the United States that employers provide birth control to those who wish to receive it.

Social institutions are *organized, patterned, and enduring sets of social structures that provide guidelines for behavior and help each society meet its basic survival needs*. Think about the fact that all societies have some form of family, education, religion, politics, and economics; in more complex societies there are also essential structures that provide science, health care, and a military. These are the institutions that provide the rules, roles, and relationships to meet human needs and guide human behavior. They are the units through which organized social activities take place, and they provide the setting for activities essential to human and societal survival. For example, we cannot survive without an economic institution to provide guidelines and a structure for meeting our basic needs of food, shelter, and clothing. Likewise, society would not function without political institutions to govern and protect its members. Most social units fall under one of these institutions.

Like the human body, society and social groups have a structure. Our body's skeleton governs how our limbs are attached to the torso and how they move. Like the system of organs that make up our bodies—heart, lungs, kidneys, bladder—all social institutions are interrelated. Just as an illness in one organ affects other organs, a dysfunction in one institution affects the other institutions. A heart attack affects the flow of blood to all other parts of the body. Likewise, if many people are unable to afford medical treatment, the society is less healthy, and there are consequences for families, schools, workplaces, and society as a whole.

All social institutions are interrelated, just as the parts of the body are interdependent: If the skeletal system of the body breaks down, the muscular system and nervous system are not going to be able to get the body to do what it needs to do.

The **national society**, one of the largest social units in our model, includes *a population of people, usually living within a specified geographic area, connected by common ideas and subject to a particular political authority.* It also features a social structure with groups and institutions. In addition to having relatively permanent geographic and political boundaries, a national society has one or more languages and a unique way of life. In most cases, national societies involve countries or large regions where the inhabitants share a common identity as members. In certain other instances, such as contemporary Great Britain, a single national society may include several groups of people who consider themselves distinct nationalities (Welsh, English, Scottish, and Northern Irish within the United Kingdom). Such multicultural societies may or may not have peaceful relations.

⬤ Thinking Sociologically

How might change in one national institution, such as health care, affect change in other national institutions, such as the family and the economy? Can you think of any human activities that do not fall into one of the institutions mentioned above?

Social Processes

If social structure is similar to the human body's skeletal structure, social processes are similar to what keeps the body alive—beating heart, lungs processing

This refugee mother and child from Mozambique represent the smallest social unit, a dyad. In this case, they are trying to survive with help from larger groups such as the United Nations.

oxygen, stomach processing nutrients. **Social processes** *take place through actions of people in institutions and other social units.* The process of socialization teaches individuals how to behave in society. It takes place through actions in families, educational systems, religious organizations, and other social units. Socialization is essential for the continuation of any society because through this process members of society learn the thoughts and actions needed to survive in their society. Another process, conflict, occurs between individuals or groups over money, jobs, and other needed or desired resources. The process of change also occurs continuously in every social unit; change in one unit affects other units of the social world, often in a chain reaction. For instance, change in the quality of health care can affect the workforce. A workforce in poor health can affect the economy; instability in the economy can affect families, as breadwinners lose jobs; and family economic woes can affect religious communities because devastated families cannot afford to give money to churches, mosques, or temples.

Sociologists try to identify, understand, and explain the processes that take place within social units. Picture these processes as overlying and penetrating our whole social world, from small groups to societies. Social units would be lifeless without the action brought about by social processes, just as body parts would be lifeless without the processes of electrical impulses shooting from the brain to each organ or the oxygen transmitted by blood coursing through our arteries to sustain each organ.

The Environment of Our Social World

Surrounding each social unit, whether a small family group or a large corporation, is an **environment**—*the setting in which the social unit operates, including everything that influences the social unit, such as its physical and organizational surroundings and technological innovations*. Just as each individual has a unique environment, including family, friends, and other social units, each social unit has an environment to which it must adjust.

Some parts of the environment are more important to the individual or social unit than others. For example, your local church, synagogue, temple, or mosque is surrounded by its unique environment. That religious organization may seem autonomous and independent, but it depends on its national organization for guidelines and support; the local police force to protect the building from vandalism; and the local economy to provide jobs to members so that the members, in turn, can support the organization. If the religious education program is going to train children to understand the scriptures, local schools are needed to teach the children to read. A religious group may also be affected by other religious bodies, competing with one another for potential members from the community. The point is that to understand a social unit *or* the human body, we must consider the *structure* and *processes* within the unit as well as the interaction with the surrounding environment.

Perfect relationships or complete harmony among the social units is unusual. Social units, be they small groups or large organizations, are often motivated by self-interest and the need for self-preservation, with the result that they compete with other units for resources (time, money, skills, energy of members). Therefore, social units within a society are often in conflict. Whether groups are in conflict or they cooperate does not change their interrelatedness; units are interdependent and can be studied using the scientific method.

Studying the Social World: Levels of Analysis

Picture for a moment your sociology class as a social unit in your social world. Students (individuals) make up the class, the class (small group) is offered by the sociology department, the sociology department (a large group, including faculty and students) is part of the college or university, and the university (an organization) is located in a community. It follows the practices approved by the social institution (education) of which it is a part, and education is an institution located within a nation. Practices the university follows are determined by a larger accrediting agency that provides guidelines and oversight for educational institutions. The national society, represented by the national government, is shaped by global events such as technological and economic competition between nations, natural disasters, global climate change, wars, and terrorist attacks. Such events influence national policies and goals, including policies for the educational system. Thus, global issues and conflicts may shape the content of the curriculum taught in the local classroom, from what is studied to the textbooks used.

Each of these social units is referred to as a level of analysis, social groups from the smallest to the largest (two students in a discussion group to a society or global system). These levels are illustrated in the social world model at the beginning of each chapter, and their relation to that chapter's content is shown through examples in the model.

Micro-Level Analysis. A focus on *individual or small-group interaction in specific situations* is called **micro-level analysis.** The micro level is important because one-to-one and small-group interaction forms the basic foundation of all social groups and organizations to which we belong from families to corporations to societies. We are members of many groups at the micro level.

To understand micro-level analysis, consider the problem of spousal abuse, most often involving women being abused. Why does a person remain in an abusive relationship, knowing that each year thousands of people are killed by their partners and millions more are severely and repeatedly battered? To answer this question, several possible micro-level explanations can be considered. One view is that the abusive partner has convinced the abused person that she is powerless in the relationship or that she "deserves" the abuse. Therefore, she gives up in despair of ever being able to alter the situation. The abuse is viewed as part of the interaction—of action and reaction—and some partners come to see abuse as what comprises "normal" interaction.

Another explanation for remaining in the abusive relationship is that battering is a familiar part of the person's everyday life. However unpleasant and unnatural this may seem to outsiders, it may be seen by the abused as a "normal" and acceptable part of intimate relationships, especially if she grew up in an abusive family.

Another possibility is that an abused woman may fear that her children would be harmed or that she would be harshly judged by her family or church if she "abandoned" her mate. She may have few resources to make leaving the abusive situation possible. To study each of these possible explanations involves analysis at the micro level because each focuses on interpersonal interaction factors rather than on large society-wide trends or forces. Meso-level analysis leads to quite different explanations for abuse.

Meso-Level Analysis. Meso-level analysis involves looking at *intermediate-sized units smaller than the nation but larger than the local community or even the region.* This level includes national institutions (such as the economy of a country, the national educational system, or the political system within a country), nationwide organizations (such as a political party, a soccer league, or a national women's rights organization), and ethnic groups that have an identity as a group (such as Jews, Mexican Americans, or Native Americans in the United States). Organizations, institutions, and ethnic communities are smaller than the nation or global social units, but they are still beyond the everyday personal experience and control of individuals. They are intermediate in the sense of being too large to know everyone in the group, but they are not as large as nation-states. For example, state governments in the United States, provinces in Canada, prefectures in Japan, or cantons in Switzerland are at the meso level and usually more accessible and easier to change than the national bureaucracies of these countries.

In discussing micro-level analysis, we used the example of domestic violence. Recognizing that personal troubles can often be related to public issues, many social scientists look for broader explanations of spousal abuse, such as social conditions at the meso level of society (Straus, Gelles, and Steinmetz 2006). When a pattern of behavior in society occurs with increasing frequency, it cannot be understood solely from the point of view of individual cases or micro-level causes. For instance, sociological findings show that fluctuations in spousal or child abuse at the micro level are related to levels of unemployment in meso-level organizations and macro-level government economic policies. Frustration resulting in abuse erupts within families when poor economic conditions make it nearly impossible for people to find a stable and reliable means of supporting themselves and their families. The message here is that economic issues in the society must be addressed in order to decrease domestic violence.

Macro-Level Analysis. Studying the largest social units in the social world, called **macro-level analysis**, involves looking at *entire nations, global forces, and international social trends.* Macro-level analysis is essential to our understanding of how larger societal forces and global events shape our everyday lives. A natural disaster such as the recent droughts in North America and West Africa and massive hurricanes in Central America and the Caribbean may change the foods we can serve at our family dinner table, since much of what we consume comes from other parts of the world. Likewise, a political conflict on the other side of the planet can lead to war, which means that a member of your family may be called up on active duty and sent into harm's way more than 7,000 miles from your home. Each member of the family may experience individual stress, have trouble concentrating, and feel ill with worry. The entire globe has become an interdependent social unit. If we are to prosper and thrive in the world today, we need to understand connections that go beyond our local communities.

Even patterns such as domestic violence, considered as micro- and meso-level issues above, can be examined at the macro level. Violence against women (especially rape) occurs at very different rates in different societies, with some having a "culture of rape"

Analyzing to Find Solutions

(Kristof and WuDunn 2009). Consider the case in 2013 of the medical student in India who was gang raped on a bus and subsequently died. Her rape became headline news and shone a spotlight on the culture and lack of law enforcement in India that encourage violence against women. The most consistent predictor of violence against women is a macho conception of masculine roles and personality. Societies or subgroups within society that teach males that the finest expression of their masculinity is physical strength and domination tend to have more battered women (Lindow 2009).

India is far from the only nation with a culture that generates violence against women. South Africa has one of the highest levels of rape in the world, with one in four men having raped a woman, and 46% of those more than once. The men tend to show no remorse because the behavior is "accepted" by their segments of society; it is "macho" (Lindow 2009).

Understanding individual human behavior often requires investigation of the larger societal beliefs and values that support that behavior. Worldwide patterns may tell us something about a social problem and offer new lenses for understanding that problem.

Distinctions between each level of analysis are not always sharply delineated. The micro level shades into the meso level, and the lines between the meso level and the macro level are blurry on the continuum. Still, it is clear that in some micro-level social units, you know everyone, or at least every member of the social unit is only two degrees of separation away. In other words, every person in the social unit knows someone whom you also know. Try the following "Engaging Sociology" to test your understanding of levels of analysis and the sociological imagination.

We all participate in meso-level social units that are smaller than the nation but that can be huge. For example, thousands or even millions of individuals join organizations such as the Tea Party movement, Occupy Wall Street, MoveOn.org, or the environmental group 350.org. Those involved participate in dialogues online and contribute money to political organizations. People living thousands of miles from one another united financially and in spirit to support Obama-Biden or Romney-Ryan in the 2012 U.S. presidential election. We share connections with the other members of these organizations, and our lives are interconnected, even if we never meet face-to-face.

The macro level is even more removed from the individual, but its impact can change our lives. For example, decisions by lawmakers in Washington, D.C.,
can seem very distant, but decisions by Congress and the president may determine whether or not your own family has health care coverage (and of what quality) and whether the United States will lead or stymie global efforts to address climate change. These government leaders will also determine whether or not interest rates on federal student loans for U.S. students go up.

The social world model presented in each chapter illustrates the interplay of micro-, meso-, and macro-level forces related to that chapter's content.

The Social World Model and This Book

The social world engulfs each of us from the moment of our birth until we die. Throughout our lives, each of us is part of a set of social relationships that provides guidelines for how we interact with others and how we see ourselves. This does not mean that human behavior is strictly determined by our links to the social world. Humans are more than mere puppets whose behavior is programmed by social structure. It does mean, however, that the individual and the larger social world influence each other. We are influenced by, and we have influence on, our social environment. The social world is a human creation, and we can and do change that which we create. It acts on us, and we act on it. In this sense, social units are constantly emerging and changing in the course of human action and interaction.

The difficulty for most of us is that we are so caught up in our daily concerns that we fail to see and understand the social forces that are at work in our personal lives. What we need are conceptual and methodological tools to help us gain a more complete and accurate perspective on the social world. The ideas, theories, methods, and levels of analysis employed by sociologists are the very tools that will help give us that perspective. To use an analogy, each different lens of a camera gives the photographer a unique view of the world. Wide-angle lenses, close-up lenses, telephoto lenses, and special filters each serve a purpose in creating a distinctive picture or frame of the world. No one lens will provide the complete picture. Yet the combination of images produced by various lenses allows us to examine in detail aspects of the world we might ordinarily overlook. That is what the sociological perspective gives us: a unique set of lenses to see the social world around us with deeper understanding.

ENGAGING SOCIOLOGY

Micro-Meso-Macro

The distinctions between levels of analysis are gray rather than precise. Levels of analysis should be viewed as a continuum—from micro to macro social units. Clear criteria help identify groups at each level. One criterion is size (number of people) of the group. A second is the geographic range of influence:

- intimate or very close personal relationships (micro);
- social units in the local community (micro);
- social units that cover a large geographic region (like a state or commonwealth) and even nationwide groups that—despite size—are still a small portion of the entire nation (meso);
- the nation itself (macro); and
- units with global reach (macro).

A third criterion is degree of separation. If you know someone personally, that is one degree of separation. If you do not know the mayor of your town, but you know someone who knows the mayor, that is two degrees of separation. If you have a friend or a relative who knows someone who is a friend or relative of the governor in your state or province, that is three degrees of separation. Some research indicates that every person on the planet is within seven degrees of separation from every other human being. Let us see what this means for various levels of analysis in our social world.

Micro-level groups are small, local-community social units such as families and school classrooms within which everyone knows everyone else or knows someone who knows another member. So the degree of separation is usually not more than two degrees.

Meso-level groups are social units of intermediate size such as state governments (with limited geographic range), ethnic groups, and religious denominations (with large geographic range but population size that makes them a minority of the entire nation). Typically the group is large enough that members have never heard the names of many other members. Many members may have little access to the leaders, yet the group is not so large as to make the leaders seem distant or unapproachable. Almost anyone within the social unit is only three or four degrees of separation apart. Everyone in the unit is likely to know someone who knows a particular member.

Macro-level groups are large social units, usually quite bureaucratic, that operate at a national or a global level, such as national governments or international organizations. Most members are unlikely to know or have communicated with the leaders personally or know someone who knows the leaders. The "business" of these groups is of international importance and implication. A macro-level system is one in which most of the members are at least five degrees of separation from one another—that is, they know someone who knows someone who knows someone who knows someone who knows the person in question.

* * * * * * *

Engaging With Sociology:

_____

1. **Micro social units**

_____

2. **Meso social units**

_____

3. **Macro social units**

Look at the list of social units below. Identify which level each group is most likely to belong to—(1) micro, (2) meso, or (3) macro. Why did you answer as you did? The definitions above should help you make your decisions. Again, some are "on the line" because this is a continuum from micro to macro, and some units could legitimately be placed in more than one group. Which ones are especially "on the line"?

_____   Your nuclear family

_____   The United Nations

_____   A local chapter of the Lions Club or the Rotary Club

(Continued)

(Continued)

_____   Your high school baseball team

_____   India

_____   NATO (North Atlantic Treaty Organization)

_____   The First Baptist Church in Muncie, Indiana

_____   The World Bank

_____   A family reunion

_____   Google, Inc. (international)

_____   The Department of Education for the Commonwealth of Kentucky

_____   The show choir in your local high school

_____   African Canadians

_____   The Dineh (Navajo) people

_____   Canada

_____   The Republican Party in the United States

_____   The World Court

_____   A fraternity at your college

_____   The International Monetary Fund (IMF)

_____   The Ministry of Education for Spain

_____   The Roman Catholic Church (with its headquarters at the Vatican in Rome)

_____   Australia

_____   The Chi Omega national sorority

_____   Boy Scout Troop #3 in Marion, Ohio

_____   Al-Qaeda (an international alliance of terrorist organizations)

_____   The provincial government for the Canadian providence of Ontario

_____   The United States of America

See how your authors rate these at edge.sagepub.com/ballantinecondensed4e.

In seeing the social world from a sociological perspective, we are better able to understand who we are as social beings.

Throughout this book, we use the social world model as the framework for understanding the social units, processes, and surrounding environment. We look at each social unit and process. We take the unit out, examine it, and then return it to its place in the interconnected social world model so that you can comprehend the whole social world and its parts, like putting a puzzle together. Look for the model at the beginning of every chapter. We will also explain the micro-, meso-, and macro-level dimensions of issues throughout the text. Test your understanding of these concepts by identifying the levels of analysis in the following "Engaging Sociology."

When we say we know something about society, how is it that we know? What is considered evidence in sociology, and what lens (theory) do we use to interpret the data? In the next chapter, we turn to how we gather data to help us test theories to understand and influence the social world.

ENGAGING SOCIOLOGY

Micro-Meso-Macro: An Application Exercise

Imagine that there has been a major economic downturn (recession) in your local community. Identify three possible events at each level (micro, meso, and macro) that might contribute to the economic troubles in your town.

The micro (local community) level:

1. _____

2. _____

3. _____

The meso (intermediate—state, organizational, or ethnic subculture) level:

1. _____

2. _____

3. _____

The macro (national/global) level:

1. _____

2. _____

3. _____

WHAT HAVE WE LEARNED?

How can sociology help you see new aspects of your life and change society? Throughout this book you will find ideas and examples that will help answer this question. You will learn how to view the social world through a sociological lens and use the *sociological imagination*. Understanding how the social world works from the micro through the meso to the macro level helps us interact more effectively in it. Using the sociological imagination enables us to see how individual troubles can be rooted in social issues, and best addressed with an understanding of the meso or macro level. This knowledge enables us to be better family members, workers, citizens, and members of the global community.

We live in a complex social world with many layers of interaction. If we really want to understand our own lives, we need to comprehend the levels of analysis that affect our lives and the connections between those levels. To do so wisely, we need both objective lenses for viewing this complex social world and accurate, valid information (facts) about the society. As the science of society, sociology can provide both tested empirical data and a broad, analytical perspective, as you will learn in the next chapter. Here is a summary of points from Chapter 1.

KEY POINTS

- Humans are, at our very core, social animals—more akin to pack or herd animals than to individualistic cats.

- Sociology is based on scientific findings, making it more predictable and reliable than opinions or commonsense beliefs in a particular culture.

- A core idea in sociology is the sociological imagination. It requires that we see how our individual lives and personal troubles are shaped by historical and structural events outside our everyday lives. It also prods us to see how we can influence our society.

- Sociology is a social science and, therefore, uses the tools of the sciences to establish credible evidence to understand our social world. As a science, sociology is scientific and objective rather than value laden.

- Sociology has pragmatic applications, including those that are essential for the job market.

- Sociology focuses on social units or groups, on social structures such as institutions, on social processes that give a social unit its dynamic character, and on their environments.

- The social world model is the organizing theme of this book. Using the sociological imagination, we can understand our social world best by clarifying the interconnections between micro, meso, and macro levels of the social world. Each chapter of this book will examine society at these three levels of analysis.

DISCUSSION QUESTIONS

1. Think of a problem that impacts you personally (e.g., the high cost of tuition, unemployment, or divorce) and explain how you would make sense of it differently if you viewed it as (a) only a personal problem or (b) influenced by a public issue. How do possible solutions to the problem differ depending on how you view it?

2. How can sociology help you become a more informed citizen and better able to understand how government policies impact society?

3. What are three ways the sociological perspective can help you succeed in college and the workforce?

4. Think of some of the ways the social institutions of government and education are connected. Why is it in the interest of the government to support higher education? How has government support (or lack of support) impacted your college experience?

5. Imagine you would like to look at reasons behind the high college dropout rate in the United States. How might your explanations differ based on whether your analysis was on the micro, meso, or macro level? Why? Which level or levels would you focus on for your study? Why?

CONTRIBUTING TO OUR SOCIAL WORLD: What Can We Do?

At the end of this and all subsequent chapters, you will find suggestions for work, service learning, internships, and volunteering that encourage you to apply the ideas discussed in the chapter. Suggestions for Chapter 1 focus on student organizations for sociology majors and nonmajors.

At the Local (Micro) Level

- *Student organizations and clubs* enable students to meet other students interested in sociology, carry out group activities, get to know faculty members, and attend presentations by guest speakers. These clubs are usually not limited to sociology majors. If no such organization exists, consider forming one with the help of a faculty member. Sociologists also have an undergraduate honors society, Alpha Kappa Delta (AKD). Visit the AKD website at http://alphakappadelta.org/ to learn more about the society and what it takes to form a chapter.

At the Regional (Meso) Level

- *State, regional, and specialty (education, criminology, social problems) sociological associations* are especially student-friendly and feature publications and sessions at their annual meetings specifically for undergraduates. The American Sociological Association lists regional and specialty organizations and their websites, with direct links to their home pages, at www.asanet.org/about/Aligned_Associations.cfm.

At the National and Global (Macro) Levels

- *The American Sociological Association (ASA)* is the leading professional organization of sociologists in the United States. Visit the ASA website at www.asanet.org, and take a look around it. You will find many programs and initiatives of special interest to students. If you are interested in becoming a sociologist, be sure to look at the links under the heading "News on the Profession." The ASA also sponsors an Honors Program at the annual meeting that introduces students to the profession and gives them a heads-up on being successful in sociology. For more information, go to www.asanet.org/students/honors.cfm.

- *The International Sociological Association (ISA)* serves sociologists from around the world. Every four years, the ISA sponsors a large meeting (Toronto, Canada, in July 2018). Specialty groups within the ISA hold smaller conferences throughout the world during the other years. Check out www.isa-sociology.org.

$\circledS$SAGE edge™

Sharpen your skills with SAGE edge at **edge.sagepub.com/ballantinecondensed4e**

SAGE edge for Students provides a personalized approach to help you accomplish your coursework goals in an easy-to-use learning environment.

2 Examining the Social World

How Do We Know?

Science is about knowing—through careful systematic investigation. Of course there are other ways of seeking knowledge, such as finding a good library on a beach!

MICRO

● ME (MY FAMILY AND CLOSEST FRIENDS)

● LOCAL ORGANIZATIONS AND COMMUNITY

I am active in local church, school, clubs, and sports teams.

MESO

● NATIONAL ORGANIZATIONS, INSTITUTIONS, AND ETHNIC SUBCULTURES

I am active in a religious denomination, part of an educational system, and perhaps an ethnic group.

MACRO

● SOCIETY

I am a citizen of the United States, Canada, or another country.

● GLOBAL COMMUNITY

I am influenced by actions of the United Nations, the World Health Organization, or Doctors without Borders.

LEARNING OBJECTIVES

2.1 Outline the development of sociology.

2.2 Describe the key points of sociology's major theoretical perspectives.

2.3 Explain the core ideas underlying the scientific approach to understanding society.

2.4 List the basic steps of the scientific research process.

THINK ABOUT IT

Micro: Local Community	When you are trying to convince neighbors or people in your community to accept your opinion, why are facts and evidence important?
Meso: National Institutions; Complex Organizations; Ethnic Groups	How do sociologists gather accurate data about families, educational institutions, or ethnic groups?
Macro: National and Global Systems	How can theories about national and global interactions help us understand our own lives at the micro level?

et us travel to the Southern Hemisphere to meet a teenage boy, Hector. He is a 16-year-old living in a *favela* (slum) on the outskirts of São Paulo, Brazil. He is a polite, bright boy, but his chances of getting an education and a steady job in his world are limited. Like millions of other children around the world, he comes from a poor rural family that migrated to an urban area in search of a better life. However, his family ended up in a crowded slum with only a shared spigot for water and one string of electric lights along the dirt road going up the hill on which they live. The sanitary conditions in his community are appalling—open sewers, no garbage collection—which makes the people susceptible to various diseases. His family is relatively fortunate, for they have cement walls and wood flooring, but no bathroom, running water, or electricity. Many adjacent dwellings are little more than cardboard walls with corrugated metal roofs and dirt floors.

Hector wanted to stay in school but was forced to drop out to help support his family. Since leaving school, he has picked up odd jobs—deliveries, trash pickup, janitorial work, gardening—to help pay for the family's dwelling and to buy food to support his parents and six siblings. Even when he was in school, Hector's experience was discouraging. He was not a bad student, and some teachers encouraged him to continue, but other students from the city teased the *favela* kids and made them feel unwelcome. Most of his friends dropped out before he did. Hector often missed school because of other obligations—looking for part-time work, visiting a sick relative, or taking care of a younger sibling. The immediate need to put food on the table outweighed the long-term value of staying in school. What is the bottom line for Hector and millions like him? Because of his limited education and work skills, obligations to his family, and limited opportunities, he most likely will continue to live in poverty.

Sociologists are interested in the factors that influence the social world of children like Hector: family, friends, school, community, and the place of one's nation in the global political and economic structural systems. Sociologists use social theories and scientific methods to examine poverty and many other social issues. In this chapter you will learn about the theories sociologists utilize to make sense of their data and some of the different data collection methods sociologists use to collect information.

Sociological research helps us to understand how and why society operates and how we might change it. It can also help you make sense of why people in your family, neighborhood, college campus, and workplace act the way they do. You will, no doubt, find yourself in a situation where conducting a research study will help your organization or community.

This chapter will introduce you to the basic tools used to plan studies and gather dependable information

Slum dwellers of São Paulo, Brazil. Hector lives in a neighborhood with shelters made of available materials such as boxes, with no electricity or running water, and poor sanitation.

on topics of interest. It will also help you understand how sociology approaches research questions. To this end, we begin this chapter by discussing the development of sociology as a discipline and the core principles of sociology's major theoretical perspectives. We then explore sociology as a science—core ideas that underlie any science, how to collect data, ethical issues involving research, and practical applications and uses of sociological knowledge. We start with the beginnings and emergence of sociology as a field of study.

THE DEVELOPMENT OF SOCIOLOGY

Throughout recorded history, humans have been curious about how and why society operates as it does. Both religious and philosophical leaders influenced how people thought about the world and how society should operate. For example, Plato, one of the world's most famous philosophers, wrote *The Republic* around 400 BCE. In it, he outlines plans for an ideal state—complete with government, family, economic systems, class structure, and education—designed to achieve social justice. His and other philosophers' opinions were derived from abstract reflection about how the social world should work but were not tested scientifically. The first person on record to suggest a systematic approach to explain the social world was North African Islamic scholar Ibn Khaldun (1332–1406).

Khaldun was particularly interested in understanding the feelings of solidarity that held tribal groups together during his day, a time of great conflict and wars (Alatas 2006; Hozien n.d.). With this beginning came the rise of modern sociology.

The Rise of Modern Sociology

Several conditions from the 1600s to the 1800s gave rise to sociology. First, European nations were imperial powers extending their influence and control by establishing colonies in other cultures. This exposure to other cultures encouraged at least some Europeans to learn more about the people in and around their new colonies. Second, they sought to understand the rapid changes in their own societies brought about by the Industrial Revolution (which began around the middle of the 1700s) and the French Revolution (1789–1799). Finally, advances in the natural sciences demonstrated the value of the scientific method, and some wished to apply this scientific method to understand the social world.

In the early and mid-1800s, no one had clear, systematic explanations for why the old social structure, which had lasted since the early Middle Ages, was collapsing or why cities were exploding with migrants from rural areas. French society was in turmoil, members of the nobility were being executed, and new rules of justice were taking hold. Churches were made subordinate to the state, equal rights under the law were established for citizens, and democratic

The Bastille, a state prison in Paris, France, and a symbol of oppression, was seized by the common people during the French Revolution, a social upheaval that forced social analysts to think differently about society and social stability. Today, rallying points for social movements and revolutions such as Tahrir Square in Cairo, Egypt, illustrate that uprisings of the common people are still changing societies.

▶ History of Sociology   📖 Scientific Method

rule emerged. These dramatic changes marked the end of the traditional monarchy and the beginning of a new social order.

It was in this setting that the scientific study of society emerged. Two social thinkers, Henri Saint-Simon (1760–1825) and Auguste Comte (1798–1857), decried the lack of systematic data collection or objective analysis in social thought. These Frenchmen argued that a science of society could help people understand and perhaps control the rapid changes and unsettling revolutions taking place.

Comte officially coined the term *sociology* in 1838. His basic premise was that religious or philosophical speculation about society did not provide an adequate understanding of how to solve society's problems. Just as the scientists compiled basic facts about the *physical* world, so, too, was there a need to gather scientific knowledge about the *social* world. Only then could leaders systematically apply this scientific knowledge to improve social conditions.

Comte asked two basic questions: What holds society together and gives rise to a stable order in lieu of anarchy? Further, why and how do societies change? Comte conceptualized society as divided into two parts: (1) *social statics*, aspects of society that give rise to order, stability, and harmony, and (2) *social dynamics*, forces that promote change and evolution in society. Comte was concerned with what contemporary sociologists and the social world model in this book refer to as *structure* (social statics) and *process* (social dynamics). By understanding these aspects of the social world, Comte felt that leaders could strengthen society and respond appropriately to change. His optimistic belief was that sociology would be the "queen of sciences," guiding leaders to construct a better social order (Comte [1855] 2003).

Sociology continued developing as scholars contemplated further changes brought about by the Industrial Revolution. Massive social and economic transformations in the 18th and 19th centuries brought about restructuring and sometimes the demise of political monarchies, aristocracies, and feudal lords. Scenes of urban squalor were common in Great Britain and other industrializing European nations. Machines replaced both agricultural workers and cottage (home) industries because they produced an abundance of goods faster, better, and cheaper. Peasants were pushed off the land by new technologies and migrated to urban areas to find work; at the same time

a powerful new social class of capitalists was emerging. Industrialization brought the need for a new skilled class of laborers, putting new demands on an education system that had served only the elite. Families now depended on work and wages in the industrial sector to stay alive.

These changes stimulated other social scientists to study society and its problems. The writings of Émile Durkheim, Karl Marx, Harriet Martineau, Max Weber, W. E. B. Du Bois, and many other early sociologists set the stage for the development of sociological theories. Accompanying the development of sociological theory was the utilization of the scientific method—the systematic gathering and recording of reliable and accurate data to test ideas. First, we turn to sociology's major theoretical perspectives.

SOCIOLOGY'S MAJOR THEORETICAL PERSPECTIVES

A **theoretical perspective** is *a basic view of society that guides sociologists' research and analysis.* Theoretical perspectives are the broadest theories in sociology, providing overall approaches to understanding the social world and social problems. Sociologists draw on major theoretical perspectives at each level of analysis to guide their research and to help them understand social interactions and social organizations. **Theories** are *more specific statements or explanations regarding how and why two or more facts are related to each other and the connections between these facts.* A good theory also allows social scientists to make *predictions* about the social world.

Recall the description of the social world model presented in Chapter 1. It stresses the levels of analysis—smaller units existing within larger social systems. Some theories are especially useful when trying to understand micro-level interactions, while others tend to be used to make sense of macro-level structures. Either type of theory—those most useful at the micro or macro levels—can be used at the meso level, depending on the research question being asked. To illustrate four of the major theoretical perspectives on the social world, we will delve into our examination of Hector's circumstances, described at the beginning of this chapter.

▶ Three Theoretical Perspectives in Sociology

Micro- to Meso-Level Theories

If we wanted to study Hector's interactions with his friends and their influence on him or his school performance, we would turn to micro- and meso-level theories to guide our research. Two theories most often used at the micro and meso levels of analysis are symbolic interaction and rational choice theory.

Symbolic Interaction Theory. Symbolic interaction theory (also called social constructionism or interpretative theory) *sees humans as active agents who create shared meanings of symbols and events, and then interact on the basis of those meanings.* Through these interactions, we learn to share common ideas, understand what to expect from others, and gain the capability to shape society. As we interact, we make use of symbols, *actions or objects that represent something else and therefore have meaning beyond their own existence*—such as flags, wedding rings, words, and nonverbal gestures. Symbolic communication (e.g., language) helps people construct a meaningful world. Humans continually create and re-create society through their construction and interpretation of the social world. More than any other theory in the social sciences, symbolic interaction theory stresses *human agency*—the active role of individuals in creating their social environment.

George Herbert Mead (1863–1931), one of the founders of the symbolic interaction perspective, explored the mental processes associated with how humans define or make sense of situations (Mead [1934] 1962). He placed special emphasis on human interpretations of gestures and symbols (including language) and the meanings we attach to our actions. He also examined how we learn our social roles in society that include *expected behaviors, rights, obligations, responsibilities, and privileges assigned to a social status* (such as mother, child, teacher, and friend) and how we learn to carry out these roles. Indeed, as we will see in Chapter 4, he insisted that our notion of who we are—our *self*—emerges from social experience and interaction with others. Language is critical to this process, for it allows us to step outside of our own experience and reflect back on how others see us.

These ideas of how we construct our individual social worlds and have some control over them represent one approach of symbolic interactionism (known as the Chicago School). Another symbolic interaction approach (the Iowa School) makes a clear link between a person's individual identity and his or her position within organizations. This connects the micro and meso levels of the social system (Kuhn 1964). If we hold several positions—honors student, club president, daughter, sister, student, athlete, thespian, middle-class person—those positions form our *self.* We will interpret new situations in light of our social positions, some of which are very important and anchor how we see the social world. Once a core *self* is established, it guides and shapes the way we interact with people in many situations—even new social settings (Kuhn 1964). Thus, if you are president of an organization and have the responsibility for overseeing the organization, part of your self-esteem, your view of responsible citizenship, and your attitude toward life will be shaped by that position. Thus, the Iowa School of symbolic interaction places less emphasis on individual choice, but more on recognizing the link between the micro, meso, and macro levels of society (Carrothers and Benson 2003; Stryker 1980).

To summarize, the modern symbolic interaction theory emphasizes the following:

- People continually create and re-create society through interacting with one another.
- People interact by communicating with one another through the use of shared symbols.
- We learn who we are (our sense of self) and our place in society through interacting with others.

Critique of the Symbolic Interaction Theory. Each theory has its critics. Although symbolic interaction theory is widely used by sociologists today, it is often criticized for neglecting the macro-level structures of society that affect human behavior. By focusing on interpersonal interactions, large-scale social forces such as an economic depression or a political revolution that shape human destinies are given less consideration. With the focus on the ability of each individual to create his or her meaning in social situations (called *agency*), symbolic interaction has often been less attuned to important macro-level issues of social class position, social power, historical circumstances, or international conflict between societies (Meltzer, Petras, and Reynolds 1975). For example, if we focused only on how Hector interacts with his family and friends in trying to determine why he dropped out of school, we would overlook macro forces (e.g., how the lack of government supports for poor families impacted his decision to drop out of school). Another critique is that it is difficult to study abstract ideas like "the development of the self," key to symbolic interaction theory.

Despite these limitations, theorists from the symbolic interaction perspective have made significant contributions to understanding the development of social identities and interactions that underlie groups, organizations, and societies. Many of these studies will be discussed in chapters throughout the book.

Rational Choice (Exchange) Theory. According to rational choice theory, *humans are fundamentally concerned with self-interests, making rational decisions based on weighing costs and rewards of the projected outcome of an action.* Someone from this perspective might say Hector would picture the situation as if it were a mental balance sheet: For example, on the plus side, staying in school may lead to future opportunities not available to the uneducated. On the minus side, school is a negative experience, and the family needs help to feed its members now, so going to school is a "waste of time." Which side will win depends on Hector's balance sheet, and on family and friends' influence over the rewards versus costs.

Rational choice, also called *exchange theory*, has its roots in several disciplines—economics, behavioral psychology, anthropology, and philosophy (Cook, O'Brien, and Kollock 1990). Social behavior is seen as an exchange activity—a transaction in which resources are given and received (Blau 1964; Homans 1974). Every interaction involves an exchange of something valued—money, time, material goods, attention, sex, allegiance, and so on. People stay in relationships because they get something from the exchange, and they leave relationships that have more costs than benefits for them. They constantly evaluate whether there is reciprocity or balance in a relationship, so that they are receiving as much as they give. Simply stated, people are more likely to act if they see some reward or success coming from their behavior. The implication is that self-interest for the individual is the guiding element in human interaction.

In summary, rational choice theory involves the following key ideas:

- Human beings are mostly self-centered, and self-interest drives their behavior.
- Humans calculate costs and benefits (rewards) in making decisions.

- Humans are rational in that they weigh choices in order to maximize their own benefits and minimize costs.
- Every interaction involves exchanges entailing rewards and penalties or expenditures.
- A key element in exchanges is reciprocity—a balance in the exchange of benefits.
- People keep a mental ledger in their heads about whether they owe someone else or that person owes them.

Critique of the Rational Choice Theory. Rational choice theorists give little attention to micro-level internal mental processes, such as self-reflection. They see human conduct as self-centered, with rational behavior implying that people seek to maximize rewards and minimize costs. Charitable, unselfish, or

©iStockphoto.com/Varinca

According to rational choice theory, people avoid cost or pain and seek benefits. Thus, people in authority try to control others—like this small child—by imposing cost for behaviors that are unwanted. The cost for this girl of "time out" in school is both boredom and humiliation, and the authority figure—a teacher—hopes it will lead to more desired behaviors.

altruistic behavior is not easily explained by this view. Why would a soldier sacrifice his or her life to save a comrade? Why would a starving person in a Nazi concentration camp share a crust of bread with another? Proponents of rational choice counter the criticism by arguing that if a person feels good about helping another, that in itself is a reward that compensates for the cost.

Thinking Sociologically

How can symbolic interaction and rational choice perspectives help explain dating behavior? For example, how might a "hookup" mean something different to females as opposed to males? How would each of the micro theories above answer this question a bit differently?

Meso- and Macro-Level Theories

Meso- and macro-level theories consider large units in the social world: organizations (e.g., General Motors or the Episcopal Church), institutions (such as education, religion, health care, politics, or economics), societies (Canada or Mexico), or global systems (the World Trade Organization or World Bank). For example, Hector's government at the national and international levels affects his life in a variety of ways. As Brazil industrializes, the nature of jobs and the modes of communication change. Local village cultures adjust as the entire nation gains more uniformity of values, beliefs, and norms. Similarly, resources such as access to clean water may be allotted at the local level, but local communities need national and sometimes international support, as illustrated in the photo of tribal elders from Tanzania. We can begin to understand how the process of modernization influences Hector, this village in Tanzania, and other people around the globe by looking at two major macro-level perspectives: the structural-functional and conflict theories.

Structural-Functional Theory. The <u>structural-functional theory</u>, also called <u>functional theory</u>, *assumes that all parts of the social structure (including groups, organizations, and institutions), the culture (values and beliefs), and social processes (e.g., social change or child rearing) work together to make the whole society run smoothly and harmoniously.* To understand the social world from this perspective, we must look at how the parts of society (structure) fit together and

The Tanzanian village elders in this photo continue to have authority to make local (micro-level) decisions about the traditional irrigation canals being improved in their village, but their expanded water supply is possible in part because of international financial support (meso- and macro-level decisions).

how each part contributes to the maintenance of society. For instance, two functions (purposes) of the family include having children and teaching them to be members of society. These and other functions help perpetuate society, for without reproducing and teaching new members to fit in, societies would collapse.

Émile Durkheim (1858–1917) was the founder of the functionalist perspective. He theorized that society is made up of necessary parts that fit together into a working whole. Durkheim believed that individuals conform to the rules of societies because of a *collective conscience*—the shared beliefs in the values of a group (Durkheim 1947). People grow up sharing the same values, beliefs, and rules of behavior as those around them. Gradually, individuals internalize these shared beliefs and rules. A person's behavior is, in a sense, governed from within because it feels right and proper to behave in accordance with what is expected. As such, the functionalist perspective of Durkheim and subsequent theorists places emphasis on social consensus, which gives rise to stable and predictable patterns of order in society. Because people need groups for survival, they adhere to the group's rules so that they do not stand apart from it. This means that most societies run in an orderly manner, with most individuals fitting into their positions in society.

Functions (consequences of an action or behavior) can be manifest or latent. **Manifest functions** are *the planned outcomes of interactions, social organizations, or institutions.* Some of the planned consequences of the microwave oven, for instance, have been to allow people to prepare meals quickly and easily, facilitating life in overworked and stressed modern families. __Latent functions__ are *unplanned or unintended consequences of actions or of social structures* (Merton 1938, [1942] 1973). Some of the unplanned consequences of microwave ovens were the creation of a host of new jobs and stimulation of the economy, as people wrote new cookbooks and as businesses were formed to produce microwavable cookware and prepared foods ready for the microwave.

Latent functions can be functional or dysfunctional. Functional actions contribute to the stability or equilibrium of society while __dysfunctions__ are *those actions that undermine the stability or equilibrium of society* (Merton 1938). For example, by allowing people to prepare meals without using a stove or conventional oven, the microwave oven has contributed to some young people having no idea how to cook, thus making them highly dependent on expensive technology and processed foods, and in some cases adding to problems of obesity.

From a functionalist theory perspective, it is important to examine the possible functional and dysfunctional aspects of life in society in order to maintain harmony and balance.

To summarize, the structural-functional perspective

- examines the macro-level organizations and patterns in society;
- focuses on what holds societies together and enhances social continuity;
- considers the consequences or "functions" of each major part in society;
- focuses on the way the structure (groups, organizations, institutions), the culture, and social processes work together to make society function smoothly; and
- considers manifest functions (which are planned), latent functions (which are unplanned or secondary), and dysfunctions (which undermine stability).

Critique of the Structural-Functional Perspective. Some ideas put forth by functional theorists are so abstract that they are difficult to test with data. Moreover, functionalism does not explain social changes in society, such as conflict and revolution. As we try to understand the many societal upheavals in the world, from suicide bombings in the Middle East to the economic privatization movements in China, it is clear that

Although the microwave oven and fast-food restaurants have had many benefits for a society in a hurry, one dysfunction is the deterioration of health—especially due to obesity.

dramatic social change is possible. The functionalist assumption is that if a system is running smoothly, it must be working well because it is free from conflict. It assumes that conflict is harmful, even though we know that stability may come about because of ruthless dictators suppressing the population. In short, stability is not always good.

Thinking Sociologically

Describe a manifest and a latent function of the system of higher education in the United States today. Is the latent function dysfunctional? Why or why not?

Conflict Theory. In many ways, __conflict theory__ turns the structural-functional theory on its head. Conflict theorists contend that conflict is inevitable in any group or society. They claim that inequality and injustice are the source of the conflicts that permeate society. Resources and power are distributed unequally in society, so some members have more money, goods, and prestige than others. The rich protect their positions by using the power they have accumulated to keep others in their places. From the perspective of poor people such as Hector, it seems the rich get all the breaks. Most of us want more of the resources in society (money, good jobs, nice houses, and cars), causing the possibility of conflict between the haves and the have-nots. These conflicts sometimes bring about a change in society.

Modern conflict theory has its origins in the works of Karl Marx (1818–1883), a German social philosopher who lived in England during the height of 19th-century industrial expansion. Capitalism had emerged as the dominant economic system in Europe. *Capitalism* is an economic system in which individuals and corporations, rather than the state, own and control the means of production (e.g., factories). As they compete for profits, some win while others lose.

Marx recognized the plight of workers toiling in factories in the new industrial states of Europe and viewed the ruling elites and the wealthy industrial owners as exploiters of the working class. Marx wrote about the new working class crowded in urban slums, working long hours under appalling conditions, without earning enough money for decent housing and food. Few of the protections enjoyed by many (but not all) workers today—such as retirement benefits, health coverage, sick leave, the 40-hour workweek, and restrictions against child labor—existed in Marx's time.

Marx believed that two classes, the capitalists (also referred to as the bourgeoisie or "haves"), who owned the **means of production** (*property, machinery, and cash owned by capitalists*), and the workers (also referred to as the proletariat or "have-nots"), would continue to live in conflict until the workers shared more equally in the profits of their labor. The more workers came to understand their plight, the more aware they would become of the injustice of the situation. Eventually, Marx believed, workers would rise up and overthrow capitalism, forming a new, classless society. Collective ownership—shared ownership of the *means of production*—would be the new economic order (Marx and Engels [1848] 1969).

The idea of the *bourgeoisie* (the capitalist exploiters who own the factories) and the *proletariat* (the exploited workers who sell their labor) has carried over into analysis of modern-day conflicts among groups in society. For example, from a conflict perspective, Hector in Brazil and millions like him in other countries are part of the reserve labor force—a cheap labor pool that can be called on when labor is needed and disregarded when demand is low, thus meeting the changing labor needs of industry and capitalism. This pattern results in permanent economic insecurity and poverty for Hector and those like him.

Many branches of the conflict perspective have grown from the original ideas of Marx. Here we mention three contributions to conflict theory, those of American sociologists Harriet Martineau ([1837] 1962), W. E. B. Du Bois ([1899] 1967), and Ralf Dahrendorf (1959). As you can see, social conflict has been a major focus of sociological investigation.

Harriet Martineau (1802–1876), generally considered the first female sociologist, wrote several books that contribute to our understanding of modern sociological research methods and provided a critique, at the time, of failure of the United States to live up to its democratic principles, especially as they related to women. She argued that social laws influence social behavior and that societies can be measured on their social progress (including how much freedom they give to individuals, and how well they treat the most oppressed members of society). Her work represents the foundation of current feminist and conflict theories (Martineau 1838).

Another early American conflict theorist was W. E. B. Du Bois (1868–1963), the first African American to receive a doctorate from Harvard University. Du Bois, like other early sociological theorists, believed that, although research should be scientifically rigorous and fair-minded, the ultimate goal of sociological work was social improvement—not just human insight. Throughout his life, Du Bois documented and lambasted the status of black Americans, noting that African Americans were an integral part of U.S. society but not fully accepted into it.

Du Bois helped establish the National Association for the Advancement of Colored People (NAACP). He stressed the need for minority groups to become advocates for their rights—to object loudly when those in power act to disadvantage minorities—and to make society more just (Du Bois [1899] 1967). He was—and continues to be—an inspiration for many sociologists who believe that their findings should have real applications and be used to create a more humane social world (Mills 1956).

A half-century later, in 1959, Ralf Dahrendorf (1929–2009) argued that society is always in the process of change and affected by forces that bring about change. Dahrendorf refined Marx's ideas in several ways. He pointed out that capitalism had survived,

Harriet Martineau (left) published a critique of the United States' failure to live up to its democratic principles 11 years before Karl Marx's most famous work, but she was not taken seriously as a scholar for more than a century because she was female—the first feminist theorist. Karl Marx (center) is known as the founder of conflict theory. W. E. B. Du Bois (right) continued the development of conflict theory and was among the first to apply that theory to U.S. society, especially to issues of race.

despite Marx's prediction of a labor revolt, because of improved conditions for workers (e.g., unions, the establishment of labor laws, and workplace regulations). Dahrendorf also maintained that, instead of divisions based on ownership, conflict had become based on authority.

Dahrendorf noted that those with lower-status positions, such as Hector, could form interest groups and engage in conflict with those in higher positions of authority. *Interest groups*, such as the members of Hector's *favela*, share a common situation or interests. In Hector and his neighbors' case, these interests include a desire for sanitation, running water, electricity, jobs, and a higher standard of living. From within such interest groups, *conflict groups* arise to fight for changes. There is always potential for conflict when those without power realize their common position and form interest groups. How much change or violence is brought about depends on how organized those groups become.

Dahrendorf's major contribution is the recognition that conflict over resources results in a conflict not just between the proletariat and the bourgeoisie but among a multitude of interest groups including old people versus young people, rich versus poor, one region of the country versus another, Christians versus non-Christians, and so forth. This acknowledges multiple rifts in the society based on interest groups.

Whereas Marx emphasized the divisive nature of conflict, other theorists have offered a modified theory of conflict in society. American theorist Lewis Coser took a very different approach to conflict from that of Marx, arguing that it can strengthen societies and the organizations within them. According to Coser, problems in a society or group lead to complaints or conflicts—a warning message to the group that all is not well. Resolution of the conflicts shows that the group is adaptable in meeting the needs of its members, thereby creating greater loyalty to the group. Thus, conflict provides the message of what is not working to meet people's needs, and the system adapts to the needs for change because of the conflict (Coser 1956; Simmel 1955).

In summary, conflict theorists advance the following key ideas:

- Conflict and the potential for conflict underlie all social relations.
- Groups of people look out for their self-interest and try to obtain resources and make sure they are distributed primarily to members of their own group.
- Social change is desirable, particularly changes that bring about a greater degree of social equality.
- The existing social order reflects powerful people imposing their values and beliefs upon the weak.

Critique of the Conflict Theory. First, many conflict theorists focus on macro-level analysis and lose sight of the individuals involved in conflict situations, such as Hector and his family. Second, empirical research to test conflict theory is limited. The conflict perspective often paints a picture with rather broad brushstrokes.

Research to test the picture involves interpretations of broad spans of history and is more difficult to claim as scientific. Third, conflict theorists tend to focus on social stress, power dynamics, and disharmony. Conflict theory is not very effective in explaining social cohesion and cooperation. Fourth, many critics of conflict theory argue that altruism and cooperation are common human behaviors, but not recognized by conflict theory.

Thinking Sociologically

Imagine you are a legislator. You have to decide whether to cut funding for a senior citizens' program or slash a scholarship program for college students. You want to be reelected, and you know that approximately 90% of senior citizens are registered to vote and most actually do vote. You also know that less than half of college-age people are likely to vote. These constituencies are about the same size. What would you do, and how would you justify your decision? How does this example illustrate conflict theory?

Multilevel Analysis. Many contemporary theorists try to bridge the gap between micro and macro levels of analysis, offering insights relevant at each level. We examine two of these below.

Max Weber's Contributions. Max Weber (1864–1920), a German-born social scientist, has had a lasting effect on sociology and other social sciences. Weber (pronounced VAY-ber) cannot be pigeonholed easily into one of the theoretical categories or one level of analysis, for his contributions include both micro- and macro-level analyses. His emphasis on *Verstehen* (meaning deep empathetic understanding in humans) gives him a place in micro-level theory, and his discussions of power and bureaucracies give him a place in meso- and macro-level theory (Weber 1946).

Verstehen stems from the interpretations or meanings individuals at the micro level give to their social experiences. Weber argued that to understand people's behaviors, you must step into their shoes and see the world as they do. Following in Weber's footsteps, sociologists try to understand both human behavior and the meanings that people attach to their experiences. In this work, Weber is a micro theorist who set the stage for symbolic interaction theorists.

However, the goal-oriented, efficient new organizational form called bureaucracy was the focus of much of Weber's writing at the meso level. This organizational form was based on **rationality** (*the attempt to reach maximum efficiency with rules that are rationally designed to accomplish goals*) rather than relying on long-standing tradition for how things should be done. As we describe in Chapter 5, Weber's ideas about society at the meso level have laid the groundwork for a theoretical understanding of modern organizations.

Weber also attempted to understand macro-level processes. For instance, in his famous book *The Protestant Ethic and the Spirit of Capitalism* (Weber [1904–1905] 1958), he asked how capitalists (those who have money and control production) understood the world around them. His work was influenced by Marx's writings, but where Marx focused on economic conditions as the key factor shaping history and power relations, Weber argued that Marx's focus was too narrow. Weber felt that politics, economics, religion, psychology, and people's ideas are interdependent—affecting each other. In short, Weber thought that society was more complex than Karl Marx's theory that focused only on two groups—the haves and the have-nots—in conflict over economic resources. ·

Feminist Theory. Much of feminist theory has foundations in the conflict perspective. **Feminist theory** *critiques the hierarchical power structures that disadvantage women and other minorities* (Cancian 1992; Collins 2008). They note that men form an interest group intent on preserving their privileges. Feminists also argue that sociology has been dominated by a male perspective that does not give a complete view of the social world.

Some branches of feminist theory come from interaction perspectives, emphasizing the way gender socialization, cues, and symbols shape the nature of much human interaction. Thus, feminist theory moves from meso- and macro-level analysis (e.g., looking at national and global situations that give privileges to men) to micro-level analysis (e.g., looking at inequality between husbands and wives in marriage). In particular, feminist theory points to the importance of gender as a variable influencing social patterns (Brettell and Sargent 2008; Burn 2011; Kramer 2010; Lorber 2009).

Many people face inequality due to multiple factors, and it is the interplay of these factors that interests Patricia Hill Collins. An important contemporary scholar, Collins examines the discrimination and

Patricia Hill Collins, an innovative feminist scholar, has challenged sociologists to look at the ways experiences of race, social class, gender, and sexuality can intersect and reinforce one another.

oppression people face because of their race, class, gender, sexuality, or nationality, all of which are interconnected. Collins uses the term *intersectionality*, meaning individuals have multiple identities (e.g., race, class, and gender) that intersect and impact their life chances (2005, 2008).

⬤ Thinking Sociologically

To what extent are human beings free agents who can create their own social world and come up with their own ideas about how to live their lives? To what extent are our lives determined or influenced by the social systems around us and by our positions in the economic and political system?

Using Different Theoretical Perspectives

Each of the theoretical perspectives described in this chapter begins from a set of assumptions about humans. Each makes a contribution to our understanding, but each has limitations or blind spots, such as not taking into account other levels of analysis

(Ritzer 2011). Figure 2.1 provides a summary of cooperative versus competitive perspectives to illustrate how the theories differ.

The strength of a theory depends on its ability to explain and predict behavior accurately. Each theoretical perspective focuses on a different aspect of society and level of analysis and gives us a different lens through which to view our social world. The social world model helps us picture the whole system and determine which theory or theories best suits our needs in analyzing a specific social process or structure.

Thinking Sociologically

Consider the issue of homelessness in cities around the world. How could each of the theories discussed in this chapter be used to help us understand the problem of homelessness?

Scientists, including sociologists, often use theories to predict changes in society and under what conditions they are likely to occur. Theory tells the researcher what to look for and what concepts or variables need to be measured. However, explanations about the relationships between social variables need to be tested. This is where research methods—the procedures one uses to gather data—are relevant. Data must be carefully gathered and then used to assess the accuracy of theory. If a theory is not supported by the data, it must be reformulated or discarded. Theory and research are used together and are mutually dependent.

To study Hector's life in Brazil, researchers might focus on the micro-level interactions between Hector and his family members, peers, teachers, and employers as factors that contribute to his situation. For example, one theory could be that Hector's family has socialized him to believe that certain activities (for example, working) are more realistic or immediately rewarding than others (such as attending school). A meso-level focus might examine the influence of the organizations and institutions—such as the business world, the schools, and the religious communities in Brazil—to see how they shape the forces that affect Hector's life. Alternatively, the focus might be on macro-level analysis—the class structure (rich to poor) of the society and the global forces, such as trade relations between Brazil and other countries, that influence opportunities for Brazilians who live in poverty. Whatever the level of analysis, as

FIGURE 2.1 Cooperative Versus Competitive Perspectives

	Macro analysis	Micro analysis
Humans viewed as cooperative (people interact with others on the basis of shared meanings and common symbols)	*Structural-Functional Theory*	*Symbolic Interactionism Theory*
Humans viewed as competitive (behavior governed by self-interest)	*Conflict Theory* (group interests)	*Rational Choice Theory* (individual interests)

social *scientists*, sociologists utilize scientific methods of gathering evidence to disprove or to support theories about society.

IDEAS UNDERLYING SCIENCE

Throughout most of human history, people came to "know" the world by the traditions passed down from one generation to the next. Things were so because authoritative people in the culture said they were so. Often, there was reliance on magical, philosophical, or religious explanations of the forces in nature, and these explanations became part of tradition. For example, just 260 years ago, the conventional wisdom was that lightning storms were a sign of an angry god, not electricity caused by meteorological forces. As ways of knowing about the world shifted, tradition and magic as the primary means to understand the world were challenged. With advances in the natural sciences, observations of cause-and-effect processes became more systematic and controlled.

The scientific approach is based on several core ideas: First, there are real physical and social worlds that can be studied scientifically. Second, there is a certain order to the world, with identifiable patterns that result from a series of causes and effects. The world is not merely a collection of unrelated random events; rather, events occur in a systematic sequence and in patterns—that is, they are *causally* related. Third, the way to gain knowledge of the world is to subject it to empirical testing. **Empirical knowledge** *is founded on information gained from evidence (facts), rather than intuition.* **Evidence** refers to *facts and observations that can be objectively observed and carefully measured using the five senses (sometimes enhanced by scientific instruments).*

For knowledge to be scientific, it must be observable and measurable. Phenomena that cannot be subject to measurement are not within the realm of scientific inquiry. For example, the existence of God, the devil, heaven, hell, and the soul cannot be observed and measured and therefore cannot be examined scientifically. Religion, however, can be studied scientifically by looking at the role it plays in society and our lives, its impact on our values and behavior (the sociology of religion), the historical development of specific religious traditions (the history of religion), or the emotional comfort and stability it brings to people (the psychology of religion). Finally, science is rooted in **objectivity**; that is, *one must take steps to ensure that one's personal opinions or values do not bias or contaminate data collection and analysis.* Scientists are obliged not to distort their research findings so as to promote a particular point of view. Scientific research is judged first on whether it relies on careful efforts to be objective. Social scientists, like all scientists, must explain what the data reveal, not what they wish it would reveal! Researchers must be open to finding results that support *or* disprove their **hypothesis** (*an educated guess or prediction*).

Failure to meet these standards—empirical knowledge, objectivity, and scientific evidence—means that a study is not scientific. Someone's ideas can seem plausible and logical but may still not be supported by

▶ The Wisdom of Sociology 　　　 📄 Obesity and Health

the facts. This is why evidence (facts) is so important. Sociology is concerned with using accurate evidence, and it is important to know what is or is not considered accurate. Perhaps you have seen an episode of the *CSI: Crime Scene Investigation* or *Bones* series on television. The shows in these series depict the importance of careful collection of data and commitment to objective analysis. Sociologists deal with different issues, but the same sort of concern for accuracy in gathering data guides their work. When sociologists establish theories as to why society works as it does, they must test those theories using scientific methods.

HOW SOCIOLOGISTS STUDY THE SOCIAL WORLD

Suppose you have a research question you want to answer, such as "Why do boys like Hector drop out of school?" In order for your research to be scientific, you must follow the basic steps of the scientific research process.

A. Planning a Research Study
  * *Step 1:* Define a topic or problem that can be studied scientifically.
  * *Step 2:* Review existing relevant research studies and theory to refine the topic and define **variables**, *concepts (ideas) that can vary in frequency of occurrence from one time, place, or person to another* (such as age, ethnicity, religion, or level of education).
  * *Step 3:* Formulate hypotheses or research questions and determine how to define and measure the variables.

B. Designing the Research Plan and Method for Collecting the Data
  * *Step 4:* Design the research plan that specifies how the data will be gathered.
  * *Step 5:* Select a **sample**, *a group of systematically chosen people who represent a much larger group to study*.
  * *Step 6:* Collect the data using appropriate research methods.

C. Making Sense of the Data
  * *Step 7:* Analyze the data and relate it to previous findings on the topic, concluding exactly what the study says about the research question(s) from Step 3.
  * *Step 8:* Draw conclusions and present the final report, including suggestions for future research. Recommendations for actions may be part of the report.

Planning a Research Study

To study Hector's situation, the researcher uses Step 1 to define a topic or problem, including the variables to be studied. Step 2 requires the researcher to review past studies on related topics to see what has been done and how variables were defined in other studies. This review provides the basis for Step 3.

In Step 3, researchers must link concepts, such as poverty or dropping out of school, to specific measurements. For example, the researcher could hypothesize that poverty is a major cause of *favela* teenagers dropping out of school because they need to earn money for their families. Who is a dropout might be determined by school records indicating whether that child has attended school during the past six months. Poverty could be defined as having a low annual income—say less than half of the average income for that size of family in the country—or by assessing ownership of property such as cattle, automobiles, and indoor plumbing. It is important for researchers to be clear, precise, and consistent in how they measure their variables.

In order to conduct research to test a theory, researchers formulate a hypothesis, a statement they can test to determine if it is true. This is called *deductive research*. It starts with a theory that you then test. *Inductive research* starts with observations that then lead to hypothesis development and, potentially, theory formation. Researchers make an observation and then begin to collect more data to determine if what they witnessed initially was a social pattern. Once they start to notice social patterns, they can begin to analyze those patterns using appropriate existing theories, or they can create a new theory if existing ones do not provide needed explanations.

Whether you use inductive or deductive research, you must always carefully define your variables and determine how they interact with and relate to one another. The relationship between variables is central to understanding *causality*. Causal reasoning is discussed in the next "Engaging Sociology."

ENGAGING SOCIOLOGY

Being Clear About Causality

Sociology as a science tries to be very careful about language—more precise than we usually are in our everyday conversations. What do we really mean when we say that something causes something else? At the heart of the research process is the effort to find causal relationships (i.e., one variable causes another one to change). The following key terms are important in understanding how two variables (concepts that vary in frequency and can be measured) are related:

Correlation

X ←————————————→ Y

- **Correlation** *refers to a relationship between variables (such as poverty and low levels of education), with change in one variable associated with change in another.* The hypothesis above predicts that poverty and teenagers dropping out of school are related and vary together. That is, when the poverty level is high, dropping out of school is also high. If we claim that there is a correlation, however, that is only the first step. We have not yet established that change in one variable *causes* a change in the other.

Cause and Effect Variables

X ←————————————→ Y

- **Cause-and-effect relationships** *occur when there is a relationship between variables so that one variable stimulates a change in another.* Once we have determined that there is probably a relationship, or correlation (the fact that the two variables, such as poverty and dropping out of school, both occur in the same situation), we need to take the next step: analyzing which comes first and seeing if one variable causes change in another. The **independent variable** *is the variable in a cause-and-effect relationship that comes first in a time sequence and causes a change in another variable—the* **dependent variable**. If we hypothesize that poverty causes Hector and others to drop out of school, *poverty* is the independent variable in this hypothesis, and *dropping out of school* is the dependent variable, dependent on the poverty. In determining cause and effect, the independent variable must always precede the dependent variable in time sequence if we

want to try to determine whether the independent variable causes a change in the dependent variable.

Spurious Relationships

- **Spurious relationships** *occur when there is no causal relationship between the independent and dependent variables, but they vary together, often due to a third variable affecting both of them.* For example, if the quantity of ice cream consumed is highest during those weeks of the year when most drownings occur, these two events are correlated. However, eating ice cream did not cause the increase in deaths. Indeed, hot weather may have caused more people both to purchase ice cream and to go swimming, with the larger number of swimmers resulting in more drowning incidents. The connection between ice cream and drownings is a *spurious relationship*.

Controls

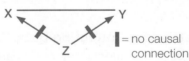

- **Controls** *are steps used by researchers to eliminate all variables except those related to the hypothesis—especially those variables that might be spurious.* Using controls helps ensure that the relationship is not spurious. Using the ice cream example, we might study beaches where lots of ice cream is sold and beaches where none is available in order to compare water death incidents. If there is no difference in death rates, the drownings cannot be caused by the ice cream.

Engaging With Sociology

1. Think of a possible cause-and-effect relationship that you would like to study.

2. Determine your independent and dependent variables.

3. What variables would you have to control for in order to determine that the relationship between your independent and dependent variables is not spurious or just a correlation?

Thinking Sociologically

Think of a research question based on a theoretical perspective. For example, you might ask how Hector's peers affect his decisions, using a micro-level theory. Then write a hypothesis and identify your variables in the hypothesis.

Designing the Research Method and Collecting the Data

Researchers must always make clear how they collect their data. Every research study should be replicable—capable of being repeated—by other researchers. So, enough information must be given to ensure that another researcher could repeat the study and compare results.

The appropriate data collection method depends on the level(s) of analysis of the research question (micro, meso, or macro) the researcher is asking. For example, if you want to answer a macro-level research question, such as the effect of poverty on students dropping out of school in Brazil, you should focus on large-scale social and economic data sources such as the Brazilian census. To learn about micro-level issues such as the influence of peers on an individual's decision to drop out of school, you will need to examine small-group interactions at the micro level. Figure 2.2 illustrates the different levels of analysis.

Designing a Method for Collecting Data. The primary methods used to collect data for research

studies include questionnaires, interviews, observational studies, secondary data analysis, content analysis, and experiments. Some methods produce *quantitative* (numerical) data while others supply *qualitative* (nonnumerical) data such as individuals' open-ended responses. Questionnaires and secondary data analysis tend to be quantitative and used when conducting macro- and meso-level studies. Interviews, observational studies, and content analysis usually produce qualitative data or a blend of quantitative and qualitative data, and are primarily used for micro-level research. Some studies include both quantitative and qualitative data.

<u>Interviews</u> *are conducted by talking directly with people and asking questions in person or by telephone.* Both unstructured and semistructured interviews, which allow respondents to answer questions in a more open-ended manner, evolve in response to what the researcher learns as the research progresses.

<u>Questionnaires</u> *contain questions and other types of items designed to solicit information appropriate to analysis of research questions* (Babbie 2014). They are convenient for collecting large amounts of data because they can be distributed by mail or sent by email to respondents.

<u>Observational studies</u> (also called field research) *involve systematic, planned observation and recording of interactions or human behavior in their natural settings (where the activity normally takes place rather than in a laboratory).* They can take different forms: (1) observations in which the researcher

FIGURE 2.2 The Social World Model and Levels of Analysis

Micro Level	
Individual	Hector
Small group	Hector's family and close friends
Local community	The *favela*; Hector's local school, church, neighborhood organizations
Meso Level	
Organizations	Brazilian corporations, Catholic Church, and local school system in Brazil
Institutions	Family; education; political, economic, and health systems in the region or nation of
Ethnic subcultures	Brazil Native peoples, African-Brazilians
Macro Level	
National society	Social policies, trends, and programs in Brazil
Globlal community of nations	Status of Brazil in global economy; trade relations with other countries; programs of international organizations or corporations

 The Nature of Science and the Scientific Method

actually participates in the activities of the group being studied or (2) observations in which the researcher is not involved in group activities but observes or videotapes the activity. It is important for observers to avoid influencing or altering group functioning and interaction by their presence.

Thinking Sociologically

If you were trying to compare how effectively two professors teach a research methods course offered in your department, what variables might you use, and what variables might you need to control? How would you set up your study? What methods would you use?

Secondary analysis *uses existing data, information that has already been collected.* Often, large data-collecting organizations, such as the United Nations or a country's census bureau, the national education department, or a private research organization, will make data available for use by researchers. Consider the question of the dropout rate in Brazil. Researchers can learn a great deal about the behavior of school dropouts as a group from analysis of information gathered by ministries or departments of education. Likewise, if we want to compare modern dropout rates with those of an earlier time, we may find data from previous decades to be invaluable. Secondary analysis can be an excellent way to do meso- or macro-level studies that reveal large-scale patterns in the social world.

Content analysis *involves systematic categorizing and recording of information from written or recorded sources.* With content analysis (a common method in historical research and study of organizations), sociologists can gather the data they need from printed materials—books, magazines, newspapers, laws, letters, comments on websites, emails, videos, archived radio broadcasts, or even artwork. They develop a coding system to classify the source content. A researcher trying to understand shifts in Brazilian attitudes toward youth poverty in *favelas* could do a content analysis of popular magazines to see how many pages or stories were devoted to child poverty in the Brazilian media each decade from the 1960s to the present. Content analysis has the advantage of being relatively inexpensive and easy to do. It is also *unobtrusive,* meaning that the researcher does not influence the participants being investigated by having direct

Census questionnaires are taken in the United States and many other countries every 10 years. Sometimes it is difficult to gather accurate data on the entire population, as in the situation with this census worker, who is counting homeless people in Penn Station in New York City.

contact with them. Furthermore, examining materials in historical sequence can be effective in recognizing patterns over time.

In experiments, *all variables except the one being studied are controlled so researchers can study the effects on the variable under study.* An experiment usually requires an experimental group, in which *subjects in the group are exposed to the variable being studied to test the effects of that variable on human behavior,* and a control group, in which *the subjects are not exposed to the variable the researcher wants to test.* The control group provides a baseline with which the experimental group can be compared.

Experiments are powerful because they are the most accurate test of cause and effect. They make it possible to control most variables (eliminating irrelevant spurious variables) and determine the sequence in which variables affect each other. By separating the sample into experimental and control groups, the researcher can see if the study's independent variable makes a difference in the behavior of people who are exposed to that variable compared with those who are not. Psychologists use lab experiments, but few sociologists use this method because many sociological questions cannot be studied in controlled settings. For example, Hector's environment in the *favela* cannot be studied in a laboratory setting.

Control and experimental research projects outside of a lab setting are more common among sociologists. For example, researchers may want to determine whether a new teaching method using technology might help children from Hector's *favela*. We can do so by comparing a control group, exposed to the usual teaching, and an experimental group, provided with the new method or experimental technology. We must ensure that the control and experimental groups of children are at the same academic level and that the teachers are equally motivated and prepared when teaching both classes. With this carefully designed research project, we can conclude that the new approach increases learning if the children in the experimental group score significantly higher on the final exam than those in the control group.

Triangulation *refers to the utilization of two or more methods of data collection to enhance the amount and type of data for analysis and the accuracy of the findings.* To study Hector's situation, a research study could use macro-level quantitative data on poverty and on educational statistics in Brazil and micro-level interviews with Hector and his peers to determine their goals and their attitudes toward education. If all findings point to the same conclusion, the researcher can feel much more confident about the study results.

Selecting a Sample. It would be impossible to interview or send a questionnaire to every school dropout in Brazil to determine why the teenage dropout rate is so high. It is possible to study a portion of that population, however. The research design process includes determining how to make sure the study includes people who are typical of the total group (or population) you want to learn about. This involves careful selection of

Social scientists aren't the only professionals who use triangulation. Journalists also consult a variety of sources, including, at times, social scientists, to put together news broadcasts.

a *sample*, a group systematically chosen to represent a much larger group.

Researchers use many types of samples. A common one, the representative sample, attempts to accurately reflect the group being studied so that the sample results can be generalized or applied to the larger group or population. In the case of studying why so many boys from Hector's *favela* drop out of school, a representative sample for a study could be drawn from all 13- to 16-year-olds in his region or city in Brazil.

The most common form of representative sample is the *random sample*. People from every walk of life and every group within the population have an equal chance of being selected for the study. By observing or talking with this smaller group selected from the total population under study, the researcher can get an accurate picture of the total population and have confidence that the findings apply to the larger group. Developing an effective sampling technique is often a complex process. In the case of Brazil, people constantly move in and out of the *favela*. Those who have just arrived may not have the same characteristics as those who have been living there a long time, but it is important to have a sample that represents the whole group being studied. Samples also must be large enough to accurately represent a population and to use statistical programs to analyze the data. If you take a methods course, you will delve further into these details of sampling and data analysis discussed below.

Making Sense of the Data: Analyzing Data and Drawing Conclusions

Once you have collected your data from your sample, you have to analyze it. Imagine that you have 100 interviews from residents of Hector's *favela*, plus a notebook full of field observation notes from "hanging out" with the youth there. What do you do with the data? Social researchers use multiple techniques to analyze data, but whatever techniques they use, they look for patterns in the data and then use theories and findings from past research on the topic to make sense of those patterns.

Presenting Your Findings. The final step in the research process is a report that presents a discussion of the results, draws conclusions as to whether or not the hypotheses were supported or answers were found for the research question, interprets the results, and makes recommendations on how to use the findings, if appropriate. As part of the presentation and discussion of results, the report may contain tables or figures presenting summaries of data to help the reader easily understand the patterns found in the data. The "Engaging Sociology" on page 44 provides useful tips on reading research tables found in journal articles and news magazines.

Ethical Issues in Social Research

What happens if a scientist conducts research that has negative impacts on the participants? It is due to this concern that most universities and other research organizations, especially those receiving public money, have human subjects review boards. The boards review the proposed research plans and methods to be used to be sure they will *not* hurt the subjects. Of special concern are research projects in medical sciences, but social scientists must also have their research reviewed.

Sociologists and other scientists are bound by the ethical codes of conduct governing research. The American Sociological Association (ASA) code of ethics outlines standards that researchers are expected to observe when doing research, teaching, and publishing. They include

- explaining the uses and consequences of the research, and gaining informed consent from respondents;
- taking steps to ensure the privacy of respondents;
- being objective, reporting findings and sources fully;
- making no promises to respondents that cannot be honored;
- accepting no support that requires violation of these principles;
- completing contracted work; and
- delineating responsibilities in works with multiple authors.

Examples of unethical research include studying people without their knowledge or consent, only including data that support the results you would like to see, and violating the confidentiality of your subjects by revealing their identity. The bottom line is that researchers must do everything they can to protect their subjects from harm.

Thinking Sociologically

What might be some ethical problems in a research project you would like to conduct? What, for example, might be the ethical issues of studying a setting or situation but not informing the people involved that you are studying them?

Putting Sociology to Work: Public Sociology

Most early sociologists—including Lester Ward, the first president of the American Sociological Association—promoted sociology as means for improving society (Calhoun 2007). As the discipline of sociology grew from its early days and became an acknowledged social science, some sociologists advocated for "pure" research disconnected from the public sphere. Throughout the history of the discipline, sociologists have debated their proper role in society.

However, like physicists, chemists, and geologists, many sociologists believe that there are both important practical applications of the discipline and many policy issues that need to be informed by good social science. Today, there is a movement to recall the roots of sociology and make sociology more "public" and of use to society. **Public sociologists** *use sociological tools to understand and inform citizens about how society operates, and to improve society*. Some help create and advocate for social policies that their research indicates will make a positive impact on society. Public sociologists—whether professors or those in a variety of professions outside academia—share a common goal: to better understand how society operates *and* to make practical use of their sociological findings (Pickard and Poole 2007).

Some public sociologists work outside of academia and use sociological knowledge and research skills to address organizational needs or problems in government, education, health care settings, social service agencies, and business organizations. They work for clients or organizations who often determine the research questions they address. Depending on their positions, they may be known as sociological practitioners, applied sociologists, clinical sociologists, policy analysts, program planners, or evaluation researchers, among other titles. They focus on pragmatic ways to improve organizations or society, sometimes recommending major changes and sometimes proposing modest policy proposals.

ENGAGING SOCIOLOGY

How to Read a Research Table

A statistical table is a researcher's labor-saving device. Quantitative data presented in tabular form are clearer and more concise than the same information presented in several written paragraphs. A good table has clear signposts to help the reader avoid confusion. For instance, Table 2.1 shows many of the main features of a table, and the list that follows explains how to read each feature.

TITLE: The title provides information on the major topic and variables in the table.

"Educational Attainment by Selected Characteristics: 2010"

HEADNOTE (or Subtitle): Many tables will have a headnote or subtitle under the title, giving information relevant to understanding the table or units in the table.

For this table, the reader is informed that it includes all persons over the age of 25 and the units will be reported in thousands.

TABLE 2.1 Educational Attainment by Selected Characteristics: 2010, for Persons 25 Years Old and Over, Reported in Thousands

Characteristic	Population (1,000)	Percent of Population—Highest Level					
		Not a High School Graduate	High School Graduate	Some College, but No Degree	Associate's Degree[1]	Bachelor's Degree	Advanced Degree
Total persons	199,928	12.9	31.2	16.8	9.1	19.4	10.5
Age							
25–34 yrs old	41,085	11.6	27.2	18.9	9.5	24.0	8.9
35–44 yrs old	40,447	11.7	28.6	16.3	10.3	21.9	11.2
45–54 yrs old	44,387	10.4	32.8	16.7	10.6	19.0	10.4
55–64 yrs old	35,359	10.4	31.3	17.3	9.2	18.6	13.1
65–74 yrs old	20,956	17.0	35.4	15.7	6.6	14.1	11.1
75 yrs or older	17,657	24.6	37.6	14.0	4.6	11.9	7.3
Sex:							
Male	96,325	13.4	31.9	16.5	8.0	19.4	10.9
Female	103,603	12.4	30.7	17.1	10.2	19.4	10.2

HEADINGS AND STUBS: Tables generally have one or two levels of headings under the title and headnotes. These instruct the reader about what is in the columns below.

In this table, the headings indicate the level of education achieved so that the reader can identify the percentage with a specified level of education.

The table also has a stub: the far-left column under "Characteristic." This lists the items that are being compared according to the categories found in the headings. In this case, the stub indicates age, sex, race, and Hispanic origin.

MARGINAL TABS: In examining the numbers in the table, try working from the outside in. The marginals, the figures at the margins of the table, often provide summary information.

In this table, the first column of numbers is headed "Population (1,000)," indicating (by thousands) the total number of people in each category who were part of the database. The columns to the right indicate—by percentages—the level of educational attainment for each category.

CELLS: To make more detailed comparisons, examine specific cells in the body of the table. These are the boxes that hold the numbers or percentages.

In this table, the cells contain data on educational achievement by age, sex, and race/ethnicity (for whites, blacks, and Hispanics).

UNITS: Units refer to how the data are reported. They could be in percentages, in number per 100 or 1,000, or in other units.

In this table, the data are reported first in raw number in thousands and then in percentages.

TABLE 2.1 Educational Attainment by Selected Characteristics: 2010, for Persons 25 Years Old and Over, Reported in Thousands (Continued)

Characteristic	Population (1,000)	Percent of Population—Highest Level					
		Not a High School Graduate	High School Graduate	Some College, but No Degree	Associate's Degree[1]	Bachelor's Degree	Advanced Degree
Total persons	199,928	12.9	31.2	16.8	9.1	19.4	10.5
Race:							
White[2]	163,083	12.4	31.3	16.7	9.2	19.6	10.7
Black[2]	22,969	15.8	35.2	19.8	9.4	13.3	6.5
Other	13,876	13.0	23.5	13.0	8.1	26.6	15.7
Hispanic origin:							
Hispanic	26,375	37.1	29.6	12.9	6.5	10.1	3.8
Non-Hispanic	173,553	9.2	31.5	17.4	9.5	20.8	11.5

Source: U.S. Census Bureau 2012b.

[1]Includes vocational degrees.

[2]For persons who selected this race group only.

*Features of the table adapted from Broom and Selznick (1963).

SOURCE: The source note, found under the table, points out the origin of the data. It is usually identified by the label "Source."

Under this table, the source note says "U.S. Census Bureau 2012b."

FOOTNOTES: Some tables have footnotes, usually indicating something unusual about the data or where to find more complete data.

In this table, two footnotes are provided so that the reader does not make mistakes in interpretation.

FACTS FROM THE TABLE: After reviewing all the above information, the reader is ready to make some interpretations about what the data mean.

In this table, the reader might note that young adults are more likely to have a college education than older citizens.

What other interesting patterns do you see?

So far, we have focused on what sociology is and how sociologists know what they know. The rest of the book examines our social world as informed by methods and theory discussed in this chapter. The next chapter explores how you can understand your culture and society at the various levels of analysis in our social world.

WHAT HAVE WE LEARNED?

The core features of *scientific* research are (1) a commitment to empirically validated evidence, facts, and information that are confirmed through systematic processes of testing using the five senses; (2) allowing us to be convinced by the evidence rather than by our preconceived ideas; (3) absolute integrity and objectivity in how we conduct and report on our research; and (4) continual openness to having our findings reexamined and new interpretations proposed. We must always consider the possibility that we have overlooked alternative explanations of the data and alternative ways to view the problem.

Science—including social science—does not consist of just facts to be memorized. Science is a process that is made possible by a social exchange of ideas, a clash of opinions, and a continual search for truth. Knowledge in the sciences is created by vigorous debate. We hope you will engage in the creation of knowledge by entering into these debates.

Theories serve as lenses to help us make sense of the data that we gather using various research strategies. The data themselves can be used to test the theories, so there is an ongoing reciprocal relationship between theory (the lens for making sense of the data) and research (the evidence used to test the theories). The most important ideas in this chapter concern what sociology considers data or evidence and how sociology uses methods to be a science. These ideas form the framework for the content of sociology.

KEY POINTS

- Attempts to understand society have existed for at least two and a half millennia, but gathering of scientific evidence to test hypotheses and validate claims is a modern idea.

- Theories are especially important to science because they raise questions for research, and they explain the relationships among facts. Sociology has four primary, overriding, theoretical perspectives or paradigms: symbolic interaction theory, rational choice theory, structural-functional theory, and conflict theory. Other perspectives, such as feminist theory, serve as correctives to the main paradigms. Most of these theories are more applicable at either the micro to meso level or the meso to macro level.

- Sociology is a science used to study society, and therefore it is essential to understand what is—and what is not—considered data or evidence. For a scientist, this means that ideas must be tested empirically, that is, scientifically.

- As social scientists, sociologists use eight systematic steps to gather data and test theories about the social world.

- The *independent variable* is the variable in a cause-and-effect relationship that comes first in a time sequence and causes a change in another variable—the *dependent variable*.

- Major methods for gathering data in sociology include questionnaires, interviews, observational studies, secondary data analysis, content analysis, and experiments.

- Quantitative data come in the form of numbers (e.g., derived from questionnaires, some secondary sources such as the Census), and qualitative data come in nonnumerical forms (e.g., derived from semistructured and unstructured interviews, observation studies).

- Use of multiple methods—triangulation—increases confidence in the findings.

- Scientific confidence in results requires representative samples, usually drawn randomly.

- Responsible research requires sensitivity to the ethics of research—ensuring that gathering scientific data does no one harm.

- Public sociologists use sociological tools to understand and inform citizens about how society operates, and to improve society.

DISCUSSION QUESTIONS

1. If you were to examine the relationship between the government and the economy in the United States today, which of the four major theoretical perspectives outlined in the chapter would be most helpful? Why?

2. Imagine you would like to conduct a sociological study of the students with whom you attended the fourth grade, to determine what key factors influenced their academic achievements. Which of the four major theoretical perspectives would you employ in your study? Why?

3. Why do research questions have to be asked in a precise way? Give an example of a precise research question. How do precise questions make it possible for you to test and measure your topic?

4. Sociologists must be continually open to having their findings reexamined and new interpretations proposed. Describe a time when you changed your mind due to new information. Was it difficult for you to change your mind? Why or why not?

5. Why is the ability to be open to new ideas and interpretations so vital to the scientific perspective? Do you think you could carry this aspect of the scientific process out successfully—no matter how you feel about a topic? Why or why not?

6. If you were to conduct a study to measure student satisfaction with a particular academic department on campus, what research method(s) would you use? Why? How would the method(s) you select vary according to (a) the size of the department and (b) the type of information you sought?

CONTRIBUTING TO OUR SOCIAL WORLD: What Can We Do?

At the Local Level

Local service organizations are found in every community and work to provide for the unmet needs of community members: housing, legal aid, medical care, elder care, and so on. United Way works with most local service organizations and may be able to let you know which ones need help in your area. Going to idealist.org is also a great way to find volunteer opportunities in your area. Volunteer to work with an organization in its applied needs assessment research, and practice the sociological principles and research methods described in this chapter. If your college or university has a service-learning office, it will offer

connections to many service opportunities, sometimes linked to specific fields of study. Many colleges and universities also offer Academic Service Learning (ASL) credit in which course assignments include such community work under the supervision of the instructor.

At the State/Meso Level

- *State agencies* often have ongoing projects to gather data for more accurate information about the state and the needs of its citizens. Go to www.nationalservice.gov/about/contact-us/state-service-commissions to find volunteer opportunities through your state government.

At the National and Global Levels

• *The U.S. Bureau of the Census* is best known for its decennial (every 10 years) enumeration of the population, but its work continues each year as it prepares special reports, population estimates, and regular publications (including *Current Population Reports*). Visit the Bureau's website at www.census.gov, and explore the valuable and extensive quantitative data and other information available. Visit your local Census Bureau office or click on www.census.gov/hrd/www/jobs/student.html to find volunteer and other opportunities for students at the Census.

Sharpen your skills with SAGE edge at **edge.sagepub.com/ballantinecondensed4e**

SAGE edge for Students provides a personalized approach to help you accomplish your coursework goals in an easy-to-use learning environment.

edge.sagepub.com/ballantinecondensed4e

SAGE edge offers a robust online environment featuring an impressive array of free tools and resources for review, study and further exploration, keeping both instructors and students on the cutting edge of teaching and learning.

PART II

Social Structure, Processes, and Control

Picture a house. First there is the foundation, then the wood frame, then the walls and roof. This provides the framework or structure. Within that structure, activities called *processes* take place—electricity to turn on lights and appliances, water to wash in and drink, and people to carry out these processes. If something goes wrong in the house, we take steps to control the damage and repair it.

Whether we are building a house or a society, the process of constructing our social world is parallel. Social structure is the framework of society with its groups and organizations; social processes are the dynamic activities of society. This section begins with a discussion of the structure of society, followed by the processes of culture and socialization through which individuals are taught cultural rules—how to function and live effectively within their society's structure. Although socialization of individuals takes place primarily at the micro level, we will explore its implications at the meso and macro levels as well.

If we break the social structure into parts, such as the wood frame, walls, and roof of a house, it is the groups and organizations (including bureaucracies) that are parts of the social structure. To work smoothly, these organizations depend on people's loyalty so that their participants do what society and its groups need to survive. However, these components do not always join together well. Things break down. Those in control of societies try to control disruptions and deviant individuals in order to maintain control and smooth functioning.

As we explore the next few chapters, we will continue to examine social life at the micro, meso, and macro levels, for each of us as an individual is profoundly shaped by social processes and structures at larger and more abstract levels, all the way to the global level.

3 Society and Culture

Hardware and Software of Our Social World

Depending on what resources are available where we live and what is considered usable and edible, we put something out to eat. It might be a juicy hamburger, dog meat, or bugs. What we consider food is influenced by the structure

MICRO

● **ME (AND MY FAMILY)**

● **LOCAL ORGANIZATIONS AND COMMUNITY**
Local soccer teams and scout troops have a microculture.

MESO

● **NATIONAL ORGANIZATIONS, INSTITUTIONS, AND ETHNIC SUBCULTURES**
Ethnic groups have a subculture.

MACRO

● **SOCIETY**
A nation has a national culture.

● **GLOBAL COMMUNITY**
Multinational organizations like the World Health Organization have a global culture.

of society, including the organization of food production, distribution, and technology, and by the culture—the ideas about what is edible. In the opening photo, an international market is bustling with activity as people shop for the kinds of foods considered nutritious and tasty in their culture.

LEARNING OBJECTIVES

3.1 Describe the structure (the "hardware") of our social world.

3.2 Illustrate how culture affects individuals.

3.3 Provide examples of microcultures, subcultures, countercultures, and global cultures.

3.4 Compare key ideas in the symbolic interactionist, functionalist, and conflict perspectives on culture.

3.5 Explain why culture (the "software") from one society does not always "fit" with the structure ("hardware") of another society.

THINK ABOUT IT

Micro: Local Community	How do microcultures (such as your fraternity, study group, or team) influence you?
Meso: National Institutions; Complex Organizations; Ethnic Groups	How do subcultures (such as your ethnic group) and countercultures (such as youth gangs) shape the character of your nation and influence your own life?
Macro: National and Global Systems	How do your nation's social structures and culture influence who you are and how you dress, eat, work, and live your life?

What do people around the world eat? Mrs. Ukita, the mom in the Ukita family, rises early to prepare a breakfast of miso soup and a raw egg on rice. The father and two daughters eat quickly and rush out to catch their early morning trains to work and school in Kodaira City, Japan. The mother cares for the house, does the shopping, and prepares a typical evening meal of fish, vegetables, and rice for the family.

The Ahmed family lives in a large apartment building in Cairo, Egypt. The 12 members of the extended family include the women who shop for and cook the food—vegetables, including peppers, greens, potatoes, squash, tomatoes, garlic, spices, and rice, along with pita bread and often fish or meat. The adult men work in shops in one of the many bazaars, while the school-age children attend school, then help with the chores.

In the Breidjing refugee camp in Chad, many Sudanese refugees eat what relief agencies can get to them—and that food source is not always reliable. Typical for the Aboubakar family, a mother and five children, is rice or some other grain, oil for cooking, dried legumes, occasionally some root plants or squash that keep longer than fresh fruits and vegetables, and a few spices. The girls and women go into the desert to fetch firewood for cooking and to get water from whatever source has water at the time. This is a dangerous trip as they may be attacked and raped or even killed outside the camps.

The Walker family from Norfolk, Virginia, grabs dinner at a fast-food restaurant on their way to basketball practice and an evening meeting. Because of their busy schedules and individual activities, they cannot always find time to cook and eat together—a behavior that would be unthinkable in most societies around the world.

Although most diets include some form of grain and starch, locally available fruits and vegetables, and perhaps meat or fish, broad variations in food consumption exist even within one society. Yet all of these differences have something in common: Each represents a society with a unique culture that includes what people eat. Food is one aspect of our way of life and what is necessary for survival. Ask yourself why you sleep on a bed, brush your teeth, or listen to music with friends. Our way of life is called culture.

Culture *refers to the way of life shared by a group of people—the knowledge, beliefs, values, rules or laws, language, customs, symbols, and material products (such as food, houses, and transportation) within a society that help meet human needs.* Culture provides guidelines for living. Learning our culture puts our social world in an understandable framework, providing a tool kit we can use to help construct the meaning of our world and behaviors in it (Bruner 1996; Nagel 1994). We compare culture to *software* because it is the human ideas and input that make the society work. Otherwise, society would just be structures, like the framework of a house.

A **society** *is an organized and interdependent group of individuals who live together in a specific geographic area; who interact more with each other than they do with outsiders; who cooperate for the attainment of common goals; and who share a common culture over time.* Most often societies are the same as the countries that make up the world. Each society includes key parts called institutions, such as family, education, religion, politics, economics, and health care or medicine, that meet basic human needs. This structure that makes up society is what we refer to here as the *hardware*, like the structure of a computer. Culture, the *software*, is learned, transmitted, shared, and reshaped from generation to generation. All activities in the society, whether educating young members, preparing and eating dinner, selecting leaders for the group, finding a mate, or negotiating with other societies, are guided by cultural rules and expectations. In each society, culture provides the social rules for how individuals carry out necessary tasks.

Society—organized groups of people—and culture—their way of life—are interdependent. The two are not the same thing, but they cannot exist without each other, just as computer hardware and software are each useless without the other.

This chapter explores the ideas of society and culture and their relation to each other, what society is and how it is organized, how it influences and is influenced by culture, what culture is, how and why culture develops, the components of culture, cultural theories, and policy issues. After reading this chapter, you will have a better idea of how you learn and make use of your society's culture.

SOCIETY: THE HARDWARE

The structures that make up society include micro-level positions (parents, students, and workers); the groups to which we belong (family, work groups, and clubs); and the larger groups, organizations, or institutions in which we participate (education, political, and economic organizations). This "hardware" (structure) of our social world provides the framework for "software" (culture) to function.

Thinking Sociologically

What major changes took place in your grandparents' lifetimes that affect the way you and your family live today?

Societies are organized in particular patterns shaped by factors including the way people procure food, the availability of resources, contact with other societies, and cultural beliefs. For example, people can change from herding to farming only if they have the knowledge, skills, and desire to do so and only in environments that will support agriculture. As societies develop, changes take place in the social structures and relationships between people. For example, in industrialized societies, relationships between people typically become more formal because people must interact with strangers and not just their relatives. It

Traditional, rural Mayan women make tortillas or "boxboles." Food preparation, as well as consumption, is a deeply communal experience among these people.

is important to note that not all societies go through all stages. Some are jolted into the future by political events or changes in the global system, and some resist pressures to become modernized and continue to live in simpler social systems.

Evolution of Societies

The Saharan desert life for the Tuareg tribe is pretty much as it has been for centuries. In simple traditional societies, individuals are assigned to comparatively few social positions or statuses. Today, however, few societies are isolated from global impact. Even the Tuareg are called on to escort adventurous tourists through the desert for a currency new to them and unneeded until recently. In 2012, al-Qaeda in the Islamic (or Arabian) Maghreb challenged the Tuareg's control over their desert homeland in a war in northern Mali, Africa. The Islamists have been pushed out, but the Tuareg continue to struggle for autonomy as a people ("Mali 'at War' With Tuareg Rebels" 2014).

In such traditional societies, men teach their sons everything they need to know, for all men do much the same jobs, depending on where they live—hunting, fishing, or farming and protecting the community from danger. Likewise, girls learn their jobs from their mothers—such as child care, fetching water, food preparation, farming, weaving, and perhaps house building. In contrast, in more complex societies, such as industrial or "modern" societies, thousands of interdependent job statuses are based on complex divisions of labor with designated tasks.

Émile Durkheim, an early French sociologist, pictured a continuum between simple and complex societies ([1893] 1947). He described simple premodern societies as held together by **mechanical solidarity**—*social cohesion and integration based on the similarity of individuals in the group, including shared beliefs, values, and emotional ties between members of the group.* Furthermore, the division of labor is based largely on male/female distinctions and age groupings; everyone fulfills his or her expected social positions. This provides the glue that holds the society together. The entire society may involve only a few hundred people, with no meso-level institutions, organizations, or subcultures. Prior to the emergence of nation-states, there was no macro level either—only tribal groupings.

According to Durkheim, as societies transformed, they became more complex through increasingly multifaceted divisions of labor and changes in the ways people carried out necessary tasks for survival ([1893] 1947). **Organic solidarity** refers to *social cohesion (glue) based on division of labor, with each member playing a highly specialized role in the society and each person being dependent on others due to interdependent, interrelated tasks.* The society has cohesion regardless of whether people have common values and shared outlooks. Prior to the factory system, for example, individual cobblers made shoes to order. With the Industrial Revolution, factories took over the process, with many individuals carrying out interdependent tasks. The division of labor is critical because it leads to new forms of social cohesion based on interdependence, not on emotional ties. Gradual changes from mechanical (traditional) to organic (modern) society also involve harnessing new forms of energy and finding more efficient ways to use them (Nolan and Lenski 2014). For example, the use of steam engines and coal for fuel triggered the Industrial Revolution, leading to the development of industrial societies.

As societies changed toward organic solidarity, they added large organizations and institutions that reached individuals and families as never before. The meso level—institutions and large bureaucratic organizations—became more influential. Still, as recently as 200 years ago, even large societies had little global interdependence, and life for the typical citizen was influenced mostly by events at the micro and meso levels. As communication and transportation around the world developed and expanded, the global level grew.

As you read about each of the following types of societies, from the simplest to the most complex, notice the presence of these variables: (a) division of labor, (b) interdependence of people's positions, (c) increasingly advanced technologies, and (d) new forms and uses of energy. Although none of these variables alone is *sufficient* to trigger evolution to a new type of society, they may all be *necessary* for a transition to occur.

According to Durkheim, then, in traditional societies with mechanical solidarity, interpersonal interaction and community life at the micro level were the most important aspects of social life. Meso- and macro-level societies developed as a result of changes toward more organic solidarity. As societies become more complex, meso- and macro-level institutions become more important and have more profound impacts on the lives of individuals.

Hunter-Gatherer Societies. In the Kalahari Desert of southwestern Africa live hunter-gatherers known as the !Kung. (The ! is pronounced with a click of the tongue.) The !Kung live a nomadic life, moving from one place to another as food supplies become available or are used up. As a result, they carry very few personal possessions and live in temporary huts, settling around water holes for a few months at a time. Settlements are small, rarely more than 20 to 50 people, for food supplies are not plentiful enough to support large, permanent populations (Lee 1984). !Kung women gather edible plants and nuts, while !Kung men hunt. Beyond division of labor by gender and age, however, there are few differences in roles or status.

In **hunter-gatherer societies**, *people rely on the vegetation and animals occurring naturally in their habitat to sustain life.* Generally, life is organized around kinship ties and reciprocity—that is, mutual assistance—for the well-being of the whole community. When a large animal is killed, people gather from a wide area to share in the bounty, and great care is taken to ensure that the meat is distributed fairly. Resources are shared among the people, but sharing is regulated by a complex system of mutual obligations. A visitor who eats food at another's hearth is expected to repay that hospitality in the future.

The !Kung are a typical hunter-gatherer society. People make their clothing, shelter, and tools from available materials or obtain goods through trade with other nearby groups. People migrate seasonally to new food sources. Population size remains small as the numbers of births and deaths in the society are balanced.

From the beginning of human experience until recently, hunting and gathering (or foraging) were the sole means of sustaining life. Other types of societies emerged only recently. Today, only a handful of societies still rely on hunting and gathering (Nolan and Lenski 2014). The hunter-gatherer lifestyle is becoming extinct.

Herding and Horticultural Societies. A semi-nomadic herding society, the Masai of Kenya and Tanzania, move camp to find grazing land for their animals and set up semipermanent shelters for the few months they will remain in one area. Settlements consist of huts constructed in a circle with a perimeter fence surrounding the compound. At the more permanent settlements, the Masai grow short-term crops to supplement their diet.

Herding societies *have food-producing strategies based on domestication of animals whose care is the central focus of their activities.* Domesticating animals has replaced hunting them. In addition to providing food and other products, cattle, sheep, goats, pigs, horses, and camels represent forms of wealth that result in more social prestige for members of the group with large herds.

Horticultural societies *are those in which the food-producing strategy is based on domestication of plants, using digging sticks and wooden hoes to cultivate small gardens.* They may also keep domesticated animals, but they focus on simple agriculture or gardening. They cultivate tree crops, such as date palms or bananas, and plant garden plots, such as yams, beans, taro, squash, or corn. This is more efficient than gathering wild vegetables and fruits. Both herding and horticultural societies differ from hunter-gatherer societies in that they make their living by cultivating food and have some control over its production (Ward and Edelstein 2014).

The ability to control food sources was a major turning point in human history. Societies became more settled and stored surpluses of food, which led to increases in population size. A community could contain as many as 3,000 individuals. More people, surplus food, and greater accumulation of possessions

A mother in Côte d'Ivoire (West Africa), carrying her load on her head, returns to the village with her daughter after gathering wood. Carrying wood and water is typically women's work in this hunter-gatherer society.

encouraged the development of private property and created new status differences between individuals and families. Forms of social inequality started to become pronounced.

The technological breakthrough that moved many societies from the horticultural to the agricultural stage was the plow, introduced more than 6,000 years ago. It marked the beginning of the agricultural revolution in Europe, the Middle East, and other parts of the world, and it brought about massive changes in social structures in many societies. The end of the horticultural stage also saw advances in irrigation systems, the fertilization of land, crop rotation, more permanent settlements, land ownership, human modification of the natural environment, higher population density (cities), and power hierarchies.

Agricultural Societies. Pedro and Lydia Ramirez, their four young children, and Lydia's parents live as an extended family in a small farming village in Nicaragua. They rise early, and while Pedro heads for the fields to do some work before breakfast, Lydia prepares his breakfast and lunch and sees that their eldest son is up and ready to go to school, while

Lydia's mother looks after the younger children. After school, the oldest boy also helps in the fields. Most of the land in the area is owned by a large company that grows coffee, but the Ramirezes are fortunate to have a small garden plot where they grow some vegetables for themselves. At harvest time, all hands help, including young children. The family receives cash for the coffee they have grown, minus the rent for the land. They plow the land with the help of strong animals such as horses and oxen, and use fertilizers and water the garden when needed.

The Ramirezes' way of life is typical of life in an agricultural society. **Agricultural societies** *rely primarily on raising crops for food, but make use of technological advances such as the plow, irrigation, animals, and fertilization to continuously cultivate the same land.* The continuous cultivation of the same land results in permanent settlements and greater food surpluses. Agricultural societies utilize energy more efficiently than foraging societies. For example, the plow circulates nutrients better than a digging stick, and when an animal pulls the plow, the farmer uses strength beyond that of a person. As increasingly sophisticated agricultural technology resulted in surplus food, the size of population centers increased to as much as a million or more.

As surpluses accumulated, land in some societies became concentrated in the hands of a few individuals. Wealthy landowners built armies and expanded their empires. During these periods, fighting for land took precedence over technological advances. War was prevalent, and societies were divided increasingly into rich and poor classes. Those who held the land and wealth could control the labor sources and acquire serfs or slaves. Thus, the feudal system was born. Serfs (the peasant class) were forced to work the land for their survival. Food surpluses also allowed some individuals to leave the land and to trade goods or services in exchange for food. For the first time, social inequality became extensive enough to divide society into social classes. At this point, religion, political power, a standing army, and other meso-level institutions and organizations came to be independent of the family. The meso level became well established.

As technology advanced, goods were manufactured in cities. Peasants moved from farming communities, where the land could not support the large population, to rapidly growing urban areas, where the demand for labor was great. It was not until the mid-1700s in

Plows, essential for agricultural societies to develop, were pushed by people and then pulled by animals and later machines. Harnessing energy ever more effectively is a prerequisite to a society becoming more complex.

England that the next major transformation of society began to take place, resulting largely from technological advances and additional harnessing of energy.

Industrial Societies. The Industrial Revolution involved the harnessing of steam power and the manufacture of gasoline engines, permitting machines to replace human and animal power. A tractor can plow far more land in a week than a horse, and an electric pump can irrigate more acres than an ox-driven pump. As a result of such new technologies, raw mineral products such as ores, raw plant products such as rubber, and raw animal products such as hides could be transformed into mass-produced consumer goods. The Industrial Revolution brought about enormous changes in occupations, the division of labor, the production of goods, products produced, and social structures.

Industrial societies *rely primarily on mechanized production resulting in greater division of labor based on expertise.* Economic resources were distributed more widely among individuals in industrial societies, but inequities between owners and laborers persisted. Wage earning gradually replaced slavery and serfdom, and highly skilled workers earned higher wages, leading to the rise of a middle class. Farmworkers moved from rural areas to cities to find work in factories, which produced consumer goods. Cities grew, and many became populated by millions of people.

Family and kinship patterns at the micro level also changed. Agricultural societies need large, land-based, extended family units to do the work of farming (recall how the Ramirez parents, grandparents, and children in Nicaragua all help out at harvest time), but industrial societies need individuals with specific skills, ability to move to where the jobs are, and smaller families to support. Family roles change. Children are an asset in agricultural societies and begin work at an early age. However, from a purely economic perspective, children become a liability in an industrial society because they contribute less to the finances of the family.

Meso- and macro-level dimensions of social life expand in industrializing societies and become more influential in the lives of individuals. National institutions and multinational organizations develop. Today, for example, global organizations such as the World Bank, the World Court, the United Nations, and the World Health Organization address social problems and sometimes even make decisions that change national boundaries or national policies. Corporations such as Nike and Gap are multinational organizations (located in many countries). Some voluntary associations—such as Doctors without Borders, which serves medical needs, and Amnesty International, which lobbies for human rights—do their work across the globe.

Perhaps the most notable characteristic of the industrial age is the rapid rate of change compared with other stages of societal development. The beginning of industrialization in Europe was gradual, based on years of population movement, urbanization, technological development, and other factors of modernization. Today, however, societal change occurs so rapidly that societies at all levels of development are being drawn together into a new age—the postindustrial era.

Postindustrial or Information Societies.

Postindustrial societies are *those that have moved from human labor and manufacturing to automated production and service jobs, largely processing information.* Postindustrial societies require workers with high levels of technical and professional education. Those without technical education are less likely to find rewarding employment in the technological revolution. This results in new class lines being drawn, based in part on skills and education in new technologies.

The shift to an information-based society has also enhanced cross-border workplaces. As your authors finished chapters for this book, they were sent to India for typesetting in the evening, and due to the time change were returned to the United States by morning. Technology, the efficiency of overnight delivery, and the lower cost of production have led many

publishing companies to turn to businesses halfway around the world for much of the book production process. As India and other developing countries increase their trained, skilled labor force, they are being called on by national and multinational companies to carry out global manufacturing processes. India has some of the world's best technical training institutes and modern **technology**—*the practical application of tools, skills, and knowledge to meet human needs and extend human abilities.* Although many people in India live in poverty, a relatively new middle class is rapidly emerging in major business centers around the country.

After World War II, starting in the 1950s, the transition from industrial to postindustrial society began in the United States, Western Europe, and Japan. This shift was characterized by movement from human labor to automated production and from a predominance of manufacturing jobs to a growth in service jobs, such as computer operators, bankers, scientists, teachers, public relations workers, stockbrokers, and salespeople. More than two thirds of all jobs in the United States now reside in organizations that produce and transmit information, thus the reference to an "Information Age." Daniel Bell describes this transformation of work, information, and communication as "the third technological revolution" after industrialization based on steam (the first technological revolution) and the invention of electricity (the second technological revolution) (Bell 1973). According to Bell, the third technological revolution was the development of the computer, which has led to this postindustrial era or Information Age. To examine this transformation, see Table 3.1 in the next "Engaging Sociology."

This Buddhist monk uses modern technology, including a laptop that can connect him with colleagues on the other side of the globe.

ENGAGING SOCIOLOGY

Demographics of Internet Users

Below is the percentage of each group of U.S. adults who use the Internet, according to a January 2014 Pew Internet and American Life Project survey. For instance, 86% of women use the Internet.

TABLE 3.1 Demographics of Internet Users

	Percentage Who Use the Internet
All Adults	87
Men	87
Women	86
Race/Ethnicity	
White, non-Hispanic	85
Black, non-Hispanic	81
Hispanic (English- and Spanish-speaking)	83
Age	
18–29	97
30–49	93
50–64	88
65+	57
Household Income	
Less than $30,000/year	77
$30,000–$49,999	85
$50,000–$74,999	93
$75,000+	99
Educational Attainment	
High school grad or less	76
Some college	91
College +	97

Source: Pew Research Center Internet and American Life Project 2014a. The Pew Research Center's Internet Project's Survey January 9–12, 2014.

Engaging With Sociology

Interview 10 people you know to find out about their Internet use, keeping records on the gender, age, race and ethnicity, educational attainment, and income bracket of each. Then compare your figures with those in Table 3.1. Are they similar? If not, what possible geographic, social class, or other factors might cause your figures to be different from those in this national survey?

Postindustrial societies rely, at least in part, on new sources of power such as atomic, wind, thermal, and solar energy and new uses of computer automation. Computer-controlled robots have taken over many jobs once carried out by humans. The control of information and the ability to develop technologies or provide services have become key sources of money and power.

Values of 21st-century postindustrial societies favor scientific and creative approaches to problem solving, research, and development, along with attitudes that support the globalization of world economies. Satellites, cell phones, fiber optics, and especially the Internet continue to transform postindustrial societies of the Information Age, linking people from societies around the world.

In a study of postmodern communities, sociologist Richard Florida links creativity to the local cultural climate and to economic prosperity. His research has important practical applications and is useful to policymakers in local communities. As his research in the next "Sociologists in Action" makes clear, the organization of society and the means of providing the necessities of life have a profound impact on values, beliefs, lifestyle, and other aspects of culture.

What will the future bring? Futurologists predict new trends based on current activities and predictions of new advances and technologies on the horizon. Among the many ideas for the future, technological advances dominate the field. Predictions include the increasing use of cell phones connecting the poorest corners of the globe with the rest of the world. One billion mobile phone users are predicted for China by 2020, with 80% of the population having cell phones. With discovery and efficient use of energy being central to sociocultural evolution, alternative energy sources from wind to solar power will become essential to meet demand. Plug-in hybrids, natural gas, and electric batteries may replace gasoline motors. One million hydrogen-fueled cars are predicted for the United States by the year 2035, and far more for Europe and Japan. Gas may be on the way out. Rechargeable batteries that run for 40 hours without interruption will run most home appliances by 2030. Brain-computer interfaces will give paralyzed people the ability to control their environments (National Institutes of Health 2012; News of Future 2012). These are just a few of the many predictions of what will affect societies and alter some human interactions.

In much of this book we focus on complex, multilevel societies, for this is the type of social environment in which most of us reading this book now live. Much of this book also focuses on social interaction and social structures, including interpersonal networking, the growth of bureaucratic structures, social inequality within the structure, and the core institutions necessary to meet the needs of individuals and society. In short, *hardware*—society—is the focus of many subsequent chapters. The remainder of this chapter will focus primarily on the social *software*—culture.

Thinking Sociologically

First, read the Sociologists in Action essay on page 62. Why do some communities attract creative people? What are some characteristics of these communities? What might be advantages—or disadvantages—to living in a creative community? Would you like to live in such a community? Why or why not? How do you think growing up in such a community would impact your choice of a career and with whom you became friends?

CULTURE: THE SOFTWARE

Cultures—the ideas and "things" passed on from one generation to the next in a society, including knowledge, beliefs, values, rules and laws, language, customs, symbols, and material products—vary greatly as we travel across the globe. Each social unit of cooperating and interdependent people, whether at the micro, meso, or macro level, develops a unique way of life with guidelines for the actions and interaction of individuals and groups within society.

As you can see, the sociological definition of culture refers to far more than "high or elite culture" shared by a select few—such as fine art, classical music, opera, literature, ballet, and theater—and also far more than "popular culture"—such as reality TV, professional wrestling, YouTube, and other mass entertainment. *Popular culture* is mass produced and consumed, and becomes part of everyday traditions through its practices, beliefs, and material objects. It influences public opinion and values. One type of pop culture is music in its many forms; for example, rap music often focuses on urban culture's politics,

SOCIOLOGISTS IN ACTION:
RICHARD FLORIDA

The Creative Class and and Successful Communities

Like the transformations of societies from the hunter-gatherer to the horticultural stage or from the agricultural to the industrial stage, our own current transformation seems to have created a good deal of "cultural wobble" within society. How does one identify the elements or the defining features of a new age while the transformation is still in progress? This was one of the questions that intrigued sociologist Richard Florida, who studied U.S. communities.

Professor Florida combined several methods of data collection (2002, 2012). First, he traveled around the country to communities that were especially prosperous and seemed to be on the cutting edge of change in U.S. society. In these communities, he did both individual interviews and focus-group interviews. *Focus-group interviews* are semistructured group interviews with seven or eight people where ideas can be generated from the group by asking open-ended questions. Professor Florida recorded the discussion and analyzed the transcript of the discussion. He also used existing (secondary) data collected by various U.S. government agencies, especially the U.S. Bureau of Labor Statistics and the Census Bureau. The collected data helped Professor Florida identify the factors that attracted creative people to certain areas: other creative people, access to technology, innovation (measured by the number of patents per capita), and diversity (measured by the percentage of gay people living in the area) (2002).

Currently, more than one third of the jobs in the United States—and almost all the extremely well-paid professional positions—require creative thinking. These include not just the creative arts but scientific research, computer and mathematical occupations, education and library science positions, and many media, legal, and managerial careers. People in this "creative class" have an enormous amount of autonomy in their work; they are given problems to solve and the freedom to figure out how to do so. Florida found that modern businesses flourish when they hire highly creative people.

Florida's research led him to collaborate with Gary Gates, a scholar who was doing research on communities hospitable to gays and lesbians. Gates and Florida were amazed to find that their lists were nearly identical. Florida found that creative people thrive on diversity—ethnic, gender, religious, and otherwise—for when creative people are around others who think differently, it tends to spawn new avenues of thinking and problem solving. Tolerance of difference and even the enjoyment of individual idiosyncrasies are hallmarks of thriving communities.

Florida is now very much in demand as a consultant to mayors and urban-planning teams, and his books have become required reading for city council members. Some elected officials have decided that fostering an environment that attracts creative people leads to prosperity because business will follow. Key elements of creative communities include local music and art festivals, organic food grocery stores, legislation that encourages interesting mom-and-pop stores (and keeps out large "box stores" that crush such small and unique endeavors), quaint and locally owned bookstores and distinctive coffee shops, provisions for bike and walking paths throughout the town, and ordinances that establish an environment of tolerance for people who are "different."

• •

Note: Richard Florida heads the Martin Prosperity Institute at the Rotman School of Management at the University of Toronto. He also runs a private creative class institute. He earned his bachelor's degree from Rutgers University and his doctorate in urban planning from Columbia University.

Keith A. Roberts

Creative, highly productive people are attracted to communities that embrace diversity and have locally owned stores like Village Lights Bookstore in Madison, Indiana.

economics, and inequality, and provides an outlet for frustrations through musical commentary. Much of pop culture has been shaped by technology, as we see in texting and social media. The very rapid change in this aspect of popular culture is illustrated in the next "Engaging Sociology."

ENGAGING SOCIOLOGY

Pop Culture and Technology Timeline

©Getty/Bernhard Lang

Digital telephones, high-speed lines for computers, digitized print media, and the World Wide Web were all invented within about the past half-century, many within the last 20 years. The following timeline shows the rapid advances of the Internet and World Wide Web in recent years; the point of this timeline is to illustrate the rapid advance of technology and the place it holds in our lives. Technology is now a primary conveyor of culture, especially pop culture.

An Internet and World Wide Web Timeline

1946: The first general-purpose computer is developed for military purposes.

1951: The first civilian computer is created.

1971: Microprocessors are produced, making possible personal computer (PC) technology.

1978: Cellular phone service begins.

1982: The National Science Foundation sponsors a high-speed communications network, leading to the Internet.

1984: Apple Macintosh introduces the first PC with graphics.

1991: The Internet opens to commercial uses; the World Wide Web is launched.

1993: The first point-and-click web browser, Mosaic, is introduced.

1996: Google makes its debut.

2001: Instant messaging services expand to allow exchanges between different service providers.

2004: Mark Zuckerberg begins Facebook while a student at Harvard University.

2005: YouTube is created by PayPal employees Chad Hurley, Steve Chen, and Jawed Karim.

2005 to present: Cloud computing enables users to run programs on many connected computers at the same time; video glasses have a head-mounted display screen and video capability; smart (computerized) watches connect to the Internet and smartphones.

The continuing rapid advances in technology have paralleled the development of shared pop culture in the United States and around the world, culture that is accessible to everyone, not just the elite. Music groups from other continents have gained audiences in the United States, with musical groups becoming instant success stories through YouTube.

Engaging With Sociology

1. Identify four of the historic innovations that you feel are particularly significant. What are some ways in which they have impacted your life?

2. Identify three positive and three negative ways these rapid advances in technology might impact less developed parts of the world.

3. How can the spread of pop culture across the globe (a) bring different societies closer together and (b) cause tensions within and between societies?

Characteristics of Culture

Cultures have certain characteristics in common. These characteristics help define culture and illustrate the purposes it serves for our societies.

All people share a culture with others in their society. Culture provides the rules, routines, patterns, and expectations for carrying out daily rituals and interactions. Within a society, the process of learning how to act is called socialization (discussed in Chapter 4). From birth, we learn the patterns of behavior approved in our society.

Culture evolves over time and is adaptive. What is normal, proper, and good behavior in hunter-gatherer societies, where cooperation and communal loyalty are critical to the hunt, differs from appropriate behavior in the Information Age, where individualism and competition are encouraged and enhance one's position and well-being.

The creation of culture is ongoing and cumulative. Individuals and societies continually build on existing culture to adapt to new challenges and opportunities. Your culture shapes the behaviors, values, and institutions that seem natural to you. Culture is so much a part of life that you may not even notice behaviors that outsiders find unusual or even abhorrent. You may not think about it when handing food to someone with your left hand, but in some other cultures, such an act may be defined as disgusting and rude.

The transmission of culture is the feature that most separates humans from other animals. Some societies of higher primates have shared cultures but do not systematically enculturate (teach a way of life to) the next generation. Primate cultures focus on behaviors relating to obtaining food, use of territory, protection, and social status. Human cultures have significantly more content and are mediated by language. Humans are the only mammals with cultures that enable them to adapt to and even modify their environments so that they can survive on the equator, in the Arctic, or even beyond the planet.

Thinking Sociologically

Imagine playing a game of cards with four people in which each player thinks a different suit is trump (a trump is a rule whereby any card from the trump suit wins over any card from a different suit). In this game, one person believes hearts is trump, another assumes spades is trump, and so forth. What would happen? How would the result be similar to a society with no common culture?

Ethnocentrism and Cultural Relativity

As scientists, sociologists must rely on scientific research to understand behavior. The scientific method calls for *objectivity*—the practice of considering observed behavior independently of one's own beliefs and values. The study of social behavior thus requires both sensitivity to a wide variety of human social patterns and a perspective that reduces bias. This is more difficult than it sounds because sociologists themselves are products of society and culture. All of us are raised in a particular culture that we view as normal or natural. Yet not every culture views the same things as "normal."

Views of premarital sex and pregnancy vary among societies (Library of Congress 2010). For example, in one 1970 study of 154 societies, about 42% of the societies encouraged premarital sex, while 29% forbade such behavior and punished those who disobeyed this rule (Ford 1970). The remainder fell in between those two extremes. As you can see, social values, beliefs, and behaviors can vary dramatically from one society to the next. These differences can be threatening and even offensive to people who judge others according to their own perspectives, experiences, and values.

The tendency to view one's own group and its cultural expectations as right, proper, and superior to others is called **ethnocentrism**—"ethno" for *ethnic group* and "centrism" for *centered on*. If you were brought up in a society that forbids premarital or extramarital sex, for instance, you might judge many Americans to be immoral. In a few Muslim societies, people who have premarital sex may be severely punished or even executed, because such behavior is seen as an offense against the faith and the family and as a weakening of social bonds. It threatens the lineage and inheritance systems of family groups. In turn, some Americans would find such strict rules of abstinence to be strange and even wrong.

Societies instill some degree of ethnocentrism in their members because ethnocentric beliefs hold groups together and help members feel that they belong to the group. Ethnocentrism promotes loyalty, unity, high morale, and conformity to the rules of society. Fighting for one's country, for instance, requires some degree of belief in the rightness of one's own society and its causes. Ethnocentric attitudes also help protect societies from rapid, disintegrating change. If most people in a society did not believe in the rules and values of their own culture, the result could be widespread dissent, deviance, or crime.

Unfortunately, ethnocentrism can lead to misunderstandings between people of different cultures. The same ethnocentric attitudes that strengthen ties between some people may encourage hostility, racism, war, and genocide against others—even others within the society—who are different. Virtually all societies tend to "demonize" their adversary—in movies, the news, and political speeches—especially when a conflict is most intense. Dehumanizing another group with labels makes it easier to torture or kill its members or to perform acts of discrimination and brutality against them. We see this in the current conflict in Syria in which both sides in the conflict feel hatred for each other. However, as we become a part of a global social world, it becomes increasingly important to accept those who are "different." Bigotry and attitudes of superiority do not enhance cross-national cooperation and trade—which is

what the increasing movement toward a global village and globalization entails. The map in Figure 3.1 challenges our ethnocentric view of the world. Note how you react.

U.S. foreign relations illustrate how ethnocentrism can produce hostility. Many U.S. citizens are surprised to learn that the United States—a great democracy, world power, and disseminator of food, medicine, and technological assistance to developing nations—is despised in many countries. Anti-U.S. demonstrations in South America, the Middle East, and Asia have brought this reality to life through television. The 10 countries with the most negative feelings according to polls are Pakistan, the Palestinian territories, Algeria, Lebanon, Egypt, Iran, Iraq, Yemen, Greece, and Serbia (Sauter, Weigley, and Hess 2013). One cause is the political dominance of the United States and the threat it poses to other people's way of life. In many places of the world, people believe U.S. citizens think only about their own welfare as their country exploits weaker nations. U.S. tourists are sometimes seen as loud-mouthed ignoramuses whose ethnocentric attitudes

FIGURE 3.1   **"Southside Up" Global Map**

Source: Map by Anna Versluis.

Note: This map illustrates geographic ethnocentrism. U.S. citizens tend to assume it is natural that the north should always be "on top." The fact that this map of the world is upside-down, where south is "up," seems incorrect or disturbing to some people. Most people think of their countries or regions as occupying a central and larger part of the world.

prevent them from seeing value in other cultures or from learning other languages.

Note that even referring to citizens of the United States as "Americans"—as though people from Canada, Mexico, Central America, and South America do not really count as Americans—is seen as ethnocentric by many people from these other countries. *America* and the *United States* are not the same thing, but many people in the United States, including some presidents, fail to make the distinction, much to the dismay of other North, South, and Central Americans. If you visit Mexico, people might ask you where you are from. Say "America," and they, too, will say they are from America. Say North America, and Mexicans will say "From Canada or the United States?"

Not all ethnocentrism is hostile; some of it is just a reaction to the strange ways of other cultures. An example is making judgments about what is proper food to eat and what is just not edible. While people everywhere eat, we can see widespread cultural differences in what people eat, as noted in the first part of this chapter. Some of the New Guinea tribes savor grasshoppers; Europeans and Russians relish raw fish eggs (caviar); Inuit children may find seal eyeballs a treat; some Indonesians eat dog; and some Nigerians prize termites. Whether it is from another time period or another society, variations in food can be shocking to us.

In contrast to ethnocentrism, **cultural relativism** *requires setting aside cultural and personal beliefs and prejudices to understand another group or society through the eyes of its members and using its own community standards.* Instead of judging cultural practices and social behavior as good or bad according to one's own cultural practices, the goal is to be impartial in learning the purposes and consequences of practices and behaviors of the group under study. Cultural relativism does not require that social scientists accept or agree with all the beliefs and behaviors of the societies or groups they study. Yet it allows them to try to understand those practices in the social and cultural contexts in which they occur.

Being tolerant and understanding is not always easy. Some behaviors or ideas in other cultures can be difficult for even the most objective observer to understand. The notion of being "on time," for example, which is so much a part of the cultures of the United States, Canada, Japan, and parts of Europe, is a rather bizarre concept in some societies. Among many

Native American people, such as the Dineh (Apache and Navajo), it is ludicrous for people to let a piece of machinery such as a cell phone govern the way one constructs and lives life. The Dineh orientation to time—that one should do things according to the natural rhythm of the body and not according to an artificial electronic mechanism—is difficult for many people outside that culture to grasp. Misunderstandings occur when some North Americans think that "Indians are always late" and jump to the erroneous conclusion that "Indians" are undependable. Native Americans, on the other hand, think whites are neurotic about letting some instrument control them (Basso 1979; Farrer 2011; Hall 1959, 1983).

● Thinking Sociologically

Small, tightly knit societies with no meso or macro level often stress cooperation, conformity, and personal sacrifice for the sake of the community. Complex societies with established meso- and macro-level linkages tend to be more individualistic, stressing personal uniqueness, individual creativity, and critical thinking. Why do you think this is the case?

The Components of Culture: Things and Thoughts

Things (material) and thoughts (nonmaterial) make up our culture. Together they provide the guidelines for our lives.

Material Culture: The Artifacts of Life. **Material culture** *includes all the human-made objects we can see or touch, all the artifacts of a group of people*—grindstones for grinding cassava root, microwave ovens for cooking, bricks of mud or clay for building shelters, hides or woven cloth for making clothing, books or computers for conveying information, tools for reshaping environments, vessels for carrying and sharing food, and weapons for dominating and subduing others.

Some material culture is from the local community; it is of micro-level origin. The kinds of materials with which homes are constructed and the materials used for clothing often reflect the geography and resources of the local area. Houses are an especially good example of material culture, since they result from local ideas of what a "home" looks like and shape the interactions and attitudes of people in the society. Likewise, types of jewelry, pottery, musical instruments, or clothing

Homes are good examples of material culture. Their construction is influenced not only by local materials but also by ideas of what a home is. Homes shape the context in which family members interact, so they can influence the nonmaterial culture—including beliefs, values, and symbols. Houses, like clothes, act as symbols that communicate levels of prestige. For a photo essay and further exploration of houses as material culture, visit **edge.sagepub.com/ballantinecondensed4e.**

reflect tastes that emerge at the micro and meso levels of family, community, and subculture. At a more macro level, national and international corporations interested in making profits work hard to establish trends in fashion and style that may cross continents and oceans.

Material culture helps drive the globalization process. Workers in Asia and Central American countries now make many of our clothes. Our shoes may come from the Philippines. The last banana you ate probably grew in Costa Rica, Guatemala, Honduras, or Panama. That romantic diamond engagement ring—a symbol that represents the most intimate tie—may well be imported from a South African mine using low-paid or even slave labor. Our cars consist of parts produced on nearly every continent.

Thinking Sociologically

Think of examples of material culture that you use daily: stove, automobile, cell phone, computer, refrigerator, clock, money, and so forth. How do these material objects influence your way of life and the way you interact with others? How would your behavior be different if one of these material objects, say iPhones or money, did not exist?

Nonmaterial Culture: Beliefs, Values, Rules, and Language.

Saluting the flag, saying a blessing before meals, flashing someone an obscene gesture, and a football coach signaling what defensive formation to run for the next play are all symbolic acts. In the case of the salute and the prayer, the acts undergird a belief about the nation or about a higher spiritual presence. In each case something is communicated, yet each of these acts refers to something more abstract than any material object.

Nonmaterial culture refers to *the thoughts, language, feelings, beliefs, values, and attitudes that make up much of our culture.* They are the invisible and intangible parts of culture that involve society's rules of behavior, ideas, and beliefs that shape how people interact with others and with their environment. Although we cannot touch the nonmaterial components of our culture, they pervade our life and influence how we think, feel, and behave. Nonmaterial culture is complex, comprising four main elements: values, beliefs, norms or rules, and language.

Values are *shared judgments about what is desirable or undesirable, right or wrong, good or bad. They express the basic ideals of any group of people.* In industrial and postindustrial societies, for instance, a good education is highly valued. That you are in college shows you have certain values toward learning and education. Gunnar Myrdal, a Swedish sociologist and observer of U.S. culture, referred to the U.S. value system as the "American creed," so much a part of the way of life that it acquires the power of religious doctrine (Myrdal 1964). We tend to take our core values for granted, including freedom, equality, individualism, democracy, free enterprise, efficiency, progress, achievement, and material comfort (Macionis 2012; Williams 1970).

Coaches and players use hand signals to cue each other into an upcoming play or to convey what defense or offense to set up—an example of nonverbal communication.

At the macro level, conflicts may arise between groups in society because of differing value systems. For example, there are major differences between the values of various Native American groups and the dominant culture—whether that dominant culture is in North, Central, or South America (Lake 1990; Sharp 1991). The conflict in values between First Nations and the national cultures of Canada, the United States, and many Latin American countries has had serious consequences. For example, cooperation is a cultural value that has been passed on through generations of Native Americans. Their group survival has always depended on group cooperation in the hunt, in war, and in daily life. The value of cooperation can place native children at a disadvantage in North American schools that emphasize competition. Native American and Canadian First Nation children experience more success in classrooms that stress cooperation and sociability over competition and individuality (Lake 1990; Mehan 1992).

Beliefs are *ideas we hold about life, about the way society works, and about where we fit into the world.* They are expressed as specific statements that we hold to be true. Many Hindus, for example, believe that fulfilling behavioral expectations of one's own social caste will lead to reward in one's next birth, or incarnation. In the next life, good people will be born into a higher social status. In contrast, some Christians believe that one's fate in the afterlife depends on whether one believes in certain ideas—for instance, that Jesus Christ is one's personal savior. Beliefs come from traditions established over time, sacred scriptures, experiences people have had, and lessons given by parents and teachers or other individuals in authority. Beliefs, based on values, influence the choices we make. For example, one value might be that the environment is worth preserving. A belief based on that value would be that humans should make efforts to curb global warming.

Values and beliefs, as elements of nonmaterial culture, are expressed in two forms: an ideal culture and a real culture. **Ideal culture** consists of *practices, beliefs, and values regarded as most desirable in society and consciously taught to children.* Not everyone, however, follows the approved cultural patterns, even though people may say they do. Sometimes our values contradict one another. **Real culture** refers to *the way things in society are actually done.* For example, family time and money are both highly valued in U.S.

society. However, in order to make money, we often have to sacrifice time with our families.

Norms are *rules of behavior shared by members of a society and rooted in the value system.* Examples include our rather routine behaviors, from saying "Hi" to people we meet to obeying traffic signs. Norms range from religious warnings such as "Thou shalt not kill" to the expectation in many societies that young people will complete their high school education. Sometimes the origins of particular norms are quite clear. Few people wonder, for instance, why there is a norm to stop and look both ways at a stop sign. Other norms, such as the rule in many societies that women should wear skirts but men should not, have been passed on through the generations and have become unconsciously accepted patterns and a part of tradition. Sometimes we may not know how norms originated or even be aware of norms until they are violated.

Norms generally fall into two categories—folkways and mores—based largely on their importance and people's response to the breach of those norms. *Folkways* are customs or desirable behaviors, but they are not strictly enforced. Examples of folkways include responding appropriately and politely when introduced to someone, speaking quietly in a library, not scratching your genitals in public, using proper table manners, and covering your mouth when you cough. Violation of these norms causes people to think you are weird or even uncouth but not necessarily immoral or criminal.

Mores are norms that most members observe because they have great moral significance in a society. Conforming to mores is a matter of right and wrong, and violations of many mores are treated very seriously. The person who deviates from mores is considered immoral or criminal. Being honest, not cheating on exams, and being faithful in a marriage are all mores.

Taboos are the strongest form of mores. They concern actions considered unthinkable or unspeakable in the culture. For example, most societies have taboos that forbid incest (sexual relations with a close relative) and prohibit defacing or eating a human corpse. Taboos are most common and numerous in societies without centralized governments to establish formal laws and to maintain jails.

Taboos and other moral codes are of the utmost importance to a group because they provide guidelines for what is right and wrong. Yet behaviors that are

Taboo: Assisted Suicide

taboo in one situation may be acceptable at another time and place. The incest taboo is an example found in all cultures, yet the application of the incest taboo varies greatly across cultures (Brown 1991). In medieval Europe, if a man and a woman were within seven degrees of relatedness and wanted to marry, the marriage could be denied by the priest as incestuous. (Your first cousin is a third degree of relatedness from you.) Of course, in Europe, exceptions were made for the royal families, where cousins often married. By contrast, the Balinese permit twins to marry because it is believed they have already been intimately bonded together in the womb (Leslie and Korman 1989). In some African and Native American societies, one cannot marry a sibling but might be expected to marry a first cousin. As Table 3.2 illustrates, the definition of what is and what is not incest varies even from state to state in the United States.

Laws are *norms formally encoded by those holding political power in society*, such as laws against stealing property or killing another person. The violator of a law is likely to be perceived not just as a weird or an immoral person but also as a criminal who deserves formal punishment. Many mores are passed into law, and some folkways are also made into laws with formal punishments imposed for their violation. Behaviors may be folkways in one situation and mores or laws in another, with gradually more serious consequences. For example, nudity or various stages of near nudity may be only mildly questionable in some social settings (the beach or certain fraternity parties) but would be quite offensive in others (a four-star restaurant or a house of worship) and against the law in some situations, incurring a penalty, or sanction.

Sanctions *reinforce norms through rewards and penalties.* Sanctions vary with the importance of the norm and can range from a parent frowning at a child who fails to use proper table manners to a prison term or death sentence. **Formal sanctions** *are rewards or punishments conferred by recognized officials.* Fines for parking illegally, failing grades for plagiarism, and expulsion for bringing drugs or weapons to school are formal negative sanctions your school might impose. Positive sanctions include honors and awards. **Informal sanctions** *are unofficial rewards or punishments such as smiles, frowns, or ignoring unacceptable behaviors.* A private word of praise by your professor after class about how well you did on your exam would be an informal positive sanction; gossip or ostracism by other students because of the clothes you wear would be an informal negative sanction. Most often, adherence to norms is ingrained so deeply that our reward is simply "fitting in."

Language is *the foundation of every culture. It conveys verbal, written, and nonverbal messages among members of society.* The mini-drama between infant and adult is played out every day around the world as millions of infants learn the language of the adults who care for them. In the process, they acquire an important part of culture, which is learned. Although many animals can communicate with a limited repertoire of sounds, the ability to speak a language is unique to humans (Phillips 2013). Language conveys verbal, written, and nonverbal messages among members of society. Simply put, without language there would be little, if any, culture. Through the use of language, members of a culture can pass on essential knowledge to children and can share ideas with other members of their society. Work can be organized, and the society can build on its experiences and plan its future. Through language, members express their ideas, values, beliefs, and knowledge, a key ingredient in the ability of humans to sustain social life.

TABLE 3.2 Incest Taboos in the United States: States That Allow First-Cousin Marriage

Alabama	Connecticut	Hawaii	New Mexico	South Carolina
Alaska	District of Columbia	Maryland	New York	Tennessee
California	Florida	Massachusetts	North Carolina	Vermont
Colorado	Georgia	New Jersey	Rhode Island	Virginia

States that allow marriage only under certain conditions such as marriage after a certain age or inability to bear children: Arizona, Illinois, Indiana, Maine, Utah, and Wisconsin.

Source: National Conference of State Legislatures 2015.

Language takes three primary forms: spoken, written, and nonverbal. There are an estimated 5,000 languages *spoken* in the world. The most common first languages are Chinese (with 1.2 billion speakers), Spanish (414 million), English (335 million), Hindi (260 million), and Arabic (237 million) (Infoplease 2014). English, on the other hand, is the top Internet language around the world with 536.9 million users (Internet World Stats 2014).

Written language enables humans to store ideas for future generations, accelerating the accumulation of ideas on which to build. It also makes possible communication over distances.

Nonverbal language consists of gestures, facial expressions, and body postures. This mode of communication may carry as much as 90% of the meaning of a message (Samovar and Porter 2003). Every culture uses nonverbal language to communicate, and just like verbal language, those cues may differ widely among cultures.

The power to communicate nonverbally is illustrated in American Sign Language, designed for the hearing challenged and the mute. Complex ideas can be transmitted without vocalizing a word. Indeed, one can argue that the deaf have a distinctive culture of their own rooted in large part in the unique sign language that serves them (discussed further in "Engaging Sociology" on page 74). In addition, technology has aided communication among the hearing impaired through text messaging.

Thinking Sociologically

Think about a time when you were trying to understand what someone was saying when you could not hear his or her words (at a concert, a bar, a loud party, etc.). How did you rely on the other person's nonverbal communication to interpret what he or she was trying to convey? How successful were you? How did you know whether or not you were successful?

Language also plays a critical role in our perceptions and in thought organization. The *linguistic relativity theory* posits that the people who speak a specific language make interpretations of their reality—they notice certain things and may fail to notice certain other things (Sapir 1929, 1949; Whorf 1956). "A person's 'picture of the universe' or 'view of the world' differs as a function of the particular language or languages that person knows" (Kodish 2003:384).

While language does not totally determine thinking, most scientists agree that it does influence thinking (Casasanto 2008; Gumperz and Levinson 1996; Levinson 2000). For example, in some Native Alaskan cultures where life is dependent on the elements, there are a number of words for snow, each giving members of the group a description that could mean life or death—wet snow, dry snow, heavy snow, melting snow. Children in each different culture will learn about the world within the framework provided by their language.

In the English language people tend to associate certain colors with certain qualities in a way that may add to the problem of racist attitudes (Levinson 2000). The definition of the word *black* includes "dismal," "boding ill," "hostile," "harmful," "inexcusable," "without goodness," "evil," "wicked," "disgrace," and "without moral light." The word *white*, on the other hand, is defined as "honest," "dependable," "morally pure," "innocent," and "without malice" (Merriam-Webster 2014; *Webster's Unabridged English Dictionary* 1989). If the linguistic relativity thesis is correct, it is more than a coincidence that bad things are associated with the *black sheep* of the family, the *blacklist*, or *Black Tuesday* (when the U.S. stock market dropped dramatically and crashed in 1929).

This association of blackness with negative images and meanings is not true of all languages. The societies that have negative images for *black* and positive images for *white* are the same societies that associate negative qualities with people of darker skin. Blackness associated with something evil is not true of many African languages (Jordan 2012). The use of *white* as a synonym for good or innocent—as in reference to a "white noise machine" or a "white lie"—may contribute to a cultural climate that devalues people of color. In essence, the language may influence our perception of color in a manner that contributes to racism. Interestingly, there is empirical evidence supporting this claim of color symbolism. Athletic teams that wear black uniforms have more penalties called on them than teams with lighter-colored uniforms (Frank and Gilovich 1988).

When grouped together, material and nonmaterial components form cultural patterns. People's lives are organized around these patterns. For example, family life includes patterns of courtship, marriage, child rearing, and care of the elderly. For additional visual support for understanding material and nonmaterial cultural

White and black as colors have symbolic meaning—with phrases like "blackballed from the club" or "black sheep of the family" indicating negative judgment associated with blackness. Research shows that teams wearing black are called for more fouls than teams wearing white.

patterns, see the table titled "Material and Nonmaterial Cultural Patterns in Sport" at **edge.sagepub.com/ Ballantinecondensed4e.**

We have seen that material artifacts and nonmaterial beliefs, values, norms, and language comprise the basic components of culture. Next, we explore the theoretical explanations for culture.

SOCIETY, CULTURE, AND OUR SOCIAL WORLD

Whether their people are eating termite eggs, fish eggs, or chicken eggs, societies always have a culture, and culture is always linked to a society. Culture provides guidelines for behaviors and actions at each level of society, from the global system to the individual family. The social world model at the beginning of the chapter, with its concentric circles, represents the micro to macro levels of society. Smaller social units such as a school operate within a larger community that is also part of a region of the country. The culture determines what takes place in each of these units. There is a social unit—or structural "hardware"—and a culture—or "software"—at each level.

Microcultures: Micro-Level Analysis

Micro-level analysis focuses on social interactions in small groups. Groups of people, if those people meet with regularity and have some common interests or purpose, will develop insider language, jokes, symbols, and ways of interacting that may differ from other groups in which those same people participate. The social unit at this level of analysis only affects a portion of one's daily life (a bowling league, a book group, or a poker club) or shapes a limited time period of one's life (such as a Boy Scout troop or a gremlin soccer team for 8-year-old girls) (Gordon 1970). The social unit at the meso or macro level affects larger groups or societies and has more long-term impacts. So a **microculture** is *a culture that develops at the micro level in groups or organizations and affects only a segment of one's life or influences a limited period of one's life.* Other classic examples from sociology include a street gang, a college sorority, and a business office.

Hospitals are communities of people who share a microculture. People in different-colored uniforms scurry around carrying out their designated tasks, part of the division of labor in the organization, each having symbolic significance indicating positions at the hospital. Hospital workers interact among themselves to attain goals of patient care. They have a common in-group vocabulary, a shared set of values, a hierarchy of positions with roles and behaviors for each position, and a guiding system of regulations for the organization—all of which shape interactions during the hours when each member works in the hospital. Yet the hospital

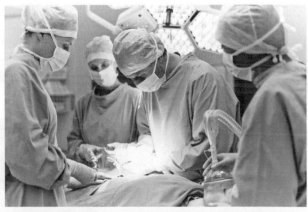

Hospitals provide one example of a microculture. Hospital employees share terminology, rules of interaction, and values regarding objectifying human body parts so that the patient is not sexualized.

microculture may have little relevance to the rest of the employees' everyday lives. Microcultures may survive over time, with individuals coming in and leaving as workers and patients, but in a complex society, no one lives his or her entire life within a microculture. The values, rules, and specialized language used by the hospital staff continue as one shift ends and other medical personnel enter and sustain that microculture.

Every organization, club, and association is a social group and therefore must have a culture (a microculture) with its own set of rules and expectations. Schools develop their own unique cultures and traditions; as students graduate and move out of that microculture, others move into it. Many microcultures exist for a limited period of time or for a special purpose. A summer camp microculture may develop but exists only for that summer. The following summer, a very different culture may evolve because of new counselors and campers. A girls' softball team may develop its own cheers, jokes, insider slang, and values regarding competition or what it means to be a good sport, but next year, the girls may be realigned into different teams, and the transitory culture of the previous year changes. In contrast to microcultures, subcultures continue across a person's life span.

Subcultures and Countercultures: Meso-Level Analysis

A subculture is the culture of a meso-level subcommunity that distinguishes itself from the dominant culture of the larger society. A **subculture** *is smaller than the nation but, unlike a microculture, is large enough to support people throughout the life span*—such as an ethnic group (Arnold 1970; Gordon 1970). Many ethnic groups within the larger society have their own subculture with their own sets of conventions and expectations. For example, picture a person who is African Canadian, Chinese Canadian, or Hispanic Canadian, living within an ethnic community that provides food, worship, and many other resources. Despite unique cultural traits, that person is still a Canadian citizen, living within the national laws, norms, and way of life. It is just that the person's life has guidelines from the subculture in addition to the dominant culture of the society.

Because the social unit, such as the ethnic groups mentioned above, plays a more long-term and pervasive role in the life span of group members than a summer camp or a sorority (microcultures), we analyze subcultures at the meso level. (Table 3.3 illustrates the connection between the social unit at each level and the type of culture at that level.)

Note that many of the categories into which we group people are not subcultures. For example, redheads, left-handed people, tall people, individuals who read *Wired* magazine, people who are single, visitors to Chicago, and DVD watchers do not make up subcultures because they do not interact as social units or share a common way of life. A motorcycle gang, a college fraternity, and a summer camp are also not subcultures because they affect only a segment of one's life (Gordon 1970; Yablonski 1959). In the United States, subcultures include ethnic groups, such as Mexican American and Korean American; restricted religious groups, such as the Orthodox Jews in New York City; and social class groups, including the elite upper class on the East and West Coasts of the United States. The superwealthy have networks, exclusive clubs, and the Social Register, which lists the names and phone numbers of the elite, so they can maintain contact with one another. They have a culture of opulence that differs from middle-class culture, and this culture is part of their experience throughout their lives.

TABLE 3.3 Level of Social Units and of Culture

Social Unit (People who interact and feel they belong)	Culture (The way of life of that social unit)
Dyads; small groups; local community	Microculture
Ethnic community or social class community	Subculture
National society	Culture of a nation
Global system	Global culture

Counterculture and the Mainstream   ▶ Subcultures and Countercultures

Many societies have subcultures based on ethnicity or religion or other historical characteristics, but broad-based subcultures with extensive social networks can emerge in other ways as well. Perhaps the most fascinating is the deaf subculture in the United States, which you can analyze in the next "Engaging Sociology" on page 74.

A give-and-take exists between subcultures and the dominant culture, with each contributing to and influencing the other. Sometimes the differences between the two lead to tension and conflict. When conflict with the larger culture becomes serious and important norms of the dominant society are violated, a different type of culture emerges.

A **counterculture** is *a group with expectations and values that contrast sharply with the dominant values of a particular society* (Yinger 1960). An example of a counterculture is the Old Order Amish of Pennsylvania and Ohio. The Amish drive horse-drawn buggies and seldom use electricity or modern machines. They reject many mainstream notions of success and replace them with their own work values and goals. The Old Order Amish prefer to educate their children in their own communities, insisting that their children not go beyond an eighth-grade education in the public school curriculum. They also do not use automobiles or conventional tractors. The Amish are pacifists and will not serve as soldiers in the national military.

Other types of countercultures seek to withdraw from society, to operate outside its economic and legal systems, or even to bring about the downfall

The Amish, a counterculture, reject important aspects of the mainstream or dominant culture—technology and consumerism—replacing them with biblical principles calling for a simple lifestyle.

of the larger society. Examples include survivalist groups such as racist militias and skinheads, who reject the principles of democratic pluralism. In the United States, the number of antigovernment "Patriot" groups who believe "that the federal government is conspiring to take Americans' guns and destroy their liberties as it paves the way for a global 'one-world government'" has increased dramatically over the past decade (Potok 2013c).

Some countercultures such as the Amish continue over time and can sustain members throughout their life cycle. Like subcultures, they operate at the meso level but reject mainstream culture. However, other countercultural groups, such as punk rock groups or violent and deviant teenage gangs, are short-lived or are relevant to people only at a certain age—operating only at the micro level.

◑ Thinking Sociologically

Describe a counterculture group whose goals are at odds with those of the dominant culture. Do you see any evidence to show that the group is influencing behavioral expectations and values in the larger society? What effect, if any, do countercultures have on your life?

Countercultures are not necessarily bad for society. According to conflict theory, which was introduced in Chapter 2, the existence of counterculture groups is clear evidence that there are contradictions or tensions within a society that need to be addressed. Countercultures often challenge the unfair treatment of groups in society that do not hold power and sometimes develop into social organizations or protest groups. Extremist religious and political groups, whether Christian, Islamic, Hindu, or any other, may best be understood as countercultures against Western or

Subcultures, such as the Orthodox Jewish faith community, impact their members throughout life—from infancy to death. Here, an Orthodox Jewish boy prepares to pray according to Jewish law by wrapping the leather strap of his *tefillin* around his arm and a *tallit* (prayer shawl) around his shoulders.

ENGAGING SOCIOLOGY

Deaf Subculture in the United States

by Thomas P. Horejes

The deaf subculture possesses its own language, norms, and social networks that are unique to the deaf. American Sign Language (ASL) has its own conversational rules and social norms such as mandatory eye gaze and appropriate facial expressions. Like other subcultures, the deaf subculture celebrates its own arts and entertainment, including deaf poetry, deaf music, deaf theater, and deaf cinema. The arts of the deaf subculture are often expressed visually through perspectives, experiences, and/or metaphors only understood by those who are fluent in ASL and a part of the deaf subculture. There are social gatherings and events by associations within the deaf subculture that host annual conferences and tournaments ranging from the Deaf World Softball Championships to the Rainbow Alliance of the Deaf (an LGBT organization). As with other subcultures, there is a deaf history and heritage that is passed on from generation to generation.

Many of the 5% to 10% of deaf children born to deaf parents are immediately enculturated into their own deaf subculture. In contrast, a large majority (90%–95%) of deaf children (including myself, born to hearing parents) start with an identity from the larger world (hearing society). As we progress throughout life, however, our identities become negotiated as we become more aware of a subculture—a deaf subculture that each of us has embraced quite differently. Some reject the deaf subculture in favor of total immersion into hearing society while others navigate in the deaf subculture, but in different ways. In addition to those born deaf, there are many individuals who become deaf later in life whether it is due to age, illness, or even prolonged exposure to loud sounds.

Regardless of how one becomes deaf, some individuals rely on technology (hearing aids or cochlear implants), communicate with hearing individuals via spoken/written English or through an ASL interpreter, and express willingness to work in the workplace dominated by members of the hearing society. Other deaf individuals become fully immersed into the deaf subculture or what they call the deaf "world." They may attempt to depart from the hearing culture by rejecting values and beliefs possessed by the hearing society such as assistive-listening devices and speech therapy, and by not placing their deaf child in hearing schools. These people typically attend only deaf plays, read about deaf history, take on jobs where communication is through sign language, and forbid any voiced English in favor of equal "access" in all aspects of their daily activities. One common denominator in shaping deaf identity and deaf subculture is language: the incorporation of sign language in the deaf individual's life.

• •

Thomas P. Horejes received his PhD at Arizona State University in justice studies and teaches sociology at Gallaudet University, the world's only university with programs and services specifically designed to accommodate students who are deaf or hard of hearing. He is the author of *Social Constructions of Deafness: Examining Deaf Languacultures in Education.*

Engaging With Sociology

1. Why does Dr. Horejes see the culture of the deaf as a subculture rather than a microculture or a counterculture?
2. Why is language the critical element in being a part of this subculture?
3. Why can a subculture exist in your own community and seemingly be invisible to you?

global influences that they perceive as threatening to their way of life. Figure 3.2 illustrates the types of cultures in the social world and the relationship between countercultures and their national culture. Countercultures, as depicted, view themselves and are viewed by others as "fringe" groups—partial outsiders within a nation.

National and Global Culture: Macro-Level Analysis

Canada is a national society, geographically bounded by the mainland United States to the south, the Pacific Ocean and Alaska to the west, the Atlantic Ocean to the east, and the Arctic to the north. The government in Ottawa passes laws that regulate activities in all provinces (which are similar to states or prefectures), and each province passes its own laws on regional matters. These geographic boundaries and political structures make up the national society of Canada.

National Society and Culture. The *national society* (introduced in Chapter 1) is a population of people, usually living within a specified geographic area, who are connected by common ideas, cooperate for the attainment of common goals, and are subject to a particular political authority. Within the nation, there may be smaller groups, such as ethnic, regional, or tribal subcultures, made up of people who identify closely with each other. Most nations have a **national culture** of *common values and beliefs that tie citizens of a nation together.* The national culture affects the everyday lives of most citizens. Within some countries of Africa and the Middle East, on the other hand, local ethnic or religious loyalties are much stronger than any sense of national culture, in part because the nation-state boundaries were originally *imposed* by foreign colonial powers. Subcultural differences divide many nations. Consider the loyalties of Shiites, Sunnis, and Kurds in Iraq to their subcultures, where the national culture struggles for influence over its citizens through laws, traditions, and military force.

In colonial America, people thought of themselves as Virginians or Rhode Islanders rather than as U.S. citizens. Even during the "War Between the States" of the 1860s, the battalions were organized by states and often carried their state banners into battle. The fact that some Southern states still call it the War Between the States rather than the Civil War communicates the struggle over whether to recognize the nation or states as the primary social unit of loyalty and identity. People in the United States today are increasingly likely to think of themselves as U.S. citizens (rather than as Iowans or Floridians), yet the national culture determines only a few of the specific guidelines for everyday life. Nonetheless, the sense of nation has grown stronger in most industrialized societies over the past century, and the primary identity is likely to be "United States" or "Canadian" citizen.

Global Society and Culture. Several centuries ago there was no "global culture," but with expanding travel, economic interdependence of different countries, international political linkages, global

FIGURE 3.2 Cultures at Various Levels in the Social World

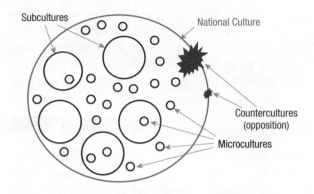

environmental concerns, and technology allowing for communication throughout the world, people now interact across continents in seconds. **Globalization** refers to *the process by which the entire world is becoming a single sociocultural entity—more uniform, more integrated, and more interdependent* (Pieterse 2004; Robertson 1997; Robertson and Scholte 2007). Globalization is a process of increased connectedness, uniformity, and interdependency across the planet (Eitzen and Zinn 2012).

Western political and economic structures lead the development of this global society, largely as a result of the domination of Western (European and U.S.) worldviews and Western control over resources. For example, the very idea of governing a geographic region with a bureaucratic structure known as a nation-state is a fairly new (Western) notion. Formerly, many small bands and tribal groupings dominated areas of the globe. However, with globalization, nation-states now exist in every region of the world.

Global culture includes *behavioral standards, symbols, values, and material objects that have become common across the globe* (International Beliefs and Values Institute 2012). We need to understand global culture to engage in human rights issues, global education, conflict resolution, sustainability, and religious and cultural understanding. For example, beliefs that monogamy is normal; that marriage should be based on romantic love; that people have a right to life, liberty, and the pursuit of happiness; that people should be free to choose their leaders; that women should have rights such as voting; that wildlife and fragile environments should be protected; and that everyone should have a cell phone and television set are spreading across the globe (Newman 2009).

During the 20th century, the idea of the primacy of individual rights, civil liberties, and human rights spread around the world, creating conflicts within nations that traditionally lack democratic institutions and processes. Backlashes against these and other Western ideas also can be seen in the acts of groups that have embraced terrorism (Eitzen and Zinn 2012; Kurtz 2007; Turner 1991a, 1991b). This has resulted in Western societies fighting terrorism when those groups see themselves as trying to preserve their culture (Morey and Yaqin 2011; Peek 2011).

Still, these trends are aspects of the emerging global culture. Even 100 years ago, notions of global cooperation and competition would have seemed quite bizarre (Lechner and Boli 2005). However, in nations all over the globe, people who travel by plane know they must stand in line, negotiate airport security, squeeze their bodies into confined spaces, and stay seated in the airplane until they are told they can get up (Lechner and Boli 2005). Regardless of nationality, we know how to behave in any airport in the world.

As the world community becomes more interdependent and addresses issues that can only be dealt with at the global level (such as global warming, pirates from Somalia and other countries, massive human rights violations as in the Syrian revolution or Sudanese war, international terrorism, global food shortages, and global financial crises), the idea of a common "software" of beliefs, social rules, and common interests takes on importance. Common ideas for making decisions allow for shared solutions to conflicts. Global culture at the macro level affects our individual lives, and its influence will only increase.

Many simple norms or beliefs about how to behave in public—like waiting in line for a train—have become accepted in cultures throughout the world.

However, global culture is not the only pattern that is new. Today, we see a counterculture at the global level. Stateless terrorist networks such as al-Shabaab, al-Qaeda, ISIS, and the Taliban reject the values of international organizations such as the World Court, the Geneva Convention, and other international systems designed to resolve disputes. Terrorists do not recognize the sovereignty of nations and do not acknowledge many values of respect for life or for civil discourse. This counterculture at the global level is a more serious threat than those at the micro and meso levels, in part because they do not fit into the global system of nations and its norms.

Thinking Sociologically

Make a list of social units of which you are a part. Place these groups into categories of microculture, subculture, national culture, and global culture. Consider which of them affects only a portion of your day or week (such as your place of work) or only a very limited time in your entire life span. Consider which groups are smaller than the nation but will likely influence you over much of your life. To what cross-national (global) groups do you belong? Do you belong to fewer groups at the national culture and global culture levels? If so, why do you suppose that is the case?

THEORIES OF CULTURE

Cultural Theory at the Micro Level

To understand our interactions with family and friends, we turn to the micro level of analysis. Although external forces at the national and global (macro) levels shape us in many ways, that is not the whole story, as we see when we examine the symbolic interaction approach to culture.

Symbolic Interaction Theory. How amazing it is that babies learn to share the ideas and meanings of complex cultures with others in those cultures. Symbolic interaction theory considers how we learn to share the meanings of symbols, whether material or nonmaterial. Cultures contain many symbols, such as rings, flags, and words that stand for or represent something. A ring means love and commitment. A flag represents national identity and is intended to evoke patriotism and love for one's country. A phrase such as *middle class* conjures up images and expectations of what the phrase means, a meaning shared with others in our group. Together in our groups and societies, we define what is real, normal, and good.

Symbolic interaction theory maintains that our humanness comes from the impact we have on each other through these shared understandings of symbols that humans have created. When people create symbols, such as a new greeting (e.g., a fist bump instead of a handshake) or a symbolic shield for a fraternity or sorority, symbols come to have an existence and importance for the group.

Symbolic interaction theory pictures humans as consciously and deliberately creating their personal and collective histories. The theory emphasizes the part that verbal and nonverbal language and gestures play in the shared symbols of individuals and the smooth operation of society. More than any other theory in the social sciences, symbolic interaction stresses the active decision-making role of individuals—the ability of individuals to do more than conform to the larger forces of the society.

Many of our definitions of what is "normal" are shaped by what others around us define as "normal" or "good." The **social construction of reality** *is the process by which individuals and groups shape reality through social interaction.* Our construction of reality, influenced by our social relations, has a profound effect on our daily lives, our life chances, and what we believe is possible in our lives. One illustration of this is the notion of what is beautiful or ugly. In the late 18th and early 19th centuries, in Europe and the United States, beaches were considered eyesores since there was nothing there but crushed stone and dangerous water. A beach was not viewed as a place to relax in a beautiful environment. Likewise, when early travelers to the West encountered the Rocky Mountains, with soaring granite rising to snow-capped peaks, the idea was that these were incredibly ugly wounds in the earth's surface. The summits were anything but appealing. Still, over time, some individuals began to redefine these crests as breathtakingly beautiful. We now see both as beautiful, but the social construction of scenery has not always been so (Lofgren 1999, 2010). So even what we experience as relaxing and peaceful in nature is shaped by how our society constructs those experiences.

This notion that individuals shape culture and that culture influences individuals is at the core of the symbolic interaction theory. Other social theories tend to focus at the meso and macro levels.

In the late 1700s and early 1800s, this mountain view would have been considered an eyesore—too ugly to enjoy. The social construction of reality—the definition of what is beautiful in our culture—has changed dramatically over the past two centuries.

Cultural Theories at the Meso and Macro Levels

How can we explain such diverse world practices as eating termites and worshipping cows? Why have some societies allowed men to have four wives, whereas others—such as the Shakers—prohibited sex between men and women entirely? Why do some groups worship their ancestors, while others have many gods, and yet others believe in a single divine being? How can societies adapt to extremes of climate and geographical terrain—hot, cold, dry, wet, mountainous, and flat? Humankind has evolved practices so diverse that it would be hard to find a practice that has not been adopted in some society at some time in history.

To explain these cultural differences, we will use two already familiar perspectives that have made important contributions to understanding culture at the meso and macro levels: structural-functional and conflict theories.

Structural-Functional Theory. Structural-functional theorists (also called functionalists) ask why members of an ethnic subculture or a society engage in certain practices. To answer, they look at how those practices contribute to the survival or social solidarity of the group or society as a whole. An example is the reverence for cattle in India. The "sacred cow" is protected, treated with respect, and not slaughtered for food. The reasons relate to India's ancient development into an agricultural society that required sacrifices (Harris 1989). Cattle were needed to pull plows and to provide a source of milk and dried dung for fuel.

Cows gained religious significance because of their importance for the survival of early agricultural communities. They must, therefore, be protected from hungry people for the long-term survival of the group. Protecting cows was functional; that is, the practice served a purpose for society.

Functionalists view societies as composed of interdependent parts, each fulfilling certain necessary functions or purposes for the total society (Radcliffe-Brown 1935). Shared norms, values, and beliefs, for instance, serve the function of holding a social group together. At a global macro level, functionalists see the world moving in the direction of having a common culture, potentially reducing "us" versus "them" thinking and promoting unity across boundaries. Synthesis of cultures and even the loss of some cultures are viewed as a natural result of globalization.

Although most cultural practices serve positive functions for the maintenance and stability of society, some practices, such as slavery, may be functional for those in power (those using child labor) but dysfunctional for minority groups or individual members of society. The fact that some societies are weak or have died out suggests that their way of life may not have been functional in the long run. Consider the case of Haiti, a country weakened in part because all the forests have been cut down to provide firewood. The resulting erosion made much of the land unusable for growing crops and led to a scarcity of food (Diamond 2005). Add to the existing poverty and hunger the devastation brought about by two earthquakes in 2010 that damaged or destroyed most buildings, a hurricane, and a cholera epidemic. The country and its people must rely on external support and donations from other countries to survive as it tries to rebuild.

The functionalist perspective has been criticized because it fails to consider how much dysfunction a society has, how much conflict a society can tolerate, and how much unity is necessary for a society to survive. Some critics argue that functional theory overemphasizes the need for consensus and integration among different parts of society, thus ignoring conflicts that may point to problems such as inequality in societies (Dahrendorf 1959).

Conflict Theory. Whereas functionalists assume consensus exists because all people in society have

Conflict theorists believe that society is composed of groups, each acting to meet its own self-interests. These protesters in this "Day Without an Immigrant" march in Los Angeles acted in support of their views toward immigration laws.

learned the same cultural values, rules, and expectations, conflict theorists do not view culture as having this uniting effect. Conflict theorists describe societies as composed of meso-level groups—class, ethnic, religious, and political groups—vying for power. Each group protects its own self-interests and struggles to make its own cultural ways dominant in the society. Instead of consensus, the dominant groups may impose their cultural beliefs on minorities and other subcultural groups, thus laying the groundwork for conflict. Conflict theorists identify tension between meso and macro levels, whereas functionalists tend to focus on harmony and smooth integration between those levels.

Actually, conflict may contribute to a smoother-running society in the long run. German sociologist Georg Simmel believed that some conflict could serve a positive purpose by alerting societal leaders to problem areas that need attention (Simmel 1955).

Conflict theorists argue that the people with privilege and power in society manipulate institutions such as religion and education. In this way, average people learn the values, beliefs, and norms of the privileged group and accept the dominant group's beliefs, self-interests, power, and advantage. The needs of the privileged are likely to be met, and their status will be secured. For instance, schools that serve lower-class children usually teach obedience to authority, punctuality, and respect for superiors—behaviors that make for good laborers and compliant workers. The children of the affluent, meanwhile, are more likely to attend schools stressing divergent thinking, creativity, and leadership, attributes that prepare them to occupy the most professional, prestigious, and highly rewarded positions in the society. Conflict theorists point to this control of the education process by those with privilege as part of the overall pattern by which the society benefits the rich.

Conflict theory can also help us understand global dynamics. Many poor nations feel that the global system protects the self-interests of the richest nations and that those rich nations impose their own culture, including their ideas about economics, politics, and religion, on the poorer nations of the Global South. Some scholars believe there is great richness in local customs that is lost when homogenized by cultural domination of the powerful nations (Ritzer 2007; Eitzen and Zinn 2012).

Conflict theory is useful for analyzing the relationships between societies (at a macro level) and between subcultures (at a meso level) within complex societies. It also helps illuminate tensions in a society when local (micro-level) cultural values clash with national (macro-level) trends. Conflict theory is not as successful, however, in explaining simple, well-integrated societies in which change is slow to come about and cooperation is an organizing principle.

THE FIT BETWEEN HARDWARE AND SOFTWARE

Computer software cannot work with incompatible machines. Some documents cannot be easily transferred to a different piece of hardware, although sometimes a transfer can be accomplished with significant modification in the formatting of the document. The same is true with the hardware of society and the software of culture. For instance, consider the size of families: the value (software) of having a large extended family, typical in agricultural societies, does not work well in the structure (hardware) of industrial and postindustrial societies that are mostly urban and crowded. Children in urban settings are generally a liability compared to those who work on the farm in agricultural societies. In short, there are limits to what can be transferred from one type of society to another, and the change or "formatting" may mean the new beliefs transferred to a different social setting are barely recognizable.

Attempts to transport U.S.-style "software" (culture)—individualism, capitalism, freedom of religion, and democracy—to other parts of the world illustrate that these ideas are not always successful in other settings. The hardware of other societies may be able to handle more than one type of software or set of beliefs, but there are limits to the adaptability. Thus, we should not be surprised when our ideas are transformed into something quite different when they are imported to another social system. If we are to understand the world in which we live and if we want to improve it, we must first fully understand other societies and cultures.

Thinking Sociologically

Some anthropologists argue that *team sports*, groups playing each other in coordinated competition, were first developed by Native American groups. Yet team sports are now a core component of U.S. society. How does participating in team sports help prepare people to successfully navigate life in the United States? For example, what lessons learned through playing on an organized team might be relevant to life in the business world?

Because there is such variation among societies and cultures in what they see as *normal*, how do we learn our particular society's expectations? The answer is addressed in the next chapter. Each society relies on the process of socialization to teach the culture to its members. Humans go through a lifelong process of socialization to learn social and cultural expectations. The next chapter discusses the ways in which we learn our culture and become members of society.

Difference Between Culture and Society

WHAT HAVE WE LEARNED?

Individuals and small groups cannot live without the support of a larger society, the hardware of the social world. Without the software—culture—there could be no society, for there would be no norms to guide our interactions with others in society. Humans are inherently social and learn their culture from others. Furthermore, as society has evolved into more complex and multileveled social systems, humans have learned to live in and negotiate conflicts among multiple cultures, including those at micro (microcultures), meso (subcultures), and macro (societal and global cultures) levels. Life in an Information Age society demands adaptability to different sociocultural contexts and tolerance of different cultures and subcultures. This is a challenge to a species that has always had tendencies toward ethnocentrism.

KEY POINTS

- *Society* refers to an organized and interdependent group of individuals who live together in a specific geographic area, interact with each other more than with outsiders, cooperate to attain goals, and share a common culture over time. Each society has a culture, the way of life shared by a group of people, including ideas and "things" that are passed on from one generation to the next; the culture has both material and non-material components.

- Societies evolve from very simple societies to more complex ones, from the simple hunter-gatherer society to the information societies of the postindustrial world.

- The study of culture requires that we try to avoid ethnocentrism (judging other cultures by the standards of our culture). Instead, we should use the view of cultural relativism, so that we can understand culture from the standpoint of those inside it.

- Just as social units exist at various levels of our social world, from small groups to global systems, cultures exist within different levels of the social system—microcultures, subcultures, national cultures, and global cultures. Some social units at the micro or meso level stand in opposition to the dominant national culture, and they are called countercultures.

- Various theories offer different lenses for understanding culture. While symbolic interaction illuminates the way humans bring meaning to events (thus generating culture), the functionalist and conflict paradigms examine cultural harmony and conflict between cultures, respectively.

- The metaphor of hardware (society's structure) and software (culture) describes the interdependent relationship of society and culture, and as with computers, there must be some compatibility between the structure of a society and the culture. If there is none, either the cultural elements that are transported into another society will be rejected, or the culture will be "reformatted" to fit the society.

DISCUSSION QUESTIONS

1. Think about the evolution of societies described in this chapter. In which type of society (hunter-gatherer, herding, horticultural, agricultural, industrial, or postindustrial) would you prefer to live? Why? In which would you most likely be (a) economically successful and (b) content? Why?

2. This chapter points out that today material culture "drives the globalization process." Look around at what your classmates are wearing and carrying and come up with some examples that support that point.

3. Think of a subculture to which you belong. What are the norms, values, and material artifacts that distinguish members of your subculture from those who do not belong to it?

4. Every classroom has norms of behavior. Some are mores, and some are folkways. Describe two of each in a typical classroom at your school. How are both enforced? How do you help enforce these norms?

5. Are you part of a counterculture? Why or why not? In what ways might a counterculture benefit a society?

CONTRIBUTING TO OUR SOCIAL WORLD: What Can We Do?

At the Local and National Levels

- *Ethnic group* organizations and clubs focus on the interests of specific ethnic groups: Arab Americans, Chinese Americans, Italian Americans, Polish Americans, and so on. You may have one or more on your own campus. Contact one of these groups (of your own background or of a background that differs from your own). Arrange to attend one of the group's meetings, and learn about the subculture and activities in which its members are involved. To find an ethnic association on campus, call your campus activities office. To find one in your local area, try Googling the name of the ethnic group, "club," and the name of your town or city.

- *Immigrant aid groups* are ethnically oriented organizations that assist recent immigrants in dealing with adjustment to life in a new country. Contact one of these groups, and explore the possibility of volunteering or serving as an intern. You should be able to determine if one is in your area by Googling the name of your town or city, the name of the ethnic group, and "immigrant aid group."

At the Global Level

- *The United Nations Permanent Forum on Indigenous Issues* assists indigenous people around the world who face threats to their cultures, languages, and basic rights as the process of globalization accelerates. We have experienced this in North America in relation to Native American and Inuit populations, but it is occurring throughout the world. Visit the forum's website at http://undesadspd.org/IndigenousPeoples.aspx, and contact the forum about the possibility of volunteering.

- *Cultural Survival* is an example of a leading nongovernmental organization (NGO) engaged in action-oriented programs. The organization partners with indigenous people to "defend their lands, languages, and cultures." Look at its website (www.culturalsurvival.org) for internship and volunteer opportunities.

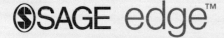

Sharpen your skills with SAGE edge at **edge.sagepub.com/ballantinecondensed4e**

SAGE edge for Students provides a personalized approach to help you accomplish your coursework goals in an easy-to-use learning environment.

4 Socialization

Becoming Human and Humane

Whether at the micro, meso, or macro level, our close associates and various organizations teach us how to be human and humane in our society. We learn skills, as well as values such as loyalty and compassion, by watching others.

MICRO

- ME (MY FAMILY AND CLOSEST FRIENDS)

- LOCAL ORGANIZATIONS AND COMMUNITY
  Families and friends serve as agents of socialization.

MESO

- NATIONAL ORGANIZATIONS, INSTITUTIONS, AND ETHNIC SUBCULTURES
  Citizens are socialized for national loyalty and patriotism.

MACRO

- SOCIETY
  Political parties and religious denominations transmit values.

- GLOBAL COMMUNITY
  People are socialized for tolerance and respect across borders.

LEARNING OBJECTIVES

4.1 Summarize the nature versus nurture debate and the sociological perspective on it.

4.2 Predict the impact of isolation and neglect on children.

4.3 Defend the position that groups at each level in our social world have a stake in how we are socialized.

4.4 Describe how we develop a "self" through interacting with others.

4.5 Explain how micro-and meso-level agents of socialization influence individuals.

4.6 Discuss how macro-level agents of socialization can impact children today.

4.7 Identify policy questions that rely on an understanding of socialization.

THINK ABOUT IT

Micro: Local Community	What does it mean to have a "self"? How have your family, local religious congregation, and schools shaped who you are?
Meso: National Institutions; Complex Organizations; Ethnic Groups	How do various subcultures or organizations of which you are a member (your ethnic group, political party, or religious affiliation) influence your position in the social world?
Macro: National and Global Systems	What would you be like if you were raised in a different country? How might globalization or other macro-level events—such as a terrorist attack on your country—impact you and your sense of self?

Phoebe Prince was a 15-year-old immigrant from Ireland. She and her family had recently settled in South Hadley, Massachusetts, and she enrolled in the high school. Unfortunately, she made a mistake! She dated a popular senior on the football team. This was not acceptable to a clique of girls who had it out for Phoebe. These "mean girls" sent her threatening text messages, threw things at her, called her "Irish slut" and "whore" on social networking sites such as Facebook and Twitter, and engaged in other bullying behaviors. Other students and even faculty who were aware of the bullying did nothing. After months of such treatment, one day the "mean girls" threw a can at Phoebe—and she went home and hung herself (Crime Library 2012).

Phoebe's story and stories of hundreds of other bullied and abused children point to a problem in the process of socialization, both in what the victim is experiencing and in what the perpetrators are doing. In this chapter we examine the process of socialization, how it involves development of our "self," and what can happen when socialization goes wrong.

Socialization is *the lifelong process of learning to become a member of the social world, beginning at birth and continuing until death.* It is a major part of what the family, education, religion, and other institutions do to prepare individuals to be members of their social world. In Phoebe's case, she had a negative socialization experience from peers, resulting in a damaged self-concept.

From the day they are born, infants are interactive, ready to be socialized into membership in the social world. As they cry, coo, or smile, they gradually learn that their behaviors elicit responses from other humans. This **interaction** is *the exchange of verbal and nonverbal messages.* These form the basic building blocks of socialization through which a child learns its culture and becomes a member of society. This process of interaction shapes the infant into a human being with a social self—the perception we have of who we are.

Three main elements provide the framework for socialization: human biological potential, culture, and individual experiences. Babies enter this world unsocialized, totally dependent on others to meet their needs, and completely lacking in social awareness and an understanding of the rules of their society. Despite this complete vulnerability, they have the potential to learn the language, norms, values, and skills needed in their society. Socialization is necessary not only for the survival of the individual but also for the survival of society and its groups. The process continues in various forms throughout our lives as we enter and exit various positions—from school to work to retirement to death.

In this chapter, we explore the nature and importance of socialization and how individuals become

Socialization starts at the beginning of life as babies interact intensively with their parents, observing and learning what kinds of sounds or actions elicit response from the adults.

socialized. We also look at development of the self, who or what socializes us, macro-level issues in the socialization process, and a policy example illustrating socialization. First, we briefly examine an ongoing debate: Which is more influential in determining who we are—our genes (nature) or our socialization into the social world (nurture)?

NATURE *VERSUS* NURTURE—OR *BOTH* WORKING TOGETHER?

What is it that makes us who we are? Is it our biological makeup or the family and community in which we grow up? One side of the contemporary debate regarding nature versus nurture seeks to explain the development of the self and human social behaviors—violence, crime, academic performance, mate selection, economic success, gender roles, and other behaviors—by examining biological or genetic factors (Harris 2009; Winkler 1991). Sociologists call this sociobiology, and psychologists refer to it as evolutionary psychology. Researchers in these fields claim that our human genetic makeup wires us for social behaviors (Pinker 2002; Wilson et al. 1978).

The idea is that we perpetuate our own biological family and the human species through our social behaviors. Human groups develop power structures, are territorial, and protect their kin. Examples of behaviors that sociobiologists see as rooted in the genetic makeup of the species include a mother ignoring her own safety to help a child, soldiers dying in battle for their comrades and countries, communities feeling hostility toward outsiders or foreigners, and people defending property lines against intrusion by neighbors. Sociobiologists say that these behaviors continue because they result in an increased chance of survival of the family, one's group, and the species as a whole (Lerner 1992; Pinker 2002; Wilson 1980, 1987).

Most sociologists believe that sociobiology and evolutionary psychology explanations have flaws. Sociobiology is a *reductionist* theory; that is, it often reduces complex social behaviors to single inherited traits such as an altruism gene, an aggression gene, or any other behavioral gene. However, evidence for such inherited traits is weak, at best. Sociologists point to the fact that there are great variations in the way members of different societies and groups behave. People born in one culture and raised in another adopt social behaviors common to the culture in which they grow up, not based on inherited traits (Gould 1997). If a specific social behavior is genetic, then it should be present regardless of the culture in which humans are raised. What sets humans apart from other animals is not so much our biological heritage but our ability to learn the ways of our culture through socialization.

Most sociologists recognize that individuals are influenced by biology, which limits the range of human responses and creates certain needs and drives, but they believe that nurture is far more important. Some sociologists propose theories that consider both nature and nurture. Alice Rossi, former president of the American Sociological Association, has argued that we need to build both biological and social theories—or biosocial theories—into explanations of social processes such as parenting (Rossi 1984). One group of sociologists has developed an approach called evolutionary sociology, which takes seriously the way our genetic makeup—including a remarkable capacity for language—shapes our range of behaviors. However, biological research also shows that living organisms are often modified by their environments and the behaviors of others around them—with even biological or genetic structure changing due to social interaction and experiences (Dobbs 2013; Machalek and Martin 2010).

In short, biology influences human behavior, but human action and interaction can also modify biological traits. For example, the nutritional history of grandparents can affect the metabolism of their grandchildren, and what grandparents ate was largely shaped by cultural ideas about food (Freese, Powell, and Steelman 1999; "The Ghost in Your Genes" 2009). Our cultural values shape what we eat today and whether we share food with the less privileged in our society. The bottom line is that *socialization* is key in the process of "becoming human and becoming humane."

THE IMPORTANCE OF SOCIALIZATION

If you have lived on a farm, watched animals in the wild, or seen television nature shows, you probably have noticed that many animal young become independent shortly after birth. Horses are on their

Why Socialize?

feet in a matter of hours, and by the time turtles hatch from eggs, their parents are long gone. Many species in the animal kingdom do not require contact with adults to survive because their behaviors are inborn and instinctual. Generally speaking, the more intelligent the species, the longer the period of gestation and of nutritional and social dependence on the mother and family. Humans clearly take the longest time to socialize their young. Even among primates, human infants have the longest gestation and dependency period, generally 6 to 8 years. Chimpanzees, very similar to humans in their DNA, take only 12 to 28 months. This extended dependency period for humans—what some have referred to as the *long childhood*—allows each human being time to learn the complexities of culture. This suggests that biology and social processes work together.

Normal human development involves learning to sit, crawl, stand, walk, think, talk, and participate in social interactions. Ideally, the long period of dependence allows children the opportunity to learn necessary skills, knowledge, and social roles through affectionate and tolerant interaction with people who care about them. Yet what happens if children are deprived of adequate care or even human contact? The following section illustrates the importance of socialization by showing the effect of deprivation and isolation on normal socialization.

Isolated and Abused Children

What would children be like if they grew up without human contact? Among the most striking examples are the few cases we know of severely abused and neglected children whose parents kept them isolated in cellars or attics for years without providing even minimal attention and nurturing. When these isolated children were discovered, typically they suffered from profound developmental disorders that endured throughout their lives (Curtiss 1977; Davis 1947). Most experienced great difficulty in adjusting to their social world's complex rules of interaction, which people normally start to learn from infancy onward.

In case studies comparing two girls, Anna and Isabelle, who experienced extreme isolation in early childhood, Kingsley Davis found that even minimal human contact made some difference in their socialization (Davis 1947). Both "illegitimate" girls were kept locked up by relatives who wanted to keep

their existence a secret. Both were discovered at about age 6 and moved to institutions where they received intensive training. Yet the cases were different in one significant respect: Prior to her discovery by those outside her immediate family, Anna experienced virtually no human contact. She saw other individuals only when they left food for her. Isabelle, on the other hand, lived in a darkened room with her deaf-mute mother, who provided some human contact. Anna could not sit, walk, or talk and learned little in the special school in which she was placed. When she died from jaundice at age 11, she had learned the language and skills of a 2- or 3-year-old. Isabelle, on the other hand, did progress. She learned to talk and played with her peers. After 2 years, she reached an intellectual level approaching normal for her age but remained about 2 years behind her classmates in skill and competency levels. By age 14, she was attending regular school and participating in social activities (Davis 1940, 1947).

Contemporary cases of children neglected or abused in their family settings or forced into slavery, prostitution, or fighting wars reinforce the importance of early social interaction. Although not totally isolated, these children also experience problems and disruptions in the socialization process. They have to deal with socially toxic abusive, violent, and dead-end environments with harmful developmental consequences for children (War Child 2014). Consider the case of child soldiers. A recent video, *Invisible Children*, went viral on YouTube, showing the plight of these children kidnapped by Joseph Kony's Lord's Resistance Army into a world of drugs, sex, and violence (Terra

This family in Papua New Guinea shares a playful moment together as they interact with one another. Even in such carefree moments, parents act as socializing agents for their children.

Long-term Consequences of Child Abuse and Neglect

Networks 2013). Most will have a difficult time integrating back into society—if they have a chance to do so—although there are organizations trying to help them.

These cases illustrate the devastating effects on socialization of isolation, neglect, and abuse early in life. Humans need more from their environments than food and shelter. They need positive contact, a sense of belonging, affection, safety, and someone to teach them knowledge and skills. This is children's socialization into the world, through which they develop a self. Before we examine the development of the self in depth, however, we consider the complexity of socialization in the multilevel (micro, meso, and macro) social world.

SOCIALIZATION AND THE SOCIAL WORLD

Ram, a first grader from India, had been in school in Iowa for only a couple of weeks. The teacher was giving the first test. Ram did not know much about what a test meant, but he rather liked school, and the red-haired girl next to him, Elyse, had become a friend. He was catching on to reading a bit faster than she, but she was better at the number exercises. They often helped each other learn while the teacher was busy with a small group in the front of the class. The teacher gave each child the test, and Ram saw that it had to do with numbers. He began to do what the teacher had instructed the children to do with the worksheet, but after a while, he became confused. He leaned over to look at the page Elyse was working on. She hid her sheet from him, an unexpected response. The teacher looked up and asked what was going on. Elyse said that Ram was "cheating." Ram was not quite sure what that meant, but it did not sound good. The teacher's scolding of Ram left him baffled, confused, and entirely humiliated.

This incident was Ram's first lesson in the individualism and competitiveness that govern Western-style schools. He was being socialized into a new set of values. In his parents' culture, competitiveness was discouraged, and individualism was equated with selfishness and rejection of community. Athletic events were designed to end in a tie so that no one would feel rejected. Indeed, a well-socialized person would rather lose in a competition than cause others to feel bad because they lost. Like Ram, each of us

learns the values and beliefs of our culture. In Ram's case, he moved from one cultural group to another and had to adjust to more than one culture within his social world.

At the micro level, most parents teach children proper behaviors to be successful in life, and peers influence children to "fit in" and have fun. In fact, the process of socialization in groups allows the self to develop as individuals learn to interact with others in their culture. Interaction theory, focusing on the micro level, forms the basis of this chapter, as you will see. At the meso level, religious denominations and political groups teach their versions of the truth, and educational systems teach the knowledge and skills considered by leaders as necessary for functioning in society. At the nationwide macro level, television ads encourage viewers to be more masculine or feminine, buy products that will make them better and happier people, and join the military. From interactions with our significant others to dealing with government bureaucracy, most activities are part of the socialization experience that teaches us how to function in our society.

Keep in mind that socialization is a lifelong process. Even your grandparents are learning how to live at their stage of life. The process of socialization takes place at each level of analysis, linking the parts. Groups at each level have a stake in how we are socialized because they all need trained and loyal group members to survive. Organizations need citizens who have been socialized to devote the time, energy, and resources that these groups need to survive and meet their goals. For example, volunteer and charitable organizations cannot thrive unless people are willing to volunteer their energy, time, skills, and money. Lack of adequate socialization means social organizations will not receive the support they need to thrive—or even, possibly, survive.

Most perspectives on socialization focus on the micro level because socialization takes place in each individual. However, meso- and macro-level theories add to our understanding of how socialization prepares individuals for their roles in the larger social world. *Structural-functionalist perspectives* of socialization tend to see organizations at different levels supporting each other. For example, families often organize holidays around patriotic themes, such as a national independence day, or around religious celebrations. These activities can strengthen family members' commitment to the nation and buttress the moral values emphasized in churches, temples, and mosques. All these values, in turn, help prepare individuals to support national political and economic systems.

At the meso level, the purposes and values of organizations or institutions sometimes directly contrast with one another or conflict with other parts of the social system. From the *conflict perspective*, the linkages between various parts of the social world are based on competition with or even direct opposition to another part. Socialization into a nation's military forces, for example, stresses patriotism and ethnocentrism, sometimes generating conflict and hostility toward other groups and countries. Demands from various organizations for people's time, money, and energy may leave little to give to our religious communities or even our families. Each organization and unit competes to gain our loyalty in order to claim some of our resources.

Conflict can occur in the global community as well. For example, religious groups often socialize their members to identify with humanity as a whole ("the family of God"). However, in some cases, nations do not want their citizens socialized to identify with those beyond their borders. Leaders of nations may seek to persuade Christians to kill other Christians, Jews, or Muslims whom they define as "the enemy." If religion teaches that all people are "brothers and sisters" and if religious people object to killing, the nation may have trouble mobilizing its people to arms when the leaders call for war.

Conflict theorists believe that those who have power and privilege use socialization to manipulate individuals to support the power structure and the self-interests of the elite. Those in power also have significant influence on the socialization of others through schools and political institutions. Although individuals may not realize it, most have little control over their futures. For example, parents decide how they would like to raise their children and what values they want to instill in them, but as their children enter school, parents must share the socialization process with school personnel. One reason why some parents choose to homeschool their children is to control external influences on the socialization process.

Whether we stress harmony in the socialization process or conflict rooted in power differences, the development of a sense of self through the process of socialization is an ongoing, lifelong process. Let us now focus on the micro level: How does the *self* develop?

Thinking Sociologically

Although the socialization process occurs primarily at the micro level, it is influenced by events at each level in the social system. Give examples of family, community, subcultural, national, or global events that influenced how you were socialized or how you might socialize your child.

DEVELOPMENT OF THE SELF: MICRO-LEVEL ANALYSIS

A baby is born with the potential to develop a *self*, but that self can evolve in many directions. Think of a baby you have observed; what influences that baby from birth? Can you see how those influences contribute to the developing self? The main product of the socialization process is *the self*. Fundamentally, **self** refers to *the perceptions we have of who we are*. Throughout the socialization process, our self develops largely from the way others respond to us—praising us, disciplining us, ignoring us. The development of the self allows individuals to interact with other people and to learn to function at each level of the social world.

Humans are not born with a sense of self. It develops gradually, beginning in infancy and continuing throughout adulthood. Selfhood emerges through interaction with others. Individual biology, culture, and social experiences all play a part in shaping the self. The hereditary blueprint each person brings into the world provides broad biological outlines, including particular physical attributes, temperament, and a maturational schedule. Each person is also born into a family that lives within a particular culture, illustrating that nature is shaped by nurture. This hereditary blueprint, in interaction with family and culture, helps create each unique person, different from any other person yet sharing the types of interactions by which the self is formed.

Most sociologists, although not all (Irvine 2004), believe that we humans are distinct from other animals in our ability to develop a self and to be aware of ourselves as individuals or objects. Consider how we refer to ourselves in the first person—*I* am hungry, *I* feel foolish, *I* am having fun, and *I* am good at basketball. We have a conception of who we are, how we relate to others, and how we differ from and are separate from others in our abilities and limitations. We have an awareness of the characteristics, values, feelings, and attitudes that give us our unique sense of self (James [1890] 1934; Mead [1934] 1962).

Thinking Sociologically

Who are some of the people who have been most significant in shaping your *self*? How have their actions and responses helped shape your self-concept as musically talented, athletic, intelligent, kind, assertive, clumsy, or any of the other hundreds of traits that might make up your self?

The Looking-Glass Self and Role-Taking

Ty: "Hi! What's up?" (Ty has had his eye on this girl in his class, so he approaches her before class.)

Valerie: "Nothin' much."

Ty: "So what do you think of our sociology class?"

Valerie: "It's OK." (She turns around, spots a friend, and walks away.) "Hey Julie, did you get your soc assignment done?"

Ty is left to reflect on how to interpret Valerie's response. Take this common interaction and apply it to interactions you have had. First you approach someone and open a conversation (or someone approaches you); second, the person takes you up on the conversation—or not; third, you evaluate the individual's response and modify your behavior based on your interpretation. These steps make up the *looking-glass self*, and they are repeated many times each day. We now explore these seemingly simple interactions that are key in developing our *self* and in our socialization process.

The looking-glass self idea is part of *symbolic interaction theory*, and offers important insights into how individuals develop the self. Two of the major scholars in this approach were Charles H. Cooley ([1909] 1983) and George Herbert Mead ([1934] 1962). Cooley believed that the self is a social product, shaped by interactions with others from the time of birth. He likened interaction processes to looking in a mirror wherein each person reflects an image of the other.

Each to each a looking-glass

Reflects the other that doth pass. (Cooley [1909] 1983:184)

For Cooley, the **looking-glass self** is *a reflective process that develops the self based on our interpretations and on our internalization of the reactions of others* ([1909] 1983). In this process, Cooley believed that there are three principal elements: (1) We imagine how we appear to others, (2) others judge our appearance and respond to us, and (3) we react to that feedback. We experience feelings such as pride or shame based on this imagined judgment and respond based on our interpretation. Moreover, throughout this process, we actively try to manipulate other people's view of us to serve our needs and interests. This is one of the many ways we learn to be boys or girls—the image we see reflected back to us lets us know whether we have behaved in ways socially acceptable according to gender expectations. The issue of gender socialization in particular will be discussed in Chapter 9. Of course, this does not mean our interpretation of the other person's response is correct, but our interpretation does determine how we respond.

Our self is influenced by the many "others" with whom we interact, and each of our interpretations of their reactions feeds into our self-concept. Recall that the isolated children failed to develop this sense of self precisely because they lacked interaction with others.

Taking the looking-glass self idea a step further, Mead explained *that individuals take others into account by imagining themselves in the position of that other*, a process called **role-taking**. When children play mommy and daddy, doctor and patient, or firefighter, they are imagining themselves in another's shoes. Role-taking allows humans to view themselves from the standpoint of others. This requires mentally stepping out of our own experience to imagine how others experience and view the social world. Through role-taking, we begin to see who we are from the standpoint of others. In short, role-taking allows humans to view themselves as objects, as though they were looking at themselves through the eyes of another person. For Mead, role-taking is a prerequisite for the development of our sense of self.

Many stereotypes—rigid images of members of a particular group—surround young African American males in the United States. How these images

ENGAGING SOCIOLOGY

Black Men and Public Space

By Brent Staples

My first victim was a woman—white, well dressed, probably in her early twenties. I came upon her late one evening on a deserted street in Hyde Park, a relatively affluent neighborhood in an otherwise mean, impoverished section of Chicago. As I swung onto the avenue behind her, she cast back a worried glance. To her, the youngish black man—broad, six-feet two-inches tall, with a beard and billowing hair, both hands shoved into the pockets of a bulky military jacket—seemed menacingly close. After a few more quick glimpses, she picked up her pace and was running in earnest. Within seconds, she disappeared into a cross street.

That was more than a decade ago. I was 22 years old, a graduate student newly arrived at the University of Chicago. It was in the echo of that terrified woman's footfalls that I first began to know the unwieldy inheritance I'd come into. . . . It was clear that she thought herself the quarry of a mugger, a rapist, or worse. Suffering a bout of insomnia, however, I was stalking sleep, not defenseless wayfarers. . . . I was surprised, embarrassed, and dismayed all at once. Her flight . . . made it clear that I was indistinguishable from the muggers who occasionally seeped into the area from the surrounding ghetto. I soon gathered that being perceived as dangerous is a hazard in itself. I only needed to make an errant move after being pulled over by a policeman. Where fear and weapons meet—and they often do in urban America—there is always the possibility of death.

In that first year, my first away from my hometown, I was to become thoroughly familiar with the language of fear. At dark, shadowy intersections, I could cross in front of a car stopped at a traffic light and elicit the thunk, thunk, thunk, thunk of the driver—black, white, male, or female—hammering down the door locks. On less-traveled streets after dark, I grew accustomed to but never comfortable with people crossing to the other side of the street rather than pass me.

After dark, on the warren-like streets of Brooklyn where I live, I often see women who fear the worst from me. They seem to have set their faces on neutral, and with their purse straps strung across their chests bandolier style, they forge ahead as though bracing themselves against being tackled. I understand, of course, that . . . women are particularly vulnerable to street violence, and young black males are drastically overrepresented among the perpetrators of that violence. Yet these truths are no solace against the kind of alienation that comes of being ever suspect. . . .

Over the years, I learned to smother the rage I felt at so often being taken for a criminal. Not to do so would surely have led to madness. I now take precautions to make myself less threatening. I move about with care, particularly late in the evening. . . . On late-evening constitutionals, I employ what have proved to be excellent tension-reducing measures: I whistle melodies from Beethoven and Vivaldi and the more popular classical composers. Even steely New Yorkers hunching toward nighttime destinations seem to relax, and occasionally they even join in the tune. Virtually everybody seems to sense that a mugger wouldn't be warbling bright, sunny selections from Vivaldi's Four Seasons. It is my equivalent of the cowbell that hikers wear when they know they are in bear country.

Engaging With Sociology

1. Brent Staples goes out of his way to reassure others that he is harmless. What might be some other responses to this experience of having others assume one is dangerous and untrustworthy?

2. How might one's sense of self be influenced by these responses of others?

3. How are the looking-glass self and role-taking at work in this scenario?

4. Have you ever experienced a similar situation in which you felt fear or others fearing you? If so, how does that affect you?

Source: Staples 2001. Reprinted with permission from Brent Staples.

---

influence the young men and their social world is the subject of the above "Engaging Sociology" feature. Think about the human cost of stereotypes and their effect on the socialization process as you read the essay. If one's sense of self is profoundly influenced by the ways others respond to you, how might the identity of a young African American boy be affected by public images of black males?

Mead also argued that role-taking is possible because humans have a unique ability to use and respond to symbols ([1934] 1962). *Symbols*, first described in Chapter 2, are actions or objects that represent something else and therefore have meaning beyond their own existence. Language and gestures are examples, for they carry specific meaning for members of a culture. Symbols such as language allow us to give names to objects in the environment and to infuse those objects with meanings. Once the person learns to symbolically recognize objects in the environment, the self can be seen as one of those objects. This starts with possessing a name that allows us to see our self as separate from other objects. If we said the name LeBron James, most listeners would immediately think of the same person: an extraordinary athlete who largely turned around the fortunes of the Miami Heat professional basketball team to win back-to-back NBA championships.

In the process of symbolic interaction, we take the actions of others and ourselves into account. We may blame, encourage, praise, punish, or reward ourselves. An example would be a basketball player missing the basket because the shot was poorly executed and thinking, "What did I do to miss that shot? I'm better than that!" Reflexive behavior, being able to look at oneself and one's behaviors as though from the outside looking in, includes the simple act of taking mental notes or mentally talking to one's self.

Parts of the Self

According to the symbolic interaction perspective, the self is composed of two distinct but related parts—dynamic parts in interplay with one another (Mead [1934] 1962). The most basic element of the self is what George Herbert Mead refers to as the *I, the spontaneous, unpredictable, impulsive, and largely unorganized aspect of the self.* The *I* initiates behavior without considering the possible social consequences. We can see this at work in the "I want it now" behavior of a newborn baby or even a toddler. Cookie Monster on the children's television program *Sesame Street* illustrates the *I* in every child, gobbling cookies at every chance and insisting on more *now*.

The *I* continues as part of the self throughout life, tempered by the social expectations that surround individuals. In stages, humans become increasingly influenced by interactions with others who instill society's rules. Children develop the ability to see their *self* as others see them (role-taking), allowing them to critique the behavior that was initiated by the *I*. Mead called this reflective capacity of the self the *Me*. The *Me* is *the part of the self that has learned the rules of society through interaction and role-taking, and it controls the I and its desires.* Just as the *I* initiates the act, the *Me* gives direction to the act. In a sense, the *Me* channels the impulsive *I* in an acceptable manner according to societal rules and restraints, yet meets the needs of the *I* as best it can. When we stop ourselves just before saying something and think to ourselves, "I'd better not say that," it is our *Me* monitoring and controlling the *I*. Notice that the *Me* requires the ability to take the role of the other, to anticipate the other's reaction.

Stages in the Development of the Self

The process of developing a social self occurs gradually and in stages. Mead identified three critical stages—(1) the imitation stage, (2) the play stage, and (3) the game stage—each of which requires the unique human ability to engage in role-taking (Mead [1934] 1962). In the **imitation stage**, *children under 3 years old are preparing for role-taking by observing others and imitating their behaviors, sounds, and gestures.* The **play stage** involves *a child, usually from 3 to 5, having the ability to see things (role-take) from the perspective of one person at a time: simple role-taking or play-acting.* Listen to children who are 3 to 5 years old play together. You will notice that they spend most of their time telling each other what to do. One of them will say something like "You be the mommy, and José can be the daddy, and Julie, you be the dog. Now you say, 'Good morning, Dear,' and I'll say, 'How did you sleep?' and Julie, you scratch at the door like you want to go out." They will talk about their little skit for 15 minutes and then enact it, with the actual enactment taking perhaps 1 minute. Small children mimic or imitate role-taking based on what they have seen as they learn and practice future roles (Handel, Cahill, and Elkin 2007).

Society and its rules are initially represented by **significant others**—*parents, guardians, relatives, siblings, or important individuals whose primary and sustained interactions are especially influential.* That is

Childhood Development   Socialization in Sports

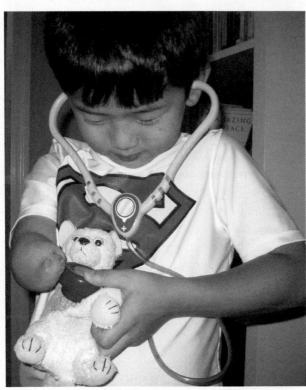

This child is learning both adult roles and empathy with others through imitation and play.

why much of the play stage involves role-taking based on these significant people in the child's life. The child does not yet understand the complex relations and multiple role players in the social world outside the immediate family. Children may have a sense of how their mommy or daddy sees them, but children are not yet able to comprehend how they are seen by the larger social world. Lack of role-taking ability is apparent when children say inappropriate things such as "Why are you so fat?"

The third stage in the process of developing a social self, the **game stage**, *is when a child develops the ability to take the role of multiple others concurrently and conform to societal expectations.* The child goes beyond the significant other such as the parent to value the opinion of all peers or expectations of the community.

Have you ever watched a team of young children play T-ball (a pre–Little League baseball game in which the children hit the ball from an upright rubber device that holds the ball), or have you observed a soccer league made up of 6-year-olds? If so, you have seen Mead's point illustrated vividly. In soccer (or football), 5- or 6-year-old children will not play

their positions despite constant urging and cajoling by coaches. They all run after the ball, with little sense of their interdependent positions. Likewise, a child in a game of T-ball may pick up a ball that has been hit, turn to the coach, and say, "Now what do I do with it?" Most still do not quite grasp throwing it to first base, and the first-base player may actually have left the base to run for the ball. It can be hilarious for everyone except the coach, as a hit that goes 7 feet turns into a home run because everyone is scrambling for the ball.

Prior to the game stage, the vision of the whole process is not possible. When children enter the game stage at about age 7 or 8, they are developmentally able to play the roles of various positions and enjoy a complex game. Each child learns what is expected and the interdependence of roles because she or he is able, at this stage, to respond to the expectations of several people simultaneously (Hewitt and Shulman 2011; Meltzer 1978). This allows the individual to coordinate his or her activity with others.

In moving from the play stage to the game stage, children's worlds expand from family and day care to neighborhood playmates, school, and other organizations. *This process gradually builds up a composite of societal expectations that the child learns from family, peers, and other organizations,* what Mead refers to as the **generalized other**. The child learns to internalize the expectations of society—the generalized other—over and above the expectations of any "significant others." Behavior comes to be governed by abstract rules ("no running outside of the baseline" or "no touching the soccer ball with your hands unless you are the goalie") rather than guidance from and emotional ties to a "significant other." Children become capable of moving into new social situations such as school, organized sports, and (eventually) the workplace to function with others in both routine and novel interactions. Individuals are active in shaping their social contexts, the self, and the choices they make about the future.

The common human experience of feeling embarrassed illustrates how the generalized other becomes internalized into one's conception of self. Making an inappropriate remark at a party or having another call undue attention to one's appearance can cause embarrassment. Feeling embarrassed may occur when one violates a social norm and then thinks about how others view that behavior.

©Ana Abejon/E+/Getty Images

Very young children who play soccer do not understand the role requirements of games. They all—including the goalie—want to chase after the ball. Learning to play positions is a critical step in socialization.

According to this role-taking view, we see ourselves as objects from the standpoint of others, and we judge ourselves accordingly. Very young children, however, do not feel embarrassment when they do things such as soiling their pants or making inappropriate comments because they have not incorporated the *generalized other*. They have not yet learned the perspective of others. The capacity to feel embarrassed is not only an indicator of having internalized the generalized other but also a uniquely human outcome of our role-taking ability (Hewitt and Shulman 2011; Koschate-Reis 2009).

As we grow, we identify with new in-groups such as a neighborhood, a college sorority, or the military. We learn new ideas and expand our understanding. Some individuals ultimately come to think of themselves as part of the global human community. Thus, for many individuals, the social world expands through socialization. However, some individuals never develop this expanded worldview, remaining narrowly confined and drawing lines between themselves and others who are different. Such narrow boundaries often result in prejudice against others.

Thinking Sociologically

Who are you? Write down 15 or 20 roles or attributes that describe who you are. How many of these items are characteristics associated with the *Me*—nouns such as *son, mother, student*, and *employee*? Which of the items are traits or attributes—adjectives such as *shy, sensitive, lonely, selfish*, and *vulnerable*? How do you think each of these was learned or incorporated into your conception of your *self*?

The Self and Connections to the Meso Level

In the preceding "Thinking Sociologically" exercise, we asked you to think about how you see yourself and what words you might use to portray yourself. If you were describing yourself for a group of people you did not know, we suspect that you would use mostly nouns describing a status or a social position within the society: *student, employee, athlete, violinist, daughter, sister, Canadian, Lutheran*, and so forth. To a large extent, our sense of who we are is rooted in social positions that are part of organizations and institutions in the society (Kuhn 1964; Stryker 1980). This is a key point made by what is referred to as the Iowa School of symbolic interaction: The *self* is relatively stable because we develop a core self—a stable inner sense of who we are regardless of the immediate setting in which we find ourselves. This core often centers on the most important social positions we hold in the larger structure of society. Your sense of core self may shape your sexual behavior, the honesty with which you conduct business with others, and whether you are willing to cheat on an exam—even though you may not be around other people of your moral or political persuasion at the time (Kuhn 1964; Stryker 1980, 2000; Stryker and Stratham 1985; Turner 2003).

The Chicago School of symbolic interaction emphasizes the role of the *I* and focuses on individuals' involvement in their own development and their agency in creating their world. The Iowa School places somewhat more emphasis on the *Me*—on the role of others and the external social environment in shaping us (Carrothers and Benson 2003).

Socialization Throughout the Life Cycle

In all societies, individuals move from one stage to the next in the socialization process: birth, naming ceremonies or christenings, starting school at age 5 or 6, officially joining a church or temple at early puberty, obtaining a driver's license at about age 16, becoming eligible for military draft, being able to vote at age 18 and drink alcohol at age 21, getting married, having children, developing a career, and retiring from the workforce. Most social scientists emphasize the importance of *rites of passage*—celebrations or

Aging Population

public recognitions when individuals shift from one status to another. The importance of this shift resides in how others come to perceive the individual differently, the different expectations that others hold for the person, and changes in how the person sees himself or herself.

As noted earlier, socialization is a lifelong process—with many small and large passages. Infants begin the socialization process at birth. In childhood, one rite of passage is a child's first day at school—entrance into the meso-level institution of education. This turning point marks a child's entry into the larger world. The standards of performance are now defined by the child's teachers, peers, friends, and others outside the home. Adolescence is an important stage in Western industrial and postindustrial societies, but this stage is far from universal. Indeed, it is largely an invention of complex societies over the past two centuries, characterized by extensive periods of formal education and dependency on parents (Papalia and Feldman 2011). Adolescence is, in a sense, a structurally produced mass identity crisis because Western societies lack clear rites of passage for adolescents. Teens come to view themselves as a separate and distinct group with their own culture, slang vocabulary, clothing styles, and opinions about appropriate sexual behavior and forms of recreation.

Most of our adult years are spent in work and home life, including marriage and parenting roles. It is not surprising, then, that graduation from one's final alma mater (whether it be high school, college, or graduate school), marriage, and acceptance of one's first full-time job serve as rites of passage into adulthood in modern societies.

Thinking Sociologically

Find someone who has grown up in a different culture and ask her or him about rites of passage from adolescence to adulthood where she or he was raised. How are the patterns similar to or different from your own?

Even the retired and elderly members of society are constantly undergoing socialization and resocialization in the process of developing their sense of self. The type of society influences the socialization experience of the elderly and how they carry out their roles, as well as their status in society. Consider the changes that have taken place in the lifetimes of those born before 1945, as described by one elder:

> We were born before television, before polio shots, frozen foods, Xerox, plastic contact lenses, Frisbees, and the Pill. We were born before credit cards, split atoms, laser beams and ballpoint pens; before pantyhose, dishwashers, clothes dryers, electric blankets, air conditioners in our homes, drip-dry clothes and before man walked on the moon.... We never heard of FM radio, artificial hearts, word processors, yogurt, and guys wearing earrings. For us time sharing means togetherness—not computers and condominiums. (Grandpa Junior 2006)

The elderly are vitally important to the ongoing group in more settled agricultural societies. They are the founts of wisdom and carry group knowledge, experiences, and traditions valued in societies where little change takes place. In industrial and postindustrial countries, the number of the elderly is growing rapidly as medical science keeps people alive longer, diets improve, and diseases are brought under control. As of 2013, the average life expectancy in the United States was 76 for men and 81 for women ("U.S. Life Expectancy" 2013). Yet, in modern societies, social participation by the elderly often drops after retirement.

Retirement is a rite of passage to a new status, like that of marriage or parenthood, for which there is little preparation. As a result, retired people sometimes feel a sense of uselessness when they abruptly lose their occupational status. Retirees in Western societies generally have many years of life yet to live. The most socially satisfied retirees tend to develop hobbies, enjoy sports, or have new jobs they can pursue after they retire.

Dying is the final stage of life (Kübler-Ross 1997). Death holds different meanings in different cultures: passing into another life, a time of judgment, a waiting for rebirth, or a void and nothingness. In some religious groups, people work hard or do good deeds because they believe that they will be rewarded in an afterlife or with rebirth to a better status in the next life on earth. Thus, beliefs about the meaning of death can affect how people live their lives and how they cope with dying and death.

Some retirees, rather than taking up hobbies, decide on a part-time job, like this man who enjoys people and is now a "greeter" at Walmart. Others take on a postretirement job because they need the income.

Death rituals differ depending on the culture and religion of the group. A celestial burial master feeds the body of a dead Tibetan to the vultures in northwest China's Qinghai province. In Tibetan regions, where people believe in rebirth and thus no need to preserve the body, they speak of this practice as "giving alms to the birds." For a photo essay and further exploration of death rituals, visit **edge.sagepub.com/ballantinecondensed4e.**

Each stage of the life cycle involves socialization into new roles in the social world. Many social scientists have studied these developmental stages and contributed insights into what happens at each stage (Clausen 1986; Erikson 1950; Freud [1923] 1960; Gilligan 1982; Handel et al. 2007; Kohlberg 1971; Papalia and Feldman 2011; Piaget 1989). For example, some sociologists focus their research on the study of old age (gerontology), and death and dying.

Death ends the lifelong process of socialization, a process of learning social rules and roles and adjusting to them. When the individual is gone, society continues. New members are born, are socialized into the social world, pass through roles once held by others, and eventually give up those roles to younger members. Cultures provide guidelines for each new generation to follow. The social world perpetuates itself and outlives the individuals who populate it.

Thinking Sociologically

How were you socialized to view death and dying? What have you learned in your family about how to cope with death? Is death a taboo topic for your family?

The Process of Resocialization

If you have experienced life in the military, a boarding school, a convent, a mental facility, or a prison, or had a major transition in your life such as divorce or the death of a spouse or child, you have experienced resocialization. **Resocialization** is *the process of shedding one or more social positions and taking on others, which*

involves learning new norms, behaviors, and values suitable to the newly acquired status (Goffman 1961). Resocialization may take place in a **total institution**—*a place that cuts people off from the rest of society and totally controls their lives in the process of resocialization.* These include prisons, mental hospitals, monasteries, concentration camps, boarding schools, and military barracks. Bureaucratic regimentation and the manipulation of residents for the convenience of the staff is part of the routine (Goffman 1961).

We often associate resocialization with major developmental stages in adult life—leaving home to go to college, marriage, having a baby, divorce, retirement, and widowhood. Changes in status present opportunities to move in new and often exciting directions, such as going to college. Resocialization can also mean adjusting to living alone, raising children alone, loneliness, and possible financial problems.

Sometimes, resocialization occurs when individuals are forced to correct or reform behaviors defined as undesirable or deviant. Prison rehabilitation programs provide one example. However, research suggests that the difficulty in resocializing prisoners is rooted in the nature of the prison environment itself. Prisons are often coercive and violent environments, which may not provide the social supports necessary for bringing about positive change in a person's attitudes and behaviors.

Although resocialization is the goal of self-help groups such as Alcoholics Anonymous, Gamblers Anonymous, Parents Anonymous, drug rehabilitation groups, and weight loss groups, relapse is a common problem among participants. Some public sociologists work on trying to understand why there are such high rates of reversion to previous patterns of behavior. Former prison inmates are at especially high risk of repeating a crime, so public sociologists want to know what might make the resocialization "stick." In the next "Sociologists in Action" feature, David Kirk shows how he used lessons from the aftermath of hurricane Katrina to solve a puzzle and make policy recommendations.

There are multiple individuals, groups, and institutions involved in the socialization process. These socialization forces are referred to as agents of socialization.

AGENTS OF SOCIALIZATION: THE MICRO-MESO CONNECTION

Agents of socialization are *the transmitters of culture— the people, organizations, and institutions that help us define our identity and teach us how to thrive in our social world.* Agents are the mechanism by which the self learns the values, beliefs, and behaviors of the culture. Agents of socialization help new members find their place, just as they prepare older members for new responsibilities in society. At the micro level, one's family, one's peer group, and local groups and organizations help people know how they should behave and what they should believe. At the meso level, formal sources of learning (e.g., education and religion) and informal sources of learning (e.g., the media and books) are all agents that contribute to socialization. They transmit information to children and to adults throughout people's lives.

Thinking Sociologically

As you read this section, make a list of socializing agents. Indicate two or three central messages each agent of socialization tries to instill in people. Are there different kinds of messages at the micro, meso, and macro levels? Do these messages conflict, and if so, why?

In early childhood, the family acts as the primary agent of socialization, passing on messages about respect for property and authority, and the value of love and loyalty (Handel et al. 2007). Peer groups are also important, especially during the teenage years. Some writers even argue that the peer group is most important in the socialization process of children and teens (Aseltine 1995; Harris 2009). Each agent has its own functions and is important at different stages of the life cycle, but meso-level institutions play a more active role as one matures. For example, schools and religious bodies become more involved in socialization as children become 6 years old and older, compared with when they were preschool age.

Lessons from one agent of socialization generally complement those from other agents. Parents work at home to support what school and religion teach. However, at times, agents provide conflicting lessons. For example, family and faith communities often give teens messages that conflict with those of peer groups regarding sexual activity and drug use. This is an example of mixed messages given by formal and informal agents.

Formal agents of socialization are *official or legal agents (e.g., families, schools, teachers, religious organizations) whose purpose it is to socialize the individual into the values, beliefs, and behaviors of the culture.* For example, a primary goal of families is to teach children to speak and to learn proper behavior. In addition, schoolteachers educate by giving formal instruction, and religious organizations provide moral instruction. (These formal agents of socialization will be discussed in Chapters 10–11.)

As children become teenagers, peers become increasingly important socializing agents, shaping their norms, values, and attitudes.

 Macrosociology vs. Microsociology

SOCIOLOGISTS IN ACTION:
DAVID S. KIRK

Using Evidence-Based Research to Inform Public Policy: Resocialization Lessons From Hurricane Katrina

I have spent much of my professional career using the tools of sociology to examine the myriad consequences of criminal justice policies in the United States. Part of my focus has been on the influence of communities on the *resocialization* of ex-prisoners. Research reveals that on leaving prison ex-prisoners tend to be geographically concentrated in a relatively small number of neighborhoods within metropolitan areas; they often return to the very same neighborhoods and find themselves surrounded by the socializing agents that helped lead them to criminal behavior in the first place. Thus, it is not surprising that large proportions of ex-prisoners end up back in prison within just three years.

If criminal behavior is influenced by the types of neighborhoods we live in, then it seems counterproductive to prisoner reintegration for ex-offenders to return to the same locales where they got into trouble. The hope for ex-prisoners is that they will become *resocialized*, shedding their criminal identity as they learn the norms, behaviors, and values of law-abiding citizens.

These well-known facts about crime and justice in the United States serve as the backdrop of my research on prisoner reentry, the process of leaving prison and returning to the community. The tragedy of Hurricane Katrina, which devastated the gulf coasts of Louisiana and Mississippi in August 2005, afforded me a unique opportunity to examine what would happen if ex-prisoners did not return home to their old neighborhoods upon exiting prison. Katrina provided a natural experiment for investigating the importance of residential change because it forced some people to move who otherwise would not have. Residential change may serve as a catalyst for sustained behavioral change by providing an opportunity for individuals to separate from the former contexts and associates that facilitated their prior criminal behavior. A fresh location enhances resocialization efforts.

As I had hypothesized, prisoners exiting incarceration following Hurricane Katrina were much less likely to reside in the New Orleans neighborhoods where they resided prior to incarceration. Among those who did return to the same parish (a parish is the equivalent of a county) where they resided prior to incarceration, 26% were reincarcerated within one year of release from prison. By comparison, only 11% of offenders who moved to a new parish faced reincarceration one year after leaving prison. Based on these results, I concluded that separating individuals from their former residential environment reduces their likelihood of recidivism. Moving allows an individual to separate from the peers and routine activities that contributed to his or her criminal behavior in the past.

One critical component of disseminating information about scientific discoveries is to communicate the implications of the research. For instance, in most states, prisoners released on parole are legally required to return to their county of last residence, contributing to a return to old neighborhoods. So, parole policies, while designed to enhance public safety, may in fact undermine it. One implication of my research that I have discussed with key policy makers is that removing the institutional barriers to residential change may enhance public safety by lessening repetition of crime. Additionally, providing incentives for individuals to move to new neighborhoods, such as public housing vouchers, may benefit public safety. Thus, in my experience, redesigning public policies is part of a methodical process that involves good science, communication of results, and further testing in a real-world environment.

• •

David S. Kirk, PhD, is an associate professor in the Department of Sociology and a faculty research associate of the Population Research Center at the University of Texas at Austin. This excerpt is adapted from Sociologists in Action: Sociology, Social Change, and Social Justice *(Sage 2013).*

Informal agents of socialization are *unofficial agents that shape values, beliefs, and behaviors in which socialization is not the express purpose.* Examples include the media, books, advertising, and the Internet. They bring us continuous messages even though their primary purpose is not socialization but entertainment or selling products. Children watch countless advertisements on television, many with messages about what is good and fun to eat and how to be more attractive, more appealing, smarter, and a better person through the consumption of products. This bombardment is a particularly influential part of socialization for children and teenagers.

Thinking Sociologically

What confusion might be created for children when the formal and informal agents of socialization provide different messages about values or acceptable behaviors? Is this contradiction something that parents should be concerned about? Why or why not?

Micro-Level Socialization

Perhaps the most important micro-level formal agent of socialization is our own family—parents, siblings, and other family members. One way in which families teach children what is right and wrong is through rewards and punishments, called *sanctions*. Children who lie to their parents may receive a verbal reprimand or a slap on the hand, be sent to their rooms, have "time out," or receive a spanking, depending on differences in child-rearing practices among families. These are examples of negative sanctions. Conversely, children may be rewarded for good behavior with a positive sanction, such as a smile, praise, a cookie, or a special event. The number and types of sanctions dispensed in the family shape the socialization process, including development of the self and the perceptions we have of who we are and even whether we are good and clever or bad and stupid. Note that family influence varies from one culture to another.

In Japan, the mother is a key agent in the process of turning a newborn into a member of the group, passing on the strong group standards and expectations of family, neighbors, community, and society through the use of language and emotion. The child learns the importance of depending on the group and therefore fears being cast out. The need to belong creates

pressure to conform to expectations, and the use of threats and the fear of shame help socialize children into Japanese ways (Hendry 1987; Holloway 2001).

Nonconformity is a source of shame in Japan. The resulting ridicule is a powerful means of social control. In some cases, the outcast is physically punished by peers. Thus, to bring shame on oneself or the family is behavior to be avoided. In the most extreme cases, young people have committed suicide because they did not conform to group expectations and felt profoundly ashamed as a result.

In contrast to the values of conformity and fitting into the group espoused in many Asian countries, in the United States, most parents teach their children to value friendliness, cooperation, orientation toward achievement, social competence, responsibility, and independence. However, subcultural values and socialization practices may differ within the

© Tibor Bognar/Corbis

A Japanese mother helps her son at Heian Shinto Shrine during *Shichi-go-san Matsuri*, also called the Seven-Five-Three Festival, a celebration with prayers of long life for children aged 3 to 7.

diverse groups in the U.S. population. Conceptions of what makes a "good person" or a "good citizen" and varied goals of socialization bring about differences in the process of socialization around the world.

Meso-Level Socialization

Meso-level agents also work to socialize people into specific cultural values and roles they must learn to fulfill. Education and religion are two obvious influences—both being institutions with primary responsibility for socialization. We will discuss those in more detail in Chapters 10 and 11; here we illustrate meso-level socialization influences with a focus on social class and the media.

Social Class. Our education level, our occupation, the house we live in, what we choose to do in our leisure time, the foods we eat, and our religious and political beliefs are just a few aspects of our lives affected by socialization. Applying what we know from sociological research, the evidence strongly suggests that socialization varies by **social class**, or *the wealth, power, and prestige rankings that individuals hold in society* (Paxton and Pearce 2009). Meso-level patterns of distribution of resources, based in part on the economic opportunities created by state and national policies, affect who we become, as we see below.

Upper-middle-class and middle-class parents in the United States usually have above-average education and managerial or professional jobs. They tend to pass on to their children the skills and values necessary to succeed in the subculture of their social class. Subcultures, you will recall, operate at the meso level of the social system. Subcultural values such as autonomy, creativity, self-direction (the ability to make decisions and take initiative), responsibility, curiosity, and consideration of others are especially important for middle-class success and are part of middle-class subculture (Kohn 1989). If the child misbehaves, for example, middle-class parents typically analyze the child's reasons for misbehaving, and punishment is related to these reasons. Sanctions often involve instilling guilt and denying privileges.

Working-class parents tend to pass on to children their cultural values of respect for authority and conformity to rules, lessons that will be useful if the children also have blue-collar jobs (Kohn 1989). Immediate punishment with no questions asked if a rule is violated functions to prepare children for

This parent passes on a love for the piano to his young son. Because of the social class of this father, his son is likely to receive many messages about creativity, curiosity, and self-direction.

positions in which obedience to rules is important to success. They are expected to be neat, clean, well-mannered, honest, and obedient students and workers (MacLeod 2008). Socialization experiences for boys and girls are also often different, following traditional gender-role expectations of the working-class subculture.

Members of each class, as you can see, socialize their children to be successful in their social class and to meet expectations for adults of that class. Schools, like families, participate in this process and socialize children to adapt to the settings in which they grow up and are likely to live. Children's social class position on entering school, in turn, has an effect on the socialization experiences they have in school (Ballantine and Hammack 2012). The result is the *reproduction of class*, as young people are socialized to enter into the social class of their parents. Social class, however, is only one of many influencing agents of socialization. As we saw in *Black Men and Public Space* (p. 90), race and ethnicity are very important factors in socialization, as is gender. We discuss gender socialization in more detail in Chapter 9, but note here that race, class, and gender act as structural constraints on some members of the population, as they receive different messages about who they are and how they should behave. Therefore, it is important to recognize the interplay of these variables in people's lives.

Electronic Media. Television and computers are important informal agents of socialization at the meso level. They are intermediate-sized social units—larger than a local community, but smaller than a nation. They impact both nation-states and global agencies at the macro level by shaping public attitudes, and they affect family notions of what is normal or not normal at the micro level. In developed countries, there is scarcely a home without a television set, and over 78% of homes have computers and Internet access (New Media Trend Watch 2013).

Researchers have collected nearly five decades of information on how television has become a way of life in homes. By the time an average child in the United States reaches age 18, he or she will have spent more time watching television than doing any other single activity besides sleeping. On average, children in the United States between ages 8 and 18 spend 3 hours a day watching television, 1 hour and 11 minutes watching videos or DVDs, 1 hour and 44 minutes with audio media, 1 hour using computers, and 49 minutes

The children above illustrate how computer games and other electronic devices influence the socialization process of even young children.

playing video games, with a total media exposure in a typical day of 8 hours and 33 minutes. Ninety-five percent of teens are online (Madden et al. 2013). More than 75% of teens own cell phones, and text an average of 60 times a day (Ahuja 2013; Pew Research Center Internet & American Life Project 2012). The next "Engaging Sociology" feature shows the total media exposure of children by several variables. Examine this issue in more depth by answering the questions following Tables 4.1 and 4.2.

The moguls of the mass media—a meso-level social system—are able to influence socialization within the most intimate of environments. "Children [in the United States] use computers at very young ages. Over 80% of children under age 5 use the Internet weekly" (Kessler 2011).

Parents who play an active role in helping children understand the content of television and computer games can have a powerful effect on mitigating media's negative impacts and enhancing the positive aspects of media. The media usage habits of parents can also influence how their children respond to media (Jordan et al. 2006; National Consumers League 2013).

An alarming concern with Internet socialization is its role in radicalizing some young people and involving them in terrorism. The Tsarnaev brothers—Tamerlan and Dzhokhar—were apparently well-adjusted teens while in high school, but they were deeply influenced by Internet exchanges and by political websites. Eventually they teamed together to plot the Boston Marathon bombings on April 15, 2013. Three people were killed, and roughly 280 people were injured, many losing limbs. The actions of these young men were spawned when they adopted ideologies deeply antagonistic to the United States through Internet socialization. In a country that values free speech, controlling such antisocial influences is a real dilemma (Crary and Lavoie 2013).

Perhaps the most important aspect of television and computers is something that we do not fully understand but that has frightening potential. For the first time in human history, we have powerful agents of socialization in the home from a child's birth onward. Time spent watching television or playing computer games means less time spent engaging in interaction with caregivers and peers. Intimate family bonds formed of affection and meaningful interaction are being altered by the dominant presence of electronic media in the home. In addition, those who control

ENGAGING SOCIOLOGY

Media Exposure and Socialization

Examine Tables 4.1 and 4.2 and respond to the questions below.

TABLE 4.1 Total Media Exposure

		Average Hours per Day
Age	8 to 10 years old	7:51
	11 to 14 years old	11:53
	15 to 18 years old	11:23
Gender	Boys	11:12
	Girls	10:17
Race	White	8:36
	Black	12:59
	Hispanic	13:00
Parent education	High school or less	11:26
	Some college	11:30
	College graduate	10:00

TABLE 4.2 Average Amount of Time per Day Spent With Each Medium (8- to 18-year-olds)

Medium	1999	2009
Television	3:47	4:29
Music/audio	1:48	2:31
Computer	:27	1:29
Video games	:26	1:13
Print	:43	:38
Movies	:18	:25
Total media exposure	7:29	10:45
Multitasking proportion	16%	29%

Engaging With Sociology

1. Considering the data in Tables 4.1 and 4.2, how would you describe television-watching and other media-engaged patterns among different groups?
2. Are the trends in media exposure over the first decade of the 21st century a matter of concern? Why or why not?
3. How might media time affect other aspects of socialization of children?
4. What might be the social consequences of ethnic minorities (blacks and Hispanics) and those children whose parents do not have a college education having so much higher media exposure each day, compared to whites and those with more education?
5. Do your conclusions indicate any cause for concern about the use of media in your society? Why or why not?

Source: Kaiser Family Foundation 2010; Rideout, Foehr, and Roberts 2010.

the flood of mass media messages received by children may have very different interests and concerns than parents.

Without a doubt, a significant part of the informal socialization process occurs with the assistance of electronic equipment that shares the home with parents and siblings and that commands a significant portion of a child's time and attention. We also know that macro forces, such as globalization, have influenced school curricula and media content. We move next to a discussion of some of the national and global processes that influence socialization.

SOCIALIZATION AND MACRO-LEVEL ISSUES

Sense of Self in the New Global Context

Immigration patterns and ethnic conflicts around the world have resulted in a fairly new phenomenon: transnationalism. **Transnationalism** is *the process by which immigrants have multinational social relations that link together their original societies with their new locations. This means that an individual or a family has national loyalty to more than one country* (Levitt 2001, 2007; Levitt and Waters 2006). Often, it occurs after the migration of war refugees, whose roots lie in their country of origin and whose close family members may continue to live there.

Consider transnational children raised in war-torn countries. In the Palestinian territories, especially Gaza, and in Israeli settlements along the border, children grow up with fear and hatred that result in major influences on their socialization. Some war refugees spend childhoods in refugee camps and may never return to their native countries. For people experiencing transnationalism, there are conflicting messages about culturally appropriate behaviors and the obligations of loyalty to family and nation. Events of a national or global nature directly impact how an individual is socialized—with some of the socializing influences being from outside one's country of residence.

However, one need not migrate to another country to experience global pressures. The Internet and cell phones have increasingly created a sense of connectedness to other parts of the world and an awareness of global interdependencies (Brier 2004; Roach 2004). Some commentators have even suggested that the Internet is a threat to the nation-state as it allows individuals to develop friendships, loyalties, and norms that are not in the interests of the state (Drori 2006). Ideas of social justice or progress may be shaped not just by the government that rules the country but by international human rights organizations and ideas obtained from media that cross borders, such as the Internet. In recent uprisings in some Middle Eastern and North African countries, social networking kept movement participants in touch with others in the uprisings and with outside media and supporters. So socialization can include agents beyond the local community and even beyond national boundaries.

As more people have access to the Internet, they also have access to international information and friendships across borders and boundaries. Figure 4.1 on Internet use around the world illustrates not only variability of access but also how widespread this

FIGURE 4.1   Internet Users per 100 People

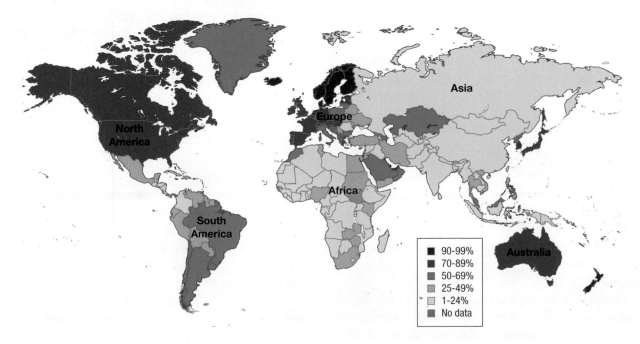

Source: World Bank 2013b.

access has become. One interesting question is how access or lack of access will influence the strength of "us" versus "them" feelings between citizens of different countries, insofar as sense of self is connected to belonging to a group—to a sense of "us."

At a time when people lived in isolated rural communities and did not interact with those unlike themselves, there was little price to pay for being bigoted or chauvinistic toward those who were different. However, we now live in a global village where we or our businesses will likely interact with very different people in a competitive environment. If we hold people in low regard because they are unlike us or because we think they are destined for hell, there may be a high cost for this animosity. Among other problems, terrorism is formented when people feel alienated. Therefore, training in cultural sensitivity toward those "others" has become an economic and political issue.

The reality is that children today live in a globalized world. Increasing numbers of children around the world learn multiple languages to enhance their ability to communicate with others. Some college campuses require experiences abroad as part of the standard curriculum because faculty members and administrators feel that a global perspective is essential in our world today and as part of a college education. Global sensitivity and tolerance of those once considered "alien" has become a core element of our day (Robertson 1992; Snarr and Snarr 2008).

Sometimes, global events can cause a different turn—away from tolerance and toward defensive isolation. When 19 young men from Saudi Arabia and other Middle Eastern countries crashed planes into the World Trade Center in New York City and into the Pentagon in Washington, DC, the United States was shocked and became mobilized to defend itself and its borders. The messages within schools and from the government suddenly took a more patriotic turn. So this event and other terrorist acts, clearly tragedies rooted in global political conflicts, can intensify the boundaries between people and loyalty to the nation-state. Global forces are themselves complex and do not always result in more tolerance.

Indeed, the only thing that we can predict with considerable certainty is that in this age of sharing a small planet, the socialization of our citizens will be influenced by events at the macro level, whether national or global.

Thinking Sociologically

When might people feel animosity toward different people is OK, and when might animosity be against their interests? What would you do to change feelings of animosity?

POLICY AND PUBLIC SOCIOLOGY

Should preschoolers living in poverty be socialized in day care settings? Should adolescents work while going to school? Should we place emphasis in high school and college on in-group loyalty and patriotism or on developing a sense of global citizenship? Should new parents be required to take child-rearing classes? How should job-training programs be structured? How can communities use the talents and knowledge of retirees? Can the death process be made easier for the dying person and the family? These are all policy questions—issues of how to establish governing principles that will enhance our common life.

These policy questions rely on an understanding of socialization—how we learn our beliefs and our positions on issues facing society. For example, making decisions about how to provide positive early-childhood education experiences at a time when young children first learn the ways of their culture depends on understanding the socialization they receive at home and at school. The quality of child care we provide for young children will affect not only how effective our future workforce is but also whether the children turn out to be productive citizens or a drain on society. These are all questions public sociologists can help to answer.

Now that we have some understanding of the process of socialization, we look at the next level in the process of interaction and how individuals become members of small groups, networks, and large complex organizations.

WHAT HAVE WE LEARNED?

Human socialization is pervasive, extensive, and lifelong. We cannot understand what it means to be human without comprehending the impact of a specific culture on us, the influence of our close associates, and the complex interplay of pressures at the micro, meso, and macro levels. Indeed, without social interaction, there would not even be a self. We humans are, in our most essential natures, social beings. The purpose of this chapter has been to open our eyes to the ways in which we become the individuals we are. We move now to a discussion of how we use our socialization in interactions with groups and organizations to be a part of society.

KEY POINTS

- Human beings come with their own biological makeup, but most of what makes us uniquely human we learn from our culture and society—through socialization. Humans who live in isolation from others do not receive the socialization necessary to be part of culture and are sometimes barely human.

- The self consists of the interaction of the *I*—the basic impulsive human with drives, needs, and feelings—and the *Me*. We develop a reflective self through role-taking to see how others might view us.

- The self is profoundly shaped by others, but it also has agency—that is, it can be an initiator of action and a maker of meaning.

- The self develops through stages, from mimicking others (the play stage) to more intellectually sophisticated abilities to role-take and to see how various roles complement each other (the game stage).

- The self is modified as it moves through life stages, and some of those stages require major resocialization—shedding old roles and taking on new ones as one enters new statuses in life.

- A number of agents of socialization are at work in each of our lives, communicating messages relevant at the micro, meso, or macro level of social life. At the meso level, for example, we may receive different messages about what it means to be a "good" person depending on our ethnic, religious, or social-class subculture.

- Some of these messages may be in conflict with each other, as when global messages about tolerance for those who are different conflict with a nation's desire to have absolute loyalty and a sense of superiority.

DISCUSSION QUESTIONS

1. Cooley's idea of the "looking-glass self" helps us understand that how we think other people view us influences our view of ourselves. How has your sense of your ability to succeed in college been influenced by the feedback you have processed from those around you (particularly teachers, peers, and family members)?

2. Socialization occurs throughout the life cycle. Into what role have you been socialized most recently?

Who were the primary agents in this socialization process? Did you find the process relatively easy or difficult? Why?

3. Sociological studies have shown that middle-class and working-class parents tend to socialize their children differently. Explain the differences and describe how they relate to how you were socialized by your family of origin.

4. How has your socialization been influenced by television and video games? Do you think the extent to which these informal agents of socialization influence children these days has a positive or a negative impact on our society? Why?

5. If you were asked to create a government policy to promote positive socialization experiences that would strengthen our society, what might you propose? Why?

CONTRIBUTING TO OUR SOCIAL WORLD: What Can We Do?

At the Local Levels

- In every community, numerous opportunities exist for volunteer work helping children from economically and otherwise disadvantaged backgrounds to succeed in school. *Opportunities to help disadvantaged children succeed in school include tutoring or mentoring in the local schools.*

- *Head Start centers for poor preschool children* often have opportunities to do something concrete to help children. An education faculty member at your college can give you contact information, or go to the association's website at www.nhsa.org.

- *Help in a local Boys and Girls Club* that provides socialization experiences for children through their teens. You can find a club near you by going to www.bgca.org/whoweare/Pages/FindaClub.aspx.

- *Take service learning course credits.* Locate the service learning office at your college or university to learn about service learning programs on your campus that help disadvantaged children.

At the National and Global Levels

- Literacy is a vital component of socialization, yet remains an unmet need in many parts of the world, especially in the less-developed countries of Africa and Asia. *World Education* provides training and technical assistance in nonformal education in economically disadvantaged communities worldwide. Go to the organization's website at www.worlded.org to learn about its wide variety of projects and volunteer/work opportunities.

- *CARE International* (www.care-international.org) and *Save the Children* (www.savethechildren.org) provide funding for families to send children to school and to receive specialized training.

- *Free The Children* (www.freethechildren.com), an organization that empowers young people to help other young people, has built more than 650 schools and schoolrooms for children in various parts of the world. Go to the organization's website to learn how you can work with others to help create more educational opportunities for children.

- *UNESCO (the United Nations Educational, Scientific, and Cultural Organization)* promotes literacy around the world in many ways. Learn more about its efforts at www.unesco.org/new/en/education. Opportunities exist for fundraising, internships, and eventually jobs with these organizations.

Sharpen your skills with SAGE edge at **edge.sagepub.com/ballantinecondensed4e**

SAGE edge for Students provides a personalized approach to help you accomplish your coursework goals in an easy-to-use learning environment.

5 Interaction, Groups, and Organizations

Connections That Work

Human interactions result in connections—networks—that make life more ful-filling and our economic efforts more productive. These connections link every-thing from small micro groups to large bureaucratic organizations.

MICRO

ME (MY FAMILY AND CLOSEST FRIENDS)

LOCAL ORGANIZATIONS AND COMMUNITY
Networks form in local organizations like civic and alumni groups.

MESO

NATIONAL ORGANIZATIONS, INSTITUTIONS, AND ETHNIC SUBCULTURES
Ethnic organizations, political parties, and religious denominations are important to many people.

MACRO

SOCIETY
Citizens of a nation develop connections and a common identity.

GLOBAL COMMUNITY
The United Nations, international courts, and transnational corporations influence our lives.

LEARNING OBJECTIVES

5.1 Demonstrate the impact social networks can have on the lives of individuals.

5.2 Provide examples of how verbal and nonverbal interaction guides our behavior.

5.3 Describe the needs primary and secondary groups meet for members of society and the overall society.

5.4 Show how the characteristics of bureaucracy apply to formal organizations.

5.5 Explain why networking with people from different cultures has become increasingly important.

THINK ABOUT IT

Micro: Local Community	How does interaction with family and friends affect who you are and what you believe?
Meso: National Institutions; Complex Organizations; Ethnic Groups	Is bureaucratic red tape necessary and inevitable?
Macro: National and Global Systems	What are some ways national trends, such as the decline in the percentage of U.S. citizens who smoke, influence your quality of life? What are some ways networks across the globe affect your daily life, your education, and your chosen profession?

As we wrote these words, Kathleen, one of the authors of this book, turned to CNN.com on her smartphone and saw that the relatives of a U.S. woman just killed in Syria were able, while at their home in Michigan, to identify her body via a picture posted online (Watkins 2013). Likewise, people online all over the world were able to follow the recent protests and uprisings in nations such as Iran, Tunisia, Yemen, Egypt, and Bahrain. Peaceful demonstrators and violent fighters used their cell phones, blogs, Twitter, and Facebook to send pictures and video footage documenting these events. Some have referred to this as "the Twitter Revolution." Cyberspace links people around the world in seconds in ways that few governments can stop (Stone and Cohen 2009). The information superhighway is opening new communication routes and allowing individuals with common interests to network instantly.

By contrast, Jeanne, another of the authors of this book, took a leave of absence in the mid-1980s to conduct some research in Japan. A benefit of that leave was that she escaped the distractions of ringing phones and she could concentrate. Fax was almost unknown, and email hardly existed for the civilian population. In 2007, she taught on Semester at Sea. Even in the middle of the ocean, she was in instant contact with her office, publisher, and family over the international Internet superhighway. She could insert earphones into her laptop computer and have a Skype conversation by voice or pick up a mobile phone and call her family or coauthor. What a change in 25 years! Technology is creating a smaller world, connected through global networks.

This chapter lays the groundwork for understanding how we fit into the structure of our social world—exploring the link between the individual and the social structure. The process starts when we are born and continues with group activities as we join playgroups, preschool, and kindergarten classes. It broadens as we become members of larger organizations and bureaucracies within universities, workplaces, national political parties, and national and international religious organizations. First, we consider how networks and connections link individuals and groups to different levels of analysis. Then, we focus on micro-level interactions, meso-level groups, and meso- and macro-level organizations and bureaucracies. Finally, we consider macro-level national and global networks.

NETWORKS AND CONNECTIONS IN OUR SOCIAL WORLD

©REUTERS/Eric Gaillard

No longer are paper and pencil the sole tools of learning. From as early as kindergarten on, students use electronic devices and the Internet at school.

Try imagining yourself at the center of a web, such as a spider's web. Attach the threads that spread from the center first to family members and close friends, on out in the web to peers, then to friends of friends. Some thread connections are close and direct. Others are more distant but connect more and more people in an ever-expanding web.

Have you ever used the Six Degrees of Kevin Bacon search tool? Perhaps you have heard that just about any actor can be connected to Kevin Bacon in six or fewer steps. It is also true that the typical person in the United States is now fewer than six steps (or degrees removed) from any other person in the country. Stanley Milgram and his associates studied social networks by selecting several target people in different cities (Korte and Milgram 1970; Milgram 1967; Travers and Milgram 1969). Then, they identified "starting persons" in cities more than 1,000 miles away. Each starting person was given a folder with instructions and the target person's name, address, and occupation, as well as a few other facts. The starting person was instructed to mail the folder to someone he or she knew on a first-name basis who lived closer to or might have more direct networks with the target person than the starting person had. The number of links in the chain to complete delivery ranged from 2 to 10, with most having 5 to 7 intermediaries. This is the source of the reference to "six degrees of separation" and the original inspiration for the Kevin Bacon game.

More recently, research by scientists at Facebook and the University of Milan showed that the average number of acquaintances separating any two people in the world is now 4.74. Within the United States the separation was only 4.37 people (Markoff and Sengupta 2011). Clearly, networks are powerful linkages and create a truly small world.

Our **social networks**, then, *refer to individuals linked together by one or more social relationships, connecting us to the larger society.* Our social networks provide us with social capital, access to people who can help us get jobs or favors. Networks begin with micro-level contacts and exchanges between individuals in private interactions and expand to small groups and then to large (even global) organizations (Granovetter 2007; Tolbert and Hall 2008). The stronger people's networks, the more influential they can be in a person's life (see Figure 5.1).

Networks at the Micro, Meso, and Macro Levels

As noted above, networks span the micro, meso, and macro levels of analysis. For example, at the *micro*

This woman takes a "selfie" with a mobile phone in front of activists during a rally near the Ukrainian Elections Commission. Within seconds her friends throughout the world could see her at this rally through her Facebook page.

level, you develop close friends in college—bonds that may continue for the rest of your life. You introduce your friends from the student government to your roommate's friends from the soccer team, and the network expands and your social capital increases. These acquaintances may have useful information about which professors to take, what campus organizations to join, and how to get a job in your field. You most likely carry out all of these interactions both in person and online.

When you graduate from your university, you will be part of the university's alumni association, and this may become important to you for social contacts, business connections, or help with settling in

FIGURE 5.1   Networks: A Web of Connections

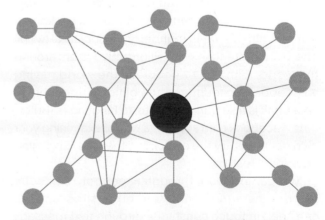

The blue circle represents an individual—perhaps you—and the yellow dots represent your friends and acquaintances. The lines represent personal relationships between individuals. Your network, then, looks a bit like a spider's web.

a new location. When people refer to the Old Boy network, they are talking about contacts made through general association with people such as alumni. Men have used networks quite successfully in the past, and networks of working women—New Girl networks—are expanding rapidly. One of the reasons for the persistent inequality in our society is that members of certain groups may not have access to these privilege-enhancing networks.

Thinking Sociologically

Map your social network web (as far as you can). What advantages do you get from your network? How might this network help you to advance in your chosen career?

Network links create new types of organizational forms at the *meso level*. These networks often cross societal, racial, ethnic, religious, and other lines that divide people. Networks also link groups at different levels of analysis. In fact, you are linked through networks to (1) micro-level college, athletic, and faith communities; (2) meso-level formal, complex organizations such as a political party or national fraternity and ethnic or social class subcultures; and (3) the macro-level nation of which you are a citizen and global entities such as the United Nations. These networks may open opportunities, but they also may create obligations that limit your freedom to make your own choices. As we move from micro-level interactions to larger meso- and macro-level organizations, interactions tend to become more formal. Formal organizations will be explored in the latter half of this chapter.

Probably the most famous networking site is Facebook, and it became even more well-known with the film about its founder, *The Social Network*. There are more than 901 million active users around the world, with 1 in 7.7 people in the world having a Facebook account and 125 billion "friendships." Facebook is also translated into 70 languages (Bullas 2012; Facebook.com 2011). As a way of examining your own networks, try the exercise in the next "Engaging Sociology" feature.

We can network through Facebook, LinkedIn, Twitter, Instagram, Vine, and other sites, and we can keep in touch constantly through text messaging. However, this means that people spend more time interacting with a piece of technology and may feel less comfortable interacting face-to-face with someone. Likewise, online courses are in one sense less intimate—the instructor and the student may never meet face-to-face. Yet, through the Internet, more people can take college-level courses than ever before. We are only beginning to understand the implications of this technology on human interaction and on interpersonal skills.

THE PROCESS OF INTERACTION: CONNECTIONS AT THE MICRO LEVEL

Each morning as you rouse yourself, you consider what the day might bring. You evaluate what is in store for you, what roles you will play during the day, and with whom you are likely to interact.

Should you wear the ragged but comfy jeans and T-shirt? Perhaps that will not work today, since there is that class trip to the courthouse. Something a bit less casual is in order. Then, you are meeting with your English professor to discuss the last essay you wrote. What approach should you take? You could act insulted that she failed to think of you as a future J. K. Rowling, Veronica Roth, or Suzanne Collins. Maybe a meek, mild "Please tell me what I did wrong, I tried so hard" approach would work. She seems a nice, sympathetic sort. After class, there is a group of students who chat in the hall. It would be nice to meet them. What strategy should you use? Tell a joke? Make small talk? Talk to the students individually so you can get to know each before engaging the whole group? Each of these responses is a strategy for interaction, and each might elicit different reactions.

The Elements of Social Interaction

"Let's have a drink!" Such a simple comment might have many different meanings. We could imagine two thirsty children playing together, men going to a bar after work, a couple of friends getting together to celebrate an event, fraternity brothers at a party, or a couple on a date. In all these cases, **social interaction** consists of *two or more individuals purposefully relating to each other*.

"Having a drink," like all *interaction*, involves action on the part of two or more individuals, is directed

ENGAGING SOCIOLOGY

Networking via Facebook

If you are on Facebook, go to your Facebook account and note the number of friends you have listed. Then, look at them carefully to see if you can answer the following questions:

1. What is the age range of the friends on your list?
2. What is the gender composition of your list?
3. How many members of each of the following racial or ethnic groups are on your list:

   __ African Americans
   __ Whites
   __ Hispanics
   __ Asians
   __ Other racial or ethnic group (or some combination)
   __ International contacts

4. What is the socioeconomic status of your friends?
   __ Blue collar (families in which the primary wage earner works for an hourly wage)
   __ Middle class (families in which the primary wage earner earns a salary of less than $100,000 per year)
   __ Professional (families in which the primary wage earner earns a salary of $100,000 to $500,000 per year)
   __ Highly affluent corporate executive (families in which the primary wage earner earns a salary of $500,000 to $10 million per year)
   __ Upper class (families in which much of the wealth is inherited and annual income is in the multimillions)

* * * * * * * *

Engaging With Sociology

- Now look at the data you have collected. What have you learned about your own networks?
- How much socioeconomic, age, and racial and ethnic diversity do the data reveal about your networks?

toward a goal that people hope to achieve, and takes place in a social context that includes cultural norms and rules governing the situation, the setting, and other factors shaping the way people perceive the circumstances. The action, goal, and social context help us interpret the meaning of statements such as "Let's have a drink."

The norms governing the particular social context tell us how to behave. Recall from Chapter 3 that *norms* are rules that guide human interactions. People assume that others will share their interpretation of a situation. These shared assumptions about proper behavior provide the cues for your own behavior that become a part of your social self. You look for cues to proper behavior and rehearse in your mind your actions and reactions. In the "Let's have a drink" scenario, the dress, mannerisms, speech, and actions you

consider appropriate depend on expectations from your socialization and past experience in similar situations. You will, no doubt, have learned to dress and act differently depending on whether you are having the drink with an old friend or a potential romantic partner. In turn, you will expect that the person with whom you are drinking will be making the same sort of decisions on what to wear and how to behave when you get together.

Although most people assume that talking, or *verbal communication*, is the primary means of communication between individuals, words themselves are actually only a part of the message. In most contexts, they make up less than 7% of the communication, with body language 55% and tone of voice 38% (Debenham 2014). We communicate primarily through **nonverbal communication**—*interactions without words using*

In North America, friends interact at a close distance, 1.5 to 4 feet—as in the photo on the left. A more formal setting calls for a distance of 4 to 12 feet, which can feel cold and intimidating, as in the photo on the right.

facial expressions, the head, eye contact, body posture, gestures, touch, walk, status symbols, and personal space (Cherry 2012; Givens 2012). We learn these important elements of communication through socialization as we grow up.

People who travel to a country other than their own often use gestures as they try to be understood. Like spoken language, however, nonverbal gestures vary from culture to culture. Communicating with others in one's own language can be difficult enough. Add to this the complication of individuals with different language, cultural expectations, and personalities using different nonverbal messages, and misunderstandings are likely. Although one may master another written and verbal language, nonverbal messages are the hardest part of another language to master because they are specific to a culture and learned through socialization.

Consider the following example: You are about to wrap up a major business deal. You are pleased with the results of your negotiations, so you give your hosts the thumb-and-finger A-OK sign. In Brazil, you have just grossly insulted your hosts—it is the equivalent of giving them "the finger." In Japan, you have asked for a small bribe. In the south of France, you have indicated the deal is worthless. Intercultural communication takes more than knowing the language of a different culture.

Another example of nonverbal communication involves personal space. Most people have experienced social situations, such as parties, where someone gets too close. One person backs away, the other moves in again, and the first backs away again—into a corner or a table with nowhere else to go. Perhaps the person approaching was aggressive or rude, but it is also possible that the person held different cultural norms or expectations in relation to personal space.

The amount of personal space an individual needs to be comfortable or proper varies with the cultural setting, gender, status, and social context of the interaction. Individuals from Arab countries are often comfortable at very close range. However, people from Scandinavia generally need a great deal of personal space. Consider the following four categories of social distance and social space based on a study of middle-class people in the United States, though there may be some variation within the middle class depending on ethnicity. Each category applies to particular types of activity (Hall and Hall 1992):

1. *Intimate distance:* from zero distance (touching, embracing, kissing) to 18 inches. Children may play together in such close proximity, and adults and children may maintain this distance, but between adults, this intimate contact is reserved for private and affectionate relationships.
2. *Personal distance:* from 18 inches to 4 feet. This is the public distance for most friends and for informal interactions with acquaintances.
3. *Social distance:* from 4 feet to 12 feet. This is the distance for impersonal business relations, such as a job interview or class discussions between students and a professor. This distance implies a more formal interaction or a significant difference in the status of the two people.
4. *Public distance:* 12 feet and beyond. This is the distance most public figures use for addressing others, especially in formal settings and in situations in which the speaker has a very high status.

 Verbal vs. Non-Verbal Communication

When the Pope speaks, it is not only the Vatican Security that keeps people at a formal distance; it is a sense of awed respect for the office: 12 feet or more is the standard distance kept between public figures and other people.

Personal space also communicates one's position in relation to others. The higher the position, the greater the control of space. In social situations, individuals with higher positions spread out, prop their feet up, put their arms out, and use more sweeping gestures.

Thinking Sociologically

Describe a time when you experienced miscommunication. Who was involved? What happened? How can what you read in this chapter help you to explain why the miscommunication occurred?

Theoretical Perspectives on the Interaction Process

Sociologists study interactions, including verbal and nonverbal communication, to better understand why people behave the way they do. Symbolic interactionists and rational choice theorists examine how and why people communicate with one another. As you will see, their different perspectives lead them to focus on different aspects of interactions and come up with distinctive conclusions as to why they occur.

Symbolic Interaction Theory. With whom do you interact? What determines whether the interaction will continue or stop? How do you know how to behave and what to say around each other? What other processes are taking place as you talk to each other? Why do you act differently with different people?

Symbolic interactionism is based on the idea that humans create society through interacting with one another. We act toward people and objects on the basis of the meanings those things have for us. The meanings are derived by individuals as they interact with others. Together, through our interactions with one another, we agree that objects, gestures, and phrases, like "Let's have a drink," symbolize certain things. Likewise, the word *hello* can signify the beginning of a conversation and *goodbye* the end of one because we agree on the meanings of those words and agree to act accordingly. Symbols are the key to understanding human life, and we go about the task of fitting our actions together through our shared perceptions and meanings of those symbols. Through our mental manipulation of symbols and interpretation of meaning, we *define situations* and determine how we should act in a given situation or how we should make sense of it (Charon 2010; Hewitt and Shulman 2011). More than any other theory in the social sciences, symbolic interactionism stresses the agency—the active decision-making role—of humans within their societies (Charon 2010; Hewitt and Schulman 2011).

Have you ever laughed at a joke you did not hear or understand because those around you laughed? In ambiguous situations, humans look to others to see how they have made sense of the situation or interaction taking place—do people around us look frightened, annoyed, bored, or amused? When in doubt, we tend to follow the cues of those around us. Once one person defines the situation and acts, especially if that person is highly regarded or very self-confident, others will often accept that response as "normal." This is how social interaction is involved in the **social construction of reality**—*the process by which individuals and groups shape reality through social interaction.* This imposed notion of reality then takes on a life of its own, often constraining and even coercing people to conform (Berger and Luckmann 1966; Hewitt and Shulman 2011; O'Brien 2011; Ritzer 2013). For example, our career goals tend to be influenced by those with whom we interact. If you had been a woman in the United States in the 1910s, you would be unlikely to think you could pursue a career in the "male" field of engineering.

However, socially constructed constraints can be challenged by individuals and lead to different realities, which, in turn, begin to influence people's

Autonomy and Social Media

perceptions of what is true and what is possible. For example, until recently, it seemed impossible for gay artists to gain acceptance in the hip-hop community. If you were gay, the choice seemed to be to choose a different genre or keep your sexual orientation hidden. This began to change when Frank Ocean publicly proclaimed that his first love was a man and his announcement drew support, rather than condemnation, from many other prominent hip-hop artists.

A different approach to interaction analysis—called *dramaturgy*—analyzes life as a play or drama on a stage, with scripts and props and scenes to be played. The play we put on creates an impression for our audience. In everyday life, individuals learn new lines to add to their scripts through the socialization process, including influence from family, friends, films, and television. They perform these scripts for social audiences to maintain certain images, much like the actors in a play.

Consider the following familiar example: Every day in high schools around the world, teenagers go on stage—in the classroom or the hallway with friends and peers and with adult authorities who may later be giving grades or writing letters of reference. The props

Depicted here are Japanese yen. Your local department store or restaurant will not accept yen in exchange for the piece of furniture or the meal you just consumed, any more than it would accept Monopoly money. We exchange goods and services based on some pieces of paper because we have a general agreement that this is "good currency"—a social construction of reality. For a photo essay and further discussion of money as a social construction, visit **edge.sagepub.com/ballantinecondensed4e.**

these students use include their style of clothing, a backpack, a smartphone, and a smile or a "cool" look. The set is the classroom, the cafeteria, and perhaps the athletic field. The script is shaped by the actors: Teachers and coaches may establish an authoritarian relationship with students; classmates engage in competition for grades; peers seek social status among companions. The actors include hundreds of teens struggling with issues of identity, changing bodies, and attempting to be accepted and avoid humiliation. Each individual works to assert and maintain an image through behavior, clothing, language, and friends.

Each part or character an individual plays and each audience requires a different script. For example, interacting with peers at a bar differs from meeting a professor in her office. As we perform according to society's script for the situation, we take into consideration how our actions will influence others. By carefully managing the image we project—a process called *impression management*—we try to create an impression that works to our advantage. Most of the time, we engage in front-stage behavior. This is the largely scripted behavior we use with strangers or casual acquaintances. A poor or unacceptable performance, such as wearing out-of-style clothes or spilling our lunch, is embarrassing both for us and for our audience. We learn to develop strategies to cover up weaknesses or failures, such as laughing at a joke even though we do not understand it.

Sometimes we avoid situations that will require us to play a role with which we are unfamiliar or uncomfortable. Have you ever avoided interacting with a certain group of people because you were unsure of how to act when around them or decided against trying out for a team or a theater production or running for office because you were afraid you might not make it or it was not an "in" thing to do? We learn to avoid those performance activities that are likely to result in humiliation or failure or that contradict the image we have worked to create.

At home or with close friends with whom we are more intimate, we engage in "backstage behavior," letting our feelings show and behaving in ways that might be unacceptable for other audiences (Goffman 1967, [1959] 2001). We feel that with them we can relax and be our "true" selves, without possible negative repercussions. So, as you can see, dramaturgical analysis, and its front- and backstage concepts, can help us to better understand our interactions and how our behavior changes with the setting.

Thinking Sociologically

Describe some ways in which your life feels like a dramatic production. Identify front-stage and backstage behaviors you carry out on a daily basis.

Rational Choice Theory. Rational choice or exchange theorists look at a different aspect of interaction—why relationships continue, considering the rewards and costs of interaction for the individual. They argue that the choices we make are guided by reason ("rational choices"). If the benefits of the interaction are high and if the costs are low, the interaction will be valued and sustained. Every interaction involves calculations of self-interest, expectations of reciprocity (a mutual exchange of favors), and decisions to act in ways that have current or eventual payoff for the individual (Smelser 1992).

Reciprocity is a key concept for rational choice theorists. The idea is that if a relationship is imbalanced over a period of time, it will become unsatisfying. As theorists from this perspective see human interaction, each person tends to keep a mental ledger of who "owes" whom. If I have done you a favor, you owe me one. If you have helped me in some way, I have an obligation to you. If I then fail to comply or even do something that hurts you, you will likely view it as a breach in the relationship and have negative feelings toward me. Moreover, if one person has more power in the relationship, there is an imbalance in what each brings to the relationship.

In the study of families, scholars use the "principle of least interest," which states that the person with the least interest in the relationship has the most power. The person with the least interest is the person who brings more resources (financial, physical, social, personal) to the relationship and receives less. That person could easily leave. The person who offers less to the relationship or who has fewer assets is more dependent on the relationship. This person is likely to give in when there is a disagreement, so the person with less interest gets her or his way.

Sometimes a person may engage in a behavior where there is little likelihood of reciprocity from the other person—as in cases where the behavior is altruistic or self-giving. Rational choice theorists would argue that there is still a benefit. It might be enhanced feelings of self-worth, positive recognition from others, hope for a place in heaven, or just the expectation of indirect reciprocity. This latter notion is akin to the idea of "paying it forward": The person you help might

not help you, but if you are in a similar situation, you could hope for and expect someone to come to your assistance (Gouldner 1960; Turner 2003).

Social Status: Individuals' Link to Groups

As you will recall from Chapter 4, a **social status** is *a social position in society.* We interact with others and they react to us based in part on the statuses we hold. We interact differently when in the daughter status with our parents, in a student status with our professor, or in friend status with our peers. Each individual holds many statuses, and this combination held by any individual is called a *status set*: for instance, daughter, sister, worker, teammate, and student.

Statuses affect the type of interactions individuals have. In some interactions (as with classmates), people are equals. In other situations, individuals have interchanges with people who hold superior or inferior statuses. If you are promoted to supervisor, your interaction with former peers and subordinates will change. Consider the possible interactions shown in Figure 5.2, in which the first relationship is between equals and the others are between those with unequal statuses.

With a friend, these status relationships are constantly being negotiated and bargained: "I'll do what you want tonight, but tomorrow I choose." By contrast, when individuals are in dominant or subordinate positions, power or deference affects their interactions. Gender, power, and hierarchical relationships are important in determining interaction patterns. The more powerful person, such as one who has more wealth or privilege, can interrupt in a conversation with his or her partner and show less deference in the interaction (Kim et al. 2007; Reid and Ng 2006; Wood 2008).

People have no control over certain statuses they hold. These **ascribed statuses** are *often assigned at*

FIGURE 5.2   Types of Status Relationships Experienced by You

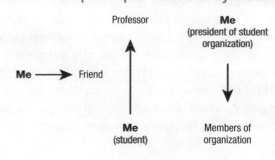

birth and do not change during an individual's lifetime. For example, while a few people undergo sex change operations, for most people sex is an ascribed characteristic. Ascribed statuses are assigned to a person without regard for personal desires, talents, or choices. In some societies, the caste or social position into which one is born (e.g., "Untouchables" or "Dalits" in India) is an ascribed status because it is usually impossible to change within one's lifetime.

Achieved status, on the other hand, *is chosen or earned by the decisions one makes and sometimes by personal ability.* Attaining a higher education, for example, improves an individual's occupational opportunities and thus his or her achieved status. Being a guitarist in a band is an achieved status, and so is being a criminal, for both are earned positions based on the person's own decisions and actions.

At a particular time in life or under certain circumstances, one of an individual's statuses may become most important and take precedence over others; this is called a **master status**. Whether it is an occupation, parental status, or something else, it dominates and shapes much of an individual's life, activities, self-concept, and position in the community for a period of time. For a person who is very ill, for instance, that illness may occupy a master status, needing constant attention from doctors, influencing social relationships, and determining what that person can do in family, work, or community activities.

Thinking Sociologically

What are your statuses? Which ones are ascribed, and which are achieved statuses? Do you have a master status? How do these statuses affect the way you interact with others in your network of relationships?

The Relationship Between Status and Role

Every status (position) in your network includes certain behaviors and obligations as you carry out the **roles**, *the expected behaviors, rights, obligations, responsibilities, and privileges assigned to a social status.* Roles are the dynamic, action part of statuses in a society. They define how each individual in an interaction is expected to act (Linton 1937). The role of a person holding the status of "college student" includes behaviors and obligations such as attending classes, studying, taking tests, writing papers, and interacting

with professors and other students. We enter most statuses with some knowledge of how to carry out the roles dictated by our culture. Through the process of socialization, we learn roles by observing others, watching television and films, reading, and being taught by family members, teachers, and others how to carry out the status.

Both statuses (positions) and roles (behavioral expectations of people holding the status) form links with other people in the social world because they must be carried out in relationships with others. For example, a father has certain obligations (or roles) toward his children and their mother. The position of father exists not on its own but in relationship to significant others who have reciprocal ties.

Your status of student requires certain behaviors and expectations, depending on whether you are interacting with a dean, a professor, an adviser, a classmate, or a prospective employer. This is because the role expectations of the status of student vary as one interacts with specific people in other statuses. In Figure 5.3, the student is the subject, and the others are those with whom the student interacts in the status of student.

Within a group, individuals may hold both formal and informal statuses. One illustration is the formal status of high school students, each of whom plays a number of informal roles in cliques that are not part of the formal school structure. A student may be known, for example, as one of the popular crowd, a jock, a nerd, a loner, a goth, a clown, a prep, or an outcast. Each of these roles takes place in a status relationship with others: teacher-student, peer-peer, coach-athlete. Social

FIGURE 5.3 Types of Interactions Students Have With Reciprocal Status Holders

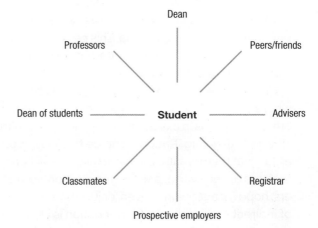

networks may be based on ascribed characteristics, such as age and sex, or on achieved status, such as education, occupation, or common interests. These links, in turn, form the basis for social interactions and group structures (Hall 2002). However, at times, individuals cannot carry out their roles as others expect them to, creating role strain or conflict.

Role Strain and Role Conflict. Most people have faced times in their lives when they simply could not carry out all the obligations of a status, such as student—write two papers, study adequately for two exams, complete the portfolio for the studio art class, finish the reading assignments for five classes, and memorize lines for the oral interpretation class, all in the same week. Every status carries role expectations, the way the status is supposed to be carried out according to generally accepted societal or group norms. Yet in these cases, individuals face **role strain**, the *tension among roles within a status*. Role strain causes the individual to be pulled in many directions by various obligations of the single status, as in the example regarding the status of "student." To resolve role strain, individuals can cope in several possible ways, such as passing the problem off lightly (and thus not doing well in classes); considering the dilemma humorous; becoming highly focused and pulling a couple of all-nighters to get everything done; or becoming stressed, tense, fretful, and immobilized because of the strain. Most often, individuals set priorities based on their values and make decisions accordingly: "I'll work hard in the class for my major and let another one slide."

Role conflict refers to *conflict between the roles of two or more social statuses*. It differs from role strain in that it is conflict *between* the roles of two or more statuses, rather than tension among roles *within* one of the statuses. For example, college athletes face role conflicts from competing demands on their time (Adler and Adler 1991, 2004). They must complete their studies on time, attend practices and be prepared for games, perhaps attend meetings of a Greek house to which they belong, and get home for a little brother's birthday. Similarly, a student may be going to school, holding down a part-time job to help make ends meet, and raising a family. If the student's child gets sick, the status of parent comes into conflict with that of student and worker. In the case of role conflict, the person may choose—or be informed by others—which status

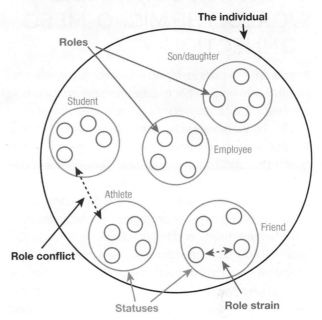

FIGURE 5.4 Role Strain and Role Conflict

Each individual has many statuses: a status set. Each status has many roles: a role set. A conflict between two roles of the same status is a *role strain*. A conflict between the roles of two different statuses is a *role conflict*.

is the master status. Figure 5.4 illustrates the difference between role strain and role conflict.

Thinking Sociologically

Using Figure 5.4 as a model, write down the statuses you hold in your social world and the roles you perform in these statuses. Then, list three examples of role conflicts and three examples of role strains that you experience.

Most statuses and accompanying roles come and go. For example, you will not always be a student. You may or may not be married at different points in your life. You will retire from your job. As people grow older, they disengage from some statuses and engage in new and different statuses and roles.

Our statuses connect us to and make us integral parts of meso- and macro-level organizations. Our place within the social world, then, is guaranteed, even obligatory, because of statuses we hold—within small groups (family and peers), in larger groups and organizations (school and work organizations), in institutions (political parties or religious denominations), and ultimately as citizens of the society and the world (citizens, and workers in global corporations). Each of these statuses connects us to a group setting.

GROUPS IN OUR SOCIAL WORLD: THE MICRO-MESO CONNECTION

Groups refer to *units involving two or more people who interact with each other because of shared common interests, goals, experiences, and needs* (Drafke 2008). As we have seen, humans are social beings. We become members of society and gain a sense of self through social interaction. Groups meet our social needs for belonging and acceptance, support us throughout our lives, and place restrictions on us. We also need groups for protection, to obtain food, to manufacture goods, and to get jobs done. Groups can be small, intimate environments—micro-level interactions with family or friends—or they can become quite large meso-level organizations. In any case, it is through our group memberships that the micro and meso levels are connected.

Not all collections of individuals are groups. For instance, your family is a group, but people shopping at a mall or waiting for a bus are not a group because they do not regularly interact or acknowledge shared common interests.

Groups form through a series of succeeding steps. Consider people forming a soccer team in a new league: The first step is initial interaction. If the interactions with the other members are rewarding and meet individuals' needs, the individuals will attempt to maintain the benefits the group provides and form a team (Mills 1984). In the second step, a collective goal emerges. For example, team members may work together to plan practice and game schedules, buy uniforms, and advertise the games. In the third and final step, the group attempts to expand its collective goals by building on the former steps and by pursuing new goals. For example, the team may reach out to new players, to coaches, and to supporters for funding.

As noted above, groups impact both society and individuals. Neither would function properly without groups. The importance of groups becomes especially clear when we consider two social problems: anomie and suicide.

Group Solidarity, Anomie, and Suicide

Who commits suicide? Did you know that the answer to this is closely related to an individual's group affiliations? Early sociologist Émile Durkheim took a unique approach to making sense of suicide trends. In *Suicide* ([1897] 1964), he discussed the social factors contributing to suicide. Using existing statistical data to determine suicide rates in European populations, Durkheim looked at variables such as sex, age, religion, nationality, and the season in which the suicide was committed. His findings demonstrate that individual problems cannot be understood without also understanding the group context in which they occur.

Durkheim found that Protestants committed suicide more often than Catholics, urban folks more often than people living in small communities, people in highly developed and complex societies more frequently than those in simple societies, and people who lived alone more than those situated in families. The key variable linking these findings was the degree to which an individual was integrated into a group, that is, the degree of social bond with others. Those who belonged to more tightly knit groups were least likely to commit suicide, while those whose lives were less tied to those of others were most likely to kill themselves. Durkheim described this type of suicide, when the individual feels little social bond to the group or society and lacks familial ties, as *egoistic suicide*.

A second type, *anomic suicide*, occurs when a society or one of its parts is in disorder, turmoil, or rapid change and lacks clear norms and guidelines for social behavior. With the rapid changes and continued breakdown of institutional structures in many modern and modernizing societies, religious and political groups may vie for power and offer contrasting definitions of reality. Social controls (police and military forces) may be strained, and leaders struggle to cope with the turmoil and lack of consensus. The result of the collapse of norms is **anomie**, *the state of normlessness that occurs when the rules for behavior in society break down under extreme stress from rapid social change or conflict* (Merton 1938). This anomie tends to lead to higher rates of suicide.

Durkheim's third type of suicide, *altruistic suicide*, differs from the others in that it involves such a strong bond and group obligation that the individual is willing to die for the group. Self-survival becomes less important than group survival (Durkheim [1897] 1964). Examples of altruistic suicide include the young suicide bombers in Iraq, Afghanistan, and Pakistan carrying out suicide missions against their country's police forces and sometimes against NATO or American military forces, which they have defined as invading forces. U.S. military Medal of Honor recipients who

Jorge Parra was one of a group of disabled workers in a General Motors plant in Colombia who were disabled while working and then fired for their inability to do the work. He and more than a dozen other injured workers went on a hunger strike, sewing their mouths closed so they could ingest only liquids. Jorge decided he would fast until death, if necessary. He had gone more than 70 days without food by January 2013, when the United Auto Workers intervened and agreed to help negotiate a solution, provided that Parra end his death fast. Jorge was willing to commit altruistic suicide—to die voluntarily for the good of his group.

sacrificed their own lives to save those of the men in their units are another example. These suicides usually include social groups that have very clear norms and high levels of consensus about values arising from their religious or political beliefs.

Durkheim's work revealed that suicide rates are strongly influenced by social and psychological factors that can operate at the meso or macro level. His findings and those of others show that groups impact our lives and even our desire to continue living (Hall 2002; Nolan, Triplett, and McDonough 2010). No individual is an island. The importance of groups and social influence from various levels in the system is an underlying theme of this text. To more fully understand the influence of groups over us, though, we must become familiar with the different types of groups in which we interact.

Types of Groups

Each of us belongs to several types of groups. Some groups provide intimacy and close relationships, whereas others do not. Some are required affiliations, and others are voluntary. Some provide personal satisfaction, and others are obligatory or necessary for survival.

Primary groups are at the most micro level and *characterized by cooperation among close, intimate,*

long-term relationships. Your family members and best friends, school classmates, and close work associates are all of primary importance in your everyday life. Primary groups provide a sense of belonging and shared identity. Group members care about you, and you care about the other group members, creating a sense of loyalty. Approval and disapproval from the primary group influence the activities you choose to pursue. Belonging to the group is the main reason for membership. The group is of intrinsic value—enjoyed for its own sake—rather than for some utilitarian value such as making money.

For individuals, primary groups provide an anchor point in society. You were born into a primary group—your family. You hold many statuses and play a variety of roles in primary relationships—those of child, sibling, partner, parent, relative, close friend, and so on. You meet with other members face-to-face or keep in touch on a regular basis and know a great deal about their lives. What makes them happy or angry? What are sensitive issues? In primary groups you share values, say what you think, let down your hair, dress as you like, and share your concerns and emotions, your successes and failures (Goffman 1967, [1959] 2001). Charles H. Cooley, who first discussed the term *primary group*, saw these relationships as the source of close human feelings and emotions—love, cooperation, and concern (Cooley [1909] 1983).

Secondary groups are *those with formal, impersonal, and businesslike relationships, often temporary, and based on a specific limited purpose or goal.* Secondary groups are usually large and task-oriented because they have a specific purpose to achieve and focus on accomplishing a goal. In the modern world, people cannot always live under the protective wing of primary group relationships. As children grow, they move from the security and acceptance of primary groups—the home and neighborhood peer group—to a secondary group—the large school classroom, where each child is one of many students vying for the teacher's (and others') approval and competing for rewards. Similarly, the job world requires formal relations and procedures: applications, interviews, contracts. Employment is based on specific skills, training, and job knowledge—competence to carry out the role expectations in the position.

Because each individual in a secondary group carries out a specialized task, communication between members is often specialized as well. Contacts with doctors, store clerks, and even professors are generally formal and impersonal parts of organizational life. Sometimes associations with secondary groups are long lasting, sometimes of short duration—as in the courses you are taking this term. Secondary groups operate at the meso and macro levels of our social world, but they affect individuals at the micro level.

As societies modernize, they evolve from small towns and close, primary relationships to predominantly urban areas with more formal, secondary relationships. In the postindustrial world, with family members scattered across countries and around the world, secondary relationships have come to play ever greater roles in people's lives. Large work organizations may provide day care, health clinics, financial planning, courses to upgrade skills, and sports leagues.

Small micro-level and large macro-level groups often occur together. Behind most successful secondary groups are primary groups. Consider the small work group within a large organization that eats together or goes out for a beer on Friday afternoons. These relationships help individuals feel a part of the larger organization, just as residents of large urban areas have small groups of neighborhood friends. Table 5.1 summarizes some of the dimensions of primary and secondary groups.

Problems in primary groups can affect performance in secondary groups. Consider the problems of a student who has an argument with a partner or roommate, or experiences a failure of his or her family support system due to divorce or other problems. Self-concepts and social skills diminish during times of family stress and affect group relationships in other parts of one's life (Drafke 2008).

Thinking Sociologically

In the past, raising children was considered a family task, done by the primary family group. Today, many children are in child care settings, often run by secondary groups. What differences do you see between the experiences a child receives in a family and in child care? What might be the advantages and disadvantages of each? Can a secondary group provide care comparable with that provided by a family? Can the secondary group provide better care than families? Why or why not?

Reference groups are *composed of members who act as role models and establish standards against which members measure their conduct.* Individuals look to reference groups to set guidelines for behavior and decision making. Successful businesses can serve as reference groups for other businesses. The term is often used to refer to models in one's chosen career field. Ethnic groups can also be reference groups. Ethnic groups can provide adolescent members with strong reference group standards by which to judge themselves. The stronger the ethnic pride and identification, the more some teens may separate themselves from contact with members of other ethnic groups (Schaefer and Kunz 2007). This can be functional or dysfunctional for the teens, as shown in the next section on in-groups and out-groups.

An **in-group** is *one to which an individual feels a sense of loyalty and belonging.* It also may serve as a reference group (any group may fit into more than one category of group). An **out-group** is *one to which an individual does not belong, but more than that, it*

TABLE 5.1 Primary and Secondary Group Characteristics

	Primary Group	Secondary Group
Quality of relationships	Personal orientation	Goal orientation
Duration of relationships	Usually long-term	Variable, often short-term
Breadth of activities	Broad, usually involving many activities	Narrow, usually involving a few largely goal-directed activities
Subjective perception of relationships	As an end in itself (friendship, belonging)	As a means to an end (to accomplish a task, earn money)
Typical examples	Families, close friendships	Coworkers, political organizations

is a group that competes with or acts in opposition to an in-group.

Membership in an in-group may be based on sex, race, ethnicity, social class, religion, political affiliation, the school one attends, an interest group such as the fraternity or sorority one joins, or the area where one lives. People tend to judge others according to their own in-group identity. Members of the in-group—for example, supporters of a high school team—often feel hostility toward or reject out-group members—boosters of the rival team. The perceived outside threat or hostility is often exaggerated, but it does help create the in-group members' feelings of solidarity. Another example might be the "preps" in a high school who control many resources because they control the school's student council and many of the leadership positions in the school. They are an in-group, but the goths, punks, or burnouts (the out-group) reject the preps and seek alternatives to the activities planned by the preps. Unfortunately, these feelings of hostility can result in prejudice and ethnocentrism, overlooking the individual differences of in-group members.

Thinking Sociologically

What are some examples of your own group affiliations? Draw a diagram of your primary groups, secondary groups, peer groups, reference groups, and in-groups and out-groups.

ORGANIZATIONS AND BUREAUCRACIES: THE MESO-MACRO CONNECTION

Our days are filled with activities that involve us with complex organizations: from the doctor's appointment to college classes; from the political rally for the issue we support to worship in a church, temple, or mosque; from paying state sales tax for our toothpaste to buying a sandwich at a fast-food franchise. Figure 5.5 on page 122 shows the institutions of society, each made up of thousands of organizations (e.g., medical organizations, educational organizations, religious groups, economic corporations, political movements, the government itself), and each following the

Even Buddhist nuns, who spend much of their lives devoted to private meditation, need the support and solidarity of a group.

cultural norms of the society. We have statuses and roles in each group, and these link us to networks and the larger social world. We now look at how the modern forms of these organizations developed.

Modern Organizations and Their Evolution

Recall from Chapter 3 the discussion of types of societies, from hunter-gatherer to postindustrial. Each type of society entails different organizational structures (Blau 1956; Nolan and Lenski 2014). The development of modern organizations and bureaucracies began with the Industrial Revolution in the 1700s and 1800s. Increasingly complex organizations required and helped create what Max Weber called the **rationalization of social life**—*the attempt to maximize efficiency by creating rules and procedures focused solely on accomplishing goals* (Weber 1947). No longer were decisions made by tradition, custom, or the whim of a despot. Instead, trained leaders planned policies to achieve organizational efficiency. Tasks became more specialized, and some manual jobs were taken over by machines. People were expected to behave in purposeful, coordinated ways to advance organizational efficiency.

Formal organizations (also called *modern "rational" organizations*), *composed of complex secondary groups deliberately formed to pursue and achieve certain goals*, were created to standardize production and increase productivity, precision, and speed. They are called "formal organizations" because of the written charters, constitutions, bylaws, and procedures

FIGURE 5.5 Our Social World: Institutions, Organizations, and Individual Status

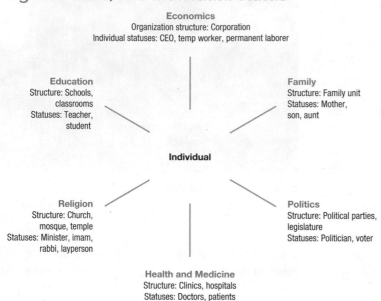

Economics
Organization structure: Corporation
Individual statuses: CEO, temp worker, permanent laborer

Education
Structure: Schools, classrooms
Statuses: Teacher, student

Family
Structure: Family unit
Statuses: Mother, son, aunt

Individual

Religion
Structure: Church, mosque, temple
Statuses: Minister, imam, rabbi, layperson

Politics
Structure: Political parties, legislature
Statuses: Politician, voter

Health and Medicine
Structure: Clinics, hospitals
Statuses: Doctors, patients

that govern them. Google, General Electric (GE), the Red Cross, the National Basketball Association (NBA), the Republican Party, and your university are all formal organizations.

Bureaucracies are *specific types of very large formal organizations that have the purpose of maximizing efficiency. They are characterized by set relations between participants, clearly laid-out procedures and rules, and pursuit of stated goals.* Bureaucratization evolved as the most efficient way of producing products economically for mass markets (Ritzer 2013).

An example of a bureaucratic organization can be found in the fast-food empires and chain "box" stores spreading all around the world. The next "Engaging Sociology" feature describes the trend toward the "McDonaldization of society"—sociologist George Ritzer's pop culture term for rationalization in organizations.

Formal Organizations and Modern Life

Think about the many organizations that regularly affect your life: the legal system that passes laws, your college, your workplace, and voluntary organizations to which you belong. Human interactions take place in formal organizations, and formal organizations require human interaction to meet their organizational needs. Some organizations, such as the local chapter of the

Rotary Club or troop of the Girl Scouts, function at the micro level. Everyone is in a face-to-face relationship with every other member of the organization. However, those local groups are part of a nationwide meso-level organization. At the macro level, the federal government in the United States is a complex formal organization that influences the lives of every citizen and organization in the nation. Meanwhile multinational corporations and entities like the United Nations are global in their reach.

Some organizations provide us with work necessary for survival. Others are forced on us—prisons, psychiatric hospitals, military draft systems, and even education—up until a certain age. Still others are organizations we believe in and voluntarily join—scouts, environmental groups, sports leagues, and religious organizations. Residents of the United States tend to join voluntary organizations at higher rates than people in many other countries (Charities Aid Foundation 2012).

Characteristics of Bureaucracy

If you have been to a Caribbean, African, Asian, or Middle Eastern market, you know that the bartering system is used to settle on a mutually agreeable price for goods. This system is more personal and involves intense interaction between the seller and the buyer, but it also takes more time and is less efficient than the buying process to which shoppers from North America are accustomed. Bartering can be frustrating to the uninitiated visitor used to the relative efficiency and predictability of bureaucracy: going to a store, selecting a product, and paying a set price. As societies become more complex, they tend to adopt bureaucratic forms of organization.

At the beginning of the 20th century, Max Weber (1864–1920) looked for the reasons behind the transition from traditional society to bureaucratic, capitalist society. He wanted to understand why bureaucracy came to dominate the forms of organization in some countries more rapidly than in others. Weber found that bureaucracies arose first in more democratic nations with capitalist, industrial economic systems.

 Characteristics of an Ideal Bureaucracy

ENGAGING SOCIOLOGY

The McDonaldization of Society

The process of rationalization described by Max Weber—the attempt to reach maximum bureaucratic efficiency—comes in a new modern version, expanded and streamlined, exemplified by the fast-food restaurant business that began to spread in the 1950s and chain "box" stores now found around the world. Efficient, rational, predictable sameness is sweeping the world—from diet centers such as Weight Watchers to Nutrisystem to 7-Eleven and from Walmart to Gap clothing stores with their look-alike layouts. Most major world cities feature McDonald's or Kentucky Fried Chicken in the traditional main plazas of train stations for flustered foreigners and curious native consumers.

The McDonaldization of society, as George Ritzer calls it, refers to several trends: First, *efficiency* is maximized by the sameness—same store plans, same mass-produced items, same procedures. Second is *predictability*, the knowledge that each hamburger or piece of chicken will appear and taste the same, leaving nothing to chance. Third, everything is *calculated* so that the organization can ensure that everything fits a standard—every burger is cooked the same number of seconds on each side. Fourth, there is *increased control* over employees and customers so there are fewer variables to consider—including substitution of technology for human labor as a way to ensure predictability and efficiency.

What is the result of this efficient, predictable, planned, automated new world? According to Ritzer, the world is becoming more dehumanized, and efficiency is replacing individual creativity and human interactions. The mom-and-pop grocery, bed and breakfasts, and local craft or clothing shops are rapidly becoming a thing of the past. This process of the McDonaldization of society, meaning principles of efficiency and rationalization exemplified by fast-food chains, is coming to dominate more and more sectors of our social world (Ritzer 2013). While there are aspects of this predictability that we all like, it also entails a loss of the uniqueness and local flavor that individual entrepreneurs bring to a community.

Some large corporations have started a movement toward "Starbuckization" to impress consumers tired of McDonaldization. For example, Starbucks, with its own music mixes, comfortable seats, and Wi-Fi, makes customers feel like they are purchasing a cultural product along with their coffee. This culture, however, is as controlled as any other McDonaldized endeavor, making

The Mall of America near Minneapolis is the largest mall in North America, with 4.3 miles of storefront footage, 520+ stores on five stories, 4.2 million total square feet, and 25 amusement park rides. Yet many of the stores look like clones of one another, and this cathedral to consumerism can feel like an experience in the McDonaldization of society.

Starbucks a McClone at its core.

McDonaldization is so widespread and influential that many modern universities are now McDonaldized. A large lecture hall is a very efficient way of teaching sociology or biology to many students at once. Similarly, massive online classes, PowerPoint presentations, multiple-choice exams, and a limited choice of textbooks for professors increase the predictability of content in course offerings. Finally, grade point averages and credit hours completed are very calculated—and efficient—ways to judge student accomplishments.

Engaging With Sociology

1. What examples of McDonaldization do you see in your community? What are the pros and cons of this pattern in your locality?

2. To what extent do you think your college is McDonaldized? Why?

3. What can you and your fellow students do to address the problem of the McDonaldization of higher education?

As these countries established systems of government and economics whereby positions were granted based on merit, rather than tradition, their economies could grow much faster. This growth, in turn, required more efficient and rational means of organization—bureaucratization (Weber 1947).

Weber's concept of the *ideal-type bureaucracy* refers to the dominant and essential characteristics of organizations designed for reliability and efficiency (Weber 1947). The term simply describes an organization with a particular set of traits, not a necessarily good or perfect organization. Any particular bureaucracy is unlikely to have all the characteristics of the ideal type, but the degree of bureaucratization is measured by how closely an organization resembles the core characteristics of the ideal type. The following shows Weber's ideal-type bureaucracy with examples related to schools today:

1. *Division of labor based on technical competence:* Administrators lead but do not teach, and instructors teach only in areas of their certification; staff are assigned positions for which their credentials make them most qualified, and recruitment and promotion are governed by formal policies.
2. *Administrative hierarchy:* There is a specified chain of command and designated channels of communication, from school board to superintendent to principal to teacher.
3. *Formal rules and regulations:* Written procedures and rules—perhaps published in an administrative manual—spell out system-wide requirements, including discipline practices, testing procedures, curricula, sick days for teachers, penalties for student tardiness, field trip policies, and other matters.
4. *Impersonal relationships:* Formal relationships tend to prevail between teachers and students and between teachers and administrative staff (superintendents, principals, counselors); written records and formal communication provide a paper trail for all decisions.
5. *Emphasis on rationality and efficiency to reach goals:* Established processes are used, based on the best interests of the school. Efficiency is defined in terms of the lowest overall cost to the organization in reaching a goal, not in terms of personal consequences.

Although the list of characteristics makes bureaucracies sound formal and rigid, informal structures allow organizational members to deviate from rules both to meet the goals of the organization more efficiently and to humanize an otherwise uncaring and sterile workplace. The *informal structure* includes the unwritten norms and the interpersonal networks that people use within an organization to carry out roles. Likewise, although bylaws, constitutions, or contracts spell out the way things are supposed to be done, people often develop unwritten shortcuts to accomplish goals. For example, the U.S. Postal Service has rules specifying that letter carriers are not supposed to walk across people's lawns; yet if they did not find shortcuts, it would take much longer for mail to be delivered.

Informal norms are not always compatible with those of the formal organization. For example, what if the norm at your organization is to do the least amount of work possible? Have you ever been pressured *not* to work hard by your coworkers? Consider the following example from a famous classical study. In the Western Electric plant near Chicago, the study found that new workers were quickly socialized to do "a fair day's work" and those who did more or less than the established norm—what the work group thought was fair—were considered "rate busters" or "chiselers" and experienced pressure from the group to conform. These informal norms help give workers a degree of power but make the formal goals of the organization harder to achieve (Roethlisberger and Dickson 1939). They also indicate a lack of clear communication or enforcement of the rules of the bureaucratic system.

Thinking Sociologically

How closely does each of Weber's characteristics of ideal-type bureaucracy describe your college or your work setting? Is your college highly bureaucratized, with many rules and regulations? Are decisions based on efficiency and cost-effectiveness, educational quality, or both? To what extent is your work setting characterized by hierarchy, and formal rules governing your work time? To what extent is it shaped by informal relationships?

Issues in Bureaucracies

Despite the fact that some informal norms and red tape can hamper bureaucratic efficiency, bureaucracies are likely here to stay. They are the most efficient form of modern organization yet devised. Nonetheless, several individual and organizational problems created by bureaucratic structures are important to understand. These deficiencies arise from our roles in organizations or our interactions with organizations. Some examples of problems that can arise in bureaucracies are decreased levels of professionalism in bureaucracies, alienation, oligarchy, and goal displacement.

Bureaucracy, some argue, can be the number-one enemy of *professionalism*, for it reduces individuals' autonomy. First, bureaucrats insist that authority rests in the person who holds an organizational status or title in the hierarchy rather than the person with the most expertise. Second, bureaucrats tend to reward people with external rewards such as bonuses rather than internal motivations, such as greater freedom in how they do their work. Third, bureaucrats focus on the needs of the organization as primary rather than on the needs of the client or professional. For example, a scientist hired by a tobacco company faced a dilemma when his research findings did not support the company position that nicotine is not addictive. They wanted him to falsify his research, which would be a violation of professional ethics. The potential clash between professionals and bureaucracy raises key concerns as universities, hospitals, and other large organizations are governed increasingly by bureaucratic principles (Roberts and Donahue 2000).

Alienation, feeling uninvolved, uncommitted, unappreciated, and unconnected to the group or the society, occurs when workers are assigned routine, boring tasks or dead-end jobs with no possibility of advancement. Marx believed that alienation is a structural feature of capitalism, with serious consequences: Workers lose their sense of purpose and become dehumanized and objectified in their work, creating a product that they often do not see completed and for which they do not get the profits (Marx [1844] 1964). Workers who see possibilities for advancement put more energy into the organization, but those stuck in their positions are less involved and put more energy into activities outside the workplace (Kanter 1977).

Thinking Sociologically

Why might giving workers increased autonomy, more participation in decision making, and stockholder shares in the company enhance commitment and productivity in your place of work? What might be some risks or downsides to such worker input and freedom?

Oligarchy, the concentration of power in the hands of a small group, is a common occurrence in bureaucratic organizations. In the early 1900s, Robert Michels, a French sociologist, wrote about the *iron law of oligarchy*, the idea that power becomes concentrated in the hands of a small group of leaders in political, business, voluntary, or other organizations. Initially, organizational needs, more than the motivation for power, cause these few stable leaders to emerge. As organizations grow, however, a division of labor emerges so that only a few leaders have

Women in many countries tend to have low-paid, dead-end jobs that result in alienation. Most, however, need the work to support themselves and their families, such as the women in these photos.

©REUTERS/Desmond Boylan

©Reuters/Sara Farid

access to information, resources, and the overall picture. This, in turn, causes leaders who enjoy their elite positions of power to become entrenched (Michels [1911] 1967).

Goal displacement occurs when the original motives or goals of the organization are displaced by new, secondary goals. Organizations are formed to meet specific goals. For example, religious organizations are established to worship a deity and serve humanity on behalf of that deity, schools are founded to educate children, and social work agencies are organized to serve needy citizens. Yet, over time, the original goals may not be met or become less important as other motivations and interests emerge. These organizations can sometimes become focused on the benefits they can bring to patrons or employees, rather than on fulfilling the goals for which they were established (Merton 1938; Whyte 1956). For example, in 2012, Pedro Espada Jr., a former New York State senator, pleaded guilty to charges of stealing money from health care clinics he ran in the Bronx. The clinics were created to care for poor people in the area, but Espada used them to enrich himself, family, and friends (Federal Bureau of Investigation 2012a).

Thinking Sociologically

In what areas of your college or workplace do you see goal displacement? In other words, where do you see decisions being driven by goals other than the original purpose of the organization?

Diversity and Equity in Organizations. In a global and diverse society, it makes sense to have a diverse workforce. The interaction of people who see things differently because of religious beliefs, ethnic backgrounds, and gender experiences increases productivity and creativity in many organizations. Having a wide range of perspectives can lead to better problem solving (Florida 2004; Molotch 2003). Successful business owners know they need to have a diverse group of employees in order to thrive. That is also one reason why colleges promote diversity on their campuses. The U.S. Supreme Court held hearings in 2013 on affirmative action programs in higher education, programs that promote diversity on campuses and prepare a diverse workforce by actively seeking qualified

underrepresented minority students for positions. Fifty large corporations, including Walmart, Pfizer, Halliburton, and American Express, joined together to write a brief in support of affirmative action programs in higher education. While these corporations gave most of their political donations to Republicans, they supported the Obama administration's arguments in favor of affirmative action, because they know a diverse workforce is good for business (Wilson 2012).

Despite efforts to diversify the workplace, women and other minorities in bureaucracies are underrepresented in upper management positions. They often find themselves with little authority and less pay than others with similar skills and credentials (Arulampalam, Booth, and Bryan 2007). It is also often much harder for minorities to even make it onto the lowest rung of bureaucratic organizations. For example, in New York City, among *equally qualified* whites, blacks, and Latinos applying for low-wage jobs, Latinos were less likely than, and blacks were *half* as likely as, white applicants to receive a job or callback. Even whites with criminal records were just as likely as, if not more likely than, black and Latino applicants *without* a criminal record to get a callback or job offer (Pager, Western, and Bonikowski 2009). These discriminatory actions are irrational and dysfunctional to organizations (Florida 2004, 2012; Molotch 2003).

NATIONAL AND GLOBAL NETWORKS: THE MACRO LEVEL

Understanding people unlike us, networking with people from different cultures, and being open to new ideas have become core competencies in our globalizing social world. Increasingly, colleges have study-abroad programs, and corporations seek multilingual employees with cultural competence in diverse settings. One young college graduate with a sociology degree found that she could use her sociology skills in leading groups of college-age students in international travel experiences. She explains this use of sociology in the next "Sociologists in Action."

Collaborating Across Cultures   ▶ Cross Cultural Communication

SOCIOLOGISTS IN ACTION:
ELISE ROBERTS

Using Sociology in International Travel and Intercultural Education

By Elise Roberts

After graduating from college with a bachelor's degree in sociology, I left the country to backpack through Mexico and Central America. My studies helped me to be more objective and aware as I experienced other societies. My international travel helped me examine my own societal assumptions and further understand how society creates so much of one's experience and view of the world. Eventually, I found a job leading groups of teenagers on alternative-education trips abroad. I was excited to get the job, but I was soon to learn that leading groups of teenagers in other countries is actually very hard work.

What struck me on meeting my first group was that I had very few students who initially understood this sociological perspective that I took for granted and that was so helpful in dealing with others. At times, my students would make fun of the way things were done in other countries, calling them "weird" or "stupid." They would mock the local traditions, until we discussed comparable traditions in U.S. culture. These students were not mean or unintelligent. In fact, they loved the places we were seeing and the people we were meeting. They just thought everything was factually, officially weird. They had been socialized to understand their own society's ways as "right" and "normal." They were fully absorbed in the U.S. society, and they had never questioned it before.

It was rewarding to apply concepts from my textbooks in the real world. My co-leaders and I learned to have fun while encouraging our students to become more socially conscious and analytical about their travel experience. We sent the groups out on scavenger hunts, and they would inevitably come back proudly announcing what they had paid for a rickshaw ride—only to learn that they had paid 10 times the local price. We would use this experience to talk about the role of foreigners, the assumptions that the local population made due to our skin color, and the culture of bartering. They had to learn to understand "odd" gestures, like pointing with the lips or side-to-side nodding. We would use these experiences to discuss nonverbal communication and gestures that we take for granted in U.S. culture.

We would encourage our novice travelers to interact with the people around them, which helped them understand the struggles facing immigrants and non-English speakers in the United States. We would force them to have conversations while standing toe-to-toe with each other, and they would finish with backaches from leaning away from one another. We would not allow them to explain their behavior with "because it's creepy to stand so close together," even though this was the consensus. "Why do you feel uncomfortable?" we would ask. "Why is this weird?" The answer has to do with social constructions of what is "normal" in any society.

Of course, while traveling internationally, one is surrounded by various other sociological issues, such as different racial or ethnic conflicts, gender roles, or class hierarchies, and learning about these issues was a part of our program as well. Without realizing it, many group conversations and meetings began to remind me of some of my favorite undergraduate sociology classes. "Study sociology!" I would say, plugging my major to the most interested students.

I have always thought that travel was an incredibly useful means not only to learn about the society and culture one is visiting but also to learn much about oneself and one's home society. For teenagers who otherwise might never step back to think about the role of being a foreigner or the traditions and social patterns they take for granted, it is even more important. Traveling abroad on my own and leading programs overseas were such extremely rich and rewarding experiences not only due to the cross-cultural exchanges and the intense personal examination that I saw in my students but also because it was fascinating and rewarding to be able to use my sociology degree every day on my job.

• •

Elise Roberts graduated from Macalester College with a major in sociology. Her post-college travels took her through Central America, the South Pacific, and many parts of Asia. She recently graduated from Columbia University with a master's degree in international social work and is a regional organizer for Witness for Peace.

With modern communication and transportation systems and the ability to transfer ideas and money with a touch of the keyboard, global networks are superseding national boundaries. Some businesses are global and can easily move their physical head-quarters from one nation to another (Ritzer 2007). This has helped many companies avoid paying millions of dollars in taxes. Apple, one of the multinational companies best at avoiding taxes, has managed to reduce its taxes by billions of dollars through "routing profits through Irish subsidiaries and the Netherlands and then to the Caribbean." This practice is now common as many corporations can move freely from nation to nation, in search of the largest profit possible (Duhigg and Kocieniewski 2013).

Profit, efficiency, and calculability are highly prized in multinational corporations. However, as these Western notions of public life are exported to other countries, a severe backlash has occurred in some nations. In many Middle Eastern Islamic countries, for example, these values clash with Muslim loyalties and priorities. The result has been high levels of anger at the United States and Western Europe. Many scholars believe that Middle Eastern anger at the United States is based not just on opposition to freedom and democracy, but also on what some Middle Easterners see as the crass greed and impersonal organizational structures we try to import

into their micro-, meso-, and macro-level worlds. They feel that their very culture is threatened (Ritzer 2007).

Radical fundamentalist movements—groups fueled by religious beliefs and socioeconomic stressors and that view the world in absolutes—are mostly anti-modernization movements turned militant (Antoun 2008; Marty and Appleby 2004). They have emerged in Christian, Jewish, Islamic, Sikh, and other groups, largely as a response to perceived threats to their ways of life (Armstrong 2000). Some aspects of global terrorism and international conflict are a response to the way the Western world organizes its social life and exports it to other parts of the world. These conflicts, in turn, have resulted in the mobilization of the armed forces in the United States. A consequence is that members of your own family might be serving abroad even as you read these pages.

Thinking Sociologically

How has global interaction been transformed during your lifetime through Internet technology? Give an example of how you can learn about what is happening in, say, Syria right now by using the Internet. Does this make you feel more connected to people there? Why or why not?

Our networks play a major role in setting norms and controlling our behaviors, usually resulting in our conformity to the social expectations of those in our network. This, of course, contributes to the stability of the entire social system because deviation can threaten the existence of "normal" patterns, as we see in the next chapter.

WHAT HAVE WE LEARNED?

Each of us has a network of people and groups that surround us. The scope of our networks has broadened with the increased complexity of societies and includes the global social world. Indeed, it is sometimes hard to recognize how far our networks reach. Although some of our social experiences are informal (unstructured), we are also profoundly affected by another phenomenon of the past

three centuries—highly structured bureaucracies. As a result of both, our experiences and personal lives are far more extensively linked to meso- and macro-level events and to people and places on the other side of the globe than were those of our parents. If we hope to understand our lives, we must understand this broad context. Although it may have been possible to live without global connections and bureaucratic systems several centuries ago, these networks are intricately woven into our lifestyles and our economic systems today. The question is whether we will control these networks or they will control us.

KEY POINTS

- People in the modern world are connected through one acquaintance to another in a chain of links, referred to as networks, that can now span the globe.

- We interpret interpersonal interactions at the micro level through unspoken assumptions based on the social context, nonverbal communication, and the physical space between people.

- Many of our behaviors are shaped by the statuses (social positions) we hold and the roles (expectations associated with a status) we play. However, our multiple-status occupancy can create role conflicts (between the roles of two statuses) and role strains (between the role expectations of a single status).

- When the norms of behavior are unclear, we may experience anomie (normlessness), and when anomie spreads in a society, suicide rates rise.

- Various types of groups affect our behavior—from primary and secondary groups to peer groups and reference groups.

- At the meso and macro levels, we find that formal organizations in the contemporary modern world have become bureaucratized. Bureaucratic organizations are ruled by rational calculation of the organization's goals rather than by tradition or emotional ties, tend to expand, are governed by impersonal formal rules, and stress efficiency and rational decision making.

- Bureaucracies often create particular issues that may make them inefficient or destructive, such as alienation, oligarchies, and goal displacement.

- In a global and diverse society, it makes sense to have a diverse workforce. Discrimination against minorities in promotion and hiring is irrational and dysfunctional for organizations.

- Some scholars think that this impersonal mode of organizing social life—so common in the West for several centuries now—is a critical factor in anti-American and anti-Western resistance movements.

DISCUSSION QUESTIONS

1. Think about your social network. How useful might it be in helping you get a job (or a better job) once you graduate from college? Why?

2. During a typical day, when do you engage in front- and backstage behavior? Why? With whom do you engage in each? Why?

3. Have you ever experienced role strain because of your status as a student? Explain why or why not. If so, how did/do you cope with it?

4. Most college students, particularly those with family, work, and/or sports team obligations, deal with role conflict. Describe a time when you dealt with a conflict between the roles you carry out. What did you do

about it? How might colleges and universities diminish role conflict among students?

5. To what primary and secondary groups do you belong? How does your involvement (or lack thereof) in primary groups on your campus impact your feelings of attachment to your school?

6. Would you rather live in a bureaucratic society or in a society without bureaucratic forms of organizations? Why?

7. How does the informal structure at your college or university impact how the school functions? Does it do more to help or hurt students? Why?

CONTRIBUTING TO OUR SOCIAL WORLD: What Can We Do?

At the Local Level

- *Tutoring and mentoring* programs help students struggling with their studies. Contact your school's Student Affairs or Tutoring Office and arrange to observe and/or volunteer in a program. Helping students build *social capital*, which includes making connections and increasing their knowledge of ways to obtain the help they need, can increase their chances of success.

- Workers' Centers for employed people not represented by unions have developed in many metropolitan areas, often with the aid of local clergy. Workers' Centers help these workers to organize and develop the social capital to obtain better wages, benefits, and workplace dignity. For a list of Workers' Centers, go to www.iwj.org/worker-center-network/locations.

At the Organizational or Institutional Level

- The social capital theory can also be applied to meso-level community organizations: *Community organizations* that work to build power and implement social change, such as *IAF* (the Industrial Areas Foundation at www.industrialareasfoundation.org), *Gamaliel* (www.gamaliel.org), and *PICO National Network* (www.piconetwork.org), provide their members with social capital. Find a group affiliated with one of these organizations near you.

- *Unions* also develop social capital for their members. Although far fewer U.S. citizens are unionized today than in past decades, membership in a union can improve the economic prospects of workers. For some workers, this can make the difference between living in poverty and obtaining a living wage. At 2.1 million members, the *Service Employees International Union (SEIU)* is the fastest growing union in North America. Internships with unions like SEIU are a great way to learn about organizing and social capital. You can find information about internships on the SEIU website (www.seiu.org).

- *The Anti-Defamation League* (www.adl.org), *the American-Arab Anti-Discrimination Committee* (www.adc.org), and *the National Association for the Advancement of Colored People* (www.naacp.org) are examples of organizations that defend the rights of minority groups. These organizations often use volunteers or interns and can provide you with the opportunity to learn about the extent to which social contacts and networks play a role in managing social conflict.

At the National or Global Level

- Well-run *microfinance organizations* can help poor people, particularly women, gain social capital and economic independence. Three well-known and respected groups are *CRS* (Catholic Relief Services at http://crs.org/microfinance), *FINCA* (www.finca.org), and Kiva (www.kiva.org). Check out their websites to learn how you can support their efforts.

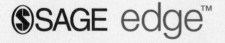

Sharpen your skills with SAGE edge at **edge.sagepub.com/ballantinecondensed4e**

SAGE edge for Students provides a personalized approach to help you accomplish your coursework goals in an easy-to-use learning environment.

edge.sagepub.com/ballantinecondensed4e

Review, practice, and **improve** your critical thinking with the tools and resources at SAGE edge.

6 Deviance and Social Control

Sickos, Weirdos, Freaks, and Folks Like Us

We often think of deviants as bad people who do not care about rules or other members of society; we contrast them to people like us. Sometimes, though, people need to commit deviant acts to change unjust social structures and to topple tyrants. Further, enforcement of conformity is often experienced as authoritarian.

MICRO

ME (MY FAMILY AND CLOSEST FRIENDS)

LOCAL ORGANIZATIONS AND COMMUNITY

People violate local ordinances and commit thefts.

MESO

NATIONAL ORGANIZATIONS, INSTITUTIONS, AND ETHNIC SUBCULTURES

People violate state laws and they commit crimes using corporations.

MACRO

SOCIETY

People commit federal crimes; the national government itself may commit crimes such as torture.

GLOBAL COMMUNITY

Crimes may result in global environmental destruction or violations of human rights across national boundaries.

LEARNING OBJECTIVES

6.1 Describe who is deviant and why.

6.2 Compare key ideas in the differential association, labeling, rational choice, structural functional, and conflict perspectives on deviance.

6.3 Provide possible explanations for why the crime rate has fallen in recent years.

6.4 Describe types of organized crime prevalent today.

6.5 Give examples of crimes committed at the national and global level today.

6.6 Discuss why you think either the structural functional or conflict perspective would be more useful in explaining the function of prisons in U.S. society today.

THINK ABOUT IT

Micro: Local Community	Are you deviant? Who says so? Why do some people in your community become deviant while others do not?
Meso: National Institutions; Complex Organizations; Ethnic Groups	What are the consequences of organized crime or occupational crime for large bureaucratic organizations?
Macro: National and Global Systems	What are the costs—and the benefits—of deviance for a nation? How can a global perspective on crime enhance our understanding of international and national criminal activities?

Wafa did not stand out from the girls around her as she grew up, but she was destined to make world headlines—as the first female suicide bomber in the Palestinian-Israeli conflict. She was the age of most university students reading this book, but she never had an opportunity to attend college. Her task was to smuggle explosives across the Israeli border for the intended bomber, her brother. Instead, on January 27, 2002, she blew up herself and an Israeli soldier. She was declared a martyr, a *sahida*, by the al-Aqsa Martyrs Brigade, and the organization took credit for the attack. The group's political leadership gave approval of her act, opening the way for other women to follow. Why did this happen? What motivated her to commit suicide and take another life in the process? Was she driven by ideology to participate in the Palestinian-Israeli struggle? Were there social and structural factors that affected her decision? Most important, was she deviant in carrying out this act, and according to whom?

Wafa Idris grew up in Palestine. She was married at a young age but did not produce children. As a result, her husband divorced her and remarried. She had no future, for who would want a barren, divorced woman in a society that values women for their purity and their childbearing ability? She was a burden to her family. Her way out of an impossible and desperate situation was to commit suicide, bringing honor and wealth to her family and redeeming herself in the process. Other women who followed Wafa have similar stories: Most shared an inability to control their own lives in the patriarchal (male-controlled) society (Gonzalez-Perez 2011; Handwerk 2004; Victor 2003).

Our question is this: Are such women deviant criminal terrorists, hapless victims of terrorist groups, mentally ill "crazies," invisible victims in a patriarchal society, or martyrs who should be honored for their acts? And who says so? Each of these views is held by someone interested in this situation. From this opening example, we can begin to see several complications that arise when defining deviance and deviants. In this chapter, we will consider who is deviant, under what circumstances, and in whose eyes.

First, we discuss **deviance**—*the violation of social norms*—and the social control mechanisms that keep most people from becoming deviant. Occasionally, most of us violate a norm, and depending on its importance and on the severity of the violation, we may or may not be seen as deviant. Wearing strange clothes may be seen as amusing and nonconformist once in a while, but you will be labeled deviant if you do so regularly. If enough people start wearing similar clothes, however, this once deviant act will no longer be deviant. Getting a tattoo or wearing skintight jeans to school are good examples of once deviant acts now considered normal behavior in many communities. We also examine **crime** in this chapter, *deviant actions for which there are formal penalties imposed by the government, such as fines, jail, or prison sentences.*

You may be surprised to learn that we are all deviant at some times and in some places and almost all of us have committed crimes. The self-test in the next "Engaging Sociology" illustrates this point.

WHAT IS DEVIANCE?

While some acts, such as murder, assault, robbery, and rape, are considered deviant in almost every time and place, some deviant acts may be overlooked or even viewed as understandable under certain circumstances, such as when a family steals water and diapers from a destroyed supermarket after a natural disaster.

Perspectives on Deviance

ENGAGING SOCIOLOGY

Who Is Deviant?

Please jot down your answers to the following self-test questions. There is no need to share your responses with others.

Have you ever engaged in any of the following acts?

1. stolen anything, even if its value was under $10
2. used an illegal drug
3. misused a prescription drug
4. used tobacco prior to age 18
5. drunk alcohol prior to age 21
6. engaged in a fistfight
7. carried a concealed knife or gun
8. used a car without the owner's permission
9. driven a car after drinking alcohol
10. forced someone to have sexual relations against her or his will
11. offered sex for money
12. damaged property worth more than $10
13. been truant from school
14. arrived home after your curfew
15. accepted or transported property that you had reason to believe might be stolen
16. taken a towel from a hotel room after renting the room for a night

All of the above are delinquent acts (violations of legal standards), and most young people are guilty of at least one infraction. However, few teenagers are given the label of *delinquent*. If you answered yes to any of the preceding questions, you committed a crime in many states. Your penalty or sanction for the infraction could range from a stiff fine to several years in prison—*if* you got caught!

Engaging With Sociology

1. Do you think of yourself as a deviant? Why or why not?
2. Are deviants only those who get caught? For instance, if someone steals your car but avoids being caught, is he or she a deviant?
3. Who is considered deviant—and by whom?

Some acts of deviance are considered serious offenses in one society but tolerated in another. Examples include prostitution, premarital or extramarital sex, gambling, corruption, and bribery. Even within a single society, different groups may define deviance and conformity quite differently. The state government may officially define alcohol consumption by 19-year-olds as deviant, but on a Saturday night at a fraternity party, the 19-year-old "brother" who does *not* drink may be viewed as deviant by his peers. What do these cases tell us about deviance?

Deviance is socially constructed and dependent on the time and social context. Members of groups in societies define (construct) what is deviant. As we noted earlier, these socially constructed definitions of deviance can change over *time* and depend on the social situation or *context* in which the behavior occurs.

If we take the same behavior and place it in a different social context, perceptions of whether the behavior is deviant may well change. For example, in Greece, Spain, and other Mediterranean countries, the clothing norms on beaches are very different from those in most of North America. Topless sunbathing by women is not at all uncommon, even on beaches designated as family beaches. The norms vary, however, even within a few feet of the beach. Women will sunbathe topless, lying only 10 feet from the boardwalk where concessionaires sell beverages, snacks, and tourist items. If these women become thirsty, they cover up, walk the 10 feet to purchase a cola, and return to their beach blankets, where they again remove their tops. To walk onto the boardwalk topless would be considered highly deviant.

Thinking Sociologically

Have you ever dressed or styled your hair in a deviant way? Why? Did you have any role models to guide you on how to do so? If so, does this mean you really were *not* being deviant? Why or why not? Who determines whether or not your clothes or hairstyle are deviant?

▶ What Is Deviance?

Miley Cyrus was purposefully deviant when she crossed the lines of appropriate behavior on television and "twerked"—a sexually provocative dance move—throughout her performance at the 2013 Video Music Awards. Perhaps chastened by the outcry that ensued, she stated in an interview at the 2014 VMAs that she had "retired" from twerking.

An individual's status or group may be defined as deviant. Some individuals have a higher likelihood of being labeled deviant because of the group into which they were born, such as a particular ethnic group, or because of a distinguishing mark or characteristic, such as a deformity. Others may escape being considered deviant because of their dominant status in society. The higher one's status, the less likely that one will be suspected of violating norms and the less likely that any violations will be characterized as "criminal." Who would suspect that a respectable, white-collar husband and father is embezzling funds from his company?

The looting that happened following Hurricane Katrina was addressed differently depending on whether it was done by whites or African Americans (Huddy and Feldman 2006; Thompson 2009). The media showed photos of black "looters" who "stole

Deviance is socially constructed. Is this man deviant by virtue of his appearance? Why or why not? For a photo essay and further thinking about deviance as social construction, visit **edge.sagepub.com/ballantinecondensed4e.**

food," but the same media described whites who "broke into grocery stores" in search of food as "resourceful." Likewise, gays and lesbians are often said to be deviant and accused of flaunting their sexuality. Heterosexuals are rarely accused of "flaunting" their sexuality, regardless of how overtly flirtatious or underdressed they may be. So one's group membership or ascribed traits may make a difference in whether or not one is defined as deviant.

Deviance can be functional for society. As structural functionalists point out, deviance serves vital functions by setting examples of unacceptable behavior, providing guidelines for behavior necessary to maintain social order, and bonding people together through their common rejection of the deviant behavior. Deviance is also functional because it provides jobs for those who deal with deviants—police, judges, social workers, and so forth (Gans 2007). Furthermore, deviance can signal problems in society that need to be addressed and can therefore stimulate positive change. Sometimes deviant individuals break the model of conventional thinking, thereby opening society to new and creative paths of thinking. Scientists, inventors, activists, and artists have often been rejected in their time but have been honored later for accomplishments that positively affected society. Famous artist Vincent van Gogh, for example, lived in poverty and suffered from schizophrenia. During his life, his artistic gifts were overlooked, but he became recognized as a renowned painter after his death. His paintings now sell for millions of dollars. Likewise,

Some sociologists point out that crime can be "functional" because it creates jobs for people such as those above and it unifies society against the nonconformists and deviant behavior.

Nelson Mandela, Martin Luther King Jr., and Mahatma Gandhi were once considered deviant and dangerous, but today they are regarded as social justice heroes.

Thinking Sociologically

Think of examples in your life that illustrate the *relative nature of deviance*. For instance, are some of your behaviors deviant in one setting but not in another, or were they deviant when you were younger but not deviant now?

Crime: Deviance That Violates the Law

Governments create laws and impose formal sanctions—punishments—for some acts of deviance, and the social disapproval associated with being convicted of these violations results in the perpetrator being identified as "criminal." *When members of society are in general agreement about the seriousness of certain crimes*, these acts are referred to as **consensus crimes** (Brym and Lie 2007; Goodman and Brenner 2002). *Predatory crimes* (crimes—usually violent—against humans, such as premeditated murder, forcible rape, and kidnapping for ransom), described later in this chapter, are consensus crimes in most nations.

Just as what is considered deviant varies over time and place, so does what is regarded as criminal behavior. For example, at the end of the 1920s, 42 of the 48 U.S. states had laws forbidding interracial marriage (Coontz 2005). Legislatures in half of these states removed those restrictions by the 1960s, but 16 states

still had anti-miscegenation laws on the books until 1967 when the U.S. Supreme Court ruling in *Loving v. Virginia* made these laws unconstitutional. Today, this legal ban on interracial marriage has been eliminated completely, illustrating that most laws change to reflect the times and sentiments of the majority of people. Likewise, the move to legalize same-sex marriage, with 37 states and Washington, DC legally recognizing same-sex marriages as of February 2015, reflects changing views toward homosexuality (Freedom to Marry 2015).

We now look at theoretical perspectives that help explain deviance, how some deviant acts become crimes, and what policies might control or reduce crime.

WHAT CAUSES DEVIANT BEHAVIOR? THEORETICAL PERSPECTIVES

Helena is a delinquent. Her father deserted the family when Helena was 10, and before that, he had abused Helena and her mother. Her mother has all she can cope with; she is just trying to survive financially and keep her three children in line. Helena gets little attention and little support or encouragement in her school activities. Her grades have fallen steadily. As a young teen, she sought attention from boys, and in the process, she became pregnant. Now, the only kids who have anything to do with her are others who have been in trouble; her friends are other young people who

Until recently, this same-sex couple would have been considered deviant throughout the United States. Today, the federal government recognizes same-sex marriages, as do many states.

Why Deviance?

have also been labeled delinquent. Helena's schoolmates, teachers, and mother see her as a delinquent troublemaker, and it would be hard for Helena to change their views and her status.

How did this happen? Helena's situation is, of course, only one unique case. Sociologists cannot generalize from Helena to other cases, but they do know from their studies that there are thousands of teens with problems like Helena's. Below we consider some theories of deviance that help us recognize and explain patterns among delinquent teens like Helena.

Throughout history, people have proposed explanations for why some members of society "turn bad"—from biological explanations of imbalances in hormones and claims of innate personality defects to social conditions within individual families or in the larger social structure. Biological and psychological approaches focus on personality disorders or abnormalities in the body or psyche of individuals, but they generally do not consider the social context in which deviance occurs.

Sociologists place emphasis on understanding the interactions, social structure, and social processes that lead to deviant behavior, rather than on individual characteristics. They consider the socialization process and interpersonal relationships, group and social class differences, cultural and subcultural norms, and power structures that influence individuals to conform to or deviate from societal expectations. Theoretical explanations about why people are deviant influence social policy decisions and strategies to curb deviant behavior and deal with deviants.

Some theories explain particular types of crime better than others (say, theft as opposed to sexual assault), just as some illuminate micro-, meso-, or macro-level processes better than others. Taken together, these theories help us understand a wide range of deviant and criminal behaviors.

Micro-Level Explanations of Deviance

No one is born deviant. Individuals learn to be law-abiding citizens or to be deviant through the process of socialization. Why do some people learn to become deviant and others learn to follow the norms of society? Symbolic interaction and rational choice theories focus primarily on micro-level answers to this question.

Symbolic Interaction Approaches to Deviance. Symbolic interactionists focus on how our interactions with others influence whether or not we will commit deviant acts. One interactionist approach, differential association theory, describes how people learn to commit delinquent acts through their social relationships with peers and family members.

Differential Association Theory. **Differential association theory** focuses on *the process of learning deviant behavior from those with whom we interact* (e.g., family, peers, fellow employees) (Hagan 2011; Sutherland, Cressey, and Luckenbil 1992). Helena, for example, came to be surrounded by people who made dropping out of school and other delinquent acts seem normal. If her close friends and siblings were also sexually active as teens, her teen pregnancy might not be remarkable and might even be a source of some prestige with her group of peers.

According to differential association theory, the possibility of becoming deviant depends on four factors related to associating with a deviant group: the *duration* of time spent with the group, the *intensity* of interaction, the *frequency* of interaction, and the *priority* of the group in one's friendship network (Sutherland et al. 1992). If people have regular and frequent exposure to deviance among their longtime, close friends, they are likely to learn to behave in deviant ways.

Some theorists contend that life in poverty often involves immersion in a distinctive subculture in

© David H. Wells/Corbis

According to differential association theory, people who abuse drugs, like this young man, tend to learn this behavior through close associations with other illicit drug users. They come to see the drugged state as acceptable or even enjoyable and learn the techniques for using drugs.

which poor people learn delinquent behavior patterns through socialization. The values, beliefs, norms, and practices that have evolved in poor communities over time can often encourage violation of laws. Just as upper-class youth learn norms that help them to succeed in middle- and upper-class areas of society, lower-class youth may learn other behaviors that help them to survive in their poor neighborhoods but that those with privilege have defined as delinquent and criminal (Bettie 2003; Chambliss 1973). The reality is that youth from all social classes commit crimes—but those crimes may be different and be perceived differently by those around the youth.

Elijah Anderson's book *Code of the Street* (2000) describes two types of groups that coexist in poor neighborhoods: "decent people" and "street people." Street-oriented people learn a code of the street that involves hanging out on the street with peers; seeking immediate gratification through sex, violence, and drugs; and adopting a certain look with their clothes and jewelry—an image expected by the group. Peers become more important than society's social control agents. Decent families accept mainstream values and often find support systems in church communities or other organizations. In order to survive in such neighborhoods and avoid violent sanctions from street-oriented peers, however, those from decent families may dress and carry themselves in a way that conforms to the street-oriented image. The result is that other members of society, including the police, view both the street-oriented individuals and those from decent families as deviant (Anderson 2000).

As mentioned above, we know that members of all social classes commit crimes, and no socioeconomic class has a monopoly on violence, corruption, or dishonesty. However, *labeling theory*, another explanation of deviance based on the symbolic interactionist perspective, explains why some individuals and groups are more likely to be caught and punished for deviance.

Labeling Theory. **Labeling theory** *explains how people can be labeled deviant after committing a deviant act, which can then lead them to carry out further acts that reflect that label.* Labels (such as "juvenile delinquency") are symbols that have meanings affecting an individual's self-concept and the way others see the individual.

Labeling theorists define two stages in the process of becoming a deviant. **Primary deviance** is *a violation of*

Shoplifting, when done by young people without a criminal record, provides an example of primary deviance.

a norm that may be an isolated act or an initial act of rule breaking, such as a young teenager shoplifting something on a dare by friends. Most people commit acts of primary deviance. However, many of us avoid being labeled "deviant" when we commit one of these primary acts. Remember how you marked the deviant behavior test that you took at the beginning of this chapter? If you have engaged in deviant acts, you were probably not labeled deviant for the offense. If you had been so labeled, you might not be in college or taking this class.

If an individual continues to violate a norm and begins to take on a deviant identity because of being labeled as deviant, this is referred to as **secondary deviance**. Secondary deviance becomes publicly recognized, and the individual is identified as deviant, beginning a deviant career. If a teenager like Helena is caught, her act becomes known, perhaps publicized in the newspaper. She may spend time in a juvenile detention center, and parents of other teens may not want their children associating with her. Employers and store managers may refuse to hire her. Soon, there are few opportunities open to her because others expect her to be delinquent. The teen may continue performing the deviant acts and associating with delinquent acquaintances, in part because few other options are available. Society's reaction, then, is what defines a deviant person and may limit options for that person to change the label (Lemert 1951, 1972).

The process of labeling individuals and behaviors takes place at each level of analysis, from individual to society. If community or societal norms and laws define a behavior as deviant, individuals are likely to believe it is deviant. Sanctions against juvenile

Theories of Deviance

delinquents can have the effect of reinforcing the deviant behavior by (a) increasing alienation from the social world, (b) forcing increased interaction with deviant peers, and (c) motivating juvenile delinquents to positively value and identify with the deviant status (Kaplan and Johnson 1991).

A **self-fulfilling prophecy** occurs when a *belief or a prediction becomes a reality, in part because of the prediction*. A false perception of a person, perhaps based on a stereotype, can become true if it provokes behavior that fulfills that false perception or stereotype. For example, James is 8 years old and already sees himself as a "bad" kid who will end up in prison, just like his father, whom he has never met. His mother tells him he was born "bad" because he resembles his father, and his teachers and peers tell him he is "bad" because he struggles in school. In keeping with the idea of a self-fulfilling prophecy, James accepts the label and acts accordingly, refusing to do his homework and stealing other kids' lunch money. Unless someone—such as an insightful teacher—steps in to give him another image of himself, James is likely to end up in prison—not because he was born "bad" but because he was treated by others as if he were bad and learned that image of himself (Merton 1948).

Thinking Sociologically

What labels do you carry? How do you know you carry these labels? How do they affect your self-concept and behavior?

A major explanation of why certain individuals and groups are labeled as deviant has to do with their status and power in society—a concern of conflict theory. Those on the fringes, away from power—the poor, minorities, members of new religious movements, or others who in some way do not fit into the dominant system—are more likely to be labeled as deviants. On the other hand, because the powerful have the influence to define what is acceptable, they tend to avoid the deviant label. Their behavior, even when it has a negative impact on society, is less likely to be labeled as deviant or criminal.

A study by William J. Chambliss illustrates the process of labeling in communities and groups. Perhaps during your high school years you witnessed situations similar to that described in his study (Chambliss 1973). Chambliss looked at the behavior of two small peer groups of boys and at the reactions of community members to their behavior. The Saints, boys from

"good" families, were some of the most delinquent boys at Hannibal High School. Although the Saints were constantly occupied with truancy, drinking, wild driving, petty theft, and vandalism, none was officially arrested for any misdeed during the two-year study. The Roughnecks, who were from less affluent families, were constantly in trouble with the police and community residents, even though their rate of delinquency was about equal to that of the Saints.

What was the cause of the disparity in the labeling of these two groups? Community members, the police, and teachers alike labeled the boys based on their perceptions of the boys' family backgrounds and social class. The Saints came from stable, white, upper-middle-class families; were active in school affairs; and were precollege students who everyone expected would become professionals. In fact, the Saints almost all did become professionals, living up to their images in the community. On the other hand, the general community feeling was that the Roughnecks would amount to nothing. They carried around a negative label that was hard to change. Two Roughnecks ended up in prison, two became coaches, and little is known of the others. For a number of these boys, the prophecy became self-fulfilling (Chambliss 1973).

Rational Choice Approaches to Deviance. Rational choice theory, as noted in previous chapters, suggests that when individuals make decisions, they calculate the costs and benefits to themselves. They consider the balance between pleasure and pain. Turning to crime is therefore a conscious, rational, and calculated decision made after weighing the costs and benefits of alternatives.

Rational choice theorists believe that punishment—imposing high "costs" for criminal behavior, such as fines, imprisonment, or even the death penalty—is the best way to dissuade criminals from choosing the path of crime. When the cost outweighs the potential benefit and opportunities are restricted, it deters people from thinking that crime is a "rational" choice (Earls and Reiss 1994; Winslow and Zhang 2008).

Positive sanctions reward those behaviors approved by society. This is the reason why schools have honor ceremonies, companies reward their top salespeople, and communities recognize civic leadership with "Citizen of the Year" awards. All these actions enhance the rewards for conventional behavior. Negative sanctions (or punishments) increase the cost to those who deviate from the norm. They range

Rational choice theorists would note that this little girl is weighing the costs and benefits of taking cookies, and the benefits are looking pretty sweet!

from fines for traffic violations to prison sentences for serious crimes, and even death in many states, for acts considered most dangerous to society.

Social Control Theory. One of sociology's central concepts is social control—why people obey norms (Hagan 2011). A specific rational choice application, control theory focuses on why most people conform most of the time and do not commit deviant acts. If human beings were truly free to do whatever they wanted, they would likely commit more deviant acts. Yet to live near others and with others requires individuals to control their behaviors based on social norms and sanctions—in short, social control.

A perpetual question in sociology is the following: How is social order possible in the context of rapidly changing society? A very general answer is that social control results from social norms that promote order and predictability in the social world. When people fail to adhere to these norms, or when the norms are unclear, the stability and continuance of the entire social system may be threatened.

Control theory contends that people are bonded to others by four powerful factors:

1. *Attachment* to other people who respect the values and rules of the society. Individuals do not want to be rejected by those to whom they are close or whom they admire.
2. *Commitment* to conventional activities (such as school and jobs) that they do not want to jeopardize.
3. *Involvement* in activities that keep them so busy with conventional roles and expectations that they do not have time for mischief.
4. *Belief* in the social rules of their culture, which they accept because of their childhood socialization and indoctrination into those conventional beliefs.

These factors can decrease the likelihood that a person will commit deviant acts (Hirschi 1969).

Two primary forces shape our tendency to conform. The first is internal controls, those voices within us that tell us when a behavior is acceptable or unacceptable, right or wrong. The second is external controls—society's formal or informal controls against deviant behavior. Informal external controls include smiles, frowns, hugs, and ridicule from close acquaintances (Gottfredson and Hirschi 1990). Formal external controls come from the legal system through the police, judges, juries, and social workers. In both cases, the cost-benefit ratio shifts, making either conformity or deviance a rational choice. Social control comes from shifting the balance toward more pain and fewer benefits for those who deviate from norms.

Situational Crime Prevention. Applying rational choice theory to crime prevention has led to measures that focus on making it harder and less rewarding to commit crimes. For example, improved lighting, especially at night (making it harder to commit a crime unnoticed), marking goods that may be stolen (for easy tracking and recovery), and creating positive alternatives to crime (such as summer jobs for teens) make crime both harder and less appealing (Clarke 1997).

Thinking Sociologically

Imagine you have a friend who is using drugs illegally. From what you know about the above theories, how might you explain her behavior? What insights can you gain, if any, about what might lead your friend to stop using these drugs?

Meso- and Macro-Level Explanations of Deviance

While micro-level interactions can lead a person to become and to be labeled as deviant, meso- and macro-level analysis can help us gain a greater understanding of the societal factors leading to deviance. As we have noted, meso-level analysis focuses on ethnic subcultures, organizations, and institutions. Macro-level analysis focuses on national and global social systems.

Structural-Functional Approaches to Deviance.

Structural-functional theories of deviance include (1) *anomie*, the breakdown of societal norms guiding behavior, which leads to social disorganization, and (2) *strain theory*, which shows that the difference between definitions of success (goals) in a society and the means available to achieve those goals can lead to deviant behavior.

Anomie and Social Disorganization.

Sociologists use the term **anomie**, or the *state of normlessness that occurs when rules for behavior in society break down under extreme stress from rapid social change or conflict* (Merton 1968). Émile Durkheim (1858–1917) first described this normlessness as a condition of weak, conflicting, or absent norms and the changes in values that arise when societies are disorganized. As discussed in Chapter 5, this situation is typical in rapidly urbanizing, industrializing societies, at times of sudden prosperity or depression, during rapid technological change, during a war, or when a government is overthrown.

Imagine you were raised in a small village where your family and all those around you have been farmers for as far back as anyone can remember. You were raised to become one yourself and thought you would raise your children to become farmers as well. Over the past few years, though, due to climate change, the rains have not come and the fields no longer support crops. You have no choice but to leave everyone and everything you have ever known to try to find work in the nearest city. This may thrust you into a situation where norms of interaction—including mutual support and friendliness—are very different and you might feel like you are in a different country.

Millions of people are now living out similar stories. Villagers in industrializing countries in Africa, Asia, and Latin America find themselves pushed off marginally productive rural lands and pulled into rapidly expanding cities to seek better lives and means for survival. They hope to find good jobs in these urban areas, but when they arrive, they often face disappointment. Poor, unskilled, and homeless, they move into crowded apartments or shantytowns of temporary shacks and try to adjust to the new style of life, which often includes unemployment. Old village norms

The autocratic Yemeni president, Ali Abdullah Saleh, claimed that the recent protests against him were leading to anomie and general social chaos. In the picture above, Yemeni army soldiers try to stop antigovernment protesters. Saleh was deposed in January 2015 by a rebel group that has taken charge of the capital.

that have provided the guidelines for proper behavior crumble, sometimes without clear expectations emerging to take their place. The lack of clear norms in the rapidly changing urban environment leads to high levels of social disorganization and deviant behavior.

This general idea of anomie led a group of Chicago sociologists to study the social conditions of that city that correlate with deviance. The Chicago School, as the research team is known, linked life in transitional slum areas to the high incidence of crime. Certain neighborhoods or zones in the Chicago area—generally inner-city transitional zones with recent settlers—have always had high delinquency rates, regardless of the group that occupied the area. Low economic status, ethnic heterogeneity, residential mobility, family disruption, and competing value systems (because of the constant transitions) led to community disorganization. Although new immigrant groups have replaced the older groups over time, the delinquency rate has remained high because each generation of newcomers experiences anomie (Shaw and McKay 1929). The high in-migration and out-migration in these communities in itself explains the lack of stability in families. Peer group norms become influential, and models of nondeviant behavior are scarce for many teenagers and adults (Anderson 2000).

Strain Theory.

What happens when you know what your goal is but you cannot find a socially acceptable path to reach it? How do you proceed? **Strain theory** contends that *the opportunity or limitations embedded* *in the structures of society may contradict and undermine the goals and aspirations society encourages for its members, creating strains that lead to deviance.*

Strain theory suggests that the gap between an individual's or a society's *goals* and the legitimate ways of attaining those goals—*the means*—can lead to strain in the society (Merton 1968). Individuals may agree with the society's *goals* for success (say, financial affluence) but may not be able to achieve them using the socially acceptable means of achieving that success. The strain created can lead to deviance. Merton uses U.S. society as an example because it places a heavy emphasis on success as measured by wealth and social standing. He outlines five ways by which individuals adapt to the strain. Figure 6.1 shows these five types and their relationship to goals and means.

To further illustrate strain theory, we trace the choices of a lower-class student who realizes the value of an education and knows it is necessary to get ahead, but has problems finding time to study because she has to work many hours a week to help support her family.

1. *Conformity* means embracing the society's definition of success and adhering to the established and approved means of achieving success. The student works hard despite the obstacles, pulling all-nighters and trying to do well in school to achieve success and a good job placement. She uses legitimate, approved means—education and hard work—to reach goals that the society views as worthy.

2. *Innovation* refers to the use of illicit means to reach approved goals. Our student uses illegitimate means to achieve her education goals. She may cheat on exams or get papers from Internet sources. Success in school is all that matters. How she attains that success does not matter.

3. *Ritualism* involves strict adherence to the culturally prescribed rules, even though individuals give up on the goals they hoped to achieve. The student may give up the idea of getting good grades and going to college but, as a matter of pride and self-image, continues to try hard and to attend school. She conforms to expectations, but with no sense of purpose. She just does what she is told.

4. *Retreatism* refers to giving up on both the goals and the means. The student either bides her time, not doing well, or drops out, giving up on future job goals. She abandons or retreats from the goals of a professional position in society and the means to get there. She may even turn to a different lifestyle—for example, becoming a user of drugs and alcohol—as part of the retreat.

5. *Rebellion* entails rejecting socially approved ideas of success and the means of attaining that success. It replaces those with alternative definitions of success and alternative strategies for attaining new goals. Rebelling against the dominant cultural goals and means, a student may leave her family, abandon thoughts of college and a profession, and join a radical political or religious group or become a terrorist, seeking to destabilize the government and establish a new type of society.

Deviant behavior results from retreatism, rebellion, and innovation. According to Merton, the reasons why individuals resort to these behaviors lie in the social conditions that prevent access to success, not in their individual biological or psychological makeup (Merton 1968).

The structural-functional approaches to deviance focus on what occurs if deviance disrupts the ongoing social order. They explore what causes deviance, how to prevent disruptions, how to keep change slow and nondisruptive, and how deviance can be useful to the ongoing society. However, anomie and strain theories fail to account for class conflicts, inequities, and poverty, which conflict theorists argue cause deviance.

Conflict Theory of Deviance. As you will recall from previous chapters, conflict theorists assume that conflict among groups is inevitable. Conflict theory

FIGURE 6.1 Merton's Strain Theory

focuses on a meso- and macro-level analysis of deviance, looking at deviance as the result of social inequality or of the struggle among groups for power.

Wealthy and powerful elites want to maintain their control and their high positions (Domhoff 2009). They have the power to pass laws and define what is deviant, sometimes by effectively eliminating the opposition groups. The greater the cultural difference between the dominant group and other groups in society, the greater the possibility of conflict. This is because minority groups and subcultures challenge the norms of the dominant groups and threaten the consensus in society (Huizinga, Loeber, and Thornberry 1994).

Some conflict theorists blame capitalist systems for the unjust administration of law and unequal distribution of resources, arguing that the ruling class uses the legal system to further the capitalist enterprise (Quinney 2002). The dominant or ruling class defines deviance, applies laws to protect its interests, represses efforts to make laws more just, and, in effect, may force those in subordinate classes to carry out actions that the dominant class has defined as deviant. These deviant actions become necessary for survival when the affluent restrict legitimate avenues to resources. In most cases, the dominant class consists of one racial or ethnic group that distinguishes itself from the racial or ethnic groups found in the subordinate classes. So, conflict and definitions of deviance often have racial and ethnic implications as well as social class dimensions. When people believe that those in power treat them unfairly, they have less loyalty to the society and to its rules.

To reduce deviance and crime, conflict theorists believe that we must change the structure of society. For instance, legal systems in many countries claim to support equal and fair treatment for all, but when one looks at the law in action, another picture emerges as seen in the next Engaging Sociology. Recall the example of the Saints and Roughnecks; the students from powerful families and higher social classes received favored treatment. Unequal treatment of groups that differ from the dominant group—the poor, laboring class and racial or ethnic minorities in particular—is rooted in the legal, political, and occupational structures of societies.

A Multilevel Analysis of Deviance: Feminist Theories.

As we have indicated in previous chapters, feminist theories sometimes take a macro approach very akin to conflict theory, and sometimes they are more micro in approach. In either case, feminist theorists consistently argue that traditional theories do not give an adequate picture or understanding of women's situations. These theorists look for explanations of violence against women and the secondary status of most women in gender relations and social structures. Although there are several branches of feminist theory, most see the macro-level causes of abuses suffered by women as rooted in the capitalist patriarchal system.

One result of women's secondary status is that they are often victims of sexual crime, and those who commit such crimes against women do not face severe, or in some cases *any*, punishment. Criminal acts against women, including honor killings, sex trafficking, and rape, take place around the world (Bales 2004; Bales and Trodd 2008). Globally, 7 out of 10 women report being sexually assaulted at some point during their lives (United Nations 2013). In a few countries or regions in countries, the legal system is based on strict interpretations of religious books by those who practice fundamentalist interpretations of the religion, in an attempt to maintain patriarchal control over women and their bodies.

According to feminist theory, women's work in the private sphere—including housework, child care, and sexual satisfaction of their husbands—is undervalued, as are the women who carry out these roles. In some societies, women are the property of their husbands, with men's strength and physical force the ultimate means of control over women. Some branches of feminist theory argue that men exploit women's labor power and sexuality to continue their dominance.

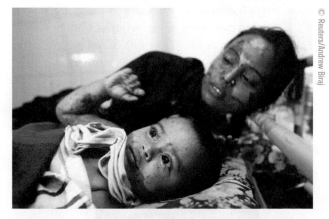

Feminist scholars point out that domestic abuse, such as that inflicted on this woman and child, disproportionately impacts women. Asma and her 11-month-old daughter Afsana were attacked with acid because she was helping her sister with a divorce.

ENGAGING SOCIOLOGY

Marijuana Use Versus Marijuana Arrests

Today, we can see evidence of disparity in treatment by comparing the treatment of black and white Americans who use marijuana in states where it is illegal. See Figures 6.2a and 6.2b.

FIGURE 6.2a Marijuana Use by Race, 2001–2010

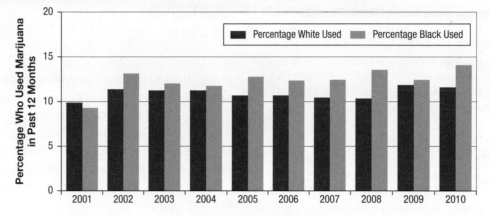

Source: Substance Abuse and Mental Health Services Administration.

FIGURE 6.2b Arrest Rates for Marijuana Possession by Race, 2001–2010

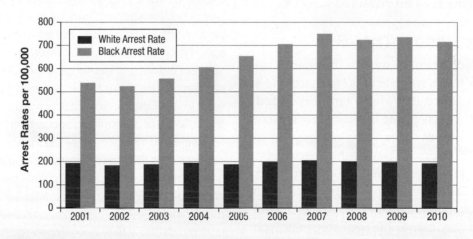

Source: FBI/Uniform Crime Reporting Program Data and U.S. Census Data.

Engaging With Sociology

1. What are the respective percentages of white and black Americans who use marijuana?

2. What are the respective percentages of white and black Americans arrested for marijuana use?

3. Of the theories described in this chapter, which offers the most convincing explanation for the discrepancy in the answers to Questions 1 and 2? Why?

The system is reproduced through new generations socialized to maintain the patriarchy and to view inequality between the sexes as "normal" and "natural."

Women who deviate from the cultural expectations of "normal" behavior are condemned. No one theory of why deviance occurs can explain all the forms of deviance. Depending on the level of analysis of the questions sociologists wish to study (micro, meso, or macro), they select the theory that best fits the data they find. In the following sections, we explore in more detail the micro-meso-macro connections as they apply to one manifestation of deviance—crime. This illustrates how the sociological imagination can be applied to deviance at each level in the social system.

● Thinking Sociologically

Meso- and macro-level social forces can be even more powerful than micro-level forces in explaining deviance. What might be the factors at the meso and macro levels that contribute to deviance such as prostitution or shoplifting? Pick a recent example of deviance now in the news. Which sociological theories help explain this deviant behavior?

CRIME AND INDIVIDUALS: MICRO-LEVEL ANALYSIS

In the United States, more than 2,800 acts are listed as federal crimes. These acts fall into several types of crime, some of which are discussed below. First, we consider how crime rates are measured.

How Much Crime Is There?

How do sociologists and law enforcement officials know how much crime occurs? Not all crime is reported to the police, and when crime is reported, the methods of collecting data may differ. Each country has its own methods of keeping crime records. For instance, the official record of crime in the United States is found in the U.S. Federal Bureau of Investigation's (FBI's) *Uniform Crime Reports* (UCR). The FBI relies on information submitted voluntarily by law enforcement agencies and divides crimes into two categories: Type I and Type II offenses. Type I offenses, also known as *FBI index crimes*, include murder, forcible rape, robbery, aggravated assault, burglary, larceny theft, motor vehicle theft, and arson. Type II offenses include fraud, simple assault, vandalism, driving under the influence of alcohol or drugs, and running away from home. In fact, there are hundreds of Type II crimes. Figure 6.3, the 2013 Crime Clock, summarizes UCR records on Type I offenses. To examine trends in crime, social scientists calculate a rate of crime, usually per 100,000.

Although the UCR data provide a picture of how much crime gets *reported* to the police and leads to

FIGURE 6.3 2013 Crime Clock

A Violent Crime occurred every	27.1 seconds
One Murder every	37.0 minutes
One Forcible Rape every	6.6 minutes
One Robbery every	1.5 minutes
One Aggravated Assault every	43.5 seconds
A Property Crime occurred every	3.7 seconds
One Burglary every	16.4 seconds
One Larceny Theft every	5.3 seconds
One Motor Vehicle Theft every	45.1 seconds

Source: U.S. Department of Justice 2014.

arrest, the FBI does not provide complete information on how much crime there is in the United States. The UCR does not show most corporate crimes or white-collar crimes, and *many* street crimes are not reported for a host of reasons. Further, sometimes a crime reported to the police does not lead to an arrest, or an arrest is made but the case is never prosecuted in court, or a prosecutor will initiate prosecution but the case never comes to trial. A majority of cases end in plea bargains—a suspect agrees to plead guilty in exchange for being given a lesser charge, perhaps because the suspect expresses feelings of guilt, because the person does not have the resources to fight the charges with a good attorney, or because the suspect is willing to exchange information for a lighter sentence. The reduction in the number of cases at each level of the criminal justice system contributes to the difficulty of determining accurate crime rates.

Self-reporting surveys—asking individuals what criminal acts they have committed—provide another way to measure crime rates. Criminal participation surveys typically focus on adolescents and their involvement in delinquency. *Victimization surveys* ask people how much crime they have experienced. The Bureau of Justice Statistics carries out the National Crime Victimization Survey each year. The NCVS indicates that the tendency to report crime to the police varies by the type of crime, with violent victimizations having the highest reporting rate.

Thinking Sociologically

Imagine that you work for the Bureau of Justice Statistics. Congress asks you to predict how many FBI agents will be needed to deal with different types of crime. How would you go about determining this, and what data sources might you use?

 Reality vs. Perception of Crime Rates in the U.S.

Although differences in crime reports are often difficult to reconcile, each measurement instrument provides a different portion of the total picture of crime. By using several data-gathering techniques (triangulation), a more accurate picture of crime begins to emerge. All data-gathering techniques indicate that the rate of violent and nonviolent crime in the United States has dropped since the mid-1990s, so we can be confident that the crime rate has really fallen. In 1990, there were 732 violent crimes per 100,000 residents, but in 2012, that number was 386 (see Figure 6.4).

The violent crime rate decreased further from June 2012 to June 2013 by the following percentage points: murders 6.9%, forcible rapes 10.6%, aggravated assaults 6.6%, and robbery offenses 1.8% (FBI 2014a). Researchers have yet to come to a consensus as to why crime has declined. Some ideas now under review include

- changing demographics—a decline in the number of young people (those most likely to commit crimes);
- rising rates of incarceration (though those rates have declined over the past few years);
- new policing strategies, including computer-assisted planning and closer focus on gun use by youth;
- greater access to abortion after the 1973 *Roe v. Wade* Supreme Court decision, which led to fewer unwanted children (relatively more likely to commit crimes due to their negative treatment); and

- the phasing out of lead in gasoline in the 1970s (lead can cause brain damage related to violent behavior) (Cohn et al. 2013).

Though crime is down, it is still the common subject of news headlines. Crime reporting is relatively inexpensive, as reporters can rely on information about index crimes that officials regularly make public. So, the crimes that grab the attention of average citizens of countries around the world tend to be violent crimes committed by individuals or small groups. The following are some examples of types of micro-level crimes.

Types of Crime

Predatory Crimes. Citizens of the United States tend to be most afraid of violent predatory crimes. Many citizens feel they cannot trust others. Some keep guns to protect themselves from this perceived danger. Some neighborhoods *are* dangerous; however, as noted above, the total violent crime victimization rate has declined over the past several decades. Below, we discuss more crimes committed by individuals—but stay tuned because most criminologists feel there are more serious crimes, to be discussed under meso- and macro-level deviance.

Crimes Without Victims. *Acts committed by or between individual consenting adults* are known as **victimless** or **public order crimes**. These can include prostitution, gambling, drug use, and public drunkenness. While these crimes do not result in specific victims, they are deemed harmful to society (and, thus, criminal)

FIGURE 6.4 U.S. Violent Crime Rate Since 1990 (per 100,000 residents)

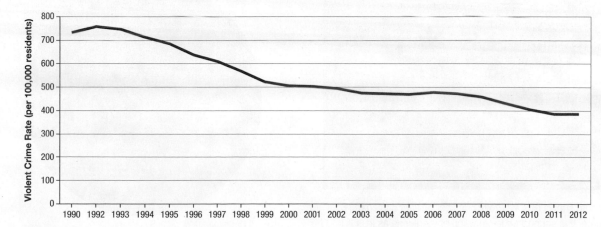

Source: FBI 2014b.

because they violate the dominant values and norms. While illegal, they may be tolerated (the police may look the other way) as long as they do not become highly visible. For example, it would be rare for police in the United States to crack down on a low-stakes monthly poker game friends play behind closed doors.

Victimless crimes involving drugs result in a variety of policies, from execution in Iran and hanging in Malaysia to legalization in Holland. As noted earlier, U.S. drug policies have led to huge numbers of people being imprisoned. Half of all drug arrests in 2010 were related to marijuana usage (American Civil Liberties Union 2013). However, proposals to legalize drugs in the United States have recently gained traction. As we write these words, 23 states and Washington, DC, allow for the medical use of marijuana, and 4 states (Colorado, Washington, Oregon, and Alaska) and Washington, DC, have legalized recreational use of the drug. A 2013 Gallup poll indicated that 58% of Americans favor decriminalization of marijuana (Nagourney and Lyman 2013).

California has the longest experience with legalization of medical marijuana—nearly two decades. Fears among some that legalization would lead to civic disorder, increased lawlessness, and drastic increases in other drug usage have not materialized. Due to careful monitoring of the age of buyers, teen use of marijuana in California has not increased since legalization in 1996 (Nagourney and Lyman 2013). Further, some scholars think more teen use of marijuana would not be a bad trend. When teens switch to marijuana, they tend to reduce alcohol usage, and alcohol is more likely to result in death from overuse or from drunk driving (Anderson and Rees 2013).

This photo shows how what we consider deviant can change over time. It is supporting legalization of marijuana as less dangerous than beer or football.

Hate Crimes

A *hate crime* is a "criminal offense against a person or property motivated in whole or in part by an offender's bias against a race, religion, disability, ethnic origin or sexual orientation" (FBI 2012b). The FBI reported 5,790 hate crimes in 2012, with the breakdown by bias indicated in Figure 6.5. Hate crimes are underreported, with many victims not believing the police can help them. From the data available, though, it is clear that hate crimes based on religion and sexual orientation have increased over the past few years (FBI 2012c; Langton, Planty, and Sandholtz 2013; Potok 2013a).

Those who commit hate crimes feel rage against the victim as a representative of a group they despise; feelings of lifestyle and economic security being threatened are part of the reason for this hatred. In the case of some white supremacy movements, philosophical, political, and even religious principles guide their group beliefs (Blee 2008). As minority groups gain notoriety *or* acceptance in society, they can face more hate crimes. For example, hate crime incidents against Muslim Americans increased after September 11, 2001, and the Boston Marathon bombing in 2013. The numbers of white supremacist groups increased dramatically after Barack Obama, the first U.S. president

FIGURE 6.5 Breakdown of the 5,790 Single-Bias Hate Crime Incidents Reported in 2012

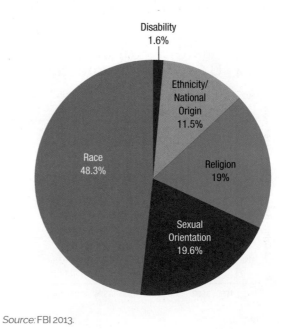

Source: FBI 2013.

These photos reveal how various subcultures can have sharply different views on what they consider deviant. They also help illustrate why hate crimes tend to increase as minority groups gain more power in society and their definitions of reality come to be normalized.

of color, was elected; and antigay hate crimes have become more common with the growing success of the same-sex marriage movement (Peek 2011).

The examples above represent only three of the many types of micro-level crimes, characterized by individual or small-group actions. We now turn to crime in organizations and institutions at the meso level. Organizations usually commit the crimes most harmful to society.

CRIME AND ORGANIZATIONS: MESO-LEVEL ANALYSIS

Crime and organized crime control efforts are part of the social structure of modern societies. First, as societies modernize, there is an almost universal tendency for crime rates to increase dramatically due to the anomie that new migrants and the poor experience in urban areas where old norms are no longer relevant (Merton 1938). Second, as societies become modernized and urban, they become more reliant on meso-level formal or bureaucratic mechanisms of control rather than small community pressures and conformity. They develop a criminal justice system.

Crimes Involving Organizations and Institutions

Jeanne, one of the authors of this book, recently got a call from a fraud office at an online retailer saying that her credit card had been compromised. Someone had ordered online items from Atlanta-based Bloomingdale's, Coach, and DSW (Designer Shoe Warehouse) using her credit card—and it was not Jeanne! How did the retailer catch it? "Unusual behavior on the account." Credit card fraud and identity theft are two types of organized crime prevalent today.

High rates of fraud can also be seen in the medical system. Approximately 20% of every Medicare dollar in 2011 went to fraud (Konrad 2012). For example, in South Florida, criminals open storefronts claiming to sell medical equipment. Often these businesses are located in dying strip malls. Once the criminals have sent in false claims for Medicare payments, sometimes amounting to millions of dollars, they close the storefronts and move on so that they cannot be traced. The federal government has had a small number of investigators in the past—hardly a match for the fast-moving get-rich-quick con artists. However, the government recently added a number of investigators, and fraud prosecutions increased 85% from 2010 to 2011. Savings from fraud will mean money put back into the health care system (Kennedy 2011).

Some crimes are committed by highly organized, hierarchically structured syndicates formed for the purpose of achieving their economic objectives through criminal behavior. On the other hand, legitimate corporations also commit crimes. Their crimes are often very serious, but the public image of such organizations is not criminal, so they are not always suspected or caught. We will look first at organized criminal organizations and then at crimes committed by people within their legitimate occupations and organizations.

▶ Top 5 Most Powerful Criminal Organizations

Organized Crime. **Organized crime** refers to *ongoing criminal enterprises by an organized group whose ultimate purpose is economic gain through illegitimate means* (Siegel 2011). Our image of this type of crime is sometimes glamorized in films such as *No Country for Old Men*, *The Godfather*, *Goodfellas*, and *Gangs of New York*. On television, *The Sopranos* is the ultimate media "mob" depiction. Despite the alluring view of these idealized stories, organized crime is a serious problem in many countries. It is essentially a counterculture with a hierarchical structure, from the boss down to the underlings. The organization relies on power, control, fear, violence, and corruption. This type of deviance is a particular problem when societies experience rapid change and anomie, and where social controls break down.

Marginalized ethnic groups that face discrimination may become involved in a quest to get ahead through organized crime. Early in U.S. history, Italians were especially prominent in organized crime, but today, many groups are involved. Organized crime around the world has gained strong footholds in countries in transition (European Commission 2014). For example, in Russia, the transition from a socialist economy to a market economy has provided many opportunities for criminal activity. The *Mafiya* is estimated to include over 100,000 people, and some estimate that the members control 70% to 80% of all private business in Russia and 40% of Russia's wealth (Lindberg and Markovic n.d.; Schmalleger 2012).

Organized crime usually takes one of three forms: (1) the sale of illegal goods and services, including gambling, loan sharking, trafficking in drugs and people, selling stolen goods, and prostitution; (2) infiltrating legitimate businesses and unions through threat and intimidation and using bankruptcy and fraud to exploit and devastate a legitimate company; and (3) racketeering—the extortion of funds in exchange for protection (i.e., not being hurt). Activities such as a casino or trash collection service often appear to be legitimate endeavors on the surface but may be cover operations for highly organized illegal crime rings.

Although the exact cost of organized crime in the United States is impossible to determine, estimates of the annual gross income of organized crime activity range from $50 billion to $90 billion per year (CNBC 2010; Siegel 2011). Internationally, criminal proceeds for all transnational organized crime are estimated at $870 billion a year (United Nations Office on Drugs and

Crime 2014b); recorded criminal activities $2.1 trillion (Bjelopera and Finklea 2012; Fedotov 2012).

Transnational organized crime takes place across national boundaries, using sophisticated electronic communications and transportation technologies. The major crime clans in the world include (a) Hong Kong–based organized crime organizations, (b) South American cocaine cartels, (c) Italian mafia, (d) Japanese *yakuza*, (e) Russian *Mafiya*, and (f) West African crime groups. Each operates across borders. Organized crime is responsible for thousands of deaths every year through drug trafficking and murders, and contributes to the climate of violence in many cities (Siegel 2011).

The value of the global illicit drug market is estimated at more than $320 billion at the retail level (based on retail prices). Add other types of crimes (transporting migrants, selling human organs, trafficking in women and children for the sex industry, and sales of weapons and nuclear material), and the estimates of profits for international crime cartels are as high as $1.5 trillion a year ("Transnational Crime in the Developing World" 2011).

Occupational Crime. Bernard (Bernie) Madoff, a well-respected investor and former chair of the NASDAQ stock exchange, developed a Ponzi scheme that was probably the largest investment fraud Wall Street has ever seen. The scheme defrauded thousands of investors, public pension funds, charitable foundations, and universities of billions of dollars, with more than $65 billion missing from investor accounts when the scam became public in 2008. Named after Charles Ponzi, the first to be caught (in 1919), Ponzi schemes involve promises of large returns on investments, paying old investors with money from new investors. Money is simply shifted among investors to make it appear as though the investments earn money ("The Madoff Case" 2009). Meanwhile, those running the scam pocket enormous sums of the money invested.

Ponzi schemes are one example of *white-collar or occupational crime*, a violation of the law committed by an individual or a group in the course of a legitimate, respected occupation or financial activity (Coleman 2006; Hagan 2011). Occupational crime can be committed by individuals from virtually any social class, and it can occur at any organizational level. However, most often this refers to white-collar crimes.

These crimes receive less attention than violent crimes because they are less visible, do not always cause obvious physical injury to identifiable people, and are frequently committed by people in positions of substantial authority and prestige. Reports of violent crimes that appear on the television news each night attract more attention. Yet occupational crime is far more costly in money, health, and lives. Victims of financial scams who have lost their life savings or workers who have lost their good health because of unsafe and illegal work conditions are well aware of this.

Sociologists divide occupational crimes into four major categories: (1) against the company, (2) against employees, (3) against customers, and (4) against the general public or other organizations (Hagan 2011).

Crimes against the company include pilfering (using company resources such as the photocopy machine for personal business) and employee theft (taking company supplies for your own use, stealing from the till, and embezzlement). Those who commit occupational crimes say they do so for several reasons. First, they feel little or no loyalty to the organization, especially if it is large and impersonal. It is like stealing from nobody, they say. Second, workers feel exploited and resentful toward the company. Stealing is getting back at the company. Third, the theft is seen as a "fringe benefit" or "informal compensation" that they deserve. Such workers may spend time on a side business while at work or take paper and ink cartridges for their printer at home. Fourth, workers may steal because of the challenge. It makes the job more interesting if they can get away with it. It is important to note that these people do not see themselves as criminals, especially compared with "street" criminals (Altheide et al. 1978).

The other three types of corporate crime benefit the company at the expense of employees or members of the larger society. *Crimes against employees* refer to corporate neglect of worker safety. In 1970, the U.S. government established the Occupational Safety and Health Administration (OSHA) to help enforce regulations to protect workers, but there are still many problems. Government agencies estimate that the death rate each year from job-related illness and injuries is *five times* the number of deaths from street crimes. For example, one out of every five cancer cases has been traced to pollutants in workplaces, and many of these cases were preventable (Bureau of Labor Statistics 2014c; Simon 2006). *Wage theft*, underpaying or not paying workers, is another

widespread corporate crime that harms millions of workers. Many employers do not pay workers their due wages by requiring them to work "off the clock," not paying them minimum wage, stealing their tips, not paying them overtime, refusing to give them their last check, or simply not paying them at all. A 2009 study revealed that almost half (43.6%) of low-wage, urban U.S. workers surveyed had experienced wage theft during the previous year (Bernhardt et al. 2009).

Neglect of worker safety is a particularly serious problem in many developing or peripheral countries trying to attract multinational corporations with low taxes, cheap labor, and few regulations. The decisions of many corporations and factory owners illustrate *rational choice theory*. Too often they decide the benefits (profit) that come from exploiting labor outweigh the costs (harm to workers). The collapse of a shoddily constructed factory building in Bangladesh that killed over 1,127 workers in 2013 is a powerful example of what can result from this type of thinking.

As *strain theorists* point out, almost all corporations have the goal of making the greatest short-term profit possible, and one (deviant) method to do that is to cut expenses at the expense of worker safety. Government regulatory agencies responsible for reducing environmental hazards and workplace dangers do not have sufficient staff to police companies for adherence to laws. Internationally, there is little oversight. Multinational corporations generally look for the cheapest labor costs and fewest environmental regulations, and governments of poor countries try to

Employees in the Rana Plaza building in Bangladesh made clothing for many multinational apparel companies who failed, along with the building owner, to ensure that they had a safe place to work. This is an example of corporate crime against employees.

attract foreign corporations to keep the poor populace employed regardless of the personal illnesses and environmental or workplace consequences.

Since the building collapse in Bangladesh, momentum is (for the moment, at least) on the side of workers' rights organizations. After the government had done nothing following several factory fires that killed hundreds of workers, the building collapse was the last straw for many workers in Bangladesh and for millions of people seeing the carnage in the media. Protesters took to the streets in Bangladesh and across the world. This organized outrage has led to promises from the Bangladesh government to raise the minimum wage for workers and ease anti-union laws. Many multinational corporations, fearing further negative exposure, have pledged to ensure better working conditions for Bangladeshi workers who make their products.

Consumers, as well as workers, can be victims of corporate crime. *Crimes against customers* involve acts victimizing patrons, such as selling dangerous foods or unsafe products, consumer fraud, deceptive advertising, and price-fixing (i.e., setting prices in collusion with another producer). The purpose of advertising is to convince customers to buy the product—appealing to their vanity, sexual interests, or desire to keep up with their neighbors. Sometimes these techniques cross the line between honesty and deception, and customers purchase defective and even dangerous products—all with the full knowledge of company officials.

Crimes against the public include acts by companies that negatively affect large groups of people. One example is hospitals or medical offices that overbill Medicare (discussed above), or insurance companies pressuring hospitals to discharge patients too early to save on costs. Surreptitiously dumping pollutants into landfills, streams, or the air is another crime against the public. Proper disposal of contaminants can be costly and time-consuming for a company, but shortcuts can cause long-term effects for the public (Coleman 2006). Pollutants from industrial wastes have caused high rates of miscarriages, birth defects, and diseases among residents.

These examples help illustrate that white-collar crime committed by company executives is by far our most serious crime problem. The economic cost of white-collar crime is vastly greater than the economic cost of street crime. White-collar criminals kill considerably more people than all violent street criminals put together (Coleman 2006).

Thinking Sociologically

Why are meso-level crimes (occupational/white-collar crimes) more dangerous and more costly to the public than micro-level crimes? Why do they get so much less attention?

NATIONAL AND GLOBAL CRIME: MACRO-LEVEL ANALYSIS

As we have seen, national boundaries continue to blur as people migrate around the globe and many corporations move headquarters across national lines in search of lower costs and higher profits. Crime syndicates, too, are multinational, as they move money, goods, and people surreptitiously across borders. Likewise, terrorist organizations have no boundaries. We now turn to the macro-level crime of terrorism.

Terrorism is *the planned use of random unlawful (or illegal) violence or the threat of violence against civilians to create (or raise) fear and intimidate citizens in order to advance the terrorist group's political or ideological goals* (U.S. Department of Defense 2011). Terrorist groups can be anarchist, state sponsored, right wing or left wing, nationalist, or religious (Rice 2013; Schmalleger 2006). Table 6.1 shows the major types of terrorist groups.

Governments can commit *state-organized crime.* Often overlooked by the public and by social scientists,

TABLE 6.1   Types of Terrorist Groups

Anarchist	Some contemporary antiglobalization groups
State sponsored	Hezbollah (Iran), Abu Nidal Organization (Syria)
Right wing	Neo-Nazis, skinheads, White supremacists; paramilitary groups in Colombia
Left wing	Revolutionary Armed Forces of Colombia (FARC); Revolutionary People's Liberation Party–Front (Turkey)
Nationalist	Irish Republican Army, Basque Fatherland and Liberty
Religious	Al-Qaeda, Hamas, ISIS (Iraq and Syria), Aum Shinrikyo (Japan)

Sources: Rice (2013); Schmalleger (2006).

this form of crime includes acts defined by law as criminal but committed by state or government officials. For example, a government might be complicit in smuggling, assassination, or torture, which is then justified in terms of "national defense." Government offices may also violate laws that restrict or limit government activities such as eavesdropping. In some countries, political prisoners, such as the Guantánamo Bay detainees held in Cuba by the United States, are imprisoned for long periods without charges, without access to lawyers, and without trials, and some have been tortured, violating both national and international laws (Center for Constitutional Rights 2013). The U.S. Supreme Court has ruled (2006 and 2008) that the U.S. administration violated the rights of these people (Global Security 2009). The Obama administration planned to shut down the Guantánamo Bay facility in 2010, but that closure has not yet occurred, and as we write these words, 122 detainees remain at "Gitmo" (Haberkorn 2014; Human Rights First 2015). Although countries may violate their own laws, it is difficult to prosecute when the guilty party is the government.

Bribery and corruption are the way of life in many governments, businesses, and police forces. The percentage of citizens who said that they had paid a bribe to obtain services is as high as 79% in Nigeria, 72% in Cambodia, and 71% in Albania. The institutions perceived

Detainees sit in a holding area at the naval base in Guantánamo Bay, Cuba, in the "temporary" detention center. It violates U.S. law, but the facility continues to hold prisoners and to operate.

to be most affected by corruption globally include political parties, the police, the judiciary, legislatures, and business (Transparency International 2012). Figure 6.6 shows an index of the perception of corruption (from 1 to 10) in various countries around the world.

 Thinking Sociologically

Sometimes government officials and even heads of state are the perpetrators of crimes. When, if ever, is it justified for a government official to violate the law of the nation?

FIGURE 6.6   Corruption Percentage Index 2013

Source: Data taken from Transparency International Corruption Perceptions Index 2013. Copyright © Transparency International. All Rights Reserved. For more information, visit http://www.transparency.org. Transparency International's Corruption Perceptions Index measures the perceived level of public sector corruption in countries and territories around the world.

The forms of global corruption are too extensive to catalog here, so we will settle for an illustration of one of the newest manifestations of global crime against people and property: cybercrime. Internet deviance or cyberspace crime is growing faster than a cybergeek can move a mouse. This new world of crime ranges from online identity theft and gambling to cybersex and pornography, to hate sites and stalking, to hacking into government and military files, to terrorist recruiting sites.

Global law enforcement gridlock due to national and international jurisdictional confusion impedes efforts to prevent such crime. For example, as many as five different U.S. agencies can be involved in preventing financial fraud on the Internet, not to mention the state and local agencies that might play a role. If the fraud involves international cybercrime, the customs services and other branches of government also may enter the investigation. The resulting confusion and lack of clear authority can play into the hands of lawbreakers. For example, most big corporations have been the victim of hacking and cybertheft from China and other nations. The federal government, however, does not yet have an effective way to make companies do all they can to safeguard their customers' information or to coordinate effective defenses against such illegal cyber intrusions from other nations ("Cybercrime: Smoking Gun" 2013; Perlroth and Sanger 2013).

Cross-National Comparison of Crimes

The vending machine was on the corner near the Ballantines' house in Japan. The usual cola, candy, and sundries were displayed, along with cigarettes, beer, whiskey, sake, and pornographic magazines. Out of curiosity, Jeanne and her family watched to see who purchased what from the machines, and not once did they see teenagers sneaking the beer, cigarettes, or porn. It turns out that the Ballantines were not the only ones watching! The neighbors also kept an eye on who did what. Because of the stigma attached to deviant behavior in Japan, teens tend to avoid violating norms, and vigilant neighbors help keep the overall amount of deviance low. The many eyes in the neighborhood remind people that deviant behavior is unacceptable and provides informal social control over those who might be tempted to commit crimes.

Japan and the United States are both modern, urban, industrial countries, but their crime rates and the way they deal with deviant behavior and crimes differ. The overall crime rate in the United States is 3 times that of Japan, and the U.S. murder rate is 10 *times* higher. Japan has 0.5 murders for every 100,000 people, whereas the United States has 5.0 per 100,000 residents (Cowen and Williams 2012; Spacey 2012).

How can these extreme differences in crime rates be explained? Researchers look at cultural differences: Japan's low violent crime rate is due in part to Japan's culturally homogeneous society and loyalty to a historic tradition of cooperation that provides a sense of moral order, a network of group relations, strong commitment to social norms, and respect for law and order. The example of vending machines in Japan illustrates this idea. In addition, guns are outlawed and much harder to come by in Japan.

Japan does not attain its lower crime rate through heavy investment in its criminal justice system. In fact, the Japanese government actually spends far less of its gross national product on the police, courts, and prisons than does the United States. For many crimes in Japan, the offender may simply be asked to write a letter of apology. This is frequently a sufficient sanction to deter the person from further violation of the law. The humiliation of writing an apology and the fear of shame and embarrassing one's family are strong enough to curb deviant behavior (Lazare 2004). Figure 6.7 provides a picture of the homicide numbers in various parts of the world.

FIGURE 6.7 Global Homicide Numbers by Country or Territory

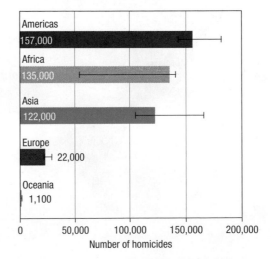

Source: United Nations Office on Drugs and Crime 2013.

Global Crimes

Increasingly, crimes are global in nature. Some scholars use the *world systems theory* to understand global crime, arguing that the cause of global crime lies in the global economy, the inequalities between countries, and the competition between countries for resources and wealth. As a result of the capitalist mode of production, an unequal relationship has arisen between core nations (the developed, wealthy nations in the Global North) and peripheral nations (the Global South). Core nations often take unfair advantage of peripheral nations. Peripheral nations, in turn, must find ways to survive in this global system, and they sometimes turn to illegal methods—such as violating global environmental standards—to achieve their goals (Chase-Dunn and Anderson 2006). Some nations, though not wealthy, have many natural resources and are semiperipheral nations. Benefiting from extensive trade, they are less vulnerable than the poorest nations. Figure 6.8 helps you see where some of these core, peripheral, and semiperipheral nations are located.

As you look at this figure, note that the developed or affluent countries are almost all located in the Northern Hemisphere. Although some poor

The U.S. "War on Drugs" has meant that the United States has pressured Mexico and other Global South nations to crack down on drug producers and traffickers. This has made drugs more scarce and mob-run drug trafficking a major source of crime and violence, negatively impacting innocent people in many nations.

countries are north of the equator, the pattern is obvious. To avoid some misleading implications of the words *developed* and *developing*, many scholars now prefer the term *Global South* to refer to less affluent nations. If you hear the phrase *Global South*, this figure should help you see why it refers to developing or poor countries.

FIGURE 6.8 Core, Semiperipheral, and Peripheral Countries of the World

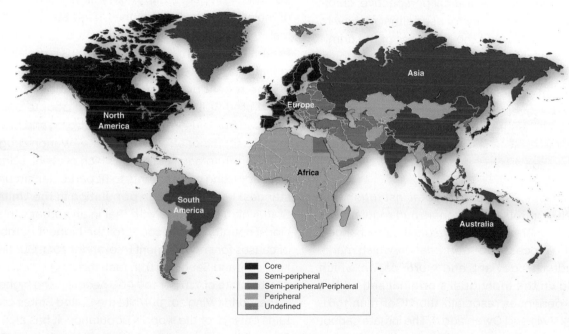

Source: Figure by Anna Versluis.

CONTROLLING CRIME: SOCIAL POLICY CONSIDERATIONS

What is the best way to control crime? While all modern societies have criminal justice systems, their crime prevention strategies vary. We now look at the mechanisms used by societies to curb deviant behavior and punish deviants.

Dealing With Crime: The Criminal Justice Process

Structural-functionalists see the justice system as a crucial means of ensuring order and social control in society. Conflict theorists, on the other hand, argue that the criminal justice system works in the interest of those in power, at the expense of the other members of society. It is in the interests of those in power to maintain the image that crime is primarily the work of outsiders and the poor. This deflects citizen discontent and hostility from the powerful, and helps them retain their positions of power (Reiman and Leighton 2010a, 2010b). Conflict theorists point out that there will always be crime in society because the powerful will make sure that some things and some people are labeled deviant.

Depending on whether one uses a structural-functional or conflict theoretical perspective, criminal justice policy generally focuses either on how to deter deviant acts or on the injustices of the criminal justice system. In the United States today, prisons provide one of the primary means of controlling individual criminal behavior. Think about which theoretical perspective, structural functionalism or conflict theory, you would use to better understand the function of prisons in U.S. society as you read the following section.

Prisons. Prisons are a form of *total institution* that completely controls the prisoners and regulates all their activities. Inmates' lives are drastically changed through the processes of *degradation*, which marks the individual as deviant, and *mortification*, which breaks down the individual's original self as the inmate experiences resocialization (Goffman 1961; Irwin 1985; Irwin and Owen 2007). The inmate cannot have any personal property. Guards allow prisoners only limited communication and often verbally abuse inmates. Uniforms and standard buzz cuts (for men) are required, and inmates have strictly controlled schedules.

In a famous study that simulated a prison situation, researchers illustrated the social organization that develops and the roles that individuals play within the prison system. College students were assigned roles as prisoners or prison guards. Within a short time, the individuals in the study were acting out their roles, and behaving in ways very different from their normal behavior, outside of the prison situation. The students playing the role of "guard" became cruel and sadistic, causing the researcher, Philip Zimbardo, to end the experiment early. Participants had taken their roles so seriously that the abuse was beginning to have alarming consequences (Zimbardo et al. 1973). The recent abuse of prisoners in Iraq and at Guantánamo Bay parallels the findings from Zimbardo's earlier study of the roles that develop in these social situations (Zimbardo 2004).

Conflict theorists believe that social class and demographic makeup of prisons reveal that prisons are mostly about controlling or "managing" minorities and poor people, not about public safety. African American males, for example, are more than 5 times more likely to be incarcerated than white men, and African American women are 2.5 times more likely than white women to be imprisoned (Fathi 2009; Sentencing Project 2014). While whites made up 63% of the overall population of the United States in 2011, just 35% of U.S. prisoners were white (Sentencing Project 2014). The makeup of U.S. prisons is presented in Table 6.2.

The recent decrease in incarceration rates in the United States stems from more people being released from prison due to overcrowding and fewer lockups for minor offenses. Still, the "War on Drugs" and "Zero Tolerance Policies" (which prevent judges from adjusting punishments to fit particular circumstances) keep the prison population in the United States high compared with that in any other Global North country, and account for the highest number of causes for imprisonment (Alexander 2011; Guerino, Harrison, and Sabol 2011). In fact, the 2013 U.S. incarceration rate of 716 per 100,000 people is the highest in the world (Wing 2013). While the United States contains only 5% of the world's population, it has 25% of the world's prisoners (Kirchhoff 2010). Nearly half (48%)

Gangs in Control of American Prisons

TABLE 6.2   Characteristics of People in Prison

	Makeup of U.S. Prison Population	Makeup of U.S. Population*	Ratio of the Population 30–34 Years Old in Prison	Chance of Spending Time in Prison During Lifetime
Black	38%	12.6%	1:13	32%
Hispanic	21%	16.3%	1:36	17%
White	35%	63.7%	1:90	6%

Source: Sentencing Project 2014.

of prisoners in federal prisons were sentenced for drug offenses (Carson and Sabol 2012). Table 6.3 compares incarceration rates among countries with the highest percentages of people in prison and among other industrialized nations.

Thinking Sociologically

Why do you think the United States has 5% of the world's population but 25% of the world's prisoners? Has this impacted your life? How and why? How do you think your age, gender, social class, and race influenced your answer?

The Purposes of Prisons. What purpose do you believe prisons serve? From the structural-functional perspective, prisons serve several purposes for society: (1) fulfilling the desire for revenge or retribution, (2) removing dangerous people from society, (3) deterring would-be deviants, and (4) rehabilitating deviants through counseling, education, and work training programs inside prisons (Johnson 2002). However, in prison, inmates are exposed to more criminal and antisocial behavior, so rehabilitation and deterrence goals are often undermined by the nature of prisons. According to a recent Bureau of Justice Statistics report, roughly 5% of prison inmates are sexually assaulted by other prisoners or prison guards, and 12% of youth in juvenile detention facilities are victims, often in gang rapes ("New Federal Report" 2010). This ongoing problem of assault, rape, and threat of violence in prison so brutalizes inmates that it becomes difficult for them to reenter society as well-adjusted citizens ready to conform to societal norms (Fathi 2009; Hensley, Koscheski, and Tewksbury 2005; Liptak 2008).

Prisons and Profits. There is money to be made by locking up prisoners. All prisons can be a source of jobs for the communities in which they are located. Traditionally run by local, state, or federal governments, for-profit companies operate increasing numbers of prisons. While privatization of prisons started in the 1980s, it has taken off in the last two decades. The number of people in private prisons has grown by 1,664% in the past 20 years, and today approximately 130,000 people are in for-profit institutions (Wade 2013a). Seven states put more than 1 of every 4 of their prisoners in private prisons (Carson and Sabol 2012; Lee 2012).

TABLE 6.3   World Comparative Rates of Incarceration (per 100,000 People), 2013

Top 10 Countries (a)		Other Industrialized Countries (b)	
United States	716	England and Wales	148
St. Kitts and Nevis	649	Australia	133
Seychelles	490	Canada	118
Virgin Islands	539	France	103
Rwanda	527	Italy	100
Cuba	510	Switzerland	87
Russia	490	Netherlands	82
Anguilla	487	Germany	78
Georgia	473	Sweden	60

Source: (a) Wing 2013; (b) International Center for Prison Studies 2014.

Prison privatization advocates claim that private businesses driven by a profit motive and competition will operate prisons more efficiently. Private prisons can save on labor costs by not paying the high benefits that states must pay to employees. Those against privatization argue that incarcerating (imprisoning) people for profit is a bad idea, morally and financially. They point out that the cost per prison often rises after the initial contract with the state (Smith 2012). Some states must incarcerate a certain number of people due to contracts with private prisons, thereby manipulating the criminal justice system (Kirkham 2012). When profit motive is the bottom line, these critics argue, quality of food, training of guards, health care, educational opportunities, and other treatment of inmates can deteriorate.

Profits are also found through inmate labor. As of 2013, 37 states had legalized the contracting of prison labor to private corporations. While prisoners in some state prisons receive minimum wage, many receive less. Some make as little as 17 cents an hour. These low wages lead to high profit margins for those invested in these companies, and business for such contracts is booming (Pelaez 2013).

As one step in an effort to revamp the U.S. criminal justice system, the Obama administration has proposed releasing low-level, nonviolent drug offenders who have not committed serious crimes. Thousands of federal offenders could be eligible for early release, easing overcrowding in the prison population (Johnson 2014). The federal government's hope is that state criminal justice systems will follow the federal lead.

The Death Penalty. Crimes of murder, assault, robbery, and rape usually receive severe penalties because citizens consider them the most dangerous crimes. The most controversial (and irreversible) method of control is for the state to put the deviant to death. The most common argument for using the death penalty, more formally known as capital punishment, is to deter people from crime. The idea is that not only will the person who has committed the crime be punished, but also others will be deterred from committing such a crime because they know that the death penalty is a possibility for them too.

However, the death penalty does not deter murder (Alarcon and Mitchell 2011; Radelet and Lacock 2009). In addition, it costs far more to use the death penalty than prison as a punishment. For example, a study in California showed that over $4 billion has been spent on 13 executions there since 1978, a cost of $308 million per execution. Because of the costs of a capital trial, various appeals processes (many of which are mandated by law to avoid mistakes), and special death row incarceration requirements, the cost is much greater than for life imprisonment (Alarcon and Mitchell 2011).

Moreover, more murders occur in states with the death penalty than in those without it. The average murder rate in death penalty states was 4.7 per 100,000 persons, while the average murder rate in states without the death penalty was 3.7 (Death Penalty Information Center 2013). Despite this, 32 states still allow the death penalty (Death Penalty Information Center 2014).

Few other Global North countries use the death penalty, and in 2007 the United Nations passed a resolution calling on all nations to abolish it as "cruel and unusual punishment" (Amnesty International 2012; UN News Center 2010). The United States is one of the few countries that utilizes the death penalty out of 198 where records are available. A total of 22 countries carried out executions in 2013, with Iran and Iraq having high numbers of executions, China's true numbers unknown but suspected to be in the thousands every year, Saudi Arabia with 79, and the United States with 39 (Amnesty International 2014). Only China and Yemen officially recorded more executions in 2010 than the United States (World Coalition 2012).

Thinking Sociologically

How can you explain the higher murder rates in U.S. states that have the death penalty? Why do you think the U.S. death penalty rate is high compared to the rate in most other countries in the world?

Race and class status relate to who receives the death penalty. In most U.S. states with capital punishment, a disproportionate number of minority and lower-class individuals are put to death. Of those executed since 1976, 56% have been white and 34% black. Yet the percentage of blacks in the total population is less than 13%. In 2013, Maryland became the 18th state to abolish the death penalty. In describing why, the governor of the state said, "Maryland has effectively eliminated a policy that is proven not to work. Evidence shows that the death penalty is not a deterrent, it cannot be administered without racial bias, and it costs three times as much as life in prison without parole" (Sutton 2013).

These problems with the death penalty have led to a search for alternative means to deter crime and spurred policy analysts to rethink assumptions about what factors are effective in controlling human behavior.

Recidivism rates—*the likelihood that someone who is arrested, convicted, and imprisoned will later be a repeat offender*—are very high. More than half of all men who do time in prison will be confined again for a crime (Quinney 2002; Siegel 2011).

Efforts to reduce recidivism include high-quality schools, preventing young people from entering the criminal justice system in the first place, and methods of treatment other than brutalizing incarceration for those who do find themselves in trouble with the law.

It is difficult to determine how best to deter crime. Not many people think that the apology technique used in Japan would work as a deterrent to crimes in other countries. On the other hand, there is a wide range of options available for dealing with crime other than harsh (and expensive) punishments. Seeing how other countries control crime can help us take a new look at our assumptions and help us come up with creative new solutions that do work. For example, is the War on Drugs having more of a positive or negative impact on crime? What can we learn from how other nations deal with drugs? How might the legalization of marijuana in some U.S. states affect incarceration rates?

Sociologists use comparative studies and evaluation of current policies to help determine the best strategies for crime and recidivism deterrence. For example, evidence shows that prison education, substance abuse, and job training programs can be used to reduce criminal justice expenses by allowing some prisoners to "earn" reduced sentences. These programs also lead to lower recidivism rates (Lawrence 2009).

Thinking Sociologically

How has what you read in this chapter affected your ideas about deviance, crime, and the criminal justice system?

One of the dominant characteristics of modern society is social inequality, and as we have seen, inequality is often an issue in criminal activity. Indeed, many of our social problems are rooted in issues of inequality. Extreme inequality may even be a threat to the deeper values of a society, especially one that stresses individualism and achievement. In the following three chapters, we look at three types of inequality: socioeconomic, ethnic or racial, and gender-based inequity.

WHAT HAVE WE LEARNED?

Deviance is socially constructed and varies across time and societies. What is considered deviant now may not be considered deviant in another place or time. All societies must fashion responses to deviant behaviors, which can threaten their stability and safety. The criminal justice system tends to be a conservative force in society because of its focus on ensuring social conformity.

To make our society run more smoothly, we must understand why deviance and crime happen. Good policy must be based on accurate information and careful analysis of the information. We must also understand that deviance and conformity operate at various levels in the social world: micro, meso, and macro. In addition, it is important to understand that there may be positive aspects of deviance for any society, from uniting society against deviants to providing creative new ways to solve problems.

KEY POINTS

- Deviance—the violation of social norms, including those that are formal laws—has both positive and negative consequences for individuals and for society.

- We can use many different sociological theories to explain deviance—rational choice (including social control); symbolic interaction's anomie and labeling theories at the micro level; structural-functional theory's differential association and strain theory; and conflict and feminist theory at the meso and macro levels.

- Many of the formal organizations concerned with crime (such as the FBI and the media) focus on crimes involving individuals—predatory crimes, crimes without victims, and hate crimes—but the focus on these crimes may blind us to occupational crimes that actually are more harmful and more costly to society.

- At the meso level, organized and occupational crimes may cost billions of dollars and pose a great risk to thousands of lives. Occupational crime may be against the company, employees, customers, or the public.

- At the macro level, national governments sometimes commit state-organized crimes, sometimes in violation of their own laws or in violation of international laws. These crimes may be directed against their own citizens (usually the minorities) or people from other countries.

- Also at the macro level, some crimes are facilitated by global networks and by global inequities of power and wealth.

- Controlling crime has generated many policy debates, from the use of prisons to the death penalty and even to alternative approaches to the control of deviance.

DISCUSSION QUESTIONS

1. List three acts that were once considered deviant but are now considered acceptable or even courageous. Have you ever committed a deviant act because you believed it was the moral thing to do? If yes, please explain why. If not, in what sort of situation might you consider carrying out a deviant act?

2. Have you ever been labeled deviant? Why or why not? How does your social class, level of education, gender, race or ethnicity, and nation of origin impact the chances you will be considered deviant in your country?

3. Which of the following theories of deviance described in the chapter—rational choice, differential association, labeling theory, anomie and social disorganization, strain theory, and conflict theory—best explains the recent increase in cheating among college students? Why?

4. Why is occupational crime not given as much attention as violent crime? What are some examples of occupational crimes that hurt millions of Americans every day? Have you ever been the victim of one of these crimes? What would you suggest policymakers do to curb these crimes?

5. How do conflict theorists explain the makeup of prisoners in the U.S. prison system? Do you agree with their explanation? Why or why not?

6. How can social capital help keep people out of prison and help former prisoners avoid returning to prison? How will your social capital help you conform (or not) to the norms of society?

CONTRIBUTING TO OUR SOCIAL WORLD: What Can We Do?

At the Local Level

- *LGBTQ groups* support lesbian, gay, bisexual, transgender, and/or queer students. The Consortium of Higher Education LGBT Resource Professionals, a national organization of college and university groups, maintains a website at www.lgbtcampus.org. Regardless of your own sexual identity/orientation, consider contacting your campus LGBT group, attending meetings, and participating in its support and public education activities.

- *Boys and Girls Clubs* provide local programs and services to promote healthy development by instilling a sense of competence, usefulness, belonging, and influence in young people. Organizations for youth like Boys and Girls Clubs need interns and volunteers to provide role models for youth. Consider volunteering to help children with homework or activities. You can find a club near you by going to www.bgca.org/whoweare/Pages/FindaClub.aspx.

At the Organizational or Institutional Level

- The extensive and rapidly growing *criminal justice system* in the United States focuses on crime prevention, law enforcement, corrections, and rehabilitation. Identify the aspect of the system that interests you most and, using faculty and community contacts, select an appropriate organization for volunteer work, an internship, or a job.

- *Criminal courts* play a central role in the administration of criminal justice, and trials are often open to the public. Attending a trial and/or contacting a judge or magistrate could provide a good introduction to the court system and some of the people who work within it.

- *Crime prevention programs* are designed to reduce crime. You can find information about such programs at the National Crime Prevention Council (www.ncpc.org/programs). In order to obtain a better understanding of what types of crime prevention programs are most effective, go to the Center for the Study and Prevention of Violence's (CSPV's) Blueprints site to find information about such programs (www.colorado.edu/cspv/blueprints).

At the National and Global Levels

- *The Polaris Project* works to reduce global trafficking in women and children (www.polarisproject.org). Volunteers participate in letter-writing campaigns, support anti-trafficking legislation, and conduct research on the problem.

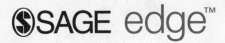

Sharpen your skills with SAGE edge at **edge.sagepub.com/ballantinecondensed4e**

SAGE edge for Students provides a personalized approach to help you accomplish your coursework goals in an easy-to-use learning environment.

PART III

Inequality

Why are you rich, while others in your sociology class or community are poor—or vice versa? Why do some people rise to the top of society with wealth, power, and prestige at their fingertips, and others languish near the bottom? Does ethnicity, race, or gender affect your position in society? What are your chances of moving out of your current social position? These are the underlying questions in the following three chapters. They focus on stratification, how individuals and groups are layered or ranked in society according to how many valued resources they possess (e.g., wealth, power, and prestige) or to which they have access. **Inequality** results from the *process of stratification through which some people "make it" and others do not.* At the very bottom of the human hierarchy are those starving and diseased world citizens who have no hope of survival for either themselves or their families. This compares with corporate executives and some world politicians or royalty who have billions of dollars at their disposal. The implications of social stratification extend from the individual all the way to global social networks.

Sometimes the basis for social stratification and inequality is one's socioeconomic status, but other characteristics such as race, ethnicity, gender, sexual orientation, nationality, religion, or age can also help determine where you fall in the social stratification system. These differences often result in strong feelings like "us" versus "them" thinking.

In this section, we focus on issues of social inequality related to social class, race, ethnicity, and gender. Chapter 7 focuses on local and global socioeconomic stratification resulting in inequality; subsequent chapters examine ethnic and gender stratification.

©REUTERS/ Romeo Ranoco

Stratification

Rich and Famous— or Rags and Famine?

Will you live under the bridge or above it—rags or riches? While hard work can often make a difference, your future success also depends on your society's system of stratification and amount of inequality.

MICRO

● ME (AND MY RAGS OR RICHES)

● LOCAL ORGANIZATIONS
AND COMMUNITY
How I am regarded by my peers.

MESO

● NATIONAL ORGANIZATIONS,
INSTITUTIONS, AND ETHNIC
SUBCULTURES
Institutions support the privileged; ethnic
subcultures are often disadvantaged.

MACRO

● SOCIETY
The privileged control resources,
health care, economic markets, and
tax rates.

● GLOBAL COMMUNITY
Rich countries have more access to
resources than poor ones.

LEARNING OBJECTIVES

7.1 Explain how the way in which
people are ranked within a
stratification system depends on
events in the society's history,
its geographic location, its level
of development in the world,
and its political philosophy.

7.2 Compare key ideas in the symbolic
interactionist, rational choice,
structural functional, and conflict
perspectives on stratification.

7.3 Describe how achieved and ascribed
characteristics impact individuals'
life chances in the United States.

7.4 Explain how family background,
socialization, marriage, and
education can impact social mobility.

7.5 Compare the pluralist and power
elite perspectives on stratification
in the United States today.

7.6 Illustrate how sociology can
help us both understand and
address inequality in society.

THINK ABOUT IT

Micro: Local Community	Why are some people in your community wealthier than others?
Meso: National Institutions; Complex Organizations; Ethnic Groups	How do institutions—such as the family, education, religion, health, politics, and the economy—help keep people in the class they were born into?
Macro: National and Global Systems	Why are some nations affluent and others impoverished? How does the fact that we live in a global society affect you and your social position?

Pomp and circumstance surrounded the April 29, 2011, royal wedding of William, the Prince of Wales (heir to the British throne) and Catherine (Kate) Middleton. All eyes in Britain and many eyes around the world were glued to their TVs and computer monitors. Thousands waited for hours to see the happy couple in person, as they lined the royal route to the palace. The wedding for this young couple included flower arrangements for $800,000, a wedding dress that cost about $400,000, and a cake for just under $80,000. The bill for the entire wedding (security included) came in at $70 million (Mawani 2011).

Members of royal families such as Prince William and Prince Harry of Britain grow up in a privileged world, with wealth, prestige, and access to power. Their lifestyles include formal receptions, horse races, polo games, royal hunts, state visits, and other social and state functions. The family has several elegant residences at its disposal. However, like most royalty, William, Harry, and now Kate Middleton also live within the confines of their elite status, with its strict expectations and limitations. They cannot show up for a beer at the local pub or associate freely with commoners. Their family problems or casual antics are subject matter for front pages of tabloids, as seen in the behavior of Prince Harry during a trip to Las Vegas that thrilled the paparazzi and dismayed the royal household. Thanks to a cell phone camera, what he did in Vegas did not stay in Vegas. While there is no official royalty in the United States, wealthy entrepreneurs, stockbrokers and bankers, and entertainment and sports figures hold positions that allow for a life of comfort similar to that of royalty.

On the other hand, rags and famine pervade the planet. Hidden from the public eye in Britain and the United States are people with no known names and no swank addresses; some have no address at all. Around the globe, wars, natural disasters, famines,

Prince William and Kate Middleton, now the Duchess of Cambridge, were married in 2011 in Westminster Abbey with all the trappings of British royalty. He is second in line to inherit the throne of England.

The United States does not have royalty with inherited thrones and titles. However, it does have enormous gaps in wealth, with some people living in splendor and luxury beyond the imagination of the average citizen.

economic crises, slavery, and human trafficking point to the presence of inequality. **Inequality** is *a social condition in which privileges, opportunities, and substantial rewards are given to people in some positions in society but denied to others.* Examples of media portrayals of suffering include refugees from the wars in Syria and South Sudan; impoverished victims of natural disasters such as Typhoon Haiyan, a record-setting strong storm on November 8, 2013, that devastated the Philippines; and famines occurring in Ethiopia, Somalia, and other poor countries. The earthquake and tsunami in Japan in March 2011 affected people of all socioeconomic levels, but poor and working-class people were most likely to live in areas vulnerable to flooding. That quake triggered 35-foot waves that left 16,447 people dead and 4,666 missing. Most victims were people who lived in the lower socioeconomic range and in poverty (Diep 2011; Vervaeck and Daniell 2011). The point is that inequality leaves many people vulnerable.

As noted in Chapter 6, climate change and economic hard times have pushed many low-income people from their rural homes to cities in hopes of finding jobs. However, with few jobs for unskilled and semiskilled workers in today's postindustrial service economies, many of the poor are left homeless. They live in abandoned buildings or sleep in unlocked autos, on park benches, under bridges, on beaches, or anywhere they can stretch out and hope not to be attacked or harassed. In the United States, cities such as Houston, Los Angeles, Washington, DC, and New York try to cope with the homeless by setting up sanitary facilities and temporary shelters, especially in bad weather. Cities also rely on religious and civic organizations to run soup kitchens and shelters.

Of the 1.9 billion children in the world, 2.2 million die every year (6,000 a day, mostly from Global South countries) from malnutrition, diseases related to unsafe water, poor sanitation, and inadequate health care. According to a recent report on the world's urban children, 1 in 3 city dwellers lives in a slum, but that ratio is as high as 6 in 10 in Africa (UN News Center 2012). These urban children grow up in poverty, with lack of electricity, clean water, education, sanitation, health care, and adequate food. They die of preventable diseases.

In some areas of the world, such as India and sub-Saharan Africa, the situation is even more desperate, and many families are starving. At daybreak, a cart traverses the city of Kolkata (Calcutta), India, picking up bodies of diseased and starved homeless people who have died on the streets during the night. Mother Teresa, who won the Nobel Peace Prize for her work with those in dire poverty, established a home in India where these people could die with dignity. She also founded an orphanage for children who would otherwise wander the streets begging or lie on the sidewalk dying. The micro and meso efforts of Mother Teresa and her fellow Missionaries of Charity are noble but only a small Band-Aid on a massive macro-level social problem.

What group of people is lower on the social hierarchy than those living in the street? That would be *slaves.* It may surprise you to know that **slavery**—*when an individual or a family is bound in servitude as the property of a person or household, bought and sold, and forced to work*—is alive and flourishing around the world (Free the Slaves 2014). An estimated 30 million people, mostly women and children from poor families in poor countries, are slaves, auctioned off or lured into slavery each year by gangs, pimps, and cross-border syndicates to work in forced labor or prostitution, as child soldiers or brides in forced marriages, or as children working on plantations or in factories (Walk Free Foundation 2013). Slavery caught the world's attention in April 2014 when the terrorist organization Boko Haram kidnapped close to 300 Nigerian schoolgirls to sell into slavery and give to men as wives. The group argues that women are the property of men and instruments of reproduction; girls, according to Boko Haram, should not receive an education, especially not a Western education.

New York, like most cities, has a large homeless population. This person seeks shelter and some sleep in a New York subway station.

A global phenomenon, slavery exists in all of the 162 countries studied by the Walk Free Foundation (2013). Mauritania has the most slaves (1 in every 25 members of the population). Next is Haiti with many children in slavery, followed by India and Pakistan. Sex trafficking is most common in South Asia and Eastern Europe (especially Ukraine), Myanmar (Burma), Laos, Nepal, and the Philippines. It is so profitable that businesspeople invest in involuntary brothels much as they would a mining operation (Bales 2007, 2012; Bales and Trodd 2008). Today, approximately 60,000 people (1 in every 5,000 members of the population) are enslaved in the United States (Walk Free Foundation 2013). Figure 7.1 provides a visual image of where most slaves are located.

The average U.S. citizen eats over 11 pounds of chocolate (that's 120 bars) a year, and 83% drink coffee (Perez 2013). However, the ugly side of treats is that over 70% of the production is from West Africa (Ivory Coast and Ghana), and most involves child labor or child slaves. Folgers, Maxwell House, Nescafé, and other major coffee companies import coffee from many plantations that use forced child labor and child slaves. Therefore, they pay very little for the coffee beans, allowing them to maintain high profit levels (Wilhoit 2014). A number of organizations including Free the Slaves, Mercy Project, Slavery Footprint, and Ark of Hope for Children work to stop and prevent child slavery. "Fair Trade Certified" products mean that production is free from abuse and exploitive labor practices, fair wages are paid, health and safety are observed, and sustainable methods are used. The two logos below are common ones for indicating that a product is fair trade.

As we write these words, at least 2.5 million people are suffering the abuse of *human trafficking*. A form of slavery, human trafficking consists of "the recruitment, transport, transfer, harbouring or receipt of a person by such means as threat or use of force or other forms of coercion, of abduction, of fraud or deception for the purpose of exploitation" (United Nations Office on Drugs and Crime [UNODC] 2014a). Most but not all victims of trafficking are women. The vast majority of trafficking (79%) results in the sexual exploitation of victims. Most other victims (18%) find themselves forced to work as slaves (UNODC 2014c).

In the slavery of the 19th century, slaves were expensive, and there was at least some economic incentive to care about their health and survival so that they could be productive workers. In the new slavery, humans are cheap and replaceable. There is little concern about working them to death, especially if they are located in remote cacao, coffee, or sugarcane plantations. By current dollars, a slave in the southern

FIGURE 7.1 Where in the World Slaves Live

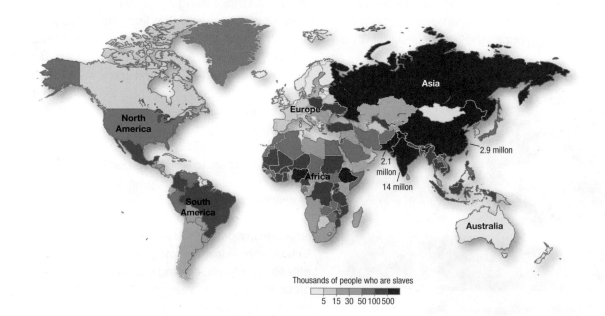

Thousands of people who are slaves

5 15 30 50 100 500

Source: Adapted from Fisher 2013. "This Map Shows Where the World's 30 Million Slaves Live" *Washington Post* October 17. Data source: Walk Free Global Slavery Index.

United States in the mid-1800s would have cost the equivalent of $40,000 today, but contemporary slaves are cheap. They can be procured from poor countries for an average of $90 (Bales 2012).

As noted, there are ongoing efforts by public sociologists among others to do away with modern-day slavery. A sociologist most at the forefront of the current movement to eradicate slavery is featured in the next "Sociologists in Action" on page 170.

⬤ Thinking Sociologically

Poor people around the world often lose control over their lives. What situations can lead to this condition, and what are some consequences for these people? What solutions would you propose?

As we can see from the examples above, our social world is stratified in ways that result in high levels of inequality. The rest of this chapter discusses (a) why stratification is important, (b) different systems of stratification, (c) the consequences of social rankings for individuals, (d) whether one can change social class positions (social mobility), (e) characteristics of major stratification systems, (f) poverty and social policies to address problems, and (g) the global digital divide.

Child laborers fill up empty cigarettes manually with locally grown tobacco in a small *bidi* (cigarette) factory at Haragach in Rangpur district, Bangladesh, in 2013.

THE IMPORTANCE OF SOCIAL STRATIFICATION

Consider your own social ranking in society. You were born into a family that holds a position in society—upper, middle, or lower class. The position of your family influences the neighborhood in which you live and where you shop, go to school, play sports, engage in the arts or other activities, and attend religious

SOCIOLOGISTS IN ACTION:
KEVIN BALES

Stopping Slavery in the 21st Century

In the following excerpt from "Confronting Slavery With the Tools of Sociology," Kevin Bales describes how he has used his sociological training to draw attention to and work to combat modern slavery, living the life of a public sociologist.

* * * * * * *

Becoming an abolitionist sociologist crept up on me. The first tiny prodding was a leaflet I picked up at an outdoor event in London. The front of the leaflet read "There are Millions of Slaves in the World Today." I was a university professor, and I confess to an unpleasant mixture of pride and hubris in my reaction to the bold title of the leaflet. Having been involved in human rights for many years, I thought, "How could this be true if I don't know about it already?"

Something began to itch in my mind . . . what if? What if there were millions of people in slavery? What if almost all of us, governments, human rights groups, the media, the public, were simply unaware? Millions of hidden slaves seemed unlikely, but my nagging thought was that if there were millions of people in slavery, then finding them was the job of a social researcher. If there were not millions of slaves, this type of literature needed debunking.

I pulled in students to help dig and sift through information, and paid one researcher to look further afield. As a faint picture of global slavery began to emerge, I came to understand why this issue was invisible. Slavery was hidden under a thick blanket of ignorance, concealed by the common assumption that it was extinct. With slavery illegal in every country, criminal slaveholders kept their activities hidden.

As I built up a picture of slavery, every new set of facts generated new questions. I began to realize that a large-scale research project was needed and I went in search of modern slavery, traveling to India, Pakistan, Thailand, Mauritania, and Brazil—often going undercover as I studied slave-based businesses in each country. The result was the book, *Disposable People: New Slavery in the Global Economy* (1999, 2004, 2012).

Some years later, I was able to build a database of slave prices over time that showed that slaves had been high-ticket capital purchase items in the past (even though occasional gluts caused prices to dip) and are normally low-cost disposable inputs today.

In 2000, I, with three others, helped found Free the Slaves, the American sister-organization of Anti-Slavery International, the world's oldest (1787) and original human rights group. Free the Slaves works with local partners to liberate slaves around the world and change the systems that allow slavery to exist. In addition to addressing the crime of enslavement, this work often involves confronting gender inequality, racism, ethnic and religious discrimination, and the negative outcomes of global economic growth. We have learned that freedom and empowerment are viral, and that freed slaves will stop at nothing to stay free and help others to liberty.

Not every part of liberation and reintegration requires sociological training, but it would be very hard to be successful without it. Without carefully constructed longitudinal surveys of villages in slavery we could never have demonstrated the "freedom dividend," the powerful and positive economic change that comes to whole communities when slavery is abolished. Without training in the empathetic understanding of a social researcher we could never have developed the "slavery lens," a way of seeing this hidden crime, that the US government now requires of all its foreign aid program workers. Without learning about the complex interplay of culture, society, economics, politics, and social vulnerability, we would never be able to build the unique methodologies of liberation tailored to specific and culturally rooted forms of slavery. And there is nothing like the ugly reality of a crime like slavery to push young sociologists to do their best work—using solid social science to change the world.

• • • • • • • • • • • • • • • • • • • •

Kevin Bales is a sociologist and professor of contemporary slavery at the Wilberforce Institute for the Study of Slavery and Emancipation (WISE) at the University of Hull, England, and cofounder of Free the Slaves in Washington, DC. This excerpt is taken from Korgen, White, and White's Sociologists in Action: Race, Class, Gender, and Intersections *(2013).*

services. Most likely, you and your family carry out the tasks of daily living in your community with people who share your social class status.

Your position in the stratification system affects the opportunities available to you and the choices you make in life. Note the social world model at the beginning of the chapter. It provides a visual image of the social world and socioeconomic stratification. The stratification process affects everything from individuals' social rankings at the micro level of analysis to positions of countries in the global system at the macro level.

Social stratification refers to *how individuals and groups are layered and ranked in society according to their access to and possession of valued resources.* The society's culture (rules, values, beliefs, and artifacts) determines and legitimizes the society's system of sorting its members.

Each society also determines what it considers to be valued resources. For example, in an agricultural society, members are ranked according to how much land or how many animals they own. In an industrial society, ownership of the *means of production* (property, machinery, and cash owed by capitalists) and occupational skills determine class status. In postindustrial information societies, education, access to technology, and information dissemination (in addition to ownership of the means of production) become key determinants in the ranking process.

What members of each society value and the criteria they use to rank other members depends on events in the society's history, its geographic location, its level of development in the world, its political philosophy, and the decisions of those in power. The more powerful individuals tend to get the best positions, the most desirable mates, and the greatest opportunities. They may have power because of birth status, personality characteristics, age, physical attractiveness, education, intelligence, wealth, race, family background, occupation, religion, or ethnic group—whatever the basis for power is in that particular society. Those with relatively high amounts of power have advantages that perpetuate their power, and they try to hold onto those advantages through laws, customs, power, ideologies, and sometimes force. Note that each level of analysis—micro, meso, and macro—adds to our understanding of the stratification process as shown below.

Micro-Level Prestige and Influence

Remember how some of your peers on the playground were given more respect than others? Their high regard may have come from belonging to a prestigious family, having a dynamic or domineering personality, being good at games, or owning symbols that distinguished them—"cool" clothing or shoes, a desirable bicycle, or expensive toys. This is stratification at work.

Property, power, and prestige are accorded to those who have **cultural capital** (*knowledge, skills, language mastery, style of dress, and values that provide a person with access to a particular status in society*) and **social capital** (*networks with others who*

Even the sports one plays—such as polo or stickball—are greatly influenced by social class and convey different kinds of social and cultural capital. Polo clearly requires a good deal of economic capital in order to play, whereas stickball requires only a ball and a straight stick.

have influence). Individual qualities such as leadership skills, an engaging personality, self-confidence, quick-wittedness, and physical attractiveness, or ascribed characteristics such as the most powerful gender or ethnic group, influence cultural and social capital. Interactions with meso-level organizations help shape the influence of these individual traits.

Meso-Level Access to Resources

Many of the resources we use come from institutions at the meso level: family, education, religion, economic and political institutions, and health care. We first learn our social status and the roles associated with it through our interactions with family members. The socialization we undergo in our families influences how we see ourselves, how others perceive us, and our access to resources such as education and jobs. For example, we learn grammar and manners from our families; that in turn affects how our teachers and peers view and judge us. Educational organizations treat children differently according to their social status, and social status is revealed through such symbols as language (e.g., if we speak standard English) and manners (e.g., not interrupting, saying please and thank you when appropriate, addressing adults by their proper titles). Our education can result

in differential access to prestigious jobs and affect our social status in society—and therefore our position in the social stratification hierarchy.

Macro-Level Factors Influencing Stratification

The global economic position of a nation affects the opportunities available to individuals in that nation, illustrating that macro-level factors also influence placement in the stratification system (see Figure 7.2). Haiti provides a powerful illustration of this fact. Located on the island of Hispaniola in the Caribbean, Haiti is the poorest country in the Western Hemisphere and one of the poorest countries in the world, with little technology, few resources, ineffective government, a very weak educational system, and an occupational structure based largely on subsistence farming. Even its forest resources are essentially gone, as desperately poor people cut down the last trees for firewood and shelters, leaving the land to erode (Diamond 2005).

The economy is in a downward cycle, pushing many already poor people still lower in the world's stratification system. The 2010 earthquake and floods added to Haitians' economic woes and misery. Residents were driven from what meager shelters they

FIGURE 7.2   Gross National Income per Capita in 2013

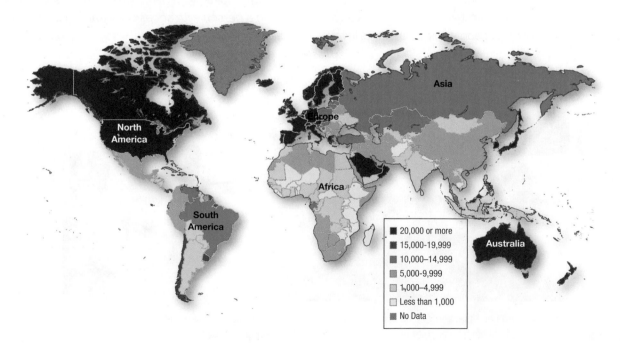

Source: World Bank.

had, and then faced a cholera epidemic from contaminated water. Haitians now have very few opportunities to get ahead and be successful. This is but one example of macro-level factors (failing economy, eroded land, lack of infrastructure such as schools and health facilities, lack of opportunity to participate in the global economy) affecting the opportunities available to people in the country.

Almost all societies stratify members, and societies themselves are stratified in the world system, so that each individual or nation experiences the world in unique ways related to its position. Stratification is one of the most powerful forces that we experience, but we are seldom conscious of how it works or how pervasive it is in our lives. This is the driving question sociologists ask when developing theories of stratification: How does it work?

⬤ Thinking Sociologically

Place yourself in the center of the social world model. Working outward from micro-level interactions toward the meso-level institutions and the macro-level global stratification system, indicate what has influenced where you fall in the stratification system.

THEORETICAL EXPLANATIONS OF STRATIFICATION

As we traverse the world, we see continuous examples of rich and poor—those who have more resources than they need and those who do not have enough to survive. Why is the distribution of resources so uneven? Is the unequal distribution inevitable, healthy, or harmful for society?

Sociologists have developed different theories to explain social stratification, based on the lens through which they view society. These explanations range from individual micro-level to national and global macro-level theories (e.g., symbolic interaction, rational choice, structural-functional, and conflict theories).

Micro-Level Theory

Our now familiar theories that relate to the micro level help us again, this time to understand differences among individuals in the stratification hierarchy.

Symbolic Interaction Theory. Have you ever been to a party where almost everyone came from a social class that had either much more or much less money than you? Even if you have not, you can probably imagine what it would be like. Awkward! Each social group has norms that members learn through the socialization process. These norms are recognized within that group and can make clueless outsiders feel like space aliens. People learn what is expected in their groups—family, peer group, social class—through interaction with others. For instance, children are rewarded or punished for behaviors appropriate or inappropriate to their social position. The socialization process transmits and perpetuates our positions in the social stratification system. Learning our position means learning values, speech patterns, consumption habits, appropriate group memberships (including political, economic, and religious affiliations), and even our self-concept. This knowledge provides us with the cultural capital necessary to interact effectively with people who share our social position.

Cultural capital (knowledge, skills, language, and values) is learned by children at home; they then bring that with them to school. Some home environments teach children to obey rules and authority, and to develop skills repairing houses and cars. Other families teach children by expanding vocabularies; developing good grammar; experiencing concerts, art, and theater; visiting historical sites; providing reading materials; and modeling engagement with reading. The higher-class parents tend to stress thinking and questioning skills as opposed to primarily obeying

©iStockphoto.com/^omazi

Look at all those forks and knives. Some people know what to do with each of them! Knowing which fork or knife to use for each course of a meal is a sign of cultural capital that can influence your chances of acceptance into elite society or success on a job interview.

authority figures. The result of this learning at home is that all children attain cultural capital that helps them interact with others at their social class level. The class difference in the types of cultural capital, though, means that children from the middle and upper classes or higher castes are more likely to get the best education, setting them up to be future leaders with better life chances. Schools place children into courses and academic groups, influenced in part by the labels children receive due to their cultural capital. In this way, children's home experiences and education help reproduce the social class systems and perpetuate the family's social class position in society (Ballantine and Hammack 2012).

Like language, other symbols can also represent social positions. Clothing, for example, sets up some people as special and privileged. In the 1960s, wearing blue jeans was a radical act by college students to reject status differences—showing solidarity with and support for the working class. Today, many young people wear expensive designer jeans that low-income people cannot afford. Drinking wine that most people do not have the means to buy, driving a Jaguar rather than a less expensive car, and living in a home that has six or eight bedrooms and is 5,000-plus square feet is an expression of *conspicuous consumption*—displaying goods in a way that others will notice and that will presumably earn the owner respect (Veblen 1902). Thus, purchased products become symbols intended to define the person as someone of high status in the stratification hierarchy.

Privacy can also symbolize affluence. For example, in most of the Global North, one symbol of middle-class "decency" is the right to bathe and do one's grooming in private. Indeed, many young people in the United States have their own bedrooms and expect no interruptions when sprucing up for the day. Homeless people in the United States do not have this luxury, and in India, bathing on the streets is not uncommon. Privacy requires money.

Rational Choice Theory. As you know, rational choice theorists focus on individuals and the way they make decisions regarding their own self-interest. From this view, people make decisions influenced by their perception of costs and benefits. Some people evaluate potential benefits with a view to the long term. They are willing to endure short-term expense or "pain" if the long-term gains are substantial. In order to take this view, one needs a sense of delayed gratification—delaying rewards or benefits until a later time. People who are

In India, many people must bathe every day in public in whatever water supply they can find. Even many people with homes do not have their own water supply. Privacy for one's grooming is a symbol of privilege for the affluent.

willing or in a position to do this—living austerely now in order to experience prosperity later—may be more likely to have upward mobility and to experience greater affluence at a later time. While your friend from high school may have a job and drive a nicer car than you can afford, you may be building debts and living in a drab dormitory in hopes of a better future. Thus, rational choice theorists would focus on how personal choices influence one's place in the social system. The idea is that one's socioeconomic position is shaped largely by individual decisions. What, though, influences those individual decisions?

In high school, many college prep students make "rational" decisions to become involved in athletic programs, student council, the Spanish Club, leadership roles in the National Honor Society, or community service because they want to list those involvements on college applications. They commit effort now—sometimes in activities that they care little about—in hopes of having a payoff in admission or scholarships to the college of their choice. Those same students become discouraged with classmates who will not help with student council activities or with building the junior class float. However, for young people whose parents did not go to college and whose past experiences do not lead them to believe that they, themselves, could ever attain a college degree, spending time decorating a float makes no sense. It is not seen as a "rational" choice. Thus, past experiences and social position can influence the way one evaluates costs and benefits.

These micro-level theories help us to understand how our daily interactions and decisions can impact our social positions (and vice versa) within society's stratification hierarchy. We now look at theories that examine the larger social structures, processes, and forces that affect stratification and inequality: structural-functional theory and various forms of conflict theory.

Meso- and Macro-Level Theories

Structural-Functional Theory. Structural-functionalists view stratification within societies as an inevitable, and generally necessary, part of the social world. The stratification system provides individuals a place or position in the social world and motivates them to carry out their roles. Societies survive by having an organized system into which each individual is born and raised, and in which each contributes to the maintenance of the society.

The basic elements of the structural-functional theory of stratification were explained by Kingsley Davis and Wilbert Moore in 1945, and their work still provides the main ideas of the theory today. Focusing on stratification by considering the rewards given to people in various occupations, they argue the following:

1. *Value of positions:* Some positions are more important to society than others. For example, society needs physicians and CEOs, both of which require specialized training. Societies must motivate talented individuals to prepare for and occupy the most important and difficult positions.
2. *Preparation requires talent, time, and money:* To motivate talented individuals to make the sacrifices necessary to prepare for difficult positions such as physician or CEO, differential rewards of income, prestige, power, or other valued goods must be offered. Thus, doctors and CEOs receive high income, prestige, and power as incentives.
3. *Unequal distribution of rewards:* The differences in rewards, such as pay for most valued positions, in turn, lead to the unequal distribution of resources—or inequality—for occupations in society. The result is that stratification is inevitable.

Look at the example of poverty. Some sociologists argue that poverty serves certain *functions* for society, thus making it difficult to eliminate (Gans 1971, 1995). Some people may actually benefit from having poor people kept poor. Consider the following points:

1. *Poverty provides us with a convenient scapegoat*—someone to blame for individual and societal problems. We can put the blame for poverty on the poor individuals themselves. That way we can ignore the meso- and macro-level causes of poverty—like economic and political systems—that would be expensive to resolve.
2. *Having poor people creates many jobs for those who are not poor,* especially in the "helping" professions such as social workers and law enforcement jobs such as police, judges, and prison workers.
3. The poor provide an easily available group of surplus laborers to do undesirable jobs when needed.
4. *The poor reinforce and legitimate our own lives and institutions.* Their existence allows the rest of us to feel superior to someone, enhancing our self-esteem.
5. *Their violation of mainstream values* helps reaffirm the values among the affluent (Gans 1971, 1995).

In the mid-20th century, structural-functional theory was the dominant theory used to explain stratification. However, it has been criticized for its inability to explain why some people in society who do not provide vital services for society (e.g., professional basketball players, hedge fund managers) receive great rewards. It also does not explain why CEOs now make so much more money compared to the typical worker than they once did. For example, in 1965, CEOs made, on average, 18 times the average worker's salary. In 2011, CEOs made 209 times the pay of the average worker (Mishel and Sabadish 2012). Functionalist explanations of stratification have also been critiqued for an inability to fully explain the conflict societies experience. This is the primary focus of conflict theory.

Conflict Theory. Conflict theorists see stratification as the outcome of struggles for dominance and scarce resources, with some individuals in society taking advantage of others. Individuals and groups act in their own self-interest by trying to exploit others, leading inevitably to a struggle between those who have advantages and want to keep them and those who want a larger share of the pie.

Conflict theorist Karl Marx (1818–1883) described four possible ways to distribute wealth, according to

(1) what each person needs, (2) what each person wants, (3) what each person earns, or (4) what each person can take. It was this fourth way, Marx believed, that was dominant in competitive capitalist societies (Cuzzort and King 2002; Marx and Engels 1955).

Marx viewed the stratification structure as composed of two major economically based social classes: the *haves* and the *have-nots*. The *haves* consist of the owners (capitalist bourgeoisie), whereas the *have-nots* are the working class (proletariat). Individuals in the same social class have similar lifestyles, share ideologies, and hold common outlooks on social life. The struggle over resources between the haves and have-nots is a cause of conflict (Hurst 2013).

The *haves* control what Marx called the *means of production*—property, machinery, and cash owned by capitalists—the valued resources in society (Marx [1844] 1964). The haves dominate because the lower-class have-nots cannot accumulate enough money and power to change their positions. The norms and values of the haves dominate the society because of their power and ability to make the distribution of resources seem "fair" and justified. Laws, religious beliefs, and educational systems spread ideas that support the domination of the haves. This keeps the *have-nots* from understanding their own self-interests and is why working-class people often support politicians whose policies really favor the wealthiest 1%. The haves' control of political structures, policies, and police or military forces ensures their continued dominance in society.

The unorganized lower-class have-nots cannot overcome their exploitation until they develop a *class consciousness*—a shared awareness that they, as a class, have interests that differ from those of the haves. They need to understand that what is good for the haves is bad for the have-nots. Marx contended that, with the help of enlightened intellectuals (like him),

Who do you think makes more money, Selena Gomez or this teacher? What does this imply about the structural-functionalist argument that societies motivate (through higher salaries) talented individuals to prepare for and occupy the most important and difficult positions?

the working class would develop a class consciousness, rise up, and overthrow the haves, culminating in a classless society in which wealth would be more equally shared (Marx and Engels 1955).

Unlike the structural-functionalists, then, conflict theorists maintain that money and other rewards are not necessarily given to those in the most important positions in the society. Can we argue that a rock star or baseball player is more necessary for the survival of society than a teacher or police officer? Yet the pay differential is tremendous. It takes most teachers (even those with a master's degree) an entire career to earn as much as many celebrities earn in a matter of months.

As you can see, not all of Marx's predictions have come true. While many nations have labor laws that require owners to pay workers a minimum wage and provide safe working conditions, and that prevent them from discriminating on the basis of race, gender, or religion, inequality still exists throughout the world. Even societies that claim to be classless, such as China, have privileged classes and poor peasants. In recent years, the Chinese government has allowed more private ownership of shops, businesses, and other entrepreneurial efforts, motivating many Chinese citizens to work long hours at their private businesses to "get ahead." The only classless societies are a few small hunter-gatherer groups that have no extra resources that would allow some members to accumulate wealth.

Some theorists criticize Marx for his focus on only the economic system, pointing out that noneconomic factors enter into the stratification struggle as well. Max Weber (1864–1920), another influential theorist, agreed with Marx that group conflict is inevitable, that economics is one of the key factors in stratification systems, and that those in power try to perpetuate their positions. However, he added two other influential factors that he argued determine stratification in modern industrial societies: power and prestige. Sometimes these are identified as the "three Ps"—property, power, and prestige.

Recent theorists suggest that using the three Ps, we can identify five classes—capitalists, managers, small business owners or the petty bourgeoisie, workers, and the underclass—rather than just the *haves* and *have-nots*. *Capitalists* own the means of production, and they purchase and control the labor of others. *Managers* sell their labor to capitalists and manage the labor of others for the capitalists. The *petty bourgeoisie*, such as small shop or business owners, own some means of production but control little of the labor of others; nevertheless, they have modest prestige, power, and property (Sernau 2010). *Workers* sell their labor to capitalists and are low in all three Ps. Finally, the *underclass* has virtually no property, power, or prestige.

In the modern world, conflict theorists argue that workers are still exploited but in different ways. As noted earlier, owners and CEOs get more income than many analysts feel is warranted by their responsibilities and education. For example, in 2013, *Forbes* magazine reported that the CEO of Kinder Morgan (an energy company), Richard Kinder, received $1.1 billion in income for the year, the highest income for billionaires that year. The money came from income on stocks and other assets. The second highest income for the year among billionaires, $288.6 million, went to Daniel Och of Och-Ziff Capital Management Group. Howard Schultz, CEO of Starbucks, received $118 million (Smith 2013).

Income is money received from work or investments while *wealth* is how much you are worth when you subtract the value of what you own from what you owe. The distribution of wealth and income in the United States has not been as uneven as it is today since before the Great Depression hit in 1929. Today, the richest 1% of U.S. households own more wealth than *all* of the bottom 90% combined (Saez 2012), and 40% of the nation's total wealth (Archer 2013). In the world, the richest 1% owns more than the other 99% of the combined world's population 2016 (Byanyima 2015).

Thinking Sociologically

How would conflict theorists explain the fact that CEOs make over 209 times the pay of the average worker and that the richest 1% in the world owns more than the combined wealth of the other 99%? Does their argument make sense? Why or why not?

The Evolutionary Theory of Stratification: A Synthesis

Evolutionary theory, developed by Gerhard Lenski, borrows assumptions from both structural-functional and conflict theories in an attempt to determine how scarce resources are distributed and how that

Theories of Stratification

distribution results in stratification (Lenski 1966; Nolan and Lenski 2014). The basic ideas are (a) to survive, people must cooperate; (b) despite this, conflicts of interest occur over important decisions that benefit one individual or group over another; (c) valued items such as money and status are always in demand and in short supply; (d) there is likely to be a struggle over these scarce goods; and (e) customs or traditions in a society often prevail over rational criteria in determining distribution of scarce resources. After the minimum survival needs of both individuals and the society are met, power determines who gets the surplus: prestige, luxury living, the best health care, and so forth. Lenski believes that privileges (including wealth) flow from having power, and prestige usually results from having access to both power and privilege (Hurst 2006).

Lenski tested his theory by studying societies at different levels of technological development, ranging from simple to complex. He found that the degree of inequality increases with technology until it reaches the advanced industrial stage. For instance, in subsistence-level hunter-gatherer societies, little surplus is available, and everyone's needs are met to the extent possible. As surplus accumulates in agrarian societies, those who acquire power also control surpluses, and they use this to benefit their friends and relations. However, they must share at least some of the wealth or fear being overthrown.

When societies finally reach the advanced industrial stage, there should be less inequality. Industrialization brings surplus wealth, a division of labor, advanced technology, and interdependence among members of a society. No longer can one individual control all the important knowledge, skills, or capital resources. The surplus can be spread to more people without diminishing that received by those who have the most. Therefore, this should eliminate the extreme gaps between haves and have-nots because resources would normally be more evenly distributed. Also, at this point in history, societies tend to have constitutions and recognize the rights of citizens, making it harder to exploit them.

Evolutionary theory takes into consideration an idea shared by the structural-functionalists and rational choice theorists—that talented individuals need to be motivated to make sacrifices. This produces motivated, competent, and well-educated people in the most important social statuses. The theory also recognizes exploitation leading to inequality, a factor that conflict theorists find in systems of stratification.

The reality is that while some inequality may be useful in highly complex societies, as functionalists have argued, extraordinary amounts of inequality may undermine motivation and productivity. The most talented people will not even try to attain the most demanding and important jobs if upward mobility seems impossible. Therefore, high levels of inequality do not make sense for a healthy industrial or postindustrial society (Nolan and Lenski 2014).

Each of the theories discussed above—symbolic interaction, rational choice, structural-functional, conflict, and evolutionary theory—provides different explanations for understanding stratification in modern societies. These theories provide the basis for micro- to macro-level discussions of stratification. Our next topic looks at some factors that influence an individual's position in a stratification system and the ability to change that position.

Thinking Sociologically

Why is the income gap between the rich and the poor currently increasing in the United States? Which theory seems most helpful in explaining this pattern? What are some possible ramifications of this widening income gap?

INDIVIDUALS' SOCIAL STATUS: THE MICRO LEVEL

You are among the world's elite. Less than 7% of the world's population has a college degree (Erickson and Vonk 2012). Being able to afford the time and money for college is a luxury beyond the financial or personal resources of almost 93% of people in the world. However, the global number of college students is expanding rapidly as countries such as China provide more higher education opportunities to support their growing economies.

In fact, enrollment of Chinese students in higher education surpassed the percentage enrolled in the United States in 2011 (People's Daily Online 2011). Because the demand for a college education far exceeds the opportunity in China, many Chinese college students are studying abroad, adding to their opportunities and enhancing China's knowledge of the world. Chinese students make up the

Average Wealth

These college graduates share the privilege of a college education with just 7% of the world's population.

largest number of international students studying in the United States—236,000 in 2013—accounting for more than a quarter of all international students (Paulson 2013).

In the United States, access to higher education is greater than in many other countries because there are more levels of entry—including technical colleges, community colleges, large state universities, and private four-year colleges. However, with limited government help, most students must have enough financial resources to cover tuition and the cost of living.

The prestige of the college that students choose can also make a difference in their future opportunities. Students born into wealth can afford private preparatory schools and tutors to increase SAT and ACT test scores that increase their chances of gaining acceptance to prestigious colleges. Such colleges offer social networking and other opportunities not available to those attending the typical state university or nonelite college (Jaschik 2013; Persell 2005). For men, attending an elite college makes a significant difference in future earnings, but for women entering a field that pays well makes more of an impact on future earnings than the college they attended (Ma and Savas 2014).

Ascribed characteristics, such as gender, can also affect one's chances for success in life. Embedded gender stratification systems may make it difficult for women to rise in the occupational hierarchy. Many Japanese women, for example, earn college degrees but leave employment after getting married and having children, in part because of gender discrimination in the workforce (Globe Women 2013). We will examine gender stratification in more depth in Chapter 9, but note that it intersects with socioeconomic status and must be viewed as part of a larger pattern resulting in inequality in the social world.

Individual Life Chances

Life chances refer to one's opportunities, depending on both achieved and ascribed statuses in society. That you are in college, probably have health insurance and access to health care, and are likely to live into your late 70s or 80s are factors directly related to your life chances. Let us consider several examples of how placement in organizations at the meso level affects individual experiences and has global ramifications.

Education. Although education is valued by most individuals, the cost of books, clothing, shoes, transportation, child care, and time taken from income-producing work may be insurmountable barriers to school attendance for many people. One's level of education affects many aspects of life, including political, religious, and family attitudes and behavior. Generally speaking, the higher the education level, the more active individuals are in political life, the more mainstream or conventional their religious affiliation, and the more likely they are to marry, remain married, and have good health.

Health, Social Conditions, and Life Expectancy. If you have a sore throat for an extended period of time, you will probably go see a doctor. Yet many people in the world will never see a doctor. Access to health care requires doctors and medical facilities, money for transportation and treatment, access to child care, and released time from other tasks. The poor sometimes do not have these luxuries. In contrast, the affluent eat better food, are less exposed to polluted water and unhygienic conditions, and are able to pay for health insurance, medical care, and drugs when they do have ailing health. As a result, they tend to live much longer than poorer people.

Examining causes of death among different classes illustrates some of the deadly results of the differences in access to health care among people at different places in the stratification hierarchy. For example, in the poor Global South, shorter life expectancies and deaths, especially among children, are due to controllable infectious diseases such as cholera, malaria, AIDS, typhoid, tuberculosis, and other respiratory ailments. In contrast, in affluent countries, heart disease, stroke, and lung cancer are the most common causes of death, and most deaths are of people above the age of 65. With improvements in immunizations, mosquito nets to prevent malaria, better sanitation and water quality, access to medicines, better nutrition, and female literacy, life expectancy rises. The chance to live a long and healthy life is a privilege available to those living in wealthy countries.

By studying Table 7.1 in the next "Engaging Sociology" feature, you can compare life expectancy with two other measures of life quality for the poorest and richest countries: the gross national product (GNP) per capita income—the average amount of money each person has per year—and the infant mortality rates (death rates for babies). Note that life expectancy in poor countries is as low as 49 years in Chad, South Africa, and Guinea-Bissau in Africa (many of the people in these countries are subsistence farmers), and as high as 89.6 years in the wealthy country of Monaco, and 84 in Macau, Japan, and Singapore. In the United States, life expectancy is 79.6 (World Factbook 2014i). Average annual income is as low as $600 in Zimbabwe and $400 in the Democratic Republic of Congo, and as high as $102,100 in Qatar and $89,400 in Liechtenstein. The average U.S. income is $52,800 a year (World Factbook 2014l). Infant mortality is as high as 117.23 deaths per 1,000 births in Afghanistan (over 1 in 10), and as low as 1.81 in Monaco and 2.13 in Japan. In the United States the estimated 2014 rate is 6.17 per 1,000 births (World Factbook 2014l).

◑ Thinking Sociologically

Explain how some specific factors at the micro, meso, and macro levels affect your life expectancy and that of your family members.

One does not have to look beyond the borders of the United States, though, to see the relationship between health and wealth. The United States has much larger gaps between rich and poor people than most other wealthy nations, and that has led to a corresponding gap in health and life expectancy among social classes much wider than that in other highly developed nations. As the video *In Sickness and in Wealth: Health in America* (2008) reveals, there is "a health-wealth gradient" in the United States, in "which every descending rung of the socioeconomic ladder corresponds to worse health." The result is that 41 other nations have higher life expectancy rates than the United States (Meyer 2012; World Factbook 2014i).

Individual life chances are determined in part by the per capita income of individuals. If a country is poor, many individuals have little disposable income. This means a life of poverty and less access to education, health, and other social conditions that determine life chances and lifestyle, discussed next.

Individual Lifestyles

Your individual lifestyle includes your attitudes, values, beliefs, behavior patterns, and other aspects of your place in the world, as shaped by socialization. As individuals grow up, the behaviors and attitudes consistent with their culture and their family's status in society become internalized through the process of socialization. Lifestyle is not a simple matter of having money. Acquiring money—say, by winning a lottery—cannot buy a completely new lifestyle (Bourdieu and Passeron 1977). This is because values and behaviors are ingrained in our self-concept from childhood. A person may gain material possessions, but that does not mean she has the lifestyle of the upper-class rich and famous. Remember the awkward party when you were around people of a different social class? Even if you suddenly made the same amount of money as those at an elegant party, you would not know the norms associated with that social class. Some examples of factors related to your individual lifestyle that tend to differ among social classes include attitudes toward achievement, family life and child-rearing patterns, religious membership, and political involvement.

Attitudes Toward Achievement. Attitudes toward achievement differ by social status and are generally closely correlated with life chances. As noted previously, motivation to get ahead and beliefs about what we can achieve are in part products of our upbringing and the opportunities we see as available to us. These attitudes differ greatly depending on the opportunity structure around us, including what our families and friends see as possible and desirable. For example, the primary concern of poor families in poor nations may be to put food on the family's table. They may view education as a luxury not appropriate for people of their social class. In Global North countries, opportunity is available for most children to attend school at least through high school and often beyond. However, some students do not learn to value achievement in school due to lack of support from their

ENGAGING SOCIOLOGY

Life Expectancy, Per Capita Income, and Infant Mortality

Analyzing the meaning of data can provide an understanding of the health and well-being of citizens around the world. A country's basic statistics including life expectancy, per capita gross national product, and infant mortality tell researchers a great deal about its economic health and vitality.

1. What questions do the data in Table 7.1 raise regarding differences in mortality and life expectancy rates around the world?

2. Considering what you know from this and previous chapters and from Table 7.1, what do you think are some differences in the lives of citizens in the richest and poorest countries?

TABLE 7.1 Life Expectancy, Per Capita Income, and Infant Mortality for Selected Poor and Rich Countries

Poor Countries	Life Expectancy (in Years)	Infant Mortality (Deaths per 1,000 Births)	Per Capita GDP ($)	Rich Countries	Life Expectancy (in Years)	Infant Mortality (Deaths per 1,000 Births)	Per Capita GDP ($)
Chad	49.4	90.3	2,500	Monaco	89.6	1.8	65,500
South Africa	49.6	41.6	11,500	Japan	84.5	2.1	37,100
Afghanistan	50.5	117.2	1,100	Singapore	84.4	2.5	62,400
Somalia	51.6	100.1	600	Hong Kong	82.8	2.7	52,700
Zambia	51.8	66.6	1,800	Switzerland	82.4	3.7	54,800
Mozambique	52.6	72.4	1,200	Sweden	81.9	2.6	40,900
Nigeria	52.6	74.1	2,800	Australia	82.1	4.4	43,000
Uganda	54.5	60.8	1,500	Canada*	81.7*	4.7*	43,100
Niger	54.7	86.3	800	France	81.7	3.3	35,700
Zimbabwe	55.7	26.6	600	United States**	79.6**	6.2**	52,800

Source: World Factbook 2014g and 2014i for infant mortality and life expectancy; *World Factbook* 2014c for per capita income.

Note: Infant mortality is per 1,000 live births.

*Canada is 14th in life expectancy and 43rd in infant mortality rates.

**United States is 42nd in life expectancy and 56th in infant mortality rates.

primary socializing agents: family, peers, and teachers (Ballantine and Hammack 2012).

Family Life and Child-Rearing Patterns. Attitudes toward achievement are not the only things that differ among socioeconomic groups. Child-rearing patterns also vary and serve to reinforce one's attitude toward achievement and social position in society. When you were growing up, were your after-school hours, weekends, and summers filled with adult-organized activities (e.g., formal lessons, youth sports, camps), or were you pretty much free to play on your own, watch TV, or hang out with friends or extended family? A family's social class location shapes the daily rhythms of family life (Lareau 2003). Upper- and middle-class parents engage in the "concerted cultivation" of their kids. They schedule their kids in multiple activities, engage in more elaborate verbal communication with them, and intervene on their behalf with teachers and other authority figures. Working-class parents, other than providing daily essentials, tend to be more hands-off, an approach that researcher Annette Lareau labeled the "accomplishment of natural growth" (Lareau 2003:238). Their kids engage in more casual, unstructured play; have fewer opportunities to hear and use extended vocabularies; and are left to fend for themselves in dealings with adults. Their parents tell them what to do with orders, rather than reasoning with them, as many middle- and upper-class parents do with their children. Their parents also tend to use more physical punishment than middle-class parents, who utilize guilt, reasoning, time-outs, and other nonphysical sanctions to control children's behavior. These differences help shape their assumptions about how authority is exercised and whether it is acceptable to challenge authority figures.

Differences in parenting behavior also lead to the "transmission of differential advantages to children" (Lareau 2003:5). Through their socialization by their parents, middle-class children are better able to navigate the educational and, later, occupational worlds than working-class children. This, in turn, influences the social class destinies of each group (Lashbrook 2009).

Religious Membership. Religious affiliation also correlates with the social status variables of education, occupation, and income. For instance, in the United States, upper-class citizens are found disproportionately in Episcopalian, Unitarian, and Jewish religious groups, whereas lower-class citizens tend to be attracted to Nazarene, Southern Baptist, Jehovah's Witness, and other holiness and fundamentalist sects. Although there are exceptions, such as Catholicism, most religious groups attract members predominantly from one social class, as Chapter 11 will illustrate (Roberts and Yamane 2012).

Political Involvement. Political party identification and general ideological beliefs affect voting, and they are, in turn, affected by social factors such as race, religion, region of the country, social class, gender, marital status, and age (Interuniversity Consortium for Political

and Social Research 2011). Throughout the world, the lower the social class, the more likely people are to vote for parties that support greater distribution of wealth, and the higher the social status, the more likely people are to be conservative on economic issues—consistent with protecting their wealth (Domhoff 2005; Kerbo 2008). However, those with lower levels of education and income tend to vote conservatively on many social issues relating to minorities and civil liberties (e.g., rights for gays and lesbians, same-sex marriage, and abortion) (Gilbert 2011; Kerbo 2008).

Money also influences who can run successful campaigns. For example, during the 2012 congressional elections, the average candidate running for a position in the House of Representatives or the Senate spent, respectively, $526,818 and $2,318,358. During the presidential campaign of 2012, President Obama and Mitt Romney (along with their allies) raised approximately a billion dollars each. This contributes to the fact that those with more money, who can help support such campaigns, also have more influence in elections (King 2012; OpenSecrets.org 2012a, 2012b).

Status Inconsistency. Some people experience high status on one trait, especially a trait achieved through education and hard work, but may experience low standing in another area. For example, a professor may have high prestige but low income. Max Weber called this unevenness in one's social standing *status inconsistency*. In societies with high levels of racism and sexism, racial minorities and women in high-status positions experience status inconsistency. If their lowest ascribed status is treated as most important, they are likely to experience discontent with the current system and become more liberal in political views (Weber 1946).

Life experiences such as hunger, unnecessary early death of family members, or pain of seeing one's child denied opportunities are all experienced at the micro level, but their causes are usually rooted in events and actions at other levels of the social world. This brings us to our next question: Can an individual move up or down in a stratification system?

Thinking Sociologically

Describe your own lifestyle and life chances. How do these relate to your socialization experience and your family's position in the stratification system? What difference do they make in your life today and for what you think you will accomplish in the future? What can you do to improve your life chances?

SOCIAL MOBILITY: THE MICRO-MESO CONNECTION

The LeBron Jameses and Peyton Mannings of the world make millions of dollars—at least for the duration of their playing careers. For professionals in the world of sport, each hoop, goal, or touchdown throw is worth thousands of dollars. These riches give hope to those in rags that if they "play hard," they too may be on the field or court making millions. The problem is that the chances of making it big are so small that such hopes are some of the cruelest hoaxes perpetrated on poor young African Americans and others in the lower or working class today. It is a false promise to think of sports as the road to wealth when chances of success are extremely limited (Dufur and Feinberg 2007; Edwards 2000).

Those few minority athletes who do "make it big" and become models for young people tend to experience "stacking," holding certain limited positions in a sport. Moreover, those young players who make it into the major leagues may have done so by going in right after high school or leaving college after a single year. This thwarts their postathletic career opportunities. When retired from playing, few black athletes rise in the administrative hierarchy in the sports of football and baseball (basketball has a better record of hiring black coaches and managers). If young people put all their hopes and energies into developing their muscles and physical skills, they may lose the possibility of moving up in the social class system, which requires developing their minds and technical skills.

Social mobility refers to *the extent of individual movement up or down in the class system, changing one's social position in society—especially relative to one's parents* (Gilbert 2011). What is the likelihood that your status will be different from that of your parents over your lifetime? Will you start a successful business? Marry into wealth? Win the lottery? Experience downward mobility due to loss of a job, illness, or inability to complete your education? What factors at different levels of analysis might influence your chances of mobility? These are some of the questions addressed in this section and the next.

The four issues that dominate the analysis of mobility are (1) types of social mobility, (2) methods of measuring social mobility, (3) factors that affect social mobility, and (4) whether there is a "land of opportunity" for those wishing to improve their lot in life.

This young street basketball player has dreams of glory on the courts. Despite many grand hoop dreams, few experience dramatic social mobility through sports.

Types of Social Mobility

Mobility can be up, down, or sideways. *Intergenerational mobility* refers to change in social class status compared with one's parents, usually resulting from education and occupational attainment. If you are the first to go to college in your family and you become an engineer, this represents intergenerational upward mobility. The amount of intergenerational mobility—that is, the number of children who move up or down in the social structure compared to where their parents are—measures the degree to which a society has an *open class system*. The more movement there is between classes, the more open the class system.

You can change positions at the same level in the stratification system. For example, you could move from your job as a postal worker and become a firefighter. This type of mobility is called *horizontal mobility*. You have changed your position, but your social prestige remains the same.

Intragenerational mobility (not to be confused with *inter*generational mobility) refers to a change in position within a single individual's life. For instance, if you begin your career as a teacher's aide and end it as a school superintendent, that is upward intragenerational mobility. However, mobility is not always up. *Vertical mobility* refers to movement up *or* down in the hierarchy and sometimes involves changing social classes. You may start your career as a waitress, go to college part-time, get a degree in computer science, and get a more prestigious and higher-paying job, resulting in upward mobility. Alternatively, you could lose a job and take one at a lower status and pay. In recent years, people at all levels of the occupational structure have experienced downward intragenerational mobility after being laid off from one job and having difficulty finding another at the same level and pay grade.

How Much Mobility Is There? Measures of Social Mobility

One traditional method of measuring mobility is to compare fathers with sons, and in more recent research with daughters. Determining the mobility of women is more difficult because they often have lower-level positions, and their mothers may not have worked full-time, but a conclusion that can be drawn is that both women's and men's occupational attainment is powerfully influenced by class origins. The level of social mobility in the United States is lower than in most other Global North nations (Gould 2012).

While the dramatic growth of the U.S. economy in the decades following World War II led to rising prosperity and upward mobility for most (particularly white, male Americans), mobility has decreased since the early 1970s. There is quite a bit of movement in the middle of the class system (between the lower-middle and upper-middle classes), but not much movement at the upper and lower ends. People born poor or wealthy tend to remain poor or wealthy when they are adults (Haskins, Isaacs, and Sawhill 2008; Pew Charitable Trusts 2012).

Factors Affecting an Individual's Mobility

Why are some people successful at moving up the ladder, while others lag behind? Mobility is driven by many factors, from your family's background to global economic variables. One's chances to move up depend on micro-level factors (e.g., cultural capital, socialization, personal characteristics, and education)—and meso- and macro-level factors (e.g., the occupational structure

and economic status of countries; population changes in the number of births, deaths, or people migrating; the numbers of people vying for similar positions; discrimination based on gender, race, or ethnicity; and the global economic situation).

Studying mobility can be a complicated process because these key variables are interrelated. Macro-level forces (such as the occupational structure and economic status in a country) are related to meso-level factors (such as access to education and type of economy) and micro-level factors (such as socialization, family background, and education level) (Blau and Duncan 1967). An individual's family background accounts for nearly half of the factors affecting what job one gets (Jencks 1979). Consider a few of the variables that can make a difference in your chances for mobility.

Family Background, Socialization, Marriage, and Education. Whether or not you marry and whom you marry can move you up or down the social class ladder. As men's wages have fallen over the past few decades and more women have joined the workforce, household incomes (rather than just male incomes) play more of a role in people's social class positions. As people increasingly tend to marry those of similar income levels, marriage makes even more of an impact on family income. Two high-income earners make much more than two low-income earners (and *much* more than one low-income or even middle-income worker) (Haskins et al. 2008; Pew Charitable Trusts 2012).

As we have noted throughout this chapter, our family background has a major influence on our chances for upward mobility on the social class ladder. For example, recent research discusses the continuing social class "word gap" between children from different classes. Disparities in vocabulary are noticeable as early as 18 months (National Public Radio [NPR] 2013). Children from higher social classes learn nuances in language whereas lower-class children learn primarily commands and short directive sentences. Professional parents use three times as many different words at home as parents in low-income families. By the time the children of professional families are 3 years old, they have a vocabulary of about 1,100 words and typically use 297 different words per hour. Children in working-class families have a 700-word vocabulary and use 217 words per hour, while children from low-income families have 500 words and use 149 per hour. These numbers represent a gap in the range of words they hear at home and illustrate the difference family background and socialization can make in education and future opportunities. A University of Chicago study recommends a "3-*Ts*" approach—tune in, talk more, take turns—to increase vocabulary (Hart and Risley 2003; NPR 2013). Because language usage at home impacts school success, that in turn plays a role in a child's chances of getting into college and climbing the stratification ladder.

Thinking Sociologically

How might your vocabulary affect your success in school? How might an expanded vocabulary affect your opportunities in life (for example, impress a potential employer)? What can you do to increase your vocabulary?

A college degree helps those at the bottom of the stratification system move up and helps those in the middle and upper classes to remain in those higher positions. This positive impact on social class position relates to the fact that, as Figure 7.3 reveals, employment rates and earnings tend to go up dramatically with a college degree. For example, in 2012, the unemployment rate was 7.5% for those with a high school degree, but just 4.0% for those with a degree from a four-year college. The median weekly earnings were $1,108 for those with a four-year degree but just $651 for those with only a high school diploma (Bureau of Labor Statistics 2014a; Pew Charitable Trusts 2012).

As Table 7.2 indicates, most people who go to college are already in the middle and upper classes. When we look at actual college degrees, however, the pattern is more extreme; 50% of college diplomas go to students in

TABLE 7.2 College Attendance by Social Class and Cognitive Ability (percent in college)

Cognitive Ability Quartile	Family Socioeconomic Status Quartile			
	Top	Third	Second	Lowest
Top	83	74	63	51
Second	69	51	42	33
Third	57	40	24	23
Lowest	35	20	13	13

Source: Gilbert 2011:149.

the top-status groups, compared with only 10% to graduates coming from the bottom half of income levels. If U.S. society were truly a **meritocracy**, *positions would be allocated in a social group or organization according to individuals' abilities and credentials.* One would expect cognitive ability to be the most important variable (Gilbert 2011).

Even when a young person is admitted to a college or university, she or he may be at a disadvantage in the classroom and alienated from past social ties. The culture of four-year colleges is typically the culture of the well-educated upper-middle class, and may be different and uncomfortable for those from other class backgrounds (Dews and Law 1995). The alienation many poor and working-class students experience at four-year colleges is explored in more detail in the next "Engaging Sociology."

FIGURE 7.3 Earnings and Unemployment Rates by Educational Attainment

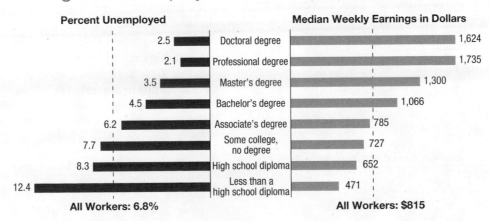

Percent Unemployed		Median Weekly Earnings in Dollars
2.5	Doctoral degree	1,624
2.1	Professional degree	1,735
3.5	Master's degree	1,300
4.5	Bachelor's degree	1,066
6.2	Associate's degree	785
7.7	Some college, no degree	727
8.3	High school diploma	652
12.4	Less than a high school diploma	471

All Workers: 6.8%   **All Workers: $815**

ENGAGING SOCIOLOGY

First-Generation College Students: Issues of Cultural and Social Capital

Socioeconomic classes develop subcultures that can be quite different from one another, and when one changes subcultures, it can be confusing and alienating. College campuses provide an example because they are dominated by middle-class cultures. First-generation college students often find themselves in a world as alien as visiting another country. Students whose parents went to college are more likely to have cultural and social capital that helps them understand their professors who are generally part of the middle-class culture. Answer the following survey questions. How might your own cultural and social capital cause you to feel at home or alienated, privileged or disprivileged, in a college environment?

A. Which of the following experiences were part of your childhood?

☐ Had a library of books (at least 50 adult books) in your childhood home

☐ Had parents who subscribed to a newspaper

☐ Had parents who subscribed to newsmagazines (*Time*, *The Economist*)

☐ Listened to music as a family, including classical or instrumental music such as harp or flute

☐ Traveled to at least 20 other states or to at least 5 other countries

☐ Took regular trips to the library

☐ Took regular trips to museums

☐ Attended plays (theater productions) and concerts

☐ Played a musical instrument

☐ Took dance lessons

☐ Listened to National Public Radio (NPR)

☐ Watched PBS (Public Broadcasting Service) on television

B. Which of the following *relationships* were part of your childhood?

☐ My parents knew at least two influential people in my community on a first-name basis—such as the mayor, members of the city council, the superintendent of schools, the governor, and the district's representative to Congress.

☐ The regional leader of my religious group—church, temple, or mosque—knew and respected my family.

☐ My parents knew, on a first-name basis, at least three CEOs of corporations.

☐ When I entered new situations in high school, it was likely that my parents were known by the coaches, music directors, summer camp directors, or others "running the show."

☐ When I came to college, one or more professors and administrators at the college knew my parents, a sibling, or another family member.

☐ I have often interacted directly and effectively (in a non-adversarial way) with authority figures.

Engaging With Sociology

1. If you experienced many of the items under A at home, you had fairly high cultural capital. If you marked most of the items under B, you had a lot of social capital. If you did not, you may find the culture of a college campus to be alien and even confusing. How well does your background match up with the cultural capital of a college?

2. Which of the following aspects of a college campus do you think might make a first-generation college student feel most alienated at your college: *economic* capital (money), *social* capital (networks with those who have resources), or *cultural* capital (knowledge of important aspects of the culture)? Why?

Source: Survey constructed in part using ideas from Morris and Grimes 1997.

Most four-year colleges have middle-class cultures—or even upper-class cultures. The environment can be quite alienating—"chilly" in more ways than one—to first-generation students who do not have social and cultural capital that fits their new environment.

Population Trends and Economic Vitality Within a Country. The economic vitality of a country affects the chances for individual mobility, since there will be fewer positions at the top if the economy is stagnant. As agricultural work decreases and technology jobs increase in most areas of the world, these changes in the composition and structure of jobs affect individual opportunity (Hurst 2013). Thus, macro-level factors such as a country's economy and its place in the global system shape the employment chances of individuals.

The U.S. nationwide baby boom following World War II resulted in a flood of job applicants and downward intergenerational mobility for the many who could not find work comparable with their social class at birth. In contrast, the smaller group following the baby boomer generation had fewer competitors for entry-level jobs. Baby boomers hold many of the executive and leadership positions today, so promotion has been hard for the next cohort. As baby boomers retire, opportunities will open up, and mobility should increase. The *fertility rates*, or number of children born at a given time, influence the number of people who will be looking for jobs.

Gender, Race, Ethnicity, and Earnings. Many women and ethnic minority groups, locked in a cycle of poverty, dependence, and debt, have little chance of changing their status. For example, African Americans tend to remain poor or fall from the middle class more often than people in other racial groups (Pew Charitable Trusts 2012). Likewise, while women have made some gains, women in the U.S. workforce are more likely than men to be in dead-end clerical and service positions with no opportunity for advancement. Overall, women still make less money than men (U.S. Department of Labor 2011). Table 7.3 shows the earnings for population groups including gender and race/ethnicity.

Women, on average, earn less money than men, but they now have more degrees than men. Women are much more likely than men (32% compared to 24%) to earn a bachelor's degree by the time they are 27. While women are still woefully underrepresented in upper-level management positions (only 4.2% of Fortune 500 CEOs are women), their increasing edge in education should, eventually, lead to more women in high-level positions in the workforce (Bureau of Labor Statistics 2013; Catalyst 2013; DeBoskey 2012).

The Interdependent Global Market. All members of an economy are vulnerable to international events and the swings in the global marketplace. If the Chinese or Japanese stock markets hiccup, it sends ripples

TABLE 7.3 Median Annual Earnings by Race/Ethnicity and Sex

Race/Gender	Earnings	Wage Ratio
White men	$46,176	100.0%
White women	37,596	81.4%
Black men	34,632	75.0
Black women	31,044	67.0
Hispanic men	30,863	66.8
Hispanic women	27,612	59.8
All men	$45,084	
All women	$36,608	
Gender wage gap for all ethnic and racial groups		81.2%

Source: Adapted from U.S. Department of Labor 2013b.

through world markets. If high-tech industries in Japan or Europe falter, North American companies in Silicon Valley, California, may go out of business, costing many professionals their lucrative positions. In ways such as these, the interdependent global economies affect national and local economies, and that in turn affects individual families.

Whether individuals move from "rags to riches" is not determined solely by their personal ambition and work ethic. As the information in this chapter indicates, mobility for the individual, a micro-level event, is linked to a variety of events at other levels of the social world. What we see and hear in the media, though, may have us believe otherwise.

● Thinking Sociologically

Think of family members or friends who have recently lost or acquired jobs. Using your sociological imagination, how can you connect those individual experiences to the national and global economy? How do you think the national and global economies will impact your experience in the marketplace after you earn your college degree?

Is There a "Land of Opportunity"? Cross-Cultural Mobility

Television shows bombard us with images of rich bachelors and the desirability of marrying a millionaire to improve our status in life. By playing a game of trivia or being challenged on an island on a TV show, we too might "strike it rich." Another possibility is that we might win the lottery by buying a ticket at our local convenience store. In reality, these quick fixes and easy get-rich-fast plans are seldom realized, and the chances of us profiting are slim indeed.

The question for this section concerns your realistic chances for mobility and whether you have a better chance to improve your status by moving to some other country. The answer is not simple. Countless immigrants have sought better opportunities in new locations. Their economic future depended on the historical period, the economic conditions, attitudes toward immigrants, their job skills, and their ability to blend into the new society.

During economic growth periods, many immigrants have found great opportunities for mobility in the United States and Europe. However, opportunities

for upward mobility have changed significantly with globalization. Multinational corporations look for the cheapest sources of labor in the Global South, countries with low taxes, few labor unions and workplace safety regulations, and many workers needing jobs. This has drained away low-skilled manufacturing jobs from Global North countries, making it even more essential to have advanced educational credentials (such as a bachelor's or master's degree).

Most jobs in the United States today focus on providing services. These service-sector jobs tend to require either a great deal of education (e.g., lawyers, computer engineers, or doctors) or minimal training (e.g., retail sales, nurse's aides, fast-food workers, or security guards). The low-skill jobs do not pay well, and labor unions, with declining memberships and political clout, have increasingly limited influence on the wages and working conditions of workers.

Although the new factories for multinational industries springing up in Global South countries such as Malaysia, Mexico, and the Philippines provide opportunities for mobility to those of modest origins, much of the upward mobility in the world is taking place among those who come from small, highly educated families with individualistic achievement-oriented values (Featherman and Hauser 1978; Rothman 2005). They are positioned to take advantage of the changing occupational structure and high-tech jobs. As the gap between rich and poor individuals widens, education becomes more important.

MAJOR STRATIFICATION SYSTEMS: MACRO-LEVEL ANALYSIS

Imagine being born into a society in which you have no choices or options in life because of your family background, age, sex, or ethnic group. You cannot select an occupation that interests you, cannot choose your mate, and cannot live in the part of town you prefer. You see wealthy aristocrats parading their advantages and realize that this will never be possible for you. You can never own land or receive the education of your choice.

This situation is reality for millions of people in the world—they are born this way and will spend their lives this way. In **ascribed stratification systems**, *characteristics beyond the control of individuals— such as family background, age, sex, and race—determine their position in society.* In contrast, **achieved stratification systems** *allow individuals to earn positions through their ability, efforts, and choices.* In an open-class system, it is possible to achieve a higher ranking by working hard, obtaining an education, and choosing an occupation that pays well.

Ascribed Status: Caste and Estate Systems

Caste systems are *the most rigid ascribed stratification systems. Individuals are born into a status, which they retain throughout life. That status is deeply embedded in religious, political, and economic norms and institutions.* Individuals born into caste systems have predetermined occupational positions, marriage partners, residences, social associations, and prestige levels. A person's caste is easily recognized through clothing, speech patterns, family name and identity, skin color, or other distinguishing characteristics. From their earliest years, individuals learn their place in society through the process of socialization. To behave counter to caste prescriptions would be to go against religion and social custom and to risk not fitting into society. That can be a death sentence in some societies.

In caste-based societies, the institution of religion works together with the family, education, economic, and political institutions to shape both expectations and aspirations and to keep people in their prescribed places in caste systems. For example, Hindu ideas dictate that violating the caste prescriptions can put one's next *reincarnation* or rebirth (in the Hindu tradition) in jeopardy. Stability in Hindu societies is maintained in part by the belief that people can be reborn into a higher status in the next life if they fulfill expectations in their ascribed position in this life.

The clearest example of a caste system is found in India, a predominantly Hindu society. The Hindu religion holds that individuals are born into one of four *varnas*, broad caste positions, or into a fifth group below the caste system, the *outcaste* group. The first and highest varna, called *Brahmans*, originally was made up of priests and scholars but now includes many leaders in society. The second varna, *Kshatriyas* or *Rajputs*, includes the original prince and warrior varna and now embraces much of the army

and civil service. The *Vaishyas*, or merchants, are the third varna. The fourth varna, the *Sudras*, includes peasants, farmers, artisans, and laborers. The final layer, below the caste system, encompasses profoundly oppressed and broken people—"a people put aside"—referred to as untouchables, outcastes, *Chandalas* (a Hindu term), and *Dalits* (the name preferred by many "untouchables" themselves). Although the Indian Constitution of 1950 granted full social status to these citizens, and a law passed in 1955 made discrimination against them punishable, deeply rooted traditions can be difficult to change. Caste distinctions are still very prevalent, especially in rural areas.

Estate systems are characterized by *the concentration of economic and political power in the hands of a small minority of political-military elite, with the peasantry tied to the land* (Rothman 2005). They existed in ancient Egypt, the Incan and Mayan civilizations, Europe, China, and Japan. In estate systems an individual's rank and legal rights are clearly spelled out, and arranged marriages and religion bolster the system. In Europe, during the Middle Ages, knights defended the realms and the religion of the nobles. Behind every knight in shining armor were peasants, sweating in the fields and paying for the knight's food, armor, and campaigns. For farming the land owned by the nobility, peasants received protection against invading armies and enough of the produce to survive. Their lives were often miserable. If the yield of crops was poor, they ate little. In a good year, they might save enough to buy a small parcel of land. A very few were able to become independent in this fashion. Today, similar systems exist in some Central and South American, Asian, and African countries on large banana, coffee, cacao, and sugar plantations.

Thinking Sociologically

What might be some advantages, for both the society and the individuals living in it, of a society where status was ascribed rather than achieved? Do you think you would enjoy living in such a society? Why or why not?

Achieved Status: Social Class in the United States

In contrast to ascribed status systems, *achieved stratification systems* maintain that everyone is born with common legal status and equality before the law. In principle, all individuals can own property and choose their own occupations. However, in practice, most achieved status systems, like the class system found in the United States, pass privilege or poverty from one generation to the next. Individual upward or downward mobility is more difficult than the ideology invites people to believe.

Social class refers to *the wealth, power, and prestige rankings that individuals hold in society.* Members of the same social class have similar income, wealth and economic position, lifestyles, levels of education, cultural beliefs, and patterns of social interaction. Our families, rich or poor and educated or unskilled, provide us with an initial social ranking and socialization experience. We tend to feel a kinship and sense of belonging with those in the same social class, and tend to live, attend school, and work with people from our social class. We think alike, share interests, and probably look up to the same people as a reference group.

Our social class position is based on the three main factors in the stratification system: (1) property, (2) prestige, and (3) power. This is the trio—the three *P*s—that, according to Max Weber, determine where individuals rank in relation to each other (Weber 1946, 1947). By *property* (wealth), Weber refers to owning or controlling the means of production. *Power*, the ability to control others, includes not only the means of production but also the position one holds. *Prestige* involves the esteem and recognition one receives, based on wealth, position, or accomplishments. Chances of being granted high prestige improve if one's patterns of behavior, occupation, and lifestyle match those valued in the society (e.g., in U.S. society today that would include scientists, physicians, military officers, lawyers, and college professors). However, recent news events—such as the Boston Marathon bombings—may increase the rankings of occupations in which people such as first responders (police and firefighters) have been portrayed as "heroes."

Although these three dimensions of stratification are often found together, this is not always so. Recall the idea of *status inconsistency*: an individual can have a great deal of prestige yet not command much wealth (Weber 1946). Consider winners of the prestigious Nobel Peace Prize such as Wangari Maathai, a Kenyan environmentalist who won the prize for starting a movement to plant trees and for her political activism; or Betty Williams and Mairead Corrigan of Northern Ireland, founders of the Community of Peace People who won for their efforts to find a peaceful end to their country's problems. None of them was rich, but each made contributions to the world that gained them universal prestige. Likewise, some people gain enormous wealth through crime or gambling, but this wealth may not be accompanied by respect or prestige.

Still, some theorists see power as the key element in systems of stratification. Conflict theorists maintain that those who hold power control the economic capital and the means of production in society (Ashley and Orenstein 2009). Consistent with Marx, many recent conflict theorists argue that a **power elite** comprising *top leaders in corporations, politics, and the military* rules society (Domhoff 2014a). These interlocking groups of elites grow up together, attending the same private schools and belonging to the same private clubs (Domhoff 2005, 2014a; Mills 1956). There is an unspoken agreement to protect each other's positions and ensure that their power is not threatened. Those not in this interlocking elite group do not hold real power and have little chance of breaking into the inner circles (Dye 2002).

Pluralist power theorists, on the other hand, argue that *power is not held exclusively by an elite group but is shared among many power centers, each of which has its own self-interests to protect* (Ritzer and Goodman 2004). Well-financed special-interest groups (e.g., the insurance industry, dairy and cattle farmers, or truckers' trade unions) and professional associations (e.g., the American Medical Association or American Bar Association) have considerable power through collective action. From the pluralist perspective, officials who hold political power are vulnerable to pressure from influential interest groups, and each interest group competes for power with others. Creating and maintaining this power through networks and pressure on legislators is the job of lobbyists. For example, in the intense U.S. debate over health care legislation, interest groups from the medical community, insurance lobbies, and citizens' groups wielded their power to influence the outcome, but because these major interests conflict and no one group has the most power, no one group attained all it wanted. Some groups wanted to nationalize health care, and others wanted to completely privatize it; the Affordable Care Act did neither. The core idea of pluralist theorists, then, is that many centers of power create at least some checks and balances on those in elite positions.

Examples of Social Classes in the United States

Imagine that you are a politician. The public is clamoring for more help for the middle class. Flash back to the most recent U.S. presidential campaign. All the candidates were talking about the middle class. Did you ever hear the politicians define what they meant? You probably did not, because the broader and more inclusive the definition, the more useful it is to politicians who are trying to appeal to a range of voters.

When given a choice among lower, middle, and upper class, almost all Americans will say they are middle class. When given a choice that includes working class, however, 45% say middle class, and another 45% define themselves as working class (Gilbert 2011). You can see sociologist Dennis Gilbert's social class model in Figure 7.4. Most social scientists measure social class by looking at the income, education, and profession of respondents. Middle class generally requires extensive education and training and a salary rather than an hourly wage—teachers, nurses, accountants, managers, and other midlevel jobs and falling at around 50% of the income distribution (Gilbert 2011).

Sometimes, social scientists break down members of the middle class into two groups: the white-collar middle class and the working class. Most white-collar workers have a college education, have professions with salaries (rather than jobs where they are paid by the hour), work in an office setting, and earn within a specified range around the median income. Members of the working class work for hourly wages, do manual labor, and do not usually have a college degree.

POVERTY AND SOCIAL POLICY

Nothing describes poverty more vividly than hunger. Stories about hunger and famine in Global South countries fill the newspapers. Around the world, nearly 870 million people, or roughly 1 in every 8 people on Earth, go to bed hungry every night. Yet chronic hunger has declined by 130 million people since 1990 (World Food Programme 2013; World Hunger Education Service 2013).

FIGURE 7.4 Gilbert's Model of Social Class

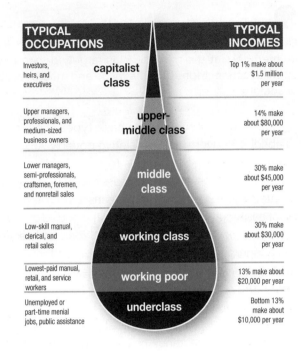

Source: Gilbert 2011:14.

One hardly expects to see hunger in rich countries, yet in the United States over 50 million people, or 1 in 6 in the U.S. population and 1 in 5 children, are hungry some of the time (Feeding America 2013; Sauter and Hess 2013). States most severely affected by food insecurity (lack of consistent access to food) include Mississippi, Arkansas, Texas, Alabama, North Carolina, Georgia, Missouri, Nevada, Tennessee, and Ohio. These states also have among the highest obesity rates due to poor diets (Sauter and Hess 2013). Households led by single women are more likely to be food insecure (36.8%). Race also influences the likelihood of food insecurity. One out of four black (25.1%) and Hispanic (26.2%) households are food insecure (Coleman-Jensen et al. 2012).

Most people living in poverty have no property-based income and no permanent or stable work, only casual or intermittent earnings in the labor market. They often depend on help from government agencies or private organizations to survive. In short, they have personal troubles in large part because they have been unable to establish linkages and networks in the meso- and macro-level organizations of our social world. They have little collective power, and therefore little representation of their interests and needs in the political system.

⬤ Thinking Sociologically

Explain how your family's ability to provide food for its members at the micro level is largely dependent upon its connectedness to the meso and macro levels of society.

Sociologists recognize two basic types of poverty: (1) absolute poverty and (2) relative poverty. **Absolute poverty**, *not having resources to meet basic needs*, means no prestige, very little access to power, no accumulated wealth, and insufficient means to survive. Some die of easily cured diseases because the bodies of those in absolute poverty are weakened by chronic and persistent hunger and almost total lack of medical attention.

Relative poverty occurs when *one's income falls below the poverty line, resulting in an inadequate standard of living relative to others in the individual's country*. In the United States, relative poverty means shortened life expectancy, higher infant mortality, and poorer health. While few people starve on the street and suffer from the easily cured diseases more common among the poor in Global South nations, food insecurity and the stress and hardships of relative poverty

lead to more health problems and earlier deaths for the poor in the United States and other Global North nations with high levels of inequality.

The *feminization of poverty* refers to the trend in which single females with children make up a growing proportion of those in poverty. In 2012, 13.6% of males and 16.3% of females in the United States lived in poverty. For women aged 18 to 64, the rate was 15.4%, and for men in this age-group 11.9% (DeNavas-Walt, Proctor, and Smith 2013). If you were raised by a single mother, chances are good that you experienced poverty. More than half (57.2%) of children under age 6 living with just a female head of household in the United States (with no husband present) were in poverty in 2011 (DeNavas-Walt, Proctor, and Smith 2012). Some of those in poverty find themselves without a home. As of January 2013, there were 610,042 homeless people in the United States (U.S. Department of Housing and Urban Development 2013). Among them, 65% were in transitional or emergency shelters, and 35% were unsheltered. Almost one out of four of the homeless (23%) were children under the age of 18. Families now make up over one third (36%) of the homeless population.

The Obama administration has made a concerted effort to combat homelessness and has used social scientific research to do so. Studies have shown that "mainstream housing, health, education, and human service programs must be fully engaged

This little boy sits at the feet of an aid worker. His family has little power to improve their situation or his life chances. Compare his circumstances to those of the little girl talking on her cell phone while riding in a limousine.

and coordinated to prevent and end homelessness" (Sullivan 2013). Research also reveals that providing a wide range of services for the homeless actually saves taxpayers money in the long run "by interrupting a costly cycle of emergency room visits, detoxes, and even jail terms" (Sullivan 2013). Thanks to strategies based on these findings, the number of both the homeless, in general, and homeless families has declined by, respectively, 6% and 8% since 2010, despite growing levels of inequality in our society.

How can we effectively address inequality? First, we must become aware of the problem. As this chapter has described, almost every society has some system of stratification. We do not all have the same chances of "making it." Most of us, though, do not fully realize the extent of the inequality in some societies including the society we call home. For example, in a recent study, a nationally representative sample of U.S. citizens were shown three charts that display different distributions of wealth ranging from somewhat equal to very unequal. When asked which of the three charts illustrated how wealth was distributed in the United States, most respondents chose the chart that actually described wealth distribution in Sweden, the nation with the *lowest level* of economic inequality in the world. The chart most often picked by respondents as an "ideal" distribution of wealth illustrated an even *more equitable* distribution of wealth than that found in Sweden (Norton and Ariely 2011). Figure 7.5 shows the actual U.S. wealth distribution plotted against the estimated and ideal distributions across all respondents. Note that the ideal distribution is closest to the results of the survey described above.

After reading this chapter, you understand that the United States has higher levels of inequality and poverty and less class mobility than most other wealthy nations. Once we understand the extent of inequality and poverty, we can start to develop ways to address these issues. We can also critique poverty reduction programs now under way in different nations and help to create more effective ones, if needed.

◑ Thinking Sociologically

Recalling what you have learned about poverty, how would you develop a plan to attack the problem of poverty within your community or nation, taking into account micro, meso, and macro levels of analysis? Consider job training, changing family values, providing child care for working parents, raising the minimum wage, or other factors. First describe the root causes of poverty and then suggest solutions.

FIGURE 7.5 Wealth Inequality in the United States: Actual, Estimated, and Perceived Ideal Percent Wealth Owned

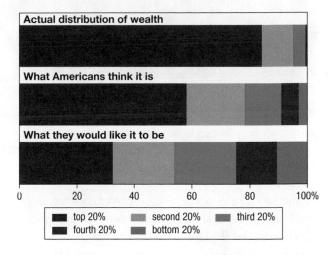

Source: Norton and Ariely 2011.

The actual U.S. wealth distribution is plotted against the estimated and ideal distributions across all respondents. Because of their small percentage share of total wealth, both the "4th 20%" value (0.2%) and the "Bottom 20%" value (0.1%) are not visible in the "Actual" distribution.

The bar labeled "What Americans think it is" represents the actual distribution of wealth in Sweden.

NATIONAL AND GLOBAL DIGITAL DIVIDE: MACRO-LEVEL STRATIFICATION

Mamadou from Niger and Eric from Ghana answer their iPhones to the sound of chimes from London's Big Ben clock tower and a Bob Marley song. In addition to English, one speaks in Kanuri and French and the other in Twi to friends and family thousands of miles away. They are the future generation of elites from the Global South, fluent in the languages of several countries, adept in computer software, and at the forefront of their countries in digital technology. Many of their fellow citizens in Niger and Ghana in Africa are not so fortunate. In their Global South subsistence lives and with insufficient education to participate in the changing economy and new technologies, they have little contact with the digital world swirling overhead through satellite connections.

Global economic and political institutions increasingly produce and transmit information through digital technology. Few tools are more important than computers, smartphones, and the Internet. In nearly every

In Laos, where many people live in grass houses such as this one (left), families do not have access to electronic devices or the Internet. Their homes and their life chances stand in stark contrast to those of the children seen here working on computers—seen as necessary equipment.

salaried and professional position, computer knowledge and ability to navigate the Internet are critical employment skills. The *digital divide* refers to the gap between those with knowledge and access to information technology and those without it. The lines of the divide are drawn by the position of the country in the world, socioeconomic status of citizens, minority group membership, and urban versus rural residence (Mehra, Merkel, and Bishop 2004).

Many individuals in Global South countries have insufficient technology and education to participate in

TABLE 7.4 World Internet Usage by Region

World Regions	Internet Penetration (% Population)	% of Total Global Internet Users
Africa	26.5	9.8
Asia	34.7	45.7
Europe	70.5	19.2
Middle East	48.3	3.7
North America	87.7	10.2
Latin America/ Caribbean	52.3	10.5
Oceania/ Australia	72.9	0.9
WORLD TOTAL	42.3	100.0

Source: Internet World Statistics 2014.

this new economy (Drori 2006; Nakamura 2004). Still, the number of Internet users in the world is increasing rapidly. In 2000 just 250 million people (around 1%) could access the Internet, but by June 2014 42.3% of the world's population had used the Internet (Renick 2011; Internet World Statistics 2014). As Table 7.4 makes clear, this varies greatly by region of the world. *Internet penetration* refers to the percentage of Internet users in each country.

Researchers have laid out three tiers in the digital divide, based on the following: (1) personal computers per 100 in the population, (2) Internet users per 100 in the population, and (3) Internet bandwidth per person. Using these standards, all developed countries plus some additional countries in the Caribbean, Eastern Europe, and the Middle East are Tier 1—the places with most access. The second tier includes Brazil, Russia, China, and some smaller countries in South America. African nations account for the majority of members in the lowest tier, reflecting the disadvantage of the continent in terms of lack of computers, computer use, and bandwidth ("The International Digital Divide" 2011). However, undersea fiber-optic cables are being laid around Africa to provide faster and more reliable Internet access (African Undersea Cables 2013).

As Internet technology expands, it brings the world to remote villages, opening new horizons and options, and changing lifestyles. Some poor countries are transitioning into the electronic age and making policies that facilitate rapid modernization. They are passing over developmental stages that rich Global North countries went through. As an illustration, consider the telephone. Most telephones in the world are cell phones, many using satellite connections. Some countries never did get completely wired for landlines and have chosen to skip that step in development. With the satellite technology now in place, some computer and Internet options are available to them without landlines (Drori 2006). Use of cell phones in poor countries has boomed, giving people access to health care and other services. By 2014, the number of mobile phones in the world was over 7 billion (enough for 96% of the world's population), with 77% of growth from smartphones (Cisco 2014). Africa had the lowest number of subscribers at 63% (Pramis 2013; Whitney 2012).

The growing use of cell phones has helped shrink the digital divide more than anything else. For example, around the world people can buy and sell goods, and send money through their cell phones. The influence is felt from the micro to the macro level, as it improves the lives of individuals, increases business in the area in which they live, and helps connect them to the global economy by allowing individuals to save and invest money in the local and global economies (Langfitt 2011).

Haiti, one of the poorest nations in the world, also provides a great example of the potential positive power of Internet technology. While only 10% of Haitians have bank accounts, 80% have cell phones. Aid agencies, after the earthquake of 2010, have been able to make use of this technology, distributing aid to far-flung refugees via their cell phones (Beaubien 2011; Partners in Prepaid 2012).

Using the Internet to promote savings and investment is one powerful means, just now being tapped, of addressing global poverty and inequality. The potential is enormous, and sociologists can help us determine how to make the most effective use of the new technologies. Digital technology is an example of one important force changing the micro- to macro-level global stratification system—a spectrum of people and countries from the rich and elite to the poor and desperate.

We leave this discussion of stratification systems, including class systems, with a partial answer to the question posed at the beginning of this chapter: Why are some people rich and others poor? In the next two chapters, we expand the discussion to include other variables in stratification systems—race, ethnicity, and gender. By the end of these chapters, the answer to the opening question—why some have riches and some have only rags—should be even clearer. Socioeconomic status is important as a measure in any society, but it is not the sole basis for stratification. In the next chapter, we look at the role of race and ethnicity in social inequality.

WHAT HAVE WE LEARNED?

The issue of social stratification calls into question the widely held belief in the fairness of our economic system. By studying this issue, we better understand why some individuals are able to experience prestige (respect) and to control power and wealth at the micro, meso, and macro levels of the social system, while others have little access to those resources. Few social forces affect your personal life at the micro level as much as stratification. That includes the decisions you make about what you wish to do with your life or whom you might marry. Indeed, stratification played a role in why you are reading this book.

KEY POINTS

- *Stratification*—the layering or ranking of people within society—is one of the most important factors shaping the life chances of individuals. This ranking is influenced by micro, meso, and macro forces and resources.

- Depending on the theoretical perspective, stratification can be viewed as either functional or destructive for society and its members.

- The United States has less social mobility and higher levels of inequality and poverty than most other Global North nations.

- For individuals, where they stand in the system of stratification is highly personal, but it is influenced by the way the social system works at the meso and macro level—due to access to education; the problems created by gender, racial, and ethnic discrimination; and the vitality of the global economy.

- People without much social capital have fewer connections to the meso and macro levels and are less likely to attain power, wealth, and prestige.

- Some macro systems stress ascribed status (assigned to one, often at birth, without consideration of one's individual choices, talents, or intelligence). Other systems purport to be open and based on achieved status (depending on one's contributions to the society and one's personal abilities and decisions).

- Poverty is a difficult social problem, one that can be costly to a society as a whole. Various solutions at the micro, meso, and macro levels have had mixed results, partially because it is in the interests of those with privilege to have an underclass to do the unpleasant jobs.

- Technology is both a contributor to and a possible remedy for inequality, as the digital divide creates problems for the poor, but electronic innovations may create new opportunities in the social structure for networking and connections to the meso and macro levels—even for those in the Global South, the poorer regions of the world.

DISCUSSION QUESTIONS

1. Were you surprised to learn that among rich nations, life expectancy in the United States is among the lowest? Explain. What sociological theory best explains this fact? Support your answer.

2. How has the social class of your parents and your upbringing influenced your success in school and your professional aspirations?

3. What is the social status of most of the people with whom you hang out? Why do you think you tend to associate with people from this social status?

4. Describe factors at the (a) micro, (b) meso, and (c) macro levels that impact your ability to move up the social class ladder.

5. How do the forces that have led to the shrinking of the middle class impact your chance of becoming (or remaining) a member of the (a) middle, (b) upper-middle, or (c) upper class after you graduate from college?

6. How can bridging the global digital divide lead to a decrease in inequality across the world? How does your ready access (or lack of access) to a computer and the Internet impact *your* life chances?

CONTRIBUTING TO OUR SOCIAL WORLD: What Can We Do?

At the Local Level

- *Volunteer to serve a meal* at an area soup kitchen. Your campus activities office should be able to help you find one in your area and even connect you with a group on campus that regularly volunteers at one.

- *Tip service people in cash.* Housekeepers in hotels and motels, maids, meal servers at restaurants, and food delivery employees may depend on tips to survive. In order to make it more likely that they receive the tips intended for them, be sure to tip in cash, rather than using a credit card.

At the Organizational or Institutional Level

- *Habitat for Humanity* pairs volunteers with current and prospective homeowners in repairing or constructing housing for little or no cost. Habitat projects are under way or planned for many communities in the United States and around the world. See the organization's website at www.habitat.org for more details and to see if you can volunteer for a project in your area.

- Founded in the early 1990s, AmeriCorps includes a variety of programs from intensive residential programs to part-time volunteer opportunities in communities across the United States. For more information, go to the organization's website at www.americorps.gov.

At the National and Global Levels

- *Peace Corps* involves a serious, long-term (two-year) commitment, but most who have done it agree that it is well worth the time and energy. The Peace Corps is an independent agency of the U.S. government, founded in 1961. Volunteers work in foreign countries throughout the world, helping local people improve their economic conditions, health, and education. The Peace Corps website (www.peacecorps.gov) provides information on the history of the organization, volunteer opportunities, and reports of former and present volunteers.

- *Grameen Bank* (www.grameenfoundation.org), a microcredit organization, was started in Bangladesh by Professor Muhammad Yunus, winner of the 2006 Nobel Peace Prize. It makes small business loans to people who live in impoverished regions of the world and who have no collateral for a loan. Consider doing a local fundraiser with friends for the Grameen Bank or other microcredit organizations, such as FINCA (www.finca.org), Kiva (www.kiva.org), and CARE International (www.care-international.org).

- *Free The Children* is a youth-focused organization whose international programs help free people across the globe from the cycle of poverty by providing clean water, schools, health care, and sanitation. You can learn more about this organization and how you can join its efforts at www.freethechildren.com.

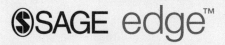

Sharpen your skills with SAGE edge at **edge.sagepub.com/ballantinecondensed4e**

SAGE edge for Students provides a personalized approach to help you accomplish your coursework goals in an easy-to-use learning environment.

8 Race and Ethnic Group Stratification

Beyond "Us" and "Them"

As human beings, we are all part of "us," but there is a tendency to define those who look or behave differently as "them." Those labeled as "them" are often separated, even dehumanized and mistreated, from "us" and from each other.

MICRO

ME (AND MY MINORITY FRIENDS)

LOCAL ORGANIZATIONS AND COMMUNITY
Locally, members of ethnic groups may experience exclusion and prejudice.

MESO

NATIONAL ORGANIZATIONS, INSTITUTIONS, AND ETHNIC SUBCULTURES
Policies in large organizations may discriminate— intentionally or unintentionally.

MACRO

SOCIETY
National laws or court rulings often set policies that relate to discrimination.

GLOBAL COMMUNITY
Racial and ethnic hostilities around the world may result in wars, genocide, and "ethnic cleansing."

LEARNING OBJECTIVES

8.1 Distinguish between racial and ethnic groups.

8.2 Describe the difference between prejudice and discrimination.

8.3 Provide examples of dominant and minority group contact in the world today.

8.4 Outline effects of prejudice, racism, and discrimination on minority and majority groups.

8.5 Describe efforts to reduce racial and ethnic inequality at the micro, meso, and macrolevels of analysis.

8.6 Provide examples of policies affecting minority and dominant group relations.

THINK ABOUT IT

Micro: Local Community	Why do people in the local community categorize "others" into racial or ethnic groups?
Meso: National Institutions; Complex Organizations; Ethnic Groups	How might your education, religion, politics, economics, and health experiences differ depending on your ethnicity?
Macro: National and Global Systems	Why are minority group members in most countries economically poorer than dominant group members? In what ways might ethnicity or race shape international negotiations and global problem solving?

DeBrun was a well-liked African American college student, actively involved in extracurricular activities. Like many college students, he enjoyed both alcohol consumption on weekends and the outrageous things that happened when people were inebriated. However, DeBrun's anger, normally kept in check, tended to surface when he was drunk. One weekend, some racial slurs were thrown around at a party, and when one of the perpetrators pushed DeBrun too far—including a sucker punch—DeBrun exploded in a fury of violence. No one died, but there were some serious injuries—the worst inflicted by the muscular DeBrun—and at one point a knife was pulled. DeBrun was expelled from the university, and felony charges were leveled against him. Because there had been a weapon—one that did not belong to DeBrun but at one point ended up in his hand—the university president would not consider readmission. The local white prosecutor, who saw a powerfully built young black man with tattoos and dreadlocks, assumed that this campus leader was a "thug" and insisted on the most severe felony charges and penalties.

DeBrun, who had no previous encounters with law enforcement, ended up with a felony record and two years in prison. Because of both state and federal laws, the felony charges meant that he no longer qualified for federal financial aid. As his family had very few resources, his hopes for a college degree were crushed. As a convicted felon, he would not be able to vote in many states for the rest of his life, his future employment prospects were greatly diminished, and his family's hopes that he would be their first college graduate were crushed. The president of the college was not a bigot, but the professors who knew DeBrun well were convinced that neither his expulsion, nor his arrest, nor his conviction as a serious felon would have occurred had he been white.

This recent incident represents a way that African American males can experience a different United States of America than middle-class white males. The cause is not necessarily personal bigotry by people in power. Differential treatment and harmful actions against minorities can sometimes occur at the individual and small-group levels, but they are particularly problematic at the meso or institutional level. In any case, life in the United States can be very different for people whose skin tone is dark.

In a recent study, sociologists interviewed black and white schoolchildren whose ages ranged from 11 to 14 and asked them "what would happen if an alien entered their room at night and turned them into black [or white] children." The majority (65%) of the white children and an overwhelming majority (93%) of the black children thought their lives would be different if their race changed (Risman and Banerjee 2013).

Would your life change if your race changed? Imagine that you were given the opportunity to choose your own racial and ethnic background. What would you do? Why? How do you think your life would be different if you chose a different racial and ethnic background?

In this chapter, we explore racial and ethnic stratification. In doing so, we look at related issues, such as the social construction of race, prejudice, racism, and discrimination. Some are micro-level issues, while others are best addressed at the meso and macro levels.

WHAT CHARACTERIZES RACIAL AND ETHNIC GROUPS?

In this section, we consider the characteristics of racial and ethnic groups and their positions within the

In the Republic of South Africa, blacks are almost three quarters of the population, but they are still considered a minority group because they face racial discrimination and have far less access to economic power and privilege than the "majority" white South Africans, who comprise 9% of the population.

stratification system. **Minority groups** *differ from other groups in some characteristics and are subject to less power, fewer privileges, and discrimination.* Like all minority groups, racial and ethnic minority groups have less power than the dominant group in society.

Minority Groups

Several factors characterize minority groups and their relations with dominant groups in society (Dworkin and Dworkin 1999). Minority groups

1. can be distinguished from the group that holds power by physical appearance, dress, language, or religion;

2. are excluded from or denied full participation at the meso level of society in economic, political, educational, religious, health, and recreational institutions;

3. have less access to power and resources within the nation and are evaluated less favorably, based on their characteristics as minority group members;

4. are stereotyped, ridiculed, condemned, or otherwise defamed, allowing dominant group members to justify and not feel guilty about unequal and poor treatment; and

5. develop collective identities to insulate themselves from the un-accepting world, which in turn perpetuates their group identity by creating ethnic or racial enclaves, intragroup marriages, and segregated group institutions such as religious congregations.

Thinking Sociologically

Based on the preceding list of minority group characteristics, explain how membership in dominant or minority groups influences people's interactions at the micro (family), meso (institutional), and macro levels of society.

Minority and majority status can change over time and among societies, and dominant groups are not always the numerical majority. In the case of South Africa, possession of advanced European weapons placed the native African Bantu population under the rule of a relatively small number of white British and Dutch descendants in what became a complex system of planned discrimination called *apartheid*. From 1948 to 1994, each major racial group in South Africa—White, Asian, Colored, and Black—had its own living area, and members carried identification cards showing the "race" to which they belonged. Racial classification and privilege were defined by the laws of the dominant group.

The Concept of Race

Race is *a socially created concept that identifies a group as "different" based on certain biologically inherited physical characteristics.* This allows members of the group to be singled out for dissimilar treatment. Most attempts at racial classifications have been based on combinations of appearance, such as skin color and shade, stature, facial features, hair color and texture, head form, nose shape, eye color and shape, height, and blood or gene type. As you will see, though, racial categories are social constructions that vary over time and place.

The Social Construction of Race. From our earliest origins in Ethiopia and around the Olduvai Gorge in East Africa, about 200,000 years ago, *Homo sapiens* slowly spread around the globe, south through Africa, north to Europe, and across Asia. Original migration patterns of early humans over thousands of years are shown in Figure 8.1. As the figure shows, most theorists believe that humans crossed Asia and the Bering Strait to North America around 20,000 BCE and continued to populate North and South America (Diamond 1999, 2005). However, continuing archaeological research indicates that indigenous human populations may have reached South America well before the figure indicates (Mann 2005). The point is that the mixing of

FIGURE 8.1   The Spread of Humans Around the World

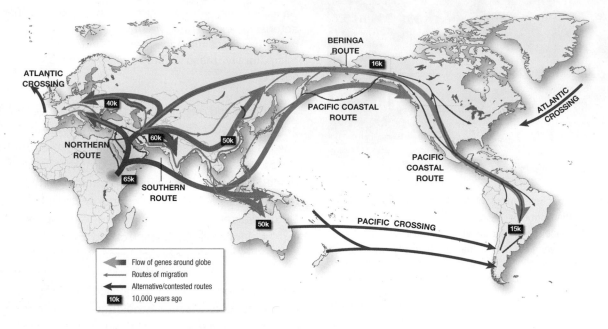

Source: Phys.org 2009.

This figure shows the historical spread of humans around the globe and the approximate time periods of the movements.

peoples over the centuries has left few if any genetically isolated people, only gradations in appearance as one moves around the world. Thus, the way societies choose to define race has come about largely through what is culturally convenient for the dominant group or race.

Throughout history, political and religious leaders, philosophers, and even scientists have struggled with the meaning and significance of race. The first systematic classification of all living phenomena was published in 1735 by Carl von Linné (Linnaeus). His hierarchy of species was actually quite complex, including monkeys, elephants, and angels, and suggested four human types: Americanus (Native Americans), Asiaticus, Africanus, and Europeanus (Cashmore and Troyna 1990). Johann Blumenbach was the first to use the word *race* in his 1775 classification system: Caucasian, Mongolian, Ethiopian, American, and Malay.

By the 19th century, race began to take on a biological meaning, and many began to use it to justify slavery and colonialism. Comte de Gobineau (1816–1882) argued that each race has specific characteristics, and he attributed the demise of societies to the mixing of the white race with other (inferior) races. His book *Essay on Inequality of the Human Races*, published in

1853–1855, earned him the title "father of modern racism." In 1899, the Brit-turned-German Houston Stewart Chamberlain ([1899] 1911) published an aristocratic, anti-Semitic work in which he argued that northern and western European populations, Teutonic in particular, were superior. He argued for racial purity, a theme the Nazis of the 1930s and 1940s adopted.

Looking through history, one can see many more examples of how racial categorizations have been misused across time and societies. For example, in the United States, Irish and Italians were once seen as distinct races that were clearly inferior to the white race. Clearly, racial categories are social, rather than biological, constructions.

In 1978, the United Nations, concerned about racial conflicts and discrimination based on scientifically inaccurate beliefs, issued a "Declaration on Race and Race Prejudice" prepared by a group of eminent scientists from around the world. This and similar statements by scientific groups point out the harmful effects of racist arguments, doctrines, and policies. The conclusion of their document upheld that (a) all people are born free and equal both in dignity and in rights, (b) racial prejudice impedes personal development, (c) conflicts (based on race) cost nations money and resources, and (d) racism foments international conflict. Racist doctrines lack any scientific basis, as all people belong to the same species and have descended from the same origin. In summary, problems arising from race relations are social, not biological, in origin. Differential treatments of groups based on "race" falsely claim a scientific basis for classifying humans.

Thinking Sociologically

How would you describe the other people in your sociology class? Do you use racial terms for everyone? Why or why not? How does your own racial background influence how much you notice the racial characteristics of others? Why?

Symbolic Interaction: The Social Construction of Race. Why are sociologists concerned about race as a concept when it has little scientific accuracy and is ill defined? The answer is its *social significance*. The social reality is that people's group membership can influence how they are treated by others and how they view themselves. Remember the *looking-glass self* concept—we see ourselves based on how we think others perceive us. Our self-concept can be greatly affected by whether or not we see ourselves as members of a dominant or minority racial group.

Strangely, we might be seen as part of a dominant group in one society and a minority group in another. For example, imagine it is 1970 and you have white parents, three white grandparents, and one black grandparent. Imagine, too, that no one would guess by your appearance that you had an ancestor who was not white. In South Africa, you would be treated as "Colored" (in between black and white). On the other hand, in many U.S. states, you would be defined as black. If you were in Brazil, you would be perceived as white (Kollack 2010).

In 1977, the U.S. Office of Management and Budget issued a directive to ensure consistent ethnic and racial categories for both statistical and administrative goals. Federal programs directed toward specific racial and ethnic groups use these categories. Many very different groups have been combined under the five government racial and ethnic categories (American Indian or Alaska Native, Asian or Pacific Islander, black, Hispanic, and white. Hispanic/Latino Americans are an ethnic group and can be of any race). For example, in North America, those racially classified as Native American or Alaska Native use 600 independent tribal nation names to identify themselves, including the Ojibwa (Chippewa), the Dineh (the Navajo), the Lakota (the Sioux), and many others. Most consider themselves very different from other "Native American" groups. Some even fought against one another in past wars. Likewise, in the U.S. Census, Koreans, Filipinos, Chinese, Japanese, and Malaysians are all identified as *Asian Americans*, but they come from very different cultures (including some that were mortal enemies). In addition, people from Brazil, Mexico, Cuba, and many other nations are grouped together in an ethnic category called *Hispanics* or *Latinos*, even though they do not think of themselves as being alike.

Before civil rights laws were passed in the United States in the 1960s, a number of states had laws that spelled out differential treatment for racial groups. These were commonly referred to as Jim Crow laws. States in the South passed laws defining who was African American or Native American. In many cases, it was difficult to determine to which category an individual belonged. For instance, African Americans in Georgia were defined as people with any ascertainable trace of "Negro" blood in their veins. In Missouri, 1/8 or more "Negro" blood was the standard, whereas in Louisiana, 1/32 Negro blood defined one as black. Differential treatment was spelled out in other states as well. In Texas, for example, the father's race determined the race of the child. Federal law now prohibits discrimination on the basis of "racial" classifications, and most state laws that are explicitly racial have been challenged and dropped, but race remains a social concept.

The Continuing Significance of Race. The civil rights legislation of the 1960s that prohibited racial discrimination in voting, housing, and employment has helped diminish discrimination. Unfortunately, though, racial discrimination still exists, and the combination of the impact of past and present discrimination has led to disparities in wealth and income among black, Hispanic, and white Americans. As Table 8.1 on page 204 makes clear, income levels for African Americans, Hispanics, and whites, even when controlling for education level, are still far apart. A clear racial economic hierarchy exists with white Americans on the top and other racial groups below. Differences in *wealth* (one's income, property, and total assets) by race are even more stark. For every dollar of wealth a white person has, Hispanic and black persons have just 7 and 6 cents,

TABLE 8.1   Income by Educational Level and Race/Ethnicity

Education	White	Black	Hispanic
Not a high school graduate	$20,457	$18,936	$19,816
High school graduate	31,429	26,970	25,998
Some college, no degree	33,119	29,129	29,836
College graduate	57,762	47,799	49,017
Master's degree	73,771	60,067	71,322
Professional degree	127,942	102,328	79,228

Source: U.S. Census Bureau 2012d.

respectively. So whites have roughly twenty times the wealth of blacks and Hispanics (Tippett et al. 2014).

As we described in Chapter 7, education is one of the key means of social mobility (despite the fact that even well-educated racial minorities make less than whites). While 52.4% of Asian Americans and 30.3% of white Americans 25 and older have a college education, only 19.8% of black and 13.9% of Hispanic Americans have college degrees (U.S. Census Bureau 2012a). This is clearly an area that must be addressed if we want to reduce racial economic inequality. Although explicit racial bias has decreased at the micro (interpersonal) level, it is still a significant determinant in the lives of African Americans, especially those in the lower class.

Thinking Sociologically

Were you aware of the race-based disparities in income and wealth? Why do you think income among races differs, even when controlling for education?

Ethnic Groups

Ethnic groups *are based on cultural factors: language, religion, dress, foods, customs, beliefs, values, norms, a shared group identity or feeling, and sometimes loyalty to a homeland, monarch, or religious leader.*

Members are grouped together because they share a common cultural heritage, often connected with a national or geographical identity. There can be many ethnic groups under one racial category (e.g., black Americans include African immigrants, West Indian immigrants, and African Americans). Visits to ethnic enclaves in large cities in the United States give a picture of ethnicity. Indian, Chinese, and Dominican neighborhoods may have non-English street signs and newspapers, ethnic restaurants, culture-specific houses of worship, and clothing styles that reflect the ethnic subculture.

As noted earlier, the U.S. government has combined many different ethnic and racial groups into singular racial and ethnic categories. When federal funds for social services were made available to Asian Americans or American Indians, these diverse people began to think of themselves as part of a larger

©iStockphoto.com/CaroleGomez

Ethnic enclaves can foster a strong sense of local community, hosting festivals from the old country and helping members develop networks in the new country. This photo depicts a street in San Francisco's Chinatown.

 The Difference Between Race and Ethnicity

grouping for political purposes (Esperitu 1992). The federal government essentially created an ethnic group by naming and providing funding to that group. If people wanted services (health care, legal rights, and so forth), they had to become a part of a particular group—such as "Asian Americans." This process of merging many ethnic groups into one broader category—called *panethnicity*—illustrates that ethnic and racial identity are socially shaped and created.

Census 2010 data show the ethnic ancestry of millions of Americans and their distribution across the United States. German ancestry makes up the largest group at almost 50 million, followed by African Americans at 41 million, Irish at 36 million, Mexicans at 32 million, and English at 30 million. (Note that if we include the panethnic category of Hispanic or Latino—which includes Mexicans and others from Latin America—they are the second largest group at 49.2 million.) Twenty million claim "American" as their ancestry. American Indians and Alaska Natives, the original Americans, make up about 5 million people (O'Connor, Lubin, and Spector 2013; U.S. Census Bureau 2013c).

Figure 8.2 shows where each ethnic group, by county, has the largest concentration, though this does not necessarily mean the group makes up more than 50% of the population of that county.

Biracial and Multiracial Populations: Immigration, Intermarriage, and Personal Identification

"Push" factors drive people from some countries and "pull" factors draw them to other countries. The most common push-pull factors today are job opportunities, the desire for security, individual liberties, and availability of medical and educational opportunities. The target countries of migrants are most often in North America, Australia, or Western Europe, and the highest emigration rates are from Africa, Eastern Europe, Central Asia, and South and Central America.

The United States was once considered to have a two-tiered racial hierarchy, black and white (which disregarded the Native American population). However, immigration into the United States from every continent has led to a more diverse population, with 13% of the current U.S. population born elsewhere (Grieco et al. 2012). With new immigration, increasing rates of intermarriage, and many more individuals claiming multiracial identification, the

FIGURE 8.2 Ancestry With Largest Population in Each County, 2010

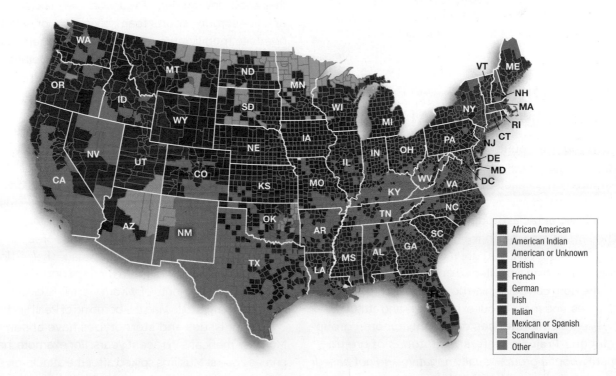

Legend:
- African American
- American Indian
- American or Unknown
- British
- French
- German
- Irish
- Italian
- Mexican or Spanish
- Scandinavian
- Other

Source: U.S. Census Bureau.

FIGURE 8.3   Percentage of the Population, by Race and Hispanic Origin: 1980-2060

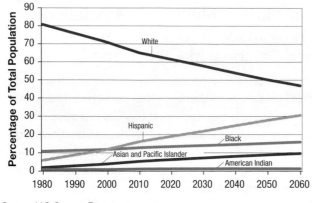

Source: U.S. Census Bureau 2014.

picture is much more complex today, and the color lines have been redrawn (DaCosta 2007; Lee and Bean 2004, 2007). In 2012, almost 1 in 5 Americans under 18 identified with two or more racial groups (Alpert 2013). Figure 8.3 illustrates the current ethnic group distribution and projections for the future for the United States.

Thinking Sociologically

Identify one dominant and one minority group in your community or on campus. Where does each group fit into the stratification system in the United States? How are the life chances of individuals in these groups influenced by factors beyond their control?

PREJUDICE: MICRO-LEVEL ANALYSIS

Have you ever found yourself in a situation in which you were viewed as different, strange, or undesirable? Perhaps you have felt the sting of rejection, not based on judgment of you as a person but solely because of the ethnic or racial group into which you were born. Then again, you may have been insulated from this type of rejection if you grew up in a homogeneous community or in a privileged group. Where and when we are born can determine how we are treated, our life chances, and many of our experiences and attitudes.

Prejudice influences dominant-minority group relations. **Prejudice** refers to *attitudes of prejudgment about a group, usually negative and not based on facts.* Prejudiced individuals lump together people

with certain characteristics without considering individual differences. Although prejudice can refer to positive attitudes and exaggerations (e.g., all Asians are good at math), in this chapter, we concentrate on the negative aspects of prejudice, and the concept of *stereotyping,* when prejudiced individuals use distorted, oversimplified, or exaggerated ideas to categorize a group of people and attribute personal qualities to them. While prejudice and stereotypes can be stimulated by events such as conflicts at the institutional level and war at the societal level, attitudes are held by individuals and can be best understood as a micro-level phenomenon.

Prejudice refers to attitudes rather than actions. **Discrimination,** on the other hand, is *differential treatment and harmful actions against minorities.* These actions at the micro level might include refusal to sell someone a house because of the religion, race, or ethnicity of the buyer or not hiring someone because of her or his minority status (Feagin and Feagin 2010). Discrimination in the legal system, such as laws that deny opportunities or resources to members of a particular group, operates largely at the meso or macro level, discussed later in this chapter.

The Nature of Prejudice

Prejudice is an understandable response of humans to their social environment. To survive, every social group or unit—sorority, sports team, civic club, or nation— needs to mobilize the loyalty of its members. Each organization needs to convince people to voluntarily commit energy, skills, time, and resources so the organization can meet its needs. As people commit themselves to a group, they invest a portion of themselves and feel loyalty to the group. This loyalty leads to a preference for the group and attempts to distinguish it from others. It is important to recognize prejudice, though, and how it can foster discriminatory actions.

In wartime, the enemy may be depicted in films or other media as villains. During World War II, American films often showed negative stereotypes of Japanese and German people. These negative images helped lead to the decision to intern more than 110,000 Japanese Americans, the majority of whom were U.S. citizens, in detention camps following the bombing of Pearl Harbor.

Similar issues and stereotypes have arisen for Muslim Americans in recent years. For example, hate crimes against Muslims spiked after the attacks on the New York World Trade Center on September 11, 2001,

After Japan bombed Pearl Harbor on December 7, 1941, more than 110,000 Japanese Americans, including those pictured here, were forcibly removed from many western states and sent to relocation camps.

and the Boston Marathon bombing on April 15, 2013 (Potok 2013b). Sociologist Saher Selod explains:

> The September 11, 2001, attacks claimed the lives of close to 3,000 Americans. The terrorists were Muslims from Saudi Arabia, United Arabs Emirates, and Egypt. These horrific events changed the lives of all Americans, including Muslim Americans and immigrants. Muslims have [since] become targets for antiterrorist laws and policies that were a part of a government-led campaign known as the "War on Terror" (Cainkar, 2009). According to a Gallup report, 43% of Americans admitted to feeling some prejudice towards Muslims, and 31% of Americans view Islam unfavorably (Gallup 2010). These rising anti-Muslim sentiments have had a direct impact on the everyday life of the Muslim population. (Selod 2016)

Explaining Racial Discrimination at the Micro Level

Why do individuals commit acts of racial discrimination? Why would people be so angry at racial minorities that they would act to harm them? The following is one theory that has attempted to explain acts of racial discrimination.

Frustration-Aggression Theory. In Greensboro, North Carolina, in 1978, a group of civil rights activists and

African American adults and children listened as a guitarist sang freedom songs. A nine-car cavalcade of white Ku Klux Klan (KKK) and American Nazi Party members arrived. The intruders unloaded weapons from the backs of their cars, approached the rally, and opened fire for 88 seconds. They left as calmly as they had arrived. Four white men and a black woman were dead (Greensboro Justice Fund 2005). According to *frustration-aggression theory*, many of the perpetrators of this and other heinous acts felt angry and frustrated because they could not achieve their work or other goals, and blamed others for their failures. Frustration-aggression theory focuses largely on poorly adjusted people who express their frustration through aggressive attacks on others.

When they cannot take out their aggression on its source and turn it on innocent victims, they are *scapegoating*. The word *scapegoat* comes from the Bible, Leviticus 16:5–22. Once a year, a goat (which was obviously innocent) was laden with parchments on which people had written their sins. The goat was then sent out to the desert to die. This was part of a ritual of purification, and the creature took the blame for the sins committed by the people. Scapegoating occurs when a minority group is blamed for the failures of others. It is often difficult to look at oneself to seek reasons for failure but easy to transfer the blame for one's failure to others. Individuals who feel they are failures in their jobs or other aspects of their lives may turn the blame toward minority groups. From within such a prejudiced mind-set, violence toward the out-group may seem acceptable. The key point is that hate groups evolve from like-minded individuals, often because of prejudice and frustration (see Figure 8.4 on page 208).

Although frustration-aggression theory can shed light on the most extreme cases of individual or small-group prejudice and racism, there is much this theory does not explain. It says little about the everyday hostility and reinforcement of prejudice that most of us experience or engage in, and it fails to deal with discrimination embedded in institutions.

Forms of Racial Prejudice

Hate groups in the United States, Europe, and many other countries justify themselves on the basis of bigoted thinking. A bigot is someone who blindly insists that certain other people are so different that they are inferior—even, perhaps, less than human. They loudly proclaim that those outside their racial or ethnic group deserve to face discrimination.

Difference Between Prejudice and Discrimination

FIGURE 8.4 Active Hate Groups in 2013

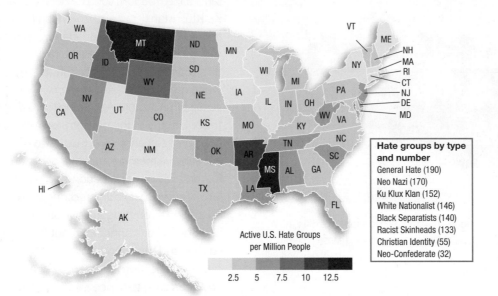

Hate groups by type and number
General Hate (190)
Neo Nazi (170)
Ku Klux Klan (152)
White Nationalist (146)
Black Separatists (140)
Racist Skinheads (133)
Christian Identity (55)
Neo-Confederate (32)

Active U.S. Hate Groups per Million People

2.5   5   7.5   10   12.5

Source: Active Hate Groups in the U.S., 2012 is reprinted with permission and originally appeared in *The Atlantic—The Geography of Hate* by Richard Florida, May 2011. Map by Zara Matheson, Martin Prosperity Institute.

Many other people are not bigoted, but simply oblivious to racial inequality and the hidden privileges that whites experience in U.S. society. They do not want to hear about the realities of racial inequality. In fact, they maintain that race no longer matters. A racial ideology that grew out of opposition to affirmative action programs in the 1980s, the *color-blind ideology* is now the dominant racial ideology in the United States (Bonilla-Silva 2009; Brunsma 2006; Korgen and Brunsma 2012). Promoters of the color-blind ideology maintain that we should all act as though we are "color-blind" when it comes to race and avoid the topic in personal interactions.

In an award-winning book, white sociologist Joe Feagin has analyzed how the "white frame"—the lens through which whites view history and understand everyday life—shapes what white people see. He documents the many ways that lens is so much a part of the socialization process that it is like water to fish—it is the unnoticed, unconscious environment in which we live. Unfortunately this frame involves assumptions that reinforce images, ideologies, interpretations, narratives, and emotional triggers that sustain white privilege. It in fact blinds white people to subtle realities so that it is entirely impossible for them to actually be color-blind (Feagin 2012). Further, for many people, their blackness or brownness is so integral to their identity that to say one is "color-blind" is to

fail to see the whole person. They feel they are being made invisible and forced to be part of the mainstream culture—to be assimilated (Dalton 2012; Dyer 2012; Feagin 2012).

Those who have a color-blind perspective on race do not notice the fact that whites in U.S. society have many "invisible" or nonobvious privileges (Rothenberg 2011). Consider the following privileges that most people who are part of the dominant group take for granted (McIntosh 2002:97–101):

- I can avoid spending time with people who mistrust people of my color.
- I can protect my children most of the time from people who might not like them.
- I can criticize our government and talk about how I fear its policies and behavior without being seen as a cultural "outsider" or not patriotic.
- I can easily buy posters, postcards, picture books, greeting cards, dolls, toys, and children's magazines featuring people of my race.
- I can arrange my activities so that I will never have to experience feelings of rejection owing to my race.

Thinking Sociologically

What is your reaction to this list? How does your own racial and ethnic background influence your reaction?

The color-blind perspective on race allows discrimination hidden within the society's institutions to remain in place. Advocates of the color-blind racial ideology reject blatant bigotry as crude and ignorant, but fail to recognize that their own actions may perpetuate inequalities at the institutional or meso level, discussed below. Note that many people without social science training see racism as just a micro-level issue—one involving individual actions or attitudes—whereas social scientists recognize racial discrimination in meso-level organizations and macro-level policies or laws as the very core of the problem of racism (Bonilla-Silva 2003).

DISCRIMINATION: MESO-LEVEL ANALYSIS

Dear Teacher, I would like to introduce you to my son, Wind-Wolf. He is probably what you would consider a typical Indian kid. He was born and raised on the reservation. He has black hair, dark brown eyes, and an olive complexion, and, like so many Indian children his age, he is shy and quiet in the classroom. He is 5 years old, in kindergarten, and I can't understand why you have already labeled him a "slow learner." He has already been through quite an education compared with his peers in Western society. He was bonded to his mother and to the Mother Earth in a traditional native childbirth ceremony. And he has been continuously cared for by his mother, father, sisters, cousins, aunts, uncles, grandparents, and extended tribal family since this ceremony. . . .

Wind-Wolf was strapped (in his baby basket like a turtle shell) snugly with a deliberate restriction on his arms and legs. Although Western society may argue this hinders motor-skill development and abstract reasoning, we believe it forces the child to first develop his intuitive faculties, rational intellect, symbolic thinking, and five senses. Wind-Wolf was with his mother constantly, closely bonded physically, as she carried him on her back or held him while breast-feeding. She carried him everywhere she went, and every night he slept with both parents. Because of this, Wind-Wolf's educational setting was not only a "secure"

A neo-Nazi protester makes a white power salute at the opening ceremony for the Illinois Holocaust Museum and Education Center in Skokie, Illinois, in 2009. The group of protesters chanted epithets expressing their hatred of Jews and other minority groups.

environment, but it was also very colorful, complicated, sensitive, and diverse.

As he grew older, Wind-Wolf began to crawl out of the baby basket, develop his motor skills, and explore the world around him. When frightened or sleepy, he could always return to the basket, as a turtle withdraws into its shell. Such an inward journey allows one to reflect in privacy on what he has learned and to carry the new knowledge deeply into the unconscious and the soul. Shapes, sizes, colors, texture, sound, smell, feeling, taste, and the learning process are therefore functionally integrated—the physical and spiritual, matter and energy, and conscious and unconscious, individual and social.

Racism in Schools

It takes a long time to absorb and reflect on these kinds of experiences, so maybe that is why you think my Indian child is a slow learner. His aunts and grandmothers taught him to count and to know his numbers while they sorted materials for making abstract designs in native baskets. And he was taught to learn mathematics by counting the sticks we use in our traditional native hand game. So he may be slow in grasping the methods and tools you use in your classroom, ones quite familiar to his white peers, but I hope you will be patient with him. It takes time to adjust to a new cultural system and learn new things. He is not culturally "disadvantaged," but he is culturally different. (Lake 1990:48–53)

Reprinted by permission of Medicine Grizzly Bear Lake, www.native healer.net

This letter expresses the frustration of a father who sees his son being labeled and discriminated against by the school system without being given a chance. *Discrimination*, introduced earlier in this chapter, refers to differential treatment and harmful actions taken against members of a minority group. It can occur at individual and small-group levels but is particularly problematic at the organizational and institutional levels—the meso level of analysis.

Thinking Sociologically

How might schools unintentionally misunderstand Wind-Wolf and other minority children in ways that have negative consequences for children's success? What might be some negative consequences of this misunderstanding?

Institutional racial discrimination is *any meso-level institutional arrangement that favors one racial group over another*; this favoritism may result in intentional or unintentional consequences for minority groups (Farley 2011). This form of discrimination results from the normal or routine part of the way an organization operates that systemically disadvantages members of one group. It can include intentional actions, such as laws restricting minorities, as well as unintentional actions that have consequences restricting minorities. Jim Crow laws, passed in the late 1800s in the United States, and laws that barred

Jews in Germany from living, working, or investing in certain places are examples of intentional discrimination embedded in organizations.

Often, though, institutional racial discrimination is done quite unintentionally. For example, in some states, local funding of schools leads to schools with racial minorities receiving fewer funds than most predominantly white schools. This type of funding policy can be supported by nonracists who simply want local control over schools. Whether intended or not, though, such a policy benefits a particular race at the expense of others. As you can see, racial discrimination does not have to be the result of a nasty or mean-spirited person bullying others; it often operates independently of prejudice (Bonilla-Silva 2003; Rothenberg 2011).

Side-effect discrimination and past-in-present discrimination are the two main types of unintentional institutional discrimination (Feagin and Feagin 1986; Rydgren 2004). **Side-effect discrimination** *refers to practices in one institutional area that have a negative impact because they are linked to practices in another institutional area; because institutions are interdependent, discrimination in one results in unintentional discrimination in others.* Figure 8.5 illustrates this idea. Each institution uses information from the other institutions to make decisions. So, discrimination in one can lead to discrimination in others.

Side-effect discrimination occurs when discrimination in the criminal justice system leads to discrimination in the employment sector. For example, in an interview conducted by one of the authors, a probation officer in a moderate-sized city in Ohio said that he had never seen an African American in his county get a not-guilty verdict and that he was not sure it was possible. He had known of cases in which minorities had pled guilty to a lesser charge even though they were innocent because they did not think they could receive a fair verdict in that city. When people apply for jobs, however, they are required to report the conviction on the application form. Employers discriminate against applicants with a criminal record, whether or not the applicant was guilty of the crime. The side-effect discrimination is *unintentional discrimination*; the criminal justice system has reached an unjust verdict, and the potential employer is swayed unfairly.

A second example of side-effect discrimination shows that the Internet also plays a role in institutionalized discrimination and privilege. For example, in

FIGURE 8.5 Side-Effect Discrimination

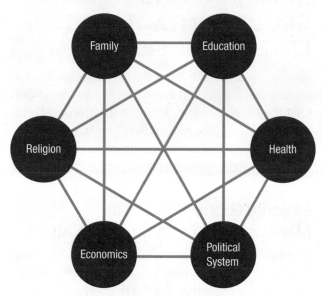

Each circle represents a different institution—family, education, religion, health, political-legal system, and economics. These meso-level systems are interdependent, using information or resources from the others. If discrimination occurs in one institution, the second institution may unintentionally borrow information or practices that result in discrimination. In this way, discrimination occurs at the meso level without awareness by individuals at the micro level.

Children play on the porch of their rustic home with no plumbing in the rural Alaska village of Akhiok, among the Aleutian Islands. Finding jobs through the Internet is not an option from this location.

Alaska, 15.2% of the population is Native, but Natives hold only 5% of state jobs, and 27.3% of Native men and 16% of Native women are unemployed (AAANativeArts 2011; U.S. Census Bureau 2011). Consider that the State of Alaska uses the Internet as its primary means of advertising and accepting applications for state jobs (State of Alaska 2006). In the early 2000s, Internet access was unavailable in the 164 predominantly Native villages in Alaska—a state so large and spread out that it is 2.2 times the size of Texas and has only 1.2 people per square mile (Denali Commission 2001; Hudson 2011). Although efforts have been made in recent years to expand Internet access, Alaska remains far behind other states in communications access, with less than half of Alaskan villages having Internet facility in 2012 (Hudson 2011, 2012).

Other options for application for state jobs include requesting applications by mail, but a person must first know about the opening. Moreover the usefulness of this process is limited by the reliability and speed of mail service to remote villages and the often short application periods for state jobs. State officials may not intentionally try to prevent Aleuts, Inupiats, Athabaskans, or other Alaska Natives from gaining access to state jobs, but the effect can be institutionalized discrimination. Here, Internet access plays a role in the participation of minorities in the social world (Nakamura 2004).

The point is that whites, especially affluent whites, benefit from privileges not available to low-income minorities. The privileged members may not purposely disadvantage others and may not be prejudiced, but the playing field is not level. The discrimination may be completely unintentional (Rothenberg 2011).

Thinking Sociologically

Imagine you run a business that is hiring people. You routinely do a criminal background check on applicants. You have just read this chapter and realize that some of that information may be a source of unintended side-effect discrimination for a minority group member. What will you do now? Why?

Past-in-present discrimination refers to *practices from the past that may no longer be allowed but that continue to have consequences for people in the present* (Feagin and Feagin 1986; Verbeek and Penninx 2009). Examples of this abound if you dig deep enough. For example, in Mississippi, during the 1950s, state expenditures to educate a white child averaged $147 per pupil, whereas the average was $34 per black pupil in segregated schools (Luhman and Gilman 1980). Such blatant segregation and inequality in use of tax dollars is no longer legal. This may seem like ancient history, yet some African Americans who were in school in the 1950s and 1960s are receiving low Social Security checks because their earning power was diminished due to their poor schooling. Today, they cannot help pay for their grandchildren to go to college. To those who received a substandard education and did not have an opportunity for college, this is not ancient history; it affects their opportunities today.

Another example can be seen in the economic inequality between whites and blacks. The great disparity in wealth between white and black Americans relates to the legal discrimination many generations of black Americans experienced that stymied efforts to amass and pass down wealth to future generations. Events from the past continue to echo into our current times, creating barriers for some citizens and clear paths for others. The next "Engaging Sociology" feature explores how discrimination can occur at different levels and in intentional or unintentional ways.

In the United States, we have a president who had both a black and a white parent. It is also true, as Table 8.2 indicates, that only two senators (out of 100) are black in the 2015–2016 Congress.

We have also seen in Table 8.1 on page 204 that college-educated African Americans earn $10,000 per year less than white college graduates. Whites with a professional degree earn, on average, $128,000 per year ($25,000 per year more than blacks with the same degree), while Hispanics with the same degree earn, on average, $79,000 (U.S. Census Bureau 2012a). This means that over a 40-year career, whites could earn $1 million more than blacks and nearly $2 million more than Hispanics with the same degree credentials. African Americans and other minorities also continue to have higher unemployment than whites. As long as these and other examples of discrimination exist, we must acknowledge and take steps to address racial inequality.

Thinking Sociologically

How do the different types of discrimination, as discussed above, help us understand world conflicts, such as the intense hostility between Palestinians and Jews in Israel? Explain.

DOMINANT AND MINORITY GROUP CONTACT: MACRO-LEVEL ANALYSIS

Meso-level analysis is essential to understanding the primary issues of racism in contemporary Global North countries, but ultimately the tone for interracial relationships is set at the macro level. The first question is how those in power decide to structure relationships between racial and ethnic groups.

Majority Group Policies to Manage Racial and Ethnic Relations

Dominant-minority relations depend on the time, place, and circumstances. However, majority groups tend to structure or manage the majority and minority relationships with one of five policies.

Genocide is *the systematic effort of one group, usually the dominant group, to destroy a minority group.* Examples of race- and ethnicity-based genocide exist throughout history. In the thirteenth century, Mongols under Genghis Khan (named Temüjin at birth) destroyed entire nations in their path. Germany's Adolf Hitler sent Jews, Gypsies, and other non-Aryan groups into concentration camps to be gassed in the 1930s and 1940s. In Rwanda, in the mid-1990s, members of the Hutu tribe committed mass murders of people from the Tutsi tribe. More recently, the terrorist group ISIS tried to wipe out the Yazidis, a religious minority group, in Iraq. Genocide has existed at many points in history, and it still exists today. These examples illustrate the lethal consequences of racism, one group at the meso level systematically killing off another, often a minority, to gain or secure control and power.

Subjugation refers to *the subordination of one group to another that holds power and authority.* Haiti and the Dominican Republic are two countries

TABLE 8.2 Representation in the U.S. Congress, 2015–2016

	Native American	Asian	Black	Hispanic
Senate	0	1 (1%)	2 (2%)	4 (4%)
House	2 (0.5%)	12 (2.7%)	43 (10%)	33 (7.5%)
% of Population	0.9%	4.8%	12.6%	16.3%

Source: Manning 2014.

ENGAGING SOCIOLOGY

Using and Relating Key Concepts

Figure 8.6 indicates the levels at which discrimination can operate and how such acts can be intended or unintended.

FIGURE 8.6   Understanding Key Concepts

	Micro Level	Meso and Macro Level
Conscious and Intended	*Prejudice and individual acts of direct discrimination*	*Direct institutional discrimination*
Unconscious and Unintended	*Color-blind perspective*	*Indirect institutional discrimination* Side-effect discrimination Past-in-present discrimination

Engaging With Sociology

1. Define and give an example of the term(s) or concept(s) in each box above.

2. Identify ways that each of these elements of intergroup conflict might foster the others.

3. Describe how you might take steps to counter each of the various types of discrimination.

---

sharing the island of Hispaniola in the Caribbean. Because many Haitians are poor, they are lured by promises of jobs in the sugarcane fields of the Dominican Republic. However, many are forced to work long hours for little pay and not allowed to leave until they have paid for their housing and food, which may be impossible to do on their low wages.

Slavery is one form of subjugation that has existed throughout history. When the Roman Empire defeated other lands, the captives became slaves. This included ancient Greeks, who also kept slaves at various times in their history. African tribes enslaved members of neighboring tribes, sometimes selling them to slave traders, and slavery has existed in Middle Eastern countries such as Saudi Arabia. As mentioned in the opening story for this chapter, with "in Chapter 7," slavery is flourishing in many parts of the world today (Bales 2000, 2007, 2012).

Segregation, a specific form of subjugation, separates minorities from the dominant group and deprives them of access to the dominant institutions. Jim Crow laws, instituted in the southern United States after the

National Archives and Records Administration

One of the most horrific results of discriminatory racial or ethnic policies was the Holocaust, the murder of 11 million people, including 6 million Jews, by the Nazi government in Germany under Adolf Hitler. This photo is difficult to view, but this is the consequence of bigotry that leads to genocide.

Civil War, legislated separation between racial groups—separate facilities, schools, and neighborhoods

(Alexander 2010; Feagin and Feagin 2010; Massey and Denton 1998).

Population transfer refers to *the removal, often forced, of a minority group from a region or country.* Generally, the dominant group wants land, or resources. For example, Native Americans in the United States were removed to reservations. The Cherokee people were forced to walk from Georgia and North Carolina to new lands west of the Mississippi—a "Trail of Tears" along which 40% of the people perished—so that whites in these states could have access to Cherokee land. As noted above, during World War II, Japanese Americans were forcibly moved to "relocation centers" and had their land and property confiscated.

Assimilation refers to *the structural and cultural merging of minority and majority groups in society.* It is often a voluntary process during which members of minority groups choose to adopt the values, norms, and institutions of the dominant group. Assimilation is more likely to occur when the minority group is culturally similar to the dominant group. For instance, in the United States, the closer a group is to being white and English speaking, the faster its members will be assimilated into the dominant group, adopting the culture and blending in biologically through intermarriage. While some assimilation happens naturally when different groups interact in housing, schooling, employment, political circles, family groups, friendship, and social relationships, some assimilation policies in certain times and places have forced ethnic minorities to change their cultural attributes (e.g., language, religion, or style of eating) in order to avoid ridicule or even death (Marger 2012).

Forced assimilation occurs when members of a minority group are compelled to suppress their cultural identity. For example, in the late 1800s and early 1900s, Native American children were forced to leave their families and go to white-run boarding schools. There, they had to cut their hair, attend Christian religious services, dress as whites did, and speak only in English.

Pluralism occurs when *each ethnic or racial group in a country maintains its own culture and separate set of institutions, but has recognized equality in the society.* For example, Switzerland has four dominant cultural language groups: French, German, Italian, and Romansh (or Rumantsch). The government and schools use and teach all of these official languages. Each group respects the rights of the other groups to maintain a distinctive language and way of life. In Malaysia, three groups share power—Malays, Chinese, and Indians. Although the balance is not completely stable because Chinese and Indians have higher levels of education and hold more political and economic power than the native Malays, most Malaysians want to maintain a pluralistic society. While tensions do exist in both nations, both Switzerland and Malaysia represent examples of pluralist societies. Legal protection of smaller or less powerful groups is often necessary to have pluralism. In the United States, religious pluralism (at least among religions practiced by white Americans), as a policy, was embraced by the nation's first president, George Washington.

The five policies toward minorities are summarized in Figure 8.7.

Thinking Sociologically

Think of examples from current news stories of positive and harmful intercultural contact. Where do your examples fit on the continuum from genocide to pluralism? What is your reaction to each? How do your experiences of intercultural contact influence your reaction to these examples?

Minority Reactions to Prejudice, Discrimination, and Racism

How have minority groups dealt with their status? Five different reactions are common: assimilation,

FIGURE 8.7 Types of Dominant-Minority Group Relations

Most Hostile to "Minorities"				Most Accepting of "Minorities"
Genocide	**Subjugation**	**Population Transfer**	**Assimilation**	**Pluralism**
Extermination of minorities	Oppression, slavery	Removal to new location	Cultural blending of groups	Groups share in legitimacy and power

Discrimination

The picture of a U.S. McDonald's (left) helps illustrate that the United States is a pluralistic society. The "McDonald's" on this sign is in the Hmong language. This pluralism is very long-standing in the United States. After George Washington was elected president of the new nation, he received a letter from a Jewish congregation in Newport, Rhode Island (right), asking about his policies on pluralism or multiculturalism (though those words had not been coined yet). In response in 1790, Touro Synagogue—the oldest synagogue in the country—received a handwritten letter signed by President Washington (now proudly on display at the synagogue) embracing an open and "liberal" policy to all American citizens, regardless of origin or religious affiliation.

acceptance, avoidance, aggression, and change-oriented actions directed at the social structure. The first four are micro-level responses; they do not address the meso- and macro-level issues.

Micro-Level Coping Strategies. Assimilation involves blending into the dominant culture. *Passing*, a form of assimilation, is one means of avoiding the prejudice and discrimination associated with minority group membership. Some minority group members, if their appearance allows them to do so, attempt to *pass* as members of the dominant group. This strategy usually involves abandoning their own culture and turning their back on family roots and community ties, an often costly strategy in terms of self-esteem. This often severs them from a part of their identity, so the personal cost of assimilation can be high. People who select this coping strategy must deny their minority background and live with the fear that it will be exposed.

Acceptance is another reaction to minority status. Some members of minority groups have learned to live with their minority status and do not challenge the system. They may or may not hold deep-seated hostility, but they ultimately conclude that change in the society is not very likely, and acceptance of their situation may be the rational means to survive within the existing system.

There are many possible explanations for acceptance. For example, religious beliefs allow poor Hindus in India to believe that if they accept their lot in life, they will be reincarnated in a higher life-form. If they rebel, they can expect to be reincarnated into a lower life-form. Their religion is a form of social control. In other cases, members of minority groups believe that they are, in fact, inferior and should be treated that way. Socialized in a society that treats them as second-class citizens, they begin to accept this image of themselves. Others may simply fear the negative consequences of refusing to accept their minority status.

Avoidance entails coping with minority group status through shunning all contact with the dominant group. This can involve an active and organized attempt to leave the culture or live separately as some political exiles have done. For example, in the United States, Marcus Garvey organized a Back-to-Africa movement in the 1920s, encouraging blacks to give up on any hope of justice in American society and to return to Africa. Today, some Native Americans on reservations avoid contact with other Americans and do all they can to live as their ancestors once did—before the intrusion of white people onto their land. For example, among some groups of isolated Apaches in New Mexico and Arizona, nearly half of

"My Nority" Spoken Word Poem

the older population speaks no English and has no need or desire to learn it. They live according to traditional cultural ways in rather isolated desert climates (Farrer 2011).

Aggression resulting from anger and resentment over minority status and from subjugation may lead to retaliation or violence. Direct confrontation can be very costly to those lacking political or economic power. Thus, aggression often takes one of two forms, indirect aggression or displaced aggression. Indirect aggression includes biting assertiveness in the arts—literature, art, racial and ethnic humor, and music—and in job-related actions such as inefficiency and slowdowns by workers. Displaced aggression, on the other hand, involves hostilities directed toward individuals or groups other than the dominant group, such as happens when youth gangs attack other ethnic or racial gangs in nearby neighborhoods. They substitute aggression against the dominant group by acting out against other minority groups. The arts can represent indirect aggression or efforts toward social change.

The four responses discussed thus far address the angst and humiliation that individual minorities feel. Each strategy allows an individual to try to cope, but none addresses the structural causes of discrimination. The final strategy involves *change-oriented action*.

Meso- and Macro-Level Efforts to Bring About Change: Resistance. Passing, acceptance, and

The Penumbra Theatre in St. Paul, Minnesota, uses the performing arts to promote social change. It fosters laughter at socially absurd norms and ideas, often a form of biting commentary. As the theater company tells the story of African Americans in the United States, the performers carry out their mission to use theater to "teach, criticize, comment, and model."

avoidance are forms of adaptation to the existing structures. Aggression, if not used strategically, can also work to support the status quo by creating opposition to changes that would help the minority group. Yet rather than accepting the current system and adapting to it, minority groups may choose strategic resistance. Resistance to the white framing of what life is like in the United States can take place through offering positive definitions of one's racial or ethnic group and preserving pride in one's culture (Feagin 2012). This is what was at work in the "black is beautiful" theme that emerged early in the civil rights movement. That movement led to more books and films that relate the stories of courage, stamina, and contribution by minority groups. These media images provide a challenge and an alternative to those developed through the white perceptions of minority groups and U.S. history.

Efforts to change cultural attitudes toward minority groups have been complemented by work within the legal system to challenge unjust laws. The National Association for the Advancement of Colored People (NAACP) sought to bring about legal changes through lawsuits that created new legal precedents supporting racial equality. Often, these lawsuits addressed side-effect discrimination—a meso-level problem. Many other associations for minorities—including the Anti-Defamation League (founded by Jewish leaders) and La Raza Unida (a Mexican American organization)—also seek to address problems both within organizations and institutions (meso level) and in the nation as a whole (macro level).

One of the most important efforts to bring change in the United States has been nonviolent resistance. The model for nonviolent resistance by minority groups comes from Mahatma Gandhi who, from 1915 to 1947, led the struggle for India's independence from Britain. Although Britain clearly had superior weapons and armies, Indian boycotts, sit-ins, and other forms of resistance eventually led to British withdrawal as the ruling colonial power. This strategy has been used by workers and students to bring about change in many parts of the world.

In the United States, Martin Luther King Jr. followed in the nonviolent resistance tradition of Gandhi. King's strategy involved nonviolent popular protests, economic boycotts, and other challenges to racially discriminatory norms of the society. His nonviolent disruptive efforts brought attention to the plight of black

▶ Are People Willing to Fix Racism? A Social Experiment

Mahatma Gandhi, leader of the Indian civil disobedience revolt, led nonviolent protests against unjust laws such as a march to collect salt, an illegal act.

people in the United States and created the political pressure needed to pass the civil rights legislation of the 1960s.

King (who majored in sociology in college) and many other public sociologists (e.g., W. E. B. Du Bois) have used their training to address issues of discrimination through empowerment and change. Their efforts to strategically counter the power of the dominant group have helped create a more equitable society for all residents of the United States.

⬤ Thinking Sociologically

The preceding discussion presents five types of responses by minorities to the experience of discrimination and rejection. Four of these are at the micro level, and one is at the meso and macro levels. Why do you think most of the coping strategies of minorities are at the micro level?

Theoretical Explanations of Dominant-Minority Group Relations

Dominant-minority group relations take place on the micro, meso, and macro levels. Therefore, we must utilize a wide variety of theoretical perspectives in order to fully understand these types of group interactions. For example, psychological and social-psychological theories are most relevant when examining prejudice in individuals and small groups. To understand discrimination embedded in institutions, studying meso-level organizations is helpful, and to understand the pervasive nature of prejudice and stereotypes over time in various societies, cultural explanations are useful. Finally, we must turn to macro-level theories to understand national and global group relations.

Structural-Functional Theory. Some functionalists point out that prejudice, discrimination, and institutional racism are dysfunctional for society, resulting in loss of human resources, costs to societies due to poverty and crime, hostilities between groups, and disrespect for those in power. For example, Durkheim divided social inequalities into *internal* (based on people's natural abilities) and *external* (those forced upon people). He argued that the existence of *external inequality* in an industrial society indicates that its institutions are not functioning properly. Because an industrial society needs all its members doing what they do best in order for it to function most effectively, external inequality—like racial discrimination—that prevents some people from fulfilling their innate talents damages all of society. Prejudice, discrimination, and institutional racism, then, are dysfunctional for society, resulting in loss of human resources, costs to societies due to poverty and crime, hostilities between groups, and disrespect for those in power (Schaefer 2012).

However, other functionalists note that maintaining a cheap pool of laborers (e.g., members of a minority group) who are in and out of work serves several purposes for society. Not only does this minority group function to provide a ready labor force for dirty work or menial unskilled jobs, but these laborers also serve other functions for society. Having minority groups makes possible occupations that service the poor, such as social work, public health, criminology, and the justice and legal systems. The oppressed buy goods others do not want—day-old bread, old fruits and vegetables, and secondhand clothes (Gans 1971, 1994). In short, having a supply of people in desperate need at the bottom of the social structure, according to some analysts, has some useful functional aspects, and this makes change more difficult.

Conflict Theory. Conflict theorists argue that creating a less powerful group protects the dominant group's advantages. Because privileges and resources are usually limited, those who have them want to keep them. One strategy used by privileged people, according to conflict theory, is to perpetrate prejudice and discrimination against minority group members. For example, in the 1840s, as the United States set out to build a transcontinental railroad, large numbers of laborers emigrated from China to do the hard manual work. When the railroad was completed and competition for jobs became intense, the once-welcomed Chinese became targets of bitter prejudice, discrimination, and sometimes violence. Members of these minority groups banded together in towns or cities for protection, founding the Chinatowns we know today (Kitano, Aqbayani, and de Anda 2005). Non-Chinese Asian groups suffered discrimination as well, because the bigoted generalizations were applied to all Asians (Winders 2004).

Karl Marx argued that exploitation of the lower classes is built into capitalism because it benefits the ruling class. Unemployment creates a ready pool of labor to fill the marginal jobs, with the pool often made up of identifiable minority groups. This pool allows people to remain in their higher-level positions and prevents others from moving up in the stratification system and threatening their jobs. Three critical factors contribute to animosity between groups, according to one conflict theorist (Noel 1968): First, if two groups of people can each be identified by their appearance, clothing, or language, then "us" versus "them" thinking and ethnocentrism may develop. However, this by itself does not mean there will be long-term hostility between the groups. Second, if the two groups conflict over scarce resources that both want, hostilities are very likely to arise. The resources might be the best land or cattle, the highest-paying jobs, access to the best schools for one's children, energy resources such as oil, or positions of prestige and power. If the third element is added to the mix—one group having much more power than the other—then intense dislike between the two groups and misrepresentation of each group by the other is fairly certain to occur.

The group with more power uses that power to ensure that its members (and their offspring) get the most valued resources. However, because they do not want to see themselves as unfair and brutish people, they develop stereotypes and derogatory characterizations of "those other people" so that it seems reasonable and justified not to give "them" access to the valued resources. Discrimination (often at the macro level) comes first, and bigoted ideology comes later to justify the discrimination (Noel 1968). Thus, macro- and meso-level conflicts can lead to micro-level attitudes.

Split labor market theory, a branch of conflict theory, characterizes the labor market as having two main types of jobs. The primary market involves clean jobs, largely in supervisory roles, and provides high salaries and good advancement possibilities, whereas the secondary market involves undesirable, hard, and dirty work, compensated with low hourly wages and few benefits or career opportunities. Competition for lesser jobs pits minorities against each other and low-income whites against minorities. By encouraging division and focusing antagonism between worker groups, employers reduce threats to their dominance and get cheaper labor in the process. Workers do not organize against employers who use this dual system because they are distracted by the antagonisms that build up among themselves—hence, the *split labor market* (Bonacich 1972, 1976). This theory maintains that competition, prejudice, and ethnic animosity serve the interests of the powerful owners of capital because that atmosphere keeps the laboring classes from uniting.

Conflict theory has taught us a great deal about racial and ethnic stratification. However, conflict theorists often focus on people with power quite intentionally oppressing others to protect their own self-interests. They often depict the dominant group as made up of nasty, power-hungry people. As we have seen in the meso-level discussion of side-effect and past-in-present discrimination, racial discrimination is often subtle and unconscious and can continue even without conscious ill will among those in the dominant group.

Thinking Sociologically

Do you think the split labor market perspective is useful when examining the racial and ethnic hierarchy in the United States? Why or why not? Can you see any evidence on your campus or in your local community to support the split labor theorists' view of racial and ethnic stratification?

POLICIES GOVERNING MINORITY AND DOMINANT GROUP RELATIONS

The dominant ethnic group in northern Sudan is Arabs—led by President Omar al-Bashir and his armies. In South Sudan, a newly formed country, the citizens are dark-skinned Africans who have a very different culture. Until a tenuous peace was brokered by the United Nations, the southern Sudanese people were tortured and killed and their villages burned by the more powerful northern Sudanese. While the hope was that the new border would separate warring factions, skirmishes continue to threaten the peace. In this case, macro-level policies from the United Nations and world powers intervened to stop the atrocities, but this has not eliminated the meso-level causes of conflict—ethnic differences and resources such as land and oil reserves. Remember that conflict over resources is usually the cause of animosity between groups.

War, famine, and economic dislocation force families to migrate to new locations where they can survive and perhaps improve their circumstances. Refugees may end up in a new country, perhaps on a new continent. The degree of acceptance children and their families find in their newly adopted countries varies depending on the government's policies, the group's background, economic conditions in the host country, and whether the refugee group poses a threat to residents (Rumbaut and Portes 2001). Some formerly refugee-friendly countries are closing their doors to immigration because of the strain on their economy and threats of terrorism. In this section, we consider policies that can reduce conflict when dominant and minority groups come into contact and interact.

Policies to Reduce Prejudice, Racism, and Discrimination

In the preceding pages, we considered some of the costs to individuals, groups, societies, and the global community inflicted by discriminatory behavior and policies. Discrimination's influence is widespread, from slavery and subjugation to unequal opportunities in education, work and political arenas, and every other part of the social world. If one accepts the premise that discrimination is destructive to both individuals and societies, then ways must be found to address the root problems effectively.

From our social world perspective, we know that no problem can be solved by working at only one level of analysis. A successful strategy must bring about change at every level of the social world—individual attitudes, organizational discrimination, cultural stereotypes, societal stratification systems, and national and international structures. However, most current strategies focus on only one level of analysis. Figure 8.8 shows some of the programs enacted to combat prejudice, racism, and discrimination at the individual, group, societal, and global levels.

Individual or Small-Group Solutions. Programs to address prejudice and stereotypes through human relations workshops, and group encounters, can achieve goals at the micro level. Two groups with strong multicultural education programs are the Anti-Defamation League and the Southern Poverty Law Center's Teaching Tolerance program. Both groups provide schools and community organizations with literature, videos, and other materials aimed at combating intolerance and discrimination toward others. Schools can also create interracial friendship opportunities with racially integrated classrooms where

FIGURE 8.8   Problems and Solutions

Types of Problems at Each Level	Types of Solutions or Programs at Each Level
Individual level: stereotypes and prejudice	Therapy, tolerance-education programs
Group level: negative group interaction	Positive contact, awareness by majority of their many privileges
Societal level: institutionalized discrimination	Education, media, legal-system revisions
Global level: deprivation of human rights	Human rights movements, international political pressures

▶ Racial Inequalities in the Justice System   ▣ Racism on the Rise?

The photo above shows a section of the wall built to keep undocumented immigrants from crossing the U.S.-Mexico border and entering the United States. Some believe that walls of this sort foster "us" versus "them" thinking.

students of different racial and ethnic backgrounds interact regularly (Cheng and Xie 2013; Ellison and Powers 1994).

Group Contact. Some social scientists advocate organized group contact between dominant and minority group members to improve relations and break down stereotypes and fears. Although not all contact reduces prejudice, many studies have shown the benefits of structured contact. Some essential conditions for success are equal status of the participants, noncompetitive and nonthreatening contact, and projects or goals on which to cooperate (Farley 2011).

In a classic study of group contact, social psychologists Muzafer Sherif and Carolyn Sherif and their colleagues ran summer camps for 11- and 12-year-old boys and studied how they interacted with one another under varying circumstances. On arrival, the boys were divided into two groups that competed periodically. The more fierce the competition, the more hostile the two cabins of boys became toward each other. The experimenters tried several methods to resolve the conflicts and tensions:

1. *Appealing to higher values (be nice to your neighbors):* This proved to have very limited value.
2. *Talking with the natural leaders of the groups (compromises between group leaders):* The group leaders agreed, but their followers did not go along.
3. *Bringing the groups together in a pleasant situation (a mutually rewarding situation):* This did not reduce competition; if anything, it increased it.
4. *Introducing a superordinate goal that could be achieved only if everyone cooperated:*

This technique worked. The boys were presented with a dilemma: The water system had broken, or a fire needed to be put out, and all were needed to solve the problem. The groups not only worked together, but their established stereotypes eventually began to fade away. Such a situation in a community might arise from efforts to get a candidate elected, a bill passed, or a neighborhood improved. At the global macro level, representatives from hostile countries could sit together to solve issues that threatened all nations (Sherif and Sherif 1953).

Students can be actively engaged in this level of change even while undergraduates by confronting and challenging bigotry and stereotypes, as is illustrated in the next "Sociologists in Action."

Positive group contact experiences can be effective in improving relations in groups at a micro level by breaking down stereotypes, but to solidify the positive gains, we must also address institutionalized inequalities.

Institutional and Societal Strategies to Improve Group Relations. Sociologists contend that institutional and societal approaches to reduce discrimination get closer to the core of the problems and affect larger numbers of people than do micro-level strategies. Changes at the macro level that can impact stratification include legislation and government programs that enforce laws mandating racial and ethnic equality. For example, laws requiring equal treatment of minorities, such as the Civil Rights Act of 1964 that prohibited discrimination on the basis of race, religion, sex, or nation of origin, have resulted in increased tolerance and opened doors once closed to minorities. The U.S. Civil Rights Commission and the Equal Employment Opportunity Commission are government organizations that protect rights and work toward equality for all citizens.

In the United States, executive action to end discrimination has been taken by a number of presidents. In 1948, Harry Truman moved to successfully end military segregation, and subsequent presidents have urged the passage of civil rights legislation and equal employment opportunity legislation. Affirmative action laws, first implemented during Lyndon Johnson's administration, have been used to fight pervasive institutional racism (Crosby 2004; Farley 2011).

SOCIOLOGISTS IN ACTION:
ANNA MISLEH

Challenging Bigotry Toward the Roma

In the spring of 2013, a group of students from St. John's University in Queens, New York, were involved in a study-abroad program in Rome, Italy, and performed weekly service work in a Roma (Gypsy) population to better understand an ethnic group that experienced discrimination. In the process we learned we could raise awareness of the discrimination of the Roma and its impact. We worked one-on-one with Roma children living in Monachina, a settlement camp of Roma that is not officially recognized, but is tolerated, by the Italian government. Through our work at the camp, interviewing Italians knowledgeable about the Roma, and interacting closely with one of the families at Monachina, my peers and I were able to better understand the Roma lifestyle and the discrimination they face in Rome.

The Roma who reside in Rome, and other European cities, have come from dozens of different countries. Most have fled political unrest in their home countries. The Roma at the Monachina camp, for example, migrated to Rome in the early 1990s when the country of Yugoslavia dissolved and ethnic wars broke out across the area.

Italians were not pleased by the arrival of the Roma. Generally, Italians stereotype them as inferior, lazy, dirty, uncooperative, and unwilling to assimilate into Italian culture. This has led to a self-fulfilling prophecy. The discrimination the Roma face prevents them from obtaining reputable jobs, owning property, receiving a good education, and generally integrating into Italian society.

Our response to this discrimination of the Roma was to raise awareness. We invited students from several U.S. universities to meet the Roma with us. Through this experience, they gained a deeper understanding of the Roma and how they are an oppressed minority group in Italian society. They were able to see that the stereotype of all Roma being lazy pickpockets was far from the truth. We also took time to discuss with them how this discrimination negatively impacts Italian society, as well as all other European countries that host Roma populations. Being seen only as a societal nuisance hurts both the life chances of the Roma and their ability to fully contribute to the societies in which they live.

After experiencing the plight of the Roma population firsthand, my peers and I were able to use our sociological imagination to relate what we saw to the social issue of racial and ethnic discrimination. Sociology has taught me that a well-functioning society has institutions that support and respect the rights and dignity of all its members. Seeing the discrimination against the Roma in Rome has brought this truth home to me in a very real way, and made me more aware that racial and ethnic discrimination hurts everyone in a society—not just its direct victims.

• •

Anna Misleh is a student at St. John's University in Queens, New York, studying sociology with minors in social justice, Spanish, and theology. She is a leader in the Ozanam Scholars social justice scholarship program at St. John's.

Affirmative Action. One of the most contentious policies in the United States has been affirmative action. The following discussion addresses the goals and forms of policies under the umbrella of "affirmative action." As a societal policy for change, affirmative action actually involves three different policies:

Strict affirmative action, its simplest and original form, involves taking affirmative or positive steps to make sure that unintentional discrimination does not occur. It requires, for example, that an employer who receives federal monies must advertise a position widely and not just through internal or friendship networks. If the job requires an employee with a college education, then by federal law, employers must recruit through minority and women's colleges as well as state and private colleges in the region. If employers are hiring in the suburbs, they are obliged to contact unemployment agencies in poor and minority communities as well as those in their affluent neighborhoods.

After taking these required extra steps, employers are expected to hire the most qualified candidate who applies, regardless of race, ethnicity, sex, religion, or other external characteristics. The focus is on providing opportunities for the best-qualified people. For many people, this is the meaning of affirmative action, and it is inconceivable that this could be characterized as "reverse discrimination," for members of the dominant group will be hired if they are, in fact, the most qualified. These policies do not overcome the problem that qualified people who have been marginalized may be competent but do not have the traditional paper credentials that document their qualifications (Gallagher 2004).

A *quota system*, the second policy, is a requirement that employers *must* hire a certain percentage of minorities. For the most part, quotas are now unconstitutional. They apply only in cases where a court has found a company to have a substantial and sustained history of discrimination against minorities and where the employment position does not have many educational requirements (such as sweeping floors and cleaning toilets).

Preference policies, the third form, have created the most controversy. Preference policies are based on the concept of equity, the belief that sometimes people must be treated differently in order to be treated fairly. These policies were enacted to level the playing field, which was not rewarding highly competent people because of institutional racism. To overcome these inequalities and achieve certain objectives (e.g., a diverse workforce to serve a diverse population), employers and educational institutions take account of race or sex by making special efforts to hire and retain workers or accept students from groups that have been underrepresented. In many cases, these individuals bring qualifications others do not possess. Consider the following examples.

A goal of the medical community is to provide access to medical care for underserved populations. There is an extreme shortage of physicians on the Navajo reservation. Thus, a Navajo applicant for medical school might be accepted, even if her scores are slightly lower than those of another candidate's, because she speaks Navajo and understands the culture. One could argue that she is more qualified to be a physician on the reservation than someone who

knows nothing about Navajo society but has a slightly higher grade point average or test score. Some argue that tests should not be the only measure to determine the merit of applicants.

Likewise, an African American police officer may have more credibility in an African American neighborhood and may be able to defuse a delicate conflict more effectively than a white officer who scored slightly higher on a paper-and-pencil placement test. Thus, being a member of a particular ethnic group can actually make one more qualified for a position.

Many colleges and universities admit students because they need an outstanding point guard on the basketball team, an extraordinary soprano for the college choir, or a student from a distant state for geographic diversity. These students are shown preference by being admitted with lower test scores than some other applicants because they are "differently qualified." Many colleges also give preference to children of former graduates. In order to achieve gender balance, male students tend to be given preference, even if more qualified females apply. The controversy about whether minority students should be given preference follows this same reasoning. Consider the following example.

A landmark case filed in a Detroit district court in 1997 alleged that the University of Michigan gave unlawful preference to minorities in undergraduate admissions and in law school admissions. In this controversial case, the court ruled that these undergraduate admissions were discriminatory because numbers rather than individualized judgments were used to make the admission determination (University of Michigan Documents Center 2003). Consider the next "Engaging Sociology" feature and decide whether you think the policy was fair and whether only race and ethnicity should have been deleted from the automatic preferences allowed.

In 2013, the Supreme Court in the case of *Fisher v. University of Texas*, No. 11-345, upheld the 1997 ruling, but said that affirmative action was permissible, in order to achieve the goal of a diverse student body. In the deciding opinion, however, Justice Kennedy wrote that universities must "verify that it is necessary for a university to use race to achieve the educational benefits of diversity . . . and that the university could [not] achieve sufficient diversity without using racial classifications" (Liptak 2013). In April 2014, the Supreme Court went further, upholding a ban on affirmative action for racial or ethnic groups that was approved

ENGAGING SOCIOLOGY

Preference Policies at the University of Michigan

To enhance diversity on the campus—a practice that many argue makes a university a better learning environment and enhances the academic reputation of the school—many colleges have preference policies in admissions. However, the University of Michigan was sued by applicants who felt they were not admitted because others replaced them on the roster due to their racial or ethnic background.

The University of Michigan is a huge university where a numbering system is needed to handle the volume (tens of thousands) of applicants; the admissions staff cannot make a decision based on personal knowledge of each candidate. Thus, they give points for each quality they deem desirable in the student body. A maximum of 150 points is possible, and a score of 100 would pretty much ensure admission. The university feels that any combination of points accumulated according to the following formula will result in a highly qualified and diverse student body.

For academics, up to 110 points are possible:

- 80 points for grades (a particular grade point average in high school results in a set number of points; e.g., a 4.0 results in 80 points, and a 2.8 results in 56 points)
- 12 points for standardized test scores (ACT or SAT)
- 10 points for the academic rigor of high school (so all students who go to tougher high schools earn points)
- 8 points for the difficulty of the curriculum (e.g., points for honors curriculum vs. keyboarding courses)

For especially desired qualities, including diversity, up to 40 points are possible for any combination of the following (but no more than 40 in this "desired qualities" category):

- Geographical distribution (10 for Michigan resident; an additional 6 for underrepresented Michigan counties)

- Legacy—a direct relative has attended Michigan (4 points for a parent; 1 point for a grandparent or sibling)
- Quality of submitted essay (3 points)
- Personal achievement—a special accomplishment that was noteworthy (up to 5 points)
- Leadership and service (5 points each)
- Miscellaneous (only one of these can be used):

  __ Socioeconomic disadvantage (20 points)

  __ Underrepresented racial or ethnic minority (black, Hispanic, or Native American) (20 points; disallowed by the court ruling)

  __ Men in nursing (5 points)

  __ Scholarship athlete (20 points)

  __ Provost's discretion (20 points; usually the son or daughter of a large financial donor or of a politician)

In addition to race or ethnicity, athleticism, socioeconomic disadvantage, having a relative who is an alum, and being the child of someone who is noteworthy to the university are also considered. Some schools also give points for being a military veteran. The legal challenge to this admissions system was based only on the points given for race or ethnic background, not on the other reasons for which some students are given preference.

* * * * * * *

Engaging With Sociology

1. Does this process seem reasonable as a way to get a diverse and highly talented incoming class of students? Why or why not?

2. Does it significantly advantage or disadvantage some students? Explain.

3. Should there be preferences for predominantly white students—such as "legacy" students, whose family members attended the university? Why or why not?

4. How would you design a fair system of admissions, and what other factors would you consider?

by 58% of Michigan voters, arguing that a lower court did not have the authority to overturn the referendum. Thus, publicly funded colleges in Michigan cannot

grant preferential treatment on the basis of race, sex, color, ethnicity, or national origin (Mears 2014). So now all such policies are illegal in Michigan.

The question remains: Should preferences be given to accomplish diversity? Some people feel that programs involving any sort of preference for minorities are unfair and should not be allowed. Others believe that such programs do much more good than harm. They have encouraged employers, educational institutions, and government to look carefully at hiring policies and minority candidates, and many more competent minority group members are working in the public sector as a result of these policies. What is the truly equitable thing to do? This is the policy issue that interests public sociologists.

Thinking Sociologically

Imagine that you are coordinating efforts to improve minority relations and opportunities for all groups in your community. How might you approach this task, and what specific steps might you take, based on your reading above?

Global Movements for Human Rights

The rights granted to citizens of any nation used to be considered the business of each sovereign nation, but after the Nazi Holocaust, German officers were tried at the Nuremberg Trials, and the United Nations passed the Universal Declaration of Human Rights. Since that time, many international organizations have been established, often under the auspices of the United Nations, to deal with health issues, world poverty and debt, trade, security, and many other issues affecting world citizens—the World Health Organization, the World Bank, the World Trade Organization, and numerous regional trade and security organizations.

The United Nations and privately funded advocacy groups speak up for international human rights as a principle that transcends national boundaries. The most widely recognized private group is

Some human rights movements focus on international justice issues in countries around the world. Amnesty International is one such movement that has strong support on many college campuses.

Amnesty International, a watchdog group that lobbies on behalf of human rights and supports political prisoners. When Amnesty International was awarded the Nobel Peace Prize in 1997, the group's visibility dramatically increased. Some activist sociologists have formed groups such as Sociologists Without Borders, or SSF (*Sociólogos Sin Fronteras*; www.sociologistswithout borders.org), a transnational organization committed to the idea that "all people have equal rights to political and legal protections, to socioeconomic security, to self-determination, and to their personality."

Everyone can make a positive difference in the world, and one place to start is in our own communities (see "Contributing to Our Social World"). We can counter prejudice, discrimination, and socially embedded racism in our own groups by teaching children to see beyond "us" and "them" and by speaking out for fairness and against stereotypes and discrimination.

> Socioeconomic inequality and racial and ethnic stratification create many problems for a society. However, a full understanding of inequality also requires insights into discrimination based on gender. We turn to issues of gender inequality in Chapter 9.

WHAT HAVE WE LEARNED?

If there is competition over resources in a society, groups tend to form. Groups with the most power become dominant, and those with less power become minority groups. Those with the most power stratify their society in a way that ensures that their group has more access to power, money, and status. Racial and ethnic prejudice and discrimination at the micro, meso, and macro levels work to uphold dominant-minority group relations.

KEY POINTS

- Race is a social construction.

- Racial and ethnic stratification are common throughout the world. Racial and ethnic minority groups have less power and less access to resources than majority groups.

- Prejudice operates at the micro level of society while discrimination can occur at the micro, meso, and macro levels.

- The racial ideology of color-blindness does not acknowledge the reality of racial discrimination.

- At the meso level, institutionalized discrimination operates through two processes: side-effect and past-in-present. These forms of discrimination are unintended and unconscious—operating quite separately from any prejudice of individuals in the society.

- The policies of the dominant group may include genocide, subjugation, population transfer, assimilation, or pluralism.

- The costs to society from racial discrimination are high, including loss of human talent and resources.

- The coping devices used by minorities include five main strategies: assimilation, acceptance, avoidance, aggression, and organizing for societal change. Only the last of these addresses the meso- and macro-level causes.

- Policies to address problems of prejudice and discrimination range from individual and small-group efforts at the micro level to institutional, societal, and even global social movements.

- Affirmative action includes three different sets of policies that are quite distinct and have different outcomes.

DISCUSSION QUESTIONS

1. Have you ever experienced being stereotyped because of your race or ethnicity? Why or why not? How can racial stereotypes harm societies, as well as groups and individuals?

2. What is the difference between the color-blind perspective on race and blatant bigotry? Why is it often so difficult to recognize and address racial discrimination in the United States today?

3. Give two examples, respectively, of both side-effect discrimination and past-in-present discrimination. How have they impacted you and your life chances? Why?

4. We know that efforts to reduce prejudice, racism, and discrimination must take place at all levels (micro, meso, and macro). Most organizations, though, must choose one level on which to focus their particular efforts. If you were going to start an organization to decrease racial or ethnic prejudice, would you focus on the micro, meso, or macro level? Why? Explain what your organization would do.

5. Do you agree with preferences for college applicants at the University of Michigan who were scholarship athletes or the sons or daughters of a large donor or a politician, but not for racial or ethnic minority applicants? Why or why not? Was the Supreme Court correct in ruling that a referendum passed by voters in Michigan should trump concerns about diversity? Why?

CONTRIBUTING TO OUR SOCIAL WORLD: What Can We Do?

At the Local Level

- *African American, Arab American, and Native American student associations* are examples of student organizations dedicated to fighting bigotry and promoting understanding and the rights of racial minorities. Identify one of these groups on your campus and arrange to attend a meeting. If appropriate, volunteer to help with its work.

At the Organizational or Institutional Level

- *The Leadership Conference on Civil and Human Rights* is a national coalition dedicated to combating racism and its effects. It maintains a website that includes a directory of its membership of more than 200 organizations (www.civilrights.org). There you can find a "take action" link that will help you to explore ways in which you can participate in its efforts.

- *Teaching Tolerance* (www.splcenter.org/center/tt/teach.jsp), a program of the Southern Poverty Law Center, has curriculum materials for teaching about diversity and a program for enhancing cross-ethnic cooperation and dialogue in schools. Check into internship opportunities in local primary and secondary schools, and explore ways in which the Teaching Tolerance approach can be incorporated into the curricula in your school district with local teachers and administrators.

At the National and Global Levels

- The *Anti-Defamation League* (www.adl.org) acts to "stop the defamation of the Jewish people and to secure justice and fair treatment to all." Members of this organization develop and implement educational programs on interfaith/intergroup understanding, scrutinize and call attention to hate groups, monitor hate speech on the Internet, and mobilize communities to stand up to bigotry throughout the United States and abroad. Job listings, summer internships, and opportunities in Israel and other locations are listed on the ADL website.

- *National Relief Charities* strives "to help Native American people improve the quality of their lives by providing opportunities for them to bring about positive changes in their communities." To do so, it partners with tribal and other groups on the ground in the tribal regions of the Plains and Midwest. You can find out how to support the work of this group and its partners by going to www.nrcprograms.org/site/PageNavigator/index.

- *Cultural Survival and the UN Permanent Forum on Indigenous Issues* (www.cs.org and www.un.org/esa/socdev/unpfii) provide opportunities for combating racism globally.

- Consider purchasing only Fair Trade Certified (packages are clearly marked as such) coffee, and especially chocolate, and encouraging your school to sell Fair Trade Certified products. You can learn more about Fair Trade Certified products and issues by reading this article—www.nytimes.com/2012/09/28/business/

media/green-mountain-coffee-begins-fair-trade-campaign-advertising.html—and looking at educational materials provided by the Fair Trade Resource Network at www.fairtraderesource.org.

- *Amnesty International* campaigns against abuses of human rights. It relies heavily on volunteers organized into chapters, many of them campus-based. You can join the organization and learn how to participate in its action through its website at www.amnesty.org. Consider joining or starting a chapter on your campus.

$SAGE edge™

Sharpen your skills with SAGE edge at **edge.sagepub.com/ballantinecondensed4e**

SAGE edge for Students provides a personalized approach to help you accomplish your coursework goals in an easy-to-use learning environment.

©REUTERS/ Pierre Marsaut

9 Gender Stratification

She/He—Who Goes First?

Social inequality is pervasive in gender relations, and although in some societies women are treated with deference, they are rarely given first access to positions of significant power or financial reward. The men often "go first."

MICRO

● **ME (AND MY GENDER GROUPS)**

● **LOCAL ORGANIZATIONS AND COMMUNITY**
Peers, neighbors, teachers, and religious congregations socialize us into gendered expectations.

MESO

● **NATIONAL ORGANIZATIONS, INSTITUTIONS, AND ETHNIC SUBCULTURES**
Organizations and institutions limit access to many positions based on gender.

MACRO

● **SOCIETY**
National policies provide sex-based privileges.

● **GLOBAL COMMUNITY**
Gender status is determined by laws and power structures; the United Nations champions equal rights for women.

LEARNING OBJECTIVES

9.1 Describe the difference between sex and gender.

9.2 Identify agents of gender socialization.

9.3 Give example(s) of meso- and macro-level gender stratification.

9.4 Illustrate the relationship between minority status and gender and sexual orientation.

9.5 Discuss costs and consequences of gender stratification.

9.6 Predict social policies that could decrease gender stratification.

THINK ABOUT IT

Micro: Local Community	How does being female or male affect your thoughts, behaviors, and opportunities? Why do some people face violence in their homes and communities because of their sexuality?
Meso: National Institutions; Complex Organizations; Ethnic Groups	Can anything be done in our organizations and institutions to make men and women more equal?
Macro: National and Global Systems	Why do women have second-class status in many societies?

As women around the world wake up to International Women's Day, each woman, no matter where she lives, holds the same basic goals: a trusting and happy relationship; the option of having healthy, educated children with a fair chance in life; enough food on the table; self-respect; access to health care; and whatever individual desires are relevant in her society. Consider the following example from a Global North country that illustrates the problems some women face in meeting basic goals.

Jocelyn, who lives in the United States, is now retired and having trouble making ends meet. After training in nursing, including a master's degree, she married and dropped her career to raise her family. The marriage did not work out, and 15 years after college she found herself with no credit, two children, little job experience, and mounting expenses. She was a conscientious and hard worker, but with two children and meager child support from their father, she could not put much away for retirement. Nursing does not pay well in her town in the Midwest, but there had been few other career options for females in the early 1960s when she was getting her education.

Moreover, two decades does not build a very large retirement annuity, and she had never been able to buy an adequate home on her income. If she had been a typical male with a master's degree, her lifetime earnings would have been $1 million more in cumulative income (Catalyst 2014c; Julian and Kominski 2011). Her life chances were clearly affected by the fact that she was a female.

Due to changes in gender roles and opportunities over the past 50 years, Jocelyn's granddaughter, Emma, will have a range of opportunities that were beyond consideration for her grandma. Ideas about sex, gender, and appropriate roles for women and men not only transform over time, but they also vary a great deal from one society to the next. Some practices of your own society may seem very strange to women and men in another society. Gender identities and roles are not stagnant; they change over time, reflecting the economic, political, and social realities of the society. For instance, women in today's India, with the exception of some rural areas, seldom commit *sati* (suicide) on their husband's funeral pyre (Greenan 2013; Ziel 2013); however, before the practice of *sati* was outlawed, it was a common way to deal with widows who no longer had a social role or means of support (Ahmad 2009).

In this chapter, we explore the concepts of sex, gender, and sexuality. Although gender refers to a range of social behaviors, more emphasis will be on women's status and roles than on men's as this is generally more relevant to our concern about stratification and minorities. At the micro level, we consider gender socialization or how girls and boys learn to be women and men in their respective societies. At the meso and macro levels we consider gender stratification, or placement of women and men in the society's stratification system. A discussion of costs and consequences of gender stratification plus policy implications will end this chapter.

SEX, GENDER, AND THE STRATIFICATION SYSTEM

You name it, and some society has probably done it! Gender relations are no exception. Variations around the world show that most roles and identities are not biological but rather socially constructed. In Chapter 7, we discussed factors that stratify individuals into social groups (castes and classes), and in Chapter 8, we discussed the roles that race and ethnicity play in stratification. Add the concepts of sex and gender, and we have a more complex and complete picture of how class, race and ethnicity, and gender together influence the experiences that make us who we are and our positions in society. Consider the following examples from societies that illustrate some unusual human social constructions based on sex and gender. These examples show that gender roles are created by humans to meet the needs of their societies. We will then move to more familiar societies.

Societies have developed cultural norms over time that cause gender behaviors to differ widely. The Wodaabe, herders and traders in the Sahel region of Africa, would be defined as effeminate by most Western standards. Men take great care in doing their hair, applying makeup, and dressing to attract women. They also gossip with each other while sipping their tea. The women tend to the animals, plant gardens, and prepare for the next move of this nomadic group (Beckwith 1993; Human Planet 2012).

Women of the Tchambuli tribe in New Guinea (also called Chambri) seem unacceptably aggressive, assertive, businesslike, and competitive to people of the Arapesh tribe in New Guinea, where gentleness and nonaggression are the rule for both women and men. Men of the Tchambuli, on the other hand, exhibit expressive, nurturing, and gossipy behavior (Dahlberg 1981; Mead [1935] 1963; Turnbull 1962). Each tradition has evolved over time to meet the basic human needs and to provide order to society.

Each person, in all these diverse societies, knows how to behave appropriately.

Under the Taliban rule in Afghanistan, women could not be seen in public without total body covering that met strict requirements. Anyone not obeying could be stoned to death. Women could not hold public positions or work outside their homes. If they became ill, women could not be examined by a physician because all doctors were male. Instead, they had to describe their symptoms to a doctor through a screen (Makhmalbaf 2003; Trust in Education 2013).

Certain tasks must be carried out by individuals and organizations in each society for members to survive. Responsibilities include raising children, providing people with the basic necessities (such as food, clothing, and shelter), leading, defending the society, and resolving conflicts. One's sex and age are often used to determine who holds what positions and who carries out what tasks. Each society develops its own way to meet its expectations and its own interpretations of right and wrong gender role behaviors. This results in gender role variations from one society to the next. If the genders are identified as fundamentally different, distinguishing symbols such as dress, head coverings, and hairstyle become important for each gender's identity.

Sex and Sexuality

At birth, when doctors say, "It's a . . . !" they are referring to the distinguishing primary characteristics that determine sex—that is, the penis or vagina. **Sex**

Wodaabe men in Niger, Africa, go to great pains with makeup, hair, and jewelry to ensure that they are highly attractive, a pattern thought by many people in other parts of the world to be associated with females.

Muslim girls in some parts of the world cover their faces when in public. The display of skin, even in a classroom, would be immoral to many Muslims. However, in other Muslim countries such coverings would be unusual.

is *a biological term referring to ascribed genetic, anatomical, and hormonal differences between males and females.* This is actually only partially true. *Sex* is also a term that categorizes people using "*socially agreed upon* biological criteria for classifying persons as females or males" (West and Zimmerman 1987:127). In other words, occasionally this binary male-female categorization by biological criteria is not clear. Occasionally, babies are born with ambiguous genitalia, not fitting the typical definitions of male or female (the *intersexed*). Germany has recently recognized "intersex" as a third group, an indeterminate gender option; Australian laws also acknowledge the intersex status (Agius 2013).

People with sex anomalies may have special status, such as the transgendered Hijras (or Aravanis) in India. These unique people are called on for special religious observances and other ceremonial occasions (Gannon 2009). Whether male, female, or intersexed, anatomical differences at birth and chromosomal typing before birth result in attempts by people in various cultures to clearly categorize people based on their sex. The word *sex* when applied to a person refers largely to elements of one's anatomy.

Transgender refers to "identification as someone who is challenging, questioning, or changing gender from that assigned at birth to a chosen gender—male-to-female, female-to-male, transitioning between genders, or gender 'queer' (challenging gender norms)" (Kinsey Institute for Research in Sex, Gender, and Reproduction 2012; Lorber and Moore 2007:6). Transgendered individuals interest sociologists because of their ambiguous life—living on the boundaries. The reason many societies go to great lengths to assign a sex to an infant is that sex constitutes a major organizing principle. Surgeries to clarify the sex of an infant are done mainly because of stigma and psychological reasons for those who do not fit socially approved categories. Despite emphasis on "achieved status" in modern societies, society's expectations guiding roles and statuses are largely ascribed—determined by a person's sex. Our attraction to others is expressed by our sexuality and our sexual identity. Most people fall into the category of heterosexual (other sex), homosexual (same sex), bisexual (both sexes), or "varied" (such as transgendered). In most societies our sexual identities follow the prevailing belief that a "normal" girl or boy will be sexually attracted to and eventually have sex with someone of

the other sex (Lorber and Moore 2007). However, as we have seen, sex is not always a straightforward distinction and is as social as it is biological.

Sexuality refers to *culturally shaped meanings both of sexual acts and of how we experience our own bodies—especially in relation to the bodies of others.* Strange as it may seem, sexuality is socially constructed. A sex act is a "social enterprise," with cultural norms defining what is normal and acceptable in each society, how we should feel, and hidden assumptions about what the act means (Steele 2005). Even what we find attractive is culturally defined. For a period, in China, men found tiny feet a sexual turn-on—hence, the bound feet of women. In some cultures, legs are the attraction, and in others, men are fascinated by breasts. Likewise, the ideal male body as depicted in popular magazines in contemporary Western cultures is "over 6 feet tall, 180 to 200 pounds, muscular, agile, with straight white teeth, a washboard stomach, six-pack abs, long legs, a full head of hair, a large penis (discreetly shown by a bulge), broad shoulders and chest, strong muscular back, clean shaven, healthy, and slightly tanned if White, or a lightish brown if Black or Hispanic" (Lorber and Moore 2011:89–90). We grow up learning what is appealing.

As individuals mature, they are expected to adopt the behaviors appropriate to their anatomical features as defined by their society. In addition to the physical sex differences between males and females, a few other physical conditions are commonly believed to be sex linked, such as a prevalence of color blindness, baldness, learning disabilities, autism, and hemophilia in males. Yet some traits that members of society commonly link to sex are actually learned through socialization. There is little evidence, for instance, that emotions, personality traits, or ability to fulfill most social statuses are determined by inborn physical sex differences. However, the social messages urging people to conform to expectations for their sex category are strong. What is defined as normal behavior for a male, a female, or an intersexed person in one society could get one killed in another.

Gender

Gender refers to *a society's notions of masculinity and femininity—socially constructed meanings associated with being male or female—and how individuals construct their identity in terms of gender* within these constraints. Gender identity, then, is how individuals form their identity using the categories of sex and gender and negotiate the constraints they entail. The examples at the beginning of this section illustrate some differences in how cultures are structured around gender.

Statuses are positions within the structures of society, and roles are expected behaviors within those statuses (Rothenberg 2010). **Gender roles**, then, are those *commonly assigned tasks or expected behaviors linked to an individual's sex-determined statuses* (Lips 2010, 2013). Members of each society learn the structural guidelines and positions expected of males and females (West and Zimmerman 1987). Our positions, which affect access to power and resources, are embedded in institutions at the meso level with culture defining what is right and wrong. There is not some global absolute truth governing gender or gender roles. While both vary across cultures, gender is a learned cultural idea, and gender roles are part of the structural system of roles and statuses in a society.

In summary, although the terms *sex*, *sexuality*, and *gender* are often used interchangeably, they do have distinct meanings. Individuals who negotiate the meanings attached to gender and sexuality are *doing gender*, a process discussed later in this chapter ("Doing Gender" 2011; West and Zimmerman 1987).

Sex, Gender, and Sexuality: The Micro Level

"It's a boy!" brings varying cultural responses. In many Western countries, that exclamation results in blue blankets, toys associated with males (footballs, soccer balls, and trucks), roughhousing, and gender socialization messages. In some Asian societies, boys are sources for great rejoicing, whereas girls may be seen as a burden. Abortion rates in some countries are much higher when ultrasound tests show that the fetus is female ("Gendercide" 2010). In China and India, *female infanticide* (killing of newborn girl babies) is sometimes practiced in rural areas, in part because the cost to poor families of raising a girl, including paying a dowry, diminishes the value of girls. In China, the male preference system has been exacerbated by the government's edict that most couples may have only one child, although this has changed for some couples in some areas of China. As a result of

This extended family helps illustrate the growing sex imbalance in some parts of the world, such as China and India. When families care more for sons than daughters in medical treatment, eventually there are fewer girls in the society.

government policy and female infanticide and abortion, a sex imbalance is growing and causing other consequences such as a shortage of brides.

At the micro level we can trace stages in an individual's life as a female or male: early childhood socialization, school and community activities and experiences, adult statuses and roles of females and males, and so on through the life cycle. At each stage, there are messages that reinforce appropriate gender behavior. Cultural traditions learned from birth guide individuals into proper gender roles. These gender expectations are inculcated into children by parents, siblings, grandparents, neighbors, peers, and even day care providers. If we fail to respond to the expectations of these significant people in our lives, we may experience negative sanctions: teasing, isolation and exclusion, harsh words, and stigma. Therefore, children usually learn to conform, at least in their public behavior.

Through the lifelong process of gender socialization, we are grouped by sex in many of these social settings: boys versus girls, us versus them. Even if our parents are not highly traditional in their gender expectations, we still experience many expectations to conform from peers, school, and other sources.

With adulthood, the differential treatment and stratification of the sexes take new forms. Men traditionally have more networks and higher status, as well as greater access to resources outside the home. This has resulted in many women around the world

Gendercide

having less power and depending more on husbands or fathers for resources. The subtitle of this chapter asks, "Who goes first?" When it comes to the question of who walks through a door first, the answer is that in many Western societies, *she* does—or at least, formal etiquette would suggest this is proper. The strong man steps back and defers to the weaker female, graciously holding the door for her, and women are served first at restaurants. This seems little compensation for the fact that doors are often closed to women at the meso and macro levels of society.

Language can be powerful in shaping the behavior and perceptions of people, as discussed in Chapter 3. Women often end sentences with tag questions, ending a declarative statement with a short tag that turns it into a question: "That was a good idea, don't you think?" This pattern may cause male business colleagues to think women are insecure or uncertain about themselves, preventing a woman from getting the job or the promotion. The women themselves may view it as an invitation to collaboration and dialogue. On the flip side, when women stop using these "softening" devices, they may be perceived as strident, harsh, or "bitchy" (Sandberg 2013; Wood and Reich 2006). Women also tend to use more words related to psychological and social processes, while men prefer more discussion of objects and impersonal topics (Newman et al. 2008). The same adverb or adjective, when preceded by a male or female pronoun, can take on very different meanings. When one says, "He's easy" or "He's loose," it does not generally mean the same thing as when someone says, "She's easy" or "She's loose." Likewise, there are words such as *slut* or *bitch* for women with no equivalents for men. The word *spinster* is supposed to be the female synonym for *bachelor*, yet it has very different connotations. Even the more newly coined *bachelorette* is not usually used to describe a highly appealing, perhaps lifelong role. What might be the implications of these differences?

Those who invoke the biological argument that women's options to participate in public affairs and politics are limited by pregnancy, childbirth, or breastfeeding ignore the fact that in most societies, these biological roles are time limited and women play a variety of social roles in addition to keeping the home and hearth. They also ignore those societies in which males are deeply involved in nonaggressive and nurturing activities such as child rearing.

Thinking Sociologically

Until recently, words like *mankind* and phrases like "all men are created equal" were commonly used. Today, some people always write *he* first when writing "he and she." Others sometimes put *she* first. How do these examples—and others you can think of—reveal how language relates to gender roles?

Sex, Gender, and Sexuality: The Meso Level

In most societies, sex and age stipulate when and how we experience *rites of passage*—rituals and ceremonies in institutions that mark a change of status in the family and community—the meso levels of society. These rites include any ceremonies or recognitions that admit one to adult duties and privileges (Brettell and Sargent 2012). Rites of passage are institutionalized in various ways: religious rituals such as the Jewish male bar mitzvah or the female bat mitzvah ceremonies; education celebrations such as graduation ceremonies, which often involve caps and gowns of gender-specific colors or place females on one side of the room and males on the other; and different ages at which men and women are permitted to marry. Other institutions also segregate us by sex. For example, in traditional Greek Orthodox Christian churches and Orthodox Jewish synagogues, men sit on one side of the sanctuary and women on the other.

Empowerment of Women. Thirty village women gather regularly to discuss issues of health, crops, their herds, the predicted rains, goals for their children, and how to make ends meet. They are from a subsistence farming village in southern Niger on the edge of the Sahara desert. Recently, a microcredit organization was established with a small grant of $1,500 from abroad. With training from CARE International, an international nongovernmental organization (NGO), the women selected a board of directors to oversee the loans. Groups of five or six women joined together to explain their projects to the board and request small loans. Each woman is responsible for paying back a small amount on the loan each week once the project is established and bringing in money. Typical microcredit participants are women with several children, living at or below poverty, and sharing shelter with other families. With loans, women can make and sell items and build businesses to feed, clothe, and educate children (Foundation for Women 2012). A loan of between $20 and $50 from the microcredit organization is a tremendous sum considering that for many of these women it is equivalent to six months' earnings. Strong social norms are instituted to encourage repayment. Participation in the program encourages women and grants them economic and social capital otherwise unavailable to them.

With the new possibilities for their lives, these women have big plans: For instance, one group acquired a press to make peanut oil, a staple for cooking in the region. Currently, people pay a great deal for oil imported from Nigeria. Another group bought baby lambs, fattened them, and sold them for future festivals at a great profit. Yet another group plans to set up a small bakery. Women are also discussing the possibility of making local craft products to sell to foreign Fair Trade organizations such as Ten Thousand Villages (a Fair Trade organization that markets products made by villagers and returns the profits back to the villagers).

Some economists and social policymakers claim that grassroots organizations such as microcredits may be the way out of poverty for millions of poor families, and that women are motivated to be small-business entrepreneurs to help support their families and buy education and health care for their children. Muhammad Yunus, the founder of Grameen Bank—a microcredit lender for the very poor—received the Nobel Prize for Peace in 2006.

Critics suggest such organizations work on a micro level to address what are really macro-level national and international problems of inequality (Mayoux 2008). For better or worse, microloans also may shift relations between husbands and wives, leaving men in a less powerful position within marriages, and changing gender dynamics. While this has led to more respect for women in some areas, this shift of power has also left some women vulnerable to criticisms, harassment, and isolation (Business Insider 2012). Most economists agree that microlending works best alongside macro-level initiatives seeking to address national economic problems.

Microcredit banks have provided a variety of opportunities for public sociologists to make a positive impact. For example, the next "Sociologists in Action" feature on page 236 describes how one class of sociology undergraduate students raised awareness

Catarina lives in Guatemala. She started a weaving business— and turned her life around—with the help of a microfinance loan from FINCA.

of how meso-level organizations—banks—can impact people at the micro level.

◐ Thinking Sociologically

How might the lack of women in positions of authority in organizations and institutions—the meso level of society—influence females' roles at the micro level? How might it influence their involvement at the macro level?

Sex, Sexuality, and Gender: The Macro Level

People around the world go to school, drive a car, and work, but in some parts of the world, school, driving, and work are forbidden for women. Fourteen-year-old Malala Yousafzai, a girl from northwest Pakistan, was shot and severely wounded by a Taliban gunman for both going to school and speaking out for other girls to have educational opportunities (Mehsud 2012). The Taliban, a regional organization that extends beyond the local boundaries, is opposed to girls going to school. Malala gained worldwide fame, and since her recovery has spoken out about the right for education for all children. In 2014, she became the youngest person ever to win the Nobel Peace Prize.

When we turn to the national and global level, we witness inequality between the sexes quite separate from any form of personal prejudice or animosity toward women. Patterns of social action embedded in the entire social system may influence women and men, providing unrecognized privileges or disadvantages. This is called *institutionalized privilege* or *disprivilege*.

SOCIOLOGISTS IN ACTION:
DONNA YANG, CHRISTIAN AGURTO, MICHELLE BENAVIDES, BRIANNE GLOGOWSKI, DEZIREE MARTINEZ, AND MICHELE VAN HOOK

Sociology Students Engage With Microfinance

Students at William Paterson University describe their participation in a microcredit organization and how they used the sociological tools they gained in their Principles of Sociology course. They educated their classmates about Kiva, a microfinance project designed to aid women and diminish poverty globally, and raised money for the organization's efforts.

Kiva is an international microfinance organization dedicated to helping ordinary people across the globe become lenders to beginning entrepreneurs. Using various sociological concepts, we sought not only to raise money for Kiva loans but also to generate awareness about microfinance's ability to empower women and help fight poverty. The website, www.kiva.org, is designed to facilitate partnerships between people willing to donate and low-income entrepreneurs seeking financial services. Kiva loans typically range from $25 to $3,000, and are temporarily financed by Kiva users who have browsed the profiles of potential entrepreneurs uploaded on the website.

Although *gender inequality* was central to our Kiva project, we used two other key sociological ideas: using a sociological eye and promoting social activism. We recognized patterns of inequality intersecting along both class and gender lines. Social stratification has created hierarchies through which women are marginalized economically, politically, and socially. Microfinance programs such as Kiva seek to mitigate this unequal access to wealth by creating greater accessibility for low-income individuals, mostly women, to financial services. As a group, we felt passionate about Kiva because of its commitment to improve society by providing more equal lending opportunities.

We raised more than $150 toward a group loan for the communal bank "Mujeres Progresistas" (Progressive Women) in Cuenca, Ecuador. This bank is composed of 11 women, and our specific loan was distributed to 2 women—both mothers of four seeking loans to help finance their personal businesses in order to help support their families. Maria Huerta invested this money in buying chickens and chicken feed to begin running a chicken farm. Maria Suqui used her loan to help establish a snack shop through which she hopes to earn enough money to eventually own a home.

In order to promote awareness about our project and Kiva's initiatives, we created informational pamphlets and distributed them to students on our college campus. The pamphlets explained microfinance, how Kiva utilizes this process of lending to help low-income individuals around the globe, and how students can get involved. This project helped us to realize the importance of sociology, its applicability within everyday life, and our obligation to act as socially conscious individuals in order to help promote greater social justice.

• •

Note: This excerpt is adapted from Korgen and White's The Engaged Sociologist: Connecting the Classroom to the Community *(2013).*

Over the past decade, the number of women in governing roles has increased in many parts of the globe. Although women are still denied the right to vote in Saudi Arabia, in most elections in the United Arab Emirates, and in the Vatican, voting is a universal right for most. In the United States, women have voted in federal elections for more than 90 years, following the passage of the Nineteenth Amendment in 1920

In 2013, nineteen women served as the head of their nations, including Angela Merkel (left), the chancellor of Germany, and Ellen Johnson Sirleaf (right), the president of Liberia and the first elected female head of state in Africa.

prohibiting voter discrimination on the basis of sex. As of 2014, however, just 20 of 100 senators and 79 of 435 representatives in the House were women—and that was an all-time high. Women comprise just 18.5% of all national representatives in the U.S. Congress (Center for American Women and Politics 2014).

The nation with the highest percentage of women in the national parliament or congress is Rwanda (sub-Saharan Africa) with 63.8% women—one of only two countries to reach or surpass 50%. Canada is 61st among nations, and the United States, tied with Sao Tome and Principe, ranks 101st—well below Global North countries like Sweden (#4), Spain (#11), Denmark (#16), and Germany (#22) and trailing Global South countries like Afghanistan (#45), Iraq (#57), and Saudi Arabia (#90) (Inter-Parliamentary Union 2014). Nations like Rwanda, with political systems that stress proportional representation and have adopted gender quotas for government positions, have more women in political offices (Yoon 2011a, 2011b). Without such systems and quotas, democratization of governmental systems is sometimes linked to a *decrease* in representation by women, a sad reality for those committed to establishing democracy around the world (Yoon 2005). Globally, women's access to power and prestige is highly variable, with some African and northern European countries having a position of leadership when it comes to gender equity in government (see Table 9.1). As you study Table 9.1, on page 238 note that researchers find the needs and interests of women are not fully represented unless a critical mass of female representatives is reached, and that critical mass is usually about 35% (Yoon 2011b).

Thinking Sociologically

What factors might explain why the United States and Canada have low rankings in representation of women in their governments?

Cross-cultural analyses confirm that gender roles that have evolved over centuries can be transformed by sweeping government reforms, economic upheaval, or wars. In many societies, though, gender roles are passed down from one generation to the next. The fact that women in China generally work outside the home whereas women in some Muslim societies hardly venture from their homes is due to differences in cultural norms about proper gender roles dictated by traditions, religious beliefs, and governments, and learned through the socialization process.

GENDER SOCIALIZATION: MICRO- AND MESO-LEVEL ANALYSES

"Sugar and spice and everything nice—that's what little girls are made of. Snips and snails and puppy dog tails—that's what little boys are made of." As the verse implies, different views of little girls and little boys start at birth, based on gender and stereotypes about what is biologically natural. Behavioral expectations stem from cultural beliefs about the nature of men and women, and these expectations guide socialization from the earliest ages and in intimate primary group settings.

TABLE 9.1 Women in National Governments (Selected Countries), 2014

	Country	Lower Chamber (House of Representatives) or Single Chamber	Upper Chamber (Senate)
1	Rwanda	63.8	38.5
2	Andorra	50.0	—
3	Cuba	48.9	—
4	Sweden	45.0	—
5	Seychelles	43.8	—
6	Senegal	43.3	—
7	Finland	42.5	—
8	Nicaragua	42.4	—
9	Ecuador	41.6	—
10	South Africa	40.8	35.2
11	Iceland	39.7	—
11	Spain	39.7	—
13	Norway	39.6	—
14	Belgium	39.3	50
15	Mozambique	39.2	—
22	Germany	36.5	27.5
27	New Zealand	33.9	—
45	Afghanistan	27.7	27.5
53	Australia	26.0	38.2
57	Iraq	25.2	—
61	Canada	25.1	39.6
74	United Kingdom	22.6	23.4
90	Saudi Arabia	19.9	—
101	United States	18.2	20.0

Source: Inter-Parliamentary Union 2014. www.ipu.org. Reprinted with permission of the Inter-Parliamentary Union.

Note: To examine the involvement of women in other countries or to see even more recent figures, go to http://www.ipu.org/wmn-e/classif.htm.

Gender role socialization is the process by which people learn the cultural norms, attitudes, and behaviors appropriate to their gender. That is, they learn how to think and act as boys or girls, women or men. Socialization reinforces the "proper" gender behaviors and punishes the improper behaviors. This process, in turn, reinforces gender stereotypes. In many societies, traits of gentleness, passivity, and dependence are associated with femininity, whereas boldness, aggression, strength, and independence are identified with masculinity. For instance, in most Western societies, aggression in women is considered unfeminine, if not inappropriate or disturbing (Sandberg 2013). Likewise, the gentle, unassertive male is often looked on with scorn or pity, stigmatized as a "wimp."

Stages in Gender Socialization

Bounce that rough-and-tumble baby boy and cuddle that precious, delicate little girl. Thus begins gender socialization, starting at birth and taking place through a series of life stages, discussed in Chapter 4 on socialization. Examples from infancy and childhood show how socialization into gender roles takes place.

Infancy. Learning how to carry out gender roles begins at birth. Parents in the United States describe their newborn daughters as soft, delicate, fine featured, little, pretty, cute, awkward, and resembling their mothers. They depict their sons as strong, firm, alert, and well coordinated (Lindsey 2011). Although gender stereotypes have declined in recent years, they continue to affect the way we handle and treat male and female infants.

Clothing, room decor, and toys also reflect notions of gender. An interesting fact is that only a century ago pink was considered the "manly" color and self-respecting men were steered away from the very soft feminine color—blue ("Finery for Infants" 1893). A trade publication, *Earnshaw's Infants' Department*, published an article in June 1918 that advises parents: "The generally accepted rule is pink for the boys, and blue for the girls. The reason is that pink, being a more decided and stronger color, is more suitable for the boy, while blue, which is more delicate and dainty, is prettier for the girl." In 1927, *Time* magazine printed a chart showing sex-appropriate colors for children: pink is for boys—blue for girls (Maglaty 2011). Moreover, prior to the 20th century both boys and girls in the United States were dressed mostly in frilly dresses until they were about 6 (Maglaty 2011).

Childhood. Once they are out of infancy, research shows that boys receive more encouragement than girls to be independent and exploratory. More pressure is put on boys to behave in "gender-appropriate" ways, with an emphasis on achievement, autonomy, and aggression (Kramer and Beutel 2014). Boys are

 Gender Socialization/Roles

Children, like the girl in this picture, begin to conform to gender expectations once they are old enough to understand that their sex is permanent.

socialized into this "boy code" that provides rigid guidelines for their behavior.

On the other hand, girls are trained to express aggression in more subtle ways: through gossip, rumors, name-calling, backbiting, and excluding other girls from social activities (Beran 2012). Friendship and needing to belong are the weapons—rather than the "sticks and stones" used by boys. This form of bullying is subtle and hard to detect, but it can have long-lasting effects on girls (Beran 2012; Girls Health 2009; Simmons 2002).

Names for children also reflect stereotypes about gender. Boys are more often given strong, hard names that end in consonants. The top 10 boys' names include Jackson, Aiden, Liam, Lucas, Noah, Mason, Jayden, Ethan, Jacob, and Jack. Girls are more likely to be given soft pretty names with vowel endings such as most of the top 10: Sophia, Emma, Olivia, Isabella, Mia, Ava, Lilly, Zoe, Emily, and Chloe (BabyCenter 2013).

Alternatively, girls may be given feminized versions of boys' names—Roberta, Jessica, Josephine, Nicole, Michelle, Donna, Charlotte, Georgia, or Antonia. Sometimes traditional boys' names are given to girls without first feminizing them. Names such as Lynn, Stacey, Tracey, Faye, Dana, Jody, Lindsay, Robin, Carmen, Kelly, Kim, Beverly, Ashley, Dana, Carol, Shannon, and Leslie used to be names exclusively for men, but within a decade or two after they were applied to girls, parents stopped using them for boys (Kean 2007). So a common name for males may for a time be given to either sex, but then, it is given primarily to girls. The pattern rarely goes in the other direction. Once feminized, the names seem

to have become tainted and unacceptable for boys (Lieberson, Dumais, and Bauman 2000).

As children are rewarded for performing proper gender roles, these roles are reinforced, setting the stage for gender-related interactions, behaviors, and choices in later life. We now turn to meso-level agents of gender socialization.

Meso-Level Agents of Gender Socialization

Clues to proper gender roles surround children in materials produced by corporations (books, toys, games), in technology and mass media images, in educational settings, and in religious organizations and beliefs. In Chapter 4, we learned about agents of socialization. Those agents play a major role in teaching children proper gender roles. The following examples demonstrate how organizations and institutions in our society teach and reinforce gender assumptions and roles.

Corporations. Corporations create many materials that help socialize children into conduct socially approved for their gender. Publishers, for example, produce books that present images of expected gender behavior. The language and pictures in preschool picture books, elementary children's books, stories for teenagers, and school textbooks are steeped in gender role messages, reflecting society's expectations and stereotypes. In a recent study of children's books published in the United States during the 20th century, researchers found males more frequently represented than females throughout the entire time period (McCabe et al. 2011). Studies on more recent books have found some change in this pattern—even an overcorrection in some cases—but many children's books still show stereotyped images of females, especially those with animal or other types of nonhuman characters (Anderson and Hamilton 2005; Diekman and Murmen 2004; Houlis 2011).

Producers of toys and games also contribute to traditional messages about gender. Wall posters and store-bought toys fill rooms in homes of children in the Western world, and it is usually quite clear which are boys' rooms and which are girls' rooms. Each toy or game prepares children for future gender roles. Choices ranging from college major to occupational choice appear to be affected by these early choices and childhood learning experiences (Deerwester

Mattel's Barbie dolls have been criticized for their extremely traditional and highly sexualized images of young women. The boy at the right looks at toys marketed for boys, and the message he receives is very different.

2013). The bottom line is that gender portrayals are unequal and the females presented in books, video games, and toys tend to be in stereotypical roles—supporting, needing rescue, or sexually alluring.

Mass Media. Mass media comes in many forms—magazines, ads, films, music videos, Internet sites—and is a major agent of socialization into gender roles. We can see its influence all around us, even during a typical weekend evening for many boys. It is Friday night, and a group of adolescent males gather to play games. Their two favorites are the card game *Magic: The Gathering* (MTG or Magic) and the online game *World of Warcraft* (WoW). WoW is played with many online players, and the individual players can sit in front of their computers alone, interacting only online. Popular video games that primarily attract boys include *Grand Theft Auto: Vice City* (adventure), *Halo 2* (action), *Gran Turismo 3: A-Spec* (driving), and *Madden NFL* (sports). One study found that over 80% of characters in video games are male (Williams et al. 2009). Research shows that adolescents identify with characters in video games, and often view them as role models (Mou and Peng 2009). Girls are generally missing or peripheral to the play. Notice the next time you are around people playing video games that the fighting characters are typically male and often in armor. When fighting women do appear, they are usually clad in skin-revealing bikini-style attire—odd clothing in which to do battle! (Martins et al. 2009).

Some recent action films include adventurous and competent girls and women, helping to counter images of sexy and helpless females. *The Hunger Games* heroine, Katniss Everdeen, has become a brave idol for teenage girls; Mattel has even made a Barbie version of the heroine. *The Girl With the Dragon Tattoo* and other films in that series present an extremely clever and unique heroine in Lisbeth. Despite these new examples of young women in strong leadership roles, highly competent females are still seen less frequently than men in the media.

Thinking Sociologically

Why are video and role-playing games primarily a boy thing? Where are the girls? What effect might girls' and boys' different activities have on their futures? What are some current examples of video games that show gender-specific roles? What do they reveal about appropriate behavior for men and women? What are the potential repercussions of these images for individuals and society?

Young men and women, desiring to fit in, can be influenced in harmful ways by messages from the media. For instance, the epidemic of steroid use or hormones among boys to stimulate muscle growth results from a desire to be successful in sports and have an appealing body image. Professional athletes set an example, and the dark side of steroids is often overlooked: acne, mood swings, depression, elevated suicide attempts, aggressive behavior, high blood pressure, heightened sex characteristics, and liver damage (Global Sports Development 2013). Adolescent girls are more prone to dieting, binging, and purging (Stephen et al. 2014). Dieting among girls, driven in part by ads, is a health concern in the United

States and some other countries (Taub and McLorg 2010). Studies show that between 40% and 60% of children age 6 to 12 are worried about their weight. Eighty percent of 10-year-olds have dieted. Over half (53%) of 13-year-old girls and more than three out of four (78%) 17-year-old girls have issues with their bodies (Hepworth 2010; Roberts 2012).

Television is another part of the media that works as a powerful socializing agent. Children born after 2005 in the United States spend—on average—35 hours watching TV per week, a 12% increase over the previous 9 years. Television presents a simple, stereotyped view of life, from advertisements to situation comedies to soap operas. Women in soap operas and ads, especially those working outside the home, are often depicted as having problems in carrying out their role responsibilities (Boston Women's Health Book Collective 2006). Even the extraordinary powers of superheroes on Saturday morning television depict the female characters as having gender-stereotyped skills such as superintuition.

Films and television series in the United States seldom feature average-size or older women (although a greater variety of ages and body types is seen in British Broadcasting Corporation and other British productions). Most U.S. films feature stars who are attractive and thin, presenting an often unattainable model for young women (Taub and McLorg 2010). Overweight women are almost entirely comic figures on U.S. television.

In addition to watching television, the average child in the United States also spends approximately 10 hours a week using other electronic devices. In part, because of this sedentary lifestyle, children today are much more likely to be overweight, even obese (Joint Center for Political and Economic Studies 2013; Mercola 2013). Ironically, this makes it harder for them to live up to the stereotypical buff male and slender female body images they see in the media.

Like most U.S. glamour stars, Paris Hilton (left—arriving at the MTV Movie Awards) must conform to the image of very thin, shapely femininity. By contrast, an older not-particularly-thin actor, Stephanie Cole (right), plays the leading role in the BBC series *Waiting for God*—a comedy about people in an assisted living nursing home.

⬤ Thinking Sociologically

Think of recent images of popular men and women you have seen in the media. What type of body images do they portray? How might these meso-level depictions affect young men and women individually at the micro level?

Educational Systems. Girls and boys often have very different experiences in school. As noted in the examples below, education systems socialize children through classroom, lunchroom, and playground activities; students' popularity and recognition; sports and Title IX programs; and teachers' attitudes and expectations. In academics, girls are achieving at a higher level than boys overall. According to a recent study, girls have better social and behavioral skills than boys and are more likely to study, whereas boys have lower engagement in school and weaker preparation (DiPrete and Buchmann 2013). However, in subjects that lead to high-paying jobs, there is a lag for some girls, such as high-level physics and math courses. Research indicates, however, that girls are equally represented with boys in physics courses in communities where women are employed in STEM (science, technology, engineering, and math) fields and girls have a model for pursuing STEM courses. Thus, girls may excel in physics and other STEM courses in communities where traditional gendered status is not the norm (Riegle-Crumb and Moore 2013). Pursuing a STEM career does not necessarily require stellar math scores, but some girls are socialized to believe they are not good in math and therefore do not take higher-level courses or expect to do well on tests (Wade 2013b).

In sports, boys are encouraged to join competitive team sports and girls to support them. Some argue that this simulates hierarchical adult roles of boss/secretary and physician/nurse. Girls' and boys' separate experiences in grade school and middle school reinforce boundaries of "us" and "them" in classroom seating and activities, in the lunchroom, and in playground activities, as girls and boys are seated, lined up, and given assignments by sex (Sadker and Sadker 2005). Those who go outside the boundaries, especially boys, are ridiculed by peers and sometimes teachers, reinforcing stereotypes and separate gender role socialization (Sadker and Sadker 2005; Thorne 1993).

Part of the issue of male-female inequality in schools is tied to the issue of *popularity*, which seems to have less to do with being liked than with being known and visible. If everyone knows a person's name, she or he is popular. At the middle school level, there are more ways by which boys than girls can become known. In sports, even when there are both boys' and girls' basketball teams, many spectators come to the boys' contests and very few to the girls' games. Thus, few people know the female athletes by name. In fact, a far more visible position is cheerleader—standing on the sidelines cheering for the boys' teams, and sometimes for girls' teams—because those girls are at least seen. One effort is to redefine cheerleading as a legitimate sport in its own right (Eder, Evans, and Parker 1995; Hu 2007; Milner 2006). The bottom line is that there are far more visible positions for the boys than for girls in middle and high school, allowing them to be recognized and become leaders.

Title IX of the U.S. Education Amendments of 1972 was a major legislative attempt to level the educational and sports playing field. Passed in order to bar gender discrimination in schools receiving federal funds, this legislation mandates equal opportunity for participation in school-sponsored programs (Lindsey 2011). The law has reduced or eliminated blatant discrimination in areas ranging from admissions and health care to counseling and housing, sex-segregated programs, financial aid, dress codes, and other areas of concern. However, the biggest impact of Title IX legislation has been in athletics.

Women's athletic programs and scholarship opportunities have grown since 1972 but still lag behind those for men. By 2011, the number of girls competing in high school sports had climbed to almost 3.2 million, yet that is still 1.3 million more boys than girls participating in high school sports. In collegiate sports, the number of female athletes has grown from fewer than 30,000 to about 200,000. Men's sports, though, both bring in and receive more money and have more airtime on TV (Dusenbery and Lee 2012). Participation in athletics, especially team sports, is important because sports can foster skills in teamwork, strategic thinking, and anticipating counteractions by a competitor, useful skills in business and government.

Religious Organizations. Religious organizations serve as agents of gender socialization by defining, reinforcing, and perpetuating gender roles and cultural beliefs. Religious teachings provide explanations of proper male and female roles. Although the specific teachings vary, the three major monotheistic religions

⬤ Middle School Peer Pressure

High school and college athletics are much less reliable paths for women to become known since so few people come to the games. Even at this professional Lynx game with a team that twice won the national title, there is a sparse attendance (left). By contrast, women in very sexy outfits can become celebrities when they perform as cheerleaders in front of 80,000 fans at men's sporting events (right).

that affirm that there is only one God—Christianity, Islam, and Judaism—are traditionally patriarchal, stressing separate female and male spheres (Kramer and Beutel 2014).

Some interpretations of the Adam and Eve creation story in the Hebrew Bible (the Old Testament in the Christian Bible) state that man was created first and that men are, therefore, superior. Because Eve, created from the rib of man, was a sinner, her sins keep women forever in an inferior, second-class position. For these and other reasons, in some branches of these religions, women are restricted in their roles. They cannot be priests in Catholic churches and cannot vote on business matters in some religious organizations. However, recent work by scholars points out that women played a much broader role in religious development than is often recognized (Hunter College Women's Studies Collective 2005). Increasingly, denominations are granting women greater roles in the religious hierarchies, ministries, and priesthood.

Women in Judaism lived for 4,000 years in a patriarchal system where men read, taught, and legislated while women followed (Lindsey 2011). Today, three of the five main branches of Judaism allow women equal participation, illustrating that religious practices do change over time. However, Hasidic and Orthodox Jews have a division of labor between men and women following old laws, with designated gender roles for the home and religious life.

Some Christian teachings have treated women as second-class citizens, even in the eyes of God. For this reason, some Christian denominations have excluded women from a variety of leadership roles and told them they must be subservient to their husbands. Other Christians point to the admonition by Saint Paul that, theologically speaking, the distinction between men and women is not relevant and that women and men are not spiritually different.

Traditional Hindu religion painted women as seductresses, strongly erotic, and a threat to male spirituality and asceticism. To protect men from this threat, women were kept totally covered in thick garments and veils and seen only by men in their immediate families. Today, Hinduism comes in many forms, most of which honor the woman's domestic sphere of life—as mothers, wives, and homemakers—while accepting women in public roles (Lindsey 2011).

Traditional Islamic beliefs also portrayed female sexuality as dangerous to men, although many women in Islamic societies today are full participants in the public and private sphere. The Quran (also spelled Qur'an or Koran), the Muslim sacred scripture, has a few passages that seem to favor men, but most of the text actually supports women's rights (Aslan 2011). Still, aspects of the traditional Sharia law, strict Islamic law, have carried over in several countries and among some groups. It has been used to punish women accused of violating rules about gender behavior (Proudman 2012; Mydans 2002).

Women in strict literalist Muslim societies such as Algeria, Iran, Syria, and Saudi Arabia are separated from men (except for fathers and brothers) in work and worship. They generally remain covered. *Purdah*, which means curtain, refers to practices of seclusion and separate worlds for women and men in Islamic cultures. Screens in households and veils in public enforce female modesty and prevent men from seeing women where this is dictated (Ward and Edelstein 2014). In the days of Muhammad, only his wives wore such veils for privacy, and there were no commandments in the Quran instructing women to be covered, so these patterns are more cultural and national than Islamic. In any case, today some women argue that the veil they wear is for modesty, for cosmetic purposes, or to protect them from the stares of men.

Meso-level religious systems influence how different societies interpret proper gender roles and how sometimes these belief systems change with new interpretations of scriptures. (Further discussion of the complex relationship between religion and gender appears in Chapter 11.) From family and education to media and religion, meso-level agents of socialization reinforce "appropriate" gender roles in each society.

Thinking Sociologically

What are some of the books, toys, games, television shows, school experiences, religious teachings, and peer interactions that have influenced your gender role socialization? In what ways did they do so?

GENDER STRATIFICATION: MESO- AND MACRO-LEVEL PROCESSES

The phrase *glass ceiling* generally applies to processes that limit the progress of women and other minorities to the highest job or status positions because of invisible barriers that bar promotion within an organization. Although they may have superior skills or experience, they are passed over (Berrey 2013). "The *glass ceiling* keeps women from reaching the highest levels of corporate and public responsibility, and the 'sticky floor' keeps the vast majority of the world's women stuck in low-paid jobs" (Hunter College Women's Studies Collective 2005:393). This discrimination results in a loss of talent, and lower salaries for women, who make up

almost half of the workforce and are the main or equal breadwinners in 4 out of 10 families. Although there are high-profile women serving as CEOs and in government leadership positions in the United States, they occupy only 4.6% of both the Fortune 500 and the Fortune 1000 CEO positions (Catalyst 2014b). Women now represent 52.2% of the U.S. PhDs (Council of Graduate Schools 2014) and 67% of college graduates, but they earn only about 80 cents for every dollar earned by men, a 23% wage gap. This holds across occupations (DeBoskey 2012; Hegewisch et al. 2014; Matson 2013).

Men, on the other hand, often face the "glass escalator," especially in traditionally female occupations. Even if they do not seek to climb in the organizational hierarchy, occupational social forces push them up the job ladder to the higher echelons (Williams 2013). The next "Engaging Sociology" provides an exercise to think about how our ideas may subtly maintain the glass ceiling and the glass escalator by defining "leadership" in the same way that we define masculinity.

Women and Men at Work: Gendered Organizations

"How can I do it all—marriage, children, education, career, social life?" This is a question that many college students ask. They already anticipate a delicate balancing act. Work has been central to the definition of masculinity in U.S. society, and for the past half-century women have been joining the workforce in greater numbers (Kramer and Beutel 2014). Today, 57.7% of women over 16 are in the workforce, compared to 70.2% of all men (Catalyst 2014a). For example, women who are personal financial advisers earn 58.7% of what men in that occupation earn. The pattern of unequal pay is true in a number of Global North countries (20-First 2010).

Among countries of the Global North, Sweden has the highest percentage of working women; more than 8 out of 10 women participate in the labor force. Yet even in Sweden, with its parental leave and other family-friendly policies, women and men feel pressures of work and family responsibilities (Eshleman and Bulcroft 2010). Dual-career marriages raise questions about child rearing, power relations, and other factors in juggling work and family.

Every workplace has gendered relationships: ratios of female to male workers; gender reflected in subordinate-supervisor positions; and distribution

ENGAGING SOCIOLOGY

Masculinity and Femininity in Our Social World

1. Mark each characteristic with an *M* or an *F* depending on whether you think it is generally defined by society as a masculine or feminine characteristic.

   _ achiever

   _ aggressive

   _ analytical

   _ caring

   _ confident

   _ dynamic

   _ deferential (defers to others; yields with courtesy)

   _ devious

   _ intuitive

   _ loving

   _ manipulative

   _ nurturing

   _ organized

   _ passive

   _ a planner

   _ powerful

   _ sensitive

   _ strong

   _ relationship-oriented (makes decisions based on how others will *feel*)

   _ rule oriented (makes decisions based on *abstract procedural rules rather people's feelings*)

2. Next, mark an *X* just to the right of 10 characteristics that you think are the essential qualities for a leadership position in a complex organization (business, government, etc.). You might want to ask 20 of your acquaintances to do this and then add up the scores for "masculinity," "femininity," and "leadership trait."

3. Do you (and your acquaintances) tend to view leadership as having the same traits as those marked "masculine" or "feminine"? What are the implications of your findings for the "glass ceiling" or "the glass escalator"?

4. How might correlations between the traits of leadership and gender notions help to explain the data on income in Table 9.2?

of positions between men and women. This, in turn, affects our experiences in the workplace. Consider the example of mothers breast-feeding their babies. Must they quit their jobs or alter their family schedules if the workplace does not provide a space for breast-feeding? Some workplaces accommodate family needs, but many do not.

Using data from the Organisation for Economic Co-operation and Development, *The Economist* constructed a "glass-ceiling index" using these five indicators: the number of men and women, respectively, with college educations; female labor-force participation; the gender wage gap; the proportion of women in senior positions in corporations and professions; and net child care costs compared to incomes. Cross-national comparisons indicate that New Zealand, Norway, Sweden, and Canada have the best conditions for working women. Nations that scored least

women-friendly in employment were Japan and South Korea where few women can reach top jobs. Among the 26 nations that were studied, the United

TABLE 9.2 U.S. Income by Educational Level and Sex—Full-Time Workers

Education	Men	Women
Not a high school graduate	$23,036	$15,514
High school graduate	$35,468	$24,304
College graduate (bachelor's)	$69,479	$43,589
Master's degree	$90,964	$58,534
Doctorate	$114,347	$83,708
Professional degree	$150,310	$89,897

Source: U.S. Census Bureau 2012d.

FIGURE 9.1 Ratio of Women's to Men's Earnings for Selected Occupations, 2010

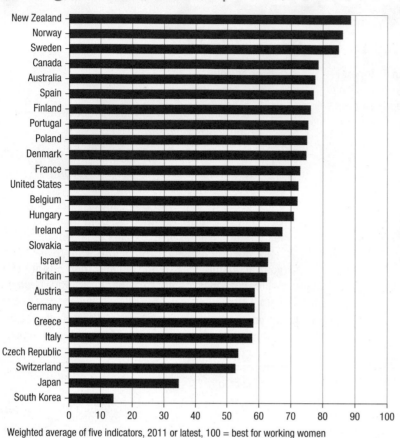

Weighted average of five indicators, 2011 or latest, 100 = best for working women

Source: "The Glass Ceiling Index" 2013. *The Economist,* March 7, 2013. Copyright © The Economist Newspaper Limited, London 2013. Reprinted with permission.

States rated 12th for women's employment conditions (Khazan 2013). The results of the ranking appear in Figure 9.1.

Institutionalized Gender Discrimination

Gender stratification at the meso level—like race and ethnic stratification—can occur quite independently of any overt prejudice or ill will by others. It becomes part of the social system, and we are not even conscious of it. *Discrimination* is often built into organizations and cultural expectations and includes both intentional actions and unintentional actions or structures that have consequences harmful to minorities. It is embedded in institutions.

You will recall from the previous chapter that **side-effect discrimination** involves *practices in one institutional area that have negative impact because they are linked to practices in another institutional area. Institutions are interdependent, so discrimination in one can result in unintentional discrimination in others.* For example, when roles of women in family life are determined by rigid gender expectations, women find it more difficult to devote themselves to gaining job promotions. In addition, as long as little girls learn through socialization to use their voices and to hold their bodies and to gesture in ways that communicate deference, employers assume a lack of the self-confidence necessary for major leadership roles. If women are paid less than men, despite the same levels of education (see Table 9.2), they are less likely to have access to the best health care or to be able to afford a $40,000 down payment for a house, unless they are married. This makes women dependent on men in a way that most men are not dependent on women.

A factor affecting differences in incomes is the type of academic degrees that men and women receive (e.g., engineering rather than education). However, even when these differences are factored in, men still make considerably more on average than women with identical levels of experience and training.

Past-in-present discrimination, discussed in Chapter 8, refers to *practices from the past that may no longer be allowed but that continue to affect people today.* For example, in a Midwest appliance industry investigated by one of the authors, there is a sequence of jobs one must hold to be promoted up the line to foreman. This requirement ensures that the foreman understands the many aspects of production at the plant. One of the jobs involves working in a room with heavy equipment that cuts through and bends metal sheets. The machine is extremely powerful and could easily cut off a leg or hand if the operator is not careful. Because of the danger, the engineers designed the equipment so it would not operate unless three levers were activated at the same time. One lever was

This little girl looks cute, but not very powerful or confident. When women tilt their heads—either forward or to one side—they also look like they lack confidence, and this hurts their chances of promotion in the corporate world.

triggered by stepping on a pedal on the floor. The other two required reaching out with one's hands so that one's body was extended. When one was spread-eagled to activate all three levers, there was no way one could possibly have a part of one's body near the blades.

It was brilliant engineering, but there was one unanticipated problem: The hand-activated levers were 5 feet, 10 inches off the ground and 5 feet apart. Few women had the height and arm span to run this machine, and therefore no women had yet made it through the sequence of positions to the higher-paying position of foreman. The equipment cost millions of dollars, so it was not likely to be replaced. Neither the engineers who designed the machine nor the upper-level managers who established the sequence of jobs to become foreman had deliberately tried to exclude women. Indeed, they were perplexed when they looked at their employee figures and saw so few women moving up through the ranks. The cause of women's disadvantage was not mean-spirited men but features of the system that had unintended consequences resulting in past-in-present discrimination. A machine built in the past to service workers at that time is still in use and now disqualifies women for an important job. The barriers women face, then, are not just matters of socialization or other micro-level social processes. The nature of sexism is often subtle yet pervasive in the society, operating at the meso and macro levels as institutional discrimination.

Men often get defensive and angry when people talk about sexism in society because they feel they are being attacked or asked to correct past injustices. However, the empirical reality is that the playing field is not level for men and women. Most men do not do anything to intentionally harm women, and they may not feel prejudiced toward women, but sexism operates so that men are given privileges they never asked for and may not even recognize.

Gender Differences in Internet Use

Internet-related gender stratification exhibits itself not just in terms of *whether* a person uses the Internet but also in terms of *how* a person uses the Internet. In the United States, women tend to use social networking sites 12% more than men (women 74%, men 62%) (Pew Research Center Internet and American Life Project 2014b), with the intent of keeping up with family and friends. Women's use focuses on personal growth, maintaining a social group, and getting information about products and brands. Globally, women account for 47.9% of visitors to social networking sites, and spend 30% more time on social networking sites than men (ComScore 2010; Morrison 2010).

Men tend to use the Internet to gather information and to exchange ideas, gain job skills, and form and maintain professional networks. Thus, women use social media more than men for their private lives, and men are more likely to use the Internet for engaging in the public sphere. The difference also reflects dissimilarities in the professional positions men and women tend to hold. Men's greater use of the Internet

In some countries, there is a huge gender digital divide, and research shows that women and men tend to use computers in different ways. These women in Afghanistan are learning computer skills.

to enhance their careers relates to the preponderance of men in upper-level management positions. In the United States, where women have recently caught up with or outpaced their male peers in education, the direction of U.S. usage parallels that of other Global North countries and may predict the future for other countries (Madden and Zickuhr 2011).

Thinking Sociologically

Ask several people from different generations and different genders how they use computer technology and the Internet and how they learned these skills. What do you conclude from their responses about the impact of gender on Internet use? How do your findings compare to those discussed in the book? Why?

GENDER STRATIFICATION: MICRO- TO MACRO-LEVEL THEORIES

Recent research by some biologists and psychologists has considered whether there are innate differences in the makeup of women and men. For instance, males produce more testosterone, a hormone found to be correlated with aggression. Research shows that in many situations, males tend to be more aggressive and concerned with dominance, whether the behavior is biologically programmed or learned or both. Other traits, such as nurturance, empathy, and altruism, show no clear gender difference (Fausto-Sterling 1992; Sapolsky 2011).

Although biological and psychological factors are part of the difference between females and males, our focus here is on the major contribution that *social factors* make in the social statuses of males and females in human society (DiPrete and Buchmann 2013). This section explores social theories that explain gender differences.

Symbolic Interaction Theory: Micro-Level Analysis

Traditional notions of gender are hard to change. Confusion over proper masculine and feminine roles creates anxiety and even anomie in a society. People want guidelines. Thus, many believe it is best to adhere to traditional notions of gender that are reinforced by religious or political dogmas, making those

ideas appear sacred, absolute, and beyond human interference. Others believe the male prerogatives and privileges of the past were established by men to protect their rights and should be challenged. Change in concepts of gender can be hard to bring about precisely because they are rooted in the meaning system and status and power structures present in the social world.

Symbolic interactionists look at gender as socially constructed. Sex is the biological reality of different "plumbing" in our bodies, and interactionists are interested in how those physical differences come to be symbols, resulting in different social rights and rewards. The meaning assigned to one's sex is connected to notions of masculinity and femininity. The symbolic interaction perspective has been forceful in insisting that notions of proper gender behavior are not intrinsically related to a person's sex. Rather, gender is a socially created or constructed idea.

More than any other theory, symbolic interaction stresses the idea of *human agency*—the notion that humans not only are influenced by the society in which they live but also actively help create it (Charon 2010; Hewitt and Shulman 2011).

Through interaction, people do gender, and although this process begins at a micro level, it has implications all the way to the global level. The next section explores meso- and macro-level forces that shape gender and stratification based on sex.

Thinking Sociologically

How do you *do gender*? How did you learn these patterns of behavior? How do you think people would react if you did not follow the behavior patterns assigned to your gender? How comfortable would you feel when violating those gender norms? Why?

Structural-Functional and Conflict Theories: Meso- and Macro-Level Analyses

Meso and macro-level theories provide the big picture related to gender issues. When the government passes laws that affect women (or men), like abortion or birth control laws, they affect individual women at the micro level. Likewise, laws related to child custody, payment of child support, and other laws related to marriage and divorce are made by state and national governmental offices and enforced by courts. In the following sections we visit our familiar theories as they relate to gender issues.

Structural-Functional Theory. From the structural-functional perspective, each sex has a role to play in the interdependent groups and institutions of society. Some early theorists argued that men and women carry out different roles and are, of necessity, unequal because of the needs of societies and practices that have developed since early human history. Social relationships and practices that have proven successful in the survival of a group are likely to continue and to be reinforced by society's norms, laws, and religious beliefs. Thus, relationships between women and men believed to support survival are maintained. In traditional hunter-gatherer, horticultural, and pastoral societies, for instance, the division of labor and social roles are based on sex and age. The females often take on the primary tasks of child care, gardening, food preparation, and other duties near the home. Men do tasks that require movements farther from home, such as hunting, fishing, and herding.

As societies industrialize, roles and relationships change due to structural changes in society. Émile Durkheim described a gradual move from traditional societies held together by *mechanical solidarity* (the glue based on shared beliefs, values, and traditions) to modern societies united through *organic solidarity* (social coherence based on division of labor, with each member playing a highly specialized role) (Durkheim [1893] 1947). According to early functionalists, gender-based division of labor exists in modern societies because it is efficient and useful to have different but complementary male and female roles. They believed this helps members of society to accomplish essential tasks and maintains societal stability (Lindsey 2011).

Today, more children are being raised by single moms than married couples, and the turnover in partners has created complex families not seen before (Aulette 2010; Coontz 2011). Fewer people are marrying, and those who do tend to be older than in previous decades. Increasing numbers of women do not have children (about 20% now, compared to just 10% in the 1970s) (Angier 2013). In addition, many families today thrive with two adult partners of the same sex.

Conflict Theory. Conflict theorists view gender relations through the lens of power. Men are the *haves*—controlling the majority of power positions and most wealth—and women are the *have-nots*. By keeping women in subordinate roles, males control the means of production and protect their privileged status.

A classical conflict explanation of gender stratification is found in the writings of Karl Marx's colleague, Friedrich Engels ([1884] 1942). In traditional societies, where size and strength were essential for survival, men were often dominant, but women's roles were respected as important and necessary to the survival of the group. Men hunted, engaged in warfare, and protected women. Over time, male physical control was transformed into control by ideology, by the dominant belief system itself. Capitalism strengthened male dominance by making more wealth available to men and their sons. Women became dependent on men, and their roles were transformed into "taking care of the home" (Engels [1884] 1942).

Ideologies based on traditional beliefs and values have continued to be used to justify the social structure of male domination and subjugation of women. It is in the interest of the dominant group, in this case men, to maintain a position of privilege. Conflict theorists believe it unlikely that those in power by virtue of sex, race, class, or political or religious ideology will voluntarily give up their positions as long as they are benefiting from them. By keeping women in traditional gender roles, men maintain control over institutions and resources (Collins 1971).

Feminist Theory. Feminist theorists agree with Marx and Engels that gender stratification is based on power struggles, not biology. On the other hand, some feminist theorists argue that Marx and Engels failed to consider fully a key variable in women's oppression: patriarchy. Patriarchy involves a few men dominating and holding authority over all others, including women, children, and the less powerful men (Arrighi 2000; Lindsey 2011). According to feminist theory, no matter what the economic or political system, women will continue to be oppressed by men until patriarchy is eliminated. There is a range of feminist theories. However, all feminist theories argue for bringing about a new and equal ordering of gender relationships to eliminate the patriarchy and sexism of current gender-stratification systems (Kramer and Beutel 2014).

Feminist theorists try to understand the causes of women's lower status and seek ways to change the systems to provide more opportunities, to improve the standard of living, and to give women control over their bodies and reproduction. Feminist theorists also feel that little change will occur until group consciousness

Men are much more likely than women to play cards, games, or sports together and develop networks that enhance their power and their ability to "close deals." When women are not part of the same networks, they are denied the same insider privileges.

is raised so that women understand the system that limits their options and do not blame themselves for their situations (Sapiro 2003).

As societies become technologically advanced and need an educated workforce, women of all social classes and ethnic groups around the world are likely to gain more equal roles. Women are entering institutions of higher education in record numbers, and evidence indicates they are needed in the world economic system and the changing labor force of most countries. Countries in which women are not integrated into the economic system generally lag behind other countries. Feminist theorists examine these global and national patterns, but they also note the role of patriarchy in micro-level interpersonal situations—such as domestic violence.

Violence against women perpetuates gender stratification, as is evident in the intimate environment of many homes. Because men have more power in the larger society, they often have more resources within the household as well (an example of side-effect discrimination). Women are often dependent on the man of the house for his resources, meaning they must yield on many decisions. Power differences in the meso- and macro-level social systems also contribute to power differentials and vulnerability of women in micro-level settings. In addition, women have fewer options when considering whether to leave an abusive relationship. Although there are risks of staying in an abusive relationship, many factors enter into a woman's decision to stay or leave; rational choice theory has been used by some researchers to evaluate the

gains and losses from staying versus leaving (Copp et al. 2013; Estrellado and Loh 2013).

In summary, feminist analysis finds gender patterns embedded in social institutions of family, education, religion, politics, economics, and health care. If the societal system is patriarchal, ruled by men, the interdependent institutions are likely to reflect and support this system. Feminist theory helps us understand how patriarchy at the meso and macro levels can influence patriarchy at the micro level and vice versa.

Thinking Sociologically

Imagine you were asked to reduce domestic violence in your society. How would you address it differently if you looked at it as a social issue, rather than just as a problem for the individuals directly affected by it?

The Interaction of Class, Race, and Gender.

Some feminist theorists look at the ways in which discrimination related to class, race, and gender intersects in society (Anderson and Collins 2010). In the process, some groups of people face multiple forms of oppression that reinforce one another.

Zouina is Algerian in her background and ethnicity, but she was born in France to her immigrant parents. She lived with them in a poor immigrant suburb of Paris until she was forced to return to Algeria for an arranged marriage to a man who already had one wife. That marriage ended, and she returned to her "home" in France. Since she returned to France, Zouina has been employed wherever she can find work. The high unemployment rate and social and ethnic discrimination, especially against foreign women, makes life difficult.

The situation is complex. Muslim women from Tunisia, Morocco, and Algeria living in crowded slum communities outside Paris face discrimination in the workplace and their communities (Lazaridis 2011). Expected to be both good Muslim women and good family co-providers—which necessitates working in French society—they face ridicule when they wear their *hijabs* (coverings) to school or to work. However, they encounter derision in their community if they do not wear them. They are caught between two cultures, and may be the scapegoats for frustrated young men who cannot find work.

Because of high unemployment in the immigrant communities, many youth roam the streets. Gang rapes by North African youth against young women

 Violence Against Women—It's a Man's Issue

have been on the rise in France and elsewhere abroad. The victims of these rapes face rejection and disdain in their immigrant community, and in their original African communities (Killian 2006).

In another example, "many women of color . . . are burdened by poverty, child care responsibilities, and the lack of job skills. These burdens, largely the consequence of gender and class oppression, are then compounded by the racially discriminatory employment and housing practices women of color often face, as well as by the disproportionately high unemployment among people of color" (Crenshaw 1991:1245–46). Table 9.3 shows the median earnings of workers in the United States by race and sex and helps illustrate how racism and sexism can reinforce one another and lead to the "double marginalization" of women of color.

These examples illustrate that race, class, and gender have crosscutting lines that may affect one's status in the society. Women of color can face the triple status determinants of being poor (class), women (gender), and of color (race or ethnicity). Lesbians and women identifying as bisexual, transgender, or queer face yet another form of oppression that intersects with the other three.

Sexual orientation, age, nationality, and other factors also have the effect of either diminishing or increasing minority status of specific women, and theorists are paying increasing attention to these intersections (Rothenberg 2010). Chapter 8 discussed the fact that race and class lines may be either crosscutting or parallel. In the case of gender, there are always crosscutting lines with race and social class. However, gender always affects one's prestige and privilege within that class or ethnic group. Thus, to get a full picture, these three variables—race, class, and gender—need to be considered simultaneously.

Thinking Sociologically

How have race, class, and gender intersected in your life and impacted your life chances? Do you think your experience is common among other members of your local community? Why or why not?

Gender, Homosexuality, and Minority Status

We have already learned that sex, gender, and sexuality are complex concepts. *Heterosexism* is an assumption that every person is heterosexual, legitimizing heterosexuality as the only normal lifestyle and marginalizing persons who do not identify as heterosexual (Gender Equity Resource Center 2013). Heterosexism operates at all levels of society; it can be seen at the micro level in the United States where it is strongest in small towns and rural areas where LGBTQs (lesbian, gay, bisexual, transgender, and queer individuals) experience housing discrimination, property damage, and employment discrimination (Swank, Fahs, and Frost 2013).

Homophobia—intense fear and hatred of homosexuality and homosexuals, whether male or female—is highly correlated with and perhaps a cause of people holding traditional notions of gender and gender roles (Shaw and Lee 2005). This concept, which operates on the micro level, was coined by a psychologist who noted that intense hatred of LGBTQs is due to a personality disorder or illness (Weinberg 1972).

Despite some fear and hostility, homosexuality and transgendered people have always existed. They have been accepted and even required for certain positions at some times and places, and rejected or outlawed in others. In some societies, homosexuals and transgendered individuals have been placed in a separate sexual category with special roles. For example, the *Hijras* in India and some other areas in South Asia are usually physiological males who have feminine gender identity. Many live in *Hijra* communities and have designated roles in Indian festivals and celebrations.

Some societies ignore the existence of LGBTQ members of the community. Some consider them to

TABLE 9.3 Median Usual Weekly Earnings of Workers by Race, Sex, and Percentage of Men's Earnings by Women, Fourth Quarter 2014

Race and Ethnicity	Male	Female	Women's % of Men's Earnings
Asian American	$1,067	$826	77.4
White	907	738	81.4
African American	667	602	90.3
Hispanic or Latino	631	544	86.2

U.S. Department of Labor 2014.

have psychological illnesses or forms of depraved immorality. Some societies even consider these forms of sexuality a crime (as in 38 out of 54 African nations today and in most states in the United States during much of the 20th century). To be accused of homosexuality can result in the death penalty in Sudan, Somalia, Mauritania, and the northern part of Nigeria (Nossiter 2014). In each case around the world, the government or dominant religious group determines the status of homosexuals. The reality is that deviation from a society's gender norms, such as attraction to a member of the same sex, may cause one to experience minority status.

Some members of the LGBTQ community deviate from traditional notions of masculinity and femininity and therefore from significant norms of many societies. This may result in hostile reactions and stigma from the dominant group. Indeed, homosexual epitaphs are often used to reinforce gender conformity, particularly among men, and to intimidate anyone who would dare to be different from the norm. Because in many societies women are economically dependent on men, their status in society is typically based on their relationship with men. Therefore, lesbians—women who are attracted to other women—are in some instances perceived as a threat to men's power (Burn 2011; Ward and Edelstein 2014).

The mass media have begun to include LGBTQ characters in films such as *Behind the Candelabra* (2013), *Dallas Buyers Club* (2013), *In Bloom* (2013), *Beginners* (2011), *A Single Man* (2009), *Milk* (2008),

A transsexual (*Hijra*) dances at a gathering in Bangladesh, where a group met in the capital to demand government action to provide legal protection from persecution. *Hijras* are treated as social outcasts, and typically earn a living by singing, dancing, and other performances.

Shelter (2007), and *Brokeback Mountain* (2005). Television shows with positive images of lesbians and gays—such as *Ellen, Will and Grace, Pretty Little Liars, Glee, Modern Family, Grey's Anatomy, Chicago Fire,* and *The Good Wife*—have also become popular. In addition, there are many well-known lesbian and gay news commentators and show hosts, reflecting an increased level of acceptance of LGBTQ people in many nations.

Gallup polls reveal that U.S. public acceptance of lesbians and gays is up 19 points in the past 12 years to 59% today (Newport and Himelfarb 2013). Over half (52%) of all Americans and 69% of 18- to 34-year-olds say they would vote in favor of laws legalizing same-sex marriage (Saad 2013). As of March 2015, 37 states and Washington, DC, legally recognize same-sex marriage (Freedom to Marry 2015). In 2013, Walmart initiated partner benefits for same-sex couples. It is among the 62% of Fortune 500 companies that now offer health insurance and other "marriage" benefits to same-sex couples ("Same-Sex Couples" 2013). Despite these indications of greater openness in attitudes, in 2014 it was still legal in 29 states to fire someone based on his or her sexuality (Edelson 2014). Note how meso-level institutions such as government and religion control personal relationships—even trying to restrain whom one can love.

The point here is not to argue for or against same-sex marriage but to note that gays and lesbians do not have many of the rights that heterosexuals have, a discrepancy based on sexual preferences. Heterosexuals in the United States have a variety of rights—ranging from insurance coverage and inheritance rights for lifelong partners to jointly acquired property, hospital visitation rights as family, rights to claim the body of a deceased partner, and rights to have the deceased prepared for burial or cremation. The U.S. federal government confers 1,138 rights on heterosexuals that they normally take for granted, but often, these rights do not extend to same-sex partners in a long-term committed relationship. Most states also bestow more than 200 specific rights to persons who "marry," but because many states do not allow same-sex marriages, many same-sex couples do not have these same rights (Wolfson 2015). A number of other countries, including Canada and many European countries, have legalized same-sex marriage, reducing the number of inequities in rights.

In short, macro-level cultural notions about gender and sexuality influence institutions such as family, politics, economics, and religion. At the micro level, gender is very personal and private, but also a public issue with macro-level implications.

⬤ Thinking Sociologically

What are some societal changes that have influenced the dramatic changes over the past decade in attitudes in the United States toward same-sex marriage? Have they impacted your perspective on this issue? Why or why not?

COSTS AND CONSEQUENCES OF GENDER STRATIFICATION

The consequences of gender stratification affect every level of society. They impact life chances for individuals and how institutions, nations, and the global society function. As illustrated in the following examples, sex- and gender-based stratification limits individual development and causes problems in education, health, work, and other parts of the social world.

Psychological and Social Consequences: Micro-Level Implications

For both women and men, rigid gender stereotypes can be very constraining (see the "Engaging Sociology" feature on leadership and gender on page 245). Individuals who hold highly sex-typed attitudes feel compelled to behave in stereotypic ways, ways that are consistent with the pictures they have in their heads of proper gender behavior (Kramer 2010). However, individuals who do not identify rigidly with masculine or feminine gender types tend to have a broader repertoire of acceptable behaviors and know how to cope with changing situations (Cheng 2005). They are more flexible in thoughts and behavior, score higher on intelligence tests, have greater spatial ability, and have higher levels of creativity. Because they allow themselves a wider range of behaviors, they have more varied abilities and experiences and become more tolerant of others' behaviors.

High masculinity in males sets up rigid standards for male behavior and has been correlated with anxiety, guilt, and neuroses, whereas less rigid masculine expectations are associated with emotional stability, sensitivity, warmth, and enthusiasm. Rigid stereotypes and resulting sexism can limit our activities, behaviors, and perspectives.

Results of Gender Role Expectations. Women in many societies are expected to be beautiful, youthful, and sexually interesting and interested, while preparing the food, caring for the children, keeping a clean and orderly home, bringing in money to help support the family, and being competent and successful in their careers. Multiple, sometimes contradictory, expectations for women can cause stress and even serious psychological problems. The resulting strain contributes to depression and certain health problems such as headaches, nervousness, and insomnia (Slaughter 2012; Wood 2008).

Gender expectations also affect women's self-concepts and body images. As noted earlier, beautiful images jump out at us from billboards, magazine covers, and TV and movie screens. Some of these images are unattainable for most women because they have been created through surgeries, eating disorders, and the use of airbrushing on photographs. Disorders, including anorexia and bulimia nervosa, relate to societal expectations of the ideal woman's appearance (Taub and McLorg 2010). In the United States, close to 24 million people suffer from eating disorders. Women are more likely to have eating disorders, but men are less likely to seek help when they do have a problem, resulting in serious health problems including death (James 2013).

Thinking Sociologically

How much time, energy, and money do you spend on your physical appearance? Why? From what socializing agents did you learn how to judge your physical appearance? Overall, how have those socializing agents impacted how you view yourself?

Men die earlier than women, in part due to environmental, psychological, and social factors. Problems in Global North countries such as heart disease, stroke, cirrhosis, cancers, accidents, and suicides are linked in part to the role expectations that males should appear tough, objective, ambitious, unsentimental, and unemotional—traits that require men to assume great responsibility and suppress their feelings (Leit, Gray, and Pope 2002; Tull 2012). So gender expectations can have a substantial cost for men as well as for women.

Societal Costs: Meso- and Macro-Level Implications

Gender stratification creates costs for societies around the world in a number of ways. *Poor educational achievement* of female children leads to the loss of human talents and resources, a serious cost for societies. *Social divisiveness*—"us" versus "them" thinking based on sex—can create alienation, if not hostility, and this can result in physical or emotional aggression, discrimination, and violence against women.

Human capital—the resources of the human population—is central to social prosperity in societal systems. Yet resistance to expanding women's public sphere and professional roles is often strong. For example, Japanese women make up close to 50% of the workforce, but only 10.1% hold managerial positions and many leave the workplace when they marry (Fackler 2007). Japan and Korea have the highest gender wage gap at 39% difference, the largest wage gap among Global North countries (Catalyst 2014c). Although Japanese women score higher in science than boys and are almost half of university graduates, few can break through the glass ceiling they face in the job market (Hewlett 2013).

CHANGING GENDER STRATIFICATION AND SOCIAL POLICY

Is it better for a woman in the Global South to have a poor-paying job and poor working conditions, or no job? On the one hand, few wage-paying jobs are available in some countries, and most of the positions in manufacturing and assembly positions that do become available are held by women. Yet women in factories around the globe face dangerous conditions and low pay. Sweatshops exist because poor women and sometimes men have few other job options to support their families and because people in rich countries want to buy the cheap products that perpetuate the multinational corporate system. For example, over one million Mexicans work in *maquiladoras* (foreign-owned manufacturing and assembly plants) in Mexican border towns for very low wages.

The maquiladoras are owned by U.S., European, and Japanese conglomerates and hire primarily unskilled young women. Wages are 18% of what U.S. workers receive (Stevenson 2013). The products are mostly shipped to the United States (Rosenberg 2012). The hours worked per week range from 50 to 75. Some maquiladoras pay $40 to $50 for a 60-hour week ("Misery of the Maquiladoras" 2011). Many multinational corporations based in the Global North exploit workers in the Global South to make their products.

One result is exploitation of women workers in other parts of the world. Another is loss of income for workers in the United States, including men. Manufacturers within the United States are starting to hire after the economic recession, but the wages they are offering are $10 to $15 an hour less than before the recession (Kelber 2012). So the "race to the bottom" by multinationals (seeking the lowest price for labor) is affecting earnings of men and women in the United States. We really live in an interconnected world.

What can be done about the abusive treatment of women workers around the world? This is a tough issue: Governments have passed legislation to protect workers, but governments also want the jobs and tax dollars that multinational corporations bring and therefore do little to enforce regulations. International labor standards are also difficult to enforce because multinational corporations are so large and located in many different parts of the world. Trade unions have had little success attracting workers to join because companies squash their recruiting efforts immediately.

One way activist groups protest for fair wages and conditions for workers is to adopt practices that have worked for other groups facing discrimination in the past. Consider the following strategies used by groups to combat unfair labor practices: holding nonviolent protests, including sit-down strikes and walkouts; encouraging companies to help the communities in which their factories are located; using the Internet to carry the message to others; carrying out boycotts against companies that mistreat employees; employing the arts, storytellers, and teachers to mobilize resistance; and building on traditions of student, community and religious activism (Collins 2008; Maquila Solidarity Network 2014). Most of these strategies require organized movements, but such efforts may antagonize the

Women in Thailand produce shoes for extremely low pay. These jobs are better than no employment at all, but before pressures from Global North societies changed their cultures, most people were able to feed their families on farms in small villages.

companies so much that they move to other countries. It is a delicate balance. To be successful, the fair labor effort must be as globalized as the corporations whose practices they wish to impact.

⬤ Thinking Sociologically

Take a look at the clothing in your closet and your drawers. Figure out where it was made either by reading the labels or by looking up the companies' factories on the Internet. Would you be willing to pay more for that clothing so that other people could have better conditions? Why or why not? What about your friends? How can the plight of workers across the globe impact you and other workers in your nation?

At women's conferences around the world, policymakers debate how to create solutions to women's problems. Most United Nations member countries have at least fledgling women's movements fighting for the improved status of women and their families. The movements attempt to change laws and other social practices that negatively impact women. One example is the Better Factories movement in Cambodia (Kampuchea), sponsored by the International Labour Organization, that works to address worker problems, especially garment workers (International Labour Organization 2014). Such efforts are but one example of how organized people can impact society and work together to address gender discrimination.

> Inequality based on class, race, ethnicity, and gender takes place at all levels of analysis and is often entrenched at the meso level within the institutions found in every society—family, education, religion, government, economics, and health care. Complex societies incorporate other institutions as well, including science and technology, sports, and the military. We turn now to a discussion of institutions in our social world.

WHAT HAVE WE LEARNED?

At the beginning of this chapter, we asked how being born female or male affects our lives. Because sex is a primary variable on which societies are structured and stratified, our sex affects our public and private sphere activities, our health, our ability to practice religion or participate in political life, our opportunities for education, and just about everything we do.

KEY POINTS

- Whereas sex is biological, notions of gender identity and gender roles are socially constructed and learned, and vary across cultures.

- Notions of gender are first taught in micro settings—in the intimacy of the home—but reinforced at the meso and macro levels.

- While "she" may go first in micro-level social encounters (served first in a restaurant or the first to enter a doorway), "he" goes first in meso and macro settings—with the doors open wider for men to enter leadership positions in organizations and institutions.

- Greater access to resources at the meso level makes it easier to have entre to macro-level positions, but it also influences the respect one receives in micro settings.

- Much of the gender stratification today is unconscious and unintended—not caused by angry or bigoted men who purposefully oppress women. Gender inequality is rooted in institutionalized privilege and disprivilege.

- Various social theories shed different light on the issues of inequality in gender roles assigned to various sexes.

- For modern postindustrial societies, there is a high cost for treating women like a minority group—individually for the people who experience it and for the society, which loses many potential contributions from women.

DISCUSSION QUESTIONS

1. Describe some of the ways socializing agents (e.g., family, peers, the media, religion, schools) encouraged you to conform to traditional gender norms. Do you think you will encourage (or have you encouraged) your own children to conform to traditional gender norms? Why or why not?

2. Give two examples of side-effect gender discrimination that lead to economic inequality between men and women.

3. How does gender socialization influence who runs for office and for whom we vote? How are female politicians treated by the media, compared to male politicians? How has that impacted your own perception of female politicians?

4. How does gender discrimination harm society? What could be done on your campus to improve the status of women or men? How might you join these efforts?

5. What are your career goals? Do they follow traditional gender roles? Why or why not? How has your gender socialization impacted your career plans?

6. More women than men are now in college. How do you think this fact will impact gender roles on campus and in the larger society?

CONTRIBUTING TO OUR SOCIAL WORLD: What Can We Do?

At the Local Level

- *To learn about gender discrimination on your campus,* schedule an interview with the director or other staff members of the human resources or affirmative action offices on your campus to learn about your school's policies regarding gender discrimination. What procedures exist for hiring? Do women and men receive the same salaries, wages, and benefits for equal work? Explore the possibility of working as a volunteer or an intern in the office, specifically in the area of gender equity.

At the Organizational and National Levels

- *The National Organization for Women (NOW)* is the world's leading advocate for gender equity. It deals with issues such as reproductive rights, legislative outreach, economic justice, ending sex discrimination, and promoting diversity. Several internship programs are listed on the organization's website, www.now.org, along with contact information, state and regional affiliates, and the National NOW Action Center (http://now.org/about/job-and-internships).

- *Sociologists for Women in Society (SWS)*, an organization that "works to improve women's lives through advancing and supporting feminist sociological research, activism and scholars," provides many resources for students. SWS provides students with scholarships, opportunities to be mentored, and an award to recognize students who improve the lives of women through activism. Visit the SWS website at www.socwomen.org.

- *The NEW Leadership Institute at the Center for American Women and Politics is an annual six-day residential summer program* that "educates college women about the important role that politics plays in their lives and encourages them to become effective leaders in the political arena." To learn more about NEW Leadership and to find out how to apply to the program, go to www.cawp.rutgers.edu/education_training/NEWLeadership/newleadership_about.php.

At the Global Level

- *MADRE*, an international women's rights organization, works primarily in less developed countries. You can find numerous opportunities for working on issues of justice, human rights, education, and health on its website at www.madre.org.

- *Equality Now*, an international nongovernmental organization, provides many venues for those interested in promoting equality for women and curbing gender violence and discrimination. You can find more about this organization at www.equalitynow.org.

- *The United Nations Inter-Agency Network on Women and Gender Equality* works on global issues, including violence against women and women's working conditions. Its WomenWatch website at www.un.org/womenwatch contains news, information, and ideas for contributing to the worldwide campaign for women's rights.

⑤SAGE edge™

Sharpen your skills with SAGE edge at **edge.sagepub.com/ballantinecondensed4e**

SAGE edge for Students provides a personalized approach to help you accomplish your coursework goals in an easy-to-use learning environment.

PART IV

Institutions

Picture a house, a *structure* in which you live. Within that house there are the action and activities that bring the house alive—the *processes*. Flip a switch, and the lights go on because the house is well wired. Adjust the thermostat, and the room becomes more comfortable as the structural features of furnace or air-conditioning systems operate. If the structural components of the plumbing and water heating systems work, you can take a hot shower when you turn the knob. These actions taken within the structure make the house livable. If something breaks down, you need to get it fixed so that everything works smoothly.

Institutions, too, provide a *structure* for society, a framework that promotes stability. *Processes* are the action dimension within institutions—the activities that take place. They include the inter-actions between people, decision making, socialization, and other actions in society. These processes are often dynamic and can lead to significant change within the structure—like a decision about whether new home owners should remodel their kitchen. Institutions are meso-level structures because they are larger in scope than the face-to-face social interactions of the micro level, and yet they are smaller than the nation or the global system. However, each institu-tion includes processes at all levels of analysis, micro to macro, as we shall see from the examples in the following chapters.

Institutions such as family, education, religion, politics, economics, and health care include certain patterns and expectations at each level of analysis that differ in each society. They are interdependent and mutually supportive, just as the plumbing, heating system, and electricity in a house work together to make a home functional. However, a breakdown in one institution or conflict over limited resources between institutions affects the whole society, just as a malfunction in the electrical system may shut the furnace off and cool down the water heater.

THE IMPORTANCE OF INSTITUTIONS

Institutions are not anything concrete that you can see, hear, touch, or smell. The concept of *institutions* is a way of describing and understanding how society works. For example, the institution of family meets certain needs found in almost all societies. Family as an institution refers to the behavior of thousands of people, which—taken as a whole—forms a social structure. Think of your own family. It has unique ways of interacting and raising children, but it is part of a community with many families. Those many families, in turn, are part of a national set of patterned behaviors we call "the family." This pattern meets the basic needs of the society for producing and socializing new members and providing an emotionally supportive environment. In this way, family processes occur at each level of analysis. Table IV.1 illustrates the impact of social institutions in society at each level of analysis.

TABLE IV.1   The Impact of Institutions at Each Level of Analysis

	Family	Education	Economic Systems	Political Systems	Religion	Medicine
Macro (National and global social systems and trends)	Kinship and marriage structures, such as monogamy versus polygamy; global trends in family, such as choice of partners rather than arranged marriages	National education system; United Nations Girls' Education Initiative	Spread of capitalism around the world; World Bank; International Monetary Fund; World Trade Organization	National government; United Nations; World Court; G7 (most powerful seven nations in the world)	Global faith-based movements and structures; National Council of Churches; World Council of Churches; World Islamic Council; World Jewish Congress	National health care system; World Health Organization; transnational pandemics
Meso (Institutions, complex organizations, ethnic subcultures, state/provincial systems)	The middle-class family; the Hispanic family; the Jewish family	State/provincial department of education; American Federation of Teachers*	State/provincial offices of economic development; United Auto Workers*	State/provincial governments; national political parties; each state or province's supreme court	National denominations/movements (e.g., United Methodist Church or American Reform Judaism)	HMOs; Minnesota Nurses Association; American Medical Association
Micro (Local "franchises" of institutions)	Your family; local parenting group; local Parents Without Partners; county family counseling clinic	Your teacher; local neighborhood school; local school board	Local businesses; local chamber of commerce; local labor union chapter	Neighborhood crime watch program; local city or county council	Your local religious study group or congregation	Your doctor and nurse; local clinic; local hospital

* These organizations are national in scope and membership, but they are considered meso level here because they are complex organizations *within* the nation.

Thinking Sociologically

Using Table IV.1, try placing other institutions (mass media, science, sports, the military) in the framework. Where do organizations you belong to fit into the institutional structure?

Institutions do not dictate exactly how you will carry out the roles within your micro-level individual family. However, they do specify certain needs families will meet and statuses (spouse/partner, parent, child) that will relate to each other in certain mutually caring ways and filling certain seminegotiable roles. An institution provides a blueprint (much like a local builder needs a blueprint to build a house), and in your local version of the institution you may make a few modifications to the plans to meet your individual micro-level needs. Still, through this society-encompassing structure and interlocking set of statuses, the basic needs for individuals at the micro level and for society at the macro level are met.

Institutions, then, *are organized, patterned, and enduring sets of social structures that provide guidelines for behavior and help each society meet its basic survival needs*. While institutions operate mostly at the meso level, they also act to integrate micro and macro levels of society. Let us look more deeply at this definition.

1. *Organized, patterned, and enduring sets of social structures* means that institutions are not bricks and mortar of buildings but refer to a complex set of groups or organizations, statuses within those groups, and norms of conduct that guide people's behavior. These structures ensure socialization of children, education of the young, sense of meaning in life, companionship, and production and distribution of needed goods (food, clothing, automobiles, cell phones, computers) for the members of the society. If this patterned behavior were missing, these needs might not be addressed. At the local level, we may go to a neighborhood school, or we may attend worship at a congregation we favor. These are local organizations—local franchises, if you will—of a much more encompassing structure (education and religion) that provides guidelines for education or addresses issues of meaning of life for an enormous number of people. The

Catholic Church in your town, for example, is a local "franchise" of an organization transnational in scope and global in its concerns.

2. *Guidelines for behavior* help people know how to conduct themselves and obtain basic needs in their society. Individuals and local organizations carry out the institutional guidelines in each culture, and the exact ways they do so vary by locality. In local "franchises" of the political system, people know how to govern and how to solve problems at the local level because of larger norms and patterns provided by the political institution. Individual men and women operate a local hospital or clinic (a local "franchise" of the medical institution) that follows a national blueprint of how to provide health care. The specific activities of a local school, likewise, abide by the guidelines and purposes of the larger goals of "formal education" in a given nation.

3. *Meeting basic survival needs* is a core component of institutions because societies must meet needs of their members; otherwise the members die or the society collapses. Institutions, then, are the structures that support social life in a large bureaucratized society. Common to all industrialized societies are family, education, religion, economics, politics, and health care. The first five of these are discussed in the following chapters.

4. *Integrating micro and macro levels of society* is also critical because one of the collective needs of society is coherence and stability—including some integration between the various levels of society. Institutions help provide that integration for the entire social system. They do this by meeting needs at the local franchise level (food for the family at the grocery, education at the local school, health care at the local clinic) while, at the same time, they coordinate national and global organizations and patterns.

Again, if all this sounds terribly abstract, that is because institutions *are* abstractions. You cannot touch institutions, yet they are as real as air, love, or happiness. In fact, in the modern world institutions are as necessary to life as is air, and they help provide love and happiness that make life worth living.

THE DEVELOPMENT OF MODERN INSTITUTIONS

If we go all the way back to early hunting and gathering societies, there were no meso or macro levels to their social experience. People lived their lives in one or two villages, and while a spouse might come from another village or one might move to a spouse's clan, there was no national or state governance, and certainly no awareness of a global social system. In those simpler times, family and community provided whatever education was needed, produced and distributed goods, paid homage to a god or gods, and solved conflicts and disputes through a system of familial (often patriarchal) power distribution. One social unit such as the family served multiple functions.

As societies have become more complex and differentiated, multiple levels of the social system and various new institutions have emerged. Sociology textbooks in the 1950s identified only "five basic institutions": family, economic systems, political systems, religion, and education (formal public education only having been created in the mid-19th century). These five institutions were believed to be the core structures that met the essential needs of individuals and societies in an orderly way.

Soon thereafter, *medicine* moved from the family, and small-town doctors became part of a larger institution. Medicine has become bureaucratized in hospitals, medical labs, professional organizations, and other complex structures that provide health care. *Science* is also now something more than flying kites in thunderstorms in one's backyard. It is a complex system that provides training, funding, research institutes, peer review, and professional associations to support empirical research. New information is the lifeblood of an information-based or postindustrial society. Science, discussed in Chapter 14, is now an essential institution. Although it is arguable whether sports are an essential component for social viability, sports have clearly become highly structured in the past 50 years, and many sociologists consider sports an institution. The mass media and military also fall into the category of institutions in more advanced countries. There are gray areas as to whether or not something is considered an institution, but the questions to ask are (a) whether the structure meets basic needs of the society for survival, (b) whether it has become a complex organization providing routinized structures and guidelines for society, and (c) whether it is national or even global in its scope, while also having pervasive local (micro) impact.

THE CONNECTIONS AMONG INSTITUTIONS

The Great Recession of 2007–2009 illustrates how institutions can impact one another. Many individuals in the United States became unemployed as credit for companies dried up and companies reduced their payrolls. Their families then also faced various stresses that come with an unemployed breadwinner. In turn, the government faced pressure, as citizens expected political leaders to intervene and find ways to bring the nation out of an economic recession. At the same time, religious congregations experienced increased demands at their food banks and soup kitchens *and* declining contributions from religious congregants who lost their jobs. Funding for schools also suffered during the Great Recession, as tax revenues fell.

Connections among meso-level institutions are a common refrain in this book. As you read these chapters, notice that change in one institution affects others. Sociologists studying the legal system, mass media, medicine, science, sports, or the military as institutions would raise questions similar to those raised in the institutions discussed in the following three chapters. We begin our examination of institutions with the family and education. In Chapter 10 we diverge from our model of discussing the micro, meso, and macro levels and focus primarily on the micro-to-meso connection. These institutions also have an important macro-level function, but family and education are institutions that play a particularly significant role in socialization at the micro level. Chapter 11 (religion) examines all three levels. Chapter 12 (political and economic institutions) focuses more on the meso-to-macro connection.

edge.sagepub.com/ballantinecondensed4e

Get the edge on your studies.

Read the chapter and then take advantage of the open-access site to

- take a **quiz** to find out what you've mastered;
- test your knowledge with key term **flashcards;** and
- watch **videos** to capture key chapter content.

©Getty/Hinterhaus Productions

10 Family and Education

Institutionalizing Socialization

Through the institutions of the family and education, we are socialized and learn to participate in the larger world. The whole society benefits when these two institutions work in tandem.

MICRO

ME (AND MY FAMILY AND SCHOOL)

Family is the basic unit within a community.

Schools teach necessary knowledge and skills for success in community and society.

LOCAL ORGANIZATIONS AND COMMUNITY

Families socialize children into social roles so they can function in society.

Schools teach children in the community.

MESO

NATIONAL ORGANIZATIONS, INSTITUTIONS, AND ETHNIC SUBCULTURES

Families follow the norms and laws of society's institutions.

Educational institutions receive support and guidelines from state and national organizations.

MACRO

SOCIETY AND GLOBAL COMMUNITY

Families and educational institutions follow patterns and sometimes the laws of their societies.

Some international organizations support families and schools in the world.

LEARNING OBJECTIVES

10.1 Discuss how definitions of families are socially constructed and change over time.

10.2 Illustrate different patterns of mate selection.

10.3 Provide examples of how families interact with other institutions.

10.4 Describe controversial issues concerning the family today.

10.5 Explain the formal and informal structures of schools.

10.6 Present evidence that schools contribute to the reproduction of social class.

THINK ABOUT IT

Micro: Local Community	What did you learn—both formally and informally—from your family and school experiences that make you who you are today?
Meso: National Institutions; Complex Organizations; Ethnic Groups	How does the institution of state or national government influence family and education?
Macro: National and Global Systems	How do family and education influence the nation and vice versa? Why and in what ways are these institutions becoming globalized?

Baby Tambara could be any one of us. Baby Tambara is born into a family in some community and country in the world. What will be her fate? Will she be rich, well fed, loved, educated, and successful, or will she be one of the billions of world citizens living in poverty, hungry, with little chance for education or success? The two institutions introduced in this chapter shed light on how Baby Tambara is introduced into her social world. Macro-level factors like whether her country is in the Global North or South and what her opportunities in her country are will affect her future life. Her state or province and her ethnic background—factors at the meso level—also influence her life chances. In this chapter we focus primarily on the micro level, and how that shapes Baby Tambara's socialization experiences, launches her into contact with the organizations in her life, and helps her become a productive member of her society.

Family is where socialization starts. It provides Baby Tambara with her initial grounding in the world, meeting her basic needs for food, clothing, shelter, and social interaction. She would not survive long without these necessities. It is in the family that she will also begin to learn language, survival skills, and the values and beliefs needed in her social world.

If Baby Tambara is fortunate, she will start her education sometime between ages 3 and 6. Here she will learn her ABCs and 1-2-3s, enabling her to function in a literate society and eventually develop the skills necessary to make a living in her society. Our personal interactions with these institutions—our family and our schools—are involved from birth and early childhood through adulthood to the end of life.

Once again, you will be asked to apply the theories with which you are now familiar to the discussion of these institutions. Briefly, *structural-functional theory* focuses on the purposes each institution serves for society. *Conflict theory* considers the tensions between different institutions, and the way people with power use institutions to protect their interests and their privileges. *Symbolic interaction theory* considers the socialization process and interactions that result from individuals learning proper behaviors and expectations in their social worlds. *Rational choice theory* studies how individuals weigh the costs and benefits of their options when making decisions. *Feminist theory* advocates for seeing the woman's point of view when doing research.

This chapter focuses primarily on micro-level socialization experiences as it provides an overview of how the institutions of family and education contribute to our learning to be a member of society. We now follow Baby Tambara through her early socialization process.

FAMILY: HOW DO WE MAKE PEOPLE?

Let us assume that Baby Tambara (whose name would change, depending on where she was born) has been born into a family in Niger, Africa, one of the poorest countries on earth. Baby Tambara will have many relatives to watch over her and teach her the ways and beliefs of the group. However, she may not have access to school as education has little to do with her immediate needs and family's expectations. Each of the children in her large family has chores appropriate for his or her age and gender. The older girls help their mother with the youngest children, the household chores, preparing meals, fetching water, and caring for the animals. Most likely, they, and eventually Baby Tambara, will be married at a young age to a man who has several wives. They will then care for his herds and many children.

But let us imagine another scenario: Baby Tambara has been born into a Swedish family, one of two children. When she is a few months old she will spend part of her day in a day care center while her parents work and her brother attends school. She will spend most of her years to adulthood in some type of schooling, learning the knowledge and skills she needs to enter the workforce and be successful in this Global North country—and she will have opportunities to pursue her choice of a career.

What a difference! Families come in many shapes, sizes, and color combinations. We begin our exploration of the institution of family with a discussion of what family is.

What Is a Family?

Who defines what constitutes a family—individuals, the government, religious groups? Is a family just Ma, Pa, and the kids? Let us consider several definitions. The U.S. Census Bureau says "a group of two or more people (one of whom is the householder) related by birth, marriage, or adoption and residing together; all such people (including related subfamily members) are considered as members of one family" (U.S. Census Bureau 2013b). Thus, a family in the United States might be composed of siblings, cousins, a grandparent and grandchild, or other groupings. Some sociologists define family more broadly, such as "two or more individuals who maintain an intimate relationship that they expect will last indefinitely—or in the case of parent and child, until the child reaches adulthood—and who usually live under the same roof and pool their incomes and household labor" (Cherlin 2010:14). This definition would include same-sex couples and many cohabiting heterosexuals as families. Some religious groups define family as a mother, father, and their children, whereas others include several spouses, multiple generations, or several siblings living under the same roof.

The definition and the typical composition of family are changing as societies and social norms change (Angier 2013). The *traditional* composition of married parents and biological children living in an intact family comprises 64% of U.S. families today, with 24% of children living with the mother only (Child Trends Data Bank 2014). Figure 10.1 on page 268 illustrates changes in family structures from 1960 to 2013.

In recent decades, the definition of family has broadened in many areas of the world to include families with parents of the same sex, like these two families.

As noted earlier, the family is often referred to as the most basic institution of any society. First, it is the place where we learn many of the norms for functioning in the larger society. Second, most of us spend our lives in the security of a family. People are born and raised in families, and many will die in a family setting. Through good and bad, sickness and health, most families provide for our needs, both physical and psychological. Therefore, families meet our primary, our most basic, needs. Third, major life events—marriages, births, graduations, promotions, anniversaries, religious ceremonies, holidays, funerals—take place within the family context and are celebrated with family members. Family is where we invest the most emotional energy and spend much of our leisure time.

The family is capable of satisfying a range of social needs—sexual regulation; reproduction and replacement of members of society as children are born; socialization of children into society, religion, and other institutions; emotional support, protection, and sense of belonging; economic support; and so forth. Family carries out functions necessary for individual and societal survival (Benokraitis 2012).

Types of Families and Marriages. In Global North societies, most individuals are born and raised in the **family of orientation**, *the family into which we are born or adopted.* This family consists of parent(s) and possibly grandparents and sibling(s); here individuals receive early socialization and learn the language, norms, core values, attitudes, and behaviors of the community and society. A **family of procreation** *is the*

FIGURE 10.1   Living Arrangements of Children Under 18: 1960–2013

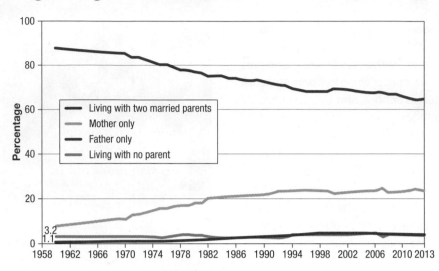

Source: Child Trends Data Bank 2014. *Family Structure* July 2014.

In the mountains of Nepal, the Chepang family lives a simple life; the children learn many survival skills, and their most basic needs, physical and psychological, are met.

family we create ourselves. We find a life mate and/or have children. The transmission of values, beliefs, and attitudes from our family of orientation to our family of procreation generally preserves and stabilizes the family system. We *make people* in families—not just biologically, but socially. In the family, we take an organism that has the potential to be fully human, and we mold this tiny bit of humanity into a caring, compassionate, productive person—at least that is the ideal plan. Yet, the Ma-Pa-and-kids monogamous model familiar in many industrialized parts of the world is not as typical as it appears. From a worldwide perspective, it is only one of several structural models of family.

Extended families include *two or more adult generations that share tasks and living quarters.* This may include brothers, sisters, aunts, uncles, cousins, and grandparents. In most extended family systems, the eldest male is the authority figure. This is a common pattern around the world, especially in agricultural societies. Some ethnic groups in the United States, such as Mexican Americans and some Asian Americans, live in extended monogamous families with several generations under one roof. This is financially practical and helps group members maintain their traditions and identity.

As societies become more industrialized and fewer individuals and families engage in agriculture, the **nuclear family**, consisting of *two parents and their children—or any two of the three*—becomes more common. A worldwide movement toward more nuclear families is under way because of urbanization, fewer arranged marriages, and growing equality between men and women (Burn 2011; Goode 1970).

No matter what form it takes in a society, the family, like all of the other major institutions, is interdependent at the meso level with each of the other institutions. For example, if the health care institution is unaffordable or not functioning well, families may not get the care they need to prevent serious illness.

If the economy goes into a recession and jobs are not available, families experience stress, abuse rates increase, and marriages are more likely to become

Families vary a great deal from one culture to another; this polygynous family from Tibet illustrates one variation. If the members of a family work well together, they provide support, a sense of identity, and feelings of belonging and caring. For a photo essay and further exploration about what it means for a family to work well, visit edge.sagepub.com/ballantinecondensed4e.

unstable. In worst-case scenarios, families who lose their incomes may become homeless.

Family Dynamics: Micro-Level Processes

The process of finding a mate is not random. Your partner was or will not be randomly selected from the entire global population. What factors enter into your mate selection?

Mate Selection: How Do New Families Start? At the most micro level, two people get together to begin a new family unit. In 2011 the world population passed 7 billion people, and as of early 2015 it had topped 7.2 billion (U.S. Census Bureau 2015). Even in Global North societies, where we think individuals have free choice of marriage partners, mate selection is not an entirely individual choice. Indeed, mate selection is highly limited by geographical proximity, ethnicity, age, social class, and a host of other variables. As we shall see, micro- and macro-level forces influence each other even in a process as personal as mate selection.

Choice of Marriage Partners. Monogamy and polygamy are the main forms of marriage found around the world. Monogamy refers to *marriage of two individuals* and is the most familiar form of marriage in industrial and postindustrial societies. Polygamy, *marriage of one person to more than one partner at the same time,*

is most often found in agricultural societies where multiple spouses and children mean more help with the farmwork.

A number of cultural rules—meso- and macro-level expectations—govern the choice of a mate in any society. Most are unwritten societal norms. They vary from culture to culture, but in every society we learn them from an early age. One of the cultural rules is **exogamy**, *norms governing the choice of a mate that require individuals to marry outside of their own immediate group.* The most universal form of exogamy is the *incest taboo,* including restrictions against father-daughter, mother-son, and brother-sister marriages. Some countries, including about half the U.S. states, forbid first cousins to marry (see Table 3.2 on page 69). Others, such as some African groups and many Syrian villages, encourage first-cousin marriages to solidify family ties and property holdings.

Exogamy also alleviates sexual jealousy within groups. For example, if father and son became jealous about who was sleeping with the wife/mother/sister, relationships would be destroyed and parental authority sabotaged. Likewise, if the father was always going to the daughter for sexual satisfaction, the mother-daughter bond would be severely threatened (Williams, Sawyer, and Wahlstrom 2013). No society can allow this to happen to its family system. Any society that has failed to have an incest taboo self-destructed long ago.

On the other hand, norms of **endogamy** *require individuals to marry inside certain human boundaries, whatever the societal members see as protecting the homogeneity of the group.* The purpose is to encourage group bonding and solidarity, and to help minority groups survive in societies with different cultures. Endogamous norms may require individuals to select mates of the same race, religion, social class, ethnic background, or clan (Williams et al. 2013). Examples of strictly endogamous religious groups include the Armenian Iranians, Orthodox Jews, Old Order Amish, Jehovah's Witnesses, and the Parsis of India. Such practices result in less biologically diversified groups, but protect the minority identity (Belding 2004).

Most people also choose a mate with similar social characteristics—age, race, place of residence, educational background, political philosophy, moral values, and psychological traits—a practice called *homogamy.* Going outside the expected and accepted group in mate selection can make things tough for newlyweds

▶ Attraction and Mate Selection

who need family and community support. Few take this risk. For instance, in the United States, close to 90% marry people with similar religious values (Williams et al. 2013). So cultural norms of societies limit individual decisions in a way that most individuals do not consciously recognize. Yet today some of these norms are weakening as the rapidly rising number of interracial marriages in the United States reveals. Still, the question remains: How do we settle on a life partner?

Finding a Mate. In most societies, mate selection takes place through arranged marriages, free-choice unions, or some combination of the two. Whether marriages are arranged or entered into freely, both endogamy and exogamy limit the number of possible mates. In either case, micro-level mate selection is shaped by meso- and macro-level cultural rules of the society.

Arranged marriages involve *a pattern of mate selection in which someone other than the couple—elder males, parents, a matchmaker—selects the marital partners*. This method of mate selection is most common in traditional, often patriarchal, societies. Marriages create and strengthen economic arrangements and political alliances between family groups. Daughters serve as valuable commodities in negotiations to secure these ties between families (Burn 2011). Beauty, youth, talent, and pleasant disposition bring a high bride price and a good match. Should the young people like each other, it is icing on the cake. Daughters must trust that their families will make the best possible matches for them. Most often, the men hold the power in this vital decision.

Kako and Hiroshi of Japan will meet for the first time for tea after a matchmaker works with their families to find a suitable mate. If they get along and do not object to the match, the wedding will be planned. Today, about 30% of marriages in Japan are still arranged this way ("Getting Married in Japan" 2012). Abdul's father has arranged a marriage for him with a girl from a nearby village. This marriage will solidify bonds between the families and the villages, reducing the chance of future conflict. Love in his culture has nothing to do with such arranged marriages, but political and economic factors matter big time! Thus, some marriages are based on individual choice and love, and some are based on what is good for the family and community group.

Where arranged marriages are the norm, love has a special meaning. The man and woman may never have set eyes on each other before the wedding day,

but respect and affection generally grow over time as the husband and wife live together. People from societies with arranged marriages are assured a mate and have difficulty comprehending marriage systems based on love, romance, and courtship—factors believed to be insufficient grounds for a lifelong relationship. They are bewildered about how people can meet possible mates in free-choice systems. Why would anyone want to place themselves in a marriage market, with all the uncertainty and rejection? Such whimsical and unsystematic methods would not work in many societies, where the structure of life is built around family systems.

Free-choice marriage is *a pattern of mate selection in which the partners select each other based primarily on romance and love*. The idea that each person has the right to choose a partner with minimal interference from others has become increasingly prevalent as societies around the world become more Westernized, women gain more rights and freedoms, and families exert less control over their children's choice of mates (Eshleman and Bulcroft 2010). Sonnets, symphonies, rock songs, poems, and plays have been written to honor romantic love and the psychological and physiological pain and pleasure that the mating game brings. However impractical romance may seem, in industrial and postindustrial societies people generally value love and individualism and tend to have high marriage rates, low fertility rates, and high divorce rates.

Starting with the assumption that eligible people are most likely to meet and be attracted to others who have similar values and backgrounds, sociologists

©AP Photo/Prakash Hatvalne

Child marriage is especially common in parts of West Africa, South Asia, and East and Central Africa. In some countries, as many as 1 out of every 10 girls is married by the time she is 15 years old, and nearly half are married by age 18.

have developed various mate selection theories, several of which view dating as a three-stage process—a series of sequential decisions (see Figure 10.2).

1. *Stimulus:* We meet someone to whom we are attracted by appearance, voice, dress, similar ethnic background, sense of humor, or other factors. Something serves as a stimulus that makes us take notice. Of course, sometimes the stimulus is simply knowing the other person is interested in us.

2. *Value comparison:* We are more likely to find someone compatible if she or he affirms our own beliefs and values toward life, politics, religion, and roles of men and women in society and marriage. If our values are not compatible, the person does not pass through our filter. We look elsewhere.

3. *Roles and needs stage:* Another filter comes when the couple explores roles of companion,

FIGURE 10.2 Mate Selection "Filtering"

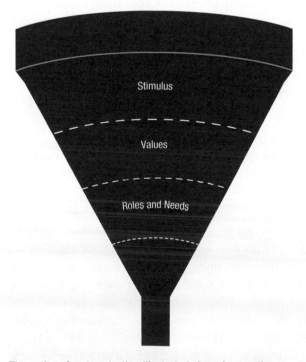

The notion of mate selection illustrated above is sometimes referred to as a filter theory, like filtering specks of gold. The first filter holds out the large stones, the second filter holds back pebbles, and the third filter stops sand, but the flakes of gold come through. Each stage in the mate selection process involves filtering some people out of the process. There may be filter factors such as religious similarities or common ethnicity.

parent, housekeeper, and lover. This might involve looking for common needs, interests, and favored activities. If the roles and needs are not complementary, desire for a permanent relationship wanes.

Thinking Sociologically

Conduct a small survey of dating and married couples you know. Ask them about how they became involved in their relationship and their process of deciding to get together or marry. How do their comments mesh with the three-stage process described above?

Who Holds the Power? Power relations in individual families, another micro-level issue shaped by cultural norms at the macro level, affect the interactions and decision making in individual families. Two areas that have received particular sociological attention are decision making in marriage and household division of labor.

Decision Making in Marriage. Cultural traditions establish the power base in society and family: patriarchy, matriarchy, or egalitarianism. The most typical authority pattern in the world is *patriarchy*, or male authority. *Matriarchy*, female authority, is rare. Even when the lineage is traced through the mother's line, males usually dominate decision making.

Egalitarian family patterns—in which power, authority, and decision making are shared between the spouses and perhaps with the children—are emerging, but they are not yet a reality in many households. For example, research indicates that in many U.S. families, decisions concerning vacation plans, car purchases, and housing are reached democratically, but males generally have a disproportionate say in major decisions such as whether to move to a new city or buy a new home (Lindsey 2011). However, social scientists find no evidence that there are any inherent intellectual or personality foundations for male authority as opposed to female authority (Kramer 2010; Ward and Edelstein 2014).

Who Does the Housework? The *second shift*, a term coined by Arlie Hochschild, refers to the housework and child care that employed women do after their "first-shift" jobs (Hochschild 1989). While the gap in household work for men and women has diminished in recent decades, it still exists. On an average day, 83% of women compared to 65% of men spend some time doing household activities, and the only area where men spend more time than women is on lawn and garden care (Bureau of Labor Statistics 2014b). Further, men spend just 7% of their time doing child care activities while women spend 14% of their day caring for children (Parker and Wang 2013). The next "Engaging Sociology" shows the breakdown in hours spent by men and women at various household activities.

Although recent research shows a narrowing of the gap in time spent by men and women on household tasks, such factors as the ages of children, how many years the mother has worked outside the home, and socioeconomic status of the family influence how involved men are and how much real "free time" each experiences. When women do have free time, it is much more likely to be interrupted than men's free time (Kan, Sullivan, and Gershuny 2011; Mattingly and Sayer 2006; Saxbe, Repetti, and Graesch 2011).

A positive relationship exists between equity in households and successful marriages. Husbands who do an equitable share of the household chores actually report higher levels of satisfaction with the marriage, and such couples are less likely to divorce (Dockterman 2014; Lorillard 2011). The success or failure of a marriage depends in large part on patterns that develop early in the marriage for dealing with the everyday situations including power relationships and division of labor.

The Family as an Institution: Meso-Level Connections

We experience family life at a very personal level, but the sum total of hundreds of thousands of families interacting in recognizable patterns results in *family as an institution* at the meso level. In this section, we look at the structure and parts of family as an institution, and the family in relation to two other institutions—economics and health care. Some of the changes in family have resulted from—or caused—changes in other institutions.

Family and Economics: Who Supports the Family?

The answer to this question has been changing in many countries as women have joined the paid workforce. The following discussion outlines two types of family support patterns: dual-career families and families who must rely on government support for survival.

Dual-Worker Families. In many Global North societies, government and industry support dual-worker families with various family-friendly policies: readily available child care facilities, parenting leaves for childbirth and illness, and flexible work hours or telecommuting (working from one's home). These policies allow families to combine both work and family lives with some time for leisure thrown in. The United States has been slower than many other Global North countries to adopt family-friendly policies. The U.S. government passed the Family and Medical Leave Act in 1993, which requires employers with 50 or more employees to grant 12 weeks of unpaid leave to workers who request it in order to care for the arrival of a child, serious health issues in the immediate family, or serious medical conditions (U.S. Department of Labor 2013a).

However, many corporations in the United States have been slow to respond to dual-career family needs. A few businesses are experimenting with family-friendly policies such as flextime (allowing individuals to schedule their own work hours within certain time frames) and job sharing (allowing individuals to split a job, with one family member working in the morning and the other in the afternoon).

In comparison to other countries, however, the government in the United States does little to ensure that women can take time off to have a baby and not lose their jobs. Figure 10.3 on page 274 indicates the legal requirements of maternal leave in several countries.

Thinking Sociologically

What are the challenges facing dual-worker families? What social policies might relieve some of the stress on families with two working parents?

Families and Poverty in the United States. The family is the primary economic unit of consumption, so what happens when economic times are tough? In the past several years much of the world economy has been troubled, resulting in employment instability and uncertainty, economic strain, and even poverty. In 2014, the poverty threshold was $23,850 for a U.S. family of four and $11,670 for a single person (U.S. Department of Health and Human Services 2014). Table 10.2 shows the percentage of individuals and families living in poverty.

Low-income families, especially single-parent families headed by women, are particularly hard-hit and often have to struggle for survival. In some

ENGAGING SOCIOLOGY

Household Tasks by Gender

In many families, household tasks are highly gendered. As recently as the 1980s, wives and daughters spent two or three times as much time as fathers and sons in household tasks such as cleaning and laundry and yard work. However, the tides have been shifting, and while they are not entirely equal, they are more balanced.

Engaging With Sociology

1. What is the division of labor (by gender) for household maintenance in your family?
2. How did it evolve?
3. Is it considered fair by all participants?
4. How does it compare to the data in Table 10.1?

TABLE 10.1 Percentage of Men and Women Who Engage in Some Type of Household Task Each Day

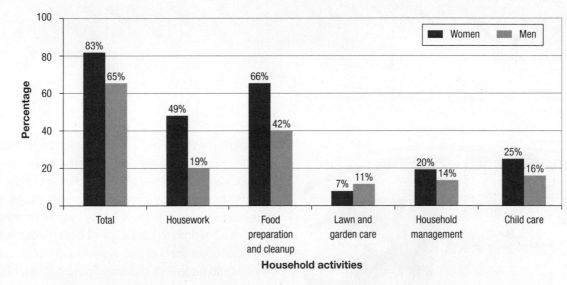

Source: Bureau of Labor Statistics 2014b.

cases, families are so financially devastated that they become homeless—an especially difficult situation for children.

The *feminization of poverty*, discussed in earlier chapters, is a global problem. It occurs where single motherhood is widespread and where there are few policies to reduce poverty, especially for this group (Williams et al. 2013). Single mothers, whether in capitalist or socialist countries, have some common experiences, including dual roles as workers and mothers, lower earnings than men, irregular paternal support payments, and underrepresentation in policy-making bodies. What differ around the world are governmental policies that help mothers with child support, child care, health care, maternity leave, and family allowances.

TABLE 10.2 Families in Poverty by Type of Family: 2013

Poverty Status and Family Type	Total Percentage Below Poverty Level
Total (all) families	11.2% (9.1 million)
Married-couple families	5.8% (3.5 million)
Single female householder	30.6% (4.6 million)
Single male householder	15.9% (1.0 million)

Source: DeNavas-Walt and Proctor 2014.

FIGURE 10.3   Total Duration of Paid Leave After Childbirth: Selected Countries

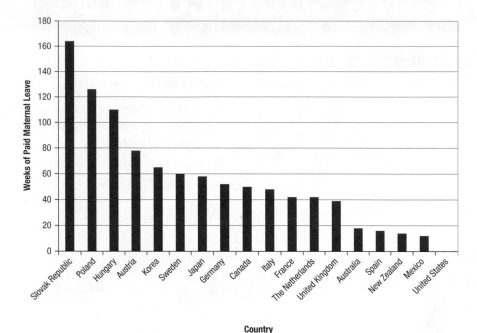

Source: Organisation for Economic Co-operation and Development (OECD) 2014.

This young woman sits at the wheel of her car with all of her possessions inside and her children in the backseat. These are not conditions that make for effective parenting.

Single mothers are as prevalent in Sweden as in the United States, but U.S. single mothers are many times more likely to be poor because of fewer support systems from the state (Casey and Maldonado 2012). For single teens, early motherhood, lack of education, and insufficient income lead to a multiproblem family pattern. Table 10.3 shows the change over three decades in births to unmarried women.

Health Care and the Family. When you feel terrible and need to see a doctor, whom do you call? Chances are you turn to a member of your family for help. From the time we are babies until the time we die, most of us rely on family members to help us take care of our health needs. Parents take their infants for regular exams and immunizations. Most parents can also tell you of emergency room visits with their children to take care of high fevers, broken bones, or other sorts of injuries and illnesses. Imagine what would happen if children could not rely on their families to take care of their medical needs. It is not a pleasant thought!

It is through our families that most of us relate to the health care system on a micro level. Before modern medicine, family members nursed one another. Today, family members help us interact with health care personnel and organizations. When you were a child, it is likely that your parents signed you up for health care insurance coverage. You might still be covered by a parent. The Affordable Care Act (ACA) now allows parents to include grown children on their health care plans until they turn 26.

As you age, you may turn to a spouse or grown children to help you manage your health care. At times, we all need someone we can rely on to pick us up from a procedure when the doctor does not allow us to drive, visit us when we must remain in the hospital, or pick up our medicine from the pharmacy. Health care may be a major billion-dollar business today, but our personal

TABLE 10.3   Percentage of Births to Unmarried and Married Women: United States

Year	Births to Unmarried Women (%)	Births to Married Women (%)
2012	40.7	59.3
2000	33.2	66.8
1995	32.2	67.8
1990	28.0	72.0
1985	22.0	78.0
1980	18.4	81.6

Source: Centers for Disease Control and Prevention 2014; ChildStats .gov 2013; DeParle and Tavernise 2012.

interactions with it on the micro level usually involve our families.

Moreover, if the family is not functioning smoothly, it affects the health care system. The related stress can make members fall ill. Likewise, if the health care system is not working (e.g., if there are not enough doctors, hospitals, or medicine), families experience enormous stressors. These two institutions are highly interdependent.

As you can see, families can be studied at each level of analysis: as interdependent micro-level social units with family members in the immediate household; as meso-level institutions that can be seen as economic units; and as part of the macro-level social system in which government sees family units as key economic units. Many individual family issues that seem very intimate and personal are actually affected by cultural norms and forces at other levels (such as migration, urbanization, and economic conditions). Likewise, decisions of individuals at the micro level affect meso- and macro-level social structures (such as size of families). Individual families are, in essence, local franchises of a larger social phenomenon.

Family Issues: Same-Sex Marriage and Divorce

Because family is the basic institution in which all of us get our start and most have a lifelong relationship, it is no wonder certain issues gain attention from the micro to macro levels. Here we mention two of these issues that crosscut levels of analysis: same-sex marriage and civil unions, and divorce.

Same-Sex Marriage and Civil Unions. A hotly debated macro-level issue concerning the family is the official status of same-sex couples. National macro-level policy decisions affect rights and benefits for micro-level partnerships, but there is intense disagreement over whether this issue is about human rights or about divinely determined rights and wrongs. As same-sex relationships become more widely acknowledged and accepted in the Global North, increasing numbers of gay and lesbian couples live together openly as families. Denmark was the first country to recognize same-sex unions in 1989, granting legal rights to such couples (Freedom to Marry 2014). Some countries, however, punish openly gay individuals. Uganda almost passed a bill authorizing the death penalty for homosexuals, but it was deterred by international condemnation. Nigeria has passed a bill outlawing homosexuality, and mobs have attacked homosexuals (Goodstein 2012).

In the United States, support for same sex marriage has rapidly increased (see Figure 10.4 on page 276). Thirty-seven states and Washington, DC, allow same-sex marriage, and the federal government recognizes same-sex marriages from states where they are legal (Freedom to Marry 2015). The U.S. Census Bureau reports over 600,000 same-sex couples in the United States, or about 1% of all couple households (U.S. Census Bureau 2013d). Most scholars acknowledge that this is probably an underreporting because of the stigma of reporting that one is gay or lesbian. One out of every nine unmarried cohabiting couples is gay or lesbian, and one quarter of these couples are raising children (Benokraitis 2012; James 2011).

This couple celebrates after hearing that their marriage and those of other same-sex couples will be legally recognized in their state.

 Divorce

FIGURE 10.4 Changing Attitudes of U.S. Adults Toward Same-Sex Marriage, 2001–2012

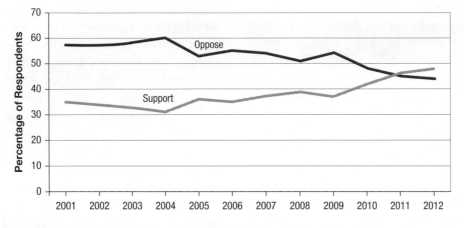

Source: Adapted from Newport, F. (2012, May 8). *Half of Americans Support Legal Gay Marriage.* Gallup Politics.

One reason many people in the *LGBTQ* community are so intent on the legalization of same-sex marriage is that same-sex partnerships or civil unions are "insufficiently institutionalized," making them somewhat less stable and creating ambiguity about their roles and rights (Cherlin 1978; Stewart 2007). They argue that, if we actually believe that stable relationships and families make for a healthier and more stable society, families with same-sex adults need public recognition.

Those opposed to the legalization of same-sex marriage argue that marriage has been a function of the church, temple, and mosque for centuries. Religious groups have defined marriage for most of Western history (England Church Records 2014). Some opponents argue that because same-sex unions do not propagate the species, they do not serve the society.

Divorce: Contract Breaking. Although most cultures extol the virtues of family life, the reality is that not all partnerships work. There is lack of support, trust is violated, abuse is present, and relationships deteriorate. So we cannot discuss family life without also recognizing the often painful side of family life that results in contract breaking.

Some commentators view divorce rates as evidence that the family is losing importance. There are costs to adults who suffer guilt and failure, to children from divided homes, and to the society that does not have the stabilizing force of intact lifelong partnerships. Many children around the world, including in the United States, grow up in homes without both natural parents present (U.S. Census Bureau 2013a).

Others argue that marriage is not so much breaking down as adapting to a different kind of social system. Indeed, more people today express satisfaction with marriage than at any previous time period, and 6% of currently married couples reach their 50th wedding anniversary, 35% their 25th, and 50% their 15th anniversary (U.S. Department of Commerce 2011). As recently as the late 19th century, the average length of a marriage was only 13 years—mostly because life expectancy was relatively short. "'Til death do us part" was not such a long time then as it is today, when average life expectancy in Global North countries reaches into the 80s (Coontz 2005).

Divorce rates in the United States have been dropping since the early 1980s (Cherlin 2010; Clarkson 2011). The divorce rate dropped from 5.9 per 1,000 citizens in 1979 to 3.6 per 1,000 people in 2011 (Centers for Disease Control and Prevention 2013). It is now the lowest it has been since 1970, as can be seen in Figure 10.5. Despite this, the United States still has one of the highest rates of divorce in Global North countries (Centers for Disease Control and Prevention 2013).

● **Thinking Sociologically**

Micro-level issues of divorce are often rooted in the personalities and relationships of the individuals involved. Talk with friends and family members who have divorced about micro-level factors that contributed to the dissolution of their marriages. Now, based on information from this chapter, make a list of meso-level factors (e.g., religious, economic, legal, educational) that contribute to or reduce divorce rates. What connections do you see between the micro and meso factors?

FIGURE 10.5   Divorce Rates in the United States, 1950–2011

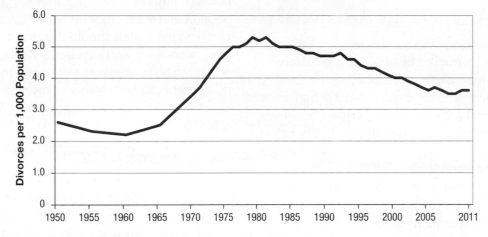

Source: Centers for Disease Control and Prevention 2013.

Many find the emotional aspects of divorce most difficult. Divorce is often seen as a failure, rejection, or even punishment. Moreover, a divorce often involves splitting with more than just a spouse. It often entails separating from some family and friends, a religious community, and other social contexts in which your identity is tied to your marriage (Amato 2000). No wonder divorce is so wrenching. Unlike simple societies, most modern ones have no ready mechanism for absorbing people back into stable social units such as clans.

Adjustment to divorced status varies by gender: Men typically have a harder time emotionally adjusting to singlehood or divorce than women. Divorced men must often leave not only their wives but also their children, and whereas many women have support networks, fewer men have developed or sustained friendships outside marriage. Finances, on the other hand, are a bigger problem for divorced women and their children than for men. Women are more likely to be living in poverty than men across all racial and ethnic groups in the United States (Reason 2011). Single mothers are twice as likely to be in poverty as

single fathers, and over 35% experience food insecurity (not enough food) (Gray 2012). Support from the noncustodial parent can help relieve the poverty, yet 29% of custodial parents receive no help at all, 30% receive some of what is owed, and 41% receive full child support (Child Trends 2013). Many children move to new houses and locations, leave one parent and friends, and must make adjustments to new schools and to reduced resources. Children in families with high levels of marital conflict, however, may be better off long-term if their parents divorce (Booth and Amato 2001; Sobolewski and Amato 2007).

Overall, children have an easier time with divorce if they can remain in their home and in their familiar school, keep both parents in their lives, and maintain their friendship networks. Grandparents, too, can provide stability during these traumatic times.

As we have seen, family is a diverse and complex social institution. Families prepare the next generation. They talk—and many pray—together about what happens after death. They provide care for disabled, infirm, or sick members. As a basic institution, the family plays a role in the vitality of the entire nation.

EDUCATION: WHAT ARE WE LEARNING?

Schooling—learning skills such as reading and math via systematic instruction by a trained professional—is a universal means of socialization; yet it is a luxury some children will never know. In most urban areas around the world and in all areas of affluent countries, formal education has become a necessity. Education of the masses in a school setting is a modern concept that developed when literacy and math skills became essential for societies with democratic forms of government and for many jobs (even if just to read instructions for operating machinery). In this part of the chapter, we focus on micro-level interactions in educational organizations, what happens in schools after the school bell rings, and whether education is the road to opportunity.

The Ins and Outs of Local Schools: Micro-Level Interactions

The process of education takes place at the micro level in the classrooms, in the corridors, and on the playgrounds of local schools through the everyday drama of teaching and learning. Schools are important organizations in local communities, a source of pride and a unifying symbol of identity, and large employers that impact the economic vitality of the area. Much sociological analysis has focused on interpersonal exchanges within the classroom and on the school as a social setting within a community at the micro level. Sociologists look at statuses and roles in educational settings and at the informal norms and interaction patterns that evolve in those settings. We will begin by reviewing the statuses and roles connected to in-school interactions.

Statuses and Roles in the Education System. Students, teachers, staff, and administrators hold statuses, or positions, in educational systems. Individuals hold statuses only during their tenure in the organization. The roles associated with each status bring both obligations and challenges. When those in each status agree on expected behaviors (role expectations), schools function smoothly. When they do not agree, conflicts can arise.

Students and the Peer Culture of Schools. In a private Rwandan secondary school, students crowd onto benches. They are quiet, respectful, and very hardworking. They know that they are in a privileged position, and many students are lined up to take their place on the bench should they not carry out their roles, work hard, and succeed. Although they have no written texts, students write down the lectures in their notebooks and memorize the material. In some countries such as Rwanda, going to high school is a privilege. In others such as the United States, it is a necessary part of life that many students resist. The culture—including the sets of outlooks and attitudes of students—impacts the learning environment.

Schools expand student skills and knowledge, but the experience of being a student can be quite different for each student. Consider a child whose family has recently immigrated to the United States and does not yet understand English or the norms of interaction within her new school. She may feel that her culture is being denigrated because her language and ethnic history is ignored or even scorned. This would not be an environment in which she would feel safe or respected, both of which are needed for learning to occur.

There are many dynamics within a school that may undermine students' capacity to learn. The role expectations for students can be complicated by variables such as ethnicity, gender, and socioeconomic standing. Health status can also impact students' ability to receive a good education. Sick children tend to miss more days of school than healthy children. Children with more highly educated and affluent parents tend to be healthier than those with less educated

In Rwandan secondary schools, as many as 45 students may be in a classroom with little more than wooden benches and tables. They value school and are diligent students, knowing it may be an escape from poverty.

parents and those who live in poverty (Bloom, Jones, and Freeman 2013).

In turn, education levels impact health. Those with higher levels of education are less likely to have heart attacks, strokes, hypertension, high cholesterol, emphysema, diabetes, asthma, and ulcers. They also miss fewer days of work, just as healthier students tend to be absent from school less often than sick children (Picker 2014).

Gender issues make schooling complex. Research for several decades showed that boys were given many privileges, were favored by teachers, and scored higher in many academic areas than girls. However, researchers point out the incredible gains in recent years made by females, who tend to study more and be more compliant in school than boys. In Global South countries, however, the picture is not rosy. For example, for every 100 boys, there are 66 girls in primary and secondary school in Afghanistan, 69 in the Central African Republic, and 68 in Chad (World Bank 2013d). Studies show, though, that schooling has a very positive influence on the life chances of women, their children, and the whole society.

Some of the benefits of educating girls include "higher wages, greater agricultural productivity, and faster economic growth . . . [and] health benefits" (Sperling 2006:274). More educated girls and women

- have lower fertility rates,
- are less likely to die in childbirth,
- are less likely to have their infants die,
- are less likely to contract HIV/AIDS,
- have increased labor force participation and earnings,
- provide better health care and education to their children,
- lift households out of poverty, and
- pass these benefits on to the next generation (World Bank 2014b).

One indicator of girls' success in education in the United States is the "feminization" of higher education. Since 1980, more women in the United States have gone to and graduated from college than men. In 2012, 71% of women entered college right after high school versus 61% of men. This gender pattern held true for all U.S. racial groups: whites (72% vs. 62%), blacks (69% vs. 57%), Hispanics (76% vs. 62%), and Asians (86% vs. 83%) (Lopez and Gonzalez-Barrera 2014).

Schoolgirls in Kenya wait for classes to begin. Children like this, whose parents can afford to send them to school, will have more life chances than those who cannot attain an education. Conflict theorists point out that inequality is deeply embedded in the institution of education.

An estimated 18% of youth between the ages of 16 and 24—mostly racial and ethnic minorities and especially boys—are disconnected without postsecondary education and sometimes without a high school degree. They are neither in school nor employed. When students drop out of high school, they have few legal means to make a living wage. This and other factors, including racial profiling, have led to one of every three African American boys eventually spending time in prison (Children's Defense Fund 2013). This is a failure of institutions in our society that has long-term consequences, including rates of college education (as seen in Table 10.4). The experience of being a student is clearly not the same for all, with gender, ethnicity, race, health, and socioeconomic factors shaping the experience.

TABLE 10.4   College Attendance Rates

Race	College Attendance Rate
Asian	92.2%
White, non-Hispanic	72%
Hispanic	64%
Black	56%
Males	66%
Females	72%

Source: National Center for Education Statistics 2012; U.S. Department of Education 2012.

Teachers: The Front Line. Teachers in the classroom occupy the front line in implementing the goals of the school, the community, and the society. Teachers serve as gatekeepers, controlling the flow of students, activities, resources, and privileges. One scholar estimated that teachers have more than a thousand interchanges a day in their roles as classroom managers (Jackson 1968).

For teachers, getting students to cooperate or take responsibility can be challenging. Some students try to wrest control from teachers and gain some freedom from the rules of the classroom or the school. Both students and teachers develop strategies to cope with pressures and difficult situations. Student coping strategies range from complete compliance to outright rebellion. Teachers try to elicit cooperation and participation from students by creating a cost-benefits ratio that favors compliance. Manipulating the classroom can be an effective means of control: putting students at specific tables or in a circle, breaking up groups of chattering friends, or leading a discussion while standing beside the most disruptive child.

As primary socializers and role models for students, teachers are expected to support and encourage students and, at the same time, judge their performance—giving grades and recommendations. This creates role strain, which can interfere with the task of teaching and contribute to teacher burnout. U.S. teachers are held accountable for students' progress as measured on standardized tests. This can cause stress for teachers and an overemphasis on teaching what will help students earn high scores on the standardized tests (Dworkin and Tobe 2012). While teachers play a role in how students do on these tests, other factors, such as the influence of students' families and peers, also influence test scores.

In some other nations of the world, like Japan, teachers are treated with great respect and honor. They receive salaries and respect commensurate with those in industry and professions such as law and medicine (Ballantine and Hammack 2012). In Europe, many high schools are organized like universities. Teachers think of themselves as akin to professors. In contrast, studies in Australia and the United States show that teachers in those nations feel they are unappreciated and not respected (Saha and Dworkin 2006). We may learn something from Finland, which tops other OECD nations in test scores. Finland has very competitive teaching programs, and all teachers,

even in primary schools, must have a master's degree. Teachers have higher than average salaries, freedom to create their own curriculum, and high status in their society ("How Finnish Schools Shine" 2012).

⬤ Thinking Sociologically

Who should enforce high teacher standards, and who should create curricula for public schools? The federal, state, or local government? Teacher unions? Interest groups or parents? Explain your answers and describe how to carry out what you envision.

Administrators: The Managers of the School System. Key administrators—superintendents, assistant superintendents, principals and assistant principals, and headmasters and headmistresses—hold the top positions in the educational hierarchy of local schools. They are responsible for a long list of tasks: issuing budget reports; engaging in staff negotiations; hiring, firing, and training staff members; meeting with parents; carrying out routine approval of projects; managing public relations; preparing reports for boards of directors, local education councils, legislative bodies, and national agencies; keeping up with new regulations; and many other tasks. They are the CEOs of local schools.

The Informal System: What Really Happens Inside Schools? It is the first day of high school, and the teacher asks a question. Should you respond or let someone else answer? If you respond, the teacher might be impressed, but the other students might think you are showing off or "brownnosing." What if you answer incorrectly and sound foolish? Does that scenario sound familiar to you?

The informal system of schooling includes the unspoken, unwritten, and implicit norms of behavior that we learn, whether in kindergarten or in college. These norms may be created or enforced by teachers or by the student peer culture. The informal system does not appear in written goal statements or course syllabi, but nevertheless it influences our experience in school in important ways. Dimensions of the informal system include the hidden curriculum, the educational climate, the value climate, power dynamics, and coping strategies in the classroom.

The *hidden curriculum* refers to the implicit "rules of the game" that students learn in school (Snyder 1971). It includes everything not explicitly taught, such as unstated social and academic norms. Students

 Formal vs. Informal Education

have to learn and respond to these rules to be socially accepted and succeed in the education system (Snyder 1971).

In many societies, children begin learning what is expected of them in preschool and kindergarten, providing the basis for schooling in the society (Neuman 2005). Kindergarten teachers teach children to follow rules, to cooperate with each other, and to accept the teacher as the boss who gives orders and controls how time is spent (Gracey 1967). All this is part of what young children learn. Sometimes being tardy has a bigger impact on grades than whether one has actually learned the material. Teachers instill these lessons in students even though it is not part of the formal curriculum of reading, writing, and arithmetic. These less formal messages form an alternative set of "three *R*s"—rules, routines, and regulations. It is through the hidden curriculum that students learn the expectations, behaviors, and values necessary to succeed in school and society, but the hidden curriculum is also a social and economic agenda that maintains class differences.

Four-year-old preschoolers recite the Pledge of Allegiance. Developing patriotism is part of the implicit and informal curriculum of schools—and sometimes part of the formal curriculum.

Thinking Sociologically

What are some examples of the hidden curriculum you learned in your K–12 education? How has this training impacted how you act now in college?

Structure and Functions of Education: Meso-Level Analysis

Organizational requirements of education systems at a meso level can influence the personal student-teacher relationship at the micro level. Bureaucratic systems provided a way to document and process masses of students coming from different backgrounds in an efficient and cost-effective way. Yet the very structure that facilitates mass education may put constraints on individual classrooms and students with different learning styles and problems.

Bureaucratic Structure of Education. Recall Weber's bureaucratic model of groups and organizations, discussed in Chapter 5. The points below show how bureaucracy applies to schools:

1. Schools have a division of labor among administrators, teachers, students, and support personnel. The roles associated with the statuses are part of the school structure. Individual teachers or students hold these roles for a limited time and are replaced by others coming into the system.

2. The administrative hierarchy incorporates a chain of command and channels of communication.

3. Specific rules and procedures in a school cover everything from course content to discipline in the classroom and use of the schoolyard.

4. Personal relationships are downplayed in favor of formalized relations among members of the system, such as placement on the basis of tests and grades.

5. Rationality governs the operations of the organization; people are hired and fired on the basis of their qualifications and how well they do their jobs (unless or until they attain tenure) (Weber 1947).

Not all children fit into neat cubbyholes that bureaucratic structures invariably create. Some children's special needs—such as personal problems or learning difficulties—are not met (Kozol 2006; Sizer 1984; Waters 2012). In schools, these feelings cause passivity, apathy, alienation, or acting out among students, which in turn labels students as "bad" and frustrates teachers' efforts to educate. These children view school not as a privilege but as a requirement imposed by an adult world. Caught between the demands of an impersonal bureaucracy and individual goals for their students, teachers cannot always give every child the personal help she or he needs. Thus, we see that organizational requirements of education systems at a meso level can influence the personal student-teacher relationship at the micro level.

Functions of Education. Formal education in schools serves certain crucial purposes in society, especially as societies modernize. The functions of education as a social institution are outlined in Figure 10.6. Note that some functions are planned and formalized (*manifest functions*), whereas others are unintended and unorganized—the informal results of the educational process (*latent functions*). Latent functions of schooling are often just as important to the society as manifest functions. For example, imagine what would happen to productivity if schools did not give parents release time from child care responsibilities so that they could perform other roles.

The means of carrying out the manifest functions do not go unchallenged, especially when decisions about what should be taught, and how, are discussed. Consider conflicts that occur routinely in many local communities over what to teach in sex education and science courses, as well as over content thought to contain obscenity, sex, nudity, political or economic

Education provides hope in this refugee camp in the Central African Republic. The adults created this school for children, even though families often lack food. They view education as a functional necessity for the future of their children.

bias, profanity, slang or nonstandard English, racism or racial hatred, and antireligious or presumed anti-American sentiment. For example, Family Friendly Libraries, an online grassroots interest group that started in Virginia, argues that the popular *Harry Potter* books should be banned from school libraries. The members of this group believe the series promotes the religion of witchcraft (DeMitchell and Carney 2005). Each year the American Library Association studies the most frequently challenged books. In 2013, they included *Captain Underpants* (Dav Pilkey), *The Bluest Eye* (Toni Morrison), *The Absolutely True Diary of a Part-Time Indian* (Sherman Alexie), *Fifty Shades of Grey* (E. L. James), *The Hunger Games* (Suzanne Collins), *A Bad Boy Can Be Good for a Girl* (Tanya Lee Stone), *Looking for Alaska* (John Green), *The Perks of Being a Wallflower* (Stephen Chbosky), *Bless Me, Ultima* (Rudolfo Anaya), and *Bone* (Jeff Smith). (To see a more complete list and reason they were banned, see www.ala.org/bbooks/frequentlychallengedbooks/top10.)

These battles over curriculum are so fierce because the vast majority of U.S. schoolchildren attend public schools, one institution where differences of opinion are played out because parents can have a say about the curriculum. We now turn to how both public and private schools can produce and reproduce inequality from one generation to the next.

Education, the Family, and Inequality. The social institutions of family and education impact each other in many ways, some of which we have already mentioned. When children enter kindergarten or primary school, they bring their prior experience, including

FIGURE 10.6   Key Functions of Formal Education (Schools)

Manifest Functions (intended; formalized)

- Teach students the skills necessary to become educated, effective participants of society.
- Socialize children to be productive members of society.
- Select individuals for key positions in society.
- Promote social participation, change, and innovation.
- Enhance personal independence and social development.

Latent Functions (unintended; informal)

- Confine and supervise underage citizens.
- Weaken parental controls over youths.
- Provide opportunities for peer cultures to develop.
- Provide contexts for the development of friendships and mate selection.

socialization experiences and cultural capital from a parent or parents, brothers, sisters, and other relatives (Jaeger 2011). Family background, according to many sociologists, is the single most important influence on children's school achievement. Children succeed in large part because of what their parent(s) do to support them in their educations (Jaeger 2011).

Most families stress the importance of education, but they do so in different ways. Often, teachers' perceptions of their students and behavior toward them are influenced by their interactions with parents. Middle- and upper-class parents are more likely to ask about their children's progress, consult with teachers on strategies to help them learn better at home and in the classroom, and make it clear that they want teachers to focus on their children. Parents from lower-socioeconomic-status families tend to be less involved in their children's schooling, with less time to help with homework and fewer interactions with teachers. Language barriers (for new immigrants), lack of time (for single parents and those working many hours per week), and views toward teachers (as authority figures who should be left alone to do their job) are some of the reasons many lower-income parents do not play an active role in their children's schooling (Cheung and Pomerantz 2012). Children who must make educational decisions on their own have a greater likelihood of doing poorly or dropping out of school (Jaeger 2011).

As noted earlier, wealthier students also tend to be healthier students—another advantage in the educational institution. Healthier children do better academically. Children from low-income families tend to have less access to nutritious food and safe areas to play. Providing a variety of healthy food choices at school and devising ways to make exercise fun and available for all students can impact the health gap between poor and wealthier students, as well as educational inequality. Recognizing the connection between health and educational achievement, as well as the obesity epidemic, the Obama administration in 2012 established higher nutritional standards for school lunches, ensuring that low-income students who rely on free or reduced-price lunches have healthy meals to eat (Nixon 2012).

Thinking Sociologically

Provide some examples of links between academic success in schools and at least two other social institutions.

Computer skills are increasingly essential in societies and schools, yet some children come from families without access to computers. Children who have computers at home have a significant advantage.

Education Issues: The Road to Opportunity?

Elite preparatory (prep) schools in England, Japan, the United States, and many other countries traditionally have been the training ground for the sons and daughters of the elite. Because elite schools are very expensive and highly selective, affluent members of society have the most access to them and thereby learn class privilege and advantage (Howard and Gaztambide-Fernandez 2010; Persell and Cookson 1985; Wade 2012). Only about 8% of U.S. students attended private K–12 schools in 2011 (Ewert 2013). Elite schools perpetuate elevated prestige and "reproduce social class."

When elites of society protect their educational advantages, the result is **reproduction of class**—*the socioeconomic positions of one generation passing on to the next.* This process takes place in part through the socialization of young people into adult work roles and compliance with the modern economic and political institutions and their needs. Schools teach students from lower socioeconomic positions to obey authority and accept the dominant ideology that justifies social inequality. If citizens believe that those with the best educations and jobs in their society personally earned them, they are not motivated to change the system. By promoting the legitimacy of the system, schools serve the interests of the privileged (Bowles and Gintis 2002; Collins 2004).

Critics of the increasing efforts to promote school choice and more charter schools (publicly funded independent schools) fear that public schools might be left with the least capable students and teachers, further stratifying an already troubled system. Students often

Education and Gender

©iStockphoto.com/michaeljung

gain entrance into charter schools through a lottery for which some, but not all, parents register. This can result in a "creaming process" that leaves traditional public schools with students whose parents are less involved in their educational process. This leads us to our next issue—can schools bring about equality in societies?

Thinking Sociologically

Consider the community in which you went to high school. Do you think the education there enhances upward social mobility and serves all students and the community, or serves the affluent, reproducing social class and training people to fulfill positions at the same level as their parents, or some combination? Explain.

Can Schools Bring About Equality in Societies?

Equal opportunity exists when all people have an equal chance of achieving high socioeconomic status in society regardless of their class, ethnicity, race, or gender (Riordan 2004). James Coleman describes the meaning and goals of equal educational opportunity:

- to provide a common curriculum for all children regardless of background;
- to allow children from diverse backgrounds to attend the same school; and
- to provide equality within a given locality (Coleman 1968, 1975, 1990).

Equal opportunity means that children are provided with equal facilities, financing, and access to school programs. Schools in poor neighborhoods or in rural villages in the United States and around the world, however, often lack the basics—safe buildings, school supplies and books, and funds to operate. Lower-class minority students who live in these areas fall disproportionately to the bottom of the educational hierarchy. Many children face what seem to be insurmountable barriers to educational success: lack of health care and immunizations, hunger, school absence due to illness or homelessness, pressure to drop out to help the family, and, in some cases, even transportation to get to school (Kozol 2012; Noguera 2011). These conditions at home and in neighborhoods affect children's achievement in school and on standardized test scores (Boger and Orfield 2009; Coleman 1990).

Who Gets Ahead and Why? The Role of Education in Stratification. Any school or educational institution is supposed to be a **meritocracy**, *a social group or organization in which people are allocated to positions according*

Does it matter how one gets to school? These children who live near Inle Lake in Myanmar (Burma) take a gondola school bus—the only option for them. For a photo essay and further exploration about transportation to and from school, visit edge .sagepub.com/ballantinecondensed4e.

to their abilities and credentials, as in level of education attained. This, of course, is consistent with the principles of a meritocratic social system where the most qualified person is promoted and decisions are impersonal and based on "credentials" (Charles, Roscigno, and Torres 2007). Still, in societies around the world, we see evidence that middle-class and elite children receive more and better education than equally qualified poor children. Children do not attend school on an equal footing, and in many cases, meritocracy does not exist at all.

Three practices that tend to lead to inequality in schools—testing, tracking, and funding—illustrate how schools reproduce and perpetuate social class and social stratification systems. They also give clues as to what might be done to mitigate inequality in education.

Assessing Student Achievement: Testing. Testing is one means of placing students in schools according to their achievement and merit, and of determining academic progress. Yet many scholars, including sociologists of education, argue that standardized test questions, the vocabulary employed, and testing situations disadvantage lower-class, minority, and immigrant students. These disadvantages often result in lower scores among these students, relegating them to lower tracks in the education system (Gardner 1987, 1999; Smith 2008).

Moreover, higher-income parents have the means to seek educational opportunities outside of school that give their children a further edge over other students on standardized tests through travel, going to museums, mixing with members of the elite, and providing opportunities outside of school such as tutoring, test prep, and summer programs

(Buchmann, Condron, and Roscigno 2010). Table 10.5 in the next "Engaging Sociology" shows differences in ACT (American College Test) and SAT (Scholastic Assessment Test) scores depending on sex, race, and ethnic group. Answer the questions posed as you engage with the sociological data below.

ENGAGING SOCIOLOGY

Test Score Variations by Gender and Ethnicity

Evaluate your testing experiences and compare them to those of other groups: (see Table 10.5).

TABLE 10.5   ACT and SAT Scores by Sex and Race/Ethnicity

ACT Scores: 2013	Average	SAT Scores: 2013	Average
Composite, total scores	20.9	SAT Writing, all students	488
Male*	21.2	Male	482
Female*	20.9	Female	493
White	22.2	White	515
African American	16.9	Black/African American	417
American Indian/Alaska Native	18	American Indian/Alaska Native	462
Hispanic	18.8	Hispanic	442
Asian American	23.5	Asian/Pacific Islanders	528
SAT Scores: 2013	Average		
SAT Critical Reading, all students	496	SAT Math, all students	514
Male	496	Male	531
Female	494	Female	499
White	528	White	535
Black/African American	428	Black/African American	428
Hispanic	450	Hispanic	461
Asian/Pacific Islanders	518	Asian/Pacific Islander	595
American Indian/Alaska Native	482	American Indian/Alaska Native	489

Source: ACT 2013; College Board 2013.

* No male/female scores listed for 2012 ACT; scores reflect 2011 data.

Engaging With Sociology

1. Do you think your scores were an accurate measure of your ability or achievement? Why or why not?

2. Do you think your race or ethnicity, social class, or gender affected your scores? Why or why not?

3. Have your scores affected your life chances? Are there ways in which you have been privileged or disprivileged in the testing process?

4. What might be some causes of the variation in test scores between groups or categories of students?

Student Tracking. Judgments by school administrators, counselors, and teachers affect children for a lifetime. *Ability grouping* places students into different-level groups within classes. *Tracking* separates students into different-level classes within a school. Each of these groups has the goal of allowing educators to more effectively address the needs of students of different abilities.

Many sociologists of education have argued against tracking, pointing out that it contributes to the stratification process that perpetuates inequality. Research finds that levels at which students are tracked correlate with factors such as the child's background and ethnic group, language skills, appearance, and other socioeconomic variables (Rosenbaum 1999; Wells and Oakes 1996). Students from lower social classes and minority groups tend to be clustered in the lower tracks and complete fewer years of school (Lucas and Berends 2002; Oakes et al. 1997). In other words, track placement is not always a measure of a student's ability. It can be arbitrary, based on teachers' impressions or questionable test results. Even language differences between teachers and students can affect placement.

On the other hand, tracking provides many benefits for teachers and students. In tracked classes, teachers do not have to slow down to help some students catch up, while trying to make sure that their more advanced students are not bored. Students tend to make more progress when working in groups with similar academic aptitudes.

Thinking Sociologically

Were you tracked in any subjects? What effect, if any, did this have on you? What effect did tracking have on friends of yours? How might (a) a conflict theorist and (b) a functionalist describe tracking's impact on society?

The family and education are two of the first institutions that children encounter and that follow them throughout life. Both institutions have a primary concern with the process of socialization. Despite those who lament the weakening of the family, the institution of the family is here to stay because it is crucial to the survival of both individuals and societies. Although it takes many forms around the world and adapts to changes in other parts of the social world, it is resilient, shaping the way we partner, make people, and socialize children. Likewise, education systems prepare children and adults through the process of socialization to fill roles necessary to societal survival. Education also plays a role in the opportunities children have available to them in the society.

WHAT HAVE WE LEARNED?

Our happiest and saddest experiences are integrally intertwined with family. Families provide the foundation through which individuals' needs are met, and they help prepare children for the demands of society. Societies depend on the family as the unit through which to funnel services. It provides the base from which other institutions—education, religion, politics, economics, and health care—carry out their functions.

The educational institution has a vested interest in stability but is also viewed as a means to reduce inequality by training children for upward mobility in society. Schools foster patriotism and loyalty toward political systems. It should not be surprising, therefore, that most schools do more to enhance stability than to create change that might threaten those who have power, privilege, and influence. Still, many families put faith in schools providing their children with the means to succeed in society. Schools work largely with young minds in the socialization process—carrying out what powerful policy makers feel is important.

KEY POINTS

- Families are diverse entities at the micro level, having many forms in different societies; they help carry out needs for societies to replace and train members.

- The family is sometimes called the most basic unit of society, providing the core unit for pairing into groups (partner taking), for making and socializing new members of society (people making), and sometimes for contract breaking.

- The process of partner taking involves rules of exogamy, endogamy, free choice or arranged marriage, and polygamy or monogamy.

- Power within a partnership—distribution of tasks and decision making—is determined within each family, guided by societal norms.

- The structure of the family has changed in recent years, with more single-parent families, more couples cohabiting outside of marriage, and the legalization of same-sex marriages in a majority of the U.S. states.

- Education is one of the primary institutions of society, focusing on the socialization of children and adults into their cultures so that they become contributing members.

- At the micro level, various statuses and roles interact within a school, and schools develop their own cultures that may or may not enhance learning.

- What we learn in schools goes far beyond the formal curriculum. We also learn a "hidden curriculum" in school that helps socialize us into our roles in society.

- At the meso level, education can be understood as a formal organization that works toward certain goals (bureaucracy) but that has many of the dysfunctions of other bureaucracies.

DISCUSSION QUESTIONS

1. Does (or did) your family expect you to marry someone of a particular (a) race or ethnicity, (b) social class, (c) educational background, or (d) religion? Why or why not? How do you think endogamous norms impact (a) individual marriages and (b) society?

2. What are arguments for and against monogamy versus polygamy as a form of marriage? Which might be more stable and why?

3. A majority of Americans and a strong majority of young Americans (those below 30) now support same-sex marriage. What are some cultural and structural changes that have led to this increase in support for marriage equality over the past decade?

4. What are examples of the "hidden curriculum" in schools? Describe your own school experience with the formal and informal systems.

5. Do you think there should be tracking in schools? Why or why not? How has tracking (or an absence of tracking) in your schools impacted your education and sense of yourself as a student? How does tracking in schools impact society?

6. How do schools produce and reproduce inequality? If you had the power and desire to use the school system to reduce inequality, what policies would you implement? What do you think the chances are of your policies actually being put into place? Why?

CONTRIBUTING TO OUR SOCIAL WORLD: What Can We Do?

At the Local Level

- *Support groups for married or partnered students* respond to the needs of an ever-increasing number of undergraduate students living on or near campus with spouses, partners, and children. If your campus has a support group, arrange to attend a meeting and work with members to help them meet the challenges associated with their family situation. If such a group does not exist, consider forming one.

- Is there *day care available on your campus*? Day care on campus can be invaluable for parents. If there is, look at the cost and availability of care for the children of faculty, staff, and students. If there is not a day care, look at the possibilities of creating, funding, and staffing one. How might it benefit the college or university, as well as the families it will serve?

- Some colleges and universities have established programs called *FIGs (First-Year Interest Groups)* to assist first-year students as they adjust to college and help them form a community with other students. Learn more about FIGs at schools such as the University of Wisconsin (http://figs.wisc.edu/). If your school does not have this program, try to initiate one.

At the Organizational or Institutional Level

- *House builders* have begun to change how they design some houses in order to meet the needs of multigeneration households. Contact your local *Habitat for Humanity chapter* (www.habitat.org) and ask if you can help the organization create more homes suitable for such households. You can find some ideas for such homes at www.newhomesource.com/resourcecenter/articles/multigenerational-living-is-back-with-a-new-twist.

- Most primary schools welcome *reading and math tutors,* volunteers, and service learning students who can read to young students and tutor them in reading and math. Contact a faculty member on your campus who specializes in early-childhood education and investigate the opportunities for such volunteer work.

- *Volunteers of America* (www.voa.org) chapters organize to provide low-income and homeless children with school supplies and backpacks every year through "Operation Backpack." You can learn more about the program and how to locate your local VOA chapter at the VOA website or by Googling "VOA," "operation backpack," and the name of your state.

At the National and Global Levels

- *Voices for America's Children* is a multi-issue advocacy group for children with member organizations across the nation. The organization strives to improve the lives of children and their families, particularly those most at risk. You can learn about the issues on which this group is working and join its efforts, if you would like to do so, by going to its website at www.raisingofamerica.org/?q=advocacy/voices-americas-children.

- *Teach for America* (www.teachforamerica.org), a national organization, modeled along the lines of AmeriCorps and Peace Corps, places recent college graduates in short-term (approximately 2-year) assignments teaching in economically disadvantaged neighborhood schools. "Teach for America is the national corps of outstanding recent college graduates and professionals of all academic majors and career interests who commit 2 years to teach in urban and rural public schools and become leaders in the effort to expand educational opportunity. . . . [Its] mission is to build the movement to eliminate educational inequity by enlisting our nation's most promising future leaders in the effort."

- *Teaching abroad* provides an opportunity to make a difference in the lives of children. Consider teaching English abroad through one of many organizations that sponsor teachers. Visit www.globaltesol.com, www.teachabroad.com, www.jetprogramme.org, and related websites.

$SAGE edge™

Sharpen your skills with SAGE edge at **edge.sagepub.com/ballantinecondensed4e**

SAGE edge for Students provides a personalized approach to help you accomplish your coursework goals in an easy-to-use learning environment.

edge.sagepub.com/ballantinecondensed4e

Review, practice, and **improve** your critical thinking with the tools and resources at SAGE edge.

- Review the **eFlashcards**
- Take the **practice quiz** to assist in your mastery of course material
- Explore the **video and multimedia**
- Access full-text **SAGE journal articles**

©REUTERS/Bazuki Muhammad

11 Religion

The Social Meaning of Sacred Meaning

Religion takes many forms and is expressed in many ways, but it is always about a sense of meaning and purpose in life. That meaning and actions associated with the meaning affect many aspects of daily life.

MICRO

● **ME (AND MY FAITH COMMUNITY)**

● **LOCAL ORGANIZATIONS AND COMMUNITY**
People find meaning and support in a local church, temple, or mosque.

MESO

● **NATIONAL ORGANIZATIONS, INSTITUTIONS, AND ETHNIC SUBCULTURES**
Religious groups and denominations influence family life, government, education, and the economy.

MACRO

● **SOCIETY**
Religious groups foster national social movements and influence the national culture.

● **GLOBAL COMMUNITY**
Transnational religious organizations cross national borders, and religious outreach programs span the globe.

LEARNING OBJECTIVES

11.1 Explain the components and functions of religion.

11.2 Discuss the process of becoming religious.

11.3 Describe how the United States became a "denominational society."

11.4 Compare the functionalist and conflict perspectives on religion.

11.5 Predict the future role of religion in the modern world.

THINK ABOUT IT

Micro: Local Community	How do various local religious congregations interact with the local community in your town?
Meso: National Institutions; Complex Organizations; Ethnic Groups	How does the institutionalization of a religion help it survive? Why do ethnic groups often have specific religions or branches of religions?
Macro: National and Global Systems	How do religions foster solidarity and conflict within your country? How do religions help solve world problems (war, poverty, hunger, disease, bigotry) or help create them?

Abu Salmaan, a Muslim father and shopkeeper in Syria, prays frequently in keeping with the commands of the Quran, the holy book of his faith. Like his neighbors, when he hears the call to prayer, he goes to the village square, faces Mecca, and prostrates himself, with his head to the ground, to honor God and to pray for peace. Doing this five times a day is a constant reminder of his ultimate loyalty to God. As part of the larger Abrahamic religious tradition (which includes Judaism, Christianity, and Islam), he believes in one God and accepts the Hebrew Bible and the authority of Jeremiah, Isaiah, Amos, and Jesus as prophets. He believes that God also revealed Truth through another voice—that of Muhammad. He is devoted, worshipping as commanded by the Quran, cherishing his family as directed by his scriptures, giving generously to charities, and making business decisions based on the moral standards of a God-loving Muslim.

Tuneq, knowledgeable Netsilik Inuit (Eskimo) hunter that he is, apologizes to the soul of the seal he has just killed. He shares the meat and blubber with his fellow hunters, and he makes sure that every part of the seal is used or consumed—skin, bones, eyes, tendons, brain, and muscles. His Inuit religion provides rules that help enforce an essential ecological ethic among these arctic hunters to preserve the delicate natural balance. His faith has taught Tuneq that, if he fails to honor the seal by using every morsel or if he violates a rule of hunting etiquette, an invisible vapor will come from his body and sink through the ice, snow, and water. This vapor will collect in the hair of Nuliajuk, goddess of the sea. In revenge, she will call the sea mammals to her so the people living on the ice above will starve.

Before going to bed, Nandi Nwankwo from Nigeria sets out a bowl of milk and some food for the ancestors who, he believes, are present outside the family's dwelling at night. Respected ancestors protect family members, but they are also a powerful and even frightening force in guiding social behavior. Children learn that they must behave or the ancestors will punish them.

These are but a few examples from the world's many and varied religious systems. What they have in common is that each system provides directions for appropriate and expected behaviors and serves as a form of social control for individuals within that society. Religious sanctions that encourage conformity are strong. Indeed, they are made *sacred*, a realm of existence different from mundane everyday life. Religion, according to Catholic priest and sociologist Andrew Greeley, pervades the lives of people of faith (Greeley 1989). It cannot be separated from the rest of the social world. Members of societies believe so strongly in their religions that conquests and wars throughout history have been based on spreading or defending the faith. Sociologists are interested in these relationships—in the way social relationships and structures affect religion and in the consequences of religion for individuals and for society.

In this chapter, we explore religion as a complex social phenomenon that interrelates with other processes and institutions of society. Religion, like education and the family, has a strong impact on socialization, and thus a deep connection to the micro level, but it also impacts national trends and global movements, so we will also look at religion's meso and macro links. We investigate what religion does for individuals, how individuals become religious, and how religion and modern societies interact.

WHAT DOES RELIGION DO FOR US?

What do people have to gain from religious practices, beliefs, and organizations? Religion helps explain the meaning of life, death, suffering, injustice, and events beyond our control. As sociologist Émile Durkheim pointed out, humans generally view such questions as belonging to a realm of existence different from the mundane or profane world of our everyday experience (Durkheim [1915] 2002). He called this separate dimension the *sacred realm*. This sacred realm elicits feelings of awe, reverence, and even fear. It is viewed as being above normal inquiry and doubt. Religious guidelines, beliefs, and values dictate "rights and wrongs," provide answers to the big questions of life, and instill moral codes and ideas about the world in members of each society or subculture. For these reasons, religions can have enormous control over people's attitudes and behavior (Ammerman 2009; Durkheim [1915] 2002).

Religion is more than a set of beliefs about the supernatural. It often *sacralizes* (makes sacred and unquestionable) the culture in which we live, the class or caste position to which we belong, the attitudes we hold toward other people, and the morals to which we adhere. Religion impacts our lifestyles, gender roles, and social status. Around the world, billions of people believe that they have found the Truth—the ultimate answers—in their religions. Many are willing to die for their faith.

Thinking Sociologically

Consider your own religious tradition. Which of the purposes or functions of religion mentioned above does your religious faith address? If you are not part of a faith community or do not hold religious beliefs of a particular group, are there other beliefs or groups that fulfill these functions for you?

Components of Religion

Religion normally involves at least three components: (1) a faith or worldview that provides a sense of meaning and purpose in life (the *meaning system*), (2) a set of interpersonal relationships and friendship networks (the *belonging system*), and (3) a stable pattern of roles, statuses, and organizational practices (the *structural system*) (Roberts and Yamane 2012).

The meaning system operates mostly at the micro level; the belonging system is also critical at the micro level but part of various meso-level organizations as well; and the structural system tends to have its major impact at the meso and macro levels. These components of religion may reinforce one another and work in harmony toward common goals, or there may be conflict among them.

Meaning System. The *meaning system* of a religion includes the ideas and symbols it uses to provide a sense of purpose in life and to help explain why suffering, injustice, and evil exist. It provides a big picture to account for events that would otherwise seem chaotic and irrational. For example, although the loss of a family member through death may be painful, many people find comfort and hope in their religion's teachings on the meaning of life and death.

Meaning systems of religion reflect the needs of the societies in which the religion is practiced. Because each culture has different problems to solve, the precise needs reflected in each society's meaning system vary. In agricultural societies, the problems revolve around growing crops and securing the elements necessary for crops—water, sunlight, and good soil. Among the Zuni of New Mexico and the Hopi of Arizona, for example, water for crops is a critical concern. These Native American people typically grow corn in a climate that averages roughly 10 inches of rain per year, so it is not surprising that the central focus of their religious dances and of their supernatural beings—*kachinas*—is to bring rain. In other societies, the death rate is so high that high fertility has been necessary to perpetuate the group. Thus, fertility goddesses take on great significance. In some other societies, strong armies and brave soldiers have been essential to preserve the group from invading forces; hence, gods or rituals of war have been prominent.

Belonging System. Belonging systems are profoundly important in most religious groups. A *belonging system* refers to the interpersonal networks and emotional ties that develop among adherents of a particular faith. Many people remain members of religious groups not so much because they accept the meaning system of the group but because that is where they find their belonging system—their friendship and kinship network. A prayer group may be the one area in their lives in which people can be truly open about their personal pain and feel safe to expose their vulnerabilities. This builds bonds and belonging. For many religious people, their religious group is a type of extended family that tends to become more important as their own families age. The religious groups that have grown the fastest in recent years are those that have devised ways to strengthen the sense of belonging and to foster friendship networks within the group.

Structural System. A religion involves a group of people who share a common meaning system. However, if each person interprets the group's beliefs in his or her own way and if each attaches his or her own meanings to the symbols, the meaning system becomes so individualized that *sacralization* of common values can no longer occur. Therefore, almost all religions (the Unitarian Universalist religion is an exception) have developed a system of control and screening of new revelations. Religious leaders in designated statuses have the authority to interpret theology and define the essentials of the faith.

Buddhist monks pray at Bayon Temple in Angkor Thom, Cambodia. Their religious system gives them a sense of meaning and purpose in life, but also provides social ties.

Religious groups also need methods of designating leaders, raising funds to support their organizations, and ensuring continuation of the group. To teach the next generation the meaning system, members need to develop a formal structure to determine the content and form of their educational materials, and then they must produce and distribute them. If the religion is to survive past the death of a charismatic leader, it must undergo institutionalization. In other words, it must establish a *structural system* of established statuses, norms, ways to access resources, and routine procedures for addressing problems.

Because religion is one institution in the larger society, it is interdependent and interrelated with the political, economic, family, education, health, and information systems. Changes in any one of these areas can bring change to religion, and changes in religion can bring changes to other institutions of society.

Although some people dislike the idea of organized religion, one insight of sociology is that a group cannot survive in the modern world unless it undergoes *routinization of charisma*. That is, religious organizations must develop established roles, statuses, groups, and routine procedures for replacing leaders after a death, making decisions, and obtaining resources in order to survive more than a generation (Weber 1947).

At the local level, a formal religious structure develops, with committees doing specific tasks, such as overseeing worship, maintaining the building, recruiting religious educators, and raising funds. These committees report to an administrative board that works closely with the clergy (the ordained ministers) and has much of the final responsibility for the life and continued existence of the people who regularly gather for religious services, referred to as the *congregation*. The roles, statuses, and committees make up the structural system. The structure is every bit as important as the meaning system if the group is to thrive.

Like any other formal organization in society, meso-level religious structures consist of individuals and committees doing specialized tasks. Contemporary branches of Christianity in the United States, for example, may have national commissions on global outreach, evangelism, worship, world peace, social justice, and so forth. In addition, bishops, presbyters, or other leaders provide guidelines for pastors who lead their own congregations. Most religious organizations are, among other things, bureaucracies. The formal organization may be caught up in some of the dysfunctions that can plague any organization: goal displacement, the iron law of oligarchy, alienation, and other problems discussed in Chapter 5. In any case, the three systems—meaning, belonging, and structure—usually go together, as illustrated in Figure 11.1.

● Thinking Sociologically

Think about the meaning, belonging, and structural systems of a religion with which you are familiar. How do these elements influence—and how are they influenced by—the larger social world, from individual to national and global systems?

BECOMING PART OF A FAITH COMMUNITY: MICRO-LEVEL ANALYSIS

We are not born religious, although we may be born into a religious group. We learn our religious beliefs through socialization, just as we learn our language, customs, norms, and values. Our family usually determines the religious environment in which we grow up, whether it is an all-encompassing message or closer to a one-day-a-week commitment. We start imitating religious practices, such as praying before bed or saying grace before dinner, before we understand these practices intellectually. Then, as we encounter the unexplainable events of life, religion is there to provide meaning. Gradually, religion becomes an ingrained part of many people's lives.

It is unlikely that we will adopt a faith not practiced in our society. For instance, if we were born in most parts of India, we would be raised in and around the Hindu, Muslim, and Sikh faiths. In most Arab countries, we would become Muslim; in South American countries, we would likely become Catholic or evangelical Christian; and in many Southeast Asian countries, Buddhist. Although our religious affiliation may seem normal and typical to us, no religion has a majority of the people in the world as its adherents, and we may in fact be part of a rather small minority religious group when we think in terms of the global population. Table 11.1 on page 296 shows this explicitly.

Learning the meaning system of a religious group is both a formal and an informal process. In

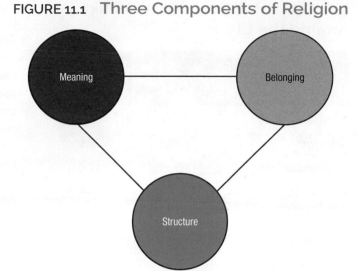

FIGURE 11.1   Three Components of Religion

some cultures, religious faith pervades everyday life. For the Amish, farming without machines or the use of electricity is part of their Christian teachings, which affect their total lifestyle. Formal teaching in most religions takes place primarily in the temple, church, or mosque. The formal teaching may take the form of bar or bat mitzvah classes, Sunday school, or parochial school. Informal religious teaching occurs when we observe others "practicing what they preach."

Again, the meaning (believing) and belonging systems are linked in important ways. Most people do not belong to a religious group because they accept its belief system, at least initially. Rather, they come to believe because they want to belong and are socialized to feel they are an integral part of the group (Greeley 1972; Roberts and Yamane 2012). Research

The bat mitzvah, shown here, is an initiation ceremony into the faith for Jewish girls.

TABLE 11.1   Religious Membership Around the Globe

Religion	Membership (in Millions)	Percentage of World Population
Christian (Total)	2,319.8	33.1
Muslim	1,609.2	22.9
Roman Catholic	1,200.9	17.0
Hindu	967.2	13.8
Nonreligious	679.0	9.7
Buddhist	504.8	7.2
Chinese Folk	437.1	6.2
Protestant	430.6	6.0
Independent	356.7	5.0
Orthodox	277.6	3.8
Other Ethnoreligious	247.5	3.5
Atheist	136.3	1.9
Unaffiliated	110.1	1.6
Sikh	24.8	0.4
Jewish	15.0	0.2
Spiritist	13.7	0.2
Taoist	8.5	0.1
Confucianist	8.2	0.1
Baha'i	7.5	0.1
Jain	5.5	0.1
Shintoist	2.8	a
Zoroastrian	0.2	a

Source: World Almanac (2014). Adapted from "World Adherents of Religions by Continental Area 2012," p. 701 in *The World Almanac and Book of Facts.* Copyright © 2014 by Infobase Learning.

Note: Numbers add up to more than the total world population because many people identify themselves with more than one religious tradition. Thus, the percentages will also add up to more than 100%. Percentages are rounded.

a = Less than 0.05%.

on people who switch religious affiliations or join new religious movements (NRMs) indicates that loyalty to a friendship network usually comes first, followed by commitment to the meaning and structural systems.

In many cases, accepting a new meaning system is the final stage rather than the initial stage of change (Roberts and Yamane 2012).

There is more fluidity in religious membership now than at any other time in history. Historically, most people remained part of the same religious group for a lifetime. Roughly 28% of U.S. citizens have either left the religious group in which they were raised for another religion or no longer have any religious affiliation (Pew Forum on Religion and Public Life 2012b). Increase in interreligious marriages plays a role in changing religions, as 37% of current marriages involve spouses with different religious affiliations. Most often, the change is to a different branch of the same umbrella religion (e.g., from one form of Christianity to another) (Pew Forum on Religion and Public Life 2012b).

Because changing religious groups occurs most often through change of friendship networks or marriage, religious groups frequently try to control the boundaries and protect their members from outside influences. The Amish in the United States have done this by living in their own communities and attempting to limit schooling of their children by outside authorities. To help perpetuate religious beliefs and practices, most religious groups encourage endogamy, marrying within the group. For example, Orthodox Jews have food taboos and food preparation requirements that limit the likelihood that they will share a meal with "outsiders." In order to have a wedding in the Catholic Church, Catholics who want to marry a non-Catholic must receive permission from their local bishop to marry "despite the disparity of cult" between them.

Religious groups also try to socialize members to make sacrifices of time, energy, and financial resources on behalf of their faith. If one has sacrificed and devoted one's resources and energy for a cause, one is likely to feel a commitment to the organization—the structural system (Kanter 2005; Sherkat and Ellison 1999). Single young people in their late teens and early twenties who are members of the Church of Jesus Christ of Latter-Day Saints (Mormons) are strongly encouraged to devote two years of their lives to missionary work. They must save money in advance to support themselves. This sacrifice of other opportunities and investment of time, energy, and resources in the church creates an intense commitment to the organization. Few of them later feel that they wasted those years or that the investment was unwise. So, commitment to the structural system is connected to strong commitment to the meaning and belonging systems.

An Amish family enjoys a trip to the beach. Amish faith influences every aspect of their lives, including their beach attire.

The survival of a religious group depends in part on how committed its members are and whether they share freely of their financial and time resources. Most religious groups try, therefore, to socialize their members into commitment to the meaning system, the belonging system, and the structural system of their religion.

Thinking Sociologically

How did you or individuals you know become committed to a faith tradition? Did you (or they) think about the process as it occurred, or were you (or they) born into it? If you left a religious organization, why did you leave?

Symbols and the Creation of Meaning: A Symbolic Interactionist Perspective

Dina is appalled as she walks past the laundromat. The *gaje* (the term Roma use to refer to non-Roma) just do not seem to understand cleanliness. These middle-class North American neighbors of hers are very concerned about whether their clothes are *melalo*—dirty with dirt. In contrast, they pay no attention to whether they are *marime*—defiled or polluted in a spiritual sense. She watches in disgust as a woman not only places the clothing of men, women, and children in a single washing machine but also includes clothing from the upper and lower halves of the body together. No respectable Roma (sometimes called Gypsies by outsiders) would allow such mixing, and if it did occur, the cloth could be used only as rags. The laws of spiritual purity make clear that the lower half

of the body is defiled. Anything that comes in contact with the body below the waist or that touches the floor becomes *marime* and can never again be considered *wuzho*—truly "clean." Food that touches the floor becomes filthy and inedible.

Ideally, a Roma woman would have separate washtubs for men's upper-body clothing, men's lower-body clothing, women's upper-body clothing, women's lower-body clothing, and children's clothing. Roma know too well that the spirit of Mamioro brings illness to homes that are *marime*. The lack of spiritual cleanliness of non-Roma causes Roma to minimize their contact with these *gaje*, to avoid sitting on a chair used by a *gaje*, and generally to recoil at the thought of assimilation into the larger culture (Sutherland 1986, 2001; Sway 1988).

How we make sense of the world takes place through meaning systems, as illustrated in the above example. Roma interpret objects and actions in ways that differ from members of the larger society, and the different meanings result in different behaviors and sometimes distancing from "outsiders."

Symbolic interaction theory focuses on how we make sense of and construct our worlds. Think about how you feel attracted to, or perhaps put off by, someone who wears a cross, a yarmulke worn by Orthodox Jewish men to cover the crown of the head, or a head scarf worn by Muslim women. When we see religious symbols, we react to them based on our experiences with and understanding of the religion they symbolize. Religious meaning systems—the worldview or conceptual framework by which people make sense of life and cope with suffering and injustice—are made up of three elements: myths, rituals, and symbols.

A Romanian Roma woman uses different tubs to wash upper- and lower-body clothing and men's and women's apparel separately so that they will not become spiritually defiled.

Myths are *stories that transmit values and embody ideas about life and the world.* When sociologists of religion use the word *myth*, they are not implying that the story is untrue. A myth may relate historical incidents that actually occurred, fictional events, or abstract ideas, such as reincarnation. Regardless of the literal truth or fiction of these stories, myths transmit values and a particular outlook on life. If a story, such as the Exodus from Egypt of ancient Hebrew people, elicits some sense of sacredness, communicates certain attitudes and values, and helps make sense of life, then it is a myth. The Netsilik Eskimo myth of the sea goddess Nuliajuk (explained in the second story that opened this chapter) reinforces and makes sacred the value of conservation in an environment of scarce resources. It provides messages for appropriate behavior in that group. Thus, whether a myth is factual or not is irrelevant. Myths are always "true" in some deeper metaphorical sense. Indeed, stories that do not carry truth or deep meaning are simply not "myths."

Rituals are *ceremonies or repetitive practices, often used to invoke a sense of awe of the divine and to make certain ideas sacred.* Ceremonies may include music, dancing, kneeling, praying, chanting, storytelling, and other symbolic acts. A number of religions, such as Islam, emphasize devotion to orthopraxy (conformity of behavior) more than orthodoxy (conformity to beliefs or doctrine) (Preston 1988; Tipton 1990). Praying five times a day while facing Mecca, mandated for the Islamic faithful, is an example of orthopraxy.

Often, rituals involve acting out myths. In almost all Christian churches, the cleansing of the soul is enacted by immersing people in water or pouring water on the head during baptism. Likewise, Christians frequently reenact the last supper of Jesus (Communion or Eucharist) as they accept their role as modern disciples. The group environment of the ritual is important. Ethereal music, communal chants, and group actions such as kneeling or taking off one's shoes when entering the shrine or mosque create an aura of separation from the everyday world and a mood of awe so that the beliefs seem eternal and beyond question. They become sacralized. Rituals also make ample use of symbols.

A **symbol** is an *object or an action that represents something else and therefore has meaning beyond its own existence* (e.g., flags and wedding rings). Because religion deals with the transcendent—a realm that

Removal of shoes before entering a mosque is a ritual expression of respect for the sacred among Muslims. Hundreds of Iraqi Shiite Muslim pilgrims have arrived to pray at this mosque in northern Baghdad.

cannot be experienced or proven with the five senses—sacred symbols are a central part of religion. They have a powerful emotional impact on the faithful and reinforce the sacredness of myths.

Sacred symbols store an enormous amount of information and can deliver that information with powerful immediacy. Seeing a cross, for example, can flood a Christian's consciousness with a whole series of images, events, and powerful emotions concerning Jesus and his disciples. Tasting the bitter herbs during a Jewish Seder service is meant to elicit memories of the story of slavery in Egypt, recall the escape under the leadership of Moses, and send a moral message to the celebrant to work for freedom and justice in the world today. The mezuzah, a plaque consecrating a house, fixed to the doorpost of a Jewish home, is a symbol reminding the occupants of their commitment to obey God's commandments and reaffirming God's commitment to them as a people. Because symbols can elicit strong feelings, they are used extensively in rituals to represent myths.

Myths, rituals, and symbols are usually interrelated and interdependent (see Figure 11.2). Together, they form the meaning system and reinforce rules of appropriate behavior. They can also limit social relationships among different groups. As noted earlier, the Roma revulsion at the filthy *marime* practices of middle-class Americans, like the Kosher rules for food preparation among the Jews, creates boundaries between "us" and "them" that nearly eliminate prospects of marriage or even of close friendships outside the religious community. Some scholars think that these rituals and symbolic meanings are the key reason why Roma and Jews have survived for millennia as distinct groups without being assimilated or absorbed into dominant cultures. The symbols and meanings have created barriers that prevent the obliteration of their cultures.

Symbolic interactionists stress that humans create, shape, and interpret the meaning of events. Clearly, no other institution focuses as explicitly on shaping and interpreting the meaning of life and its events as religion.

Thinking Sociologically

In a religious tradition with which you are familiar, how do symbols and sacred stories reinforce a particular view of the world or a particular set of values and social norms?

Seeking Eternal Benefits: A Rational Choice Perspective

Rational choice theorists maintain that people decide whether or not they should join or leave a religious group by asking: What are the benefits, and what are the costs? Do the benefits outweigh the costs? The benefits, of course, are nonmaterial when it comes to religious choices—feeling that life has meaning, belonging to a community, gaining a sense of communion with God, confidence in an afterlife, and so forth (Finke and Stark 2005; Warner 1993).

The rational choice approach views churchgoers as consumers out to meet their needs or obtain a "product." It depicts churches as entrepreneurial establishments, or "franchises," in a competitive market, with "entrepreneurs" (clergy) as leaders. Competition for members leads churches, for example, to "market"

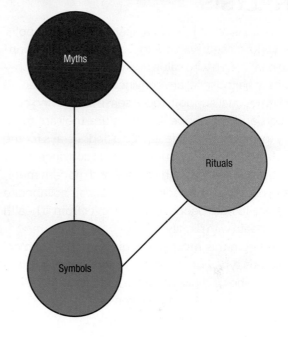

FIGURE 11.2   The Meaning System of Religion Is Composed of Three Interrelated Elements

their religion to consumers. Converts, and religious people generally, are regarded as active and rational agents pursuing self-interests. In order to grow, churches must meet "consumer demand" (Finke and Stark 2005; Jelen 2002). Religious groups produce religious "commodities" (rituals, meaning systems, a sense of belonging, symbols, and so forth) to meet the "demands" of consumers (Christiano, Swatos, and Kivisto 2008).

Competitive enterprises, churches, temples, and mosques must make investments of effort, time, and resources to attract and keep potential buyers. There are many religious entrepreneurs seeking to increase the number of people in their congregations. The challenge for the various groups is to beat the competition by meeting the demand of the current marketplace (Finke and Stark 2005). For instance, because the U.S. Constitution separates church from state, organized religions have to offer their product on an open market, in competition with other religions. Religious pluralism and spiritual diversity increase the rates of religious activity as each group seeks to increase its market share and meet the needs of individuals in the society (Finke and Stark 2005; Iannaccone and Bainbridge 2010).

▶ My First Steps in Becoming Religious

RELIGION AND MODERN LIFE: MESO-LEVEL ANALYSIS

Cassandra is a chaplain at a hospital in Minneapolis. She works closely with doctors and other professionals in health care who value her work. Many of the physicians at her hospital are convinced that when people have emotional support, feel a sense of love and connection, and have hope for the future, they are more likely to improve their health. Cassandra prays for the people she counsels, but she also is convinced that God often works through science and modern medicine. The clergy and medical professionals collaborate as a team to help people either recover from ill health or face death with dignity.

We begin this meso-level discussion by exploring various types of religious organizations and then examining how religion as an institution interacts with other institutions. As you will see, different religions structure themselves in various ways.

Types of Religious Organizations

The unique history of religious organizations in the United States led Andrew Greeley to describe the country as a "denominational society" (Greeley 1972). In doing so, he stressed that the nation is religiously diverse in two senses: multiple religious groups living side by side with no single faith tradition being dominant, and church and state given their own autonomous realms by the U.S. Constitution (Stark and Finke 2000).

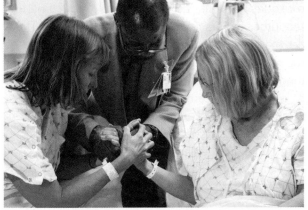

Chaplains, members of the religious institution, often work closely with professionals in another institution—health care. Here we see a hospital chaplain at work.

Denominations and Denominationalism. In the United States and most other Western countries, local congregations tend to be part of larger centralized organizations. These *centralized coordinating bodies or associations that link local congregations with a similar history and theology* are called **denominations**.

In the long history of human society, denominationalism is a unique and rather recent way of organizing religion (Ammerman 2006). For most of human history religion was diffused through all of life. Under these conditions, religion and the rest of life have been seamless and undifferentiated (Bellah 1970). Over time, religion gradually became distinct from other social institutions in most Western societies, particularly in the political or governmental structures. The result is that specifically religious organizations arose.

Initially, a single religious organization dominated a particular geographic area. For several centuries the Roman Catholic Church was the dominant religious group in Europe. Eventually, however, the religious sphere itself came to be diverse. The Reformation Era (1517–1648) launched Protestantism and brought about the emergence of different, oppositional Christian groups with different beliefs and organizational structures. Most of them were splinter groups that broke away from Catholicism, such as the Lutherans (Gorski 2000).

Each religious group attempted to become the official government-approved church in its territory. Conflict rather than peaceful coexistence came to characterize Europe, and many people were forced to flee the lands in which they were raised because of their faith.

Some of those driven out of Europe for religious reasons were followers of the Calvinist Puritan movement. The Puritans played a major role in the founding of the New England colonies and, in so doing, created religious establishments of their own. Four of the colonies (Rhode Island, Delaware, New Jersey, and Pennsylvania) had no state-sponsored church. Ultimately no single religious group established dominance or control in North America. This development led to necessary peaceful coexistence: religious pluralism and official separation of church and state.

Freedom of religion and prohibition of a state-endorsed church are key conditions for denominationalism. When scholars refer to the United States as a "denominational society," they mean a society characterized by religious congregations united into denominations that are presumed equal under the law and that generally treat other religious bodies with an attitude of mutual respect (Greeley 1972). As a consequence of this organizational pattern of religious pluralism, there are hundreds of denominations in the United States. Indeed, the *Handbook of Denominations in the United States* lists 31 different Baptist denominations alone (Mead, Hill, and Atwood 2005). Denominationalism has become a global phenomenon. The *World Christian Encyclopedia* reports 33,830 denominations within Christianity worldwide (Barrett, Kurian, and Johnson 2001; Roberts and Yamane 2012).

Although diversity within Protestantism was a key force for denominationalism, it has become fully incorporated by all major religious groups in the United States. Some scholars have even identified Jewish "denominationalism" in reference to the four branches of Judaism—Orthodox, Conservative, Reform, and Reconstructionist (Jewish Outreach Institute 2008). The Nation of Islam and American Society of Muslims are distinctively American Islamic denominations (though the former is often viewed negatively by traditional Muslims). There are also denominations of Islam that are more global (Sunni and Shiite are the largest). Buddhism and Hinduism also have different branches or schools, though, like Islam, they were brought to America in large numbers only recently, so it remains to be seen whether there will be an evolution of those branches into recognizable denominations.

Denominational Structures and the Micro-Meso Connection.

The organizational structures of denominations vary. Most, however, are congregational, episcopal, or presbyterian (Ammerman 2006; Roberts and Yamane 2012). Note that these are *not* the same as churches by those names, but rather the organizational structure (or "polity") of a number of churches.

In a *congregational* polity or structure, the authority of the local congregation is supreme. For example, the thousands of Baptist and United Church of Christ congregations in the United States hire and fire their own ministers, control their own finances, own their own property, decide whether to ordain women, and make other decisions about the congregation themselves (Ammerman 1990, 2009).

The *episcopal*—also called "hierarchical"—pattern of governance places ultimate authority over local churches in the centralized hands of bishops (the word

episcopal means "governed by bishops"). Each of the Roman Catholic Church's nearly 20,000 U.S. congregations (or "parishes") is geographically defined. They are clustered into a "diocese" under the authority of the local bishop and, ultimately, the Bishop of Rome—the Pope. In an episcopal structure, a bishop, in consultation with his or her executive staff, decides who will be the priest or minister of the local church. A committee of the local congregation may be consulted, but the bishop has the final say. Christian churches that have some form of episcopal organization include Anglican, Episcopalian, Eastern Orthodox, Methodist, African Methodist Episcopal (AME), AME Zion, and some Lutherans. So, the local United Methodist church building in your community is actually owned by the larger denomination and is only maintained by the local congregation, and a bishop decides who will be the minister for the community.

Presbyterian polity, quite simply, is a middle ground between episcopal (with a bishop having tremendous power) and congregational (where the congregation has total authority). In presbyterian polity, authority is shared so that neither a single local congregation nor the hierarchy can trump the other. The Presbyterian Church is the best example of this compromise position. Presbyterian structure usually involves a local board in a congregation that can make decisions—called Sessions. There are also organizations composed of groups of congregations at regional and national levels that, in order of regional to national, are typically called Presbyteries, Synods, and then the National Assembly. Almost all Reformed churches use this approach: Dutch Reformed, Swiss Reformed, and the Presbyterian Church, which is an offshoot of the Scottish Reformed tradition. Table 11.2 on page 302 provides some examples of which churches tend to follow which polity.

While denominational structure or polity strongly affects the structure of a local congregation and how it works, the social environment can also cause a certain amount of adaptation. The tendency to assimilate to the organizational patterns in the social environment impacts religious groups as much as it does individuals. Most mosques in the United States are relatively new, with almost all founded after 1970. According to the Islamic scholar Ihsan Bagby, "Most of the world's mosques are simply a place to pray. . . . A Muslim cannot be a member of a particular mosque" because mosques belong to God, not to the people (Bagby

TABLE 11.2   Polity or Organizational Structures of Selected Churches

Congregational Polity	Episcopal Polity	Presbyterian Polity
United Church of Christ (Congregational)	Roman Catholic	Reformed Churches
National Baptist	Episcopal	Dutch Reformed
Southern Baptist	Anglican	Swiss Reformed
Christian Church (Disciples of Christ)	United Methodist	French Reformed
Churches of Christ	African Methodist Episcopal	Church of Scotland
Unitarian Universalist	Evangelical Lutheran	Presbyterian Church USA

2003:115). The role of the imam—the leader of a mosque—is simply to lead prayers five times a day and to run the services on the Sabbath, including delivery of a sermon. Unlike many Christian and Jewish leaders in the United States, an imam does not run an organization and does not need formal training at a seminary.

Mosques in the United States cannot depend on government funding and need to adapt to the congregational model: recruiting members who will support them. Many have constructed buildings with multiple meeting spaces and become community centers rather than simply a place to pray. They have also begun to put more emphasis on religious education (which had been managed largely by extended families). Religious holidays are celebrated at the mosque rather than with families, and life cycle celebrations (births and marriages) are events for the congregation. This is a major change in the role of the mosque as it adapts to its environment and becomes more like other congregations in the United States.

New Religious Movements (NRMs) or Cults. New **religious movements**, or **NRMs**, *arise to meet specific needs not met through traditional religious organizations. If NRMs survive for several generations, become established, and gain some legitimacy, they become new religions rather than a new denomination of an existing faith. Cult* was once the common term for this kind of movement, but the media and the public have so completely misused the word that its meaning has become unclear and often negative. Most sociologists of religion now prefer to use the term *NRM* to describe these religious forms (Christiano et al. 2008).

NRMs are either imported into a country as immigrants enter from other lands or founded on a new revelation by a charismatic leader. They are usually out of the mainstream religious system, at least in their early

days. Christianity, Buddhism, and Islam all began as NRMs or cults. The estimated number of NRMs in North America at the turn of the century was between 1,500 and 2,000 (Melton et al. 2009; Nichols, Mather, and Schmidt 2006). An NRM usually originates with a charismatic leader, someone who claims to have received a new insight, usually straight from God. For example, Reverend Sun Myung Moon founded an NRM called the Unification Church, whose members are often referred to as *Moonies*. While claiming to be a part of Christianity, the Unification Church has its own additional scripture to complement the Bible, and Reverend Moon has a standing in the Unification Church equal to Jesus—an idea offensive to most Christian groups.

Some sensational NRMs have ended in tragedy: In 1997, the members of the Heaven's Gate NRM committed group suicide. They believed supernatural beings were coming to take them away in a flying saucer and that they had to kill themselves so that their souls could board the spaceship (Wessinger 2000). Most new religious groups, however, are not dangerous to members. Furthermore, most religious groups now accepted and established were stigmatized as strange or evil when they started. Early Christians, for example, were characterized by Romans as dangerous cannibals. In the 19th century and early decades of the 20th century in the United States, Roman Catholics were depicted in the media as dangerous, immoral, and anti-American (Bromley and Shupe 1981). When we encounter media reports about NRMs, we should remember that not all cults are like the sensational ones.

Religion and Other Social Institutions

The dominant religion(s) in any society generally supports the dominant political system and ideology of the society. It also closely relates to the economic and

 Religion and Academic Achievement

education systems and legitimates the family system through sacred rites of passage for marriage, birth, and death. Religion interacts with the health system, as well. For example, those who regularly attend religious services are healthier (and happier) than those who do not (Newport 2012a).

Religion not only supports other institutions but may also experience support or pressure from these other institutions. The Catholic Church, for example, has faced increasing criticism from international organizations, political movements, governments, religious groups, and educational institutions for its ban on artificial birth control. Due to AIDS and rapid population growth, especially in poor Catholic nations, many interested parties have encouraged the Catholic Church to ease the strict ban. In 2010, faced with mounting pressures and high death rates in Africa, Pope Benedict XVI indicated some openness to accepting the use of condoms among married couples to prevent the spread of AIDS (BBC News 2010). If the Church does not change and adapt with the times, it must expend considerable effort to defend its position in order to keep from losing credibility in the eyes of members and nonmembers alike. We will now consider the relationship between religion and two other social institutions: politics and economics.

Religion and Political Systems. Jan, a Swede, belongs to a state religion: Lutheranism. He was raised a Lutheran and does not really think about the possibility of other religious beliefs, although there is a growing Pentecostal movement in Sweden. The Nwankwo family, mentioned in the chapter opening, practices an ancient tribal religion, also with no thought that another religious belief might have

something better to offer. Most of us are raised in a particular belief system from childhood and adhere to that religion because it is part of the custom and tradition most familiar to us. We seldom question our "choice" until we interact with members of different religions.

In a pure **theocracy**, or rule by God, *religious leaders, like those in Iran, rule society in accordance with God's presumed wishes.* In other nations, political, rather than religious, leaders govern, but an official state religion receives support from tax money. Sweden, Britain, and Italy are examples of societies with state religions. In China, citizens have some limited freedom to practice certain religions, but the Chinese government gives itself the right to select religious leaders (like the Dalai Lama and Catholic bishops serving in China). Some countries, such as the former Soviet Union, have outlawed religion altogether so that nothing competes with loyalty to the nation. The continuum in Figure 11.3 shows the possible relationships between church and state.

Although religion often reinforces the power of the state, it may also be a source of conflict and tension on issues regarding morality, justice, and legitimate authority. Even in the United States, which professes separation between church and state matters, religious groups seek to influence policies such as prayer in school, selection of textbooks and reading matter, and abortion laws. In some countries, religious groups strongly oppose the government and seek to undermine the authority and power of political leaders. In Nazi Germany, for example, some church leaders formulated the Barmen Declaration in opposition to Hitler. Many Christian groups in South Africa opposed apartheid. In some parts of Latin America, church

FIGURE 11.3 Links Between Religion and the State

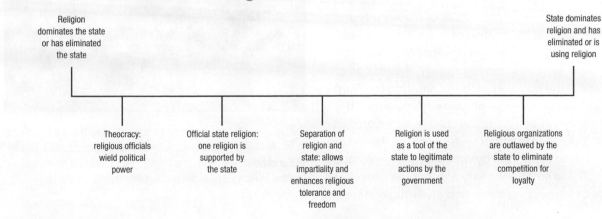

leaders work for human rights and more equitable distribution of land and resources.

Indeed, depending on the organizational structures, religion can provide a source of authority that offers a real challenge to the power of the state when that government has become oppressive. The Roman Catholic Church was one of the first truly transnational organizations, external to any one nation and including representation from many countries. It must be sympathetic to the circumstances of people in many nations, for its membership and its organizational reach span the globe. It cannot align itself with the economic and political interests of one nation or set of nations without risking the alienation of tens of millions of members in another part of the world (Roberts and Yamane 2012).

In Poland during the 1970s and 1980s, the citizenry often felt colonized by a foreign power—the Soviet Union. The communist government in Poland was extremely unpopular, but the people had no real way to make the government more responsive to their needs. The Catholic Church became a major power broker in negotiations between unions and the government in Poland (Tamney 1992). The global nature of the Catholic Church influenced the role bishops could play in the Polish situation. Because Polish bishops were ultimately responsible to the Pope and had a source of support external to the nation, they experienced a good deal of independence from the communist party in power.

In simple homogeneous societies, religion serves as a kind of glue, making sacred the existing social system by offering it supernatural legitimacy. In complex and heterogeneous societies, on the other hand, no single religion can provide the core values of the culture. In such circumstances, an alternative form of religion called civil religion frequently evolves. **Civil religion** *is the set of beliefs, rites, and symbols that sacralize the values of the society and place the nation in the context of transcendent meaning, often giving it divine significance* (Yamane 2007). The beliefs, symbols, and rituals (e.g., the Pledge of Allegiance, the national anthem, saluting the flag) serve to create a sense of sacredness about the nation and for what that nation stands. Although civil religion lacks the structural system of organized religion, it is often supported by various types of patriotic groups. These small voluntary associations develop intense belonging systems, and civil religion tends

to strengthen the sense of belonging citizens feel as members of that society (Bellah 1992; Roberts and Yamane 2012).

Civil religion in the United States is not explicitly Christian, for it must appeal to those who are non-Christian as well. It often refers to God (e.g., God bless America), however, as it acts to legitimize the U.S. political system by treating national holidays (e.g., the Fourth of July) like religious events (with days off of work and special ceremonies) and national documents (e.g., the Constitution and the Declaration of Independence) as sacred texts. Civil religions attempt to give the nation and the government supernatural blessing and authority (Bellah 1970).

Civil religion blends reverence for the nation with more traditional symbols of faith. The above picture, for example, shows a chapel at Punchbowl, the Pacific cemetery for U.S. military personnel, located in Hawaii. Note the relative prominence of the flags beside the altar.

Thinking Sociologically

How does civil religion manifest itself in your country? Give specific examples.

Religion and Economics. Why do most of us study hard, work hard, and strive to get ahead? Why are you sacrificing time and money now—taking this and other college courses—when you might spend that money on an impressive new car? Our answers probably have something to do with our moral attitudes about work, about people who lack ambition, and about the proper way to live. Max Weber provided an answer to this question with his research on the relationship between the Protestant work ethic and capitalism. He gathered information by studying many documents, including the diaries of Calvinists (a branch of Protestantism), sermons and religious teachings, and other historical papers (Weber [1904–1905] 1958).

Weber noted that the areas of Europe where the Calvinists had the strongest followings were the same areas where capitalism had grown the fastest. Weber argued that four elements in the Calvinist Protestant faith created the moral and value system necessary for the growth of capitalism: predestination, a calling, self-denial, and individualism.

1. *Predestination* meant that one's destiny—whether one would eventually go to heaven or hell—was predetermined. Nothing anyone did would change what was to happen. Because God was presumed to be perfect, he was not influenced by human deeds or prayer. Those people who were chosen by God were referred to as the *elect* and were assumed to be a small group. Therefore, people looked for signs of their status—salvation or damnation. High social status was sometimes viewed as a sign of being among the elect. This view motivated people to succeed in *this* life, so that they would appear to be headed toward salvation in the next.

2. The *calling* referred to the concept of doing God's work. Each person was put on earth to serve God, and each had a task to do in God's service. One could be called by God to any occupation, so the key was to work very hard and with the right attitude. Because work was a way to serve God, laziness or lack of ambition came to be viewed as a sin. These ideas helped create a society in which people's

self-worth and their evaluation of others were tied to a work ethic. The Calvinists, therefore, worked hard.

3. *Self-denial* involved living a simple life. If one had a good deal of money, one did not spend it on a lavish home, expensive clothing, or various forms of entertainment. Such consumption would be offensive to God. Therefore, people worked hard and began to accumulate resources, saving or investing in a business. This self-denial was tied to an idea that we now call *delayed gratification*, postponing the satisfaction of one's present wants and desires in exchange for a future reward. The reward they sought was in the afterlife. Because Calvinists believed in predestination, they did not expect to *earn* salvation through this way of life, but they believed that they could demonstrate to themselves and others that they were among the elect.

4. *Individualism* meant that each individual faced his or her destiny alone before God. Previous Christian theology had emphasized group salvation, the idea that an entire community would be saved or damned together. The stark individualism of Calvinistic theology stressed that each individual was on his or her own before God. Likewise, in the emerging capitalist economic system, individuals were on their own. The person who thrived was an individualist who planned wisely and charted his or her own course. Religious individualism and economic individualism reinforced one another (Weber [1904–1905] 1958).

The Protestant ethic that resulted from these elements stressed hard work, simple living, and rational decision making by individualists. Businesspeople and laborers spent long hours working at their calling, and reinvested profits into new equipment or expansion of the company. The rise of individualism allowed people to focus on their own efforts to accumulate and reinvest wealth—and not feel guilty for doing so. The growth of the Calvinist Protestant church led to major changes in cultural values, which, in turn, helped transform the economy into a capitalistic system (Weber [1904–1905] 1958).

Gradually, the capitalistic system, stimulated by the Protestant ethic, spread to other countries and to other religious groups. Many of the attitudes about work and delayed gratification no longer have a supernatural focus, but they are part of the larger cultural value system nonetheless. They influence our feelings about people who are not industrious and our ideas about why some people are poor. In fact, some religious groups see individuals as responsible for their own fate, believing that the poor and jobless should solve their own problems rather than depend on government aid (Davidson 2008). This view was expressed by Mitt Romney in the 2012 presidential election, and a large number of Americans share it (Brooks 2012; Rubin 2012).

Weber recognized that other factors also had to be present for capitalism to develop, but he believed that the particular set of moral values and attitudes that Calvinism instilled in the people was critical. Whereas Marx argued that religion encouraged workers to stay in their places and allowed the capitalists to exploit the system and maintain their elite positions, Weber focused on the change brought about in the economic system as a result of religious beliefs and values.

Religion interacts with the economy in other ways as well. First, religion is a major part of the economy. In the United States, more than 322,485 religious congregations received donations in June 2013. Of the total estimated charitable contributions ($316.23 billion) in the United States in 2012, 32% went to religious organizations (School of Philanthropy 2013). In most countries, religions (a) employ clergy and other people who serve the church, (b) own land and property, and (c) generate millions through collections and fundraising. Some of this money goes to salaries and the upkeep of buildings, some to charitable and advocacy activities, and some to investments. In the United States, televangelism and megachurches (congregations with upwards of 10,000 members) are multi-million-dollar industries with sophisticated marketing strategies. The televangelism industry, for example, involves the sale of books, CDs, and DVDs and donations of hundreds of millions of dollars by listeners. These megachurches become corporations and use information from the corporate world (e.g., how to structure their organization and market their product) to increase their chances of success. Indeed, many televangelists and megachurches preach a version of the "gospel of prosperity"—that God wants people to be prosperous and even wealthy. They argue that worshipping God in their style and giving to their church will contribute to wealth. This embracing of the search for wealth fits with the interests of capitalists and capitalism.

Religion interacts with and impacts the other major social institutions in society, but the interaction between religion and society is a two-way street. While religions can influence other social institutions, religions also find themselves influenced by the society in which they exist.

RELIGION IN SOCIETY: MACRO-LEVEL ANALYSIS

As an integral part of society, religion meets the needs of individuals and of the social structure. In this section, we explore some functions of religion in society, the role of religion in supporting stratification systems, and various conflicts within societies and in the global system.

The Contribution of Religion to Society: A Functionalist Perspective

Regardless of their personal belief or disbelief in the supernatural, sociologists of religion acknowledge that religion has important social consequences. Functionalists contend that religion has some positive consequences—helping people answer questions about the meaning of life and providing part of the glue that helps hold a society together. Let us

Megachurches, such as this one in Illinois, which sometimes draw 20,000 to 30,000 worshippers on a weekend, offer high-entertainment worship and a range of other services. These churches are run—and marketed—like a business.

look at some of the social functions of religion, keeping in mind that the way religion affects society varies depending on the structure of the society and the time period.

Social Cohesion. Religion helps individuals feel a sense of belonging and unity with others, a common sense of purpose with those who share the same beliefs. It serves to hold social units together and gives the members a sense of camaraderie. You will recall that Durkheim's widely cited study of suicide stresses the importance of belonging to a group, such as a congregation (Durkheim [1897] 1964). Research shows that communities with religious homogeneity and a high rate of congregational membership have lower rates of suicide (Ellison, Burr, and McCall 1997; Lotfi, Ayar, and Shams 2012). In societies with competing religions, or religions inconsistent with other values of society, however, religions may reduce cohesion and even be a source of conflict and hatred (Bainbridge and Stark 1981). As mentioned earlier, societies with competing religions often develop a civil religion—a theology of the nation—that serves to bless the nation and to enhance conformity and loyalty.

Legitimating Social Values and Norms. Functionalists note that religion often sacralizes social norms—grounds them in a supernatural reality or a divine command that makes them larger than life. Whether those norms have to do with care for the vulnerable, the demand to work for peace and justice, the immorality of extramarital sex, the sacredness of a monogamous heterosexual marriage, or proper roles for men and women, the foundations of morality from scripture create feelings of absoluteness. This lends stability to society: Agreement on social control of deviant behavior is easier, and society needs to rely less on coercion and force to get citizens to follow social norms. Of course, the absoluteness of the norms also makes it more difficult to change them as the society evolves. This inflexibility is precisely what pleases religious conservatives and distresses theological liberals, with the latter often seeking new ways to interpret the norms.

Social Change. Depending on the time and place, religion can work for or against social change. Some religions fight to maintain the status quo or return to norms from an earlier era. This is true of many literalist and absolutist religious groups—whether they are branches of Christian, Jewish, Hindu, or Islamic faiths—that seek to simplify life in the increasingly complex industrial world. Other religious traditions support or encourage change. For example, Japan made tremendous strides in industrialization in a short time following World War II, in part because the Shinto, Confucian, and Buddhist religions provided no obstacles and, in fact, supported the changes needed to move their economy forward. In the United States, African American religious leaders led the civil rights movement in the 1950s and 1960s, utilizing the established networks and communication channels created by African American religious organizations (Farley 2011; Lincoln and Mamiya 1990; McAdam 1999, 2003).

Thinking Sociologically

Which religious groups in your community have a stabilizing influence, and which ones have a disruptive influence? Which faith communities make the existing system seem sacred and beyond question? Which push for more social equality and less ethnocentrism toward others? Are there mosques, temples, or churches that oppose the government's policies, or do they foster unquestioning loyalty?

The Link Between Religion and Stratification: A Conflict Perspective

At times, religions reinforce socially defined differences between people, giving sacred legitimacy to racial prejudice, gender bias, and other inequalities. Conflict theory considers the ways in which religion relates to stratification and the status of minority groups. Our religious ideas and values and the way we worship are shaped not only by the society into which we are born but also by our family's position in the stratification system. Religion serves different primary purposes for individuals, depending on their positions in the society. People of various social statuses differ in the type and degree of their involvement in religious groups.

The Class Base of Religion. Conflict theorist Karl Marx states clearly his view of the relationship between religion and class—religion perpetuates the prevailing power structure (Marx [1844] 1963). For the proletariat or working class, religion is a sedative, he asserts, a narcotic that dulls people's sensitivity to and understanding of their desperate situation. He labels religion the "opiate of the people." Faith provides workers an escape from reality—from the tedium and suffering in everyday life. At the same time, it helps those in power discourage workers from rebelling, as it promises life in the hereafter if they work hard and contentedly. Some religions justify the positions of those who are better off by saying they have earned it.

Because the needs and interests of socioeconomic groups differ, most societies have class-based religions. With some exceptions (e.g., Catholics and Muslims) in the United States, religious affiliation tends to correlate with social class measures such as education, occupation, and income (Pyle 2006; Smith and Faris 2005). Table 11.3 indicates the specific links between denominational affiliation and socioeconomic measures in the United States today. Some religious traditions tend to attract lower- and working-class worshippers because they focus on the problems and life situations faced by people in the lower social classes. People with higher social status attend worship more regularly and know more about the historical and social context of scriptures than do people with less education and income, but people with lower socioeconomic status are more likely to pray and read scripture daily (Roberts and Yamane 2012).

Max Weber referred to this pattern of people belonging to religious groups that espouse values and characteristics compatible with their social status as *elective affinity* (Weber 1946). For example, people in laboring jobs usually find obeying the rules of the workplace and adhering to the instructions of the employer or supervisor essential for success on the job (Bowles and Gintis 1976; MacLeod 2008). Likewise, the faith communities of the poor and the working class tend to stress obedience, submission to "superiors," and the absoluteness of religious standards. The values of the workplace are reenacted and legitimated in churches to help socialize children to adapt to noncreative laboring jobs.

Many people in affluent congregations are paid to be problem solvers and break the mold of conventional thinking. They will not do well professionally if they merely obey rules. Instead, they must help create rules while trying to solve organizational or management problems (Bowles and Gintis 1976). It is not surprising, then, that the denominations of the affluent (Unitarian Universalist, Jewish, Episcopalian, Presbyterian, and United Church of Christ) are more likely to value tolerance of other perspectives, religions, or values and

to view factors that limit individual opportunity (e.g., institutional racism and sexism) as evil. They tend to embrace tolerance of differences and condemn rigidity, absolutism, and conventionalism. Their religious communities are likely to encourage each member to work out his or her own theology, within limits, and value divergent thinking and a streak of independence (Roberts and Yamane 2012; Roof 1999).

Whatever the particular belief, one's religion and one's social status are correlated to everything from life expectancy, the likelihood of divorce, and mental health to attitudes regarding sexual behavior, abortion, and fetal stem cell research.

Thinking Sociologically

How do the social class and religious affiliation of people you know relate to this discussion? How do denominations in your community whose members have higher-than-average levels of education (Unitarians, Jews, Episcopalians, Presbyterians, and members of the United Church of Christ) differ from those with less educated members?

Racial Bias, Gender Prejudice, and Religion.

Most religious groups profess to welcome all comers. Many, however, have practiced discrimination against some group at some time, often related to political and economic factors in the society. It is important to recognize that religion has multiple and even contradictory effects on societies. For example, most Christian denominations have formal statements that reject racial prejudice as un-Christian. The meaning system teaches tolerance. However, informal group norms in a local congregation—the belonging system—may be tolerant of ethnic jokes and may foster distrust of certain races. Among whites in the United States, for instance, active church members have historically displayed more prejudice than inactive church members or the unchurched (Chalfant and Peck 1983; Roberts and Yamane 2012).

The structural system of religion can also play a role in supporting prejudice and discrimination. Promotions to larger churches are usually awarded to well-liked ministers, who have growing, harmonious congregations and financially sound organizations. Such ministers are sometimes reluctant to speak out forcefully on issues such as racial or gender equality, for fear of offending their parishioners. Bishops may not promote a minister or priest to a larger church if

TABLE 11.3   Socioeconomic Profiles of American Religious Groups

Religious Group	Education Level (in Percentages)		Annual Household Income (in Dollars)
	% With at Least a College Degree	No High School Degree	% Over 100,000
Hindu	74	4	43
Jewish	59	3	46
Episcopal Church in USA	57	1	35
Unitarian	51	3	26
Buddhist	48	3	22
Presbyterian USA	47	7	28
Orthodox	46	6	28
United Church of Christ	42	4	18
Atheist	42	8	28
United Methodist	35	8	22
Disciples of Christ	35	10	20
Evangelical Lutheran in America	30	6	17
Nondenominational	29	6	18
Latter-Day Saint (Mormon)	28	8	15
Catholic	26	17	19
Muslim	24	21	16
Southern Baptist	21	15	15
Seventh-Day Adventist	21	24	11
Religious but Unaffiliated	17	21	12
American Baptist	14	23	8
Assemblies of God	12	24	8
Other Pentecostal	11	26	7
Jehovah's Witness	9	19	9
Black Baptist	8	19	8

Source: Pew Forum on Religion and Public Life 2008:78–80, 84–86. Published by the Pew Forum on Religion and Public Life, www.pewforum.org.

his or her current congregation is racked with dissention and donations have declined. Even though the denomination's meaning system may oppose prejudice, the structural system may reward clergy who do not defend that meaning system and who allow bigotry to remain unchecked (Campbell and Pettigrew 1959; Roberts and Yamane 2012).

Women have often been the most active members of Christian congregations and appear to be more spiritual than men, as discussed in the next "Engaging Sociology" on page 310. In some denominations, they hold leadership positions (Chaves 2004). Many Christian and Jewish denominations, for example, have female ministers and rabbis (Chaves 2004;

Religious Tolerance 2012). Several Christian denominations allow women to become bishops.

More conservative denominations and conservative members within more moderate denominations oppose moves to grant women leadership positions. The Anglican Church of England suffers from an internal division among progressives who support and social conservatives who oppose ordaining women to be bishops, with both groups vociferously arguing for their side (Jourdan 2013). Similar divisions exist within the Catholic Church, but because of the organizational structure of the Church, there is less open debate. In 2012, 59% of Catholics in the United States supported the ordination of women priests (Levitt

ENGAGING SOCIOLOGY

Women and Spirituality

Figure 11.4 indicates that there is a spirituality gap.

FIGURE 11.4 The Spirituality Gap

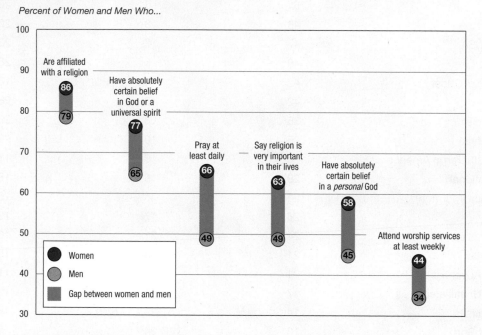

Percent of Women and Men Who...

Source: Pew Research Center, "The U.S. Religious Landscape Survey," February 2008. http://religions.pewforum.org/. Reprinted with permission.

*　*　*　*　*　*　*

Engaging With Sociology

1. Are you convinced by this evidence that women are more spiritual than men? Why or why not?

2. If so, why do you think this is the case? If not, why do the data seem to suggest less involvement of men?

3. Is the message of religious communities and faith traditions (altruism, self-sacrifice, trusting others) less in tune with the everyday experiences of men than of women?

2012). However, the Pope and Bishops of the Roman Catholic Church have taken a strong position in opposition, threatening excommunication and categorizing any attempt by a woman to be ordained as a grave crime against the church—in the same category as crimes committed by priests who sexually abuse children (Donadio 2010).

While most mainline Christian denominations now have official statements on the equality of women and formal policies against discrimination in ordaining or hiring women pastors, the official meaning system does not tell the whole story. Again, religious structures play a role. Local congregational search committees who screen and hire new ministers usually care deeply about the survival and health of the local church. Studies show that often members of these committees are themselves not personally opposed to women in the pulpit, but they believe that others in their church would be offended if they hired a woman and would stop coming and giving money to the church. Thus, the local belonging and structural systems of the religion may perpetuate unequal treatment of clergywomen, even if the meaning system says they are equal (Chaves 2004; Lehman 1985).

As noted above, some religions may reinforce and legitimize social prejudices, while others may be powerful forces for change and for greater equality in a society. Religion elicits strong emotions and influences people's definition of reality. Religion has promoted social strife, but it has also been the motivation for altruism and service to others, and a major contributor to social solidarity.

Thinking Sociologically

From what you know about the status of racial and ethnic minority groups, LGBTQ people, and women in your society, how are the problems they face in religion and other institutions (education, politics, economics, health care) similar?

RELIGION IN THE MODERN WORLD

Name almost any religion, and a group representing that belief system can probably be found in the United Kingdom, the United States, Canada, Kenya, and several other countries where religious diversity is the norm. In the United States, religious pluralism has been a founding principle since Roger Williams founded the state of Rhode Island in 1636 and advocated religious toleration and separation of church and state. This makes for a complex religious pattern. In this section we look at the vitality of major religions in North America, with empirical data that track religious trends over time (Pew Forum on Religion and Public Life 2012b; Stark 2000).

In order to make sense of religious trends, we must first define the variables we want to measure. For example, if we want to know whether being highly religious is correlated with other social factors or with specific behaviors, how do we measure religiosity? This question is discussed in "Engaging Sociology" on page 312.

Is Religion Dying or Reviving in North America?

Depending on the survey, 16% to 20% of Americans report no religious affiliation, with higher numbers of younger than older people reporting a lack of affiliation (Grossman 2012; Pew Forum on Religion and Public Life 2012a). On the other hand, 65% of people in the United States say that religion is "very important" to them and the percentage is especially high—80%—for Muslim Americans (Gallup 2009). Indeed, even among those not affiliated with a religious community, roughly half say that spirituality is important to their lives—calling themselves spiritual but not religious (Pew Forum on Religion and Public Life 2012a). Spirituality is a more individual experience of feeling there is something sacred in life beyond the realm of the everyday empirical world, while religion is a communal or social expression of that outlook. In any case, it is safe to say that religion and spirituality still have a significant influence in U.S. society.

Religion has somewhat less influence in Canadian life. Well over half of Canadians regularly engage in some form of religious activity over the course of a year, and a third claim to attend worship services monthly. Close to half (44%) say religion is very important in their lives (Clark and Schellenberg 2008). While the Canadian indicators have dropped a bit over the last several years, the indicators of religious commitment in both the United States and Canada are higher than those in most other religiously pluralistic nations.

Religious affiliation in the United States today is also high in comparison to earlier periods in U.S. history. In the days of colonial America, only about 17% of the population belonged to a church. Religious membership rose fairly steadily from the 1770s until the 1960s. Although there has been a modest decline since the 1970s, self-reports of membership in a faith community have fluctuated between 64% and 70% for the past two decades (Newport 2010). Another measure of religious strength is belief in God. Gallup poll results for the past three decades indicate that 92% of the U.S. population believes in God or a universal spirit or higher power (Newport 2012b). Tables 11.4 and 11.5 show the results from Gallup polls regarding indicators of the importance of religion in people's lives.

Attendance at worship in a church, temple, or mosque is also an indicator of religious involvement. While attendance rates vary by faith community,

ENGAGING SOCIOLOGY

Determining What It Means to Be "Religious"

- Study the list of items in Table 11.4. Do measures such as belief in God, church membership, and frequency of attendance seem like good measures of one's religiosity? Why might the answer to this question indicate something other than the depth of one's religious faith?

- Attendance at Sabbath worship varies greatly, with Mormons and members of the conservative Church of Christ reporting weekly attendance at about 67% to 68%; Muslims at 56%; mainline Methodists, Presbyterians, Lutherans, and Roman Catholics at 43% to 45%; and Jews at 15%. Given the fact that attendance varies so much by religious group, does this mean that members of some groups are less religious, or does it mean attendance is not a very good measure of religiosity for some groups?

- Is asking whether religion is very important in one's life, whether one believes religion answers problems in life, or how much confidence one has in religious organizations a good indicator of a person's religiosity? (See Table 11.5 for indications of how stable "importance in life" has been over time.) What might be some misleading dimensions of using one or more of these measures to indicate "religiosity"?

- Some scholars have argued that how religious beliefs affect one's behavior is a good indicator of religiosity. So in studying Islam, Judaism, or some forms of Christianity, one measure of religiosity has been how much one gives to charitable causes—both to one's faith community and to people living in poverty. Is this measure an accurate way to understand levels of religious influence in the society? Why or why not?

- Imagine you have been asked to conduct a study to determine the religiosity of various demographic groups in the United States. How would you define religiosity?

TABLE 11.4   Leading Religious Indicators (in Percentages)

Belief in God	92[a]
Member of a church, temple, or mosque	63[b]
Say they attend worship services regularly	43[c]
Religion *very important* in life	55[a]
Pray daily	58[d]
High confidence in organized religion	44[e]

Sources:

a. Newport 2012b.

b. Newport 2009.

c. Newport 2010.

d. Pew Forum on Religion and Public Life 2009.

e. Saad 2012.

TABLE 11.5   How Important Is Religion in Your Life (in Percentages)?

	Very[a]	Fairly	Not Very
2012	58	23	19
2000	59	29	12
1992	58	29	12

Source: Adapted from Gallup 2013.

a. These figures vary by religious affiliation. Note, for example, that Muslims rated among the highest—at 80% *very important*—in a 2009 Gallup survey.

Gallup polls indicate self-reports of attendance has been fairly steady in the United States for more than 70 years at 37% to 49% of the population, hovering close to 40% in 2013 (Newport 2013). (See Figure 11.5.) Figure 11.6, however, shows that there are significant geographical variations in rates of affiliation with a religious group.

Religion in the United States has adjusted to changes in society and taken on new forms. For example, the number of Protestants in the United States

FIGURE 11.5   Weekly Attendance at Church, Synagogue, or Mosque in the United States: Annual Averages

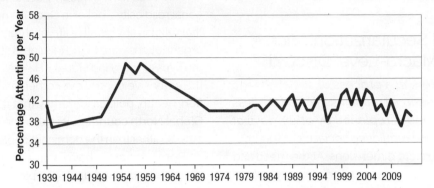

Source: Newport, Frank. 2013. "In U.S., Four in 10 Report Attending Church in Last Week." December 24. Reprinted with permission from Gallup.

FIGURE 11.6   Percentage of U.S. Population Affiliated With a Church, Mosque, or Temple

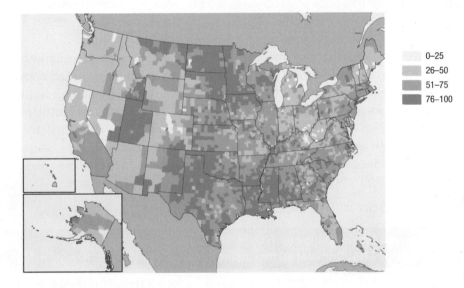

0–25
26–50
51–75
76–100

Source: Religious Congregations and Membership Study 2010.

Note: This map is based on data reported by local congregations and includes both members and other regular attendees; it does not represent weekly attendance. The numbers indicate overreporting (people report attendance at higher rates than they actually attend), but that does not change the overall geographical pattern of religious affiliation.

has declined from two thirds of the population to less than half (48%) in the past 30 years, as the country has become more religiously diverse. This decline stems in part from decreasing numbers of white Protestant families (due to the changing ethnic composition of the country) and an increase in the number who no longer affiliate with any faith community (Pew Forum on Religion and Public Life 2012a, 2012b). The latter half of the 20th century also saw a wide range of religious groups forming and growing in North America,

from the occult and astrology to New Age spirituality and Zen Buddhism, which seemed to represent a resurgence of religious commitment.

Demographic changes in the makeup of the United States and Canada have influenced the religious landscape. Although two out of every three native-born U.S. citizens are Protestant, two out of every three Christian immigrants are Catholic. This influx of Catholic immigrants has helped the Catholic Church maintain the membership of a steady percentage of

U.S. citizens. Some other religious faiths are represented among those new U.S. residents as well (Pew Forum on Religion and Public Life 2012b).

Religion and Secularization: Micro-, Meso-, and Macro-Level Discord

Secularization refers to *a process of social change through which traditional religious thinking has less public influence and is replaced by other ways of explaining reality and regulating social life.* It has both meso/macro and micro dimensions. At the meso and macro levels, religion becomes one of many institutions in the society—no longer having authority in governing, health, and other realms. Secularization at the micro level involves a movement away from supernatural and sacred interpretations of the world and toward decisions based on empirical evidence and logic. Before the advent of modern science and technology, religion helped explain our social and physical world. However, the scientific method, its emphasis on logical reasoning, and the fact that there are many different religions rather than one have challenged religious and spiritual approaches to the world. As part of micro-level secularism, we might expect to see most individuals working out their own faith systems rather than adhering to the faith affirmations of their denomination or religious leaders. If secularization

were uniform, it might look like the pattern indicated in Table 11.6.

However, we have seen that most indicators of traditional religiosity—belief in God, attendance, affirmation that religion affects all of life, and confidence in religious organizations—are high. Religion is still a strong force in the lives of many individuals. However, it does not have the extensive control over other institutions of education, health, politics, or family that it once did. In most Global North countries, it is just one institution among others, rather than the dominant one.

Some scholars have argued that secularization is an inevitable and unstoppable force in the modern postindustrial world (Dobbelaere 2000; Gorski and Altinordu 2008). Others argue that secularization is far from inevitable and that it has almost reached its limit (Gardom 2011; Stark 2000). Our social world model helps us understand that, like religion, secularization is a complex phenomenon that occurs at several levels and affects each society differently (Yamane 1997; Chaves and Gorski 2001).

Secularization may be occurring at the societal level, but the evidence noted above suggests that this is not so pervasive at the individual level in North America (Chaves and Gorski 2001). When religious faith guides people's everyday lives—their conduct on the job, their political choices, their sexual behavior, or their attitudes toward race relations—then secularization at

TABLE 11.6 Secularization in the Social World

	Institutional Differentiation (Separation of Religion So It Does Not Dominate Other Institutions)	Decision Making
Macro Level	In the larger society, government, education, and the economic institutions are independent and autonomous from religious organizations.	Decision making about social policies uses logic, empirical data, and cost/benefit analysis rather than scripture, theological arguments, or proclamations of religious authorities.
Meso Level	**Organizations** look to other social associations for accepted practices of how to operate, not to religious organizations and authorities.	Decision making about an organization's policies is based on analyses of possible consequences, rather than on scripture, theological arguments, or proclamations of religious authorities.
Micro Level	**Individuals** emphasize being "spiritual rather than religious," formulate their own meaning system or theology, and may believe that spirituality has little to do with other aspects of their lives.	Decision making among individuals is based on individual self-interest without concern for the teachings of the religious group or the clergy.

Source: From *Religion in Sociological Perspective*, 4th edition by Keith A. Roberts and David Yamane. Copyright © 2004 Wadsworth, a part of Cengage Learning, Inc.

Despite the process of secularization in some parts of the world, the sense of awe before the holy remains strong for many people. This enormous Buddha at the Yungang Buddhist Caves at Wuzhou Mountain in China has been a source of veneration for generations.

the micro level is weak and religious influence is strong. Faith still matters to many people.

Secularization is more obvious at the meso and macro levels. For example, religiously affiliated organizations (e.g., Catholic nursing homes, Presbyterian colleges, Jewish social service foundations) make most, though not all, of their decisions about how to deliver services or whom to hire or fire based on systematic policies designed for organizational efficiency, not religious dogma. Likewise, policies in the society at large are usually made with little discussion of the theological implications. In morally ambiguous cases, policy makers defend positions with human rights arguments, rather than ideas on what is sinful—again suggesting that society has become secular at the macro level (Chaves 1993; Roberts and Yamane 2012; Yamane 1997). On the other hand, debates about prayer in schools, abortion, same-sex marriage, and economic inequality; the involvement of religious leaders in political issues; and the influence of religion

in presidential politics indicate a continuing impact of religion on the meso and macro levels in U.S. society. *Secularization* even at the macro level is not complete.

In short, most sociologists of religion believe that religion continues to be a particularly powerful force at the individual level while secularization is more pervasive at the societal levels (Roberts and Yamane 2012; Sommerville 2002). At the global level, no particular theological authority has the power to define reality or determine policies, and secularization is well established. Perhaps this is one reason why conservatives of nearly every religious faith are leery of global processes and global organizations, such as the United Nations. Our global political organizations are governed by rational-legal (secular) authority, not religious doctrines.

● Thinking Sociologically

What might be the results if a society is secularized at the meso and macro levels but much less so at the micro level? Is this a problem? Does it create problems for decision making and social coherence? Is separation of church and state, with government policies based on secular calculations of the interests of the nation, a good idea or a bad idea? Why or why not?

Religion: Fostering War or Peace?

Can religion bring peace to the world? Most religious systems advocate living in harmony with other

Although religious faith is very strong at the micro level in the United States, public policy and the operation of organizations and government are secularized—based on principles of pluralism and rational deliberation. A town council prays as it opens its monthly meeting following a Supreme Court ruling approving city council prayers if there is a long tradition of having prayer. Was that a wise decision? For a photo essay and further exploration about controversies over secularization and social policy, visit edge.sagepub.com/ballantinecondensed4e.

humans and with nature, yet peace has not been the reality. Although Christianity, Judaism, and Islam embrace a world of peace and justice, Christian denominations often foster nationalistic loyalty—with displays of the flag and even pledges of allegiance to the flag during worship. This endorsement of national pride can foster "us" versus "them" thinking and undermine peace.

Congregations that take peace activities seriously may decline in membership and financial stability if seen as "anti-American," whereas those that foster in-group or nationalistic sentiments can attract large numbers. So, as noted earlier, the structural system may actually undermine the message of the meaning system because growth and financial vitality are major concerns for many local church leaders. Despite the rhetoric, fiscal concerns that require keeping the members happy can actually trump claims to worship the "Prince of Peace." The linking of nationalistic loyalty to religion can also lead to the conflation of nation and God and, in some cases, the perception that leaders are divinely chosen.

Liberal theologies suggest that God may speak to people through a variety of channels, including the revelations of other religious traditions. While religious leaders may feel that their theology provides the fullest and most complete expression of God's Truth, some hold that other faiths also provide paths to salvation. This pluralism has resulted in more tolerance,

FIGURE 11.7 Lines of Differentiation Between "Us" and "Them"

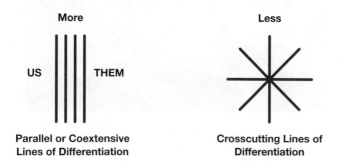

Likelihood of Hostilities

More | Less
US | THEM

Parallel or Coextensive Lines of Differentiation

Crosscutting Lines of Differentiation

Note: Imagine that each line represents a division in society between groups based on religion, ethnicity, political party, economic status, language spoken, skin color, or other factors. Parallel lines of differentiation divide people in each conflict along the same lines. *Crosscutting lines* cut the differences, so that people who were part of "them" in a previous antagonism become part of "us" in the present discord. This lessens the likelihood of deep and permanent hostilities within a social unit.

but it may also be an indication of secularization of theology itself.

Members of fundamentalist or absolutist groups—whether they are Jewish, Muslim, or Christian—generally believe in a literal interpretation of their holy books. They usually believe that they have the only Truth, which they must defend and spread. This generates ethnocentrism and sometimes hatred, causing people to fight and die to defend their belief systems and way of life (Marty and Appleby 1991, 2004). They seldom believe in pluralism or tolerance of other beliefs. Consequently, they resist and defend themselves against threats to their beliefs and way of life (Ebaugh 2005; Stern 2003; Wessinger 2000).

Conflict between religious groups is especially intense if there are also ethnic, economic, and religious differences between the groups. On the other hand, crosscutting social categories reduces social hostilities, as Figure 11.7 illustrates. When you are in a group that includes adherents of different religions, different ethnicities, and different socioeconomic classes, it becomes much less likely that you will vilify people from those other groups. They no longer—as a category—can be seen as uniformly evil or as the enemy. This is what is meant by crosscutting divisions.

Religion has the greatest potential for reducing hatred between groups when the groups share some type of common identification. If the conflict is over ethnicity and economics, a common religious heritage can lessen the likelihood of violent confrontation. Likewise, some religious groups (including Christian, Jewish, and Muslim) have joined together in peaceful enterprises such as attempts to ban nuclear weapons or to address global poverty or climate change. These common purposes provide for cooperation and collaboration, thus lessening animosity and "us" versus "them" thinking.

Many countries today make clear separations between religion and the state because of their histories of religious hostilities. The conflicts in Europe between Protestant and Catholic religious groups were very brutal. Intense religious in-group loyalties led to a willingness to kill those following other religions or other denominations of the same faith. The horrific religious conflicts in European societies—known as the Hundred Years' War—did not reach closure until the beginning of the Enlightenment period in the mid-1600s. Acceptance of other religious traditions and separation of religion from the state were needed to restore civility (Dobbelaere 1981, 2000; Lambert 2000).

The global rise of *religious nativism*—absolutist religious groups that insist only their own view of life and the divine is Truth—appears to be a local reaction against global modernization (Fernandez 2011; Salzman 2008). Rapid global change has resulted in *anomie* as people confront

- threats to traditional cultures and religious perspectives,
- the increasing secularization of society,

- the threat to the material self-interests of religious organizations, and
- increased interdependence among nations.

All these threats have strengthened religious nativism (Fernandez 2011).

Thinking Sociologically

What specific religious beliefs or behaviors might influence the way in which religions and countries relate to one another? How might religious organizations influence international relations? For example, how might anti-Muslim prejudice by Christians influence U.S. relations with predominantly Islamic countries?

> Religion deals with issues of meaning and, like education, serves as a core socialization agent in the society. It provides socialization of members of society on important values, which sometimes makes cooperation more possible within a society. However, conflict cannot always be overcome by appeals to values, and sometimes the issues between individuals and groups come down to matters of power and access to resources. In the next chapter, we examine the influence of power and privilege in society and in our own lives. We turn now to the institutions of politics and economics.

WHAT HAVE WE LEARNED?

Religion is a powerful force in the lives of people around the world. It typically elicits passions and deep loyalties, and in so doing, it can stimulate great acts of self-sacrificing charity or horrible atrocities and intergroup bigotries. People's religious affiliation strongly relates to their nationality, ethnic and racial group, and lifestyle. Religion is the one institution in most societies that consistently professes a desire for peace and goodwill, yet there may be inconsistencies between what people say and what they do. Religion can provide us with the hope that the world's problems may be dealt with in humanitarian ways.

Religion can provide a sense of purpose to our lives, and religious symbols come to have sacred meaning. Systems of meaning, belonging, and structure are interdependent components of religion.

Humans in the modern world tend to be spiritual. They may also live in states with massive governmental bureaucracies that hold power, and they participate in economic systems that produce and distribute the goods and services needed for survival. The next institutions we will examine are politics and economics—how power relations are negotiated at each level in the social world.

KEY POINTS

- Religion makes our most important values sacred, operating through three interconnected systems: (1) a meaning system, (2) a belonging system, and (3) a structural system.

- We become committed through these three systems, by our attachment to a reference group that becomes a belonging system, by making investments in the organization (the structural system), and by holding as real the system of ideas (the meaning system).

- At the micro level, symbolic interaction theory illuminates how the meaning system works, with an interaction of myths, rituals, and symbols coming to define reality and making the values and the meaning system sacred. Rational choice theory focuses on the costs and benefits that influence the decisions individuals make about religious commitments. It also examines how religious organizations go about seeking a "market share" in the competition for members.

- Denominationalism organizes religious life when there are a plurality of religious groups and when religious authority is separated from governmental authority. New Religious Movements (NRMs) also arise in pluralistic social contexts.

- At the macro level of analysis, functionalists maintain that religions can serve as a kind of glue to help solidify the country and can meet the basic needs of the populace. In contrast, conflict theorists focus on the ways in which religion reinforces conflicts and inequalities in society, whether socioeconomic, racial, or gender.

- In the United States and Canada, secularization is dominant at the meso and macro levels but does not seem to be as strong at the micro level. This is a source of tension in societies.

- At the global level, religion can be involved in issues of war and peace (sometimes unwittingly undermining peace).

DISCUSSION QUESTIONS

1. What are some ways that religion and government are interdependent and interrelated in the United States?

2. If you are a person of faith and affiliated with a religious community, how did you become so? If you are not, explain why. How did your family members and peers influence your views toward religion?

3. What motivates you to work hard and try to succeed professionally? Think about how Weber perceived the relationship between the development of the capitalist economic system and thoughts about sacrifice and work. Does it relate to your answer to the first part of this question? Why or why not?

4. Do you think religion is more of a unifying or divisive force in (a) the United States and (b) the world today? Why? Do you have many friends from different religious groups? Why or why not?

5. What do you think might happen to society if religions did not exist? Why? How would an absence of religion impact you personally?

CONTRIBUTING TO OUR SOCIAL WORLD: What Can We Do?

At the Local Level

- *Campus religious foundations or ministries:* Most colleges and universities, including many of those not affiliated with a religion, have religious groups on campus. If you are not already a member and would like to join such an organization on your campus, contact a student representative or faculty sponsor, attend a meeting, and become involved. Most of these organizations participate in various types of outreach work, including volunteering for soup kitchens, food pantries, or thrift stores for the poor. If you attend a religiously affiliated college or university, you will find many and varied options.

At the Organizational or Institutional Level

- *College-based religious organizations.* Many religious campus organizations such as the Newman Foundation (Roman Catholic; http://newmanfnd.org), InterVarsity (Christian; www.intervarsity.org), Muslim Students

Association (MSA; http://msanational.org), and Hillel Foundation (Jewish; www.hillel.org) are branches of larger organizations. You can find out more about them and how to start or join a chapter by going to their websites.

- *American Atheists* (www.atheists.org) provides similar services to atheists. According to the group's website, "Now in its fourth decade, American Atheists is dedicated to working for the civil rights of Atheists, promoting separation of state and church, and providing information about Atheism." Volunteers assist in this work through contributions, research, and legal support.

At the National and Global Levels

Several religious groups are committed to working for justice and peace at the national and global levels.

- *Tikkun Community* (www.tikkun.org) is an interreligious organization, started by progressive members of the Jewish community, to "mend, repair, and transform the world." It is an "international community of people of many faiths calling for social justice and political freedom."

- *The American Friends Service Committee* (www.afsc .org), a Quaker organization, "includes people of various faiths who are committed to social justice, peace, and humanitarian service."

- *Catholic Relief Services* (www.crs.org) "carries out the commitment of the Catholic bishops of the United States to assist the poor and vulnerable" in over 100 countries.

- *Lutheran World Relief* (www.lwr.org) "extends the hand of Christian love to people overcoming poverty and injustice in 50 countries."

These and similar faith-based organizations sponsor many relief, peace, and justice projects around the world. You can find out more by going to their websites.

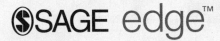

Sharpen your skills with SAGE edge at **edge.sagepub.com/ballantinecondensed4e**

SAGE edge for Students provides a personalized approach to help you accomplish your coursework goals in an easy-to-use learning environment.

12 Politics and Economics

Probing Power; Dissecting Distribution

Power probes every aspect of our lives with intimidating force, even as economic distribution cuts across the social fabric. Sociology helps us probe and dissect the sources and consequences of each.

MICRO

● ME (AND MY FAMILY)

● **LOCAL ORGANIZATIONS AND COMMUNITY**

Power struggles and finances influence how well a local fraternity or a women's civic club functions.

MESO

● **NATIONAL ORGANIZATIONS, INSTITUTIONS, AND ETHNIC SUBCULTURES**

State or provincial governments, political parties, and corporations within the state affect quality of life.

MACRO

● **SOCIETY**

National governments and court systems set rules that resolve conflicts and establish standards for conducting business.

● **GLOBAL COMMUNITY**

Cross-national organizations such as the United Nations and the World Court and global human rights movements like Amnesty International set standards for nations.

LEARNING OBJECTIVES

12.1 Describe the sociological definition of power.

12.2 Discuss the importance of power and privilege in societies.

12.3 Compare the key points of the pluralist and elite theories of power.

12.4 Explain why some people participate in political systems and others do not.

12.5 Describe the major types of governmental systems in operation today.

12.6 Provide examples of the threats political systems can face from internal and external groups vying for power.

THINK ABOUT IT

Micro: Local Community	How do people in your local community use power in constructive or destructive ways?
Meso: National Institutions; Complex Organizations; Ethnic Groups	How does the political institution interact with the economic institution? How are different ethnic groups affected by power and privilege?
Macro: National and Global Systems	How does economic instability threaten a national government? Why do struggles over power and privilege often evolve into war and terrorism?

Imagine that a nuclear disaster has occurred. The mortality rate is stunning. The survivors gather together for human support and collectively attempt to meet their basic survival needs. They come from varying backgrounds and have diverse skills. Before the disaster, some—the stockbroker and the business executive, for instance—earned more money and held higher social status than the others, but that is in the past. Faced with the new and unfamiliar situation, different skills are more immediately important for survival.

Where should this group begin? Think about the options. Some sort of organization seems essential, a structure that will help the group meet its needs. Food, shelter, and medical care are paramount. Those with experience in agriculture, building trades, and health care are likely to take leadership roles to provide these initial necessities. As time goes on, the need for clear norms and rules emerges. These survivors decide that all members must work—must contribute their share of effort to the collective survival. At first, these norms are unwritten, but gradually some norms and rules are declared more important than others and are recorded, with sanctions (penalties) attached for noncompliance. Survivors form committees to deal with group concerns, and a semblance of a judicial system emerges. One person is appointed to coordinate work shifts and others to oversee emerging aspects of this small society's life. This scenario could play out in many ways.

What is happening? A social structure is evolving. Not everyone in the group will agree with the structure, and some people will propose alternatives. Whose ideas will be adopted? Leadership roles may fall to the physically strongest, or perhaps the most persuasive, or those with the most skills and knowledge for survival. Those most competent at organizing may become the leaders, but that outcome is by no means assured.

In our world of power and privilege, a war, an invading power, or a revolutionary overthrow of an unstable government can change the form of a political system overnight, necessitating rapid reorganization. The daily news brings stories of governments overthrown by military leaders in coups, with new governments emerging to fill the gap, as has been happening in various parts of the Middle East and Africa. The opening scenario and the political activity in our modern society share a common element—power. The concept of power is critical to understanding many aspects of our social world.

In this chapter we focus primarily on the political and economic dimensions of society, since both political and economic systems enforce the distribution of power and resources in a society. Political systems involve the power relationships between individuals and larger social institutions. Economic systems produce and distribute goods and services. Not everyone gets an equal share, thus giving some citizens privileges that others do not have.

©Reuters/Jeff Haynes

U.S. Vice President Joe Biden (left) makes a point during the vice presidential debate in 2012. This debate helped determine what political party—Democrats or Republicans—would control the power of the executive branch of the U.S. government.

In this chapter, we will consider the nature of power, politics, and economics, but since economics and politics tend to be seen as mostly governing forces, we focus less on the micro level and more on the meso and macro levels of the social system. It is also true that economic systems have been explored in many chapters of this book, so we put more emphasis here on political systems and their relationship to economic systems.

Thinking Sociologically

Imagine that global climate change has caused massive flooding on your island nation (a reality for some people living on Pacific islands). Only a few people have survived. How would you construct a new social system? What are the issues you would need to resolve to build a new society?

WHAT IS POWER?

Power is an age-old theme in many great scholarly discussions. Social philosophers since Plato, Aristotle, and Socrates have addressed the issue of political systems and power. Machiavelli, an early 16th-century Italian political philosopher, is perhaps best known for his observation that "the ends justify the means." His understanding of how power was exercised in the 15th, 16th, and 17th centuries significantly influenced how monarchs used the powers of the state (the means) to obtain wealth, new territories, and trade dominance (the ends) (Machiavelli [1532] 2010).

The most common definition of power used in social sciences today comes from Max Weber, who saw **power** as *the ability of a person or group to realize its own will in group action, even against resistance of others who disagree* (Weber 1947). Building on Weber's idea of power, we can identify various power arenas. Two key arenas of power are the nation-state and the economic system. The leaders of a national government attempt to control the behavior of individuals through (a) *physical force and the threat of violence* (through a police force); (b) *symbolic control*, such as the manipulation of people (control of the media); and (c) *rules of conduct* that channel behavior toward desired patterns (laws). For example, the dictator and military in Syria have used torture, rape, and death to intimidate dissidents and their families, and the media to present the opposition as terrorists. The opposition has also used force and social media, but does not have the same degree of power.

Control of the economy is another important source of power. Conflict theorists argue that those with power over the economy can control government officials (who are dependent on campaign contributions from the wealthy) and can convince the public that what is good for the wealthy is good for everyone. The members of the middle and working classes become convinced via the media that further tax breaks and advantages to the wealthy are—in the long run—in their own self-interest. In the United States, the media is largely controlled by wealthy owners of large corporations. Six companies (Comcast, News Corp., Disney, Viacom, Time Warner, and CBS), each operated by wealthy owners, control 90% of television, radio, and newspaper outlets (Lutz 2012).

Thinking Sociologically

Weber's definition of power involves control over group action from the micro to macro levels. At what level do you have the most power? Why? Be sure to give examples.

POWER AND PRIVILEGE IN OUR SOCIAL WORLD

Power can be found at even micro levels of interaction, from individuals to family groups. In family life, relations often involve negotiation and sometimes conflict over how to run a household and spend money. Interactions between parents and children also involve power issues, as parents socialize their children. Indeed, the controversy over whether spanking is an effective discipline or an abusive imposition of pain is a question of how parents use their power to teach their children and control their behavior.

At the meso level, power operates in cities, counties, and states/provinces. Governments make decisions about which corporations receive tax breaks to locate their plants within the region. They pass laws that regulate everything from how long one's grass can grow before a fine is imposed, to how public schools will be funded. Therefore, people have an interest in influencing governments by contributing to political campaigns and helping elect the people who support their views. Interest groups such as environmental advocacy, flat tax, and gay rights organizations also wield power and try to influence the political process at the meso level.

Individual campaign workers in local communities try to influence voters at the micro level to determine who will wield power in meso and macro systems.

Power processes pervade the micro, meso, and macro levels. Locally organized groups can force change that influences politics at the local, state/provincial, national, or global level. Provincial or state laws shape what can and cannot be done at the local level. These laws may either limit or enhance the ability of citizens to protest or express their views, by determining where and when protests can occur.

Laws at the national and global levels influence state, provincial, and county politics and policies. Global treaties, for example, affect national autonomy. Reluctance to yield national autonomy is the main reason the United States and a few other countries have refused to ratify seemingly very benign global treaties, such as the Convention on the Rights of the Child (UNICEF 2005).

Power can also be understood in terms of the allocation of economic resources in a society and what factors influence patterns of resource distribution. Both economic and political systems are important in the sociologist's consideration of power distribution in any society. Let us first consider the theoretical lenses that help us understand power and politics.

THEORETICAL PERSPECTIVES ON POWER AND PRIVILEGE

Do you and I have any real decision-making power? Can our voices or votes make a difference, or do leaders hold all the power? Many sociologists and political scientists have studied these questions and found several answers to who holds power and the relationship between the rulers and the ruled.

Micro- and Meso-Level Perspectives: Legitimacy of Power

Symbolic interactionists look at how loyalty to the power of the state is created—a loyalty so strong that citizens are willing to die for the state in a war. In the early years of the United States, citizens' loyalty tended to be mostly to individual states. Even as late as the Civil War, Northern battalions fought under the flag of their own state rather than that of the United States.

Most people in the United States now tend to think of themselves as U.S. citizens more than Virginians, Pennsylvanians, or Oregonians, and they are willing to defend the whole country. National symbols such as anthems and flags help create loyalty to nations. The treatment of flags illustrates the social construction

This man no doubt feels he is expressing his patriotism, yet technically he is violating the U.S. Flag Code and "desecrating" the American flag. During the Vietnam War, protesters risked being attacked for dressing this way and "disrespecting" the flag and the country.

 Power and Resistance—Perception of Power

ENGAGING SOCIOLOGY

The Flag, Symbolism, and Patriotism

Flags have become pervasive symbols of nations, helping to create a national identity (Billig 1995). National loyalty becomes sacred, and that sacredness is imbedded in the flag as a symbol of patriotism (Durkheim 1947).

Care of the U.S. flag is an interesting example of symbolism and respect for that symbol. For example, flag etiquette instructions make it clear that flying a flag that is faded, soiled, or dirty is an offense to the flag. Other aspects of the U.S. Flag Code, which specifies what is considered official respect for or desecration of the flag, are interesting precisely because many people violate this code while they believe themselves to be displaying their patriotism (Sons of Union Veterans of the Civil War 2010).

1. The flag should *never* be used in any form of advertising. It should not be embroidered on cushions, handkerchiefs, or scarves, or reproduced on paper napkins, carry-out bags, wrappers, or anything else that will soon be discarded.

2. No *part* of the flag—depictions of stars and stripes that are in any form other than that approved for the flag itself—should *ever* be used as a costume, a clothing item, or an athletic uniform.

3. Displaying a flag after dark should not be done unless it is illuminated, and it should not be left out when it is raining.

4. The flag should never be represented flat or horizontally (as many marching bands do). It should *always* be aloft and free.

5. The flag should under no circumstances be used as a ceiling covering. (U.S. Flag Code 2008)

According to the standards established by U.S. military representatives and congressional action, any of these forms of display may be considered a desecration of the flag; yet the meaning that most citizens give to these acts may be quite different. Symbolic interactionists are interested in the meaning people give to actions and to symbols.

Engaging With Sociology

1. Do you think wearing a shirt or sweater with the U.S. stars and stripes in some sort of artistic design is an act of desecration of the flag or a statement of patriotism? Why?

2. Is it disrespectful to use a flag in advertising, to put stars and stripes on disposable napkins, or to have a flat flag covering a football field? Why might the military personnel who developed the flag code think that it *is*?

---

of meaning around national symbols. The above "Engaging Sociology" explores this issue.

Socialization of individuals at the micro level generally instills a strong sense of the legitimacy and authority of the reigning government in a particular society. This includes loyalty to a flag or other symbol that represents the nation, as illustrated above. Individuals learn their political and economic attitudes, values, and behaviors—their political socialization—from family, schools, the media, and their nation. For example, national leaders provide much of the information for newspapers and other media and can spin that information to suit their needs and manage the perceptions of the public. Governments also play a role in what is taught in schools, which shapes

attitudes of the citizenry regarding democracy, capitalism, socialism, and other political and economic systems (Glasberg and Shannon 2011).

Social Constructions of Politics: Legitimacy, Authority, and Power.

Max Weber distinguished between legitimate and illegitimate power. *Power that people consider legitimate* is **authority**, and *is recognized as rightful by those subject to it* (Weber 1947). Governments are given legitimate power when citizens acknowledge that the government has the right to exercise power over them. They adhere to a judge's rulings because they recognize that court decrees are legitimate. In contrast, illegitimate power, or coercion, includes living under force of a military regime or

FIGURE 12.1   Weber's Formula Regarding Power

Force + Consent = Power

Force < Consent = Legitimate Power (authority)

Force > Consent = Illegitimate Power (e.g., dictatorship)

being kidnapped or imprisoned without charge (see Figure 12.1). These distinctions between legitimate and illegitimate power are important to our understanding of how leaders or political institutions establish the right to lead. To Weber, illegitimate power is sustained by brute force or coercion. Authority, on the other hand, is granted by the people subject to the power (Weber 1946).

How Do Leaders Gain Legitimate Power? Generally, leaders with legitimate power gained their positions in one of three ways:

1. *Traditional authority* is passed on through the generations, usually within a family line, so that positions are inherited. Tribal leaders in African societies pass their titles and power to their sons. Japanese and many European royal lines pass from generation to generation. Usually called a monarchy, this has been the most common form of leadership throughout history. Authority is seen as "normal" for a family

or a person because of tradition. It has always been done that way, so no one challenges it. When authority is granted based on tradition, authority rests with the position rather than the person. The authority is easily transferred to another heir of that status.

2. *Charismatic authority* is power based on a claim of extraordinary, even divine, personal characteristics. Charismatic leaders often emerge at times of change when strong, new leadership is needed. For charismatic leaders, unlike traditional authority leaders, the right to lead rests with the person, not the position. Followers believe power is rooted in the personality of a dynamic individual. This is an inherently change-oriented and unstable form of leadership because authority resides in a single person. The most common pattern is that, as stability reemerges, power will become institutionalized—rooted in stable routine patterns of the organization. Charismatic leaders are effective during transitional periods but often replaced by *rational-legal* leaders once affairs of state become stable.

    Some examples of charismatic religious leaders include Jesus, Muhammad, Joan of Arc, and the founder of the Mormon Church, Joseph Smith. Charismatic political leaders include Mao Zedong in China and Mahatma Gandhi in India. Both men led their countries to independence and had respect from citizens that bordered on "awe." One charismatic leader today is Aung San Suu Kyi, pro-democracy activist and Nobel Prize winner who was imprisoned for many years by the military leadership in Myanmar (formerly known as Burma).

3. *Rational-legal authority* is the most typical type of legitimate power in modern nation-states. Authority is given not to a particular person, but to the position the person holds. Such authority is often found in political and economic bureaucracies in the modern states. For example, the president of the United States has authority due to the office he holds, just as the CEO of a corporation does. Individuals are granted authority because they have proper training or have proven their merit.

Each of these three types of authority is a "legitimate" exercise of power because the people being

©Reuters/Pawel Kopczynski

Japan's Emperor Akihito (right) and Empress Michiko leave after praying at the altar of the late Prince Tomohito. Japan has the only monarch in the world with the title *Emperor*, a position that is inherited through the family line. This is an example of traditional authority.

Aung San Suu Kyi, Nobel Prize winner and opposition leader in Myanmar (Burma), spent 15 years under house arrest after an authoritarian military junta took over the government. Released from house arrest to participate in the changing political situation in Burma, she and her party recently won 40 of 45 elected seats in the government.

governed give their consent, at least implicitly, to the leaders (Weber 1947, [1904–1905] 1958). However, on occasion, leaders overstep their legitimate bounds and rule by force. Some of those rulers, such as Muammar Gaddafi in Libya and Hosni Mubarak of Egypt, are challenged and overthrown.

Self-Interest as a Path to Legitimacy. In contemporary democratic politics, politicians and political commentators often explicitly refer to the self-interests of voters. This reflects the *rational choice perspective* that humans tend to vote for their own benefit, regardless of whether the actions of government would be fair to all citizens.

Both U.S. Republican and Democratic parties try to convince the public and donors that their policies will serve the public's self-interests. Democrats tend to argue that their government policies benefit citizens directly, with government programs for the middle and working classes, such as government support for preschool and higher education. Republicans, on the other hand, often stress that less government and lower taxes create a greater stimulus to the economy than anything the government can do. Again, the appeal is to self-interests. Members of both political parties promise to help those who support and vote for them, once they are put in positions of power.

Many voters do not understand the issues at play in elections and vote for people who support policies that would actually harm them. To make it even more complex, some people vote based on values—right to life, support for the needy, or protection of the environment, for example—because they think it is the right thing to do. The policy may not be in the person's economic self-interests—unless the person is considering the interest of his or her children and grandchildren or long-term noneconomic interests, such as a desire to build a society pleasing to God.

Macro-Level Perspectives: Who Rules?

Pluralist Model of Power. As noted in previous chapters, the pluralist model holds that power is distributed among various groups so that no one group has complete power. According to pluralists, it is primarily through interest groups that you and I influence decision-making processes. Groups such as unions or environmental organizations represent our interests and act to keep power from being concentrated in the hands of an elite few (Dahl 1961; Dye and Zeigler 1983). One current example of an interest group in the United States is the Tea Party, which began as a small group of disaffected individuals opposed to government expansion and higher taxes. With big wins in the 2010 congressional election, it has become a major determinant of Republican Party politics (Skocpol and Williamson 2012). Tea Party members have also won approximately 700 seats in state legislatures around the country. Their impact moved the Republican platform to the right and focused debates in Congress on the national debt and reducing the size of the federal government (Martin and Meckler 2012; Tanenhaus 2012).

Interest groups can influence laws and policies by mobilizing large numbers of voters or political donors. Examples include efforts to influence health care reform in the United States; combat global climate change; and reform government, business, and banking industry practices. Greenpeace, Common Cause, Earth First!, Bread for the World, Focus on the Family, the Family Research Council, the Service Employees International Union, and other consumer, environmental, religious, and political action groups have had impacts on policy decisions. According to pluralists, shared power is found in each person's ability to join groups and influence policy decisions and outcomes.

National or international nongovernmental organizations (NGOs) can have a major impact on global issues and policy making, as exemplified by the Grameen Bank and other microcredit organizations that work in the field of international development (Global Journal 2013; Yunus and Jolis 1999). NGOs exert influence on power holders because of the numbers they represent, the money they control, the issues they address, and the effectiveness of their spokespeople or lobbyists. Sometimes they form coalitions around issues of concern such as the environment, human rights, health care, or women's and children's issues. The efforts of religious, business, and labor unions for immigration reform provide an example of such a coalition. Each of these groups, with its own set of constituents, believes that immigration reform is in its best interest.

According to pluralists, multiple power centers offer the best chance to maintain democratic forms of government because no one group dominates and many citizens are involved. Although an interest group may dominate decision making on a specific issue, no one group dictates all policy. On the other hand, some theorists maintain that only a small group of elite people really have much power.

Elite Model of Power. The *power elite model* asserts it is inevitable that a small group of elite will rule societies. As we discussed in earlier chapters, they argue that this is the nature of individuals and society and that pluralists are imagining a world that does not exist. Individuals have limited power through interest groups, but real power is held by the power elite (Domhoff 2005, 2008; Dye 2002; Mills 1956). They wield power through their institutional roles and make decisions about war, peace, the economy, wages, taxes, justice, education, welfare, and health issues—all of which have a serious impact on citizens. These powerful elites attempt to maintain, perpetuate, and even strengthen their rule. Robert Michels, a well-known political philosopher, believed that elite rule is inevitable. He described this pattern of domination as the *iron law of oligarchy*. In democratic and totalitarian societies alike, leaders have influence over who is elected to succeed them and to whom they give political favors. This influence eventually leads those in elite positions to abuse their power (Michels [1911] 1967).

The social philosopher Vilfredo Pareto expanded on this idea of abuse of power, pointing out that abuse would cause a counter group to challenge the elite for power. Eventually, as the latter group gains power, its members would become corrupt as well, and the cycle—a *circulation of elites*—would continue. Corruption in many countries illustrates this pattern (Pareto [1911] 1955), as can be seen in current headlines from such various nations as Greece, Guatemala, Zimbabwe, and Bangladesh.

C. Wright Mills also argued that there is an invisible but interlocking power elite in U.S. society, consisting of leaders in military, business, and political spheres, wielding their power from behind the scenes. They make the key political, economic, and social decisions for the nation and manipulate what the public hears (Mills 1956). A wealthy few citizens of the United States form a cohesive economic-political power structure that represents their interests. Many of those who hold top positions on corporate boards or in the foreign policy-making agencies of national government attended the same private preparatory schools and Ivy League colleges—Brown, Columbia, Cornell, Harvard, University of Pennsylvania, Dartmouth, Princeton, and Yale—and created lasting connections (Domhoff 2005, 2008, 2014b; Howard 2007; Persell and Cookson 1985).

Elite theorists believe that government seldom regulates business. Instead, business co-opts politicians to support its interests by providing the financial support needed to run political election campaigns (Domhoff 2008). Pluralists, however, believe that a powerful government serves as a balance to the enormous power of the corporate world. Big business and big government are safety checks against tyranny—and each is convinced that the other is too big.

● **Thinking Sociologically**

Do you think your national society is controlled by pluralist interest groups or a power elite? Can an individual outside of a power elite help to influence policies in your nation? What makes you think so?

🖥 Classical Elite Theory

INDIVIDUALS, POWER, AND PARTICIPATION: MICRO-LEVEL ANALYSIS

Whether you have health insurance or are subject to a military draft depends in part on the political and economic decisions made by the government in power. Political systems influence our personal lives in myriad ways, some of which are readily apparent: health and safety regulations, taxation, a military draft, regulations on food and the drugs we buy, and even whether the gallon of gas pumped into our car is really a full gallon—or whether it is really gasoline. In this section, we explore the impact individuals have on the government and the variables that influence participation in political and economic policy-making processes. At the micro level, individuals decide to vote or otherwise participate in the political system. This private decision is, in turn, affected by where those individuals fall in the stratification system of society, not just by personal choices.

Participation in Democratic Processes

Citizens in democratic countries have the right to free and fair elections. Many social scientists, including sociologists, have tried to understand what influences citizens' decisions on whether and how to vote.

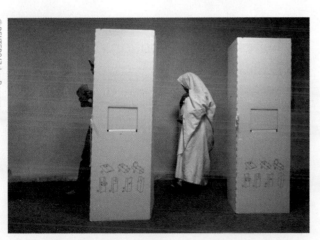

©REUTERS/Zohra Bensemra

A woman in Libya commits an act of courage as she casts her ballot during the 2012 General National Congress elections. The elections were considered a crucial step for Libya, but they occurred amid fears of violence.

Levels of Participation in Politics. As mentioned in previous chapters, wealthier people are more likely to vote. For example, they tend to

- have been socialized to believe they can make an impact on the political process,
- benefit from an educational background that allows them to understand the issues at hand and how their own self-interests are at stake,
- have the time to follow the news and political issues, and
- experience a more flexible schedule that allows them the time to vote.

Those with little money, on the other hand, tend to feel that politics has little relevance for them (apathy) or that they cannot affect the process and are disaffected by the scandals or corruption in politics (alienation from a system that does not value them). Participation in elections in the United States is the second lowest of the Global North democracies, as indicated in Table 12.1 on page 330.

Structural factors also influence voting. The recent debates over U.S. voter registration are a case in point, with some states combing their voter lists for ineligible voters or making registration and voting difficult for some citizens, usually the elderly, minorities, and people in poverty who may have problems obtaining acceptable ID. By contrast, in 22 countries voting is compulsory, a legal obligation of citizenship, and voter turnout is above 90%. Ten countries that enforce voting are Argentina, Australia, Brazil, Democratic Republic of Congo, Ecuador, Luxembourg, Nauru, Peru, Singapore, and Uruguay; it is a violation of the law not to vote (Frankal 2011; World Factbook 2011). Fines, community service, and even jail time are penalties for not voting. Elections are held over many days to ensure that people can get to the polls. Some other countries also make sure that ethnic minorities and women have a voice by structuring elections to ensure broad representation. Even inmates in prison are expected to vote in some countries.

A higher percentage than normal, 58.7% of eligible U.S. voters, turned out in the 2012 presidential election (Nonprofit Vote 2012; U.S. Elections Project 2012), and the numbers have generally been higher in the 21st century than in the three decades from 1970 to 2000 (Lederman 2012). A higher African American and Latino participation rate was a major reason why

TABLE 12.1   Average Voter Participation Over 60 Years (All Elections)

Country	Voter Participation % (All Elections for 60 Years)	Most Recent Parliamentary Election
Italy	92.5	75.2% (2013)
Iceland	89.5	81.4% (2013)
New Zealand	86.2	74.2% (2011)
South Africa	85.5	77.3% (2009)
Austria	85.1	81.7% (2008)
Netherlands	84.8	74.6% (2012)
Australia	84.4	93.2% (2010)
Denmark	83.6	87.7% (2011)
Sweden	83.3	84.6% (2010
Germany	80.6	70.8% (2009)
United Kingdom	74.9	65.8% (2010)
Argentina	70.6	79.4% (2011)
Japan	69.0	59.3% (2012)
Canada	68.4	61.4% (2011)
France	67.3	55.4% (2012)
Bolivia	61.4	94.6% (2009)
USA	48.3	58.7% (2012)
Mexico	48.1	62.5% (2012)

Source: International Institute for Democracy and Electoral Assistance 2012.

*The figures are averages of voter participation for all elections since 1945. Note that enfranchisement of women and various ethnic minorities changed in some countries during that time, so these should be viewed as very crude overall indicators of voting patterns.

Note: To see the voting participation figures for 172 countries in the world, go to www.idea.int/vt/.

voter participation was relatively high during the last few presidential elections (Sherwood 2012; Short 2009). In off-year elections—when many senators, congressional representatives, and state governors are elected—the turnout hovers in the low 40s or even below. If 40% of the eligible population votes and it is a very close election, only slightly more than 20% of the citizenry have elected the new officeholder. So voter turnout is an important issue for a society that purports to be a democracy. Figure 12.2 indicates voter turnout since 1990.

POWER AND RESOURCE DISTRIBUTION: MESO-LEVEL ANALYSIS

In Southern Africa, Bantu tribal groups provide for heirs to take on leadership when a leader dies. When there is no male heir to the position, a female from the same lineage is appointed. This woman must assume the legal and social roles of a male husband, father, and chief by acting as a male and taking a "wife." The wife is assigned male sexual partners, who become the biological fathers of her children. This provides heirs for the lineage, but the female chief is their social father because she has socially become a male. This pattern has been common practice in many southern Bantu societies and among many other populations in four separate geographic areas of Africa. Anthropologists interpret this as a means of maintaining public positions of dominance and power in the hands of males in a particular family and community (O'Brien 1977). In any case, ruling groups in society have mechanisms for ensuring a smooth transition of power to keep the controlling structure functioning.

Meso-level political institutions include state or provincial governments, national political parties, and large formal organizations within the nation. Those political institutions also influence and are influenced by other meso-level institutions: family, education, religion, health care, and economics.

Purposes of Political and Economic Institutions

We have learned that each institution serves purposes or *functions* in society. Just as family, education, and religion meet certain societal needs, so do the political and economic institutions. The following six activities are typical societal purposes (functions) of meso-level political and economic institutions. They set the stage for power and privilege carried out at the macro level in national and international arenas.

1. *To maintain social control:* We expect to live in safety, to live according to certain "rules," to be employed in meaningful work, and to participate in other activities prescribed or protected by law. Ideally, governments help clarify

FIGURE 12.2 Voter Turnout in the United States: 1990–2012 (by Percentage of Eligible Voters)

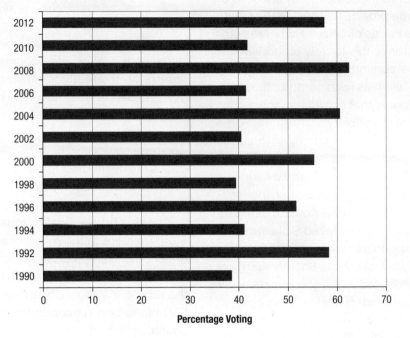

Source: U.S. Elections Project 2012.

expectations and customs and implement laws that express societal values.

2. *To serve as an arbiter in disputes:* When disputes arise over property or the actions of another individual or group, a judicial branch of government can intervene. In some systems, such as the tribal groups mentioned above, a council of elders or powerful individuals performs judicial functions. In other cases, elected or appointed judges have the right to hear disputes, make judgments, and carry out punishment for infractions.

3. *To protect citizens:* Governments are responsible for protecting citizens from takeover by external powers or disruption from internal sources.

4. *To represent the group in relations with other groups or societies:* Individuals cannot negotiate agreements with foreign neighbors. Official representatives deal with other officials to negotiate arms and trade agreements, protect the world's airways, determine fishing rights, and establish military bases in foreign lands, among other agreements.

The four functions listed thus far are rather clearly political in nature; the two that follow are areas of contention between political and economic realms.

5. *To make plans for the future of the group:* As individuals, we have little direct impact on the direction our society takes, but the official governmental body—be it elected, appointed, or imposed through force—shares responsibility with economic institutions for planning in the society. In some (but not all) socialist societies, this planning determines how many engineers, teachers, or nurses are needed. The appropriate numbers of people are then trained according to these projections. In other societies, power is much less direct. In capitalist systems, for instance, supply and demand are assumed to regulate the economic system, and there is less governmental planning in economic matters than in socialist societies. The question of who plans for the future is often a source of stress between the political and economic institutions: Are the planners elected politicians/trained public servants or private entrepreneurs?

6. *To provide for the needs of their citizens:* Governments differ greatly in the degree to which they attempt to meet the material needs of citizens. Some provide for most of the health and welfare needs of citizens, whereas others tend to leave this largely to individuals, families, local community agencies, and other institutions, such as faith communities. Not everyone agrees that providing for needs is an inherent responsibility of the state. Some people believe that the economy will produce jobs, goods, and services for the population if the government gets out of the way and lets individuals make decisions based on their self-interests. The debates over health care and welfare systems in the United States point to conflicts over who should be responsible—the state or private individuals. Should such services be coordinated by the government or left to "the invisible hand" of market forces?

The ways in which governments and economic institutions carry out these six functions are largely determined by society's dominant philosophies of power and political structures. Political and economic institutions, like family and religious institutions, come in many forms. In essence, these variations in political institutions reflect variations in human ideas of power.

Thinking Sociologically

In an era of terrorist threats, how do you think the "protecting the safety of the citizens" function has affected the ability of governments to perform other functions?

One function of governments is to provide protection from external threats—the role of the military establishment. These soldiers are in training for that role.

Systems of Power and Distribution

While *politics* refers to the social institution that determines and exercises power relations in society, *economics* is the social institution that deals with the production and distribution of goods and services. Both politics and economics focus on questions related directly to the concept of power and power relationships among and between individuals, organizations, nation-states, and societies. Economic and political systems overlap in part because those who have power also have access to resources. How goods are distributed to the members of society—a major function of economics—is often determined by who has political power.

Successful political campaigns in the United States, except at the most local level, require significant financial resources, so attaining political positions involves cultivating relationships with leaders in the economic system. Thus, there is a reciprocal relationship between economics and politics. In many countries, the government is the largest employer, purchaser of goods, controller of exports and imports, and regulator of industry and of interest rates. In the United States, many government regulatory agencies, such as the Food and Drug Administration, Department of Agriculture, and Justice Department, attempt to watch over the economic sector to protect consumers.

Government officials have a vested interest in the well-being of the economy, for should the economy fail, the state would be likely to fail as well. Recessions, depressions, and high rates of inflation put severe strains on governments that need stable economies to run properly. When problems occur, government officials are inclined to increase their roles in the economic sector. Witness the volatile world money markets from 2008 to 2012 and measures, such as bailouts, taken by many governments to stabilize their economies.

On September 29, 2008, the Dow Jones index dropped an unprecedented 777 points and fell another 782 points a week later. President Bush and Congress immediately began to look for "stimulus packages" to keep the economy from going into a deep recession. When Barack Obama became president in 2009, turning the economy around became one of the key challenges of his presidency.

A dramatic drop in financial markets indicates a loss of the population's confidence in the economy

▶ **Political Systems**

and a mass reluctance to invest in it. Lending institutions cannot loan money easily, business stagnates, unemployment rates skyrocket, and the entire government may be held responsible for a lack of economic vitality. When a country goes into a recession, the party in power is often held responsible and will not likely be reelected if the recovery takes too long. Economic recessions can destroy the careers of politicians but can also create such dissatisfaction that the entire government may be at risk of a citizen uprising. Indeed, in 2009, Dennis Blair, the U.S. director of national intelligence, declared the global economic crisis the most serious national security issue facing the nation, calling it a "bigger threat than Al Qaeda terrorists" (Haniffa 2009).

Types of Governments. The major systems of government in the world range from fascist totalitarianism to democracy. However, each culture puts its own imprint on the system it uses, making for tremendous variation in actual practice.

Authoritarian Governments. In **authoritarian governments**, *one absolute monarch or dictator or a small group of unelected people hold all of the political power*. They often have the backing of the military to keep them in power. Authoritarian regimes are common forms of government. Some are helpful to citizens—benevolent dictators—but almost all exert tremendous power and discourage dissent. The Castro brothers—Fidel and more recently Raúl—have maintained absolute political control of Cuba since 1959 (and exercised control, to various extents, over other institutions as well). While they are despised by many Cuban immigrants in the United States and subject to U.S. government embargos, they are admired by many Cubans who believe they rule in the best interests of the people. So *within* Cuba, they are popular despite autocratic rule.

Totalitarian Governments. A **totalitarian government** *is any form of government that almost totally controls people's lives*. It differs from an authoritarian

A stable economic system is essential to political stability, and extreme fluctuations in the economy threaten those in power. On September 29, 2008, the Dow Jones index dropped dramatically and the New York Stock Exchange, usually bustling with activity, emptied out.

government in that the political leaders also control the social and economic institutions. Totalitarian states are often based on a specific political ideology and run by a single ruling group or party, referred to as an *oligarchy*. Russia under Joseph Stalin, Germany under Adolf Hitler, Libya under Muammar Gaddafi, and North Korea under Kim Jong-un are examples. The state typically controls the workplace, education, the media, and other aspects of life. All actions revolve around state-established objectives. Dissent and opposition are discouraged or forcefully eliminated as we saw when Gaddafi was in power, with violent crackdowns on demonstrators. Interrogation by secret police, imprisonment, and torture are used to quiet dissenters. Terror is used as a tactic to deal with both internal and external dissent, but when it is used by the state to control the citizenry or to terrorize those of another nation, it is called *state terrorism*.

Throughout history, most people have lived under authoritarian or totalitarian systems. Under certain conditions, totalitarian regimes can turn into democratic ones, and of course, democratically elected leaders can change or ignore laws to retain their positions of power, as was the case for a number of elected leaders who changed the constitutions to allow for them to run again (Venezuela, Zimbabwe, and Russia are examples). Consider an example of a government gone totalitarian. In 1978, the Cambodian (Kampuchean) government was taken over by a radical faction, the Khmer Rouge. They relocated urban dwellers to rural areas, seized personal property, and reclassified some people as peasants, workers, or soldiers. Approximately 1.7 million people (21% of the population)—including bureaucrats, royalty, businesspeople, intellectuals with opposing views, Muslims, and Buddhist monks—were slaughtered for minor offenses. Hence, the term *Killing Fields* is used to describe the execution sites (Cambodian Genocide Program 2013). Pol Pot and the Khmer Rouge were finally overthrown in 1979. Violence still exists in Cambodia, however. The Human Rights Center reports chaos, corruption, poverty, and a reign of terror, as the military kills and extorts money from citizens. Killings, violence, and intimidation have surrounded elections, though the parliamentary elections of 2012 had somewhat fewer problems than in the past (Loy 2012).

Democratic Systems of Government. In contrast to totalitarian regimes, **democratic governments** are *characterized by accountability of the government to citizens and a large degree of control by individuals over their own lives*. Democracies always have at least two political parties that compete in elections for power and that generally accept the outcome of elections. Mechanisms for the smooth transfer of power are laid out in a constitution or another legal document. Ideal-type democracies share the following characteristics, although few democracies fit this description exactly:

1. *Citizens participate in selecting the government:* There are free elections with anonymous ballots cast, widespread suffrage (voting rights), and competition between members of different parties running for offices. Those who govern do so by the consent of the majority, but political minorities have rights, representation, and responsibilities.

2. *Civil liberties are guaranteed:* These usually include freedom of association, freedom of the press, freedom of speech, and freedom of religion. Such individual rights ensure dissent, and dissent creates more ideas about how to solve problems. These freedoms are therefore essential for a democracy to thrive.

3. *Government powers are limited by a constitution:* The government can intrude only into certain areas of individuals' lives. Criminal procedures and police power are clearly defined, thus prohibiting harassment or terrorism by police. The judicial system helps maintain a balance of power.

Children interact with a person dressed as a polar bear advocating against the proposed Keystone XL Pipeline project, near a cutout of U.S. President Obama outside the White House in 2013. Protests are a way citizens try to keep a government accountable and influence policy.

4. *Governmental structure and process are spelled out:* Generally, some officials are elected whereas others are appointed, but all are accountable to citizens. Representatives are given authority to pass laws, approve budgets, and hold the executive officer accountable for activities. The two main forms of democratic constitutional government are the parliamentary and presidential systems. In typical parliamentary governments, the head of government is a prime minister, chancellor, or premier, and there is also a president or monarch, with less power. Countries with this model include Belgium, Canada, Denmark, the United Kingdom, Japan, Sweden, Ireland, India, Israel, Pakistan, and Turkey. Examples of presidential governments include France, Italy, the United States, Germany, Argentina, Brazil, Kenya, and the Philippines.

Proportional representation means that each party is given a number of seats corresponding to the percentage of votes it received in the election. In "winner-takes-all" systems, the individual with more than 50% of the votes gets the seat. In the United States, the winner-takes-all presidential electoral system has come under attack because the winner of the nationwide presidential popular vote can lose the election. This actually happened in two presidential elections in the United States: once in 1876 and the other time in 2000. Al Gore received the most votes for president in 2000, but because of the system for electing the Electoral College, George W. Bush became the next president, as elected by the Electoral College. Defenders of this system of choosing the president argue that this protects the voice of each state, even if each individual voice is not given the same weight.

Constitutional governments may include representatives from two to a dozen or more parties, as has been the case in Switzerland. Most have four or five viable ones. In European countries, typical parties include Social Democrats, Christian Democrats, Communists, Liberals, and other parties tied to specific local or state issues, such as Green parties.

In the modern world, new challenges and issues face democracies, especially electronic technology. The Internet and other "smart" technologies can enhance democracy by providing an opportunity for people around the world to be informed citizens or hurt it by hindering thoughtful debate and civic engagement in ideas—essential ingredients of a functioning democracy (Barber 2006). The Internet, fax machines, camcorders, and other telecommunications devices have been major instruments for indigenous people, linking them to the outside world and combating oppressive governments. As one political scientist put it,

> Recent events confirm that social media is playing a significant role in modern political protests. For example, social media has helped maintain news coverage of events going on inside Syria since the civil war began there in 2011. After the Syrian government attempted to restrict non-state reporters following the outbreak of protests, members of the rebel groups and bystanders tweeted and uploaded YouTube videos of government-led violence going on there (Mackey 2011). These videos helped bolster support for the rebels both inside Syria and in some parts of the broader international community. (Castle 2016)

In representative democracies, a key contribution that these technologies bring is helping citizens stay in touch with their elected representatives. On the other hand, blogs, talk shows, webpages, and Internet discussions are often known more for sound bites and polemical attacks on opponents than for reasoned debates in which opposing sides express views.

Thinking Sociologically

How can the above issues of technology be problems for representative democracy? Which are benefits? What effect do they have on direct participatory democracy?

Types of Economic Systems. As societies become industrialized, one of two basic economic systems evolves: a planned system or a market system. Planned or centralized systems involve state-based planning and control of property, whereas market systems stress individual planning and private ownership of property, with much less governmental coordination or oversight. These basic types vary, depending on the peculiarities of the country and its economy. For instance, China has a highly centralized planned economy with government control, yet some private property and incentive plans exist, and these are expanding. The United States is a market system, yet the government puts many limitations on business enterprises and regulates the flow and value of money. Distinctions between the two major types rest on the degree of centralized planning and the ownership of property. In each type of system, decisions must be made concerning which goods to produce (and in what quantity), what to do in the event of shortages or surpluses, and how to distribute goods. Who has the power to make these decisions helps determine what type of system it is.

Market/Capitalist Economic Systems. Market or capitalist economic systems *are driven by the balance of supply and demand, allowing free competition to reward the efficient and the innovative with profits. They stress individual planning and private ownership of property.* As noted earlier, the goal of capitalism is profit, made through free competition between competitors for the available markets. Proponents of pure capitalism assume that the laws of supply and demand will allow some to profit, while others fail. Needed goods will be made, and the best product for the price will win out over the others. No planning by an oversight group is necessary, because the invisible hand of the market will ensure sufficient quality control, production, and distribution of goods. This system also rewards innovative entrepreneurs who take risks and solve problems in new ways, resulting in potential growth and prosperity.

Capitalist manufacturers try to bring in more money than they pay out to produce goods and services. As Karl Marx described, because workers are a production cost, getting the maximum labor output for the minimum wage benefits capitalists. Therefore, multinational corporations look throughout the world for the cheapest sources of labor with the fewest restrictions on employment and operations. This practice of labor exploitation leads most governments to exercise some control over manufacturing and the market, although the degree of control varies widely (Marx [1844] 1964).

Capitalism was closest to its pure form during the Industrial Revolution, when some entrepreneurs gained control of large amounts of capital and resources, and legislation to control owners and protect workers did not yet exist. Using available labor and mechanical innovations, these entrepreneurs built industries and, soon, monopolies (exclusive control over supplying certain goods). Craftspeople such as cobblers could not compete with the efficiency of the new machine-run shops, and many were forced to become laborers in new industries to survive.

As we noted in earlier chapters, Marx predicted that capitalism would cause citizens to split into two main classes: the *bourgeoisie*, capitalists who own the means of production (the "haves"), and the *proletariat*, those who sell their labor to capitalists (the "have-nots"). He argued that institutions such as education, politics, laws, and religion work to preserve the privileges of the elite (the "haves").

Members of the economic and political elite often encourage patriotism to distract the less privileged from their conflicts with the elite. According to Marx, the elite want the masses to draw the line between "us" and "them" based on national loyalty, not based on lines of economic self-interests (Gellner and Breuilly 2009). So, in Marxist thought, even patriotism is a tool of the elite to control the workers. However, Marx believed that ultimately the workers would realize their plight, develop a class consciousness, and rebel against their conditions. They would overthrow the "haves" and bring about a new and more egalitarian society.

The revolutions that Marx predicted have not occurred in most countries. Labor unions have protected workers from the severe exploitation that Marx witnessed in the early stages of industrialization in England, and capitalist governments have created and expanded a wide array of measures to protect citizens, including antimonopoly legislation, social security systems, unemployment compensation, disability programs, welfare systems, and health care systems. Therefore, most workers have not been discontent to the point of trying to overthrow their governments. Marx's vision of a small group of owners controlling the economy has borne out, however. For example, today, among all transnational companies, just 1% control 40% of all of the world's collective wealth (Coghlan and MacKenzie 2011). Fewer than 740 multinational corporations control 80% of corporate wealth. These figures are out of 37 million companies and investors and 43,060 transnational corporations in the world, each with interlocking networks (Upbin 2011).

One of the major criticisms of pure capitalism is that profit is the only value that drives the system. Human dignity and well-being, environmental protection, rights of ethnic groups, and other social issues are important only as they affect profits. This leaves some people deeply dissatisfied with capitalism.

Planned Economic Systems. In **planned (or centralized) economic systems**, *the government or another centralized group oversees production and distribution.* They de-emphasize private control of property and economic autonomy and have the government do economic planning. Matters of production and labor are, in theory, governed with the "communal" good in mind. There is deep suspicion of the exploitation that can occur when individuals all pursue their own self-interests. Those who hold this philosophy believe that the market system also results in *oligarchy*—a system run by the financial elite in the pursuit of their own self-interests. Therefore, they believe the state needs to oversee the total economy. China, Cuba, Laos, North Korea, the former Soviet Union, and several nations in Africa, Asia, and Latin America have planned economies with industry controlled by the state (Nations Online 2014).

In reality, however, no system is a perfect planned state with the complete elimination of private property or differences in privilege. China, based on a planned, government-controlled system, made rapid progress in tackling hunger, illiteracy, drug addiction, and other problems by using its strong central government to establish five-year economic development plans. Today, however, charges of corruption among those who control state-run companies and a desire for increased economic growth has led it to experiment with new economic plans, including limited private entrepreneurship, more imported goods, and trade and development agreements with other countries. China is now the largest trading nation, and its economy is expected to be the world's largest economy by 2016 (Organisation for Economic Co-operation and Development 2013).

One key criticism of planned systems is that placing both economic and political power in the hands of the same people can lead to control by a few leaders, resulting in tyranny. Multiple power centers in government, the business world, and the military can balance each other and help protect against dictatorships and tyranny (Heilbroner and Milberg 2007).

Mixed Economies. *Mixed economies*, sometimes called "democratic socialism," try to balance societal needs and individual freedoms. **Democratic socialism**, for example, refers to *collective or group planning of the development of the society, but within a democratic political system.* Private profit is less important than in capitalism, and the good of the whole is paramount. Planning may include goals of protecting the environment, wealth redistribution through progressive taxation, universal health care, or supporting families through government-subsidized health care and family leave legislation, but individuals' rights to pursue their own self-interests are also allowed within certain parameters. Mixed economies seek checks and balances so that both political and economic decision makers are accountable to the public.

Several countries, including Sweden, the United Kingdom, Norway, Austria, Canada, France, and Australia, have incorporated some democratic socialist ideas into their governmental policies, especially in public services. Many Western European democracies redistribute income through progressive tax plans that tax according to people's ability to pay. The government uses these revenues to nationalize education, health plans and medical care, pensions, maternity leaves, and sometimes housing for its citizens. Although much of the industry is privately run, the government regulates business and assesses high taxes to pay for government programs. Typically, public service industries such as transportation, communications, and power companies are government controlled.

When U.S. President Obama was first elected, he was faced with a major economic crisis caused by the deregulation of banks and the system of loans for home mortgages and businesses. He—as his Republican predecessor, George W. Bush, did before him—pushed a massive ($787 billion) stimulus plan through Congress (Espo 2009). The problem was lack of regulation of the economy, and the solution was massive support for corporations and businesses, actions that some called socialistic. Other programs and policies in the United States that follow the structure of democratic socialism include Social Security, Medicaid, Medicare, farm subsidies, federal unemployment insurance, the national parks system, public schools, environmental policies, and thousands of other programs that support and protect U.S. citizens. So despite hostility to the term *socialism*, any government program that "bails out" the economy (such as rescuing a failing bank) or that "protects consumers" is part of a mixed economy that includes some socialist policies. Note that both Republican and Democratic administrations have supported such policies, and most policies have been very popular.

Just two centuries ago, it was widely believed, perhaps rightly at that time, that democracy could not work. The notion of self-governance by the citizenry was discredited as a pipe dream. Yet this experiment in self-governance is continuing, despite some flaws and problems. In a speech to the British House of Commons in 1947, then Prime Minister Winston Churchill said that "democracy is the worst form of government, except for all those other forms that have been tried" (Churchill 2009). Some economists and social philosophers have argued that if the people can plan for self-governance, they certainly should be able to plan for economic development in a way that does not put economic power solely in the hands of a political elite.

The institutions of politics and economics cannot be separated. In the 21st century, new political and economic relationships will emerge as each institution influences the other. Both institutions ultimately have close connections to power and privilege.

NATIONAL AND GLOBAL SYSTEMS: MACRO-LEVEL ANALYSIS

Each nation-state develops its own systems of power and privilege in unique ways, depending on its history, leaders, needs, and relations with other nations. A macro-level analysis of national and global systems of governance and power includes both individual nation-states and international organizations, including terrorist groups that cross borders.

Power and the Nation-State

A *nation-state* is a political, geographical, and cultural unit with recognizable boundaries and a system of government. These boundaries change as disputes over territory are resolved by force or negotiation. For example, the boundaries of Israel have changed multiple times since the establishment of the nation in 1948.

There are officially 195 nation-states in the world today that are recognized by each other's governments in the United Nations, and 6 more with partial recognition, making 201 nation-states (Political Geography Now 2014). Only the Vatican, Taiwan, and Kosovo do not have UN representation. The number of nations increases as new independent nation-states continue to develop in Europe, Asia, Africa, and other parts of the world. One of the newest countries is South Sudan, which broke away from Sudan in 2011.

Within each nation-state, systems of power govern people through leaders, laws, courts, the tax structure, the military, and the economic system. Different forms of power dominate at different times in history and in different geographical settings.

The notions of the nation-state and of nationalism are so accepted that we rarely stop to think of them as social constructions of reality, created by people to meet group needs. In historical terms, though, nationalism is a rather recent or modern concept, emerging only after the nation-state (Gellner 1983, 1993; Gellner and Breuilly 2009). Medieval Europe, for example, knew no nation-states. One scholar writes that

> throughout the Middle Ages, the mass of inhabitants living in what is now known as France or England did not think of themselves as "French" or "English." They had little conception of a territorial nation (a "country") to which they owed an allegiance stronger than life itself. (Billig 1995:21)

Some argue that nation-states have "no precedent in history" prior to the 16th century and did not become widely acknowledged until they formed throughout Europe in the 19th century (Giddens 1987:166). This raises an interesting question: Why did nation-states emerge in Europe and then spread throughout the rest of the world? The answer to this puzzle of modern history has to do with the change to rational organizational structures (Billig 1995). It is noteworthy that today every square foot of the earth's land space is thought to be under the ownership of a nation-state. Yet, even today, a sense of nationalism or patriotism linking one's personal identity to the welfare of a nation is a foreign idea in many areas of the world. For example, people in Kenya, Pakistan, and Afghanistan have loyalty to their region, their ethnic or tribal group, their religious group, or their local community, but a sense of being Pakistani, Kenyan, or Afghani is weak for many. Yet, in places such as the United States, having a passionate sense of national loyalty for which one would die is so taken for granted that anyone lacking this loyalty is suspect or deviant. Note the earlier discussion of the role of the flag.

The nation is largely an imagined reality, something that exists because we choose to believe that it exists, but it can exert tremendous influence over us (Anderson 2006; McCrone 1998). Indeed, for some people, belonging to the nation has become a substitute for religious faith or belonging to local ethnic groups (Theroux 2012).

Revolutions and Rebellions

From the 1980s to the present, significant social and political changes have taken place throughout the world. The Berlin Wall was dismantled, leading to the reunification of East and West Germany. The government of South Africa that supported apartheid fell. The Baltic states of Estonia, Latvia, and Lithuania became independent. In Eastern Europe, political and social orders established since World War II underwent radical change. When the Soviet Union and Yugoslavia broke apart, national boundaries were redrawn. Internal strife resulted from ethnic divisions formerly kept under check by the strong centralized governments in these areas. In addition, the "Arab Spring" of 2011–2012 led a number of dictators in the Middle East to fall from power.

Were these changes related to world revolutions? **Revolution** refers to *social and political transformations of a nation that result when states fail to fulfill their*

Revolutions can involve a violent attack on governments or nonviolent events such as this protest march by Burmese monks that the government in Myanmar (Burma) brutally suppressed.

One revolution has been the Zapatista movement in southern Mexico (Chiapas). Here we see Zapatista commanders holding a Mexican flag as they attend a mass rally in Mexico City's main square. They have fought for indigenous rights, including clean water, and schooling through sixth grade for their children. The Zapatistas wear masks to avoid identification and persecution by the government, but they have become a symbol of the antiglobalization movement.

expected responsibilities (Skocpol 1979). Revolutions can be violent or peaceful, but generally result in altered distributions of power. Revolutions typically occur when the government does not respond to citizens' needs and when leadership emerges to challenge the existing regime. News reports from around the world frequently announce that nation-states have been challenged by opposition groups attempting to overthrow the regimes. This is the case in Syria and some other Middle Eastern nations today.

The Meso to Macro Political Connection

State or provincial governments and national political parties are meso-level organizations that operate beyond the local community, but with less widespread influence than national or federal governments or global systems. Still, decisions at the state or provincial government level can have major

Revolutionary Movements

impacts on political processes at the national level. Here we look at recent controversies about how to nominate and elect a president within the United States. Although the focus is on the U.S. political system, this discussion should be seen as illustrative of the tensions and peculiarities of the meso-macro link in any complex political system.

In some U.S. states, only members of the respective political parties (e.g., Democrat and Republican) can vote in their party's primary election. In other states, registered Independents can vote in either primary election and help select either party's candidate of office. In other states, Democrats and Republicans can cross over and vote in the primary for the other party.

In some U.S. states, each political party runs its own caucuses (face-to-face meetings of voters in homes, schools, and other buildings) to discuss policy and to carry out public votes. Each political party funds the process and sets the rules. Other states have primary elections run by the state government, though the methods of voting differ (see Table 12.2 for caucus and primary states). However, even states that use a primary are not all the same. In most states, delegates to the convention are selected based on the proportion of the vote won by a candidate in that state. If a candidate wins 40% of the vote, she wins 40% of the delegates. However, in some states on the Republican side, the delegate selection process is a winner-takes-all system. In such elections, even if one candidate wins by a hundred votes, he or she wins all the delegates for that state. In short, there is not uniformity. One state, New Hampshire, has in its state constitution a clause that the state *must* have the first presidential primary, and this means the state has more influence on winnowing down the presidential candidates than other states (to see the processes for various states—whether winner-takes-all or proportional—go to **edge.sagepub.com/ballantine condensed4e**.

Thinking Sociologically

Some states never get any say in the nomination of candidates because the process is completed before they vote. One state has written into its constitution that it must have the first primary election. Should these decisions be made at the state or national level? Who has the authority to tell a state it cannot put into its constitution a regulation that it must have the first presidential primary?

TABLE 12.2   Meso-Level Presidential Nomination Variations in the United States

Open	Semiclosed	States With Caucuses Rather Than Primaries
Allowing citizens to cross over to vote in the other party's election	Allowing Independents to vote in the other party's election	Controlled by the political parties rather than the state
AL MN TN	AK IL NH	AK ME NV
AR MS VT	CA IA OH	CO MN ND
ID MO VA	GA MA RI	IA WA
IN ND WA		KS NE WY
MI SC WI		
Open in the Democratic but closed in the Republican processes:	Semiclosed in the Democratic but closed in the Republican processes: KS	Texas has both a primary and a caucus
MT UT WV		

Sources: Bowen 2008; Center for Voting and Democracy 2008; Green Papers 2008a, 2008b; National Archives and Records Administration 2008; "Primary Calendar" 2008; Project Vote Smart 2008; State of Delaware 2008; "U.S. Elections Map" 2008; Voting and Democracy Research Center 2008.

Note: States that are not listed in the first two columns have closed voting systems—one can only vote if registered in that party.

In some places, state governments decide when primaries will be held, but elsewhere the political parties control the process of selecting nominees. The contentious 2008 U.S. election raised several controversial questions. Can a political party tell a state when to have its primary elections—and then punish that state if it does not obey by refusing to seat its delegates at the party convention? This is what happened in Michigan and Florida. On the other hand, can a state legislature—a meso-level political entity— tell a major national political party (also a meso-level political entity) how to run its nomination process? The answers to these questions are not clear, yet they can have profound effects on who becomes the president of the most powerful nation on earth.

In two states—Montana and Nebraska—the Republican primary is a "beauty contest" with no binding outcome. The results are purely advisory, and the delegates from that state are free to ignore the outcome of the election. The delegates are selected by party leaders in that state, not by the voters. The Democratic Party has only recently passed a national policy banning this kind of primary. On the other hand, the Democratic Party has 915 "superdelegates"—party leaders who have not been elected by the populace and who may commit their votes to anyone they please. So both parties allow delegates not representing any constituency to help choose the presidential nominee. What are the implications for a democracy when there are such irregularities?

Even selection of the Electoral College, which truly decides who will be president after the general election, is not uniform in policy across the states. Two states—Nebraska and Maine—have proportional distribution of electors, and all the others have winner-takes-all. Should there be consistency between the states in the way the Electoral College is selected? Should state elections all be proportional or winner-takes-all?

Because the Constitution grants considerable autonomy to states to make these decisions, how does the nation ever get consistency? At the state (meso) level, legislatures are very protective of their right to make their own decisions. Yet governance of the nation and the nation's relationships with the global community may be at stake. As you can see, meso-level political power can shape power at the macro level, which then influences policies relevant to individual lives. The three levels are intimately linked. The next "Engaging Sociology" raises questions about where authority for decisions resides at each level in the social system.

Global Interdependencies: Cooperation and Conflicts

The most affluent countries in the Global North are democracies, but a democratic system of government may not be functional in poor countries with different cultural values and systems (Etounga-Manguelle 2000). Despite the movement toward political liberalization, democracy, and market-oriented reforms in countries such as Chile, Mexico, Nigeria, Poland, Senegal, Thailand, and Turkey, not all of these societies are ready, willing, or able to adopt democratic forms of governance (Diamond 1992, 2009).

Foreign powers can do little to alter the social structure and cultural traditions of other societies, yet these structures are key to the successful development of democracy. If the imposed system is premature or incompatible with the society's level of development and other institutional structures, authoritarian dictatorship rather than democracy may emerge as the traditional authority structure breaks down. We can see signs of this in Afghanistan and Iraq, two nations in which the United States tried to establish democratic forms of government. Certain preconditions tend to be necessary for the successful emergence of democracy:

- High levels of economic well-being
- The absence of extreme inequalities in wealth and income
- Social pluralism, including a particularly strong and autonomous middle class
- A market-oriented economy
- Influence in the world system of democratic states
- A culture relatively tolerant of diversity and that can accommodate compromise
- A functioning and impartial media that will hold the government accountable
- A literate population (80% or more) informed about issues
- A written constitution with guarantees of free speech and freedom of assembly (Bottomore 1979; Inglehart 1997)

ENGAGING SOCIOLOGY

Political Decisions: Social Processes at the Micro, Meso, and Macro Levels

Imagine that your state legislature is considering a change in the presidential election process. Your state representatives in the Electoral College would be selected according to the percentage of the popular vote in your state going to each candidate (Republican, Democratic, Libertarian, and Green Party). (*Note*: Currently, almost all states distribute their electors on a winner-takes-all basis.)

1. Identify two possible micro-level consequences of this policy change. (For example, how might it affect an individual's decision to vote or how the local board of elections does its job?)

2. Identify three consequences at the macro level. (For example, how might the change affect how presidential candidates spend their resources and time, how might Congress respond to such an initiative, and so forth?)

3. How does this illustrate the influence of meso-level organizations on micro and macro levels of the social system? For example, is it a problem for a *national* democracy when the delegate selection system is so variable at the meso level, or does this make elections even more democratic because states can make their own autonomous decisions? Explain your answer.

4. Which system—winner-takes-all or percentage of the popular vote—would produce the fairest outcome? Why?

Thinking Sociologically

Why might some analysts believe that Iraq or Afghanistan—where the United States has attempted to set up democracies—may not be ready for a successful democratic government? Can you describe societies with which you are familiar that are—or are not—ready for democratic government? If you are not able to answer these questions, discuss why it is important for you, as a citizen of your own society, to be knowledgeable about other nations (and what you will do to become better informed).

An outside power like the United States can help establish the structures necessary to support democracy, but can seldom successfully impose those structures. If countries in the Global North want more democracies around the world, a more successful strategy would focus on supporting economic development in less affluent countries. Again, politics and economics are intertwined.

Some Global South countries see discussions of democracy as a ploy—a cover-up used by dominant affluent nations for advancing their wealth. For example, the Global North nations have combined to form a coalition of nations calling itself the Group of Seven (or the G7—the United States, Japan, Germany, Canada, France, Great Britain, and Italy). Russia was in what was called the G8, but was asked to leave because of political disputes over the country of Ukraine. The G7 uses its collective power to regulate global economic policies to ensure stability (and thereby ensure that its members' interests are secure). The G7 has the power to control world markets through the World Trade Organization, the World Bank, and the International Monetary Fund (Brecher, Costello, and Smith 2012; Kaiser Family Foundation 2010). Global South nations have responded to the G7 with an organization of poor countries that they called the G77 to create collective unity and gain enough power to determine their own destinies (Brecher et al. 2012; Eitzen and Zinn 2012; Hearn 2012). Figure 12.3 shows the location of G7 and G77 nations.

Political systems can face threats from internal sources such as disaffected citizens, the military, and interest groups vying for power, or they can be challenged by external sources such as other nations wanting land or resources or by coalitions of nations demanding change. This is the situation for North Korea and Iran, as coalitions of nations demand that they drop their nuclear enrichment programs. Sometimes these power struggles erupt into violence. The following section discusses how war, terrorism, and rebellion challenge existing systems.

Violence on the Global Level. Although some wars in the past were brutal and entire populations were slaughtered (Genghis Khan's ruthless campaigns

FIGURE 12.3   Countries of the G7, Major Emerging Economies, and Countries of the G77

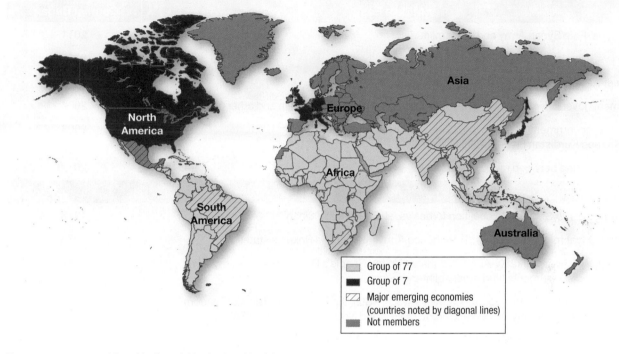

Group of 77
Group of 7
Major emerging economies
(countries noted by diagonal lines)
Not members

Source: www.g77.org, retrieved April 2008. Map by Anna Versluis.

providing one example), it is also true that in the Middle Ages gallant knights in shining armor went forth to battle with good-luck tokens from their ladies and the cause of their religion or their monarch to spur them on. They seldom died in these battles, and the daily life of the society went on as usual. Likewise, battles between First Nations in North America often resulted in four or five deaths. In contrast, since the invention of modern weaponry and chemical and nuclear weapons, no one has been safe from death and destruction in war. Weapons can destroy whole civilizations. A malfunctioning computer, a miscalculation, a deranged person, a misunderstanding between hostile factions, or a terrorist attack could kill millions of people.

War is *armed conflict occurring within, between, or among societies or groups.* It is sometimes called "organized mass violence" (Nolan 2002b:1803). War is a frequent but not inevitable condition of human existence. Many countries are now engaged in wars detrimental to their economies and morale. Some of these wars (between India and Pakistan, between the Palestinian Territories and Israel, and between rival factions in the Congo) have lasted for years. Others have been short and decisive, such as the "Desert Storm"

war with Iraq under the first President Bush. Table 12.3 on page 344 lists ongoing world conflicts as of 2013.

Why Do Nations Go to War? Leaders use moral, religious, or political ideology to legitimize war, although the cause may be conflicts over economic resources or ethnic tensions. Wars have been waged to support religions through crusades and jihads; to liberate a country from domination by a foreign power; to protect borders, resources, and cultural customs; and to capture resources, including slaves, land, and oil. War can also distract citizens from other problems in their country, and may therefore be used by politicians intent on staying in power. The United States has been involved in numerous wars spanning from the Colonial Wars (1620–1774) to the War on Terrorism (2001–present). The United States has been at war 193 out of the 237 years since the colonies declared independence. Indeed, during the entire 20th century, there were only 6 years when the United States was not engaged in some sort of military action around the world (Allison, Grey, and Valentine 2012; Noguera and Cohen 2006). On the other hand, in some cultures, war is virtually unknown. These groups, often isolated, live

The Iraq War

TABLE 12.3   Significant Ongoing Armed Conflicts, 2013

Main Warring Parties	Year Conflict Began[1]
Middle East	
Syria vs. Free Syrian Army and other militants	2011
Iraq vs. Islamic State of Iraq and Syria (ISIS)	2003
Israel vs. Palestine	1948
Yemen: government forces vs. the rebel group Shabab al-Moumineen and other militants	2004
Turkey: government forces vs. the Kurdistan Workers' Party (PKK) and Kurdistan Freedom Falcons (TAK)	2003
Libya: fighting between militia groups	2012
Asia	
Afghanistan: U.S., UK, and coalition forces vs. al-Qaeda and Taliban	1978
Burma (Myanmar) vs. Kachin Independence Army (Kachin and Rakhine states)	1988
India vs. Kashmir Harkat ul-Ansar, Northeast United People's Democratic Front, Maoist insurgents (and other splinter groups)	1947
Philippines vs. the Mindanaoan separatistis (MILK/ASG), the Bransamoro Islamic Freedom Fighters (BIFF), the New Democratic Front (NDFP), and New People's Army (NPA)	1971
National Democratic Front/New People's Army (NDF/NPA)	1969
Thailand vs. antigovernment insurgents	2004
Africa	
Algeria vs. al-Qaeda in the Islamic Maghreb	1992
Chad vs. Chadian Popular Front for Recovery (FPR)	1965
Democratic Republic of Congo vs. March 23 Movement (M23)	1990
Ethiopia vs. Ogaden National Liberation Front (ONLF)	2007
Kenya vs. Somali Islamists	1991
Nigeria vs. Boko Haram	1990
South Sudan vs. Sudan People's Liberation Army (SPLA) and Darfur	1983
Europe	
Russia vs. Chechen separatists in Chechnya; Russian and rebel forces in eastern Ukraine	1999
Latin America	
Colombia vs. Revolutionary Armed Forces of Colombia (FARC)	1964

Sources: Project Ploughshares 2013.

Note: As of 2013.

1. Where multiple parties and long-standing but sporadic conflict are concerned, date of first combat deaths is given.

in peace and cooperation, with little competition for land and resources. War is not inevitable but a product of societies and their leaders, created by societies and learned in societies.

Two familiar sociological theories attempt to explain the social factors that can lead to war. Functionalist theorists think underlying social problems cause disruptions to the system, including war, terrorism, and revolution. If all parts of the system were working effectively, they contend, these problems would not occur. Agents of social control and a smooth-running system would prevent disruptions. However, some functionalists also argue that war brings a population together behind a cause, resulting in social solidarity.

Conflict theorists see war, terrorism, and revolution as the outcome of oppression by the ruling elite and powerful countries, and an attempt to eliminate that oppression. Other conflict theorists note, however, that many businesses profit from wars because their manufacturing power is put to full use. In fact, during times of conflict more money is spent on war than on prevention of disease, illiteracy, and hunger.

Those with power have the most control over decisions to go to war, but citizens from the lower classes and racial minorities join the military, fight, and die in disproportionate numbers. They are more likely to join the military as an avenue to employment and job training. They join as enlistees who serve on the front lines and are more at risk.

All sociological theorists agree that war is not a natural or biological necessity but a social construction (Stoessinger 1993). Likewise, societies create ways to resolve disputes and avoid war.

How Might Nations Avoid War? Two primary methods used by powerful nations to avoid war include deterrence and negotiation. *Deterrence* is a theory of conflict management and a strategy aimed at preventing undesirable behavior by another group or country. Any parties contemplating action against others are deterred because the costs to them, should they strike, exceed any possible gains (Lebow 1981:83). This rational cost-benefit calculus is similar to rational choice theory with which you are familiar. This approach was paramount during the Cold War between the United States and the Soviet Union, and many argue it worked since no nuclear war ensued. Today those who advocate building defense capability as a deterrent against nuclear attacks or war align themselves with this theory.

However, many argue that deterrence will not work against terrorists because they operate under different rules of engagement. These groups are difficult to locate and willing to incur loss of lives to achieve goals. Since some current threats do not lead to the possibility of conventional warfare, deterrence has

more limited effectiveness (Kroenig and Pavel 2012; U.S. Department of Defense 2012b). Others argue that continual buildup of weapons increases mistrust and raises the potential for misunderstandings, mistakes, or disaster. Furthermore, military personnel often have a vested interest in war. The military trains for war and proves it is necessary through success in war. Business interests and economies may also profit from supporting successful wars.

The world spent $1.75 trillion on defense in 2013, with only 15 countries accounting for 79% of global defense spending. In 2013, the United States accounted for over 37% of world military spending, an estimated $640 billion. China was second, accounting for 11% of global defense spending with a budget of $188 billion. Russia was third, spending $88 billion (Keck 2014). Military spending usually comes at the expense of social programs such as education and health care, simply because there is not usually enough money to fund all these programs when the military consumes so much (Hinton 2010). Still, many people feel that protection of the citizenry is the government's most essential responsibility, and deterrence is the way to achieve security.

Negotiation is the second approach to avoiding war and involves resolving conflicts by discussions to reach agreement. For example, diplomacy and treaties have set limits on nuclear weapons and their use. President Obama has pointed out that, as well as increasing the threat of nuclear war, maintaining Cold War weapons systems is expensive and can drain weakened economies. He negotiated a treaty with Russia in 2010 that led to a reduction in deployed, long-range nuclear warheads by 30% (Sheridan and Branigin 2010; Zeleny 2009).

Many nongovernmental peace groups are active in preventing war, including protest marches, educational programs, and museum displays. The horrors depicted in the Hiroshima Peace Memorial Museum in Japan; the Killing Fields Museum in Cambodia; the Holocaust Memorial Museum in Washington, DC; the Anne Frank Museum in Amsterdam, the Netherlands; the Kigali Genocide Memorial in Rwanda; and the Korean War and Vietnam Veterans Memorials in Washington, DC, all help sensitize the public and politicians to the effects of war. Interestingly, most war memorials in the United States glorify the wars and lionize the heroes who fought in them. In Europe, many memorials stress the pathos and agony of war.

The Vietnam Veterans Memorial in Washington, DC, also sends a message about the sorrows of war. Peace advocates and veterans of the war have stood and wept together in front of that memorial.

Scholars draw several conclusions from studies of war in the past century: (a) No nation that began a major war in the 20th century emerged a clear winner; (b) in the nuclear age, war between nuclear powers could be suicidal; and (c) a victor's peace plan seldom lasts. Peace settlements negotiated on the basis of equality tend to be much more permanent and durable. Economic issues such as an inequitable distribution of resources can incite a war. Therefore, a lasting peace requires attention to at least semi-equitable distribution of resources.

As long as conflict over resources, discrimination, hunger, and poverty exist, the roots of violence are present. The world is a complex interdependent system. When the linkages between peoples are based on ideologies that stress "us" versus "them" polarities and power differentials that alienate people, then war, terrorism, and violence will not disappear from the globe.

Terrorism. "Geronimo! Bin Laden, mastermind of 9/11, is dead!" was the headline on May 2, 2011. For the 10 years since September 11, 2001, the search had been on. That was when three commercial airplanes became the missiles of terrorists, two crashing into the Twin Towers of the World Trade Center in New York City and one into the Pentagon in Washington, DC. Another crashed into the fields of Pennsylvania after the passengers heroically attacked the terrorists piloting the plane. Together more than 3,025 people from 68 nations died, and countless others were injured. This was an act of terrorism. Why did Bin Laden and his followers do it?

Terrorism refers to *the planned use of random, unlawful (or illegal) violence or threat of violence against civilians to create (or raise) fear and intimidate citizens in order to advance the terrorist group's political or ideological goals* (U.S. Department of Defense 2012a). Terrorism usually refers to acts of violence by private nonstate groups to advance revolutionary political goals, but *state terrorism* — government use of terror to control people—also proliferates. Terrorists are found at all points on the political continuum: anarchists, nationalists, religious fundamentalists, and members of ethnic advocacy groups. Worldwide, terrorist attacks rose by 43% from 2012 to 2013, killing 17,891 globally and wounding 32,577. There were almost 3,000 kidnapping and

The Vietnam Veterans Memorial in Washington, DC—like many European war memorials do—expresses and elicits a sense of the anguish and suffering of war. This man mourns the loss of a close friend and comrade.

hostage-taking victims just in 2013. Most of these terrorist activities took place outside the United States (Ackerman 2014).

What makes terrorism effective? Terrorists strike randomly and change tactics so that governments have no clear or effective way of dealing with them. This unpredictability causes public confidence in the ability of government to protect citizens and deal with crises to waver. Private terrorist groups tend to be most successful when attacking democratic governments. They seldom attack targets in oligarchic or dictatorial societies because these countries ignore their demands despite the risk to innocent civilians and hostages' lives (Frey 2004).

Why do terrorists commit hostile acts? In our anger against terrorists, we sometimes fail to look at why they commit these atrocities. Who are the terrorists, and what have they to gain? Without understanding the underlying causes of terrorism, we can do little to prevent it.

Few terrorists act completely alone. They tend to be members of or connected in some way (even if only through the Internet) to groups highly committed to an ideology or a cause—religious, political, or both. Class, ethnic, racial, or religious alienation often lies at the roots of terrorism. The ideology of terrorist groups stresses "us" versus "them" perceptions of the world, viewing "them" as evil. Those committing terrorist acts often feel victimized by more powerful forces, and sometimes, they see their lives as the only weapon they have to fight back. Many believe they have nothing to lose by committing terrorist acts, even suicidal

A protester addresses the "Bring Back Our Girls" protest group as they march to the presidential villa to deliver a protest letter to Nigeria's President Goodluck Jonathan in Abuja. The letter calls for the release of the Nigerian schoolgirls kidnapped by the Islamist militant group Boko Haram on May 22, 2014.

terrorist acts. One person's terrorist may be someone else's freedom fighter—it is in *the eye of the beholder.*

Ahmad is a 20-year-old terrorist. All his life, his family has been on the move, forced to work for others for barely a living wage, and controlled by rules made up by other people—ones that he feels are hostile to his group. When he was very young, his family's home was taken away, and the residents of his town scattered to other locations. He began to resent those who he thought had dislocated his family, put neighbors in jail, and separated him from friends and relatives. Ahmad sees little future for himself or his people, little hope for education or a career of his choosing. He feels that he has nothing to lose by joining a resistance organization to fight for what he sees as justice. Its members keep their identities secret. They are not powerful enough to mount an army to fight, so they rely on terrorist tactics against those they see as oppressors.

Ahmad puts the "greater good" of his religious and political beliefs and his group above his individual well-being. When he agrees to commit a terrorist act, he truly believes it is right and is the only way he can retaliate and bring attention to the suffering of his people. If killed, he knows he will be praised and become a martyr within his group. His family may even receive compensation for his death.

Religious and political beliefs are usually at the root of what leads terrorists to commit violent acts. Timothy McVeigh and Terry Nichols, convicted of bombing the Alfred P. Murrah Federal Building in Oklahoma City, Oklahoma, in 1995, had connections to paramilitary, antigovernment militia groups, many of which opposed government intervention in the private lives of U.S. residents. These groups are white supremacist and antigovernment (despite their fanatic pro-Americanism). Most such paramilitary groups consider themselves to be devoutly Christian, and they believe that their religion and "good intentions" justify their acts. Figure 8.4 on page 208 shows how such groups are scattered throughout the United States.

Structural explanations help predict when conditions are ripe for terrorism. Again, terrorism and war tend to be sparked by conflict and strife within and between societal systems. Ahmad learned his attitudes, hatreds, and stereotypes from his family, his friends, charismatic leaders, and media such as the Internet. These beliefs were reinforced by his leaders, religious beliefs, and schools. However, their origin was anger and economic despair.

Conflict theory explanations of terrorism lie in the unequal distribution of world resources and the oppression of minority groups. Countries such as Germany, China, and the United States and multinational corporations control immense resources and capital and have considerable economic and cultural influence and power over peripheral nations. This inequity results in feelings of alienation and hostility—and sometimes terrorism.

Terrorism, then, is a means by which those with less power can gain attention to their cause and some power in the global system, even if it involves hijackings, bombings, suicides, kidnappings, and political assassinations. Terrorists feel they are justified in their actions. The victims of these acts are understandably outraged.

Democracy comes in many forms and structures. If you want to live in a society where you have a voice, get involved in the political system and stay well informed about the policies your government is considering or has recently enacted. Political systems need diverse voices and critics—regardless of what party is currently in power—to create vibrant societies that represent the citizens.

WHAT HAVE WE LEARNED?

Political and economic systems are both sources of power and are highly interlinked. Those who have high status in one institution tend to also have high status in the other. However, some political and economic systems do a better job of producing and distributing resources, ensuring accountability of power so it is less probing, and providing checks on abuses of power.

KEY POINTS

- Power involves the ability to realize one's will, despite resistance.

- Power and economics impact our intimate (micro-level) lives, our (meso-level) organizations and institutions, and our (macro-level) national and global structures and policies.

- Leadership facilitates getting things done in any social group. It can be accomplished through raw power (coercion) or through authority (granted by the populace). Different types of leadership invest authority in the person, the position, or both.

- Various theories illuminate different aspects of political power and view policy-making processes in democracies very differently—as dominated by the power elite or as distributed among various groups so that no one group has complete power (pluralism).

- At the micro level of a political institution, individuals decide whether or not to vote or participate in politics.

- These decisions are not just individual choices but are shaped by culture and structures of the society.

- At the meso level, the political institution (when it functions well) works to resolve conflicts and to address social needs within the political system. This may be done with authoritarian or democratic structures. Within nations, meso-level political parties and policies can also have major implications for national power distribution.

- The economic system ensures production and distribution of goods in the society, and the type of economy in a society determines who has the power to plan for the future and who has access to resources.

- At the macro level, nation-states have emerged only in the past few centuries as part of modernity.

- At the global level, issues of power, access to resources, alienation, and ideology shape economic policies, war, terrorism, and the prospects for lives of peace and prosperity for citizens around the globe.

DISCUSSION QUESTIONS

1. As you were growing up, did your parents encourage you to try to influence your local community or society? Why or why not? Was their perspective on power more like the pluralist or elite theoretical perspective? Explain. How have their views about power influenced your own?

2. Is your family of origin part of what G. William Domhoff refers to as the "power elite"? What makes you think so? Are you a member of the power elite? Why or why not? If you are not, what do you think your chances are of becoming a member of the power elite, and what would you have to do? Why?

3. Do you think that large corporations have undue influence over the U.S. government? Why or why not?

4. If you had the choice, would you rather live in a society with a planned/centralized economic system, a market/capitalist economic system, or a mixed economic system? Why?

5. How do conflict theorists explain terrorism? Do you agree? Why or why not? How would you suggest the U.S. government try to stem terrorism? What theoretical perspective do you think is most helpful in terms of understanding and dealing with terrorism? Why?

CONTRIBUTING TO OUR SOCIAL WORLD: What Can We Do?

At the Local Level

- Consider getting involved in the *student government* on your campus. Most students do not know the power they have on their own campus. Organized students can have a major impact. If you would like to see something changed on your campus, establish relationships with key administrators and organize other students. Consider running for a leadership position in a student club or the student government association. Doing so will help you learn how to gain and use power and to better understand the basic principles of the democratic process.

- *Model Legislature and Model UN programs* can be found on most campuses, and are usually administered through the department of political science. Consider joining yours and gain valuable knowledge and skills in debating and governing.

- *Arrange a campus visit by a local political candidate or officeholder.* If this can be done through a sociology club, it would be especially appropriate to have the visitor discuss the political system as a social institution.

At the Organizational or Institutional Level

- *Government internships.* Consider doing an internship in your *state/provincial legislature* (www.ncsl.org/legislative-staff.aspx?tabs=856,33,816) or in *Congress* (www.senate.gov/reference/Index/Employment.htm and www.house.gov/content/educate/internships.php) with a state/provincial legislator, the governor's office (Google "governor's office," "internship," and the name of your state), or a court judge (Google "court judge," the name of your district, and "internship").

- *Special-interest parties.* Become involved in a special-interest political group such as the Green Party (www.gp.org), the Libertarian Party (www.lp.org), the Socialist Party (www.sp-usa.org), the Tea Party (www.teaparty.org), Occupy Together (www.occupytogether.org), Bread for the World (www.bread.org), People for the Ethical Treatment of Animals (www.peta.org), or any number of others.

At the National and Global Levels

- *Internships at the White House or one of the executive offices, such as the Departments of State, Agriculture, or Commerce,* can be a great learning experience. You can learn about the White House internship program and how to apply for a position at www.whitehouse.gov/about/internships. Google the name of a cabinet office to obtain contact information for the other executive offices.

- Several agencies of the *United Nations* hire interns. The general contact for relevant information is http://www.un.org/Depts/OHRM/sds/internsh.

$SAGE edge™

Sharpen your skills with SAGE edge at **edge.sagepub.com/ballantinecondensed4e**

SAGE edge for Students provides a personalized approach to help you accomplish your coursework goals in an easy-to-use learning environment.

PART Ⓥ

Social Dynamics

Social structures such as institutions tend to resist change. Nonetheless, this entire book demonstrates that societies are dynamic and changing. Institutions and organizations come alive with processes that are fluid and vibrant. Globalization, a major theme in this book, is a process bringing transformation to our social world, as shown by the very different world inhabited by our grandparents. The macro- and meso-level dimensions of society have become increasingly powerful, which is exactly why we need a sociological imagination to understand how the events in our own micro worlds are influenced by the larger society.

This section looks at some of those dynamic, fluid, and vibrant processes: population changes, urbanization, expansion of technology, social movements, and more. In periods of rapid change, understanding how and why that change occurs can help us to influence the direction those changes take in our society. From global climate change to terrorism and from new digital technologies to immigrants in our communities, we need to understand causes and consequences in order to respond constructively. To do so, we must grasp the micro-, meso-, and macro-level dimensions of change in our lives and the linkages between parts of our social world. We turn first to population dynamics.

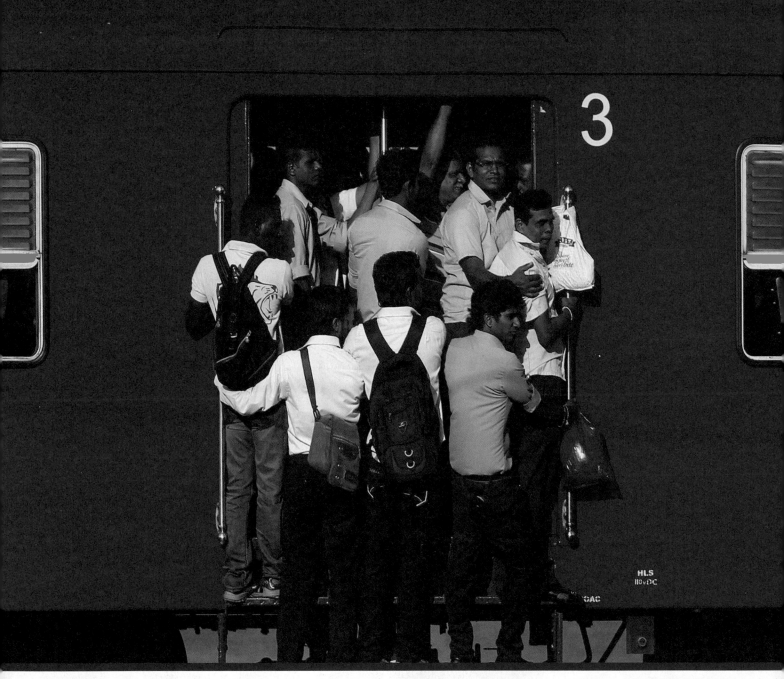

© REUTERS/ Dinuka Liyanawatte

13 Population and Urbanization

Living on Planet Earth

Humans are confined to this one moderate-sized planet on which we depend for survival. The challenges of controlling population size, migration patterns, the spread of disease, and climate change add to the need for global cooperation.

MICRO

ME (AND MY NEIGHBORS)

LOCAL ORGANIZATIONS AND COMMUNITY
Local schools and community organizations serve the local population.

MESO

NATIONAL ORGANIZATIONS, INSTITUTIONS, AND ETHNIC SUBCULTURES
Population trends influence institutions such as politics, economics, and education.

MACRO

SOCIETY
National governments set policies that influence birth incentives, birth control, and immigration.

GLOBAL COMMUNITY
Cross-national migration patterns can spread epidemics or meet pressing needs for labor.

LEARNING OBJECTIVES

13.1 Illustrate the pattern of the world's population growth over time.

13.2 Discuss the relationship between institutions and population patterns including fertility, mortality, and migration.

13.3 Describe individual decisions that affect population patterns.

13.4 Explain national and global urbanization trends.

13.5 Predict the environmental and other impacts of human movements to urban areas.

THINK ABOUT IT

Micro: Local Community	What is the population profile of your hometown: economic status of residents, ethnic and racial composition, recent immigrant groups? Where do you fit into that population profile?
Meso: National Institutions; Complex Organizations; Ethnic Groups	Why do people move from rural areas to urban areas? What problems might this pattern of movement create?
Macro: National and Global System	How do global issues relating to demographic changes, urbanization, and the environment affect your family and your local community?

When Sally Ride, the first U.S. woman in space, looked down at Earth, she, like other astronauts who have the opportunity to see the planet from far above, experienced the "overview effect." This occurs when Earth is viewed from a new angle, from the perspective of space. Ride described the impact it had on her:

Mountain ranges, volcanoes, and river deltas appeared in salt-and-flour relief, all leading me to assume the role of a novice geologist. In such moments, it was easy to imagine the dynamic upheavals that created jutting mountain ranges and the internal wrenching that created rifts and seas. I also became an instant believer in plate tectonics; India really is crashing into Asia, and Saudi Arabia and Egypt really are pulling apart, making the Red Sea wider. Even though their respective motion is really no more than mere inches a year, the view from overhead makes theory come alive. (Quoted in Beaver 2012)

Ride's perspective changed, and thus, her ability to recognize and understand the world also changed. Ride saw and noticed things she had not seen or noticed before, because of this new view of the world. In this chapter, you will learn to observe changes in the world's population from a sociological perspective and, in the process, see and notice patterns you may not have paid attention to before.

Since the emergence of *Homo sapiens* in East Africa almost 200,000 years ago, human populations have grown in uneven surges and declines due to births, deaths, and migrations. The World Population Clock (see Table 13.1) illustrates the current state of the human population. As you can see, there are now more than 7 billion people on Earth, and the number is increasing rapidly.

TABLE 13.1 Population Clock, 2013 (in Thousands)

	World	Global South	Global North
Population	7,136,796	5,890,885	1,245,911
Births per day	390,696	352,521	38,175
Births per year	142,634	128,670	13,934
Deaths per day	153	120	34
Deaths per year	55,973	43,668	12,305
Infant deaths per day	15,789	15,597	193
Natural annual increase	86,661	85,002	1,629

Source: Haub, Carl and Toshiko Kaneda, 2013. *World Population Data Sheet.* Washington, DC: Population Reference Bureau 2013.

The world's human population grew sporadically over the millennia, but the explosion of human beings on the planet in the past 2.5 centuries is stunning. If we collapsed all human history into one 24-hour day, the time period since 1750 would consume 1 minute. Yet 25% of all humans have lived during this 1-minute time period. In the 200 years between 1750 and 1950, the world's population mushroomed from 800 million to 2.5 billion. On October 12, 1999, the global population reached 6 billion. It has now expanded to over 7.2 billion with almost all of the latest growth in the Global South (Population Reference Bureau 2012a; Worldometers 2014).

Let us start by focusing on one area of our world, Kenya in East Africa. We begin here partly because East Africa, where Kenya and Tanzania are located, is believed to be home to Earth's earliest human inhabitants. Scientists believe that bones found in the dry Olduvai Gorge area are the oldest remains of *Homo sapiens* ever recovered. We also focus here because today Kenya is making human history for another reason. With a population of 45 million people, and a growth rate of 2.11% annually, Kenya has one of the most rapidly growing populations on Earth (World Factbook 2014h). Kenya is made up of many tribal groups. With different religions and value systems, the tribes have clashed in power struggles in recent years. Still, there are several themes that pervade most Kenyan subcultures, as illustrated by the following example.

Wengari, like Kenyan girls of most tribal affiliations, married in her teens. She has been socialized to believe that her main purpose in life is to bear children, to help with the farming, and to care for parents in their old age. Children are seen as an asset in Kenya. Religious beliefs and cultural value systems encourage large families. However, due to high birthrates and high death rates caused by AIDS, the working-age population has declined and cannot continue to feed the growing population. Almost half (44.8%) of the Kenyan population consists of *dependents:* people under 15 or over 65 years of age, who rely on working-age citizens to support them (World Factbook 2014h). Almost all of the dependent population consists of children under 15, rather than adults over 65 (42.1% compared to 2.7% of the population). Adding to Kenya's problems are severe droughts that kill animal herds and destroy crops. These facts, however, have little impact on the behavior of young women like Wengari, who, socialized to conform to the female role within their society, plan on having many children.

By contrast, far to the north in many of the industrialized, urbanized countries of Europe, birthrates are

Changes in the environment and in the global economy compel these Kenyan children to join the worldwide urbanization trend and move to the nearest city in search of work. Much of the socialization they receive in villages will not be relevant to their adult urban lives.

below population replacement levels, meaning population size has begun to drop. The population growth rate in Germany is 0.19%, in France 0.47%, and in the United Kingdom 0.55%. Russia, Hungary, Latvia, the Czech Republic, and many other countries in Eastern Europe are also losing population (IndexMundi 2013). Germany, the most prosperous nation in Europe, does not have enough working-age people to support the pensions of older Germans. Much of Europe faces this problem (Daley and Kulish 2013).

While Asia's share of world population may continue to hover around 60% through the next century, Europe's portion has declined sharply and will likely drop even more during the rest of the 21st century. Africa and Latin America each will gain part of Europe's portion. By 2100, Africa is expected to capture the greatest share. Countries outside of Europe growing by less than 1% annually include Japan, Australia, New Zealand, and Russia (Population Reference Bureau 2013a).

As societies develop, birthrates tend to go down. For example, typical European young people often wait until their late 20s or even 30s to start a family, postponing children until their education is complete and a job is in hand. Moreover, they have access to effective birth control options, widely used throughout their societies. Unlike many children in the Global South, most children born in Europe will survive to old age. Parents do not feel as though they must have many children in order to see some grow to maturity. **Life expectancy**, the *number of years a person in a particular society can expect to live,* is 63.5 years in Kenya (World Factbook 2014h). In Japan and some European countries, it is more than 82 years.

The overcrowding in some cities means that governments have a difficult time providing the infrastructure and services needed for the growing urban population. Rio de Janeiro, Brazil, is one example.

China, the country with the largest population in the world (1.35 billion people), had the greatest drop in population growth in the late 20th century, due to strict governmental family planning practices (World Factbook 2014c). India, the second-largest country, has a current population growth rate (increase in a country's population during a specified period of time) of 1.25% a year, just over replacement level (World Factbook 2014f).

Although some countries have birthrates below population replacement levels, the world's population continues to grow because of the skyrocketing growth rate in other countries and because of *population momentum* caused by the large number of individuals of childbearing age having children. After a baby boom, even though birthrates per couple may drop, the number of women of childbearing age becomes very high, resulting in continued growth in population size. Most of the countries with the highest growth rates are in the Global South, where societies value large families, and have less access to birth control and fewer resources to support the additional population.

⬤ Thinking Sociologically

Do you have a choice in how many children you have or will have? Explain. If you do, what factors go into your decision? How might your decision differ if you lived in a different country? Should global patterns—which include food shortages and climate change—be a consideration in the size of your family and your neighbors' families? Why or why not?

We know the information above thanks to research gained through **demography**, *the study of human populations*. When demographers speak of **populations**, they mean *all permanent societies, states, communities, adherents of a common religious faith, racial or ethnic groups, kinship or clan groups,* *professions, and other identifiable categories of people*. Demographers examine various aspects of a population, including the size, location, movement, concentration in certain geographical areas, and changing characteristics. For example, the next "Engaging Sociology" asks you to imagine that the entire world population was only 100 people and look at how it would be composed given the current distribution of certain characteristics.

With few jobs to support populations in rural areas (areas outside of cities and their surrounding suburbs), many people move to cities in hopes of finding employment. This *pattern of movement from rural areas to cities* is called **urbanization**. The second half of this chapter will consider the evolution, growth, and development of populated areas, including movements from rural areas to cities, the organization of micro-level urban life, the relationship between individuals and the city, and some problems facing cities. The previous chapters have moved from micro- to macro-level analysis, but in this chapter, because of the nature of the material and the need to explain certain issues before the micro issues make sense, we discuss macro-level patterns in world population growth first. We then describe meso-level institutional influences on population, and micro-level factors affecting population patterns.

MACRO-LEVEL PATTERNS IN WORLD POPULATION GROWTH

Above, we noted that Global North societies tend to see reduced population growth as they continue to develop. What happens before this, though? Why did the world's population grow so slowly and then, recently, so rapidly?

ENGAGING SOCIOLOGY

If the World Were 100 People

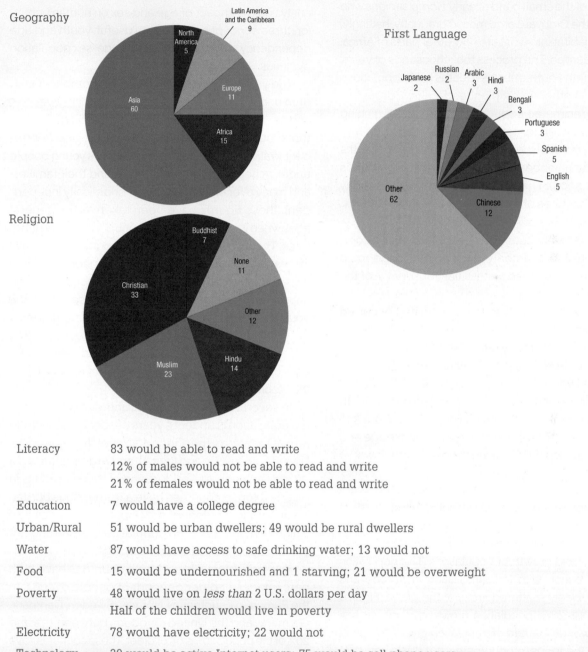

Geography

Latin America and the Caribbean 9

North America 5

Europe 11

Asia 60

Africa 15

First Language

Japanese 2

Russian 2

Arabic 3

Hindi 3

Bengali 3

Portuguese 3

Spanish 5

English 5

Other 62

Chinese 12

Religion

Buddhist 7

None 11

Christian 33

Other 12

Hindu 14

Muslim 23

Literacy	83 would be able to read and write
	12% of males would not be able to read and write
	21% of females would not be able to read and write
Education	7 would have a college degree
Urban/Rural	51 would be urban dwellers; 49 would be rural dwellers
Water	87 would have access to safe drinking water; 13 would not
Food	15 would be undernourished and 1 starving; 21 would be overweight
Poverty	48 would live on *less than* 2 U.S. dollars per day
	Half of the children would live in poverty
Electricity	78 would have electricity; 22 would not
Technology	30 would be active Internet users; 75 would be cell phone users

Engaging With Sociology

1. Did any of these facts surprise you? If so, which ones? Why? If not, where did you learn these facts before?

2. In which ways are you highly privileged compared to most others in the world?

3. Which of the factors in this list cause the most suffering?

4. If you were a public sociologist and could improve two of these factors, which ones would you focus on? Why?

Sociologists look for patterns in population growth over time to answer these demographic questions.

Patterns of Population Growth Over Time

Members of the small band of early *Homo sapiens* who inhabited the Olduvai Gorge moved gradually, haltingly, from this habitat into what are now other parts of Africa, Asia, and Europe. The process took thousands of years. At times, births outnumbered deaths and populations grew, but at other times, plagues, famines, droughts, and wars decimated populations. From the beginning of human existence, estimated as perhaps one million years ago, until modern times, the number of births and deaths balanced each other over the centuries (Diamond 2005). The large population we see today resulted from three phases of population evolution:

1. Humans, because of their thinking ability, competed satisfactorily in the animal kingdom to obtain the basic necessities for survival of the species.
2. With the agricultural revolution that occurred about 10,000 years ago and the resulting food surplus, mortality rates declined, and the population grew as more infants survived and people lived longer.
3. The biggest increase in population came with the Industrial Revolution, beginning about 300 years ago. Improved medical knowledge and sanitation helped bring the death rate down.

Industrialization not only brought about the social and economic changes in societies discussed in Chapter 3 (e.g., machines replacing human labor and mass production using resources in new ways); it also led to the rapid growth of populations. The population explosion began with industrialization in Europe and spread to widely scattered areas of the globe. Figures 13.1 and 13.2 show population growth throughout history. The worldwide *rate* of population growth reached its peak in the 1960s (Worldometers 2014). We now take a closer look at factors that impact population growth.

Predictors of Population Growth

Think for a moment about the impact that your age and sex have on your position in society and your activities. Are you of childbearing age? Are you dependent on others for most of your needs, or are you supporting others? Your status is largely due to your age and sex, and what they mean in your society. These demographic variables greatly influence your behavior and the behavior of others like you, and collectively they shape the population patterns of an entire society. In analyzing the impact of age and sex on human behavior, three concepts can be very useful: youth and age dependency ratios, sex ratios, and age-sex population pyramids.

The *youth dependency ratio* is the number of children under age 15 divided by the number between 15 and 64. The number of those older than 64 divided by those between 15 and 64 is called the *age dependency ratio*. Although many of the world's young people under 15 help support themselves and their families, and many over 64 are likewise economically independent, these figures have been taken as the general ages when individuals are not contributing to the labor force. They represent the economic burden (especially in wealthy countries) of people in the population who must be supported by the working-age population. The **dependency ratio**, then, is *the ratio of those in both the young and aged groups compared with the number of people in the productive age groups between 15 and 64 years old.* Today, 90% of those in the world between the ages of 10 and 24, many of whom are dependent, live in the Global South (Sengupta 2014).

In several resource-poor countries nearly half of the population is under 15 years of age. These include Kenya (42.1%, as mentioned above), Niger (49.8%), Uganda (48.7%), Congo (43.1%), and Afghanistan (42%) (World Factbook 2014h, j, k, d, and a). Working adults in less developed countries have a tremendous burden in supporting the dependent population, especially if a high percentage of the population is urban and not able to support itself through farming.

Similarly, most Global North countries have high percentages of older dependent people over 64. In the European countries of Norway, Sweden, Denmark, Germany, and the United Kingdom, between 15% and 20% of the population is 65 or older. These countries have low death rates, resulting in the average life expectancy at birth being as high as 82.8 in Switzerland, followed by Japan, Italy, and Spain at 82.7 years (UPI 2014).

Consider the case of Japan, which faces the problem of its "graying" or aging population. In 2014, 24.8% of its population was 65 or older, and the average life expectancy had topped 84 years (World Factbook

FIGURE 13.1 The Exponential World Population Growth From About 8000 BCE to the 21st Century

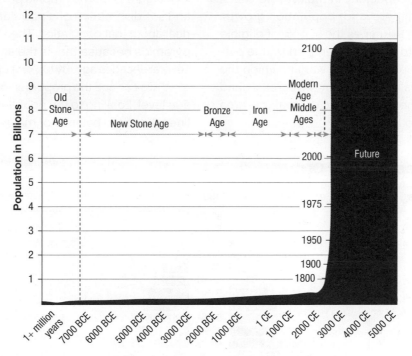

Source: Adapted from Fig. 2.12 in Abu-Lughod, Janet L. 1991. *Changing Cities: Urban Sociology.* New York: HarperCollins.

FIGURE 13.2 World Population Growth Rate, 1950–2050

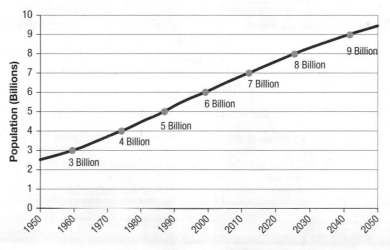

Source: U.S. Census Bureau 2012c.

2014i). The death rate is higher than the birthrate, and the population is shrinking in size. Only 13.2% of the population is under 15 years old. With a declining population and almost no influx of immigrants, there are not enough replacement workers to support the aging population. Japan may provide a glimpse into the future for other rapidly aging societies, including Germany, the United States, and China. These different societies, however, vary in their approach to immigration and population control policies, which will impact both the demographic challenges they face and how they handle them (see Figure 13.3 on page 360 for a vivid depiction of the expected transformation in one century).

The *sex ratio* refers to the ratio of males to females in the population. For instance, the more females there are, especially in their fertile years, the more potential there is for population growth. The sex ratio also determines the supply of eligible spouses. Other factors that influence marriage patterns include economic cycles, wars in which the proportion of males to females may decrease, and migrations that generally take males from one area and add them to another.

Population pyramids *are pyramid-shaped diagrams that illustrate sex ratios and dependency ratios* (see Figure 13.4). The graphic presentation of the age and sex distribution of a population tells us a great deal about that population. The structures are called pyramids because that is the shape they took until several decades ago. By looking up and down the pyramid, we can see the proportion of population at each age level. Looking to the right and left of the centerline tells us the balance of males to females at each

FIGURE 13.3 Japan Grows Old

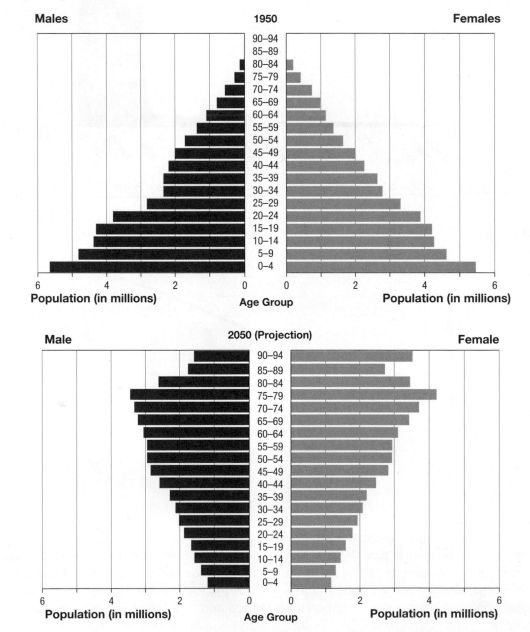

Source: Statistical Handbook of Japan 2010. 1950 pyramid is based on data from the results of the survey of the Statistics Bureau of Japan. 2050 pyramid is based on data of the National Institute of Population and Social Security Research, the Ministry of Health, Labour and Welfare.

age. The bottom line shows us the total population at each age.

The first pyramid shows the population of Germany with low birthrates and death rates. This is typical of Global North countries. The second pyramid—Uganda—is typical of Global South countries and illustrates populations with high birthrates and large dependent youth populations. As these images show,

the world population has been getting both younger (the Global South) *and* older (the Global North), resulting in large numbers of people dependent on the working-age population between 15 and 65 years of age. As Global South nations have more and more children, they create more potential parents in later years, adding momentum to the world's population growth. Fewer deaths of infants and children, due to

FIGURE 13.4 Population Pyramids in Global North (Germany) and Global South (Uganda) Countries in 2014

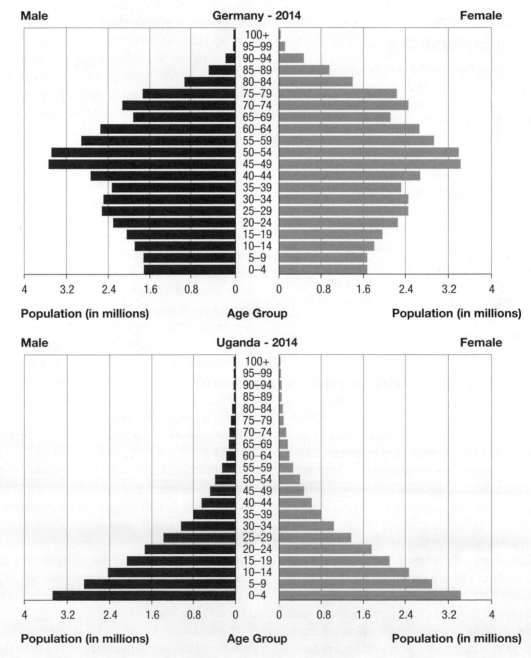

Source: SlideShare 2014.

immunizations and disease control, result in lower mortality rates, younger populations, and higher potential numbers of births in the future.

Thinking Sociologically

Consider your own country's population pyramid. You can find it at www.census.gov/population/interna tional. What can you tell about your country's level of development by studying the population pyramid? How might societies differ if they have a young versus old population?

Population Patterns: Theoretical Explanations

The earliest historical writings reveal that interest in population size is nothing new. Scriptures written many centuries ago, such as the Quran and the Bible, encourage population growth to increase the ranks of the faithful. Of course, population expansion made sense at the time these holy tracts were written, and populations grew slowly. Government leaders throughout the ages have adopted various philosophies about the best size of populations. The ancient Greek philosopher Plato argued that the ideal city-state should have 5,040 citizens and that measures should be taken to increase or decrease the population to bring it in line with this figure (Plato [350 BCE] 1960). However, the first significant scholarly analysis that addressed global population issues came from Thomas Malthus (1766–1834), an English clergyman and social philosopher.

Malthus's Theory of Population. In his *Essay on the Principle of Population*, Malthus argued that humans are driven to reproduce and will multiply excessively without checks imposed to slow population growth (Malthus [1798] 1926). He noted that an unchecked population increases geometrically: 2 parents could have 4 children, 16 grandchildren, 64 great-grandchildren, and so forth—just with a continuous average family size of 4 children. Meanwhile, the means of subsistence (food) increases at best only arithmetically or lineally (5, 10, 15, 20, 25). Therefore, population growth must be controlled. Malthus described two types of checks that control population growth—positive checks that lead to higher death rates (wars, disease, epidemics, and food shortages leading to famine), and preventative

checks that result in lower birthrates (delaying marriage and practicing abstinence). Hoping to avoid the positive checks, Malthus advocated for implementing the preventative checks. He did not approve of contraception, viewing it as immoral.

Contemporary neo-Malthusians like Paul and Anne Ehrlich favor contraception rather than simple reliance on the moral restraint that Malthus proposed. They also add to the formula of "too many people and too little food" the additional problem of a "dying planet"—caused by environmental damage. They argue that "the human predicament is driven by overpopulation, overconsumption of natural resources and the use of unnecessarily environmentally damaging technologies and socio-economic-political arrangements to service Homo Sapiens' aggregate consumption." Successfully addressing these threats and avoiding the "collapse" of global society will require dramatic cultural and political shifts across the world (Ehrlich and Ehrlich 1990, 2013:1).

Looking at the world today, we see examples of the "positive" population checks described by Malthus. War decimated the populations of several countries during the world wars and has taken its toll on other countries in Central and Eastern Europe, Africa, and the Middle East since then. Waterborne diseases such as cholera and typhus strike after floods, and the floods themselves are often caused by large populations clearing and using almost all of the trees in their environment for fuel and building materials. In 2013 and 2014 alone, famines necessitated food aid in many countries including the Central African Republic, South Sudan, Syria, Somalia, and West Africa. Bosnia may require food aid after severe flooding (World Famine Timeline 2014).

Disease has also taken a toll on the world's population. In some villages in sub-Saharan and East African countries, AIDS has wiped out large percentages of the population, and many children must fend for themselves. Orphaned children take care of their younger siblings. PEPFAR (President's Emergency Plan for AIDS Relief), begun under President George W. Bush and continued under President Barack Obama, distributes generic forms of antiviral drugs to those with AIDS, and has helped bring the death toll down by 1.2 million. Without this relief effort, the loss of life would be even more staggering in this region of the world (Aguirre 2012).

While Malthus's work raised many issues still discussed today, his pessimistic vision of the future has not come to pass. He overemphasized *environmental determinism*, the idea that we can do little about the environment because it controls our lives. Malthus and neo-Malthusians were not able to anticipate the advances in agriculture that have increased the food supply tremendously. Nor did they foresee the importance of vaccines in controlling diseases. However, they have raised important issues that have helped government leaders in many parts of the world become aware of the need to plan for and take steps to control population growth (Bell 2012).

Thinking Sociologically

What are contemporary examples of what Malthus described as "positive" checks on population growth—war, disease, famine? Are family planning and contraception (a) suitable and (b) sufficient means to solve the problem of global overpopulation by humans? Can you think of other alternatives?

Demographic Transition: Explaining Population Growth and Expansion.

Why should a change in the economic structure such as industrialization and movement from rural agricultural areas to cities have an impact on population size? The **demographic transition theory**, *which links trends in birthrates and death rates with patterns of economic and technological development, offers one explanation.*

This theory identifies four clear stages of development and posits that a fifth one is in process: These stages are illustrated in Figure 13.5.

Stage 1: Populations have *high birthrates and death rates that tend to balance each other* over time. Births may outpace deaths until some disaster diminishes the increase. This has been the pattern for most of human history.

Stage 2: Populations still have high birthrates, but death rates decline (i.e., more people live longer) because of improvements in health care and sanitation, establishment of public health programs, disease control and immunizations, and food availability and distribution. This imbalance between the continuing high number of births and the declining number of deaths means that the *population growth rate is very high.*

Stage 3: *Populations begin to level off* due to access to contraception, wage increases, urbanization, increases in education levels and the status of women, and other changes. Most industrial societies are in this stage.

Stage 4: *Birthrates and death rates are both low.* Birthrates in some Global North countries drop below replacement level, resulting in declining population. Death rates remain fairly constant and low, though lifestyle diseases caused by smoking, obesity, and lack of exercise may increase death rates in some areas.

FIGURE 13.5 Stages of Demographic Transition

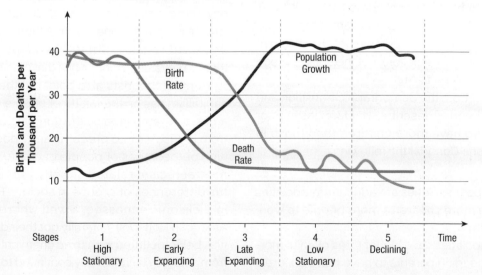

Stage 5: This stage has not yet come into full existence, but many demographers predict it will. As death rates remain stable and birthrates decline, the total population will begin to decrease for the first time. Japan and Germany are in the beginning of Stage 5.

Demographic transition theory helps explain the developmental stages and population trends in countries around the world, but it does not consider some important factors that affect the size of populations:

1. People's age at marriage determines how many childbearing years they have (late marriage means fewer years until menopause).
2. Contraceptive availability determines whether families can control their number of children.
3. A country's resources and land may determine how much population it can support.
4. The economic structure, religious beliefs, and political philosophies of a country affect attitudes toward birth control and family size.
5. Economic expansion rates influence a country's need for labor and its ability to create jobs.

The *wealth flow theory* suggests that two possible strategies operate in couples' personal decisions about family size. When wealth flows from children to parents—that is, when children are an asset working on the family farm or laboring—parents have larger families. When wealth flows from parents to children, families tend to have fewer children (Caldwell 1982). To raise a child born in 2012 to 18 years in the United States, for instance, costs an average of more than $301,970 (adjusted for inflation), not including college expenses (Willis Report 2014).

Elements of both the demographic transition and wealth flow theories describe why families in poor nations tend to have more children than those in wealthier nations. Consider the following:

1. Many poor societies are agricultural societies where more children = more people to work the farm.
2. Poor societies have higher rates of child mortality (leading parents to have more children,

because they know some are likely to die at a young age).
3. Girls in poor societies tend to leave school early (if they attend at all), and to marry at a young age, leading to early childbearing.
4. Artificial contraception tends to be less available in poor nations.

With these facts in mind, Jeffry Sachs, an economist and leading expert on world poverty, advocates (along with many other social scientists) for efforts to keep girls in school longer and to improve health care and access to contraceptives in poor nations (Sachs 2011).

Conflict Theorists' Explanations of Population Growth. Karl Marx did not agree with Malthus's idea that high fertility rates and population growth that outstrips food and resources produce poverty. He believed that social and structural factors built into the economic system—inequitable distribution and control of resources—cause poverty. Capitalist structures lead to wealth for the owners and create overpopulation and poverty for workers. Workers are expendable, kept in competition for low wages, used when needed, and let go when unprofitable to capitalists (Marx [1844] 2009).

Socialist societies, Marx argued, could absorb the growth in population so the problem of overpopulation would not exist. In a classless society, all would be able to find jobs, and the system would expand to include everyone (Magnus 2009). Marx's writing partner Friedrich Engels asserted that population growth in socialist societies could be controlled by the central government, as was done by the Chinese government when it imposed a "one child per family" policy in 1979 (Marx and Engels [1881] 1975). (The policy has gone through several revisions since that time.)

Conflict theorists also point out the impact that capitalism has on the health of people living in poor areas, as exemplified by the dumping of toxic waste from industries into predominantly poor areas with high percentages of people of color. This *environmental racism* relates directly to the social status differences of groups in society. For example, in Dickson, Tennessee, a well where the African American Holt-Orsted family got their drinking water was being polluted with toxic chemicals that leaked from a nearby landfill. They continued to use this well,

Overpopulation presents a challenge to food and water resources, and large populations damage the environment and provide little ecological recovery time. Smog from fires, factories, and automobiles (left)—called "brown haze"—routinely hovers over Cape Town, South Africa, in the morning. A billboard in Shanghai (right) advertises China's "one child per family" policy.

unaware of any problems, for nine years. Although some of the neighbors—those who were white—were notified within 48 hours after local waste treatment agencies learned of the danger (in 1993), the Holt-Orsted family was not informed and in fact was told by county officials that things were fine (Holt 2007; Huang 2011). By the time Sheila Holt-Orsted was finally informed (in 2002) that the water the family had been using for showers, cooking, and beverages was contaminated with cancer-causing agents, Sheila had breast cancer and her father had terminal prostate cancer. Four additional Holt-Orsted family members suffered from various other illnesses believed to be caused by the spills into the water supply. The family finally won their court case in 2011, but by then several family members had died from cancer (Holt 2007; Huang 2011). People of color are two to three times more likely to live in communities with hazardous waste problems. It has become a pressing issue in poor minority areas where housing was built on contaminated land (Bell 2012). A race- and class-based distribution of environmentally hazardous materials, as seen in the location of toxic dumps and landfills in predominantly poor and minority communities, occurs in countries across the world.

Of the many examples of environmental racism in the United States, consider the following: In Los Angeles, some minority schools are located in areas with high levels of airborne toxins; in Missouri, industrial-scale hog farms can be found in low-income counties; in Massachusetts, communities with high proportions of low-income minorities are 10 times more likely to experience chemical releases from industries than high-income communities. Other low-quality-of-life indicators like poor-quality drinking water and noise pollution from highways are common in low-income and minority neighborhoods (Bell 2012). One classic study in Chicago focused on the impact of efforts to make Chicago a more eco-friendly or "green" city by encouraging more recycling. However, there were substantial problems of pollution, disease risk, and other costs to the neighborhoods where the recycling plants were located (Pellow 2002). Those involved in the *environmental justice movement* work to address such problems.

In a similar vein, if you sent your old computer to a recycling center, there is a good chance it ended up in a West African dump. To save money, many electronic recycling centers in Global North nations illegally send what they take in to Global South nations like Ghana, where governments are unable or unwilling to stop dumps from taking in e-waste. In a dump in Accra, the capital of Ghana, teenage boys can be seen smashing old computers and other electronic devices so that they can sell the metals inside to local businesses. Exposed to the chemicals that leach out of the abandoned computers, they are being poisoned and injuring their health. It is sobering to realize that environmentally friendly policies (recycling or donating—rather than throwing away—electronic devices) aimed at prolonging the health of Earth and the human population have often been implemented in ways that hurt those who have the fewest resources—people living in poverty and minorities (Hugo 2010; Korgen and Gallagher 2013).

MESO-LEVEL INSTITUTIONAL INFLUENCES ON POPULATION CHANGE

Meso-level analysis focuses on institutions and ethnic subcultures within a country. In this section we examine how institutions influence birthrates and other population patterns. Populations change in three main ways: (1) *size* (overall number of people), (2) *composition* (the makeup of the population, including sex ratio, age distribution, and religious or ethnic representation in the population), and (3) *distribution* (density or concentration in various portions of the land).

The key *demographic processes* that cause population changes are **fertility** (*the birthrate*), **mortality** (*the death rate*), and **migration** (*movement of people from one place to another*). Populations change when births and deaths are not evenly balanced or when significant numbers of people move from one area to another. Migration does not change the size or composition of the world as a whole, but can affect size or makeup in a micro- (family), meso- (institution or ethnic subculture), or macro-level (national) population. Fertility is the most easily controllable factor impacting population change.

Institutions and Population Patterns

Jeanne, one of the coauthors of this book, was riding in the back of a "mammy wagon," a common means

In an urban area in Cambodia (Kampuchea), residents crowd onto this truck, a common form of transportation. With a high fertility rate and migration from rural to urban areas, crowded transportation is common.

of transport in West Africa. Crowded in with the chickens and pigs and people, she did not expect the conversation that ensued. The man in his late 20s asked if she was married and for how long. Jeanne responded, "Yes, for three years." The man continued, "How many children do you have?" Jeanne answered, "None." The man commented, "Oh, I'm sorry!" Jeanne replied, "No, don't be sorry. We planned it that way!" This man had been married for 10 years to a woman 3 years younger than him and had eight children. The ninth was on the way. In answer to his pointed questions, Jeanne explained that she was not being cruel to her husband and that birth control was what prevented children, and no, it did not make sex less enjoyable. He expressed surprise that limiting the number of children was possible and rather liked the idea. He jumped at the suggestion that he visit the family planning clinic in the city. With his meager income, he and his wife were finding it hard to feed all their children. This story helps to illustrate the fact that knowledge of and access to family planning options are not uniformly available. Institutions affect access to those services.

Demographers consider micro-, meso-, and macro-level factors in attempting to understand fertility rates around the world. We know that personal knowledge and access are key factors. Couples' decisions to use or not use contraception, their ideas about the acceptability of abortion, and whether they want to have children (and how many) can also have an impact on national and global rates of population change. So choices at the micro level make a difference at the macro level. Consider the following meso-level institutional factors affecting the size of the population.

Economic Factors and Population Patterns. Fertility fluctuates with actions in meso-level institutions such as the economy and the government. During economic depressions, for example, the rate of fertility tends to drop due to lack of family resources. Thus, meso-level structural factors—including level of economic prosperity within the nation, government policies to encourage or discourage births, changes in norms and values about sexuality within a society, and access to health care—all influence decisions within families about fertility.

Political Systems and Population Patterns. Some governments provide incentives to parents to have more children through *pronatalist policies* (those that encourage fertility), while others discourage high fertility with *antinatalist policies* (those that discourage fertility). Thus, meso-level social policies established by the political system can shape decisions of families at the micro level. Government policies can take several forms: (1) manipulating contraceptive availability; (2) promoting change in factors that affect fertility such as the status of women, education, availability of abortion, and degree of economic development; (3) using propaganda for or against having children; (4) creating incentives (maternity leaves, benefits, and tax breaks) or penalties (such as fines) for having children; and (5) passing laws governing age of marriage, size of family, contraception, and abortion.

Antinatalist policies arise out of concern over available resources and differences in birthrates among population subgroups. Singapore, a small island country in Asia, consists of one main island and many smaller islands. It is one of the most crowded places on Earth, with 7,405 people per square kilometer (compared to 34 in the United States, 4 in Canada, and 351 in Japan) (World Bank 2013c). The entire population of Singapore is urban, and 90% live in the capital city. The country has little unemployment and one of the highest per capita incomes in Asia. However, it depends on imports from other countries for most of its raw materials and food.

Some years ago, the central government in Singapore started an aggressive antinatalist plan. It made birth control widely available, and residents of Singapore who had more than two children were penalized with less health care, smaller housing, and higher costs for services such as education. As a result of these policies, Singapore now claims one of the lowest natural increase rates (the birthrate minus the death rate) in Southeast Asia, at 0.6% a year (Population Reference Bureau 2013a).

Examples of pronatalist government policies can be seen in Eastern Europe where governments are worried about the drop in birthrates. There are fewer young people to pay taxes and to do jobs needed in the society. Pronatalist policies established to raise birthrates include giving workers a day off to "have sex"; free summer camps for young couples—without condoms; cars and monetary gifts for new parents; and additional benefits for parents and their children. Abortions and even birth control have been restricted in some Eastern European countries to curb dropping population numbers (Stracansky 2013).

In the United States, it is sometimes hard to pin a simple label of antinatalist or pronatalist on the administration in power. Presidents Ronald Reagan, George H. W. Bush, and George W. Bush each implemented a "gag rule" (requiring parental notification) that limited the availability of birth control for teens in the United States. Presidents Bill Clinton and Barack Obama each eliminated the gag policy. On the other hand, President Clinton signed the Family and Medical Leave Act, which allows employees (in organizations with 50 or more employees) to take up to 12 weeks of (unpaid) leave to take care of a family member, without risk of losing their job.

While family planning programs and contraceptive use have increased in much of the world, availability and use in sub-Saharan Africa remains low. Global use of modern contraception was 57% in 2012, but 222 million Global South women who would like to control family size are not using contraception because of limited access and knowledge, fear of side effects, cultural or religious opposition, and gender-based barriers (World Health Organization [WHO] 2012a). The vast majority of the 16 million girls between 15 and 19 who give birth each year live in Global South countries (WHO 2014).

Thinking Sociologically

Do you think it is appropriate for governments to use enticements or penalties to encourage or discourage fertility decisions by couples? Why or why not? Identify several positive and several negative repercussions of either pronatalist or antinatalist policies discussed above.

Religion and Population Patterns. Religion is a primary shaper of norms and values in most societies, including those related to fertility. In some societies, children born out of wedlock are accepted into the mother's family. In other societies, a woman can be stoned to death for having a child or even sex out of wedlock.

Some religious groups oppose any intervention, such as birth control or abortion, in the natural processes of conception and birth. Roman Catholicism, for example, teaches that large families are a blessing from God and that artificial birth control is a sin. The Roman Catholic Church officially advocates natural family planning (NFP) to regulate conception, a less reliable method than artificial birth control, using

Nur Azizah binti Hanafiah, 22, receives a punishment of caning for having premarital sex with her boyfriend. Her community in the Aceh region of Indonesia follows a form of Islamic Sharia law. In some societies, she would have been stoned to death for having premarital sex.

medication, or physical barriers. Many Catholics, however, do use artificial birth control methods. In the United States, only 2% of Catholics rely on NFP while almost 70% rely on the birth control pill, an IUD (intra-uterine device), or sterilization to control their fertility (Guttmacher Institute 2013). Almost all (99%) of the sexually active women in the United States have used some form of contraception.

Education and Population. If a country wants to control population growth, providing better access to schools and raising the education level of women is a key to success. The higher women's status in society—as measured by education level and job opportunities—the lower their fertility (Population Reference Bureau 2013b). Figure 13.6 shows the relationship between education and family size in five Global South countries (Population Reference Bureau 2012b). Note that the higher the education level, the lower the fertility rate and population growth.

Lower population growth means less pressure on governments to provide emergency services, such as food and water rations, for booming populations, and more attention to services such as schools, health care, and jobs. Most population experts encourage governments and other meso-level institutions in fast-growing countries to act aggressively to control population size. Consequences of population fluctuations affect affluent parts of the world as well as poor parts.

Factors Affecting Mortality Rates

Recall that life expectancy refers to the average number of years a person in a particular society can expect to live. It indicates the overall health conditions in a country. Imagine living in Chad, Africa, where the life expectancy at birth is 49.44 years. In this low-income, largely agricultural society, families tend to have many children (4.68, on average, or 37.3 per 1,000 population). Of every 1,000 babies born alive, 90.3 will die within the first year. Over 72% of men and women live in rural areas, where most are subsistence farmers, working small plots that may not provide enough food to keep their families from starving (World Factbook 2014b). When one plot is overfarmed

FIGURE 13.6 Women's Education and Family Size—Selected Countries

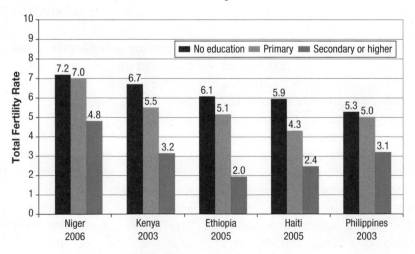

Source: Population Reference Bureau 2012b.

A sick and displaced Chadian woman watches as her malnourished infant sleeps at a health clinic run by Doctors Without Borders. This mother knows that life expectancy for her child is less than 50 years.

and the soil depleted so that plants will no longer grow, the family moves to another and clears the land, depleting more arable land. This scenario repeats itself, leading to little arable land, shortages of food, malnutrition, and a population susceptible to illnesses

FIGURE 13.7 Infant Mortality Rates Around the World (Deaths per 1,000 Live Births)

Region	Infant Mortality Rate
World	41
More affluent (Global North) countries	5
Less affluent (Global South) countries	49
Least affluent (the very poor Global South)	72
Africa	67
North America	6
Latin America	20
Asia	37
Europe	5

Source: UNICEF 2013. Levels and Trends in Child Mortality, Report 2013. Estimates Developed by the UN Inter-agency Group for Child Mortality Estimation. Copyright © 2013 by the United Nations Children's Fund.

Migration

and disease. The limited medical care that exists is mostly available in urban areas.

Some other African countries face similar situations, with life expectancy in South Africa at 49.56, Somalia at 51.58, and Zimbabwe at 55.68. Average life expectancy for sub-Saharan Africa as a whole is about 56 years (World Bank 2014a).

Why are these societies so dramatically different from Global North countries, many of which have average life expectancies into the 80s? The low life expectancy stems from lack of medical care, epidemics such as ebola, wars and civil strife, corrupt governments, droughts and famine, malnutrition, resulting susceptibility to diseases, and high infant mortality. Figure 13.7 shows the number of children who die before the age of five (per 1,000 live births) for various regions of the world. This is another key indicator of a country's overall well-being.

Migration and Mobility: Where People Move and Why

Most of us have moved one or more times in our lives, a process called migration. Perhaps we have moved to a larger house down the block, maybe to another area for a job opportunity or school, or even to another country altogether. The process of changing one's place of residence is called *geographic mobility*. Over the history of the human race, people have migrated to the far reaches of the globe. Because of adaptability to climatic and geographic barriers, humans have dispersed to more areas of the world than any other species. Even inhospitable locations such as the Arctic North and the South Pole have human settlements.

As noted in previous chapters, the *push-pull* model points out that some people are pushed from their original locations by wars, plagues, famine, political or religious conflicts, economic crises, or other factors and pulled to new locations by economic opportunities or political and religious tolerance. Most people do not leave a location unless they have been forced out or they have a viable alternative in the new location. They weigh the benefits of moving versus the costs (Weeks 2012).

Migration is often initiated at the micro level: a lucrative job offer in another location requires a move, the family dwelling becomes too small, a relative needs help, or a family member's health requires a different climate. If an opportunity arises, the individual or

A giant dust storm (left) blacked out the sky of Goodwell, Oklahoma, during the Dust Bowl of the late 1800s, *pushing* many people off their farms and out of the plains states. By contrast, the Alaskan Gold Rush of the late 1800s *pulled* thousands of migrants to that territory in search of wealth.

family may move. However, if the risks are high, if the information about migration is scarce, or if the move involves negative factors such as leaving family, individuals may decide to stay put. For rational choice theorists, assessment of costs and benefits by individuals impacts migration patterns.

Although the decision to move is often a personal or family one, the sociocultural environment also influences it. Examples of large groups of people leaving an area because of aspirations to improve their life chances, hopes of retaining a way of life, or expulsion by political, economic, or religious forces have existed throughout history. Chinese railroad workers came to the United States for economic reasons. Amish and Mennonite settlers from Europe sought religious freedom and preservation of their way of life. The Amish, a group originating in Germany, left Germany *en masse*, and members of this group now live entirely in North America. Italian immigration to the United States took place in a collective manner. When a family left Italy, it would usually move to a U.S. city where a relative or a previous acquaintance lived. Thus, residents of entire apartment buildings in the North End of Boston were from the same extended family, and entire city blocks of people came from the same town or region of southern Italy (Gans 1962). Many European countries are multicultural environments today because of immigrants from former colonies.

Those living at the receiving end have not always been welcoming, and in fact have often tried to isolate the newcomers in ghettos, preventing them from moving into other neighborhoods. Especially in difficult economic times, when competition for jobs is greatest, newcomers may find few employment opportunities (Foner 2005).

Immigrants seeking a better life often struggle in their new locations. Consider Mohammed from Senegal who traverses the streets of Verona, Italy, trying to make a living selling children's books and hoping he might have some money left to send back to his family. Mohammed speaks five languages and has a high school education, but opportunities in his homeland are limited, and he is an undocumented immigrant in Italy. European countries, especially those with former colonies, have large populations of immigrants from North Africa and the Middle East. These immigrants often face great peril in their attempts to gain entry into more prosperous nations; and once they arrive, many find themselves in crowded, unsanitary housing with little economic opportunity.

Social scientists study the impact of immigration, pointing out that immigration tends to yield significant economic gains for receiving countries. Scholars who study migration—especially long-distance migration that involves crossing into another society—point out that migrants are usually among the most hardworking, ambitious, optimistic, healthy, and well-adjusted people, for it takes considerable courage and motivation to undertake a migration to a new land. Isabel Wilkerson summarizes:

> Any migration takes some measure of energy, planning, and forethought. It requires not only the desire for something better but the willingness to act on that desire to achieve it. Thus, the people who undertake such a journey are

ENGAGING SOCIOLOGY

From South to North of the U.S. Border

by Nancy Diggs

When Luis and the group of 60 undocumented immigrants made the journey across the Arizona desert, it was March; temperatures ranged as high as the 90s during the day to freezing at night. The group was told that they would be walking in the desert for about six hours, and to bring food and water for that time. To travel quickly, they were told to carry nothing else. Their guide claimed that in order to avoid the Immigration and Naturalization Service [U.S. Citizenship and Immigration Services] they would have to change plans and march through more of the desert—a hellish two-and-a-half days, most of it without food or water. It was so hot that when they chanced upon water tanks for animals, most of them rushed to gulp down the green, slimy water. Along the path, the travelers passed the remains of one man who had not made it. Having nothing but the clothes on their backs, they were unable to bury him.

At night in the desert cold, without extra clothing or blankets, Luis and his companions huddled together for warmth. In order not to be spotted, they wore dark clothes. Smoking and whistling were also forbidden. At last they came to a highway to be crossed, where they would wait until late at night when there was no traffic. When a car stopped on the road, the guide warned everyone not to move and to keep their eyes closed so the light wouldn't reflect off the whites of their eyes.

When all was dark and quiet, the guide called another coyote (a person who helps undocumented immigrants into the United States in exchange for money), who arrived with two vans. The sound of a helicopter caused everyone to push and shove in a vain attempt to squeeze 60 people into the two vehicles.

At the next step of the journey, the immigrants were loaded into a truck trailer that was "incredibly hot," with no water. After traveling some 400 miles, the group eventually arrived in Los Angeles where they were able to buy food and drinks. After spending the night in a safe house, Luis and his group met their new U.S. coyote who sent them off in different directions. Luis took a bus to Las Vegas where his uncle lived (Diggs 2011).

Engaging With Sociology

1. What do you think may have led Luis to risk what he did to enter the United States? What circumstances might lead you to try to cross a national border without documents, as Luis did?

2. Over the past few years, hundreds of thousands of unaccompanied minors have tried to cross the U.S.-Mexico border to escape from gang-related violence in their hometowns (see www.pbs.org/news hour/updates/country-lost-kids). Their parents often encourage them to go, because they believe they will be killed if they remain. Do you think the U.S. government should let them enter and remain in the United States? Why or why not?

3. As a public sociologist, what advice would you give to government policymakers trying to deal with the undocumented migration of minors to the United States?

more likely to be either among the more educated in their homes of origin or those most motivated. (Wilkerson 2010:261)

International Migration. More than 3.1% of the world's population is "on the go" each year. That is 214 million international migrants, or 1 out of every 33 persons in the world. Half are women. These migrants change the size and characteristics of populations around the world, expanding some and emptying out others (International Organization for Migration 2012).

Many people have taken great risks to enter Global North nations illegally in search of work. Luis is one such undocumented immigrant. His story, in the above "Engaging Sociology," illustrates the hardships that many migrants must endure as they seek a better life for themselves and their families. To these migrants, a better life awaits *if* they can reach it.

In 2014, this group of immigrants from Honduras and El Salvador, most of them children, crossed the U.S.-Mexico border into Texas and were caught. The border fences cost millions of dollars but have not stopped the flow of undocumented migrants, who endure great peril to get to the United States.

International migration is especially common where political turmoil, wars, famines, or natural disasters ravage a country. *Refugees*, those "who flee in search of refuge in times of war, political oppression, or religious persecution," numbered 43.7 million in 2011, half of them children. This is a 15-year high (UNHCR 2012). Roughly 27.5 million citizens are *internally displaced*, forcibly relocated within their own countries by violent conflict or environmental disaster. In China, pollution in large cities such as Beijing is creating an environmental disaster, causing some people to move out of the cities to small towns (Wong 2013b).

The ongoing crisis in Syria has added significantly to the number of refugees. By 2013, over 1.5 million Syrians had fled the nation. Over 500,000 sought refuge in the tiny neighboring nation of Jordan, which already harbored many Palestinian refugees. Ten percent of the Jordanian population now consists of refugees, and that number increases daily (PBS Newshour 2013).

A recent study of immigrants to the United States shows people born elsewhere who later acquire U.S. citizenship are more likely than their native-born neighbors to marry, less likely to divorce, and more likely to avoid poverty. In the 10 poorest U.S. states, native-born citizens earn $0.84 to every $1 earned by naturalized citizens. In the richest states, the ratio is $0.97 to $1. One reason for this difference in earnings comes from the fact that foreign-born naturalized citizens tend to bring with them the tools and attitudes they need to be successful. They had to have the wherewithal to leave their home country, find

sponsors in the United States, navigate visa and green card requirements, and fulfill the requirements for U.S. citizenship. Those who can do all that tend to be self-reliant and willing to take risks, and have an entrepreneurial spirit (Giridharadas 2014).

Internal Migration in the United States. The rate of internal migration in the United States is high compared with that in most places in the world. Patterns of migration have primarily involved individual "pull" to economic opportunities and better housing. According to the U.S. Census, about 40% of people who move cite a housing reason, including a new or better home or apartment, a better neighborhood, cheaper housing, owning rather than renting, or establishing their own household (Demographics Livability 2014).

During different historical periods, movement directions have varied. During the 20th century, up until the 1960s, people moved out of the southern states and into northern states. This included the Great Migration of 6 million black Americans who left the rural south for northern cities. Then the pattern reversed, and the flow started going south and west. Movement starting in the 1960s and increasing in the 1970s has been toward the Sunbelt, especially to California, Arizona, Texas, and Florida. Movement to the Pacific Coast and even Alaska has also increased, due to economic opportunities in these locations.

One major form of internal migration is urbanization (U.S. Census Bureau 2012c). The second half of this chapter focuses on the urbanization of the population across the globe. Although decisions about family size and migration are individual choices, what happens at the meso and macro levels influences these decisions, as we see in the next section.

MICRO-LEVEL POPULATION PATTERNS

Understanding demography can be extremely important for comprehending social processes in your everyday life. While most Global North countries do not have massive famines or population explosions, population fluctuations influence them in many ways. Consider the life choice decisions you will make regarding education, employment, and retirement.

Keith, one of the coauthors of this book, lived in Boston, and his wife taught in a suburban school system there at a time when the fertility rate was falling. The elementary school where she taught had four first-grade classrooms, with 28 children per room—112 first graders in the school. By the next year, the school felt the decline in the fertility rate six years earlier, and the number of first graders declined. Within four years, there were only 40 first graders in her school, with two classrooms and only 20 students per class. Some school systems lost half of their student population in a few years. One year, first-grade teachers were losing their jobs or having to move to another grade, and the next year, it was second-grade teachers who were scrambling. The third year, third-grade teachers were in oversupply, and so forth. With low demand, these were not times for college students to be pursuing teaching careers. A personal decision was being influenced by population trends—and this pattern continues.

We have already mentioned the impact of the baby boom (the high fertility rates from 1946 to about 1963) and the following baby bust (the drop in fertility for more than a decade following the baby boom). The population pyramid of the United States reveals the impact on the population (see Figures 13.8 and 13.9). As we can see, the U.S. population no longer looks anything like a pyramid. From these figures, we can tell a great deal about job prospects, retirement security, career decisions, and other outcomes of demographic changes. As that bulge for the baby boomer group moves into the senior citizens' category, society will have new challenges.

Thinking Sociologically

Why do population experts predict the population pyramid will look like Figure 13.9 by 2050? What factors in society might lead to this? What kinds of problems do you think this sort of configuration might cause?

Retirement is another topic for which population patterns are critical. When Social Security was established in the United States in the 1930s, life expectancy from birth was 58 for men and 62 for women (Social Security Administration 2013). The number of people in the age-dependent categories of under 15 and over 65 was low. For each person who received Social Security in 1945, 42 workers paid Social Security taxes. Forty people, each paying $255 a year, could easily support a retired person, receiving $10,000 per year. However, the average life expectancy has shifted, and the age-dependent population has increased. Currently in the United States, nearly 14% of the population is over the age of 65, as opposed to 4% in the 1930s (World Factbook 2014l). Moreover, predictions are that by 2035, 20% of the population will be over 65. In 2013, there were just 2.8 workers contributing Social Security taxes for each person covered by Social Security (Social Security Administration 2013). When commentators and politicians say Social Security is in trouble, they refer to problems created by changes in the composition of the U.S. population.

As noted in Chapter 6, population patterns also influence rates of deviance and juvenile delinquency. Most deviant acts are committed by young people in their mid-teens to early 20s. Thus, when the baby boom

FIGURE 13.8 United States, 2010

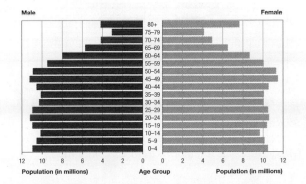

Source: Nationmaster 2011. "United States Population Pyramids" www.nationmaster.com/country/us/Age_distribution

FIGURE 13.9 United States, 2050

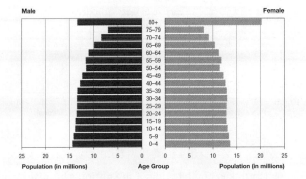

Source: Nationmaster 2011. "United States Population Pyramids" www.nationmaster.com/country/us/Age_distribution

generation was in their teens and early 20s, in the 1960s and 1970s, the overall rates of deviance climbed higher. When the birth dearth group was in their teens, overall rates of crime dropped because there were fewer teenagers. Thus, private and personal decisions by thousands of couples (micro level) may result in the crime rates for the entire country rising or falling 15 years later.

Because population trends shape your life, understanding those trends can help you use that knowledge to your advantage. To illustrate the power of demographic trends on individual decisions, the next "Engaging Sociology" provides an exercise in problem solving using information from population pyramids of U.S. cities.

ENGAGING SOCIOLOGY

Population Pyramids and Predicting Community Needs and Services

Study these three population pyramid graphs. Based on what you see, answer the following questions:

1. Which community would likely have the lowest crime rate? Explain.

2. Which community would likely have the most cultural amenities (theaters, art galleries, concert halls, and so forth)? Explain.

3. Imagine you were an entrepreneur planning on starting a business in one of these communities.

   a. Name three businesses that you think would succeed in each community. Explain.

   b. Name one business that you think would not succeed in each community. Explain.

Bloomington, Indiana

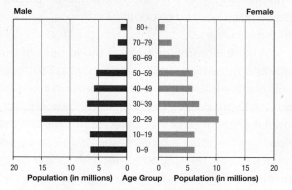

(Hint: Bloomington is the home of Indiana University located in a smallish city.)

Norfolk, Virginia

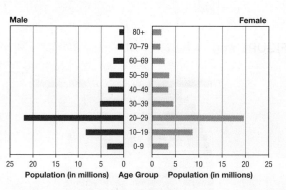

Source: U.S. Census Bureau.

(Hint: Norfolk is home to one of the nation's largest navy bases.)

Naples, Florida

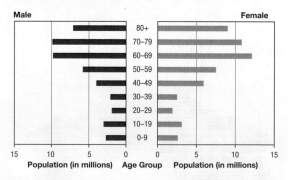

Source: U.S. Census Bureau.

(Hint: Naples is a major retirement community.)

We now turn to population changes resulting from migration from rural to urban areas. This trend has had major ramifications on all levels of our social world—impacting the lives of individuals, institutions, nations, and the global environment.

URBANIZATION: MOVEMENT FROM RURAL TO URBAN AREAS

Mumbai (Bombay), India; Caracas, Venezuela; Lagos, Nigeria; Shanghai, China; and New York City, United States, *are megacities* (cities and their surrounding metropolitan areas with more than 10 million people). They are part of a global trend that has gained momentum over several centuries—urbanization. Today, more than half of all people live in urban areas, and projections indicate that 7 out of 10 people will do so by 2050 (WHO 2013b). The U.S. Census breaks down the geographic regions of the nation into urbanized areas (of 50,000 or more), urban clusters (2,500–50,000), and rural areas (all nonurban areas). In 1900, 60.4% of Americans lived in nonurban, or rural, areas and in 1960, 36% did so. By 2010, just 19.3% of the population lived in rural parts of the country, while 80.2% resided in urban areas.

In the 1950s, the New York City metropolitan area (which comprises 30 counties, including cities and towns in the states of New York, New Jersey, Connecticut, and Pennsylvania) was the only place in the world that had 10 million people. At that time, there were 75 cities in the world with 1 to 5 million residents, mostly in the Global North. Table 13.2 shows the rapid change in this pattern with the 10 largest population centers in 2014. New York City now ranks eighth, as cities in the Global South move up in population; just three years earlier New York was ranked third largest city in the world.

As the world becomes more congested and cities continue to attract residents, cities start to merge or to become continuous urban areas without rural areas between them. Those who have driven from Boston to Washington, DC, an area sometimes called BosWash, know the meaning of *megalopolis*, a spatial merging of two or more cities along major transportation corridors (Brunn, Hays-Mitchell, and Zeigler 2011).

The move from rural to urban areas has always stemmed from the increased opportunities for employment and investment that come with living around

TABLE 13.2 The 10 Largest Population Centers (Population in Millions)

2014 Rank	Urban Center	Population
1	Tokyo, Japan	37,126
2	Jakarta, Indonesia	26,063
3	Seoul, South Korea	22,547
4	Delhi, India	22,242
5	Shanghai, China	20,860
6	Manila, Philippines	20,767
7	Karachi, Pakistan	20,711
8	New York City, USA	20,464
9	São Paulo, Brazil	20,186
10	Mexico City	19,463

Source: Worldatlas 2014.

more people. Globalization has made this more important than ever, as markets and job opportunities have become transnational. Population growth often spurs job growth. For example, in the United States, all but one of the ten urban areas with the most population growth between 2000 and 2010 also increased their number of jobs. The exception was Atlanta, which had a slight decline. While the growth in these urban areas in the United States focuses primarily in the low-density, suburban areas surrounding the cities, in other parts of the world, poor migrants to urban areas live in crowded slums. In many parts of the Global South, the rural poor, who come to cities to find opportunities, often live with no running water, electricity, or sewage disposal and lack basic services, including health care and education (Kotkin 2013; Kotkin and Cox 2011; World Bank 2013a).

The next "Engaging Sociology" feature invites you to explore some consequences of major urbanization trends in the world (Brunn et al. 2011).

Theories of Urban Development

Urban scholars who studied problems in the city of Chicago were among the first sociologists in the United States. Referred to as the Chicago School, their studies of urban ecology focused on the patterns of land use and residential distribution of people in urban areas. These theorists pictured the city's growth pattern as a series of circles. Moving out from the center, each circle was dominated by a particular type of activity and

World Urbanization Prospects   Urbanization

ENGAGING SOCIOLOGY

World Urbanization Trends

World Urbanization Prospects are reports published by the United Nations Population Division. They provide valuable data on past, present, and future urbanization trends in regions and subregions of the world. They also provide data on individual cities and urban areas. Consider the impact of major migration trends on the environment, friends and relatives left behind, dual-worker families, maintaining one's culture, the impact of new cultural ideas spreading, and many more impacts. The major findings of the most recent edition follow in Figures 13.10 to 13.12.

FIGURE 13.10   Percentage of Population Residing in Urban Areas

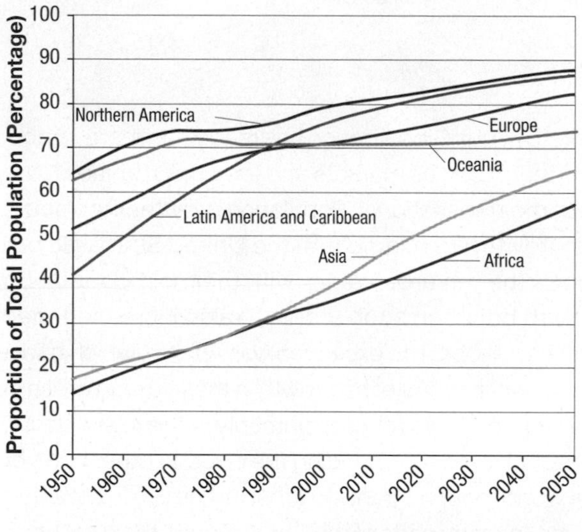

Source: United Nations, Department of Economic and Social Affairs, Population Division (2014). *World Urbanization Prospects: The 2014 Revision, Highlights.* Used by permission of the United Nations.

FIGURE 13.11   Urban and Rural Population of the World, 1950–2050

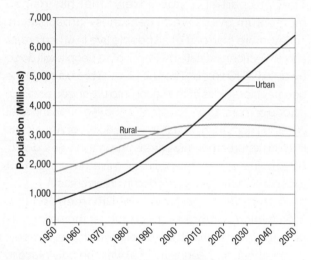

Source: United Nations, Department of Economic and Social Affairs, Population Division (2014). *World Urbanization Prospects: The 2014 Revision, Highlights.* Used by permission of the United Nations.

Engaging With Sociology: Figure 13.10

- What do you learn from these graphs about world urbanization trends? Which continents seem to be urbanizing most rapidly?

- How might these trends affect people moving to urban areas?

- What might be some effects on global climate change, the possibilities of globally transmitted diseases, political stability or instability, or the global economy?

- How might the global trend toward urbanization affect your own life?

Engaging With Sociology: Figure 13.11

- When the size of the rural population declines, how might it affect the culture of a nation?

- Identify two positive and two negative consequences of this urbanization trend for a nation.

Engaging With Sociology: Figure 13.12

- In 1950, North America had 15% of the world's population. That number has dropped to 8% and will drop again to 6% by 2050. Is this cause for concern? Why or why not?

Source: United Nations Population Division 2012.

(Continued)

FIGURE 13.12   Percentage of World's Urban Population by Region

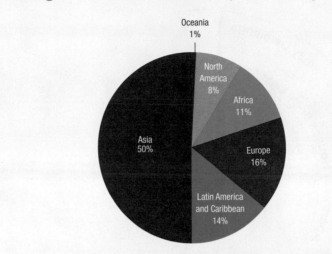

Source: United Nations, Department of Economic and Social Affairs, Population Division (2014). *World Urbanization Prospects: The 2014 Revision, Highlights.* Used by permission of the United Nations.

residential pattern, from central city ghettoes and rooming houses to working-class apartments and bungalows, to middle-class housing, to upper-class suburbs (Park, Burgess, and McKenzie [1925] 1967). See Figure 13.13 on page 378 for an illustration of this pattern.

Urban ecologists further refined the Chicago School's original ideas by exploring social, economic, political, and technological systems of cities' spatial patterns (Abu-Lughod 1991). Several processes constantly take place in urban areas: residential segregation; invasion by a new ethnic, religious, or socioeconomic group; and successive movement by that group. These processes are part of dynamic city life (Berry and Kasarda 1977).

Racial and ethnic segregation is a continuing and troubling issue in many urban areas of the United States. Despite some reductions in racism in the nation, American cities—especially northern cities—have high levels of residential segregation. This segregation affects individual networking, school composition, and access to community resources. The next "Engaging Sociology" on page 379 examines the likelihood that someone of a given race will have contacts in his or her neighborhood that cross racial lines. This figure is based on one city—Chicago, Illinois—but you can easily check the residential patterns in your city by going to www.censusscope .org/segregation.html.

In Mumbai (Bombay), India, many children have no choice but to sleep on the streets each night.

FIGURE 13.13 Burgess's Theory of City Growth

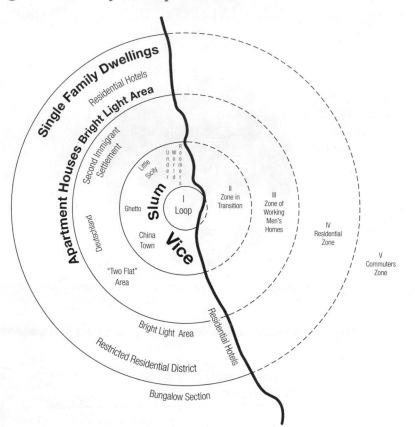

Source: Park et al. (1925) 1967:55.

Note: The Chicago School envisioned urban growth as a series of concentric circles, with ethnicity, class, residential patterns, and types of activity evolving with each ring removed from the central city.

Any effective solution to urban problems must address inequalities between groups and allocations of resources in urban areas. Some conflict theorists see growing city problems as a result of domination by elites, creating poverty and exploiting the poor (Gottdiener and Hutchison 2006). Cities produce profits for those who buy and sell property and for investors and politicians who redevelop urban areas. Sometimes, poor urban residents become displaced, so there are winners and losers in the process.

THE URBAN ENVIRONMENT AND SOCIAL POLICY: MACRO-LEVEL PERSPECTIVES

The mountains rise from the sea, dotted with pastel-colored shanties. On the drive from the port city of La Guaira up into the mountains to the capital city of Caracas, Venezuela, one sees settlements nestled into the hillsides. The poor, who have come from the country to find opportunities in the capital, make shelters in the hills surrounding Caracas, often living with no running water, electricity, or sewage disposal. The laundry list of urban problems facing governments is overwhelming: excessive size and overcrowding; shortages of services, education, and health care; slums and squatters; traffic congestion; unemployment; and effects of global restructuring, including loss of agricultural land, environmental degradation, and resettlement of immigrants and refugees (Brunn, Williams, and Zeigler 2003). This section considers several of the many problems mentioned earlier in the chapter and now facing urban areas such as Caracas.

Rural Migrants and Overcrowding

In Cairo, Egypt, a huge, sprawling graveyard full of large mausoleums, the City of the Dead, has become home to thousands of families transplanted from rural

ENGAGING SOCIOLOGY

Residential Segregation and Cross-Race Contact

The bar graph in Figure 13.14 illustrates typical contact of most residents with members of their own and other races in a metropolitan area. The Census Bureau calculates the average racial composition of neighborhoods as they are experienced by members of each ethnic group—called *exposure indices*. In this graph, the first five columns represent the average neighborhood racial composition of a person of a given race. The far right column shows the racial composition of the metropolitan area as a whole. Study the graph and answer the following questions.

FIGURE 13.14   Exposure Indices for Race and Ethnic Groups: Chicago

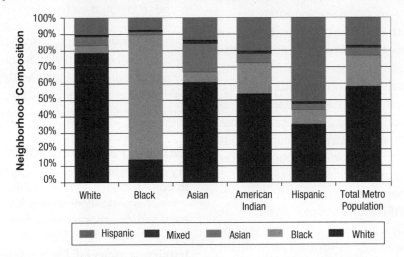

Source: "Residential Segregation and Cross-Race Contact: Chicago, Illinois." www.censusscope.org/segregation.html

Engaging With Sociology

1. How likely are whites to experience diversity in their neighborhoods compared with the diversity of the city as a whole?

2. Which group experiences the most diversity and is likely to have more opportunities to encounter people from other racial groups?

3. Which groups experience the most segregation?

4. What might be some consequences of living in a racially homogeneous neighborhood? Which group might experience more negative consequences because of the homogeneity? Why?

5. Go to www.censusscope.org/segregation.html and enter a city near you to see the exposure indices for various racial groups in that city. What do you conclude?

areas. Cities in India such as Chennai (the former colonial name was Madras), Mumbai (Bombay), and Kolkata (Calcutta) have thousands of homeless migrants living on the sidewalks, on highway medians, and in river channels that flood during the rainy season.

Overcrowding exists in cities throughout the world but causes special problems in the Global South when rural residents seek opportunities in urban areas. Poor migrants set up shacks of any material available—tin, cardboard, leaves, mud, and sticks—in settlements known as *barriadas* in Spanish, *shantytowns* in English, *bidonvilles* in French, *favelas* in Portuguese-speaking Brazil, and *bustees* in India. The majority of migrants to the city are young. They are pulled to the city in hopes of finding jobs and often have been pushed from the rural areas because of limited land on which to farm and too many mouths to feed.

As we have seen, over the past three decades, the urban populations in Africa, Asia, and Latin America have grown rapidly, and many of the largest cities in the world are now in the Global South. Rural-to-urban migration and development of megacities dominate the economic and political discussions in many countries. The newcomers spill out into the countryside, engulfing towns along the way. Refer to Figure 13.11 (page 376) for trends from 1950 to 2012 and projections through 2050, and Figure 13.12 (page 377) for the population living in urban areas by more and less developed regions of the world (United Nations Population Division 2012).

Most Global South countries have little time or money to prepare infrastructures and provide services for the rapidly increasing numbers of urban residents. Technological development, job opportunities, and basic services have not kept up with the large migrations of would-be laborers. Lack of basic services has become a major problem, resulting in contagious diseases that can cause deadly epidemics due to lack of services and poor sanitary conditions.

The study of urbanization teaches us that the social environment influences people's lives. Public sociologists can play a role in improving the conditions of urban areas, as described in the next "Sociologists in Action."

Urban Planning for Structures That Meet Human Needs

Ideal city planning is quite a task. City planners must meet citizens' needs for housing, sanitation, education, food distribution, jobs, family life, and recreation. The problem is that most urban planners do not have the luxury of starting from scratch. They must work with decaying areas, being cognizant of meaningful landmarks and treasured sites. Planners may also have to undo mistaken or inadequate planning by previous administrations.

Whether demographers, political leaders, and urban planners can keep up with the demands for even basic services in the Global South remains to be seen. This is especially true in areas of the world where poor rural people flock to cities for survival. This basic population pattern—urbanization—has consequences at the most global levels and at the most micro levels of human life. Our social world model—which looks at the connections of micro,

With few places to live, rural migrants to Egypt's largest city, Cairo, find shelter in the large ancient mausoleums in the burial grounds of the City of the Dead.

meso, and macro levels of the social system—makes us cognizant of the consequences of decisions made by millions of individuals and families. It also makes us mindful of the consequences of global trends and forces for individuals and for cities.

Thinking Sociologically

Try planning an ideal city. First, list everything you need to consider, such as how big the city should be. Now think of organization: Who will handle what? Keep in mind services, maintenance, financing, and leadership.

Intersection of Demographic and Environmental Policy

Ecosystems—streams, rivers, inland and coastal wetlands, grasslands, and forests—provide critical resources and services that sustain human health and well-being (EcoSummit 2012). Yet our ecosystems are under stress, much of it caused by human activity. Extinction of species, lack of water and water pollution, resource exploitation, collapse of some global fisheries, and new diseases are the results of this breakdown. Major storms such as Typhoon Haiyan in the Philippines and infestations such as the southern pine beetle in the New Jersey Pine Barrens have been determined by scientists to be a result of global warming (Bradsher 2013; Gillis 2013). As scientists in the Royal Society make clear,

The combination of increasing global population and increasing overall material consumption has implications for a finite planet. As both continue to rise, signs of unwanted impacts and feedback (climate change reducing crop yields and irreversible changes such as species extinction)

SOCIOLOGISTS IN ACTION:
JAY WEINSTEIN

Improving Quality of Life by Transforming Community Structure

As is true of many urban centers, Detroit, Michigan, has its share of distressed neighborhoods. Dr. Jay Weinstein has been director of an interdisciplinary team attempting to bring about economic, social, and physical restructuring of some of these areas. By developing long-term relationships in several urban neighborhoods, the team has had success working with residents and others to improve conditions. Weinstein calls this approach *relationship brokering*—bringing people together to share perspectives and to clear up misperceptions between residents, local officials, service providers, and police. These efforts have helped empower residents to take action and improve their neighborhoods.

A major project along these lines, which began in 1990, is in the Detroit suburb of Taylor. For decades, residents of Taylor and the surrounding Down River area were painfully aware of the problems of their neighborhood, known by uncomplimentary names such as "Crack Ridge," "Hooker Heaven," and "Sin City." With about 7,500 people packed into one-half square mile, most residents lived in rental units controlled by the U.S. Department of Housing and Urban Development Section 8 program (subsidized private housing). An influential local newspaper published a series of articles showing that the neighborhood had earned the labels applied to it. The articles inspired local and federal political leaders to demand action.

Weinstein and his colleagues were awarded a research grant by the City of Taylor Department of Community Development to assess the problems and make recommendations to improve the community. The fact-finding stage revealed that the residents of the neighborhood were not the main perpetrators. Instead, the area had been under siege by nonresidents who came and went, drifting from apartment to apartment, or illegally occupying residences after threatening to harm the rightful owners.

The research team recommended a plan for a thorough physical, economic, social, and political reconstruction of the neighborhood. City and federal officials accepted the recommendations of the sociological team and set out on a 10-year program of implementation. Working with residents of the neighborhood and other citizens of the city, Taylor's mayor, city council, Department of Human Resources, police department, and many others tackled the problem, with Weinstein and his colleagues' help.

Today, the neighborhood has a new name (the Villages of Taylor), a new human services center, a new residential owner (a private nonprofit corporation established by the city), and many new or redesigned buildings. The population density has been reduced by more than 20%, without one person, other than drug dealers, displaced against his or her will. The average median income of Taylor now exceeds the national average. Former secretary of Housing and Urban Development Shaun Donovan called Taylor "a model for the nation."

During his work in the Taylor neighborhood, Weinstein used triangulation (multiple methods of data collection), utilizing surveys, participant observation, census data, and other large data sets. He also used a symbolic interactionist approach to learn how residents view the community and how it operates. With this understanding of how their neighborhood functions, residents and community leaders were able to transform their neighborhood.

• •

Dr. Jay Weinstein, professor emeritus at Eastern Michigan University, specializes in urban sociology, demography, and social change. He has been a private consultant for more than 20 years, with contracts from international and local governments and nonprofit organizations. His studies have included analysis of demographic trends and changes in India, Albania, Bulgaria, and Jamaica.

are growing alarmingly...Demographic change is driven by economic development, social and cultural factors as well as environmental change. (Royal Society 2012)

Additional infrastructure problems threaten to immobilize cities in the Global South. Traffic congestion and pollution are so intense in some cities that the slow movement of people and goods reduces productivity, jobs, health, and vital services. Pollution of the streets and air are chronic problems, especially with expansion of automobile use around the world. One scientific report in 2013 made the urgency of the issue very clear:

> Warming of the climate system is unequivocal, and since the 1950s, many of the observed changes are unprecedented over decades to millennia. The atmosphere and ocean have warmed, the amounts of snow and ice have diminished, sea level has risen, and the concentrations of greenhouse gases have increased ... Continued emissions of greenhouse gases will cause further warming and changes in all components of the climate system. Limiting climate change will require substantial and sustained reductions of greenhouse gas emissions. (Intergovernmental Panel on Climate Change 2013a:3,14)

Older cities face deteriorating infrastructures, with water, gas, and sewage lines in need of replacement. In regions of China, parents confine their children to their homes, in order to keep them from breathing the outside air. In Beijing and other Chinese cities, the air has 40 times the pollutants deemed safe to breathe (Wong 2013a). In Global North countries, concern for these problems has brought some action and relief, but in impoverished countries where survival issues are pressing, environmental contamination is a low pri-

In 2013, air pollution was so thick in Beijing that people wore masks and entrepreneurs sold cans of fresh air for people to breathe.

ority. Thus, the worst air pollution is now found in major cities in the Global South, such as Mexico City, São Paulo, and several Chinese cities, including Beijing.

In order to improve Earth's ecosystems, we must rebalance consumption between the Global North and Global South; stabilize population growth, especially in Global South countries; bring those in extreme poverty (those who live on $1.25 or less per day) out of this condition; develop plans for urban growth; provide access to reproductive health and family planning; and adopt plans to reduce overall human consumption (Royal Society 2012). In order to increase the health of cities, we must also address urban crime. Rapidly growing cities can become hotbeds of deviance and crime.

Many factors create change in a society, and population dynamics are key among them. Some factors contributing to social dynamics push for innovation and change in a particular direction, and other factors retard change. The next chapter examines the larger picture of social transformation and change in our complex and multileveled social world.

WHAT HAVE WE LEARNED?

Population trends, including migration resulting in urbanization, provide a dynamic force for change in societies. Whether one is interested in understanding social problems, social policy, or factors that may affect one's own career, it is helpful to understand demographic processes. We ignore them at our peril—as individuals and as a society. If we overlook demographic patterns, family businesses can be destroyed, retirement plans obliterated, and the health of our communities sabotaged. Awareness of such patterns can enhance planning that leads to prosperity and enjoyment of our communities.

KEY POINTS

- Population analysis (called demography) looks at the composition, distribution, and size of a population and how variables of fertility, mortality, and migration impact society.

- The population of the world has increased dramatically since industrialization. Its implications for society can be viewed in population pyramids.

- Various theories explain the causes and repercussions of rapid population growth.

- Many institutions affect and are affected by fertility and mortality rates at the meso level—government, religion, the economy, education, and health care.

- Migration is also an important issue for society— whether the migration is international or internal—for it can change the size, distribution, and composition of a nation's citizenry.

- Population patterns can also affect individual decisions at the micro level, from career choices to business decisions to retirement plans.

- A major element of population migration has been urbanization. As populations become more densely concentrated, this creates a series of opportunities and problems for meeting human needs.

DISCUSSION QUESTIONS

1. Why is it important for policymakers to understand demographic trends in their communities and nation? Why should *you* be interested in such knowledge? How might it impact your understanding of and positions on issues related to (a) immigration, (b) education, (c) health care, and (d) Social Security legislation?

2. How many children (if any) do you think you would (ideally) like to have? Why? What might make this (ideal) number change?

3. What are some examples of (a) pronatalist and (b) antinatalist policies? Do you approve of such policies? Why or why not? How might your perspective differ depending on the demographics of your particular nation?

4. How is the social status of girls and women related to a society's ability to control population growth? If you were a male leader in the government of an overcrowded nation, why and how might you use this information to promote gender equality in your country? How might your ideas be perceived differently, depending on your sex?

5. What are some of the major reasons people leave their country of origin and move to another? Have you ever done so? Why? If not, under what circumstances would you be willing to leave the country in which you were born and move to another?

CONTRIBUTING TO OUR SOCIAL WORLD: What Can We Do?

At the Local Level

- The *U.S. Census Bureau* is always at work collecting, analyzing, and disseminating demographic information. It is a great source of data, ranging from information on your block to the whole nation. Invite a representative to your campus to discuss the Bureau's activities. You can check internship and job opportunities with the Census at www.census.gov/about/census-careers/opportunities/programs/student.html.

- Check out your *local department of urban planning, urban and regional development, or community development* by Googling those terms and the name of your town, county, or province. Invite a representative to your campus or visit the department's offices. Discuss how population information is used in planning and service delivery contexts. Consider an internship with one of the organizations you find in your area.

At the Organizational or Institutional Level

- *The Population Association of America (PAA)* "is a non-profit, scientific, professional organization that promotes research on population issues," according to its website. At www.populationassociation.org, you can find information on demographic issues and ways to get involved in efforts to address them.

At the National and Global Levels

- The *Population Reference Bureau* (www.prb.org/About.aspx) "informs people around the world about population, health, and the environment, and empowers them to use that information to advance the well-being of current and future generations." The organization offers fellowships for recent college graduates with a BA or a BS.

- *Planned Parenthood* (www.plannedparenthood.org) promotes family planning education and outreach programs throughout the United States. The International Planned Parenthood Federation (www.ippf.org) works in 180 nations. The organizations use volunteers and interns, as well as providing long-term employment opportunities.

- *World Vision* (www.worldvision.org/?open&lpos=facebook-sponsor_bot_Home) is "a Christian humanitarian organization, dedicated to working with children, families, and their communities worldwide to reach their full potential by tackling the causes of injustice and poverty." The organization provides many ways you can get involved in efforts to alleviate poverty and promote justice around the world.

- *The Population Council* (www.popcouncil.org) promotes family planning in order to reduce poverty, create healthier populations and communities, empower women, and improve lives across the globe. You can find fact sheets and other information at the organization's website. You can also look for possible job and internship opportunities at www.popcouncil.org/employment/index.asp.

$)SAGE edge™

Sharpen your skills with SAGE edge at **edge.sagepub.com/ballantinecondensed4e**

SAGE edge for Students provides a personalized approach to help you accomplish your coursework goals in an easy-to-use learning environment.

edge.sagepub.com/ballantinecondensed4e

Get the edge on your studies. Read the chapter and then take advantage of the open-access site to

- review the **eFlashcards** and strengthen your understanding of key terms and concepts;
- take the **practice quiz** to assist in your mastery of course material;
- explore the **video and multimedia** links for further exploration of topics; and
- access full-text **SAGE journal articles** that have been carefully selected to support and expand on the concepts.

© REUTERS/Sharif Karim

14 The Process of Change

We Can Make a Difference!

Individuals are profoundly influenced by the macro structures around them, but people are also capable of creating change, especially if they band together with others and approach change in an organized way.

MICRO

ME (AND MY FAMILY)

LOCAL ORGANIZATIONS AND COMMUNITY
Unemployment and business scandals cause personal losses.

MESO

NATIONAL ORGANIZATIONS, INSTITUTIONS, AND ETHNIC SUBCULTURES
Family instability contributes to wobble and flux— that is, change—in other institutions and increases in delinquency rates.

MACRO

SOCIETY
National government policies about trade, war, or immigration may cause change in families, the economy, or international relationships.

GLOBAL COMMUNITY
World Bank loans or United Nations poverty programs may result in change for poor nations and stimulate international trade.

LEARNING OBJECTIVES

14.1 Give examples of how change takes place at each level of analysis.

14.2 Explain how stresses and strains can lead to organizational change.

14.3 List the six factors necessary for collective behavior to occur.

14.4 Provide examples of the difference between planned and unplanned change.

14.5 Illustrate the stages of social movements.

14.6 Describe how the development of technology brings about change in societies and their environments.

THINK ABOUT IT

Micro: Local Community	What do you think needs to change in your community?
Meso: National Institutions; Complex Organizations; Ethnic Groups	How do complex organizations or ethnic groups enhance, hamper, or shape change?
Macro: National and Global Community	How does training and support from national governments for technological innovation affect the process of change in your country and in the world?

Our planet is in peril, according to evidence from the Asian subcontinent to the Arctic and from Africa to the Americas (Tollefson 2012). Seven hundred and seventy-two scientists from around the world have signed on to the statement that "the world is not ready for the impacts of climate change, including more extreme weather and the likelihood that populated parts of the planet could be rendered uninhabitable" (Intergovernmental Panel on Climate Change [IPCC] 2014). The evidence presented by the IPCC indicates a dire future with extreme weather events.

A major factor in climate change is the waste humans create. Wet, dry, smelly, and sometimes recyclable—garbage is a problem, and we are running out of space to dispose of our refuse. We dump it in the ocean and see garbage surfacing on

Smoke billows from a controlled burn of spilled oil off the Louisiana coast in the Gulf of Mexico in 2010. Millions of gallons of oil have poured into the Gulf since an April 20, 2011, offshore rig explosion killed 11 workers and ruptured British Petroleum's deep-sea well. Such environmental problems can stimulate social change.

beaches and killing fish and birds (Heyes 2012). We bury it in landfills, and the surrounding land becomes toxic. Recycling and waste reduction efforts are relatively new movements in response to the urgent pleas from environmentalists about our polluted air, land, and water sources; dying oceans; and warming planet.

Recycling, salvaging items that can be reused, is part of a social reform movement—the environmental movement. However, few issues have simple solutions. The dumping and recycling have to take place somewhere. As noted in Chapter 13, many of the recycling plants and trash dumps are located in areas where poor people and racial and ethnic minorities live—part of a practice of *environmental racism*, in which members of lower socioeconomic classes and racial and ethnic minority groups face the brunt of environmental dangers, including pollutants and disease (Bell 2012).

At the micro level, individuals can help save the planet through responsible personal actions. At the meso level, the environmental movement can encourage local and regional governments to enact policies and plans to reduce waste and pollution and address environmental racism. At the macro level, world leaders need to hold all nations accountable for, and find ways to adapt to and mitigate, global warming. Our social world is, indeed, complex and interdependent.

Turn on the morning or evening news, and there are lessons about other aspects of our changing social world. We see headlines about medical advances and cures for disease; biological breakthroughs in cloning and the DNA code; terrorist bombings in Afghanistan, Israel, Iraq, Pakistan, Ukraine, and other parts of the world; famine in drought-afflicted sub-Saharan Africa; disasters such as earthquakes, hurricanes, tsunamis, and floods; and social activists calling for boycotts of chocolate, coffee, oil companies, Walmart, or other multinational corporations. Some events seem far away and hard to imagine: thousands killed by a tidal wave in India, hundreds swept away by mud from an erupting volcano in Colombia, a massive oil spill in the Gulf of Mexico, or a rise in terrorism reflecting divisions in world economic, political, and religious ideologies. Others may impact you directly—having affordable access to health insurance, living in an area suffering from the results of a drought or severe storm, or accessing financial aid for increasing college costs. Some of these are natural events, but most are the result of human actions.

Social change refers to *variations or alterations over time in the structure, culture (including norms and values), and behavior patterns of a society.* Some change is controllable, and some is out of our hands, but change is inevitable and ubiquitous. Change can be rapid, caused by some disruption to the existing system, or it can be gradual and evolutionary. Very often, change at one level in the social world occurs because of change at another level. Micro, meso, and macro levels of society often work together in the change process but are sometimes out of sync.

In this chapter, we explore the process of change, the causes of change, and some strategies for bringing about desired change. We consider the complexity of change in our social world, explanations and theories of social change, the role of collective behavior in bringing about change, planned change in organizations, macro-level social movements, technology, and environmental actions as they affect and are affected by change.

Our social world model is based on the assumption that change, whether evolutionary or revolutionary, is inevitable and ever present in the social world. The impetus for change may begin at the micro, meso, or macro level of analysis. Studies of the change process are not complete, however, until the level under study is understood in relation to other levels in the model, for each level affects the others in multiple ways.

⬤ Thinking Sociologically

How do your activities impact the environment? Have you taken steps to address climate change? If so, what socializing agents prompted you to do so? If not, why do you think you have not?

THE COMPLEXITY OF CHANGE IN OUR SOCIAL WORLD

The Yir Yoront, a group of Australian aborigines, long believed that if their own ancestors did not do something, then they must not do it. It would be wrong and might cause evil to befall the group (Sharp 1990). However, contact with European cultures and missionaries brought new tools such as the steel axe, changing the role of men whose job it was to make stone axes. Gradually other European ways were introduced, changing the culture dramatically so that old ways were obsolete. The group's original culture disintegrated as it adopted others' ways, but a major contributor was the introduction of new technological ideas, especially the steel axe. In the 1940s, missionaries gave steel axes to the Yir Yoront women, and the hunting and gathering economy changed due to changing roles of women and men. Men, who used to control the stone axes, lost their high status in the community when they had to borrow axes and other tools from women, and thus the power structure of the community changed (BushTV 2010).

Obviously, the Yir Yoront are not a people who favored change or innovation. In contrast, *progress* is a positive word in much of Australia and in many other countries where change is seen as normal, even desirable. The traditions, cultural beliefs of a society, and internal and external pressures all affect the degree and rate of change in society (Berman 2011).

Change at the Individual Level: Micro-Level Analysis

One of the top U.S. entrepreneurs, Microsoft's Bill Gates, combines intelligence, business acumen, and philanthropy, qualities that appeal to American individualism. Gates has the power to influence others because of his fame, wealth, and personal organizational skills. He is able to bring about change in organizations through his ability to motivate people and set wheels in motion. Some people have persuasive power to influence decision making, based on expertise, wealth, privileged position, access to information, or the ability to use coercive force. Any of us, if we feel strongly about an issue, can rally others and bring about change in society. Each individual in society has the potential to be a change agent.

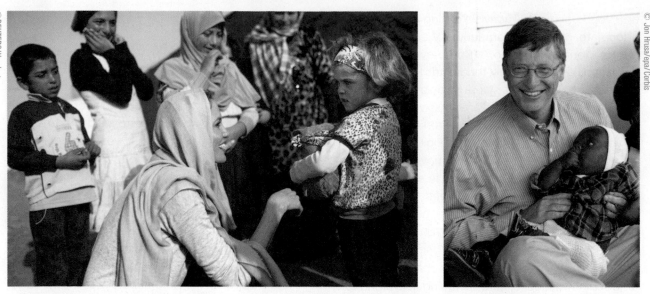

Angelina Jolie (left) has used her fame as an Academy Award–winning actress to bring attention to problems of refugees, serving as a Special Envoy and Goodwill Ambassador for the United Nations High Commissioner for Refugees. Bill Gates (right) holds a child who is receiving a trial malaria vaccine at a medical research center in Mozambique. Gates announced a grant of $168 million to fight malaria, a disease that kills more than 1 million people a year, 90% of them children. Sometimes, social change occurs because of individual initiatives.

Individuals are active agents, and they can either stimulate or resist change. Sometimes they prod organizations to change, insisting on more family-supportive policies (like an onsite day care center), better safety precautions for employees, or more environmentally friendly buildings and programs. For example, at the urging of students and others, colleges may develop more recycling programs, more energy-efficient buildings or transportation systems, and more degree programs that involve study of the environment.

Sometimes individuals are not eager to change. They must be enticed or manipulated into change by organizations. When this does occur, most organizations—schools, businesses, volunteer associations—use one or more of the following strategies to persuade individuals to accept change: They appeal to individuals' values, use persuasion by presenting hard data and logic, convince individuals that the existing benefits of change outweigh the costs, remove uncooperative individuals from the organization ("addition by subtraction"), provide rewards or sanctions for acceptance of change to alter the cost-benefit ratio, or compel individuals to change by an order from authority figures. In any case, individuals are critically important parts of any understanding of social change.

Change at the Institutional Level: Meso-Level Analysis

Global climate change, an issue connected to pollution and use of Earth's natural resources, affects people at all levels in the social system. Many meso-level organizations have developed policies and practices to reduce emission of pollutants and change the way they use resources. For example, many religious denominations have developed programs to be more "green" or "earth-friendly." The United Church of Christ is one such group, passing a resolution in July 2009 encouraging local churches to become "Earthwise Congregations." An example of one congregation within this meso-level denomination follows.

Mayflower United Church of Christ in Minneapolis was one of the first in the United States to seek the designation of an "Earthwise Congregation." The church has an action team that works on ways to help members have more energy-efficient homes, but it also brought a resolution to the congregation that by 2030, the church would be entirely carbon neutral. The resolution was approved, and fundraising began to change the heating system to solar energy. The roof of the church is now covered with 240 solar

Human Rights

panels. Within 18 months, the church reported a reduction of carbon emissions of almost 50% (Mayflower Church 2013; Riley 2014). Members of the congregation have also begun lobbying the state legislature to have more public transit, and especially more transportation that runs on electricity rather than oil-based fuels. Other United Church of Christ congregations are also taking actions, as are other communities of faith—inspired by denominational resolutions at the meso level.

Another example of meso-level change takes place at universities. Under pressure from college students, many have changed their policies about production of campus clothing. Multinational corporations like Gap and Nike, seeking higher profits, fostered the growth of sweatshops in the Global South. Many professors, students, and concerned citizens in the United States and other Global North nations began to insist that these companies establish acceptable labor and human rights conditions in their factories in the Global South. Their efforts gradually grew into an anti-sweatshop movement with strong labor and religious support and tens of thousands of active participants. College students on hundreds of campuses in the United States have taken up the anti-sweatshop cause, holding sit-ins on many campuses to force their college bookstores to ban the use of college logos on products not produced under acceptable labor conditions (Brecher, Costello, and Smith 2012). In doing so, they have helped shape the conditions for production of clothing on other continents.

Change at the National and Global Levels: Macro-Level Analysis

Change may begin also at the national level in response to some concern, or it may be stimulated by a global organization (like the United Nations or the World Bank) or by a global concern (like climate change). In this section we will discuss national and then global forces that can bring about change.

Societal-Level Change. Take a look at the impact of national policies and trends on the global environment and the constant change we bring to our planet. To illustrate the increasingly complex and biologically interdependent social world, consider that pollution of the environment by any one country now threatens other countries. Carcinogens, acid rain, and other airborne chemicals carry across national boundaries (Brecher et al. 2012). Heat-trapping gases have risen dramatically in the past several years causing pessimism about reversing the environmental effects (Borenstein 2013). People in the United States comprise about 4.5% of the world's population but emit almost a fourth of the heat-trapping gases ("Global Warming and Climate Change" 2013).

According to scientists, Earth's surface has warmed by 1 degree in the past century. That does not sound like much until one considers that during the last ice age, Earth's surface was only 7 degrees cooler than it is today. Small variations can make a huge difference, and those consequences are likely to be dire if the

As part of its "Earthwise" mission to protect the environment, this church in Minneapolis installed 240 solar panels in a commitment to be carbon neutral by 2030.

People at the local level often try to influence policies at the meso level. At this local community event, people lobby their neighbors on a state referendum in an upcoming election.

Due to global climate change, ice on which polar bears depend is disappearing, as is the habitat of many other species that are becoming endangered.

earth's surface temperature increases by another 2 or 3 degrees. Currently, massive blocks of sea ice are melting each year at a rate that equals the size of Maryland and Delaware combined ("Global Warming and Climate Change" 2013). In the Northern Hemisphere, Greenland is home to many glaciers such as the huge Petermann Glacier. Warming recently caused the Petermann Glacier to calve (break off) an iceberg twice the size of Manhattan ("Iceberg Breaks Off" 2012).

In a warmer world, there is less snowfall, resulting in smaller mountain icecaps and, thus, a smaller spring runoff of crucial fresh water. In fact, 80% of the world's population today lives in areas with shortages of water for human use (Environment 911 2012).

While some of the environmental change may be rooted in natural causes, the preponderance of evidence suggests that human activity—and the way we live our lives—is the primary cause (Gore 2012; IPCC 2013b). So national policies and cultural attitudes within a country can have consequences at many levels of our social world.

Thinking Sociologically

What do you think happens when people do not have enough water in their current location to survive? What happens when they try to move into someone else's territory to gain access to needed resources such as land and water?

This global issue requires nations to work together for change, yet some nations resist change because they feel climate control efforts will impede economic progress. The Kyoto Protocol on global warming requires commitment by nations to curb carbon dioxide and other emissions, but U.S. President Bush rejected it because it "does not make economic sense" (Lindsay 2006:310–11). As of February 2014, 191 countries and the European Union had approved the treaty. The exceptions are the United States, Afghanistan, the Vatican, and the newly formed country of South Sudan (United Nations Framework Convention on Climate Change 2014). The Obama administration has indicated support for dramatic efforts to curb climate change and global warming, but passage of a bill in Congress is still pending. There is continuing pressure on the United States to sign onto a global agreement to address climate change.

The two big quandaries are (1) the costs and benefits to various nations of participating in a solution and (2) the question of time—will nations respond before it is too late to make a difference? Currently, impoverished countries bear most of the costs and consequences of pollution, while rich nations benefit from the status quo. It is becoming increasingly clear, though, that the rich will also pay a price. Not only will they have to face pollution, increasingly severe weather and intense storms, and contaminated food supplies from around the world, but if Global South countries cannot support their populations, affluent nations will also face increasing pressure from immigration (legal or not).

Yet fixing the environmental issues will be expensive for nations and may add to economic woes by temporarily hindering economic growth. Because slow-growth economies and recessions can lead to an unhappy public and political unrest, making changes to address climate change is not easy. However, such action is crucial because nations are still the most powerful units for allocating resources and for setting policy.

Global Systems and Change. As the world becomes more interconnected and interdependent, impetus for change increasingly comes from global organizations, international and transnational government agencies, and multinational corporations. As discussed in other chapters, nongovernmental organizations (NGOs) work on such efforts as eradicating polio or controlling AIDS, Ebola, and malaria. Some promote human rights, and others support local social movements for clean water, environmental protection, and access to health. One NGO, *Sociologists Without Borders*, works transnationally to develop globally inclusive sociology curricula, advance human rights, and support the needs of vulnerable groups.

New and shifting alliances among international organizations and countries link together nations, form international liaisons, and create changing economic and political systems. The following international alliances among countries, for example, are based primarily on economic ties:

- SADC: Southern African Development Community
- NAFTA: North American Free Trade Agreement
- CAFTA-DR: Dominican Republic–Central America Free Trade Agreement
- WIPO: World Intellectual Property Organization
- G7: Group of Seven—the most affluent and most powerful countries in the world
- OPEC: Organization of the Petroleum Exporting Countries
- APEC: Asia-Pacific Economic Cooperation
- EU: European Union
- AU: African Union

Consider NAFTA, which recently had its 20th anniversary. It was initiated in 1993 to establish a free trade area between Canada, the United States, and Mexico in order to facilitate trade in the region. Promoters, including many global corporations, promised that the agreement would create thousands of new high-wage jobs, raise living standards in each of the countries, improve environmental conditions, and transform Mexico from a poor developing country into a booming new market. Opponents (including labor unions, environmental organizations, consumer groups, and

religious communities) argued the opposite—that NAFTA would reduce wages; destroy jobs, especially in the United States; undermine democratic policy making in North America by giving corporations a free rein; and threaten health, the environment, and food safety (U.S. Trade Representative 2012).

Analyses of NAFTA show mixed results. It has helped boost intraregional trade between Canada, Mexico, and the United States, but has fallen short of generating the jobs and deeper regional economic integration its advocates promised decades ago (Council on Foreign Relations 2014). Trade has increased significantly, from $290 billion in 1993 to more than $1.1 trillion in 2012. There is some indication that tariffs are down and U.S. exports have increased (U.S. Trade Representative 2012). NAFTA has been more effective in increasing trade in agricultural commodities than nonagricultural products. Some analysts argue that there is improvement in the areas of environmental protection and labor rights, but many others argue that these areas have declined. The truth is hard to determine, but there are probably both gains and losses.

In the above discussion of changes at different levels of analysis, one principle carries through all: change at one level leads to change in other levels, as it has done in the global cases of climate change and NAFTA. Changes at the macro level affect individuals, just as changes at the micro level have repercussions at the meso and macro levels.

SOCIAL CHANGE: PROCESS AND THEORIES

Something always triggers a social change. The impetus may come from within an organization or a society, a source of change known as *strain*. Sometimes, it comes from outside an organization, what sociologists call *stress*. Let us consider two examples of *strain*: (1) conflicting goals and (2) contrasting belief systems within an organization.

Conflicting goals are seen in the case of the platinum mining industry and its union workers. In the Lonmin South African platinum mines (providing materials for catalytic converters and jewelry), 44 workers died in August 2012 and 2 more died in May 2014 during strikes against the company. Two feuding unions both demanded pay hikes, and violence broke out. As we write, the company is trying to settle the dispute by going directly to the miners with a pay offer. Individual miners work in difficult, dangerous conditions to try to meet their basic needs for food and shelter for their families.

Sometimes they must live at the mines away from their families for many months, but when jobs are scarce, one does what one must. Company goals focus on the bottom line, being profitable in a competitive environment. The company argues that it cannot afford to raise wages and still be competitive, yet their profit margin has dropped as a result of the strikes (Herskovitz 2012; "Lonmin Profit Plunges" 2014). This conflict and others like it demonstrate how the needs of the workers can be at odds with those of the company, creating internal strain.

Contrasting belief systems (political, religious, economic, and social) within a society can also have a major effect on the type and rate of change. For example, some religious groups oppose stem cell research, which often uses the cells of fetuses created in test tubes. Yet other members of those same religious groups may believe this research will alleviate the suffering of loved ones and save lives. Although both sides in the organization believe they are pro-life, the internal conflicts can be disruptive and cause internal strain (Religious Tolerance 2014).

Stresses, those pressures for change that come from the organization's external environment, can be traced to several sources: the natural environment and natural disasters, population dynamics, actions of leaders, new technologies, changes in other institutions, and major historical events. For example, the natural environment can bring about either slow or dramatic change in a society.

Natural disasters such as floods, hurricanes, tsunamis, heavy snows, earthquakes, volcanic eruptions, mudslides, tornadoes, and other sudden events are not planned occurrences, but they can have dramatic consequences. Disease epidemics are often unpredictable, such as the 2010–2013 cholera epidemic in Haiti (UNICEF 2014). Natural disasters and diseases are so important as a dramatic change agent that the sociology of disasters has become a specialty field within the discipline.

Population dynamics—birthrates and death rates, size of populations, age distribution, and migration patterns—can be important contributors to external stress on organizations. Where populations are growing at extremely rapid rates, government systems may be unable to meet the basic needs of the people. Immigration due to political upheavals or motivated by anticipated economic opportunities can also create stress on the societies that receive the newcomers as they attempt to meet the immigrants' needs.

Leaders influence change through their policy decisions or the social movements they help generate. India's Mohandas K. (Mahatma) Gandhi taught the modern world nonviolent methods of bringing about change in political systems. The policies of Charles Taylor, former military dictator of Liberia, created long-term war that resulted in thousands of deaths. President Robert Mugabe of Zimbabwe locked his country in a downward spiral of economic turmoil and disease, killing thousands. These leaders' actions created internal strains in their own countries and external stressors resulting in discussions and sometimes change in the international community.

Technology also influences societal change. William F. Ogburn compiled a list of 150 social changes in the United States that resulted from the invention of the radio, such as instant access to information (Ogburn 1933). Other lists could be compiled for cell phones, automobiles, television, computers, and new technologies such as smartphones. Some of these

Natural disasters—floods, hurricanes, tornadoes, earthquakes, volcanic eruptions—can be the cause of major social changes in a community, as shown in this photo after a tsunami hit the Philippines in 2013.

The Domiz Refugee Camp in the Kurdistan Region of Iraq is home to thousands of Syrian refugees. Immigration to avoid persecution and war can stimulate massive change for people and for countries.

ENGAGING SOCIOLOGY

Technology and Change: The Automobile

At the turn of the 20th century, the "horseless carriage" was often referred to in rural areas as the "devil wagon." In the 1890s and early 1900s, some cities and counties had rules forbidding motorized vehicles. In Vermont, a walking escort had to precede the car by an eighth of a mile with a red warning flag, and in Iowa, motorists were required to telephone ahead to a town they planned to drive through to warn the community lest their horses be alarmed (Berger 1979; Clymer 1953; Glasscock 1937; Morris 1949). In most rural areas, motorists were expected to pull their cars to a stop or even to shut down the motor when a horse-drawn buggy came near. "Pig and chicken legal clauses" meant the automobile driver was liable for any injury that occurred when passing an animal near the road, even if the injury was due to the animal running away (Scott-Montagu 1904).

Roughly 85,000 motored vehicles were in use in the United States in 1911. By 1930, the number was nearly 10 million, and in 2011 the estimated number of registered passenger vehicles was 253 million (Berger 1979; Statistica 2014). Forms of entertainment began to change when people were able to be more mobile, and entertainment became available virtually any night of the week (Berger 1979; McKelvie 1926). Thus, dependence on family was lessened, possibly weakening familial bonds and oversight (Berger 1979). Even courting was substantially changed, as individuals could go farther afield to find a possible life partner, couples could go more places on dates, and two people could find more privacy. School attendance rates of rural children also increased substantially with motorized buses (U.S. Department of Interior Office of Education 1930).

As people could live in less congested areas but still get to work in a reasonable amount of time via an automobile, the suburbs began to develop around major cities. A dispersed population needs to use more gasoline, thereby creating pollution. As the wealthy moved to expensive suburbs and paid higher taxes to support outstanding schools, socioeconomic and ethnic stratification between communities increased. These are some of the *unintended consequences* of the spread of the automobile. It sometimes takes decades before we can identify the consequences of the technologies we adopt.

Engaging With Sociology

1. What might be some long-term social consequences for our individual lives and societies of the widespread use of smartphones, microwave ovens, and computer games?

2. How might the introduction of smart cars that can navigate themselves and warn us of hazards change our lives?

changes give rise to secondary changes. For example, automobile use led to paved highways, complex systems of traffic patterns and rules, and gasoline stations. The next "Engaging Sociology" explores several issues involving the automobile and change.

The diffusion or spread of technology throughout the world is likely to be uneven, especially in the early stages of the new technology. For example, computer technology has advanced rapidly, but those advances began in corporate boardrooms, on military bases, and in university laboratories. Policies of governing bodies—such as funding for school computers—determine the rate of public access. Thus, only gradually are computers reaching the world's citizenry through schools, libraries, and eventually private homes. Clearly, internal strains and external stressors give impetus to the processes of change. The question is "How do these processes take place?"

Theories of Social Change

Social scientists seek to explain the causes and consequences of social change, sometimes in the hope that change can be controlled or guided. Theories of change often reflect the events and belief systems of particular historical time periods. For example, conflict theory developed during periods of change in Europe. It gained adherents in the United States during the 1960s, when intense conflict over issues of race and ethnic relations, the morality of the Vietnam War, and changes in social values peaked. Theories such as structural functionalism that focused on social harmony were of little help.

The major social change theories can be categorized as micro-level (symbolic interaction and rational choice theories) or meso- and macro-level (evolutionary, functional, conflict, and world systems theories).

As we review these theories, many of them will be familiar to you from previous chapters. Here, we relate them to the process of change.

Micro-Level Theories of Change

Symbolic Interaction. According to symbolic interaction theory, human beings are always trying to make sense of the things they experience, figure out what an event or interaction means, and determine what action is required of them. Humans construct meanings that agree with or diverge from what others around them think. This capacity to define one's situation, such as concluding that one is oppressed, even though others have accepted the circumstances as normal, can be a powerful impetus to change. It can be the starting point of social movements, cultural changes, and revolutions.

Some sociologists believe that individuals are always at the core of any social trends or movements, even if those movements are national or global (Blumer 1986; Giddens 1986; Simmel [1902–1917] 1950). After all, it is individuals who act, make decisions, and take action. There are a number of leaders, for example, who have changed the world—for better (Mahatma Gandhi) or worse (Adolf Hitler). Neither corporations nor nations nor bureaucracies make decisions—people do. The way in which an individual defines the reality he or she is experiencing makes a huge difference in how she or he will respond to it.

Social institutions and structures are always subject to maverick individuals "thinking outside the box" and changing how others see things. Individual actions can cause riots, social movements, planned change in organizations, and a host of other outcomes that have the potential to transform society. That people may construct reality in new ways can be a serious threat to the status quo, and those who want to protect the status quo try to ensure that people will see the world the same way they do. If change feels threatening to some members who have a vested interest in the current arrangements, those individuals who advocate change may face resistance. Consider the current state of the world, in which some nations are making rapid technological advances and others are resisting modernization as a threat to their traditional political and religious way of life.

Leaders may provide opportunities for group members to participate in suggesting, planning, and implementing change in order to help create acceptance and positive attitudes toward change. Several recent street demonstrations in Egypt and Ukraine against governments in power turned violent; at different points during the demonstrations, leaders attempted to engage the opposition in talks to calm the tensions. Symbolic interactionists might see this as either an effort to build a consensus about what social change is necessary or a method to appease those wanting change in order to remain in control and maintain much of the status quo.

Rational Choice. To rational choice theorists, behaviors are largely driven by individuals seeking rewards and reduced costs. They maintain that most individuals engage in those activities that bring positive rewards and try to avoid actions that can have negative outcomes. A group seeking change can attempt to set up a situation in which the desired behavior is rewarded. The typology presented in Figure 14.1 shows the relationship between behaviors and sanctions.

Bringing about change may not, however, require a change in costs or rewards. It may be sufficient simply to change people's perception of the advantages and disadvantages of certain actions. Sometimes, people are not aware of all the rewards, or they have failed to accurately assess the costs of an action. For example, few citizens in the United States realize all the financial, health, and legal benefits of marriage. To change the marriage rates, we may not need more benefits to encourage marriage. We may do just as well to change the population's appraisal of the benefits already available.

Meso- and Macro-Level Theories of Change

Social Evolutionary Theories. Social evolutionary theories at the macro level assume that societies change slowly from simple to more complex forms. Early unilinear theories maintained that all societies moved through the same steps and that advancement or progress was desirable and would lead to a better society. These theories came to prominence during the Industrial Revolution, when European social scientists sought to interpret the differences between their own societies and the "primitive societies" of other continents. Europe was being stimulated by travel, exposure to new cultures, and a spawning of new philosophies, a period called the Enlightenment. Europeans witnessed the development of mines, railroads, ships, weaponry, cities, educational systems, and industries, which they defined as "progress" or "civilization." World travelers reported that other peoples and societies did not seem to have these developments. These reports provided the empirical evidence that early sociologist Auguste

FIGURE 14.1   Relationship Between Behaviors and Sanctions

		Sanction	
		Formal	Informal
Behavior	Positive	Bonuses, advances, fringe benefits, recognition	Praise, smile, pat on the back
	Negative	Demotion, loss of salary	Ridicule, exclusion, talk behind back

Comte used in proposing his theory of unilinear development from simple to complex societies. Unilinear theories came to legitimate colonial expansion and exploitation of other people and lands seen as less developed and "inferior."

In a more recent version of evolutionary theory, Patrick Nolan and Gerhard Lenski discuss five stages through which most societies progress: hunter-gatherer, horticultural, agrarian, industrial, and postindustrial (Nolan and Lenski 2014; see also Chapter 3). This does not mean that some stages are "better" than others. It simply means that this is the typical pattern of change resulting from new technologies and more efficient harnessing of energy. Contemporary evolutionary theories acknowledge that change takes place in multiple ways and not just in a straight line. The rapid spread of ideas and technologies means that societies today may move quickly from simple to complex, creating modern states. They skip steps or are selective about what aspects of technology they wish to adopt. For example, countries such as India and China are largely agricultural but are importing and developing the latest technology that allows them to skip over developmental steps. As noted in Chapter 7, many countries will not see landlines for phones, but instead will have cell phones even in the more remote areas.

Functionalist Theories. Functional theorists assume that societies are basically stable systems held together by the shared norms and values of their members. The interdependent parts work together to make the society function smoothly. A change in one part of the society affects all the other parts, each changing in turn until the system resumes a state of equilibrium. Change can come from external or internal sources, from stresses in contact with other societies, or from strains within.

Slow, nondisruptive change occurs as societies become more complex, and this may be a very functional adaptation. Rapid change, however, is often seen as dysfunctional or disruptive to stability by functional theorists. Because functionalists often view major change with suspicion, many sociologists have turned to conflict theories to help explain change, especially rapid or violent change.

Conflict Theories. Conflict theorists assume that societies are dynamic and that change and conflict are inevitable. According to Karl Marx, socioeconomic class conflict is the major source of tension leading to change in any society. Marx and Friedrich Engels predicted that the antagonistic relationship they saw developing between the workers (proletariat) and the owners of the production systems (bourgeoisie) in 19th-century England would lead to social

The modes of transportation for goods and people vary around the world, often reflecting the level of development of the region or country. Sometimes, technological progress has high costs, including pollution. For a photo essay and further exploration of transportation systems and modernization, visit **edge.sagepub .com/ballantinecondensed4e.**

revolution. From this, they believed a new world order would emerge in which the workers themselves would own the means of production. Thus, conflict between the owners and the workers would be the central factor driving social change (Marx and Engels [1848] 1969).

Other conflict theorists study variables such as gender, religion, politics, and ethnic or interest group problems in their analyses, feeling that these factors can also be the grounds for oppression and "us" versus "them" differences (Dahrendorf 1959). Some see conflict as useful for society because it forces societies to adapt to new conditions and leads to healthy change (Coser 1956). Conflicts over slavery and over gender inequality are examples of problems that cause stresses and strains, often resulting in an improved society.

World Systems Theory of Global Change. World systems theorists focus on how world history has influenced the status of individual countries today. Capitalist economies first appeared about 1500. Since then, except for a few isolated tribal groupings, almost all societies have been at least indirectly influenced by dominant capitalist world economic and political systems (Wallerstein 1974).

This theory divides the world system into three main parts: the core, semiperipheral areas, and peripheral areas (see Figure 14.2). Core countries include most Western European states, Australia and New Zealand, Japan, Canada, the United States, and a few others (Wallerstein 1974). Historically, they have controlled global decision making, received the largest share of the profits from the world economic system, and dominated the peripheral areas politically, economically, and culturally by controlling the flow of technology and capital into and out of those countries. Peripheral countries, most of which are in Africa, Asia, and South America, provide cheap labor and raw materials for the core countries' needs.

The semiperipheral countries hold an intermediate position, trading with both the core and the peripheral countries. Brazil, Argentina, South Africa, India, the Philippines, Iran, Mexico, and the Baltic regions of Eastern Europe are among the semiperipheral areas. Because most semiperipheral countries are industrializing, they serve as areas to which core-country businesses and multinational corporations can move for continued growth, often in partnerships, as semiperipheral states aspire to join the core countries. The core and semiperipheral countries process raw materials,

often taken from peripheral countries for little in return, and may sell the final products back to the peripheral countries. The semiperipheral countries and the peripheral countries need the trade and the resources of the core countries, but they are also at a severe disadvantage in competition and are exploited by those at the core, resulting in an uneasy relationship.

Core countries have been a major force in the development of global institutions, such as the International Monetary Fund (IMF), that facilitate and attempt to control international capital flow. By increasing the frameworks for debt restructuring for peripheral countries, the IMF attempts to restore sustainability and growth to countries that default on their loans. At least 95 countries have restructured their debt under IMF guidelines since the 1950s (Das, Papaioannou, and Trebesch 2012). However, the IMF leaves countries little economic autonomy. The restructuring plans control what countries do even within their own national boundaries, creating debt dependencies on core countries that most poorer countries can never overcome (Dollars and Sense Collective 2012; Gibler 2012; Rothkopf 2012; Stiglitz 2012).

World systems theory is a global conflict theory, with core countries exploiting the poor countries. As we might expect from conflict theory, some groups of noncore countries have increased their collective power by forming alliances such as OPEC (Organization of the Petroleum Exporting Countries), OAS (Organization of African States), and SEATO (Southeast Asia Treaty Organization). These alliances present challenges to the historically core countries of the world system because of their combined economic and political power. For example, the price we pay at the gas pump reflects, in part, the power of OPEC to set prices.

When we understand international treaties and alliances as part of larger issues of conflict over

FIGURE 14.2   World Systems Theory

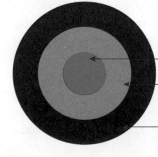

Core countries (wealthy countries of Europe, Japan, United States, Canada)

Semiperipheral countries (India)

Peripheral countries (many poor African, Asian, and Latin American nations)

resources and economic self-interests, the animosity of noncore countries toward core countries such as the United States begins to make sense. Likewise, the threat felt by the United States from countries that seem to be getting jobs once found in the United States is not entirely unfounded. The problem is an extraordinarily complex system that tends to leave the most vulnerable more at risk and the wealthiest even richer (Gibler 2012; Rothkopf 2012; Stiglitz 2012).

The climate crisis illustrates the world systems theory and rift between rich and poor nations. For example, tiny Pacific islands such as Nauru soon will be under water due to global warming and water rising. Human activity, mostly from development in Global North countries, is causing what some groups of countries call "climate injustice," and Global South nations harmed by climate change now demand compensation for damages. After decades of climate talks with little change taking place, the divide between peripheral nations and core nations is becoming more stark. This world system outlook assumes that developed Global North countries are most to blame for climate change problems and therefore should be held accountable. However, nations like India and China, in the midst of phenomenal economic growth, now contribute to increasing global carbon emissions. The causes of climate change are complex and not solely due to the actions of Global North countries (Myers and Kulish 2013).

We have discussed examples of planned change, but sometimes behavior that results in change is unplanned, even spontaneous, as described in the following section.

⬤ Thinking Sociologically

Where is your clothing made? Did a multinational corporation have it assembled in the Global South? What steps can you take to ensure that the workers who made your clothes receive tolerable working conditions and a fair wage?

COLLECTIVE BEHAVIOR: MICRO- TO MESO-LEVEL CHANGE

Individuals in local communities often come together over some issue that irritates or even enrages them, and these gatherings can evolve into mobs, riots, panics, or other forms of collective reaction to events.

It is often at the micro or local level that change movements get started. These can evolve into large statewide, national, or even global movements with implications for the larger society, but since they begin with individuals in local communities deciding to take some sort of common action, we discuss it as a micro- to meso-level event. Political demonstrations and stock market sell-offs are all forms of collective behavior that can stimulate change. In this section we introduce a form of change that typically has uncertain outcomes.

Collective behavior refers to *spontaneous, unstructured, and disorganized actions that may violate norms; this behavior arises when people are trying to cope with stressful situations and unclear or uncertain conditions* (Goode 1992; Smelser 1963, 1988). Collective behavior falls into two main types: crowd behavior and mass behavior. It often starts as a response to an event or a stimulus. It could begin with a shooting or beating, a speech, a sports event, or a rumor. The key is that as individuals try to make sense of the situations they are in and respond based on their perceptions, collective social actions emerge.

Crowd behaviors—mobs, panics, riots, and demonstrations—are forms of collective behavior in which a crowd acts, at least temporarily, as a unified group (LeBon [1895] 1960). Crowds are often made up of individuals who see themselves as supporting a just cause. Because the protesters are in such a large group, they may not feel bound by normal social controls—either internal (normal moral standards) or external (fear of police sanctions).

Crowds can stimulate change in a society, but they can also become unruly and unpredictable, so governments spend a good deal of money and time equipping and training officers to control crowds. Here a Ukrainian woman participating in a protest places carnations into the shields of anti-riot policemen standing outside the presidential office in Kiev.

Mass behavior occurs when individual people communicate or respond in a similar manner to ambiguous or uncertain situations, often based on common information from word-of-mouth rumors, websites, social networking, and television. Examples include fashions and fads, such as the ALS (Lou Gehrig's disease) "ice bucket challenge." Unlike social movements, these forms of collective behavior generally lack a hierarchy of authority and clear leadership, a division of labor, and a sense of group action.

Theories of Collective Behavior

Social scientists studying group and crowd dynamics find that most members of crowds are respectable, law-abiding citizens, but faced with specific situations, they act out (Berk 1974; Turner and Killian 1993). Several explanations of individual involvement dominate the modern collective behavior literature.

Based on principles of rational choice theory, *the minimax strategy* suggests that individuals try to minimize their losses or costs and maximize their benefits (Berk 1974). People are more likely to engage in behavior if they feel the rewards outweigh the costs. Individuals may become involved in a riot if they feel the outcome—drawing attention to their plight, the possibility of improving conditions, solidarity with neighbors and friends, looting goods—will be more rewarding than the status quo or the possible negative sanctions.

Emergent norm theory points out that individuals have different emotions and attitudes guiding their behaviors in crowds than when they act alone (Turner and Killian 1993). The theory addresses the unusual situations, involving the breakdown of norms, in which most collective behavior takes place. Unusual situations may call for the development of new norms and even new definitions of acceptable behavior. The implication of this theory is that in ambiguous situations, people look to others for clues about what is happening or what is acceptable, and norms emerge in ambiguous contexts that may be considered inappropriate in other contexts. This is the most widely used approach to understanding collective behavior (Turner and Killian 1993).

Imagine you are at an athletic event. Someone in the crowd with a very loud voice begins to taunt a player from the visiting team. Initially some people around you laugh, but as the initiator begins to chant an insult, your friends and others around you begin to join in. Chances are good that in the camaraderie of the moment, you follow suit and start chanting the insult, too—even if it is very disrespectful. Normally you would not make such an insulting remark to someone's face, but in this situation where you were anonymous, the pattern of behavior emerged and you felt compelled to follow the crowd. This would be an example of an emergent norm affecting an entire crowd.

Value-added theory (sometimes called structural-strain theory) describes the conditions for crowd behavior and social movements. Key elements are necessary for collective behavior, with each new variable adding to the total situation until conditions are sufficient for individuals to begin to act in common. At this point, collective behavior emerges (Smelser 1963). These are the six factors identified that can result in collective behavior:

1. *Structural conduciveness:* Existing problems create a climate ripe for change. Consider the example of the independent country of Ukraine, caught between Russia and Western Europe. The (now deposed) president of Ukraine stated that he planned to align Ukraine with the West, but under pressure and promises from Russia he changed his mind. This change angered many Ukrainians.

2. *Structural strain:* The social structure is not meeting the needs and expectations of the citizens, which creates widespread dissatisfaction with the status quo—the current arrangements. Ukrainians who felt the country would fare better if aligned with Western Europe demonstrated in the capital of Kiev.

3. *Spread of a generalized belief:* Common beliefs about the cause, effect, and solution of the problem evolve, develop, and spread. Charges spread that the pro-Russian president was corrupt, lived opulently, and had stolen money belonging to the Ukrainian people to support his lifestyle.

4. *Precipitating factor:* A dramatic event or incident occurs to incite people to action. The Ukrainian president left the capital Kiev in fear after the guards defending him left their posts. President Putin of Russia amassed Russian troops on the Ukrainian border, charging that the president of Ukraine had been rightfully elected and that Crimea should be part of Russia. Russian troops then entered

 Collective Behavior Civil Disturbances

Crimea, and Russia officially annexed it (declared it part of Russia).

5. *Mobilization for action:* Leaders emerge and set out a path of action, or an emergent norm develops that stimulates common action. Ukrainian leaders emerged to defend Ukraine against what they saw as Russian aggression. A newly elected Ukrainian president sent troops to eastern Ukraine to defend it against Russians who want to align it with Russia.

6. *Social controls are weak:* If the police, the military, or political or religious leaders are unable to counter the mobilization, a social movement or other crowd behavior may form. Ukraine's new president, parliament, and army resisted the efforts of the pro-Russian groups (assisted by Russian troops) in eastern Ukraine to establish a separate (pro-Russian) state, but Ukrainian forces and resources are much less than Russia's. As we write these words, the outcome remains unclear.

When all six of the above factors are present, some sort of collective behavior will emerge. Those interested in controlling volatile crowds must intervene and take control when one or more of these conditions exists (Flynn 2014; Smelser 1963).

Types of Collective Behavior

Collective behavior ranges from spontaneous violent mobs to temporary fads and fashions. Figure 14.3 shows the range of actions.

Mobs are emotional crowds that engage in violence against a specific target. Examples include lynchings, killings, and hate crimes. Near the end of the U.S. Civil War, self-appointed vigilante groups roamed the countryside in the South looking for army deserters, torturing and killing both those who harbored deserters and the deserters themselves. There were no courts and no laws, just "justice" in the eyes of the vigilantes. The

All six social factors that contribute to collective behavior were present in 2014 in Kiev, Ukraine, and the results were riots in the streets, the overthrow of the Ukrainian president, and the annexation of Crimea by Russia.

members of these groups constituted mobs. The film *Cold Mountain* depicts these scenes vividly. Unless deterred, mobs often damage or destroy their target.

Riots—an outbreak of illegal violence against random or shifting targets committed by crowds expressing frustration or anger against people, property, or groups in power—begin when certain conditions occur. Often, a sense of frustration or deprivation sets the stage for a riot—hunger, poverty, poor housing, lack of jobs, discrimination, poor education, or an unresponsive or unfair judicial system. If the conditions for collective behavior are present, many types of incidents can be the precipitating factor setting off a riot. For example, in the summer of 2014, residents of Ferguson, Missouri, became outraged when a police officer shot and killed Michael Brown, an unarmed black 18-year-old. While some residents peacefully protested, others looted stores and threw rocks at police officers. The distinction between riots and mobs is illustrated in Figure 14.4 on page 402.

Panic occurs when a large number of individuals become fearful or try to flee threatening situations beyond their control, sometimes putting their lives in danger. Panic can occur in a crowd situation, such as

FIGURE 14.3 Types of Collective Behavior

Spontaneous and often violent			Less spontaneous and seldom violent
Crowd behavior			Mass behavior
Mob	Riot	Panic	Rumor	Fad	Fashion

FIGURE 14.4   The Difference Between Riots and Mobs

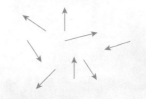

Riots involve dispersed actions expressing frustration (e.g., urban riots over poor conditions).

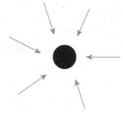

Mobs involve a group collectively focusing their action on a single individual or location (e.g., a lynch mob).

a restaurant or theater in which someone yells "Fire," or it can occur following rumors or information spread by the media. Panic started by rumors set off the run on the stock market in October 1929. A large number of actions by individuals caused the stock market crash in the United States, with repercussions around the world. In 2008, the collapse of the global investment banking and securities trader Bear, Stearns & Co. resulted in turmoil in the financial markets. Only radical intervention by the federal government abated the immediate panic. Panics can result in collapse of an organization, destruction, or even death.

Rumors are forms of mass behavior in which unsupported or unproven reports about a problem, issue, or concern circulate widely throughout the public. Rumors may spread only in a local area, but with electronic means available, rumors spread more widely and rapidly. Without authoritative information, ambiguous situations can produce faulty information on which decisions are made and actions are based. *Urban legends*, one example of widely spread but unverified messages, are unsubstantiated stories that sound plausible and become widely circulated. The people telling these stories usually believe them (Mikkelson and Mikkelson 2012). The next "Engaging Sociology" provides an example. (Go to www.snopes.com/college/college.asp for some additional entertaining urban legends about professors, exam scams, embarrassments, and other college pranks.)

Fads are temporary behaviors, activities, or material objects that spread rapidly and are copied enthusiastically by large numbers of people. Body modification, especially tattooing, appeals mostly to young people of all social classes. Tattoo artists emblazon IDs, secret society and organization emblems, fraternity symbols, and decorations to order on all parts of customers' bodies. Body modification has taken place for centuries, but it goes through fads (University of Pennsylvania 2010). Sometimes, fads become institutionalized—that is, they gain a permanent place in the culture. Other fads die out, replaced by the next hot item.

Fashions refer to a style of appearance and behavior temporarily favored by a large number of people. Examples include clothing styles, music genres, color schemes in home decor, types of automobiles, and architectural designs. Fashions typically last longer than fads but sometimes survive only a season, as can be seen in the clothing industry. Music styles such as "hardcore techno," "acid," "alternative hip-hop," and "UK 2-step garage" were popular among some groups as the previous edition of this book was being written, but a couple of years later as we finished the fourth edition, the fads were "dub step," "indie," "electropop," "screamo," "Latin-pop," and "chiptune." These styles will probably be passé by the time you read this, replaced by new fads emerging in mass behavior.

Each of these forms of collective behavior involves micro-level individual actions that cumulatively become collective responses to certain circumstances. Insofar as these various types of collective activity upset the standard routines of society and the accepted norms, they can unsettle the entire social system and cause lasting change. When we move to meso- and macro-level analyses, the established structures and processes of society become increasingly important. Much of the change at these levels is planned change.

PLANNED CHANGE IN ORGANIZATIONS: MESO-LEVEL CHANGE

The board of trustees of a small liberal arts college has witnessed recent drops in student enrollments that could cause the college to go out of business, but the college has a long tradition of fine education and

ENGAGING SOCIOLOGY

Exam Stories: Testing the Truth

College exams are quickly approaching, so it is a good time to take a look at the latest chapter in the tome of teacher-student legend and rumors. Take a look at the following examples of exam stories and think of others you may have heard of; then answer the questions at the end.

The first one was reported from Calgary, Alberta, by a civil engineering student at the University of Manitoba. This tale says a professor announced an open-book final examination in which the students could "use anything they are able to carry into the exam room." One innovative undergraduate, it is reported, carried in a graduate student who wrote his exam for him.

Another legend came from North Carolina. Supposedly, on the day before the final exam, the professor left his office unattended, with the door open and the examinations left sitting on his desk. A student who came by to ask a question found the room empty and quickly left with one of the exams. However, the professor had printed the exact number of exams that he needed, and the next morning, he counted them again before going to the classroom. Discovering that he was one short, he suspected that it had been stolen, so he trimmed a half inch from the bottom of the remaining exams. When the exam papers were turned in, the student whose paper was longer than the others' received a failing grade.

Finally, in an introductory chemistry class, two guys were taking chemistry, and they had done so well on all the quizzes that by the last week of class they each had a solid A. These friends were so confident going into the final that for the weekend before the exam they decided to party. However, after hangovers on Monday, they overslept and missed the exam. They found the professor and told him they missed the final because they had been away, had had a flat tire on the way back to campus, and were without a spare. The professor thought this over and agreed that they could make up the final. The two studied intensely that night and went in the next day for the exam. The professor placed them in separate rooms and handed each of them a test booklet and told them to begin. The first problem was simple and was worth 5 points. They were both relieved. They did the first problem and then turned the page. The next question was "Which tire? (95 points)."

Campus legends such as these help reduce the strain of college life and spread the reputations of legendary professors. Furthermore, they keep alive hopes of someday outfoxing the professors—or the students, depending on which side you are on.

1. Can you think of examples to add to this list? How do you know whether they are true or not?
2. How did you hear about the urban legends with which you are familiar? How did you learn they were not, in fact, true?
3. In what ways do such stories illustrate "collective behavior"?

Source: www.snopes.com.

---

devoted alumni. How does the college continue to serve future students and current alumni? The problem is how to plan change to keep the college solvent.

A company manufactures silicon chips for computers. Recently, the market has been flooded with inexpensive chips, primarily from Asia, where they are made more cheaply than this North American firm can possibly make them. Does the company succumb to the competition, figure out ways to meet it, or diversify its products? What steps should be taken to facilitate the change? Many companies in Silicon Valley, California, face exactly this challenge.

A Native American nation within the United States faces unemployment among its people due in large measure to discrimination by Anglos in the local community. Should the elders focus their energies and resources on electing sympathetic politicians, boycotting racist businesses, filing lawsuits, becoming entrepreneurs as a nation so they can hire their own people, or beginning a local radio station so they will have a communication network for a social movement? What is the best strategy to help this proud nation recover from centuries of disadvantage?

All these are real problems faced by real organizations. Anywhere we turn, organizations face questions involving change, questions that arise because of internal strains and external stresses. How organizational leaders deal with change will determine the survival and well-being of the organizations.

How Organizations Plan for Change

When working for an organization, we engage in the process of planning for change. Some organizations spend time and money writing long-range strategic plans and doing self-studies to determine areas for ongoing change. Sometimes, change is desired, and sometimes it is forced on the organization by *stresses* from society and more powerful organizations, or *strains* from individuals and groups within organizations pushing for new ideas. Moreover, a problem solved in one area can create unanticipated problems someplace else.

Organizational leaders must be prepared to guide their organization through planned and unplanned changes. Planned change involves strategic planning: deliberate, structured attempts, guided by stated goals, to alter the status quo of the social unit (Bennis, Benne, and Chin 1985; Ferhansyed 2008). Several important questions should be considered before undertaking planned change: How can we identify what needs to be changed? How can we plan or manage the change process successfully? What kind of systems adapt well to change? Here, we outline three of the many approaches to planned change. Keep in mind the levels of analysis as you read about change models.

Models for Planning Organizational Change. Change models fall into two main categories: (1) closed-system models, which deal with the internal dynamics of the organization, and (2) open-system models (such as our social world model), which consider the organization and its environment. *Closed-system models*, often called classical or mechanistic models, focus on the internal dynamics of the organization. The goal of change using closed models is to move the organization closer to the ideal of bureaucratic efficiency and effectiveness. An example is "time and motion studies," which analyze how much time it takes a worker to do a certain task and how it

can be accomplished more efficiently. Each step in McDonald's process of getting a hamburger to the customer has been planned and timed for the greatest efficiency (Ritzer 2013).

In some closed-system models, top executives legislate change, and it filters down to the workers. Other organizations follow a closed-system change model with an "organizational development approach." They involve participants in the organization in decision making leading to change. The leadership is more democratic and supportive of workers, and the atmosphere is transparent—open, honest, and accountable to workers and investors. This model emphasizes that change comes about through adjusting workers' values, beliefs, and attitudes regarding new demands on the organization. Many variations on this theme have evolved, with current efforts including team building and change of the organizational culture to improve worker morale. Closed-system models tend to focus on group change that occurs from within the organization.

Open-system models combine both internal processes and the external environment. The latter provides the organization with inputs (workers and raw materials) and feedback (acceptability of the product or result). In turn, the organization has outputs (products) that affect the larger society. There are several implications of this model: (1) Change is an ever-present and ongoing process, (2) all parts of the organization and its immediate environment are linked, and (3) change in one part has an effect on the other parts. The model in Figure 14.5 illustrates the open system.

FIGURE 14.5 Open Systems Model

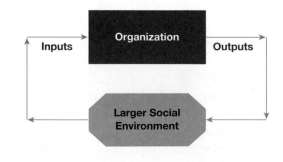

Thinking Sociologically

Using the model in Figure 14.5, fill in the parts as they relate to your college or university. For example, inputs might include students, federal student aid grants, new knowledge, and technology.

The Process of Planned Change. A huge issue in the Global South is the availability of clean drinking water. For example, in parts of Africa, women must spend as much as 6 hours a day carrying water to their homes. Because older daughters care for the younger siblings while the mother is away, many girls cannot attend school. Sometimes the water found is not clean, leading to water-related diseases and more lost school days. This, in turn, has implications for the continuation of poverty (WaterAid 2012). Scientists and public policy NGOs work to plan changes and address such problems. Consider the following example.

With global climate change, the glaciers on top of mountains such as Mount Kenya are melting. Although that mountain peak has been snow covered for more than 10,000 years, the glaciers are expected to be completely gone in approximately 20 years (Cousteau 2008). When the snow on the mountaintop disappears, the water supply for hundreds of thousands of people and animals will disappear (Maoncha 2013). One British NGO bringing about change in this area is WaterAid, launched in 1981. It has grown to become an international NGO that focuses entirely on water and sanitation issues, including hygiene. WaterAid now assists communities throughout the world to develop the most appropriate technologies for clean water, given the geographical features and changes in resources in their areas. This is an issue that requires careful planning and strategic use of resources if change is to be effective and have positive outcomes.

Using planned change, WaterAid reached 1.9 million people with safe water, 2.9 million people with sanitation, and an estimated 4.1 million people with hygiene promotion in 2013–2014 (WaterAid 2014). Some sociologists also use their understanding of social processes to improve access to safe water and water management.

The process of planned change is like a puzzle with a number of pieces that differ for each organization but must fit together for the smooth operation of the organization. The goal of most organizations is to remain balanced and avoid threats or conflict. Most organizations and countries prefer to bring about change in a slow, carefully planned way. Unplanned change can be disruptive to the system.

At the societal and global macro levels, individuals and events outside the chambers of power often stimulate change, and there is much less control over how the change evolves. We turn next to an exploration of change at the macro level.

SOCIAL MOVEMENTS: MACRO-LEVEL CHANGE

Sochi, Russia, hosted the prestigious 2014 Winter Olympics. The Olympics purport to promote peace and goodwill around the globe. The Olympic torch, a symbol of peace and goodwill, traveled from Moscow to Sochi through 2,900 towns and villages to prepare for and celebrate the event. However, its journey and the opening of the games were far from peaceful and full of goodwill. Protests about Russia's policies toward gay rights dogged the torch and pregame political

Petermann Glacier, 5 August 2009

Petermann Glacier 24 July 2011

These before and after shots of the Petermann Glacier in Greenland show a massive loss of glacier in just one calving (breaking off of chunks of ice at the edge of a glacier). For many parts of the world, glaciers are a major source of fresh water, but they are melting because of global climate change.

 Social Movements–A Primer: Toby Chow

This photo shows Russian police attacking members of the Russian punk band Pussy Riot as they mock Russian antigay policies. This was one of hundreds of protests against the Russian policy prior to and during the Winter Olympic Games in Sochi.

commentary, and major political leaders refused to attend the opening ceremonies. Russian legislation denigrating LGBTQ individuals and those spreading "propaganda" that "promotes" same-sex relationships sparked off protests and demonstrations around the world ("Sochi" 2014). Was this a social movement? We now turn to the definition of a social movement and discuss how social movements form and the results of such movements.

What Is a Social Movement?

From human rights and women's rights to animal rights and environmental protection, individuals seek ways to express their concerns and frustrations. **Social movements** are *consciously organized attempts outside of established institutions to enhance or resist change through group action*. Movements focus on a common interest of members, such as abortion policy. They have an organization, a leader, and one or more goals that aim to correct some perceived wrongs existing in society or even around the globe. Social movements are most often found in industrial or postindustrial societies although they can occur anyplace groups of people have a concern or frustration.

Social movements entail large groups of people who hold little power individually, but do have power as united groups that promote or resist social change. The problems leading to social movements often result from the way resources—human rights, jobs, income, housing, money for education and health care, and

power—are distributed. In turn, countermovements—social movements against the goals of the original movement—may develop, representing other opinions (McCarthy and Zald 1977).

Many individuals join social movements to change the world or their part of the world and affect the direction of history. In fact, some social movements have been successful in doing just that. Consider the movements around the world that have protected lands, forests, rivers, and oceans, seeking environmental protection for the people whose survival depends on these natural resources. For example, the Chipko movement (meaning "embrace") has been fighting the logging of forests by commercial industries in a number of areas in India. Villagers, mostly women, who depend on the forests, use Gandhi-style nonviolent methods to oppose the deforestation. These women have set an example for environmentalists in many parts of the world who wish to save trees (Scribd 2011).

Stages of Social Movements

Why do people become involved in social movements such as PETA (People for the Ethical Treatment of Animals), pro-choice or pro-life movements, or political demonstrations against governments and their policies? Social movements begin because of cultural conflicts in society and because people who want to create—or resist—social change come together. Movements take the time and energy of individual volunteers, and these human resources must be focused as the movement evolves.

The first stage of a social movement involves setting the purpose of the movement. Long-standing problems or very recent events may create dissatisfaction and discontent in the general public or a part of the public. This discontent can galvanize people through a single event.

Sociologists have identified several conditions that give rise to the *preliminary stage*:

a) Individuals must *share some basic values and ideals*. They often occupy similar social statuses or positions and share concerns.

b) Social movements need to have a "*preexisting communication network*" that allows alienated or dissatisfied people to share their discontent (Farley 2011). Several recent political movements, such as MoveOn.org and Crossroads GPS, were carried out primarily on the Internet.

c) A *strain* and a *precipitating event* galvanize people around the issue. Effective leadership emerges—leaders who can mobilize people, organize the movement, and garner resources to fund the movement.

d) The people in the movement develop a *sense of efficacy*, a sense of confidence that they actually can be successful and change the system. Sometimes, as in the case of the civil rights movement, a sense of efficacy comes from a religious conviction that God will not let the movement fail (Farley 2011).

The *second stage* in the development of a movement is popularization, in which individuals coalesce their efforts, define their goals and strategies, develop recruitment tactics, and identify leaders. The social movement enters the public arena. The leaders present the social problems and solutions as seen by the members of the social movement. Now the social movement enters the *third stage*, becoming institutionalized and a formal organization. This organized effort generates the resources and members for the social change efforts.

In some movements, the final *fourth stage* is fragmentation and demise. The group may or may not have achieved its goals, but fragmentation breaks apart the organization because the resources may be exhausted, the leadership may be inept or have lost legitimacy, or the leaders may be co-opted to join powerful mainline organizations. In the latter case, radical renewal movements may arise among those still strongly committed to the original cause (Mauss 1975).

Social movements sometimes focus on regional or even organizational modification, but typically, their focus is on national or global issues. For example, Amnesty International's primary interest is challenging countries with human rights violations. It publishes information on violations around the world and encourages supporters to advocate for those who face government persecution. One way to classify social movements is by their purpose or goals, as seen in the following section.

© Keith A. Roberts

Flash mobs consist of groups of people who assemble suddenly in a public place, perform an unusual act for a brief time, and then quickly disperse, often for the purposes of entertainment, satire, or artistic expression. They are often fun and sometimes have a message critiquing the society or calling for change. This church-based flash mob in Minnehaha Park (Minneapolis) sang and danced to encourage voters to support same sex-marriage legislation in the 2012 election.

Types of Social Movements

Stonewall is a gay, lesbian, and bisexual rights movement that began when patrons of a gay bar fought back against a police raid in New York in 1969. After that incident, the concern about gay rights erupted from a small number of activists into a widespread movement for rights and acceptance. Stonewall now has gone global, with chapters in many other countries and continents.

Proactive social movements advocate moving forward with a new initiative—proposing something that did not exist before. One example is the effort by the Nonhuman Rights Project to give mammals such as chimpanzees legal rights of personhood. The Supreme Court ruled in the *Citizens United* case that corporations can be considered "persons." Now the Nonhuman Rights Project and Harvard Professor Steven Wise argue that dogs, cats, elephants, and other animals should be protected with rights of persons (such as right to body integrity) since they are aware, thinking, feeling, compassionate, communicating beings (Nonhuman Rights Project 2014). Regardless of whether you think this is an idea whose time has come or a harebrained notion, it would clearly change many aspects of society and move us in an entirely new direction.

Reactive social movements resist change, reacting against something that exists or against new trends or new social policies. The Climate Change Countermovement provides an example of a reactive social movement. It comprises 91 groups that have spent more than $1 billion from 141 nonprofit organizations and think tanks trying to debunk the conservation movement and climate change claims (Brulle 2014). They aim to counter the environmental movement and the change in policies that would result if that movement were successful in passing legislation and action.

Note that both liberals and conservatives can be involved in a reactive movement. When businesses want to build a corporation or plant in an area that will wipe out a native forest or destroy a historic area, liberals can be at the forefront of fighting "progress." Whether proactive or reactive, there are five main types of social movements: expressive, social reform, revolutionary, resistance or regressive, and globalized.

Expressive movements take place in groups, but they *focus on changing individuals and saving people from lifestyles the movement considers corrupt.* Many expressive movements are religious, such as the born-again Christian movements, Zen Buddhism, Scientology, and the Christian Science Church. Expressive movements also include secular psychotherapy movements and self-help or self-actualization groups.

Social reform movements *seek to change some specific dimension of society, usually involving legislative policy modification or appeals to the courts.* Movement members generally support the society as a whole but think things could be better if attention were given to issues such as environmental protection, women's rights, same-sex marriage, "just and fair" globalization, reducing the national debt, or abortion policy.

Social reform movements are not interested in disrupting the functioning of the entire society: They have one issue they think needs reform. For example, many individuals with disabilities are given little attention, hope, or opportunity to get ahead and are institutionalized or left to languish. However, social reform movements have advocated for legislation to promote the rights of the differently abled. One such movement is Special Olympics International, begun by Eunice Kennedy Shriver in 1968 to give those with intellectual or physical disabilities an opportunity to excel in sports. Over 3 million athletes from 150 countries now participate in these games (www.specialolympics.org). The 2014 Winter Paralympic Games were held in Sochi, Russia, featuring athletes with physical, mental, and sensorial disabilities. These events bring attention to the movement and issues faced by those with disabilities. Of particular interest were the advances the movement has helped to stimulate in physical adaptations for amputees, such as ice hockey using two sticks.

Revolutionary movements *attempt to transform society to bring about total change in society by overthrowing existing power structures and replacing them with new ones; these movements often resort to violent means to achieve goals.* When we read in the paper that there has been a coup, we are learning about the ousting of an existing government such as when the military in Thailand declared martial law and seized power from the interim prime minister in May 2014.

Resistance or regressive movements *try to protect an existing system, protect part of that system, or return to what a system had been by overthrowing current*

Four Stages of Social Movements

laws and practices. They see societal change as a threat to values or practices and wish to maintain the status quo or return to a former status by reversing the change process (Eitzen and Zinn 2012; Inglehart and Baker 2001). The Taliban religious movement in Afghanistan is a regressive movement against modernization, especially against the Western pattern of giving freedom and autonomy to women. The movement was successful in gaining power in the 1990s, imposing a harsh brand of Islamic law in the sections of Afghanistan under its control. The Taliban insists that its version of Islam is pure in that it follows a literal understanding of the Muslim holy book. Members of the movement maintain that someone who commits adultery should be stoned to death; the hands or arms of thieves should be amputated; and women who deviate from the Taliban interpretation of Muslim law should be mutilated, publically beaten, and sometimes executed (Valentine 2009).

Global transnational movements are *mobilized groups that take place across societies as international organizations.* Such groups focus on issues that affect the global community, such as the status of women, child labor, the rights of indigenous peoples, environmental degradation, global warming, and disease pandemics. Free the Slaves, an antislavery movement started by sociologist Kevin Bales, provides one example of a global transnational movement. Members of this movement have researched and written about the plight of the 27 million slaves in the world, "forced to work without pay, under threat of violence and

This photo shows a statue of Nelson Mandela, who voted for the first time in South Africa in 1994. He had been a political prisoner for 26 years before becoming president of South Africa and winning the Nobel Peace Prize. Mandela provides a model for those committed to nonviolent revolutionary change.

unable to walk away" (Bales 2007; Bales and Soodalter 2010; Bales, Trodd, and Williamson 2009; Free the Slaves 2014).

The autoworkers' conflict with General Motors in Colombia is another example of a transnational or global social movement. A group of 68 autoworkers at a GM assembly plant outside of Bogotá formed a protest movement in May 2011. The issue was that a number of workers were fired when they could no longer perform their jobs due to disabling workplace injuries, including severe impairments to backs and rotator cuffs. Some of the workers will never be able to work again. Some health care companies hired by GM changed medical records to read "injuries unrelated to occupation." After 15 months of protests, 13 protesters began a hunger strike, 8 of them sewing their mouths shut. International supporters began solidarity actions to put pressure on GM to enter into negotiations, and supporters in the United States sent money, wrote letters, and even engaged in fasting or hunger strikes themselves (Witness for Peace 2012). Intervention in 2013 by the United Auto Workers temporarily ended the hunger strike, but they were not able to resolve the issue. In November 2014, several of the autoworkers in Colombia chained themselves to the gate of the U.S. Embassy in a nonviolent protest action to get the U.S. government involved, but U.S. Embassy officials refused to meet with them. In February 2015, 25 injured workers from Colombia's oil sector, who are also seeking just compensation and better conditions for their fellow workers, joined the movement (ASOTRECOL 2015). As we write these words, their efforts continue. As you can see, this is a local issue in Colombia that has mobilized people in other parts of the world.

Figure 14.6 summarizes the types of movements and the focus of each, from the micro to the macro level.

FIGURE 14.6   Types of Movements

	Proactive	Reactive
Macro level	Social Reform Revolutionary Global Transnational	Resistance or Regressive
Micro level	Expressive	Expressive

Globalization and Social Movements

Social movements provide compelling evidence that humans make choices and are capable of countering macro- and meso-level forces. As Stanley Eitzen and Maxine Baca Zinn put it,

> Powerful social structures constrain what we do, but they can never control (us) entirely. Human beings are not passive actors.... Individuals acting alone, or with others, can shape, resist, challenge, and sometimes change the social structures that impinge on them. These actions constitute human agency. (Eitzen and Zinn 2012:269)

Since World War II, power in the global system has been dominated by a group of industrial giants calling themselves the Group of Eight (or the "G8"). As noted in Chapter 12, in March 2014, Russia was voted out by the other members because of its actions in Ukraine, so the group is now the G7. These nations control world markets and regulate economic and trading policies. Included among these elites are the dominant three (Japan from the East, Germany from central Europe, and the United States from the American continents). Four other important but less dominating powers include Canada, France, Great Britain, and Italy.

Although some politicians say they believe in a free market economy, uninhibited by governmental interference, government officials use international agencies to intervene regularly in the global market. The G7 nations have the most power in the World Trade Organization, the World Bank, the IMF, and other regulatory agencies that preside over the global economy. These agencies have required poor countries to adhere to their demands or lose the right to loans and other support. The policies they have imposed, however, have sometimes been disastrous for poor countries, leading to debt burdens impossible to pay off.

The IMF points out that the loans are the only way poor countries can meet the UN Millennium Development Goals, but critics argue that the loans make poor countries dependent on wealthy countries and that the loans should be forgiven (IMF 2013). They argue that if these were individuals rather than countries, we would call the poorer nations indentured servants or slaves (Brecher et al. 2012). One might think that hopelessness would reign supreme in these nations, yet social movements are arising in precisely these places and often joining forces across national boundaries (Eitzen and Zinn 2012; Ferree 2012; Muchhala 2012). Even some groups within the G7 nations—labor unions, college student groups, and religious bodies concerned about social justice—are joining the movements.

Global South nations, calling themselves the G77, have now united, rather like a labor union seeking collective unity among workers, in an attempt to gain some power and determine their own destinies (Brecher et al. 2012). Figure 12.3 on page 343 displays the location of G7 and G77 countries.

Although workers risk losing jobs by participating in protests for higher wages and better working conditions, one result of globalization has been a rise in countermovements. "Globalization from below" refers to the efforts by common people in small groups and protest movements to fight back (Della Porta, Andretta, Mosca, and Reiter 2006; Eitzen and Zinn 2012). These countermovements seek to protect workers, defend the environment, and combat the bone-crunching poverty that plagues so much of the Global South. The argument goes like this:

> It is the activity of people—going to work, paying taxes, buying products, obeying government officials, staying off private property—that continually re-creates the power of the powerful.... [The system, for all its power and resources, is dependent on common people to do the basic jobs that keep the society running.] This dependency gives people a potential power over the society—but one that can be realized only if they are prepared to reverse their acquiescence.... Social movements can be understood as the collective withdrawal of consent to established institutions. (Brecher et al. 2012:279)

The movement against globalization can be understood as withdrawing consent for globalization dominated by the most powerful nations and global corporations (Brecher et al. 2012). There are thousands of small resistance actions against what are sometimes perceived to be the oppressive policies of G7 transnational corporations (Hearn 2012). They involve micro-level actions to bring change at the macro level. Consider the following example:

> Under heavy pressure from the World Bank, the Bolivian government sold off the public water

system of its third-largest city, Cochabamba, to a subsidiary of the San Francisco–based Bechtel Corporation, which promptly doubled the price of water for people's homes. Early in 2000, the people of Cochabamba rebelled, shutting down the city with general strikes and blockades. The government declared a state of siege, and a young protester was shot and killed. Word spread all over the world from the remote Bolivian highlands via the Internet. Hundreds of e-mail messages poured into Bechtel from all over the world, demanding that it leave Cochabamba. In the midst of local and global protests, the Bolivian government, which had said that Bechtel must not leave, suddenly reversed itself and signed an accord accepting every demand of the protesters. (Brecher et al. 2012:284)

Many concerned citizens in the Global North now buy Fair Trade Certified goods such as coffee, cocoa, and fruits. This is an effort by individuals to support *globalization from below*—a different model of how to change the world. Activists believe that actions by individuals and small groups—globalization from below—can have a real impact on global problems.

Thinking Sociologically

Identify three reasons to be optimistic about why change from the bottom up can be successful. To examine a specific example of a group that approaches globalization from below, do an Internet search of the Zapatistas. What are the pros and cons of this movement? Do you think the Zapatistas have any chance of bringing change to the poor, disfranchised people of southern Mexico? Why or why not?

In summary, some social change is planned by organizations (planned change), some is initiated by groups outside the organizational structure (social movements), and some is unplanned and spontaneous (collective behavior). The most important point, however, is that actions taken by individuals affect the larger social world, sometimes even having global ramifications. Likewise, national and international changes and social movements influence the lives of individuals.

In the opening to this book, we asked whether you as an individual can make a difference. On page 412 we present an example of a "Sociologist in Action" who helps others bring about social change.

TECHNOLOGY, ENVIRONMENT, AND CHANGE

A lot is at stake for businesses, workers, environmentalists, policymakers, and others when considering the need for more energy sources. From renewable energy such as solar and wind power to gas and oil from fracking, strong opinions abound. One current example is the proposed Keystone XL Pipeline that would go from the Canadian tar sands source of oil to Texas refineries, crossing many states in the process. Proponents argue that it will be the safest, most advanced oil pipeline in North America, bringing jobs, long-term energy independence, and an economic boost to both Canada and the United States. In addition, it will enhance the relationship between the two countries (TransCanada 2014).

Opponents argue that a technology failure along the pipeline could create havoc. The popularity of the movement to stop the construction of the pipeline illustrates that controversy can sometimes inspire or revitalize a group supporting social change, as happened with the environmentalists opposing the Keystone XL Pipeline project. Increasingly, U.S. oil is coming from deposits of tar sands in Alberta, Canada. This is not conventional crude oil. It is thick, sticky sand that companies extract by shooting steam deep underground to liquefy it, or they scrape it out of sprawling surface mines. These techniques of extraction are expensive, and they produce a lot more greenhouse gases than conventional oil wells. Still, high oil prices make tar sands oil profitable. If the network, known as the Keystone XL Pipeline, is approved, some 800,000 barrels of oil would be transported to refineries in Texas via large 36-inch pipes. A break in a tar sands pipeline in Michigan in 2010 resulted in 40 miles of the Kalamazoo River being basically closed to any public use (Wheaton 2014). TransCanada, the company that owns the pipeline, has admitted that it expects about two breaks per year over the 1,700 miles of pipe (Shogren 2012).

James Hansen, a former NASA climate scientist, published an open letter to the public calling the pipeline "game over for the climate" and urged people to take action. This jump-started the environmental movement, bringing in unexpected allies—including Texas landholders—and large numbers of young people (Wheaton 2014).

SOCIOLOGISTS IN ACTION:
ELLIS JONES

Empowering Everyday People: Democratizing Access to Social Change

On April 22, 1990, something changed for me. It was a Sunday. I was a student at the University of Southern California, and a friend invited me to walk down to a fair that was going on nearby. I didn't have any plans, so I decided to join him. Apparently, it was something called "Earth Day." There were tables and booths everywhere, and people were excitedly milling about from one to the next. Every booth I visited offered me a different way to make a positive environmental impact: recycling, composting, conserving water, reusing old clothes, and the list went on and on.

At the end of that day, I felt absolutely inspired to make the world a better place. In my mind, the environmental movement had experienced a stroke of true genius. They weren't asking people to join groups, attend meetings, or organize rallies. Instead, they had opened up a completely new realm of action for people—their own everyday lives. By engaging people in micro-activism rather than asking them to commit to the much more intensive work undertaken by full-time activists, they were essentially democratizing access to social change. It was a way to expand the environmental movement to almost anyone despite their limits of time, money, skills, or circumstances.

As soon as I realized this, I imagined that thousands of others were having the same revelation at that same moment of history. The environmental movement was laying the foundation for all other social movements to do exactly the same thing! The human rights movement, the social justice movement, the animal rights movement, the feminist movement, the LGBTQ movement, and all the rest would begin to adapt this new technique to engage people everywhere in actions they could take in their own lives to contribute to some much needed social change.

Granted, no particular action would add up to much in terms of impact, but if enough people were inspired to act, the collective impact of thousands, or tens of thousands, or perhaps even millions of people would redefine what kind of changes were possible around these issues. At the same time, all of these people would now feel more invested in the outcomes that they themselves had been working toward in their own way. Rather than relying solely on a relatively small group of activists to bear the weight of these daunting social and environmental problems, now everyone could take on a piece of that responsibility.

The more I thought about this potential, the more I became convinced that what people really needed (or at least what *I* really needed) was a book that would collect as many of these possible actions as possible into a single place. I was absolutely sure that someone would write it and that I, in turn, would be first in line to buy it. Ten years later, I was a sociology graduate student at the University of Colorado Boulder. I had waited, patiently, for the imaginary author of this hypothetical book to appear and s/he had yet to step forward. In the meantime, I was teaching *Social Problems* along with a number of other mainstay sociology courses and found that my own students were constantly asking what they could actually do about all of these problems we were spending so much time reading about, discussing, and analyzing.

I had waited 10 years and decided that was long enough. So I roped in two of my closest friends (also fellow sociology grad students), and we spent the next year writing a book that collected all of the actions we could find, from every source we could get our hands on, and distilled the results into a single book. We added a section summarizing the latest data on some of the most significant social and environmental problems we seemed to be facing at the beginning of the 21st century, and the result was *The Better World Handbook: Small Changes That Make a Big Difference.* It has since sold 25,000 copies, been added to more than 300 college and university libraries worldwide, and been adopted in sociology classrooms across the country. The website (betterworldhandbook.com) has had over 550,000 unique visitors since it was created. In a very practical sense, sociology provided the three of us with the tools we needed to uncover, understand, and translate our world's social and environmental problems into a form that allows each of us to personally contribute to their resolution.

• •

Ellis Jones received his doctorate from the University of Colorado Boulder, and is now an assistant professor of sociology at College of the Holy Cross in Worcester, Massachusetts.

An exhausted oil-covered brown pelican struggled in a pool of oil on an island off the coast of Louisiana, part of the cost of a massive oil spill in 2010. Environmental disasters from oil spills have created new impetus for environmental movements.

Environmentalists opposed to the Keystone XL Pipeline have built a human chain around the White House, clogged the State Department's public comment system with more than a million emails and letters, and had themselves arrested at protests across the country. The email list of an organization called 350.org, which focuses on climate change, more than doubled to 530,000 people in less than a year. In addition, about 76,000 people have signed a "pledge of resistance," and an environmental group—the Sierra Club—raised more than $1 million in one week when they announced an anti-pipeline initiative (Wheaton 2014). The revitalized environmental movement is changing the landscape regarding the energy-versus-environment conflict (Wheaton 2014).

Technology refers to *the practical application of tools, skills, and knowledge to meet human needs and extend human abilities.* Technology and the environment cannot be separated, as we see from the debate over the Keystone XL Pipeline. The raw products that fuel technology come from the environment, the wastes return to the environment, and technological mistakes affect the environment. This section discusses briefly the development and process of technology, the relationship between technology and the environment, and the implications for change at each level of analysis.

Throughout human history, there have been major transition periods when changes in the material culture brought about revolutions in human social structures and cultures (Toffler and Toffler 1980). For example, the agricultural revolution, which resulted from the use of the plow to till the soil, established new social arrangements and created food surpluses that allowed cities to flourish. With the Industrial Revolution came machines powered by steam and gasoline, resulting in mass production, population increases, urbanization, the division of labor in manufacturing, social stratification, and the socialist and capitalist political-economic systems. Today, postindustrial technology, based on the microchip, fuels the spread of information, communication, transportation on a global level, and even exploration of outer space. It also allows us to store and retrieve masses of information in seconds. However, each wave of innovation initially affects only a portion of the world, leaving other people and countries behind and creating divisions between the Global North and the Global South.

Sociologist William Ogburn has argued that change is brought about through three processes: *discovery, invention,* and *diffusion. Discovery* is a new way of seeing reality. The material objects or ideas have been present, but they are seen in a new light when the need arises or conditions are conducive to the discovery. It is usually accomplished by an individual or a small group, a micro-level activity (Ogburn [1922] 1938, 1961, 1964).

Invention refers to combining existing parts, materials, or ideas to form new ones. There was no light bulb or combustion engine lying in the forest waiting to be discovered. Human ingenuity was required to put together something that had not previously existed. Technological innovations often result from research and the expansion of science, increasingly generated in meso-level institutions and organizations in society.

Diffusion is the spread of an invention or discovery from one place to another. The spread of ideas such as capitalism, democracy, and religious beliefs has brought about changes in human relationships around the world. Likewise, the spread of various types of music, film technology, telephone systems, and computer hardware and software across the globe has had important ramifications for global interconnectedness. Diffusion often involves expansion of ideas across the globe, but it also requires individuals to adopt ideas at the micro level.

Technology and Science

Science is *the systematic process of producing human knowledge; it uses empirical research methods to discover facts and test theories.* The question "How do

Can We Auto-Correct Humanity?

we know what we know?" is often answered: "It's science." Whether social, biological, or physical, science provides a systematic way to approach the world and its mysteries. It uses empirical research methods to discover facts and test theories. Today, technology applies scientific knowledge to solve problems. Early human technology was largely the result of trial and error, not based on scientific knowledge or principles. Humans did not understand why boats floated or fires burned. Since the Industrial Revolution, many inventors and capitalists have seen science and technology as routes to human betterment and happiness. Science has become a major social institution in industrial and postindustrial societies, providing the bases of information and knowledge for sophisticated technology.

Indeed, one of the major transformations in modern society is the result of science becoming an institution. Prior to the 18th century, science was an avocation. People like Benjamin Franklin experimented in their backyards with whatever spare cash they had to satisfy their own curiosity.

Science in the contemporary world is both a structure and a social process. *Institutionalization* is the organized, patterned, and enduring sets of social structures that provide guidelines for behavior and help the society meet its needs. Within these structures, actions are taken—the processes within the structure—that accomplish a goal such as conducting research. Innovation resulting in change will be very slow until a society has institutionalized science—providing extensive training and paying some people simply to do research. Modern science involves mobilizing financial resources and employing the most highly trained people (which, in turn, requires the development of educational institutions).

Specialization in science speeds up the rates of discovery. A researcher focuses on one area and gets much more in-depth understanding. Also, effective methods of communication across the globe mean that we do not need to wait several years for a research manuscript to cross the ocean and to be translated into another language. Competition in science (now global) means that researchers move quickly on their findings. The first to create new drugs, devices, and other inventions tend to reap the most recognition and compensation.

© REUTERS/ Fabian Bimmer

Technological innovation is now providing us with electricity through wind farms. The one depicted here is the first complete high-sea wind farm on the North Sea coast of Germany.

Thomas Edison had more than 1,000 patented inventions, including the light bulb, recorded sound, and movies, but perhaps his most influential invention was the research lab—in which people were paid to invent and to conduct research—at Menlo Park in New Jersey. This was the seminal step in the institutionalization of science.

We would not have automobiles, planes, missiles, space stations, computers, the Internet, and many of our modern conveniences without the institutionalization of science and without scientific application (technology). Science is big business, funded by industry and government. Most university researchers and some government-funded science institutes engage in *basic research* designed to discover new knowledge. Industry and some governmental agencies such as the military and the Department of Agriculture employ scientists to do *applied research* and discover practical uses for existing knowledge.

Scientific knowledge is usually cumulative, with each study adding to the existing body of research. However, radical new ideas can result in scientific revolutions (Kuhn 1970). Galileo's finding that Earth revolves around the Sun and Darwin's theory of evolution are two examples of radical new ideas that changed history. More recently, cumulative scientific knowledge has resulted in energy-efficient engines that power cars and computer technology that has revolutionized communication.

Thinking Sociologically

Imagine what your life would have been like before home computers, email, and the Internet. What would be different? (Note that you are imagining the world from only 30 years ago.) Ask your parents or grandparents what this recent past was like.

Technology and Change

A nation's research and development (R&D) is an important measure of investment in the future. For many years the biggest investors have been the European Union, the United States, and Japan, accounting in 2014 for $1.6 trillion or 78% of global R&D expenditures. However, in 2022, China is expected to surpass the United States in R&D spending. While U.S. industry continues to support R&D, the government is under pressure to pare down federal spending and thus contributes less than in previous budgets.

This lack of U.S. investment in research is especially troubling, given what we know about the relationship between economic growth, R&D, and change (Battelle 2013). For example, technological revolution in communications has resulted in fiber-optic cable and wireless microwave cell phones and satellite technologies that make it easier to communicate with people around the world. A cable starting in Europe is now circling Africa; the capabilities for high-speed Internet will enhance opportunities for businesses, health care to remote areas, and educational advances in countries that have few textbooks. We now live in a global village, a great boon for those fortunate enough to have the education and means to take advantage of it (Drori 2006).

However, changes in technology do not always have a positive effect on less affluent countries. Consider, for example, the effects of the invention of artificial sweeteners on the demand for sugar. Sugar is the major source of income for the 50 million people who work in the beet and cane sugar industries around the globe. As new technologies bring substantial benefits to many in the world, these results can also harm people in other parts of the interconnected world. Changes in technology and the economy have forced many individuals to leave their native villages in search of paid labor positions in urban factories and the tourism industry, disrupting family lives.

Rapid technological change has affected generational relationships as well. It is not uncommon for younger generations to have more technological competence than their elders, and this sometimes creates a generational digital divide in competencies regarding use of computers, cell phones, and other electronic devices. In some settings, younger people are looked to for their expertise, whereas in the past, the elders were the source of knowledge and wisdom. Often the older members of a business or group

Research and Development   Factors of Change

ENGAGING SOCIOLOGY

Making a Difference

Because bringing about change requires cooperation, working in a group context is often essential. Flexibility, openness to new ideas, and willingness to entertain alternative suggestions are also key factors in successful change making. The following steps provide a useful strategy for planning change:

1. *Identify the issue:* Be specific and focus on what is to be changed. Without clear focus, your target for change can get muddied or lost in the attempt.

2. *Research the issue and use those findings:* Learn as much as you can about the situation or problem to be changed. Use informants, interviews, written materials, observation, existing data (such as U.S. Census Bureau statistics), or anything that helps you understand the issues. That will enable you to find the information you need to thoroughly understand the issue you wish to address.

3. *Find out what has already been done and by whom:* Other individuals or groups may be working on the same issue. Be sure you know what findings and intervention have already taken place. This can also help determine whether attempts at change have been tried, what has been successful, and whether further change is needed.

4. *Change must take into account each level of analysis:* When planning a strategy, you may focus on one level of analysis, but be sure to consider what interventions are needed at other levels to make the change effective or to anticipate the effects of change on other levels.

5. *Determine the intervention strategy:* Map out the intervention and the steps to carry it out. Identify resources needed, and plan each step in detail.

6. *Evaluate the plan:* Get feedback on the plan from those involved in the issue and from unbiased colleagues. If possible, involve those who will be affected by the intervention in the planning and evaluation of the change. When feasible, test the intervention plan before implementing it.

7. *Implement the intervention:* Put the plan into effect, watching for any unintended consequences. Ask for regular feedback from those affected by the change.

8. *Evaluate the results:* Assess what is working, what is not, and how the constituents that experience the change are reacting. Sociological knowledge and skills should help guide this process.

You are now ready to make a difference!

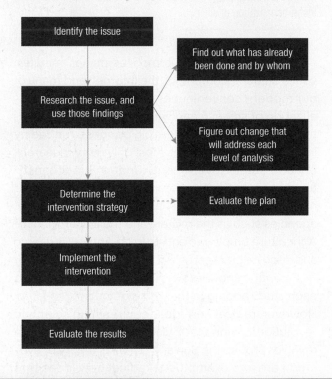

feel devalued and demoralized late in their careers because those with technical competence view the older members as "outdated has-beens."

Popular video games such as *Grand Theft Auto V* and *BioShock Infinite* plus *BioShock 2* top the sales charts (Kotaku 2013), and forms of entertainment such as the Wii-U and Nintendo 3DS further the social distance between generations. With the changes brought about by technology come changes in the nonmaterial culture—values, political ideologies, and human relationships. Clearly, technology can have a variety of social impacts—both positive and negative.

In the opening to this book, we asked whether you as an individual can make a difference. In closing, we present a final "Engaging Sociology," a plan you can follow to make a difference.

Thinking Sociologically

First, read "Engaging Sociology: Making a Difference." Then use the steps to plan how you might bring about a change that would make a difference in your community, in your country, or in the world. Go to "Contributing to Our Social World: What Can We Do?" at the end of this and other chapters to find ways in which you can be actively involved in bettering society.

WHAT HAVE WE LEARNED?

Can you change the world? The underlying message of this chapter and the text is that the choices we make facilitate change at each level in our social world. Sociology helps us to learn how to work with groups to make a difference.

As you face individual challenges to bring about change in your social world, keep in mind this message: Change at one level affects all other levels. Sociology as a discipline is focused on gathering accurate information about the society in which we live. Sociologists often use their knowledge to advocate for changes that they think will make a better society. We hope that through his book and your course you have gained important sociological insights that will help you contribute to the dialogue about how to make our social world a better, more humane place.

KEY POINTS

- Social change—variation or alteration over time in behavior patterns, culture, or structure in a society—typically involves change at one level of the social system that ripples through the other levels, micro, meso, and macro.

- *Strains* within an organization or group can induce change, as can *stresses* imposed from the outside environment.

- Sociological theories—whether micro or macro—offer explanations for the causes of change.

- At the micro level, change is often initiated through collective behavior, which can take several forms: crowds, mobs, riots, rumors, fads, and fashions.

- At the meso level, change in organizations is often managed through a planned process.

- Social movements often provide impetus for change at the macro level. Social changes can be induced at the micro level, but they can have impacts even at the global level.

- Science and technology can also stimulate change, but science has its greatest impact for change when it is institutionalized.

- Social structures constrain what we do, but individuals, especially when acting in concert with others, can challenge, resist, and change the social systems that constrain them. We can change our society through *human agency*.

DISCUSSION QUESTIONS

1. What is the latest technological device you or your family have acquired? How has it changed your life? What are the (a) intended and (b) unintended consequences of your having it?

2. Every organization must adapt to change. Describe how an organization to which you belong coped with change. Was the adaptation successful? Why or why not? What was your role? Did you feel as though you

had some influence over the adaptation strategy? Why or why not?

3. Were you aware that the United States gives far less than the 0.7% of gross national product the United Nations has requested of nations, in order to achieve the UN Millennium Development Goals to decrease poverty, illiteracy, famine, and disease? Would it be in the self-interest of the United States to contribute more or less? Why?

4. What type of social movement has helped bring about the dramatic increase in support for same-sex marriage over the past few years? Why? How do the results of this movement indicate the power of social movements to influence society at the micro, meso, and macro levels?

5. If you were to join a social movement today, which would you join? Why? What would you hope to achieve?

CONTRIBUTING TO OUR SOCIAL WORLD: What Can We Do?

At the Local Level

- *Campus-wide Movements:* A wide range of social issues, including international peace, environmental issues, human rights, and specific student concerns such as campus safety and the rising cost of higher education, may have movements represented on your campus. Consider participating in such activities. If you feel strongly about an issue for which no movement exists, consider organizing one with a few like-minded students. You can find tools to create a campus movement at www .campusactivism.org/index.php, and www.campusactiv ism.org/displayresource-471.htm.

- Many *community movements* bring about change at the local level, sometimes with national and even international effects. Check with your professors, service learning and campus activities offices, and Chambers of Commerce to find community movements in your area.

At the Organizational or Institutional Level

- *Invite a movement leader to campus.* Consider inviting movement leaders to your campus for a lecture, or organize a conference that features several experts in

a particular field. Environment, civil rights, and modern slavery are topics that have wide appeal. Professors who teach classes that cover these issues may be able to help you find a good speaker. Work with your sociology club or student government to provide funding for the speaker.

- *Volunteer Match* seeks to connect individuals with movements of interest to them. Its website (www.volunteer match.org) has suggestions for getting involved in your local area.

At the National and Global Levels

- *The Jubilee Movement* promotes international debt forgiveness for the world's poorest countries—a solution that the U.S. government has embraced in principle. Named for the principle offered in the Hebrew scriptures that creditors are to cancel all debt owed to them every jubilee year (once every 49 years), the organization sponsors legislative programs, research work, and educational outreach activities throughout the world. The website of Jubilee USA (www.jubileeusa.org/aboutus) provides information on ways in which you can get involved, and includes information about international debt, activities, and the history of the movement.

$SAGE edge™

Sharpen your skills with SAGE edge at **edge.sagepub.com/ballantinecondensed4e**

SAGE edge for Students provides a personalized approach to help you accomplish your coursework goals in an easy-to-use learning environment.

Glossary

Absolute poverty. Not having resources to meet basic needs, 192

Achieved status. Social status that is chosen or earned by decisions one makes and sometimes by personal ability, 116

Achieved stratification systems. Societal systems that allow individuals to earn positions through their ability, efforts, and choices, 189

Agents of socialization. The transmitters of culture—the people, organizations, and institutions that help us define our identity and teach us how to thrive in our social world, 96

Agricultural society. Relies primarily on raising crops for food, but makes use of technological advances such as the plow, irrigation, animals, and fertilization to continuously cultivate the same land, 58

Alienation. Feeling uninvolved, uncommitted, unappreciated, and unconnected to the group or the society, 125

Anomie. The state of normlessness that occurs when rules for behavior in society break down under extreme stress from rapid social change or conflict, 118

Arranged marriages. A pattern of mate selection in which someone other than the couple—elder males, parents, a matchmaker—selects the marital partners, 270

Ascribed statuses. Social statuses that are often assigned at birth and that do not change during an individual's lifetime; gender, race, and ethnic status group are examples, 115

Ascribed stratification systems. Societal systems in which characteristics beyond the control of the individual—such as family background, age, sex, and race—determine one's position in society, 188

Assimilation. The structural and cultural merging of minority and majority groups in society, 214

Authoritarian governments. Governments in which one absolute monarch or dictator, or a small group of unelected people, holds all of the political power, 333

Authority. Power that people consider legitimate and that is recognized as rightful by those subject to it, 325

Beliefs. Ideas about life, the way society works, and where one fits in, 68

Bureaucracies. Specific types of large formal organizations that have the purpose of maximizing efficiency; they are characterized by formal relations between participants, clearly laid-out procedures and rules, and pursuit of shared goals, 122

Caste systems. The most rigid ascribed stratification systems. Individuals are born into a status, which they retain throughout life. That status is deeply embedded in religious, political, and economic norms and institutions, 189

Cause-and-effect relationships. Occur when there is a relationship between variables so that one variable stimulates a change in another, 39

Civil religion. The set of beliefs, rites, and symbols that sacralize the values of the society and place the nation in the context of transcendent meaning, often giving it divine significance, 304

Collective behavior. Refers to spontaneous, unstructured, and disorganized actions that may violate norms; this behavior arises when people are trying to cope with stressful situations and unclear or uncertain conditions, 399

Conflict theory. Theory that focuses on social groups competing for scarce resources, 32

Consensus crimes. Crimes for which members of society are in general agreement about the seriousness, 137

Content analysis. Entails the systematic categorizing and recording of information from written or recorded sources—printed materials, videos, radio broadcasts, or artworks, 41

Control group. A group in which the subjects are not exposed to the variable the researcher wants to test, 41

Controls. Steps used by researchers to eliminate all variables except those related to the hypothesis—especially those variables that might be spurious, 39

Correlation. A relationship between variables such as poverty and low levels of education, with change in one variable associated with change in another, 39

Counterculture. A group with expectations and values that contrast sharply with the dominant values of a particular society, 73

Crime. Deviant actions for which there are formal penalties imposed by the government, such as fines, jail, or prison sentences, 134

Cultural capital. The knowledge, skills, language mastery, style of dress, and values that provide a person with access to a particular status in society, 171

Cultural relativism. Requires setting aside cultural and personal beliefs and prejudices to understand another group or society through the eyes of its members and using its own community standards, 66

Culture. The way of life shared by a group of people—the knowledge, beliefs, values, rules or laws, language, customs, symbols, and material products within a society that help meet human needs, 54

Democratic governments. Governments characterized by accountability of the government to citizens and a large degree of control by individuals over their own lives, 334

Democratic socialism. Collective or group planning of the development of society, but within a democratic political system; the good of the whole is paramount, 337

Demographic transition theory. Links trends in birthrates and death rates with patterns of economic and technological development, 363

Demography. The study of human populations, 356

Denominations. Centralized coordinating bodies or associations that link local congregations with a similar history and theology, 300

Dependency ratio. The ratio of those in both the young and aged groups compared with the number of people in the productive age groups between 15 and 64 years old, 358

Dependent variable. The variable in a cause-and-effect relationship that is affected by and comes after the independent variable in time sequence, 39

Deviance. The violation of social norms, 134

Differential association theory. Focuses on the process of learning deviant behavior from those with whom we interact, 138

Discrimination. Differential treatment and harmful actions against minorities, 206

Dysfunctions. Actions that undermine the stability or equilibrium of society, 32

Empirical knowledge. Founded on information gained from evidence (facts), rather than intuition, 37

Endogamy. Norms that require individuals to marry inside certain human boundaries, whatever the societal members see as protecting the homogeneity of the group, 269

Environment. The setting in which the social unit operates, including everything that influences the social unit, such as its physical and organizational surroundings and technological innovations, 16

Estate systems. Characterized by the concentration of economic and political power in the hands of a small minority of political-military elite, with the peasantry tied to the land, 189

Ethnic group. A group within the human species that is based on cultural factors: language, religion, dress, foods, customs, beliefs, values, norms, a shared group identity or feeling, and sometimes loyalty to a homeland, monarch, or religious leader, 204

Ethnocentrism. The tendency to view one's own group and its cultural expectations as right, proper, and superior to others, 64

Evidence. Facts and information that are confirmed through systematic processes of testing, using the five senses, 37

Exogamy. Norms governing the choice of a mate that require individuals to marry outside of their own immediate group, 269

Experiment. All variables except the one being studied are controlled so researchers can study the effects of the variable under study, 41

Experimental group. In a controlled experiment, the group in which people are exposed to the variable being studied to test its effect, 41

Expressive movements. Focus on changing individuals and saving people from lifestyles the movement considers corrupt, 408

Extended family. Two or more adult generations that share tasks and living quarters. This may include brothers, sisters, aunts, uncles, cousins, and grandparents, 268

Family of orientation. The family into which we are born or adopted, 267

Family of procreation. The family we create ourselves, 267

Feminist theory. Critiques the hierarchical power structures that disadvantage women and other minorities, 35

Fertility. Demographic processes referring to the birthrate, 366

Formal agents of socialization. Official or legal agents (e.g., families, schools, teachers, religious organizations) whose purpose it is to socialize the individual into the values, beliefs, and behaviors of the culture, 96

Formal organizations. Modern rational organizations composed of complex secondary groups deliberately formed to pursue and achieve certain goals, 121

Formal sanctions. Rewards or punishments conferred by recognized officials, 69

Free-choice marriage. A pattern of mate selection in which the partners select each other based primarily on romance and love, 270

Functional theory. See *structural-functional theory*, 31

Game stage. Stage in the process of developing a social self when a child develops the ability to take the role of multiple others concurrently (norms, values, and expectations of the generalized other) and conform to societal expectations, 92

Gender. A society's notions of masculinity and femininity—socially constructed meanings associated with being male or female—and how individuals construct their identity in terms of gender within these constraints, 232

Gender roles. Those commonly assigned tasks or expected behaviors linked to an individual's sex-determined statuses, 233

Generalized other. A composite of societal expectations that a child learns from family, peers, and other organizations, 92

Genocide. The systematic effort of one group, usually the dominant group, to destroy a minority group, 212

Global culture. Behavioral standards, symbols, values, and material objects that have become common across the globe, 75

Global transnational movements. Mobilized groups that take place across societies as international organizations seek change in the status of women, child labor, rights of indigenous peoples, environmental degradation, global warming, disease pandemics, and other issues that affect the global community, 409

Globalization. The process by which the entire world is becoming a single interdependent sociocultural entity, more uniform, more integrated, and more interdependent, 75

Goal displacement. Occurs when the original motives or goals of the organization are displaced by new secondary goals, 126

Groups. Units involving two or more people who interact with each other because of shared common interests, goals, experiences, and needs, 118

Herding societies. Societies in which the food-producing strategy is based on the society's domestication of animals, whose care is the central focus of their activities, 57

Horticultural societies. Societies in which the food-producing strategy is based on domestication of plants, using digging sticks and wooden hoes to cultivate small gardens, 57

Hunter-gatherer society. A society in which people rely on the vegetation and animals occurring naturally in their habitat to sustain life, 56

Hypothesis. An educated guess or prediction, 37

I. The spontaneous, unpredictable, impulsive, and largely unorganized aspect of the self, 91

Ideal culture. Consists of practices, beliefs, and values regarded as most desirable in society and consciously taught to children, 68

Imitation stage. A period when children under 3 years old are preparing for role-taking by observing others and imitating their behaviors, sounds, and gestures, 91

Independent variable. The variable in a cause-and-effect relationship that comes first in a time sequence and causes a change in another variable, 39

Industrial societies. Rely primarily on mechanized production, resulting in greater division of labor based on expertise, 58

Inequality. A social condition in which privileges, opportunities, and substantial rewards are given to people in some positions in society but denied to others, 167

Informal agents of socialization. Unofficial agents that shape values, beliefs, and behaviors in which socialization is not the express purpose, 98

Informal sanctions. Unofficial rewards or punishments such as smiles, frowns, or ignoring unacceptable behaviors, 69

In-group. A group to which an individual feels a sense of loyalty and belonging; it also may serve as a reference group, 120

Institutional racial discrimination. Any meso-level institutional arrangement that favors one racial group over another; this favoritism may result in intentional or unintentional consequences for minority groups, 210

Institutions. Organized, patterned, and enduring sets of social structures that provide guidelines for behavior and help each society meet its basic survival needs, 261

Interaction. The exchange of verbal and nonverbal messages, 84

Interviews. Conducted by talking directly with people and asking questions in person or by telephone, 40

Labeling theory. Explains how people can be labeled deviant after committing a deviant act, which can then lead them to carry out further acts that reflect that label, 139

Language. Conveys verbal and nonverbal messages among members of society; the foundation of every culture, 69

Latent functions. Unplanned or unintended consequences of actions or of social structures, 32

Laws. Norms formally encoded by those holding political power in society, 69

Levels of analysis. Social groups from the smallest to the largest, 12

Life expectancy. The average number of years a person in a particular society can expect to live, 356

Looking-glass self. A reflective process that develops our *self* based on our interpretations and internalization of the reactions of others to us, 89

Macro-level analysis. Analysis of the largest social units in the social world, including entire nations, global forces, and international social trends, 17

Manifest functions. The planned outcomes of interactions, social organizations, or institutions, 31

Market or capitalist economic system. An economic system driven by the balance of supply and demand, allowing free competition to reward the efficient and the innovative with profits; stresses individual planning and private ownership of property, 336

Master status. An individual's social status that becomes most important and takes precedence over other statuses, 116

Material culture. Includes all the objects we can see or touch; all the artifacts of a group of people, 66

Me. The part of the self that has learned the rules of society through interaction and role-taking, and that controls the *I* and its desires, 91

Means of production. Karl Marx's concept of property, machinery, and cash owned by capitalists, 33

Mechanical solidarity. Social cohesion and integration based on the similarity of individuals in the group, including shared beliefs, values, and emotional ties between members of the group, 56

Meritocracy. A society in which positions are allocated in social groups or organizations according to individuals' abilities and credentials, 185

Meso-level analysis. Analysis of intermediate-size social units, smaller than the nation but large enough to encompass more than the local community or region, 17

Microculture. A group that affects only a small segment of one's life or influences a limited period of one's life, 71

Micro-level analysis. Analysis with a focus on individual or small-group interaction in specific situations, 16

Migration. In terms of demographic processes, refers to the movement of people from one place to another, 366

Minority groups. Groups in a population that differ from other groups in some characteristics and are subject to less power, fewer privileges, and discrimination, 201

Mortality. In terms of demographic processes, refers to the death rate, 366

Myths. Stories that transmit values and embody ideas about life and the world, 298

National culture. Common values and beliefs that tie citizens of a nation together, 75

National society. A population of people, usually living within a specified geographic area, who are connected by common ideas, cooperate for the attainment of common goals, and are subject to a particular political authority, 15

New religious movements (NRMs). Innovative religious groups that arise to meet specific needs not met through traditional religious organizations, and that can become established religions after several generations, 302

Nonmaterial culture. The thoughts, language, feelings, beliefs, values, and attitudes that make up much of our culture, 67

Nonverbal communication. Interactions without words using facial expressions, the head, eye contact, body posture, gestures, touch, walk, status symbols, and personal space, 111

Norms. Rules of behavior shared by members of a society and rooted in the value system, 68

Nuclear family. Consists of two parents and their children—or any two of the three, 268

Objectivity. Entails steps taken to ensure that one's personal opinions or values do not bias or contaminate data collection and analysis, 37

Observational studies (also called field research). Involve systematic, planned observation and recording of interactions or human behavior in their natural settings (where the activity normally takes place rather than in a laboratory), 40

Oligarchy. The concentration of power in the hands of a small group, 125

Organic solidarity. Refers to social cohesion (glue) based on division of labor, with each member playing a highly specialized role in the society and each person being dependent on others due to interdependent, interrelated tasks, 56

Organized crime. Ongoing criminal enterprises by an organized group whose ultimate purpose is economic gain through illegitimate means, 150

Out-group. A group to which an individual does not belong and a group that competes with or acts in opposition to an in-group, 120

Past-in-present discrimination. Practices from the past that may no longer be allowed but that continue to have consequences for people in the present, 211

Planned (or centralized) economic systems. Economic systems in which the government or another centralized group oversees production and distribution, 337

Play stage. Involves a child, usually between 3 and 5, having the ability to see things (role-take) from the perspective of one person at a time; simple role-taking or play-acting, 91

Pluralism. Occurs when each ethnic or racial group in a country maintains its own culture and separate set of institutions but has recognized equality in the society, 214

Pluralist power theorists. Argue that power is not held exclusively by an elite group but is shared among many power centers, each of which has its own self-interests to protect, 190

Population pyramids. Pyramid-shaped diagrams that illustrate sex ratios and dependency ratios over time, 360

Population transfer. The removal, often forced, of a minority group from a region or country, 214

Populations. Permanent societies, states, communities, adherents of a common religious faith, racial or ethnic groups, kinship or clan groups, professions, and other identifiable categories of people, 356

Postindustrial society. A society that has moved from human labor and manufacturing to automated production and service jobs, largely processing information, 59

Power. Ability of a person or group to realize its own will in groups, even against the resistance of others, 323

Power elite. Power held by top leaders in corporations, politics, and military, 190

Prejudice. Attitudes or prejudgment about a group, usually negative and not based on facts, 206

Primary deviance. A violation of a norm that may be an isolated act or an initial act of rule breaking, 139

Primary groups. Groups characterized by close, intimate, long-term contacts, cooperation, and relationships, 119

Public order crimes. See *victimless crimes*, 147

Public sociologists. Strive to better understand how society operates and to make practical use of their sociological findings, 43

Questionnaires. Contain questions and other types of items designed to solicit information appropriate to analysis of research questions, 40

Race. A socially created concept that identifies a group as "different" based on certain biologically inherited physical characteristics. This allows members of the group to be singled out for dissimilar treatment, 201

Rational choice (exchange) theory. A theory that focuses on humans as fundamentally concerned with self-interests, making rational decisions based on weighing costs and rewards of the projected outcome, 30

Rationality. The attempt to reach maximum efficiency with rules that are rationally designed to accomplish goals, 35

Rationalization (of social life). The attempt to maximize efficiency by creating rules and procedures focused solely on accomplishing goals, 121

Real culture. The way things in society are actually done, 68

Recidivism rates. The likelihood that someone who is arrested, convicted, and imprisoned will later be a repeat offender, 159

Reference groups. Groups composed of members who act as role models and establish standards against which members evaluate their conduct, 120

Relative poverty. Occurs when one's income falls below the poverty line, resulting in an inadequate standard of living relative to others in the individual's country, 192

Reproduction of class. The socioeconomic positions of one generation passing on to the next, 283

Resistance or regressive movements. Try to protect an existing system, protect part of that system, or return to what a system had been by overthrowing current laws and practices. They see societal change as a threat to values or practices and wish to maintain the status quo or return to a former status by reversing the change process, 408

Resocialization. The process of shedding one or more positions and taking on others; it involves learning new norms, behaviors, and values suitable to the newly acquired status, 95

Revolution. Social and political transformations of a nation that result when states fail to fulfill their expected responsibilities, 339

Revolutionary movements. Attempt to transform society to bring about a total change in society by overthrowing existing power structures and replacing them with new ones; these movements often resort to violent means to achieve goals, 408

Rituals. Ceremonies or repetitive practices, often to invoke a sense of awe of the sacred and to make certain ideas sacred, 298

Role conflict. Conflict between the roles of two or more social statuses, 117

Role strain. Tension among roles within a social status, 117

Role-taking. The process by which individuals take others into account by imagining themselves in the position of the other, 89

Roles. The expected behaviors, rights, obligations, responsibilities, and privileges assigned to a social status, 116

Sample. A group of people systemically chosen for research who represent a much larger group, 38

Sanctions. Rewards and penalties that reinforce norms, 69

Science. The systematic process of producing human knowledge; it uses empirical research methods to discover facts and test theories, 413

Secondary analysis. Uses existing data, information that has already been collected in other studies—including data banks such as the national census, 41

Secondary deviance. Occurs when an individual continues to violate a norm and begins to take on a deviant identity *because* of being labeled as deviant, 139

Secondary groups. Groups characterized by formal, impersonal, and businesslike relationships; often temporary, based on a specific limited purpose or goal, 119

Secularization. A process of social change through which traditional religious thinking has less public influence and is replaced by other ways of explaining reality and regulating social life, 314

Self. Refers to the perceptions we have of who we are, 88

Self-fulfilling prophecy. Occurs when a belief or a prediction becomes a reality, in part because of the prediction, 140

Sex. A biological term referring to ascribed genetic, anatomical, and hormonal differences between males and females, 231

Sexuality. Culturally shaped meanings both of sexual acts and of how we experience our own bodies—especially in relation to the bodies of others, 232

Side-effect discrimination. Practices in one institutional area that have a negative impact because they are linked to practices in another institutional area; because institutions are interdependent, discrimination in one results in unintentional discrimination in others, 210

Significant others. Parents, guardians, relatives, siblings, or important individuals whose primary and sustained interactions with the individual are especially influential, 91

Slavery. When an individual or a family is bound in servitude as the property of a person or household, bought and sold, and forced to work, 167

Social capital. One's networks with others who have influence, 171

Social change. Variations or alterations over time in the behavior patterns, culture (including norms and values), and structure of society, 389

Social class. The wealth, power, and prestige rankings that individuals hold in society; a large group with similar rankings, 99

Social construction of reality. The process by which individuals and groups shape reality through social interaction, 77

Social institutions. Organized, patterned, and enduring sets of social structures that provide guidelines for behavior and help each society meet its basic survival needs, 14

Social interaction. Consists of two or more individuals purposefully relating to each other, 110

Social mobility. The extent of individual movement up or down in the class system, changing one's social position in society—especially relative to one's parents, 183

Social movements. Consciously organized attempts outside of established institutional mechanisms to enhance or resist change through group action, 406

Social networks. Refer to individuals linked together by one or more social relationships, connecting us to the larger society, 109

Social processes. Take place through actions of people in institutions and other social units or structures, 15

Social reform movements. Seek to change some specific dimension of society, usually involving legislative policy modification or appeals to the courts, 408

Social status. A social position in society, 115

Social stratification. How individuals and groups are layered or ranked in society according to their access to and possession of valued resources, 171

Social structure. The stable patterns of interactions, statuses, roles, and institutions that provide stability for the society and bring order to individuals' lives, 14

Social units. Interconnected parts of the social world ranging from small groups to societies, 14

Social world model. The levels of analysis in our social surroundings as an interconnected series of small groups, organizations, institutions, and societies, 12

Socialization. The lifelong process of learning to become a member of the social world, beginning at birth and continuing until death, 84

Society. An organized and interdependent group of individuals who live together in a specific geographical area and who interact more with each other than they do with outsiders; they cooperate for the attainment of common goals and share a common culture over time, 54

Sociological imagination. The recognition of the complex and interactive relationship between micro-level individual experiences and macro-level public issues, 8

Sociology. The scientific study of social life, social change, and the social causes and consequences of human behavior, 6

Spurious relationships. Occur when there is no causal relationship between the independent and dependent variables, but they vary together, often due to a third variable affecting both of them, 39

Strain theory. Contends that the opportunity or limitations embedded in the structures of society may contradict and undermine the goals and aspirations society encourages for its members, creating strains that lead to deviance, 142

Stratification. See *social stratification*, 171

Structural-functional theory. Assumes that all parts of the social structure (including groups, organizations, and institutions), the culture (values and beliefs), and social processes (social change or child rearing) work together to make the whole society run smoothly and harmoniously, 31

Subculture. The culture of a meso-level subcommunity that distinguishes itself from the dominant culture of the larger society, 72

Subjugation. The subordination of one group to another that holds power and authority, 212

Symbolic interaction theory (also called social constructionism or interpretative theory). Sees humans as active agents who create shared meanings of symbols and events, and then interact on the basis of those meanings, 29

Symbols. Actions or objects that represent something else and therefore have meaning beyond their own existence. Flags and wedding rings are examples, 29

Technology. The practical application of tools, skills, and knowledge to meet human needs and extend human abilities, 59

Terrorism. The planned use of random, unlawful (or illegal) violence or threat of violence against civilians to create (or raise) fear and intimidate citizens in order to advance the terrorist group's political or ideological goals, 152

Theocracy. Religion in which religious leaders rule society in accordance with God's presumed wishes, 303

Theoretical perspective. A basic view of society that guides sociologists' research and analysis, 28

Theories. Statements or explanations regarding how and why two or more facts are related to each other and the connections between these facts, 28

Total institution. A place that cuts people off from the rest of society and totally controls their lives in the process of resocialization; examples are prisons and boot camps, 95

Totalitarian government. Any form of government that almost totally controls people's lives, 333

Transnationalism. The process by which immigrants create multinational social relations that link together their original societies with their new locations; this usually entails national loyalty to more than one country, 102

Triangulation. The utilization of two or more methods of data collection to enhance the amount and type of data for analysis and the accuracy of the findings, 42

Urbanization. The pattern of movement from rural areas to cities, 356

Values. Nonmaterial shared judgments about what is desirable or undesirable, right or wrong, good or bad; they express the basic ideals of any culture, 67

Variables. Concepts (ideas) that can vary in frequency of occurrence from one time, place, or person to another, 38

Victimless crimes. Acts (also called *public order crimes*) committed by or between consenting adults, 147

War. Armed conflict occurring within, between, or among societies or groups, 343

References

AAANativeArts. 2011. "Facts About Alaskan Natives." Retrieved April 19, 2011 (www.aaanativearts.com/alaskan-natives/index.html).

Abu-Lughod, Janet L. 1991. *Changing Cities: Urban Sociology.* New York: HarperCollins.

Abu-Lughod, Janet L. 2001. *New York, Chicago, Los Angeles: America's Global Cities.* Minneapolis: University of Minnesota Press.

Ackerman, Spencer. 2014. "Global Terrorism Rose 43% in 2013 Despite Al-Qaida Splintering, US Reports." *The Guardian.* Retrieved May 22, 2014 (www.theguardian.com/world/2014/apr/30/global-terrorism-rose-despite-al-qaida-splintering).

ACT. 2013. "National and State Scores." Retrieved September 12, 2014 (http://www.act.org/newsroom/data/2013).

Adler, Patricia A. and Peter Adler. 1991. *Backboards and Blackboards: College Athletes and Role Engulfment.* New York: Columbia University Press.

Adler, Patricia A. and Peter Adler. 2004. "The Gloried Self." Pp. 117–26 in *Inside Social Life,* 4th ed., edited by Spencer E. Cahill. Los Angeles: Roxbury.

African Undersea Cables. 2013. *Many Possibilities.* Retrieved February 13, 2014 (http://manypossibilities.net/african-undersea-cables/).

Agius, Silvan. 2013. "Third Gender: A Step Toward Ending Intersex Discrimination." Retrieved January 16, 2014 (Spiegel.de/international/Europe/third-gender-option-in-germany-a-small-step-for-intersex-recognition-a-917650.html).

Aguirre, Jessica Camille. 2012. "Generic Drugs Make Dent in Global AIDS Pandemic." NPR, July 13. Retrieved July 3, 2013 (www.npr.org/blogs/health/2012/07/11/156612196/generic-drugs-make-dent-in-global-aids-pandemic).

Ahmad, Nehaluddin. 2009. "Sati Tradition—Widow Burning in India: A Socio-legal Examination." *Web Journal of Current Legal Issues,* 2 WEB JCLI. Retrieved April 7, 2011 (http://webjcli.ncl.ac.uk-/2009/issue2/almad2/html).

Ahuja, Masuma. 2013. "Teens Are Spending More Time Consuming Media, on Mobile Devices." *Washington Post,* March 13. Retrieved December 6, 2013 (http://articles.washingtonpost.com/2013-03-13/news/37675597_1_teens-cellphones-video-games).

Alarcon, Arthur L. and Paula M. Mitchell. 2011. "Executing the Will of the Voters? A Roadmap to Mend or End the California Legislature's Multi-Billion Dollar Death Penalty Debacle." *Loyola of Los Angeles Law Review* 44(June):S41.

Alatas, Syed Farid. 2006. "Ibn Khaldun and Contemporary Sociology." *International Sociology* 21(6):782–95.

Alexander, Michelle. 2010. *The New Jim Crow: Mass Incarceration in the Age of Color Blindness.* New York: The New Press.

Alexander, Michelle. 2011. "More Black Men Are in Prison Today Than Were Enslaved in 1850." October 10. Retrieved April 15, 2012 (www.huffingtonpost.com/2011/10/12/michelle-alexander-more-Black-men-are-in-prison-today-than-were-enslaved-in-1850_n_1007368.html).

Allison, William T., Jeffrey G. Grey, and Janet G. Valentine. 2012. *American Military History: A Survey From Colonial Times to the Present,* 2nd ed. Boston: Pearson.

Alpert, Emily. 2013. "More Americans Consider Themselves Multiracial." *Los Angeles Times,* June 13. Retrieved June 17, 2013 (www.latimes.com/news/local/la-me-multiracial-growth-20130613,0,6580186.story).

Altheide, David, Patricia A. Adler, Peter Adler, and Duane Altheide. 1978. "The Social Meanings of Employee Theft." P. 90 in *Crime at the Top,* edited by John M. Johnson and Jack D. Douglas. Philadelphia: Lippincott.

Amato, Paul R. 2000. "The Consequences of Divorce for Adults and Children." *Journal of Marriage and the Family* 62(November):1269–87.

American Civil Liberties Union. 2013. *The War on Marijuana in Black and White.* Retrieved June 5, 2013 (www.aclu.org/files/assets/aclu-thewaronmarijuana-rel2.pdf).

American Library Association. 2014. "Frequently Challenged Books of the 21st Century: 2013." Retrieved September 9, 2014 (http://www.ala.org/bbooks/frequentlychallengedbooks/top10).

American Sociological Association. 2009. *21st Century Careers With an Undergraduate Degree in Sociology.* Washington, DC: Author.

Ammerman, Nancy. 1990. *Baptist Battles: Social Change and Religious Conflict in the Southern Baptist Convention.* New Brunswick, NJ: Rutgers University Press.

Ammerman, Nancy. 2006. "Denominationalism/Congregationalism." Pp. 353–72 in *Handbook of Religion and Social Institutions,* edited by Helen Rose Ebaugh. New York: Springer.

Ammerman, Nancy. 2009. "Congregations: Local, Social, and Religious." Pp. 562–80 in *Oxford Handbook of the Sociology of Religion,* edited by Peter Clarke. New York, Oxford: Oxford University Press.

Amnesty International. 2012. "Death Penalty 2011: Alarming Levels of Executions in the Few Countries That Kill." March 27. Retrieved April 16, 2012 (www.amnesty.org/en/news/deasth-penalty-2011-alarming-level-executions-few-countries--kill-2012-03-27).

Amnesty International. 2014. "Death Penalty 2013: Small Number of Countries Trigger Global Spike in Executions." Retrieved April 25, 2014 (www.amnesty.org/en/news/death-penalty-2013-small-number-trigger-global-spike-executions-2014-03-27).

Anderson, Benedict. 2006. *Imagined Communities: Reflections on the Origin and Spread of Nationalism*, Rev. ed. London: Verso.

Anderson, D. Mark and Daniel I. Rees. 2013. "The Legalization of Recreational Marijuana How Likely Is the Worst-Case Scenario?" *The Journal of Policy Analysis and Management*. Retrieved October 17, 2013 (http://dmarkanderson.com/Point_Counterpoint_07_31_13_v5.pdf).

Anderson, David A. and Mykol Hamilton. 2005. "Gender Role Stereotyping of Parents in Children's Picture Books: The Invisible Father." *Sex Roles: A Journal of Research* 52(3/4):145.

Anderson, Elijah. 2000. *Code of the Street: Decency, Violence, and the Moral Life of the Inner City*. New York: Norton.

Anderson, Margaret and Patricia Hill Collins. 2010. *Race Class and Gender: An Anthology*, 7th ed. Belmont: Wadsworth.

Angier, Natalie. 2013. "The Changing American Family." *New York Times*. November 25. Retrieved January 17, 2014 (www.nytimes.com/2013/11/26/health/families.html?_r=0).

Antoun, Richard T. 2008. *Understanding Fundamentalism: Christian, Islamic, and Jewish Movements*, 2nd ed. Walnut Creek, CA: AltaMira.

Archer, Dale. 2013. "Could America's Wealth Gap Lead to a Revolt?" *Forbes*, September 4. Retrieved January 4, 2014 (www.forbes.com/sites/dalearcher/2013/09/04/could-americas-wealth-gap-lead-to-a-revolt/).

Armstrong, Karen. 2000. *The Battle for God*. New York: Knopf.

Arnold, David O., ed. 1970. *The Sociology of Subcultures*. Berkeley, CA: Glendessary.

Arrighi, Barbara A. 2000. *Understanding Inequality: The Intersection of Race, Ethnicity, Class, and Gender*. Lanham, MD: Rowman & Littlefield.

Arulampalam, Wiji, Alison L. Booth, and Mark L. Bryan. 2007. "Is There a Glass Ceiling Over Europe? Exploring the Gender Pay Gap Across the Wages Distribution." *Industrial and Labor Relations Review* 60(1):163–86.

Aseltine, Robert H., Jr. 1995. "A Reconsideration of Parental and Peer Influences on Adolescent Deviance." *Journal of Health and Social Behavior* 36(2):103–21.

Ashley, David and David Michael Orenstein. 2009. *Sociological Theory*, 7th ed. Boston: Allyn & Bacon.

Aslan, Reza. 2011. *No god but God: The Origins, Evolution, and Future of Islam*, updated ed. New York: Random House.

ASOTRECOL. 2015. "Injured Colombian General Motors Workers." Retrieved February 15, 2015 (www.asotrecol.org/).

Association of American Colleges and Universities and Hart Research Associates. 2013. *It Takes More Than a Major: Employer Priorities for College Learning and Student Success*. Washington, DC. Retrieved May 22, 2013 (www.aacu.org/leap/documents/2013_EmployerSurvey.pdf).

Aulette, Judy Root. 2010. *Changing American Families*. Boston: Allyn & Bacon.

Babbie, Earl. 2014. *The Basics of Social Research*, 6th ed. Belmont, CA: Thomsen/Wadsworth.

BabyCenter. 2013. "100 Most Popular Baby Names of 2013." *Choosing a Name*, December. Retrieved January 16, 2014 (www.babycenter.com/top-baby-names-2013).

Bagby, Ihsan. 2003. "Imams and Mosque Organization in the United States: A Study of Mosque Leadership and Organizational Structure in American Mosques." Pp. 113–34 in *Muslims in the United States*, edited by Philippa Strum and Danielle Tarantolo. Washington, DC: Woodrow Wilson International Center for Scholars.

Bainbridge, William S. and Rodney Stark. 1981. "Suicide, Homicide, and Religion: Durkheim Reassessed." *Annual Review of the Social Sciences of Religion* 5:33–56.

Bales, Kevin. 1999. *Disposable People: New Slavery in the Global Economy*, Updated ed. Berkeley: University of California Press.

Bales, Kevin. 2000. *New Slavery: A Reference Handbook*, 2nd ed. Santa Barbara, CA: ABC-CLIO.

Bales, Kevin. 2004. *Disposable People: New Slavery in the Global Economy*, 2nd ed. Berkeley: University of California Press.

Bales, Kevin. 2007. *Ending Slavery: How We Free Today's Slaves*. Berkeley: University of California Press.

Bales, Kevin. 2012. *Disposable People: New Slavery in the Global Economy*, 3rd ed. Berkeley: University of California Press.

Bales, Kevin. 2013. "Confronting Slavery With the Tools of Sociology." In *Sociologists in Action: Race, Class, Gender, and Intersections*, edited by Shelley White, Jonathan White, and Kathleen Odell Korgen. Thousand Oaks, CA: Sage.

Bales, Kevin and Ron Soodalter. 2010. *The Slave Next Door: Human Trafficking and Slavery in America Today*. Berkeley: University of California Press.

Bales, Kevin and Zoe Trodd. 2008. *To Plead Our Own Cause: Personal Stories by Today's Slaves*. Ithaca, NY: Cornell University Press.

Bales, Kevin, Zoe Trodd, and Alex Kent Williamson. 2009. *Modern Slavery: The Secret World of 27 Million People*. Oxford, UK: Oneworld Press.

Ballantine, Jeanne H. and Floyd M. Hammack. 2012. *The Sociology of Education: A Systematic Analysis*, 7th ed. Upper Saddle River, NJ: Prentice Hall.

Barber, Benjamin R. 2006. "The Uncertainty of Digital Politics: Democracy's Relationship With Information Technology." Pp. 61–69 in *Globalization: The Transformation of Social Worlds*, edited by D. Stanley Eitzen and Maxine Baca Zinn. Belmont, CA: Wadsworth.

Barrett, David, George Kurian, and Todd Johnson, eds. 2001. *World Christian Encyclopedia*, 2 vols. New York: Oxford University Press.

Basso, Keith H. 1979. *Portraits of the Whiteman: Linguistic Play and Cultural Symbols Among the Western Apache*. Cambridge, UK: Cambridge University Press.

Battelle. 2013. "2014 Global R&D Funding Forecast." December. Retrieved February 24, 2014 (www.battelle.org/docs/tpp/2014_global_rd_funding_forecast.pdf).

BBC News. 2010. "Pope Condones Condom Use in Exceptional Cases—Book." Retrieved July 11, 2013 (www.bbc.co.uk/news/world-europe-11804398).

Beaubien, Jason. 2011. "In Haiti, Cell Phones Serve as Debit Cards." NPR, January 30. Retrieved June 8, 2013 (www.npr.org/2011/01/30/133305663/in-haiti-cell-phones-serve-as-debit-cards).

Beaver, David. 2012. "Sally Ride: Beauty of the Earth Is Only Half of It." The Overview Institute. Retrieved June 29, 2013 (www.overviewinstitute.org/featured-articles/45-sally-ride-beauty-of-the-earth-is-only-half-of-it).

Beckwith, Carol. 1993. *Nomads of Niger*. New York: Harry N. Abrams.

Belding, Theodore C. 2004. "Nobility and Stupidity: Modeling the Evolution of Class Endogamy." Retrieved August 7, 2008 (http://arxiv.org/abs/nlin.AO/0405048).

Bell, Daniel. 1973. *The Coming of Post-Industrial Society: A Venture in Social Forecasting*. New York: Basic Books.

Bell, Michael Mayerfeld. 2012. *An Invitation to Environmental Sociology*, 4th ed. Thousand Oaks, CA: Sage/Pine Forge.

Bellah, Robert N. 1970. "Civil Religion in America." Pp. 168–215 in *Beyond Belief: Essays on Religion in a Post-Traditionalist World*. New York: Harper & Row.

Bellah, Robert N. 1992. *The Broken Covenant: American Civil Religion in Time of Trial*. Chicago: University of Chicago Press.

Bennis, Warren G., Kenneth D. Benne, and Robert Chin. 1985. *The Planning of Change*, 4th ed. New York: Holt, Rinehart Winston.

Benokraitis, Nijole V. 2012. *Marriages and Families: Changes, Choices, and Constraints—2010 Census Update*, 7th ed. Englewood Cliffs, NJ: Prentice Hall.

Beran, Tanya. 2012. "Bullying: What Are the Differences Between Boys and Girls?" *Education.com*, January 24. Retrieved January 17, 2014 (www.education.com/reference/article/Ref_Bullying_Differences).

Berger, Michael L. 1979. *The Devil Wagon in God's Country: The Automobile and Social Change in Rural America, 1893–1929*. Hamden, CT: Archon.

Berger, Peter L. and Thomas Luckmann. 1966. *The Social Construction of Reality*. Garden City, NY: Doubleday.

Berk, Richard A. 1974. *Collective Behavior*. Dubuque, IA: Brown.

Berman, Bruce J. 2011. "Of Magic, Invisible Hands and Elfs: How Not to Study Ethnicity in Africa." Presented at the ECAS4, Uppsala, Sweden, June 14–18.

Bernhardt, Annette, Ruth Milkman, Nik Theodore, Douglas Heckathorn, Mirabai Auer, James DeFilippis, Ana Luz González, Victor Narro, Jason Perelshteyn, Diana Polson, and Michael Spiller. 2009. *Broken Laws, Unprotected Workers*. Retrieved June 3, 2013 (http://labor.ucla.edu/publications/reports/brokenlaws.pdf).

Berrey, Ellen. 2013. "Breaking Glass Ceilings, Ignoring Dirty Floors: The Culture and Class Bias of Diversity Management." *American Behavioral Scientist*, October 11. Retrieved January 17, 2014 (http://abs.sagepub.com/content/easrly/2013/10/11/0002764213503333.abstract).

Berry, Brian J. L. and John Kasarda. 1977. *Contemporary Urban Ecology*. New York: Macmillan.

Bettie, Julie. 2003. *Women Without Class: Girls, Race, and Identity*. Berkeley: University of California Press.

Billig, Michael. 1995. *Banal Nationalism*. Thousand Oaks, CA: Sage.

Bjelopera, Jerome P. and Kristin M. Finklea. 2012. "Organized Crime: An Evolving Challenge for U.S. Law Enforcement." Congressional Research Service. Retrieved April 13, 2012 (www.fas.org/sgp/crs/misc/R41547.pdf).

Blau, Peter M. 1956. *Bureaucracy in Modern Society*. New York: Random House.

Blau, Peter M. 1964. *Exchange and Power in Social Life*. New York: John Wiley.

Blau, Peter and Otis Dudley Duncan. 1967. *The American Occupational Structure*. New York: John Wiley.

Blee, Kathleen M. 2008. "White Supremacy as Extreme Deviance." Pp. 108–17 in *Extreme Deviance*, edited by Erich Goode and D. Angus Vail. Thousand Oaks, CA: Pine Forge.

Bloom, Barbara, Lindsey I. Jones, and Gulnur Freeman. 2013. "Summary Health Statistics for U.S. Children: National Health Interview Survey, 2012." *Vital and Health Statistics* 10, no. 258. Retrieved February 6, 2015 (http://www.cdc.gov/nchs/data/series/sr_10/sr10_258.pdf).

Blumer, Herbert. 1986. *Symbolic Interactionism: Perspective and Method*. Berkeley: University of California Press.

Boger, John Charles and Gary Orfield. 2009. *School Resegregation: Must the South Turn Back?* University of North Carolina Press.

Bonacich, Edna. 1972. "A Theory of Ethnic Antagonism: The Split Labor Market." *American Sociological Review* 37(October):547–59.

Bonacich, Edna. 1976. "Advanced Capitalism and Black-White Race Relations in the United States: A Split Labor Market Interpretation." *American Sociological Review* 41(February):34–51.

Bond, Jeff. 2010. "The Anthropology of Garbage." *Columns*, March. Retrieved August 15, 2013 (www.washington .edu/alumni/columns/march10/garbage.html).

Bonilla-Silva, Eduardo. 2003. *Racism Without Racists: Color-Blind Racism and the Persistence of Racial Inequality in the United States.* Berkeley: University of California Press.

Bonilla-Silva, Eduardo. 2009. *Racism Without Racists: Color-Blind Racism and the Persistence of Racial Inequality in America,* 3rd ed. Lanham, MD: Rowman & Littlefield.

Booth, Alan and Paul R. Amato. 2001. "Parental Predivorce Relations and Offspring Postdivorce Well-Being." *Journal of Marriage and the Family* 63(February):197–212.

Borenstein, Seth. 2013. "U.S. Scientists Report Big Jump in Heat-Trapping CO2." March 5. Retrieved June 20, 2013 (phys.org/news/2013-03-scientists-big-heat-trapping-co2.html).

Boston Women's Health Book Collective. 2006. *Our Bodies, Ourselves: Menopause.* New York: Touchstone.

Bottomore, Tom. 1979. *Political Sociology.* New York: Harper & Row.

Bourdieu, P. and J. C. Passeron. 1977. *Reproduction in Education, Society and Culture.* London: Sage.

Bowen, Debra. 2008. "History Behind California's Primary Election System." Retrieved March 21, 2008 (www.sos .ca.gov/elections/elections_decline.htm).

Bowles, Samuel and Herbert Gintis. 1976. *Schooling in Capitalist America.* New York: Basic Books.

Bowles, Samuel and Herbert Gintis. 2002. "Schooling in Capitalist America Revisited." *Sociology of Education* 75(1):1–18.

Bradsher, Keith. 2013. "Kerry Calls Typhoon a Warning of Climate Change." *New York Times,* December 18. Retrieved March 18, 2014 (www.nytimes.com/2013/12/19/world/asia/typhoon-haiyan-philippines-aid.html).

Brecher, Jeremy, Tim Costello, and Brendan Smith. 2012. "Globalization and Social Movements." Pp. 272–90 in *Globalization: The Transformation of Social Worlds,* 3rd ed., edited by D. Stanley Eitzen and Maxine Baca Zinn. Belmont, CA: Wadsworth.

Brettell, Caroline B. and Carolyn F. Sargent. 2012. *Gender in Cross-Cultural Perspective,* 6th ed. Englewood Cliffs, NJ: Prentice Hall.

Brier, Noah Rubin. 2004. "Coming of Age." *American Demographics* 26(9):16.

Bromley, David G. and Anson D. Shupe, Jr. 1981. *Strange Gods: The Great American Cult Scare.* Boston: Beacon.

Brooks, David. 2012. "Thurston Howell Romney." *New York Times,* September 17. Retrieved September 18, 2012 (www.nytimes.com/2012/09/18/opinion/brooks-thurston-howell-romney.html?_r=0).

Broom, Leonard and Philip Selznick. 1963. *Sociology: A Text With Adapted Readings,* 3rd ed. New York: Harper & Row.

Brown, Donald E. 1991. *Human Universals.* Philadelphia: Temple University Press.

Brulle, Robert J. 2014. "Institutionalizing Delay: Foundation Funding and the Creation of U.S. Climate Change Counter-Movement Organizations." *Climactic Change* 122(4):681–94.

Bruner, Jerome. 1996. *The Culture of Education.* Cambridge, MA: Harvard University Press.

Brunn, Stanley D., Maureen Hays-Mitchell, and Donald J. Zeigler. 2011. *Cities of the World: World Regional Urban Development,* 4th ed. Lanham, MD: Rowman and Littlefield.

Brunn, Stanley D., Jack F. Williams, and Donald J. Zeigler. 2003. *Cities of the World: World Regional Urban Development,* 3rd ed. Lanham, MD: Rowman & Littlefield.

Brunsma, David. 2006. *Mixed Messages: Doing Race in the Color-Blind Era.* Boulder, CO; Lynne Rienner.

Brym, Robert J. and John Lie. 2007. *Sociology: Your Compass for a New World,* 3rd ed. Belmont, CA: Wadsworth.

Buchmann, Claudia, Dennis J. Condron, and Vincent J. Roscigno. 2010. "Shadow Education, American Style: Test Preparation, the SAT and College Enrollment." *Social Forces* 89(2): 435–61.

Bullas, Jeff. 2012. "20 Interesting Facts, Figures and Statistics Revealed by Facebook." Jeffbullas.com. Retrieved September 25, 2012 (www.jeffbullas .com/2012/04/30/20-interesting-facts-figures-and-statistics-revealed-by-facebook/).

Bureau of Labor Statistics. 2013. "America's Young Adults at 25: School Enrollment, Training, and Employment Transitions Between Ages 23 and 25 Summary." March 1. Retrieved June 12, 2014 (www.bls.gov/news.release/nlsyth.nr0 .htm).

Bureau of Labor Statistics. 2014a. "Earnings and Unemployment Rates by Educational Attainment." *Current Population Survey.* Retrieved January 28, 2015 (www.bls.gov/emp/ep_chart_001.htm).

Bureau of Labor Statistics. 2014b. "Economic News Release: American Time Use Survey—2013 Results." Retrieved September 8, 2014 (www.bls.gov/news.release/atus .nr0.htm).

Bureau of Labor Statistics. 2014c. "Injuries, Illnesses, and Fatalities." Retrieved September 4, 2014 (www.bls.gov/iif/).

Burn, Shawn Meghan. 2011. *Women Across Cultures: A Global Perspective,* 3rd ed. New York: McGraw-Hill.

BushTV. 2010. "Kowanyama Keeping Culture Alive." Retrieved September 12, 2014 (http://www.youtube.com/watch?v=QCcBaVEUFlo).

Business Insider. 2012. "Hundreds of Suicides in India Linked to Microfinance Organizations." Retrieved January16, 2014 (www.businessinsider.com/hundreds-of-suicides-in-India-linked-to -microfinance-organizations-2012-2).

Byanyima, Winnie. 2015. "Richest 1% Will Own More Than All the Rest by 2016." January 19. Oxfam International, January 19. Retrieved January 29, 2015 (www.oxfam.org/en/pressroom/pressreleases/2015-01-19/richest-1-will-own-more-all-rest-2016).

Cainkar, Louise A. 2009. *Homeland Insecurity: The Arab American and Muslim American Experience After 9/11.* New York: Russell Sage Foundation.

Caldwell, John C. 1982. *Theory of Fertility Decline*. New York: Academic Press.

Calhoun, Craig, ed. 2007. *Sociology in America: A History*. Chicago: University of Chicago Press.

Cambodian Genocide Program. 2013. "The CGP, 1994–2013." Yale University. Retrieved June 28, 2013 (www.yale.edu/cgp/).

Campbell, Ernest Q. and Thomas F. Pettigrew. 1959. *Christians in Racial Crisis*. Washington, DC: Public Affairs Press.

Cancian, Francesca M. 1992. "Feminist Science: Methodologies That Challenge Inequality." *Gender and Society* 6(4):623–42.

Carrothers, Robert M. and Denzel E. Benson. 2003. "Symbolic Interactionism in Introductory Textbooks: Coverage and Pedagogical Implications." *Teaching Sociology* 31(2):162–81.

Carson, E. Ann and William J. Sabol. 2012. December. "Prisoners in 2011." Bureau of Justice Statistics. Retrieved June 2, 2013 (www.bjs.gov/content/pub/pdf/p11.pdf).

Casasanto, Daniel. 2008. "Who's Afraid of the Big Bad Whorf? Crosslinguistic Differences in Temporal Language and Thought." *Language Learning* 58(1):63–79.

Casey, Timothy and Laurie Maldonado. 2012. "Worst Off—Single-Parent Families in the United States: A Cross-National Comparison of Single Parenthood in the U.S. and Sixteen Other High-Income Countries." *The Women's Legal Defense and Education Fund*, December. Retrieved October 4, 2014 (www.legalmomentum.org/sites/default/files/reports/worst-off-single-parent.pdf).

Cashmore, Ellis and Barry Troyna. 1990. *Introduction to Race Relations*. London: Routledge.

Castiello, Umberto, Cristina Becchio, Stefania Zoia, Cristian Nelini, Luisa Sartori, Laura Blason, Giuseppina D'Ottavio, Maria Bulgheroni, and Vittorio Gallese. 2010. "Wired to Be Social: The Ontogeny of Human Interaction." *PLoS ONE* 5(10). Retrieved October 19, 2010 (www.plosone.org/article/info%3Adoi%2F10.1371%2Fjournal.pone.0013199).

Castle, Jeremiah. 2016. "Social Media and Political Protests." Pp. 442–43 in *Our Social World*, 5th ed., edited by Jeanne H. Ballantine, Keith A. Roberts, and Kathleen O. Korgen. Thousand Oaks, CA: Sage.

Catalyst. 2013. "Women CEOs of the Fortune 500." January 3. Retrieved June 7, 2013 (www.catalyst.org/knowledge/women-ceos-fortune-500).

Catalyst. 2014a. "Statistical Overview of Women in the Workplace." Equity in Business Leadership, March 3. Retrieved September 2, 2014 (http://www.catalyst.org/knowledge/statistical-overview-women-workplace).

Catalyst. 2014b. "Women CEOs of the Fortune 1000." Equity in Business Leadership, August 27. Retrieved September 2, 2014 (http://www.catalyst.org/knowledge/women-ceos-fortune-1000).

Catalyst. 2014c. "Women's Earnings and Income." Equity in Business Leadership, March 24. Retrieved May 11, 2014 (http://www.catalyst.org/knowledge/womens-earnings-and-income).

Center for American Women and Politics. 2014. "Historical Information About Women in Congress." Retrieved September 4, 2014 (http://www.cawp.rutgers.edu/fast_facts/levels_of_office/Congress-HistoricalInfo.php).

Center for Constitutional Rights. 2013. "Report: Torture and Cruel, Inhuman, and Degrading Treatment of Prisoners at Guantanamo Bay." March 19. Retrieved April 25, 2014 (http://ccrjustice.org/learn-more/reports:-torture-and-cruel,-inhuman,-and-degrading-treatment-prisoners-quantanamo).

Center for Voting and Democracy. 2008. "Understanding Super Tuesday: State Rules on February 5 and Lessons for Reform." Retrieved March 21, 2008 (www.fairvote.org/?page=27&pressmode=showspecific&showarticle=185).

Centers for Disease Control and Prevention. 2013. "National Marriage and Divorce Rate Trends." Retrieved February 26, 2014 (www.cdc.gov/nchs/nvss/marriage_divorce_tables.htm).

Centers for Disease Control and Prevention. 2014. "Unmarried Childbearing." Retrieved May 12, 2014 (www.cdc.gov/nchs/fastats/unmarry.htm).

Chalfant, H. Paul and Charles W. Peck. 1983. "Religious Affiliation, Religiosity, and Racial Prejudice: A New Look at Old Relationships." *Review of Religious Research* 25(December):155–61.

Chamberlain, Houston Stewart. [1899] 1911. *The Foundations of the Nineteenth Century*, translated by John Lees. London, New York: John Lane.

Chambliss, William J. 1973. "The Saints and the Roughnecks." *Society* 11(December):24–31.

Charities Aid Foundation. 2012. "World Giving Index 2012," December. Retrieved June 15, 2013 (www.cafonline.org/PDF/WorldGivingIndex2012WEB.pdf).

Charles, Camille Z., Vincent J. Roscigno, and Kimberly C. Torres. 2007. "Racial Inequality and College Attendance: The Mediating Role of Parental Investments." *Social Science Research* 36(1):329–52.

Charon, Joel. 2010. *Symbolic Interactionism: An Introduction, and Interpretation, an Integration*, 10th ed. Englewood Cliffs, NJ: Prentice Hall.

Chase-Dunn, Christopher and E. N. Anderson. 2006. *The Historical Evolution of World-Systems*. New York: Palgrave Macmillan.

Chaves, Mark. 1993. "Denominations as Dual Structures: An Organizational Analysis." *Sociology of Religion* 54(20):147–69.

Chaves, Mark. 2004. *Congregations in America*. Cambridge, MA: Harvard University Press.

Chaves, Mark and Philip S. Gorski. 2001. "Religious Pluralism and Religious Participation." *Annual Review of Sociology* 27:261–81.

Cheng, Cecilia. 2005. "Processes Underlying Gender-Role Flexibility: Do Androgynous Individuals Know More or Know How to Cope?" *Journal of Personality* 73(3):645–73.

Cheng, Siwei and Yu Xie. 2013. "Structural Effect of Size on Interracial Friendship." *Proceedings of the National Academy of Sciences*, April 15.

Cherlin, Andrew. 1978. "Remarriage as an Incomplete Institution." *American Journal of Sociology* 84(3):634–50.

Cherlin, Andrew J. 2010. *The Marriage-Go-Round: The State of Marriage and the Family in America Today*. New York: Random House.

Cherry, Kendra. 2012. "Understanding Body Language." *About .com Psychology*. Retrieved September 25, 2012 (http:// psychology.about.com/od/nonverbalcommunication/ ss/understanding-body-language.htm).

Cheung, Cecilia Sin-Sze and Eva M. Pomerantz. 2012. "Why Does Parents' Involvement Enhance Children's Achievement? The Role of Parent-Oriented Motivation." *Journal of Educational Psychology* 14(3):820–32.

Child Trends. 2013. "Child Support Receipt." Retrieved February 19, 2014 (www.childtrends.org/wp-content/ uploads/212/07/84_Child_Support_Receipt.pdf).

Child Trends Data Bank. 2014. *Family Structure July 2014*. Retrieved November 3, 2014 (www.childtrends .org/?indicators=family-structure).

Children's Defense Fund. 2013. "Cradle to Prison Pipeline Campaign." Retrieved January 15, 2014 (www .childrensdefense.org/programs-campaigns/cradle- to-prison-pipeline/).

ChildStats.gov. 2013. "America's Children: Key National Indicators of Well-Being, 2013." Retrieved February 25, 2014 (www.childstats.gov/americaschildren/fam- soc2.asp).

Christiano, Kevin J., William H. Swatos, Jr., and Peter Kivisto. 2008. *Sociology of Religion: Contemporary Developments*, Rev. ed. Walnut Creek, CA: AltaMira.

Churchill, Winston. 2009. *Churchill by Himself: The Definitive Collection of Quotations*, edited by Richard Langworth. Jackson, TN: Public Affairs.

Cisco. 2014. "Cisco Visual Networking Index: Global Mobile Data Traffic Forecast Update, 2013." Retrieved May 10, 2014 (www.cisco.com/c/en/us/solutions/collateral/ service-provider/visual-networking-index-vni/white_ paper_c11-520862.html).

Clark, Warren and Grant Schellenberg. 2008. "Who's Religious?" *Statistics Canada*. Retrieved January 30, 2013 (http:// www.statcan.gc.ca/pub/11-008-x/2006001/9181-eng .htm#half).

Clarke, Ronald R., ed. 1997. *Situational Crime Prevention: Successful Case Studies*, 2nd ed. New York: Harrow and Heston.

Clarkson, Lamar. 2011. "Divorce Rates Falling, Report Finds." *CNN Living*, May 19. Retrieved June 6, 2012 (http://arti cles.cnn.com/2011-05-19/living/divorce.rates.drop_1_ divorce-rate-divorce-laws-marriage?_s=PM:LIVING).

Clausen, John A. 1986. *The Life Course: A Sociological Perspective*. Englewood Cliffs, NJ: Prentice Hall.

Clymer, Floyd. 1953. *Those Wonderful Old Automobiles*. New York: Bonanza.

CNBC. 2010. "Mob Money: An American Greed." July 7. Retrieved February 8, 2013 (www.cnbc.com/ id/37593299/mob_money).

Coghlan, Andy and Debora MacKenzie. 2011. "Revealed—The Capitalist Network That Runs the World." *NewScientist*. Retrieved June 23, 2013 (www.newscientist.com/arti cle/mg21228354.500-revealed--the-capitalist-net- work-that-runs-the-world.html).

Cohn, D'Vera, Paul Taylor, Mark Hugo Lopez, Catherine A. Gallagher, Kim Parker, and Kevin T. Maass. 2013. "Gun Homicide Rate Down 49% Since 1993 Peak; Public Unaware." Pew Research Social & Demographic Trends, May 7. Retrieved June 1, 2013 (www.pewsocialtrends .org/2013/05/07/gun-homicide-rate-down-49-since- 1993-peak-public-unaware/).

Coleman, James S. 1968. "The Concept of Equality of Educational Opportunity." *Harvard Education Review* 38(Winter):7–22.

Coleman, James S. 1975. "What Is Meant by 'an Equal Educational Opportunity'?" *Oxford Review of Education* 1(1):27–29.

Coleman, James. 1990. *Equality and Achievement in Education*. Boulder, CO: Westview.

Coleman, James William. 2006. *The Criminal Elite: Understanding White Collar Crime*, 6th ed. New York: Worth.

Coleman-Jensen, Alisha, Mark Nord, Margaret Andrews, and Steven Carlson. 2012. "Household Food Security in the United States in 2011." ERR-141, U.S. Department of Agriculture, Economic Research Service, September. Retrieved January 28, 2015 (www.cbpp.org/cms/index .cfm?fa=view&id=2226).

College Board. 2013. "SAT Total Group Profile Report." Retrieved May 16, 2014 (http://media.collegeboard.com/digitalSer vices/pdf/research/2013/TotalGroup-2013.pdf).

Collins, Patricia Hill. 2005. *Black Sexual Politics: African Americans, Gender and the New Racism*. New York: Routledge.

Collins, Patricia Hill. 2008. *Black Feminist Thought: Knowledge, Consciousness, and the Politics of Empowerment*. New York: Routledge.

Collins, Randall. 1971. "A Conflict Theory of Sexual Stratification." *Social Problems* 19(Summer):2–21.

Collins, Randall. 2004. "Conflict Theory of Educational Stratification." *American Sociological Review* 36:47–54.

ComScore. 2010. "Social Networking Sites Reach a Higher Percentage of Women Than Men Worldwide." July 28. Retrieved May 25, 2012 (www.comscore.com/ Press_Events/Press_Releases/2010/7/Social_ Networking_Sites_REach_a -Higher_Percentage_of_ Women_than_Men).

Comte, Auguste. [1855] 2003. *The Positive Philosophy of Auguste Comte*, freely translated and condensed by Harriet Martineau. Whitefish, MO: Kessinger.

Cook, Karen S., Jodi O'Brien, and Peter Kollock. 1990. "Exchange Theory: A Blueprint for Structure and

Process." Pp. 158–81 in *Frontiers of Social Theory: The New Syntheses*, edited by George Ritzer. New York: Columbia University Press.

Cooley, Charles Horton. [1909] 1983. *Social Organization: A Study of the Larger Mind.* New York: Schocken Books.

Coontz, Stephanie. 2005. *Marriage, a History: From Obedience to Intimacy, or How Love Conquered Marriage.* New York: Viking.

Coontz, Stephanie. 2011. "What Is the 'Traditional American Family'? Interview With Stephanie Coontz." *The Mother Company*, November 22. Retrieved May 25, 2012 (www.themotherco.com/2011/1/what-is-the-traditional-family/).

Copp, Jennifer E., Peggy C. Giordano, Monica A. Longmore, and Wendy D. Manning. 2013. "Stay/Leave Decision-Making in Non-Violent and Violent Dating Relationships." 2013 Working Paper Series. *Center for Family and Demographic Research.* Retrieved January 17, 2014 (www.bgsu.edu/organizations.cfdr).

Coser, Lewis A. 1956. *The Functions of Social Conflict.* New York: Free Press.

Council on Foreign Relations. 2014. "NAFTA's Economic Impact." Retrieved February 23, 2014 (www.cfr.org/trade/naftas-economic-impact/p15790).

Council of Graduate Schools. 2014. "Doctoral Degrees by Field and Gender, 2012." Retrieved May 11, 2014 (www.aei-ideas.org/2013/09/women-earned-majority-of-doctoral-degrees-in-2012-for-4th-straight-year-and-outnumber-men-in-grad-school-141).

Cousteau, Jacques-Yves. 2008. "The Great Ocean Adventure." Lecture at Hanover College, January 15.

Cowen, Nick and Nigel Williams. 2012. "Comparisons of Crime in OECD Countries." *Civitas Crime.* Retrieved May 2, 2013 (www.civitas.org.uk/crime/crime_stats_oecdjan2012.pdf).

Crary, David and Denise Lavoie. 2013. "As Boston Buries Its Dead, More Evidence Gathered." AP, April 23. Retrieved August 23, 2014 (http://bigstory.ap.org/article/more-details-sought-mute-boston-bomb-suspect).

Crenshaw, Kimberlé. 1991. "Mapping the Margins: Intersectionality, Identity Politics, and Violence Against Women of Color." *Stanford Law Review* 43(6):1241–99.

Crime Library. 2012. "Worst Cases of Bullying." Retrieved October 5, 2012 (www.gtrutv.com/library/crime/photo-gallery/worst-cases-of-bullying.html?curPhoto=3).

Crosby, Faye J. 2004. *Affirmative Action Is Dead; Long Live Affirmative Action.* New Haven, CT: Yale University Press.

Cultural Survival. 2010. "Wodaabe." Retrieved July 7, 2013 (www.culturalsurvival.org/publications/cultural-survival-quarterly/cameroon/wodaabe).

Curtiss, S. 1977. *Genie: A Psycholinguistic Study of a Modern-Day "Wild Child."* New York: Academic Press.

Cuzzort, R. P. and Edith W. King. 2002. *Social Thought Into the Twenty-First Century*, 6th ed. Belmont, CA: Wadsworth.

"Cybercrime: Smoking Gun." 2013. *The Economist*, February 23. Retrieved June 2, 2013 (www.economist.com/news/china/21572228-evidence-mounting-chinas-government-sponsoring-cybertheft-western-corporate).

DaCosta, Kimberly McClain. 2007. *Making Multiracials: State, Family, and Market in the Redrawing of the Color Line.* Stanford, CA: Stanford University Press.

Dahl, Robert A. 1961. *Who Governs?* New Haven, CT: Yale University Press.

Dahlberg, Frances. 1981. *Woman the Gatherer.* New Haven, CT: Yale University Press.

Dahrendorf, Ralf. 1959. *Class and Class Conflict in Industrial Societies.* Palo Alto, CA: Stanford University Press.

Daley, Suzanne and Nicholas Kulish. 2013. "Germany Fights Population Drop." *New York Times*, August 13. Retrieved March 17, 2014 (www.nytimes.com/2013/08/14/world/europe/germany-fights-population-drop.html).

Dalton, Harlon. 2012. "Failing to See." Pp. 15–18 in *White Privilege*, edited by Paula S. Rothenberg. New York: Worth.

Das, Udaibir S., Michael G. Papaioannou, and Christoph Trebesch. 2012. "Sovereign Debt Restructurings 1950–2010: Literature Survey, Data, and Stylized Facts." International Monetary Fund, August. Retrieved September 8, 2014 (www.un.org/esa/ffd/ecosoc/debt/2013/IMF_wp12_203.pdf).

Davidson, James D. 2008. "Religious Stratification: Its Origins, Persistence, and Consequences." *Sociology of Religion* 69(4):371–95.

Davis, Kingsley. 1940. "Extreme Social Isolation of a Child." *American Journal of Sociology* 45:554–65.

Davis, Kingsley. 1947. "A Final Note on a Case of Extreme Isolation." *American Journal of Sociology* 52:432–37.

Death Penalty Information Center. 2013. "FBI Releases Report Including State Murder Rates for 2012: DPIC Analysis Posted October 28, 2013." Retrieved April 25, 2014 (www.deathpenaltyinfo.org/studies-fbi-releases-report-including-state-murder-rates-2012).

Death Penalty Information Center. 2014. "States With and Without the Death Penalty." Retrieved April 25, 2014 (www.deathpenaltyinfoorg/states-and-without-death-penalty).

Debenham, Lucy. 2014. "Communication—What Percent Is Body Language?" August 18. Retrieved August 29, 2014 (www.bodylanguageexpert.co.uk/communication-what-percentage-body-language.html).

DeBoskey, Bruce. 2012. "Women Changing the Face of Philanthropy." *The Denver Post*, July 22. Retrieved April 25, 2013 (www.denverpost.com/business/ci_21124380/women-changing-face-philanthropy).

Deerwester, Karen. 2013. "Boy Toys or Girl Toys: Children Are What They Play." *Examiner*, November 8. Retrieved January 16, 2014 (www.examiner.com/article/boy-toys-or-girl-toys-children-are-what-they-play).

Della Porta, Donatella, Massimillano Andretta, Lorenzo Mosca, and Herbert Reiter. 2006. *Globalization From Below: Transnational Activists and Protest Networks.* Minneapolis: University of Minnesota Press.

DeMitchell, Todd A. and John J. Carney. 2005. "Harry Potter and the Public School Library." *Phi Delta Kappan* (October):159–65.

Demographics Livability. 2014. "Why Do People Move? Here Are the Top Reasons for Relocation." June 12. Retrieved September 8, 2014 (http://livability.com/blog/demo graphics/why-do-people-move-here-are-top-rea sons-relocation).

Denali Commission. 2001. "Telecommunications Inventory Survey." Retrieved June 29, 2006 (www.commonwealth .north.org/transcripts/denalicom.html).

DeNavas-Walt, Carmen and Bernadette D. Proctor. 2014. "Table 4. Families in Poverty by Type of Family: 2012 and 2013." *Income and Poverty in the United States: 2013.* U.S. Census Bureau, Current Population Reports, September.

DeNavas-Walt, Carmen, Bernadette D. Proctor, and Jessica C. Smith. 2012. "Income, Poverty, and Health Insurance Coverage in the United States: 2011." U.S. Census Bureau *Current Population Reports*, September. Retrieved February 6, 2013 (http://www.census.gov/ prod/2012pubs/p60-243.pdf).

DeNavas-Walt, Carmen, Bernadette D. Proctor, and Jessica C. Smith. 2013. "Income, Poverty, and Health Insurance Coverage in the United States." U.S. Census Bureau *Current Population Reports*, September. Retrieved September 5, 2014 (http://www.census.gov/ prod/2013pubs/p60-245.pdf).

DeParle, Jason and Sabrina Tavernise. 2012. "For Women Under 30, Most Births Occur Outside Marriage." *New York Times*, February 17. Retrieved June 5, 2012 (www.nytimes.com/2012/02/18/us/for-women- under-30-most-births-occur-outside-marriage .html?pagewanted=all).

Dews, C. L. Barney and Carolyn Leste Law, eds. 1995. *This Fine Place So Far From Home: Voices of Academics From the Working Class.* Philadelphia: Temple University Press.

Diamond, Jared M. 1999. *Guns, Germs, and Steel: The Fates of Human Societies.* New York: Norton.

Diamond, Jared. 2005. *Collapse: How Societies Choose to Fail or Succeed.* New York: Viking.

Diamond, Larry. 1992. "Introduction: Civil Society and the Struggle for Democracy." Pp. 1–28 in *The Democratic Revolution: Struggles for Freedom and Pluralism in the Developing World,* edited by Larry Diamond. New York: Freedom House.

Diamond, Larry. 2009. *The Spirit of Democracy: The Struggle to Build Free Societies Throughout the World.* New York: Times Books/Henry Holt & Co.

Diekman, Amanda B. and Sarah K. Murmen. 2004. "Learning to Be Little Women and Little Men: The Inequitable Gender Equality of Nonsexist Children's Literature." *Sex Roles: A Journal of Research* 50(5/6):373.

Diep, Francie. 2011. "Fast Facts About the Japan Earthquake and Tsunami." *Scientific American,* March 14. Retrieved May 13, 2012 (www.scientificamerican.com/article .cfm?if=fast-facts-japan).

Diggs, Nancy Brown. 2011. *Hidden in the Heartland.* East Lansing: Michigan State University Press.

DiPrete, Thomas A. and Claudia Buchmann. 2013. *The Rise of Women: The Growing Gender Gap in Education and What It Means for American Schools.* New York: Russell Sage Foundation.

Dobbelaere, Karel. 1981. *Secularization: A Multidimensional Concept.* Beverly Hills, CA: Sage.

Dobbelaere, Karel. 2000. "Toward an Integrated Perspective of the Processes Related to the Descriptive Concept of Secularization." Pp. 21–39 in *The Secularization Debate,* edited by William H. Swatos, Jr. and Daniel V. A. Olson. Lanham, MD: Rowman & Littlefield.

Dobbs, David. 2013. "The Social Life of Genes." *Pacific Standard,* September 3. Retrieved December 17, 2013 (www.psmag .com/health/the-social-life-of-genes-64616/).

Dockterman, Eliana. 2014. "Chore Wars: How the Division of Domestic Duties Really Affects a Couple's Sex Life." *Time,* February 18. Retrieved February 28, 2014 (http:// healthland.time.com/2014/02/18/chore-wars-how- the-division-of-domestic-duties-really-affects-a-cou ples-sex-life/#ixzz2udTcoUJ0).

"Doing Gender." 2011. *Creative Sociology.* August 10. Retrieved May (http://creativesociology.blogspot .com/2011/08/doing-gender.html).

Dollars and Sense Collective. 2012. Pp. 81–91 in *Globalization: The Transformation of Social Worlds,* 3rd ed., edited by D. Stanley Eitzen and Maxine Baca Zinn. Belmont, CA: Wadsworth.

Domhoff, G. William. 2005. "The Class-Domination Theory of Power." *Who Rules America,* 6th ed. Retrieved May 16, 2012 (www2.ucsc.edu/whorulesamerica/power/class_ domination.html).

Domhoff, G. William. 2008. "Who Rules America.net: Power, Politics, and Social Change." Retrieved March 24, 2008 (http://sociology.ucsc.edu/whoruleeesamerica).

Domhoff, G. William. 2009. *Who Rules America: Challenges to Corporate and Class Dominance,* 6th ed. Upper Saddle River, NJ: Prentice Hall.

Domhoff, G. William. 2014a. *Who Rules America: The Triumph of the Corporate Rich,* 7th ed. New York: McGraw-Hill.

Domhoff, G. William. 2014b. "Who Rules America Today?" YouTube, April 7. Retrieved November 6, 2014 (www .youtube.com/watch?v=k31RJC4Om98).

Donadio, Rachel. 2010. "Vatican Revises Abuse Processes but Causes Stir." *New York Times*, July 15. Retrieved July 12, 2013 (www.nytimes.com/2010/07/16/world/ europe/16vatican.html).

Drafke, Michael. 2008. *The Human Side of Organizations.* Englewood Cliffs, NJ: Prentice Hall.

Drori, Gili S. 2006. *Global E-Litism: Digital Technology, Social Inequality, and Transnationality.* New York: Worth.

Du Bois, W. E. B. [1899] 1967. *The Philadelphia Negro: A Social Study.* New York: Schocken.

Dufur, Mikaela J. and Seth L. Feinberg. 2007. "Artificially Restricted Labor Markets and Worker Dignity in

Professional Football." *Journal of Contemporary Ethnography* 36(5):505–36.

Duhigg, Charles and David Kocieniewski. 2013. "How Apple Sidesteps Billions in Taxes." *New York Times*, April 28. Retrieved May 31, 2013 (www.nytimes.com/2012/04/29/business/apples-tax-strategy-aims-at-low-tax-states-and-nations.html?pagewanted=all&_r=0).

Durkheim, Émile. [1893] 1947. *The Division of Labor in Society*, translated by George Simpson. New York: Free Press.

Durkheim, Émile. [1895] 1982. *The Rules of the Sociological Method*, edited by Steven Lukes and translated by W. D. Halls. New York: Free Press.

Durkheim, Émile. [1897] 1964. *Suicide*. Glencoe, IL: Free Press.

Durkheim, Émile. [1915] 2002. In *Classical Sociological Theory*, edited by Craig Calhoun. Malden, MA: Blackwell.

Durkheim, Émile. 1947. *Elementary Forms of Religious Life*. Glencoe, IL: Free Press.

Dusenbery, Maya and Jaeah Lee. 2012. "Charts: The State of Women's Athletics, 40 Years After Title IX." *Mother Jones*, June 22. Retrieved May 2, 2013 (www.motherjones.com/politics/2012/06/charts-womens-athletics-title-nine-ncaa).

Dworkin, Anthony Gary and Rosalind J. Dworkin. 1999. *The Minority Report: An Introduction to Racial, Ethnic, and Gender Relations*, 3rd ed. Fort Worth, TX: Harcourt Brace.

Dworkin, Anthony Gary and Pamela F. Tobe. 2012. "Teacher Burnout in Light of School Safety, Student Misbehavior, and Changing Accountability Standards." Pp. 199–211 in *Schools and Society: A Sociological Approach to Education*, edited by Jeanne H. Ballantine and Joan Z. Spade. Thousand Oaks, CA: Sage Pine Forge.

Dye, Thomas, R. 2002. *Who's Running America? The Clinton Years*. Upper Saddle River, NJ: Prentice Hall.

Dye, Thomas and Harmon Zeigler. 1983. *The Irony of Democracy*. North Scituate, MA: Duxbury Press.

Dyer, Richard. 2012. "The Matter of Whiteness." Pp. 9–14 in *White Privilege*, edited by Paula S. Rothenberg. New York: Worth.

Earls, Felton M. and Albert J. Reiss. 1994. *Breaking the Cycle: Predicting and Preventing Crime*. Washington, DC: National Institute of Justice.

Ebaugh, Helen Rose Fuchs. 2005. *Handbook of Religion and Social Institutions*. New York: Springer.

EcoSummit. 2012. "Ecological Sustainability: Restoring the Planet's Ecosystem Services." *Fourth International Ecosummit*. Retrieved July 31, 2012 (www.ecosummit2012.org/).

Edelson, Josh. 2014. "Most Americans Think It's Illegal to Fire Someone for Being Gay. They're Wrong." *Bloomberg Businessweek*, June 26. Retrieved September 6, 2014 (www.businessweek.com/articles/2014-06-23/discrimination-at-work-is-it-legal-to-fire-someone-for-being-gay).

Eder, Donna, Catherine Colleen Evans, and Stephen Parker. 1995. *School Talk: Gender and Adolescent Culture*. New Brunswick, NJ: Rutgers University Press.

Edwards, Harry. 2000. "Crisis of the Black Athlete on the Eve of the 21st Century." *Society* 37(3):9–13.

Ehrlich, Paul and Anne Ehrlich. 1990. *The Population Explosion*. New York: Simon and Schuster.

Ehrlich, Paul R. and Anne H. Ehrlich. 2013. "Can a Collapse of Global Civilization Be Avoided?" *Proceedings of the Royal Society B* 280. Retrieved July 3, 2013 (http://rspb.royalsocietypublishing.org/content/280/1754/20122845.full.pdf).

Eitzen, D. Stanley and Maxine Baca Zinn. 2012. "Changing Global Structures: Resistance and Social Movements." Pp. 269–71 in *Globalization: The Transformation of Social Worlds*, 3rd ed., edited by D. Stanley Eitzen and Maxine Baca Zinn. Belmont, CA: Wadsworth.

Ellison, Christopher G., J. A. Burr, and P. L. McCall. 1997. "Religious Homogeneity and Metropolitan Suicide Rates." *Social Forces* 76(1):273–99.

Ellison, Christopher G. and Daniel A. Powers. 1994. "The Contact Hypothesis and Racial Attitudes Among Black Americans." *Social Science Quarterly* 75(2):385–400.

Engels, Friedrich. [1884] 1942. *The Origin of the Family, Private Property, and the State*. New York: International Publishing.

England Church Records. 2014. "Introduction." Retrieved September 10, 2014 (https://familysearch.org/learn/wiki/en/England_Church_Records#Introduction).

Environment 911. 2012. "Causes of Water Shortages." Retrieved February 8, 2013 (www.environment911.org/221.Causes_of_Water_Shortages).

Erickson, Fritz and John A. Vonk. 2012. "100 People: A World Portrait." Retrieved January 4, 2014 (www.100people.org/statistics_100stats.php).

Erikson, Erik H. 1950. *Childhood and Society*. New York: Norton.

Eshleman, J. Ross and Richard A. Bulcroft. 2010. *The Family*, 12th ed. Boston: Allyn & Bacon.

Esperitu, Yen Le. 1992. *Asian American Panethnicity: Bridging Institutions and Identities*. Philadelphia: Temple University Press.

Espo, David. 2009. "$797 Billion Stimulus Plan Ok'd in Victory for Obama." *Los Angeles Daily News*, February 14. Retrieved February 24, 2009 (www.dailynews.com/search/ci_11703066).

Estrellado, Alicia F. and Jennifer (M. I.) Loh. 2013. "Factors Associated With Battered Filipino Women's Decision to Stay in or Leave an Abusive Relationship." *Journal of Interpersonal Violence*, November 7. Retrieved January 17, 2014 (http://jiv.sagepub.com/content/early/2013/11/07/0886260513505709.abstract).

Etounga-Manguelle, Daniel. 2000. "Does Africa Need a Cultural Adjustment Program?" Pp. 65–77 in *Culture Matters: How Values Shape Human Progress*, edited by Lawrence E. Harrison and Samuel P. Huntington. New York: Basic Books.

European Commission. 2014. "EU Anti-Corruption Report." February 3. Retrieved April 25, 2014 (http://ec.europa.eu/dgs/home-affairs/e-library/documents/policies/organized-crime-and-human-trafficking/corruption/docs/acr_2014_en.pdf).

Ewert, Stephanie. 2013. "The Decline in Private School Enrollment." *SEHSD Working Paper Number FY12-117*. U.S. Census Bureau, January. Retrieved July 10, 2013 (www.census.gov/hhes/school/files/ewert_private_school_enrollment.pdf).

Facebook.com. 2011. "Facebook Facts." Retrieved March 6, 2011 (www.facebook.com/press/info/php?statistics).

Fackler, Martin. 2007. "Career Women in Japan Find a Blocked Path." *New York Times*, August 6. Retrieved November 8, 2009 (www.nytimes.com/2007/08/06/world/asia/06equal.html).

Farley, John E. 2011. *Majority-Minority Relations*, 6th ed. Englewood Cliffs, NJ: Prentice Hall.

Farrer, Claire R. 2011. *Thunder Rides a Black Horse: Mescalero Apaches and the Mythic Present*, 3rd ed. Long Grove, IL: Waveland.

Fathi, David C. 2009. "Prison Nation." Human Rights Watch, April 9. Retrieved April 15, 2009 (www.hrw.org/en/news/2009/04/09/prison-nation).

Fausto-Sterling, Anne. 1992. *Myths of Gender: Biological Theories About Women and Men*, 2nd ed. New York: Basic Books.

Feagin, Joe R. 2012. *The White Frame: Centuries of Racial Framing and Counter-Framing*, 2nd ed. New York: Routledge.

Feagin, Joe R. and Clairece Booher Feagin. 1986. *Discrimination American Style: Institutional Racism and Sexism*. Malabar, FL: Krieger.

Feagin, Joe R. and Clairece Booher Feagin. 2010. *Racial and Ethnic Relations*, 9th ed. Englewood Cliffs, NJ: Prentice Hall.

Featherman, David L. and Robert Hauser. 1978. *Opportunity and Change*. New York: Academic Press.

Federal Bureau of Investigation. 2012a. "Former New York State Senate Majority Leader Pedro Espada, Jr. Pleads Guilty to Tax Fraud and Will Not Challenge Jury Conviction for Stealing From Bronx Health Clinics." New York Field Office, October 12. Retrieved June 2, 2013 (www.fbi.gov/newyork/press-releases/2012/former-new-york-state-senate-majority-leader-pedro-espada-jr.-pleads-guilty-to-tax-fraud-and-will-not-challenge-jury-conviction-for-stealing-from-bronx-health-clinics).

Federal Bureau of Investigation. 2012b. "Hate Crime—Overview." Retrieved January 26, 2015 (http://www.fbi.gov/about-us/investigate/civilrights/hate_crimes/overview).

Federal Bureau of Investigation. 2012c. "Hate Crime Statistics 2011." Retrieved June 1, 2013 (www.fbi.gov/news/stories/2012/december/annual-hate-crimes-report-released/annual-hate-crimes-report-released).

Federal Bureau of Investigation. 2013. "Latest Hate Crime Statistics: Annual Report Shows Slight Decrease." Retrieved January 26, 2015 (http://www.fbi.gov/news/stories/2013/november/annual-hate-crime-statistics-show-slight-decease).

Federal Bureau of Investigation. 2014a. "FBI Releases Preliminary Semiannual Crime Statistics for 2013." Retrieved April 25, 2014 (www.fbi.gov/news/press-releases-fbi-releases-preliminary-semiannual-crime-statistics-for-2013).

Federal Bureau of Investigation. 2014b. "Uniform Crime Report: Crime in the United States 2012." Retrieved April 26, 2014 (www.fbi.gov/about-us/cjis/ucr/crime-in-the-u.s/2012/crime-in-the-u.s.-2012/crir).

Fedotov, Yury. 2012. "Briefing: Fight Against Transnational Organized Crime and Drug Trafficking." Retrieved April 18, 2013 (www.unodc.org/unodc/en/speeches/briefing-to-member-states-toc-7-february-2012.html).

Feeding America. 2013. "Hunger in America." Retrieved January 5, 2014 (http://feedingamerica.org/hunger-in-america.aspx).

Ferhansyed. 2008. "Fundamental Terminology of Planned Change." Retrieved December 21, 2009 (http://organizationdevelopment.wordpress.com/2008/08/10/fundamental-terminology-of-organization-development).

Fernandez, Eleazar S. 2011. *Burning Center, Porous Borders: The Church in a Globalized World*. Eugene, OR: Wipf and Stock.

Ferree, Myra Marx. 2012. "Globalization and Feminism: Opportunities and Obstacles for Activism in a Global Arena." Pp. 291–320 in *Globalization: The Transformation of Social Worlds*, 3rd ed., edited by D. Stanley Eitzen and Maxine Baca Zinn. Belmont, CA: Wadsworth.

"Finery for Infants." 1893. *New York Times*, July 23. Retrieved May 8, 2012 (http://query.nytimes.com/mem/archive-free/pdf?res=F20E17FB3B5F1A738DDDAA0A94DF405B8385F0D3).

Finke, Roger and Rodney Stark. 2005. *The Churching of America, 1776–1990: Winners and Losers in Our Religious Economy*, 2nd ed. New Brunswick, NJ: Rutgers University Press.

Fisher, Max. 2013. "This Map Shows Where the World's 30 Million Slaves Live." *Washington Post*, October 17. Retrieved February 17, 2014 (www.washingtonpost.com/blogs/worldviews/wp/2013/10/17/this-map-shows-where-the-worlds-30-million-slaves-live-there-are-60000-in-the-u-s/).

Flavin, Jeanne. 2004. "Employment, Counseling, Housing Assistance . . . and Aunt Yolanda? How Strengthening Families' Social Capital Can Reduce Recidivism." *Fordham Urban Law Journal* 3(2):209–16.

Florida, Richard. 2004. *Cities and the Creative Class*. New York: Routledge.

Florida, Richard. 2012. "Creative Class Group." March 2. Retrieved March 5, 2012 (www.creativeclass.com/richard_florida).

Flynn, Simone I. 2014. "Social Movement Theory: Value-Added Theory." *Research Starters*. Retrieved February 24, 2014 (http://connection.ebscohost.com/c/essays/36268048/social-movement-theory-value-added-theory).

Foner, Nancy. 2005. *In a New Land: A Comparative View of Immigration.* New York: New York University Press.

Ford, Clennan S. 1970. *Human Relations Area Files: 1949–1969—A Twenty Year Report.* New Haven, CT: Human Relations Area Files.

Foundation for Women. 2012. "Eliminating Global Poverty through Microcredit." Retrieved May 21, 2012 (www.foundationforwomen.org/).

Frank, Mark G. and Thomas Gilovich. 1988. "The Dark Side of Self- and Social Perception: Black Uniforms and Aggression in Professional Sports." *Journal of Personality and Social Psychology* 54(1):74–85.

Frankal, Elliot. 2011. "Compulsory Voting Around the World." *The Guardian,* October 4. Retrieved May 21, 2014 (guardian.co.uk/politics.guardian.co.uk).

Freedom to Marry. 2014. "The Freedom to Marry Internationally." Retrieved September 10, 2014 (http://www.freedomtomarry.org/landscape/entry/c/international).

Freedom to Marry. 2015. "States." Retrieved February 9, 2015 (http://www.freedomtomarry.org/states).

Freese, J., B. Powell, and L. C. Steelman. 1999. *Rebel Without a Cause or Effect: Birth Order and Social Attitudes.* Washington, DC: American Sociological Association.

Free the Slaves. 2014. "About Slavery: Slavery Map." Retrieved September 14, 2014 (www.freetheslaves.net/sslpage.aspx?pid=375).

Freud, Sigmund. [1923] 1960. *The Ego and the Id.* New York: Norton.

Frey, Bruno S. 2004. *Dealing With Terrorism: Stick or Carrot?* Cheltenham, UK: Edward Elgar.

Gallagher, Charles. 2004. "Transforming Racial Identity Through Affirmative Action." Pp. 153–70 in *Race and Ethnicity: Across Time, Space and Discipline,* edited by Rodney D. Coates. Leiden, Holland: Brill.

Gallup. 2009. "Muslim Americans: A National Portrait." The Muslim West Facts Project. Retrieved September 24, 2012 (www.gallup.com/strategicconsulting/153572/REPORT-Muslim-Americans-National-Portrait.aspx).

Gallup. 2013. "Religion." Retrieved January 30, 2013 (http://www.gallup.com/poll/1690/religion.aspx).

Gallup Center for Muslim Studies. 2010. "In U.S., Religious Prejudice Stronger Against Muslims." Retrieved January 22, 2013 (www.gallup.com/poll/12312/religious-prejudice-stronger-against-muslims.aspx).

Gannon, Shane Patrick. 2009. *Translating the Hijra: The Symbolic Reconstruction of the British Empire in India.* PhD thesis, University of Alberta.

Gans, Herbert J. 1962. *The Urban Villagers: Group and Class in the Life of Italian-Americans.* New York: Free Press.

Gans, Herbert J. 1971. "The Uses of Poverty: The Poor Pay All." *Social Policy* 2(2):20–24.

Gans, Herbert J. 1994. "Positive Functions of the Undeserving Poor: Uses of the Underclass in America." *Politics and Society* 22(3):269–83.

Gans, Herbert J. 1995. *The War Against the Poor.* New York: Basic Books.

Gans, Herbert J. 2007. "No, Poverty Has Not Disappeared." Reprinted in *Sociological Footprints,* edited by Leonard Cargan and Jeanne Ballantine. Belmont, CA: Wadsworth.

Gardner, Howard. 1987. "The Theory of Multiple Intelligences." *Annual Dyslexia* 37:19–35.

Gardner, Howard. 1999. *Intelligence Reframed: Multiple Intelligences for the 21st Century.* New York: Basic Books.

Gardom, James. 2011. "The End of Secularisation." *Cambridge GodThink,* March 30. Retrieved July 12, 2013 (http://godthink.org.uk/2011/03/30/the-end-of-secularisation/).

Gellner, Ernest. 1983. *Culture, Identity, and Politics.* Cambridge, UK: Cambridge University Press.

Gellner, Ernest. 1993. "Nationalism." Pp. 409–11 in *Blackwell Dictionary of Twentieth Century Thought,* edited by William Outhwaite and Tom Bottomore. Oxford, UK: Basil Blackwell.

Gellner, Ernest and John Breuilly. 2009. *Nations and Nationalism,* 2nd ed. Ithaca, NY: Cornell University Press.

Gender Equity Resource Center. 2013. "Definition of Terms: Heterosexism." Retrieved February 10, 2014 (http://geneq.berkeley.edu/lgbt_resources_definiton_of_terms#heterosexism).

"Gendercide: The War on Baby Girls." 2010. *The Economist,* March 4. Retrieved May 2, 2010 (www.economist.com/node/15606229).

"Getting Married in Japan." 2014. Retrieved September 8, 2014 (http://japanese.about.com/library/weekly/aa080999.htm).

"The Ghost in Your Genes." 2009. BBC's *Science and Nature.* Retrieved November 12, 2009 (www.bbc.co.uk/sn/tvradio/programmes/horizon/ghostgenes.shtml).

Gibler, John. 2012. "Mexico's Ghost Towns." Pp. 68–72 in *Globalization: The Transformation of Social Worlds,* 3rd ed., edited by D. Stanley Eitzen and Maxine Baca Zinn. Belmont, CA: Wadsworth.

Giddens, Anthony. 1986. *The Constitution of Society.* Berkeley: University of California Press.

Gilbert, Dennis. 2011. *The American Class Structure in an Age of Growing Inequality,* 8th ed. Thousand Oaks, CA: Sage.

Gilligan, Carol. 1982. *In a Different Voice: Psychological Theory and Women's Development.* Cambridge, MA: Harvard University Press.

Gillis, Justin. 2013. "In New Jersey Pines, Trouble Arrives on Six Legs." *New York Times,* December 1. Retrieved March 18, 2014 (www.nytimes.com/2013/12/02/science/earth/in-new-jersey-pines-trouble-arrives-on-six-legs.html?_r=0).

Giridharadas, Anand. 2014. "The Immigrant Advantage." *New York Times,* May 25. Sunday Review, pp. 1, 5.

Girls Health. 2009. "Bullying." *Girlshealth.gov.* Retrieved May 21, 2012 (www.girlshealth.gov/bullying/).

Givens, David B. 2012. "Nonverbal Communication." *Center for Nonverbal Studies.* Retrieved September 25, 2012 (http://center-for-nonverba-studies.org/nvcom.htm).

Glasberg, Davita Silfen and Deric Shannon. 2011. *Political Sociology: Oppression, Resistance, and the State.* Thousand Oaks, CA: Sage.

"The Glass Ceiling Index." 2013. *The Economist,* March 13. Retrieved February 10, 2014 (www.economist.com/ blogs/graphicdetail/2013/03/daily-chart-3).

Glasscock, C. B. 1937. *The Gasoline Age: The Story of the Men Who Made It.* Indianapolis, IN: Bobbs-Merrill.

Global Journal. 2013. "Top 100 NGOs." Retrieved June 28, 2013 (http://theglobaljournal.net/top100NGOs/).

Global Security. 2009. "Guantanamo Bay Detainees." Retrieved April 14, 2012 (www.globalsecurity.org/military/facility/ guantanamo-bay_detainees.htm).

Global Sports Development. 2013. "Steroid Use Among High School Athletes: Research Articles." November 12. Retrieved January 17, 2014 (http://globalsportsdevelop ment.org/steroid-use-among-high-school-athletes/).

"Global Warming and Climate Change." 2013. *New York Times,* January 8. Retrieved February 5, 2013 (http:// topics.nytimes.com/top/news/science/topics/global warming/index.html).

Globe Women. 2013. "WEXPO: Women's Online Marketplace." Retrieved January 23, 2013 (http://www .wexpo.biz/).

Goffman, Erving. 1961. *Asylums: Essays on the Social Situation of Mental Patients and Other Inmates.* New York: Anchor.

Goffman, Erving. 1967. *Interaction Ritual.* New York: Anchor.

Goffman, Erving. [1959] 2001. *Presentation of Self in Everyday Life.* New York: Harmondsworth, UK: Penguin.

Gonzalez-Perez, Margaret. 2011. "The False Islamization of Female Suicide Bombers." *Gender Issues 28*(1/2): 50–65.

Goode, Erich. 1992. *Collective Behavior.* New York: Harcourt Brace Jovanovich.

Goode, William J. 1970. *World Revolution and Family Patterns.* New York: Free Press.

Goodman, Marc D. and Susan W. Brenner. 2002. "The Emerging Consensus on Criminal Conduct in Cyberspace." *International Journal of Law and Information Technology* 10(2):139–223.

Goodstein, Laurie. 2012. "Ugandan Gay Rights Group Sues U.S. Evangelist." *New York Times,* March 14. Retrieved May 27, 2012 (www.nytimes.com/2012/03/15/us/ ugandan-gay-rights-group-sues-scott-lively-an-ameri can-evangelist.html).

Gordon, Milton. 1970. "The Subsociety and the Subculture." Pp. 150–63 in *The Sociology of Subcultures,* edited by David O. Arnold. Berkeley, CA: Glendessary.

Gore, Al. 2012. "Global Warming Is Real." *EarthSky,* April 30. Retrieved September 7, 2012 (http://earthsky.org/ human-world/al-gore-at-hampshire-college-global- warming-is-real).

Gorski, Phillip S. 2000. "Historicizing the Secularization Debate: Church, State, and Society in Late Medieval and Early Modern Europe, ca 1300 to 1700." *Social Forces* (February):138–67.

Gorski, Philip and Ates Altinordu. 2008. "After Secularization." *Annual Review of Sociology* 34:55–85.

Gottdiener, Mark and Ray Hutchison. 2006. *The New Urban Sociology,* 3rd ed. Boston: McGraw-Hill.

Gottfredson, Michael R. and Travis Hirschi. 1990. *A General Theory of Crime.* Palo Alto, CA: Stanford University Press.

Gould, Elise. 2012. "U.S. Lags Behind Peer Countries in Mobility." Economic Policy Institute, October 10. Retrieved June 12, 2013 (www.epi.org/publication/usa- lags-peer-countries-mobility/).

Gould, Stephen J. 1997. *The Mismeasure of Man.* New York: Norton.

Gouldner, Alvin W. 1960. "The Norm of Reciprocity: A Preliminary Statement." *American Sociological Review* 25(2):161–78.

Gracey, Harry L. 1967. "Learning the Student Role: Kindergarten as Academic Boot Camp." Pp. 215–26 in *Readings in Introductory Sociology,* 3rd ed., edited by Dennis Wrong and Harry L. Gracey. New York: Macmillan.

Grandpa Junior. 2006. "If You Were Born Before 1945." Retrieved July 20, 2006 (www.grandpajunior.com/1945 .shtml).

Granovetter, Mark. 2007. "Introduction for the French Reader." *Sociologica* 1(Suppl.):1–10.

Gray, Emma. 2012. "Women and Poverty in the United States: 18 Essential Facts and Statistics." *The Huffington Post,* August 29. Retrieved May 5, 2013 (www.huffing tonpost.com/2012/08/29/women-and-poverty-united- states-facts-statistics_n_1838384.html#slide=more 247419).

Greeley, Andrew M. 1972. *The Denominational Society.* Glenview, IL: Scott, Foresman.

Greeley, Andrew M. 1989. *Religious Change in America.* Cambridge, MA: Harvard University Press.

The Green Papers. 2008a. "Presidential Primaries, Caucuses, and Conventions." Retrieved March 21, 2008 (www .thegreenpapers.com/P08/CO-R.phtml).

The Green Papers. 2008b. "Presidential Primaries 2008: Republican Delegate Selection and Voter Eligibility." Retrieved March 21, 2008 (www.thegreenpapers.com/ P08/R-DSVE.phtml?sort=a).

Greenan, Matthew. 2013. "New Indian Documentary on the Practice of Sati." Retrieved January 16, 2014 (http:// greenanreport.wordpress.com/2013/05/12/new- indian-documentary-on-the-practice-of-sati/).

Greensboro Justice Fund. 2005. "Courage From the Past." *GJF Newsletter* (17, Summer):1.

Grieco, Elizabeth M., Yesenia D. Acosta, G. Patricia de la Cruz, Christine Gambino, Thomas Gryn, Luke J. Larsen, Edward N. Trevelyan, and Nathan P. Walters. 2012. "The Foreign-Born Population in the United States: 2010." American Community Survey Reports. Retrieved June 17, 2013 (www.census.gov/prod/2012pubs/acs-19.pdf).

Grossman, Cathy Lynn. 2012. "Survey Finds 19% Without Religious Affiliation." *USA Today*, February 29. Retrieved September 20, 2012 (www.usatoday .com/news/religion/story/2012-07-19/no-religion-affiliation/56344976/1).

Guerino, Paul, Paige M. Harrison, and William J. Sabol. 2011. "Prisoners in 2010 (Revised)." December 15. Retrieved April 15, 2012 (http://bjs.ojp.usdoj.gov/index .cfm?ty=tp&tid=13).

Gumperz, John J. and Stephen C. Levinson, eds. 1996. *Rethinking Linguistic Relativity*. Cambridge, UK: Cambridge University Press.

Guttmacher Institute. 2013. "Contraceptive Use in the United States." August. Retrieved March 17, 2014 (www.guttm acher.org/pubs/fb_contr_use.html).

Haberkorn, Leonardo. 2014. "From Guantánamo to Uruguay, an Unlikely Journey." *The Miami Herald*, August 14. Retrieved September 15, 2014 (http://www.miamiherald .com/2014/08/14/4289381/from-guantanamo-to-uru guay-an.html).

Hagan, Frank E. 2011. *Introduction to Criminology*, 7th ed. Thousand Oaks, CA: Sage.

Hall, Edward T. 1959. *The Silent Language*. New York: Doubleday.

Hall, Edward T. 1983. *The Dance of Life*. Garden City, NY: Anchor Books/Doubleday.

Hall, Edward T. and Mildred Reed Hall. 1992. *An Anthropology of Everyday Life*. New York: Doubleday.

Hall, Richard H. 2002. *Organizations: Structures, Processes, and Outcomes*, 7th ed. Englewood Cliffs, NJ: Prentice Hall.

Handel, Gerald, Spencer Cahill, and Frederick Elkin. 2007. *Children and Society: The Sociology of Children and Childhood Socialization*. New York: Oxford University Press.

Handwerk, Brian. 2004. "Female Suicide Bombers: Dying to Kill." *National Geographic News*, December 13. Retrieved July 5, 2008 (http://news.nationalgeographic.com/ news/2004/12/1213_041213_tv_suicide_bombers.html).

Haniffa, Aziz. 2009. "Financial Crisis Bigger Than Al Qaeda, Says U.S. Intelligence Czar." *Rediff India Abroad*. February 13. Retrieved March 17, 2009 (www.rediff.com/ money/2009/feb/15bcrisis-financial-crisis-bigger-threat-than-al-qaeda-says-us-intel-chief.htm).

Hansen, Randall and Katharine Hansen. 2003. "What Do Employers Really Want? Top Skills and Values Employers Seek From Job-Seekers" (Quintessential Careers). Retrieved June 23, 2008 (www.quintcareers .com/job_skills_values.html).

Harris, Judith Rich. 2009. *The Nurture Assumption: Why Children Turn Out the Way They Do*, Revised and updated edition. New York: Free Press.

Harris, Marvin. 1989. *Cows, Pigs, War, and Witches: The Riddles of Culture*. New York: Random House.

Hart, Betty and Todd R. Risley. 2003. "The Early Catastrophe: The 30 Million Word Gap by Age 3." *American Educator* 27(1):4–9.

Haskins, Ron, Julia B. Isaacs, and Isabel V. Sawhill. 2008. *Getting Ahead or Losing Ground: Economic Mobility in America*. The Brookings Institute. Retrieved June 7, 2013 (www.brookings.edu/research/reports/2008/02/eco nomic-mobility-sawhill).

Haub, Carl and Toshiko Kaneda. 2013. *World Population Data Sheet*. Washington, DC: Population Reference Bureau. Retrieved May 25, 2014 (www.prb.org/pdf13/2013-pop ulation-data-sheet_eng.pdf).

Hearn, Kelly. 2012. "Big Oil Wreaks Havoc in the Amazon, but Communities Are Fighting Back." Pp. 313–16 in *Globalization: The Transformation of Social Worlds*, 3rd ed., edited by D. Stanley Eitzen and Maxine Baca Zinn. Belmont, CA: Wadsworth.

Hegewisch, Ariane, Claudia Williams, Heidi Hartmann, and Stephanie Keller Hudiburg. 2014. "The Gender Wage Gap: 2013." *Institute for Women's Policy Research*, March. Retrieved May 12, 2014 (www.iwpr.org/publica tions/pubs/the-gender-wage-gap-2013-differences-by-race-and-ethnicity-no-growth-in-real-wages-for-women).

Heilbroner, Robert L. and William Milberg. 2007. *The Making of Economic Society*, 12th ed. Englewood Cliffs, NJ: Prentice Hall.

Hendry, Joy. 1987. *Becoming Japanese: The World of the Preschool Child*. Honolulu: University of Hawaii Press.

Hensley, Christopher, M. Koscheski, and Richard Tewksbury. 2005. "Examining the Characteristics of Male Sexual Assault Targets in a Southern Maximum-Security Prison." *Journal of Interpersonal Violence* 20(6):667–79.

Hepworth, Kimberly. 2010. "Eating Disorders Today—Not Just a Girl Thing." *Journal of Christian Nursing*, July/ September. Retrieved January 17, 2014 (http://nursing .ceconnection.com/nu/public/modules/2224).

Herskovitz, Jon. 2012. "Militant South African Union Tells Lonmin to Pay Up." Reuters, September 7. Retrieved September 8, 2012 (www.reuters.com/article/2012/09/07/us-safrica-mines-idUSBRE8860U82012090/).

Hewitt, John P. and David Shulman. 2011. *Self and Society: A Symbolic Interactionist Approach to Social Psychology*, 11th ed. Englewood Cliffs, NJ: Prentice Hall.

Hewlett, Sylvia Ann. 2013. "What's Holding Japanese Women Back." *Time Ideas*, September 27. Retrieved January 18, 2014 (http://ideas.time.com/2013/09/27/whats-hold ing-japanese-women-back/).

Heyes, J. D. 2012. "Plastic Waste Garbage Floating in Pacific Ocean Has Increased 100-Fold." *NaturalNews.com*, May 15. Retrieved September 7, 2012 (www.naturalnews .com/035866_garbage_floating_Pacific_Ocean.html).

Hinton, Christopher. 2010. "Global Military Spending to Outpace GDP Growth in 2010." *Market Watch*, June 18. Retrieved May 10, 2011 (www.marketwatch.com/ story/worlds-militaries-see-another-budget-busting-year-2010-06-18).

Hirschi, T. 1969. *Causes of Delinquency.* Berkeley: University of California Press.

Hochschild, Arlie. 1989. *The Second Shift: Working Parents and the Revolution at Home.* New York: Viking.

Holloway, Susan. 2001. "Mothers of Japanese Preschoolers." *GSE Term Paper* 8(1). University of California, Berkeley. Retrieved April 17, 2010 (http://gse.berkeley.edu/admin/publications/termpaper/fall01/fall01/html).

Holt, Sheila. 2007. *Talk of the Nation.* National Public Radio. Interview by Cheryl Covley, March 26.

Homans, George C. 1974. *Social Behavior: Its Elementary Forms.* New York: Harcourt, Brace Jovanovich.

Houlis, Anna Marie. 2011. "Gender Stereotypes in Picture Books Are Blamed for Affecting Children." June 13. Retrieved May 23, 2012 (http://annamariehoulis.word press.com/2011/06/13/gender-stereotypes-in-pic ture-books-are-blamed-for-affecting-children/).

"How Finnish Schools Shine." 2012. *The Guardian*, May 21. Retrieved July 8, 2013 (www.guardian.co.uk/teacher-network/teacher-blog/2012/apr/09/finish-school-system).

Howard, Adam. 2007. *Learning Privilege: Lessons of Power and Identity in Affluent Schooling.* New York: Taylor & Francis.

Howard, Adam and Ruben Gaztambide-Fernandez, eds. 2010. *Educating Elites: Class Privilege and Educational Advantage.* Lanham, MD: Rowman and Littlefield.

Hozien, Muhammad. N.d. "Ibn Khaldun: His Life and Work." Retrieved May 7, 2009 (www.muslimphilosophy.com/ik/klf.htm).

Hu, Elise. 2014. "Niche Online Dating Promises a Different Site for Every Preference." *National Public Radio*, February 12. Retrieved February 18, 2014 (www.gpb.org/news/2014/02/12/niche-online-dating-promises-a-different-site-for-every-preference).

Hu, Winnie. 2007. "Equal Cheers for Boys and Girls Draw Some Boos." *New York Times*. January 14. Retrieved February 11, 2014 (www.nytimes.com/2007/01/14/nyregion/14title.html).

Huang, Al. 2011. "'Poster Child' for Environmental Racism Finds Justice in Dickson, TN." *NRDC Switchboard*, December 8. Retrieved March 14, 2014 (http://archive.is/AsHA).

Huddy, Leonie and Stanley Feldman. 2006. "Worlds Apart: Blacks and Whites React to Hurricane Katrina." *Du Bois Review* 3(1):97–113. Retrieved July 7, 2011 (http://journals.cambridge.org/action/displayAbstract?fromPage=onli ne&aid=462978).

Hudson, Heather E. 2011. "Digital Diversity: Broadband and Indigenous Populations in Alaska." *Journal of Information Policy* 1:378–93. Retrieved September 25, 2012 (jip.vmhost.psu.edu/ojs/index.php/jip/article/down load/42/37).

Hudson, Heather E. 2012. "Toward Universal Broadband in Rural Alaska." Institute of Social and Economic Research, University of Alaska, Anchorage. Retrieved September 25, 2012 (www.iser.uaa.alaska.edu/Publications/2012_11-TERRA.pdf).

Hugo, Peter. 2010. "A Global Graveyard for Dead Computers in Ghana." *New York Times Magazine*. Retrieved July 10, 2013 (www.cnn.com/2011/10/17/opinion/sachs-global-population).

Huizinga, David, Rolf Loeber, and Terence P. Thornberry. 1994. "Urban Delinquency and Substance Abuse: Initial Findings." OJJDP Research Summary. Washington, DC: Government Printing Office.

Human Planet. 2012. "Wodaabe Flirtation Festival." Retrieved January 16, 2014 (http://dsc.discovery.com/tv-shows/human-planet/videos/wodaabe-flirtation-festival.htm).

Human Rights First. 2015. "Guantanamo by the Numbers." *Fact Sheet: January 15.* Retrieved January 27, 2015 (www.humanrightsfirst.org/sites/default/files/gtmo-by-the-numbers.pdf).

Hunter College Women's Studies Collective. 2005. *Women's Realities, Women's Choices: An Introduction to Women's Studies,* 3rd ed. New York: Oxford University Press.

Hurst, Charles E. 2006. *Social Inequality: Forms, Causes and Consequences,* 6th ed. Boston: Allyn & Bacon.

Hurst, Charles E. 2013. *Social Inequality: Forms, Causes, and Consequences,* 8th ed. Pearson.

Iannaccone, Laurence and William S. Bainbridge. 2010. "Economics of Religion." Pp. 461–75 in *The Routledge Companion to the Study of Religion,* 2nd ed., edited by John Hinnells. New York: Routledge.

"Iceberg Breaks Off From Greenland's Petermann Glacier." 2012. *BBC News,* July 19. Retrieved February 8, 2013 (www.bbc.co.uk/news/world-europe-18896770).

In Sickness and in Wealth: Health in America. 2008. Unnatural Causes, July 3. Retrieved May 13, 2014 (www.youtube.com/watch?v=w98GSXBEyQw).

IndexMundi. 2013. "Population Growth Rate." Retrieved March 17, 2014 (www.indexmundi.com/united_kingdom/demographic_profile.html).

IndexMundi. 2014. "Chad Demographic Profile 2014." Retrieved September 16, 2014 (www.indexmundi.com/chad/demographics_profile.html).

Infoplease. 2014. "Most Widely Spoken Languages in the World." Retrieved August 19, 2014 (www.infoplease.com/ipa/A0775272.html).

Inglehart, Ronald. 1997. *Modernization and Post-modernization: Cultural, Economic, and Political Change in 43 Societies.* Princeton, NJ: Princeton University Press.

Inglehart, Ronald and Wayne E. Baker. 2001. "Modernization's Challenge to Traditional Values: Who's Afraid of Ronald McDonald?" *The Futurist* 35(2):16–22.

Intergovernmental Panel on Climate Change. 2013a. *Fifth Assessment Report.* Retrieved March 18, 2014 (www.ipcc.ch/report/).

Intergovernmental Panel on Climate Change. 2013b. "Working Group I Contribution to the IPCC Fifth Assessment Report." *Climate Change 2013: The Physical*

Science Basis. Summary for Policymakers, September 27. Retrieved September 27, 2013 (http://graphics8.nytimes.com/packages/pdf/science/27climate-ipcc-report-summary.pdf).

Intergovernmental Panel on Climate Change. 2014. "Climate Change 2014: Mitigation of Climate Change." Retrieved May 27, 2014 (http://www.ipcc.ch/).

International Beliefs and Values Institute. 2012. "Mission." Staunton, VA: Mary Baldwin College. Retrieved March 23, 2012 (www.ibavi.org).

International Center for Prison Studies. 2014. "World Prison Brief." Retrieved May 13, 2014 (www.prisonstudies.org/).

"The International Digital Divide." 2011. *Science Daily,* February 8. Retrieved May 18, 2012 (www.sciencedaily.com/releases/2011/02/110208121345.htm).

International Institute for Democracy and Electoral Assistance. 2012. *Voter Turnout Since 1945: A Global Report.* Retrieved June 2, 2013 (www.idea.int/vt/).

International Labour Organization. 2014. "Cambodia." Retrieved January 18, 2014 (www.ilo.org/asia/countries/cambodia/lang--en/index.htm).

International Monetary Fund. 2013. "Debt Relief Under the Heavily Indebted Poor Countries (HIPC) Initiative." January 10. Retrieved February 7, 2013 (http://www.imf.org/external/np/exr/facts/hipc.htm).

International Organization for Migration. 2012. "Global Estimates and Trends." Retrieved July 30, 2012 (www.iom.int/jahia/Jahia/about-migration/facts-and-figures/lang/en).

Internet World Statistics. 2014. "Internet Usage Statistics: The Internet Big Picture." Retrieved January 30, 2015 (http://www.internetworldstats.com/stats.htm).

Inter-Parliamentary Union. 2014. "Women in National Parliaments." Retrieved September 2, 2014 (www.ipu.org/wmn-e/classif.htm).

Interuniversity Consortium for Political and Social Research. 2011. "Voting Behavior: The 2008 Election." Retrieved May 16, 2012 (http://www.icpsr.umich.edu/icpsrweb/SETUPS2008/voting.jsp).

Irvine, Leslie. 2004. *If You Tame Me: Understanding Our Connection With Animals.* Philadelphia: Temple University Press.

Irwin, John. 1985. *The Jail: Managing the Underclass in American Society.* Berkeley: University of California Press.

Irwin, John and Barbara Owen. 2007. *The Warehouse Prison: Disposal of the New Dangerous Class.* New York: Oxford University Press.

Jackson, Philip W. 1968. *Life in Classrooms.* New York: Holt, Rinehart & Winston.

Jaeger, Mads Meier. 2011. "Does Cultural Capital Really Affect Academic Achievement? New Evidence From Combined Sibling and Panel Data." *Sociology of Education* 84(October):281–98.

James, Deanna. 2013. "The Psychology of Eating Disorders." *PsychCentral,* August 8. Retrieved January 18, 2014

(http://psychcentral.com/blog/archives/2013/08/08/the-psychology-of-eating-disorders/).

James, Susan Donaldson. 2011. "Census 2010: One-quarter of Gay Couples Raising Children." *ABC News,* June 23. Retrieved June 5, 2012 (http://abcnews.go.com/Health/sex-couples-census-data-trickles-quarter-raising-children/story?id=13850332).

James, William. [1890] 1934. *The Principles of Psychology.* Mineola, NY: Dover.

Jarrett, R. L., P. J. Sullivan, and N. D. Watkins. 2005. "Developing Social Capital Through Participation in Organized Youth Programs: Qualitative Insights From Three Programs." *Journal of Community Psychology* 33(1):41–55.

Jaschik, Scott. 2013. "Prestige vs. Major." *Inside Higher Education,* December 10. Retrieved January 4, 2014 (www.insidehighered.com/news/2013/12/10/study-examines-impact-major-vs-impact-college-prestige-womens-earnings).

Jelen, Ted, ed. 2002. *Sacred Markets, Sacred Canopies: Essays on Religious Markets and Religious Pluralism.* New York: Rowman & Littlefield.

Jencks, Christopher, ed. 1979. *Who Gets Ahead? The Determinants of Economic Success in America.* New York: Harper & Row.

Jewish Outreach Institute. 2008. "What Are the Different Denominations (Types) of Judaism?" Retrieved November 11, 2014 (www.joi.org/qa/denom.shtml).

Johnson, Kevin. 2014. "Thousands of Prisoners Could Qualify for Clemency." *USA Today,* April 21. Retrieved April 25, 2014 (www.usatoday.com/story/news/nation/2014/04/21/prisoners-clemency-holder/7962929/).

Johnson, Robert. 2002. *Hard Time: Understanding and Reforming the Prison.* Belmont, CA: Wadsworth/Thompson Learning.

Joint Center for Political and Economic Studies. 2013. "Nickelodeon: Kids Watch 35 Hours of TV/Week—MTI Stats and Studies, 12/2/2013." Retrieved January 17, 2014 (http://jcpes.wordpress.com/2013/12/02/nickelodeon-kids-watch-35-hours-of-tvweek-mti-stats-and-studies-1222013/).

Jordan, Amy B., James C. Hersey, Judith A. McDivitt, and Carrie D. Heitzler. 2006. "Reducing Children's Television-Viewing Time: A Qualitative Study of Parents and Their Children." *Pediatrics* 118(5):1303–10.

Jordan, Winthrop D. 2012. *White Over Black: American Attitudes Toward the Negro 1550–1812,* 2nd ed. (Published for the Omohundro Institute of Early American History). Chapel Hill: University of North Carolina.

Jourdan, Adam. 2013. "Divided Church of England Renews Pledge to Ordain Women Bishops." Reuters, July 8. Retrieved July 12, 2013 (http://uk.reuters.com/article/2013/07/08/uk-britain-church-women-idUKBRE9670SC20130708).

Julian, Tiffany and Robert Kominski. 2011. "Table 1: Annual Earnings by Level of Education and Work Status." *American Community Survey Reports*, September. Retrieved September 9, 2014 (http://www.census.gov/prod/2011pubs/acs-14.pdf).

Kaiser Family Foundation. 2010. "G8 Leaders to Discuss Economic Policy, Developing World, Maternal and Child Health, Haitian Rebuilding." June 25. Retrieved July 13, 2012 (http://globalhealth.Kff.org/Daily-Reports/2010/June/25/GH-062510-G8-G20-Summits.aspx).

Kan, Man Yee, Oriel Sullivan, and Jonathan Gershuny. 2011. "Gender Convergence in Domestic Work: Discerning the Effects of Interactional and Institutional Barriers From Large-Scale Data." *Sociology* 45(2):234–51.

Kanter, Rosabeth Moss. 1977. *Men and Women of the Corporation.* New York: Basic Books.

Kanter, Rosabeth Moss. 2005. *Commitment and Community.* Cambridge, MA: Harvard University Press.

Kaplan, Howard B. and Robert J. Johnson. 1991. "Negative Social Sanctions and Juvenile Delinquency: Effects of Labeling in a Model of Deviant Behavior." *Social Science Quarterly* 72(1):117.

Kean, Sam. 2007. "What's in a Name?" *New York Times*, October 28. Retrieved May 21, 2012 (www.nytimes.com/2007/10/28/magazine/28wwln-idealab-t.html).

Keck, Zachary. 2014. "US Drives Down Global Defense Spending." *The Diplomat*, April 15. Retrieved May 22, 2014 (http://thediplomat.com/2014/04/us-drives-down-global-defense-spending/).

Kelber, Harry. 2012. "Manufacturers Are Hiring Workers in America, but Offer a Sharp Drop in Wages and Benefits." *The Labor Educator*, January 2. Retrieved May 28, 2012 (www.laboreducator.org/lt120102.htm).

Kennedy, Kelly. 2011. "Health Care Fraud Prosecutions on Pace to Rise 85%." *USA Today*, August 29. Retrieved April 13, 2012 (www.usatoday.com/news/washington/story/2011-08-29/Health-care-fraud-prosecutions-on-pace-to-rise-85/50180282/1).

Kerbo, Harold R. 2008. *Social Stratification and Inequality*, 7th ed. Boston: McGraw-Hill.

Kessler, Sarah. 2011. "Study: 80% of Children Under 5 Use Internet Weekly." *Technology Live*, March 15. Retrieved April 9, 2013 (http://content.usatoday.com/communities/technologylive/post/2011/03/study-80-percent-of-children-under-5-use-internet-weekly/).

Khazan, Olga. 2013. "The Countries Where Women Have the Best Lives." *The Atlantic*, March 8. Retrieved January 17, 2014 (www.theatlantic.com/international/archive/2013/03/the-countries-where-women-have-the-best-lives-in-charts/273848).

Killian, Caitlin. 2006. *North African Women in France: Gender, Culture, and Identity.* Palo Alto, CA: Stanford University Press.

Kim, Min-Sun, Katsuya Tasaki, In-Duk Kim, and Hye-ryeon Lee. 2007. "The Influence of Social Status on Communication Predispositions Focusing on Independent and Interdependent Self-Construals." *Journal of Asian Pacific Communication* 17(2):303–29.

King, Neil, Jr. 2012. "Vote Data Show Changing Nation." *The Wall Street Journal*, November 8. Retrieved June 7, 2013 (http://online.wsj.com/article/SB10001424127887324073504578105360833569352.html#project%3DEXITPOLLS2012%26articleTabs%3Darticle).

Kinsey Institute for Research in Sex, Gender, and Reproduction. 2012. Retrieved May 20, 2012 (www.kinseyinstitute.org).

Kirchhoff, Suzanne M. 2010. "Economic Impacts of Prison Growth." Congressional Research Service, April 13. Retrieved June 2, 2013 (www.bjs.gov/content/pub/pdf/p11.pdf).

Kirkham, C. 2012. "Private Prison Corporation Offers Cash in Exchange for State Prisons." *Huffington Post*, February 14. Retrieved September 16, 2014 (http://www.huffingtonpost.com/2012/02/14/private-prisons-buying-state-prisons_n_1272143.html).

Kitano, Harry H., Pauline Aqbayani, and Diane de Anda. 2005. *Race Relations*, 6th ed. Englewood Cliffs, NJ: Prentice Hall.

Kodish, Bruce I. 2003. "What We Do With Language—What It Does With Us." *ETC: A Review of General Semantics* 60:383–95.

Kohlberg, Lawrence. 1971. "From Is to Ought." Pp. 151–284 in *Cognitive Development and Epistemology*, edited by T. Mischel. New York: Academic Press.

Kohn, Melvin. 1989. *Class and Conformity: A Study of Values*, 2nd ed. Chicago: University of Chicago Press.

Konrad, Walicia. 2012. "As Medicare Fraud Evolves, Vigilance Is Required." *New York Times*, September 11. Retrieved April 18, 2013 (www.nytimes.com/2012/09/12/business/retirementspecial/medicare-fraud-victimizes-patients-and-taxpayers.html?_r=0).

Korgen, Jeffry and Charles Gallagher. 2013. *The True Cost of Low Prices.* New York: Orbis Books.

Korgen, Kathleen Odell and David Brunsma. 2012. "Avoiding Race or Following the Racial Scripts? Obama and Race in the Recessionary Part of the Colorblind Era." In *Obama and the Biracial Factor: The Battle for a New American Majority*, edited by Andrew Jolivette. Bristol, UK: Policy Press.

Korgen, Kathleen Odell and Jonathan M. White. 2013. *The Engaged Sociologist: Connecting the Classroom to the Community*, 3rd ed. Thousand Oaks, CA: Sage.

Korgen, Kathleen Odell, Jonathan M. White, and Shelley K. White. 2013. *Sociologists in Action: Sociology, Social Change, and Social Justice*, 2nd ed. Thousand Oaks, CA: Sage.

Korte, Charles and Stanley Milgram. 1970. "Acquaintance Networks Between Racial Groups." *Journal of Personality and Social Psychology* 15:101–108.

Koschate-Reis, Miriam. 2009. "The Social Psychology of Embarrassment." Research project at the School of Psychology, University of St. Andrews. Retrieved March 31, 2012 (http://sites.google.com/site/embarrassment-project/home).

Kotaku. 2013. "The 13 Most Popular Video Games of 2013, as Purchased by You." Retrieved February 14, 2014 (http://kotaku.com/the-13-most-popular-video-games-of-2013-as-purchased-b-1487785780).

Kotkin, Joel. 2013. "America's Fastest—and Slowest—Growing Cities." *Forbes*, March 18. Retrieved July 1, 2013 (www.forbes.com/sites/joelkotkin/2013/03/18/americas-fastest-and-slowest-growing-cities/).

Kotkin, Joel and Wendell Cox. 2011. "Cities and the Census." *City Journal*, April 6. Retrieved July 1, 2013 (www.city-journal.org/2011/eon0406jkwc.html).

Kottak, Conrad Phillip. 2010. *Prime-Time Society: An Anthropological Analysis of Television and Culture*, Updated edition. Walnut Creek, CA: Left Coast Press.

Kozol, Jonathan. 2006. *The Shame of the Nation: The Restoration of Apartheid Schooling in America*. New York: Crown.

Kozol, Jonathan. 2012. *Fire in the Ashes: Twenty-Five Years Among the Poorest Children in America*. New York: Random House Crown Publishing Group.

Kramer, Laura. 2010. *The Sociology of Gender: A Brief Introduction*, 3rd ed. New York: Oxford University Press.

Kramer, Laura and Ann Beutel. 2014. *The Sociology of Gender: A Brief Introduction*, 4th ed. New York: Oxford University Press.

Kristof, Nicholas and Sheryl WuDunn. 2009. *Half the Sky: Turning Oppression Into Opportunity for Women Worldwide*. New York: Alfred A. Knopf.

Kroenig, Matthew and Barry Pavel. 2012. "How to Deter Terrorism." *The Washington Quarterly* 35(2):21–36.

Kübler-Ross, Elizabeth. 1997. *Death, the Final Stage of Growth*, Rev. ed. New York: Scribner.

Kuhn, Manford. 1964. "Major Trends in Symbolic Interaction Theory in the Past Twenty-Five Years." *Sociological Quarterly* 5:61–84.

Kuhn, Thomas. 1970. *The Structure of Scientific Revolutions*, 2nd ed. Chicago: University of Chicago Press.

Kurtz, Lester R. 2007. *Gods in the Global Village*, 2nd ed. Thousand Oaks, CA: Pine Forge Press.

Lake, Robert. 1990. "An Indian Father's Plea." *Teacher Magazine* 2(September):48–53.

Lambert, Yves. 2000. "Religion in Modernity as a New Axial Age: Secularization or New Religious Forms?" Pp. 95–125 in *The Secularization Debate*, edited by William H. Swatos, Jr. and Daniel V. A. Olson. Lanham, MD: Rowman & Littlefield.

Langfitt, Frank. 2011. "Mobile Money Revolution Aids Kenya's Poor, Economy." NPR, January 5. Retrieved June 8, 2013 (http://www.npr.org/2011/01/05/132679772/mobile-money-revolution-aids-kenyas-poor-economy).

Langton, Lynn, Michael Planty, and Nathan Sandholtz. 2013. "Hate Crime Victimization, 2003–2011." Bureau of Justice Statistics, March 21. Retrieved June 1, 2013 (www.bjs.gov/index.cfm?ty=pbdetail&iid=4614).

Lareau, Annette. 2003. *Unequal Childhoods: Class, Race, and Family Life*. Berkeley: University of California Press.

Lashbrook, Jeffrey. 2009. "Social Class Differences in Family Life." P. 224 in *Our Social World*, 2nd ed., edited by Jeanne H. Ballantine and Keith A. Roberts. Thousand Oaks, CA: Sage.

Lawrence, Alison. 2009. "Cutting Correction Costs: Earned Time Policies for State Prisoners." National Conference of State Legislatures. Retrieved June 2, 2013 (www.ncsl.org/documents/cj/earned_time_report.pdf).

Lazare, Aaron. 2004. *On Apology*. New York: Oxford University Press.

Lazaridis, Gabriella. 2011. *Security, Insecurity and Migration in Europe*. Farnham, UK: Ashgate.

LeBon, Gustave. [1895] 1960. *The Crowd: A Study of the Popular Mind*. New York: Viking.

Lebow, R.N. 1981. *Between Peace and War: The Nature of International Crisis*. Baltimore: Johns Hopkins University Press.

Lechner, Frank J. and John Boli. 2005. *World Culture: Origins and Consequences*. Malden, MA: Blackwell.

Lederman, Josh. 2012. "Voter Turnout Shaping Up to Be Lower Than 2008." *Huffington Post*, November 7. Retrieved November 11, 2012 (http://www.huffingtonpost.com/2012/11/07/voter-turnout_n_2088810.html).

Lee, Jennifer and Frank D. Bean. 2004. "America's Changing Color Lines: Immigration, Race/Ethnicity, and Multiracial Identification." *Annual Review of Sociology* 30(August):222–42.

Lee, Jennifer and Frank D. Bean. 2007. "Redrawing the Color Line?" *City and Community* 6(1):49–62.

Lee, Richard B. 1984. *The Dobe !Kung*. New York: Holt, Rinehart & Winston.

Lee, Suevon. 2012. "By the Numbers: The U.S.'s Growing For-Profit Detention Industry." *ProPublica*, June 20. Retrieved June 3, 2013 (www.propublica.org/article/by-the-numbers-the-u.s.s-growing-for-profit-detention-industry).

Lehman, Edward C., Jr. 1985. *Women Clergy: Breaking Through Gender Barriers*. New Brunswick, NJ: Transaction.

Leit, R. A., J. J. Gray, and H. G. Pope. 2002. "The Media's Representation of the Ideal Male Body." *International Journal of Eating Disorders* (doi.wiley.com).

Lemert, Edwin M. 1951. *Social Pathology*. New York: McGraw-Hill.

Lemerl, Edwin M. 1972. *Human Deviance, Social Problems, and Social Control*, 2nd ed. Englewood Cliffs, NJ: Prentice Hall.

Lenski, Gerhard E. 1966. *Human Societies*. New York: McGraw-Hill.

Lerner, Richard M. 1992. "Sociobiology and Human Development: Arguments and Evidence." *Human Development* 35(1):12–51.

Leslie, Gerald R. and Sheila K. Korman. 1989. *The Family in Social Context*, 7th ed. New York: Oxford University Press.

Levinson, Stephen C. 2000. "Yeli Dnye and the Theory of Basic Color Terms." *Journal of Linguistic Anthropology* 1:3–55.

Levitt, Judith. 2012. "Women as Priests." *New York Times,* September 29. Retrieved June 20, 2013 (www.nytimes.com/2012/09/30/opinion/sunday/women-as-priests.html).

Levitt, Peggy. 2001. *The Transnational Villagers.* Berkeley: University of California Press.

Levitt, Peggy. 2007. *God Needs No Passport: Immigrants and the Changing American Religious Landscape.* New York: New Press.

Levitt, Peggy and Mary Waters, eds. 2006. *The Changing Face of Home: The Transnational Lives of the Second Generation.* Russell Sage Foundation. Retrieved June 27, 2011 (www.russellsage.org/publications/changing-face-home).

Library of Congress. 2010. "Margaret Mead: Human Nature and the Power of Culture." July 27. Retrieved March 7, 2012 (www.loc.gov/exhibits/mead/field-sepik.html).

Lieberson, Stanley, Susan Dumais, and Shyon Bauman. 2000. "The Instability of Androgynous Names: The Symbolic Maintenance of Gender Boundaries." *American Journal of Sociology* 105(5):1249–87.

Lincoln, Erik and Laurence Mamiya. 1990. *The Black Church in the African American Experience.* Durham, NC: Duke University Press.

Lindberg, Richard and Vesna Markovic. N.d. "Organized Crime Outlook in the New Russia: Russia Is Paying the Price of a Market Economy in Blood." Retrieved January 4, 2001 (www.search-international.com/Articles/crime/russiacrime.htm).

Lindow, Megan. 2009, June 20. "South Africa's Rape Crisis: 1 in 4 Men Say They've Done It." *Time/World.* Retrieved February 27, 2012 (www.time.com/time/world/article/0,8599,1906000,00.html).

Lindsay, James M. 2006. "Global Warming Heats Up." Pp. 307–13 in *Globalization: The Transformation of Social Worlds,* edited by D. Stanley Eitzen and Maxine Baca Zinn. Belmont, CA: Wadsworth.

Lindsey, Linda L. 2011. *Gender Roles: A Sociological Perspective,* 5th ed. Englewood Cliffs, NJ: Prentice Hall.

Linton, Ralph. 1937. *The Study of Man.* New York: D. Appleton-Century.

Lips, Hilary M. 2010. *Sex and Gender: An Introduction,* 9th ed. Boston: McGraw-Hill.

Lips, Hilary. 2013. *Gender: The Basics.* Taylor and Francis.

Liptak, Adam. 2008. "U.S. Prison Population Dwarfs That of Other Nations." *New York Times,* April 23. Retrieved April 15, 2012 (www.nytimes.com/2008/04/23/world/americas/23iht-23prisons.12253738.html).

Liptak, Adam. 2013. "Justices Step Up Scrutiny of Race in College Entry." *New York Times,* June 24. Retrieved June 25, 2013 (www.nytimes.com/2013/06/25/us/affirmative-action-decision.html?pagewanted=1&_r=0&hp).

Lofgren, Orvar. 1999. *On Holiday: A History of Vacationing.* Berkeley: University of California Press.

Lofgren, Orvar. 2010. "The Global Beach." Pp. 37–55 in *Tourists and Tourism,* 2nd ed., edited by Sharon Bohn Gmelch. Long Grove, IL: Waveland Press.

Loftsdottir, Kristin. 2004. "When Nomads Lose Cattle: Wodaabe Negotiations of Ethnicity." *African Sociological Review* 8(2):55–76.

Lombard, Hamilton. 2014. "Ancestry: Who Do You Think You Are?" Stat Chat from the Demographics Research Group at UVA. Retrieved September 5, 2014 (http://statchatva.org/2014/03/13/ancestry-who-do-you-think-you-are/).

"Lonmin Profit Plunges on South Africa Platinum Strike." 2014. *BBC News,* May 12. Retrieved September 7, 2014 (www.bbc.com/news/business-27369966).

Lopez, Mark Hugo and Anna Gonzalez-Barrera. 2014. "Women Outpace Men in College Enrollment." Pew Research Fact Tank, March 6. Retrieved May 16, 2014 (www.pewresearch.org/fact-tank/2014/03/06/womens-college-enrollment-gains-leave-men-behind/).

Lorber, Judith. 2009. *Gender Inequality: Feminist Theories and Politics.* New York: Oxford University Press.

Lorber, Judith and Lisa Jean Moore. 2007. *Gendered Bodies.* Los Angeles, CA: Roxbury.

Lorber, Judith and Lisa Jean Moore. 2011. *Gendered Bodies: Feminist Perspectives,* 2nd ed. New York: Oxford University Press.

Lorillard, Didi. 2011. "What's Going on With the Venerable State of Marriage?" *GoLocal Lifestyle.* Retrieved June 4, 2012 (www.golocalprov.com/lifestyle/modern-manners-etiquette-sharing-household-chores/).

Lotfi Yaser, Ali Ayar, and Simin Shams. 2012. "The Relation Between Religious Practice and Committing Suicide: Common and Suicidal People in Darehshahr, Iran." *Procedia—Social and Behavioral Sciences* July 16–18(50):1051–60.

Loy, Irwin. 2012. "Observers: Cambodian Vote Improved but Problems Remain." *Voice of America.* Retrieved July 25, 2012 (www.voanews.com/content/observers-cambodian-elections-improved-but-problems-remain/1146999.html).

Lucas, Samuel R. and Mark Berends. 2002. "Sociodemographic Diversity, Correlated Achievement, and De Facto Tracking." *Sociology of Education* 75(4):328–48.

Luhman, Reid and Stuart Gilman. 1980. *Race and Ethnic Relations: The Social and Political Experience of Minority Groups.* Belmont, CA: Wadsworth.

Luscombe, Belinda. 2010. "Marriage: What's It Good For?" *Time* 176(November 29):48–56.

Lutz, Ashley. 2012. "These 6 Corporations Control 90% of the Media in America." *Business Insider,* June 14. Retrieved June 30 (www.businessinsider.com/these-6-corporations-control-90-of-the-media-in-america-2012-6).

Ma, Yngyi and Gokhan Savas. 2014. "Which Is More Consequential: Fields of Study or Institutional Selectivity?" *The Review of Higher Education* 37(2):221–47.

Machalek, Richard, and Michael W. Martin. 2010. "Evolution, Biology, and Society: A Conversation for the 21st Century Classroom." *Teaching Sociology* 38(1):35–45.

Machiavelli, Niccolò. [1532] 2010. *The Prince.* Hollywood, FL: Simon & Brown.

Macionis, John. 2012. *Sociology*, 14th ed. Upper Saddle River, NJ: Prentice Hall.

Mackey, Robert. 2011. "Social Media Accounts of the Protests in Syria." The Lede Weblog, *New York Times*, April 23. Retrieved October 3, 2012 (thelede.blogs.nytimes.com).

MacLeod, Jay. 2008. *Ain't No Makin' It: Aspirations and Attainment in a Low-Income Neighborhood*, 3rd ed. Boulder, CO: Westview.

Madden, Mary, Amanda Lenhart, Maeve Duggan, Sandra Cortesi, and Urs Glasser. 2013. "Teens and Technology." Pew Internet and American Life Project, March 13. Retrieved December 6, 2013 (www.pewinternet.org/Reports/2013/Teens-and-Tech/Main-Findings/Teens-and-Technology.aspx).

Madden, Mary and Kathryn Zickuhr. 2011. "65% of Online Adults Use Social Networking Sites." *Pew Internet*. Retrieved May 25, 2012 (http://pewinternet.org/Reports/2011/Social-Networking-Sites.aspx).

"The Madoff Case: A Timeline." 2009. *The Wall Street Journal*, March 12. Retrieved November 5, 2009 (http://online.wsj.com/article/SB112966954231272304.html?mod=googlenews.wsj).

Maglaty, Jeanne. 2011. "When Did Girls Start Wearing Pink?" Retrieved May 9, 2013 (www.smithsonianmag.com/arts-culture/When-Did-Girls-Start-Wearing-Pink.html).

Magnus, George. 2009. "Malthus, Marx and the Globalization Debate." *The Globalist*, February 28. Retrieved February 16, 2015 (www.theglobalist.com/malthus-marx-and-the-globalization-debate/).

Makhmalbaf, Mohsen, producer. 2003. *Kandahar: The Sun Behind the Moon* (Film).

"Mali 'at War' With Tuareg Rebels." 2014. *Aljazeera*, May 19. Retrieved August 29, 2014 (http://www.aljazeera.com/news/africa/2014/05/mali-at-war-with-tuareg-rebels-201451815152681548.html).

Malthus, Thomas R. [1798] 1926. *An Essay on the Principle of Population*. London: Macmillan.

Mann, Charles C. 2005. *1491: New Revelations of the Americas Before Columbus*. New York: Alfred A. Knopf.

Manning, Jennifer E. 2014. "Membership of the 113th Congress: A Profile." Congressional Research Service. Retrieved February 2, 2015 (www.senate.gov/CRSReports/crs-publish.cfm?pid=%260BL%2BR%5CC%3F%0A).

Maoncha, Merculine. 2013. "Sustainability: Lake Nakuru in the Great Rift Valley." *Thomson Reuters*, April 22. Retrieved February 24, 2014 (http://sustainability.thomsonreuters.com/2013/04/19/youth-perspective-lake-nakuru-in-the-great-rift-valley/).

Maquila Solidarity Network. 2014. "Support Grows for Cambodian Garment Workers After Violent Government Crackdown." January 17. Retrieved January 18, 2014 (http://en.maquilasolidarity.org/).

Marger, Martin N. 2012. *Race and Ethnic Relations: American and Global Perspectives*, 9th ed. Belmont, CA: Wadsworth.

Markoff, John and Somini Sengupta. 2011. "Separating You and Me? 4.74 Degrees." *The New York Times*, November 21. Retrieved September 25, 2012 (www.nytimes.com/2011/11/22/technolgoy/between-you-and-me-4-74-degrees.html).

Martin, Jenny Beth and Mark Meckler. 2012. *Tea Party Patriots: The Second American Revolution*. New York: Henry Holt and Company.

Martineau, Harriet. [1837] 1962. *Society in America*. Garden City, NY: Doubleday.

Martineau, Harriet. 1838. *How to Observe Manners and Morals*. London: Charles Knight & Co.

Martins, Nichole, Dmitri C. Williams, Kristen Harrison, and Rabindra A. Ratan. 2009. "A Content Analysis of Female Body Imagery in Video Games." *Sex Roles* 61:824–36.

Marty, Martin E. and R. Scott Appleby, eds. 1991. *Fundamentalism Observed*. Chicago: University of Chicago Press.

Marty, Martin E. and R. Scott Appleby, eds. 2004. *Accounting for Fundamentalism: The Dynamic Character of Movements*. Chicago: University of Chicago Press.

Marx, Karl. [1844] 1963. "Contribution to the Critique of Hegel's Philosophy of Right." Pp. 43–59 in *Karl Marx: Early Writings*, translated and edited by T. B. Bottomore. New York: McGraw-Hill.

Marx, Karl. [1844] 1964. *The Economic and Philosophical Manuscripts of 1844*. New York: International Publishers.

Marx, Karl and Friedrich Engels. [1848] 1969. *The Communist Manifesto*. Baltimore: Penguin.

Marx, Karl and Friedrich Engels. 1955. *Selected Work in Two Volumes*. Moscow: Foreign Language Publishing House.

Marx, Karl and Friedrich Engels. [1881] 1975. "Friedrich Engels to Karl Kautsky in Vienna." In *Selected Correspondence*. Moscow: Progress Publishers.

Massey, Douglas S. and Nancy A. Denton. 1998. *American Apartheid: Segregation and the Making of the Underclass*. Cambridge, MA: Harvard University Press.

Matson, John. 2013. "Women Are Earning Greater Share of STEM Degrees, but Doctorates Remain Gender-Skewed." *Scientific American Magazine*, April 23. Retrieved January 18, 2014 (www.scientificamerican.com/article.cfm?id=women-earnings-greater-share-stem-degrees-doctorates-remain-skewed).

Mattingly, Marybeth and Liana C. Sayer. 2006. "Under Pressure: Trends and Gender Differences in the Relationship Between Free Time and Feeling Rushed." *Journal of Marriage and Family* 68(1):205–21.

Mauss, Armand. 1975. *Social Problems as Social Movements*. Philadelphia: Lippincott.

Mawani, Vrushti. 2011. "Marriage Majestic: William-Kate Wedding to Cost $70 Million." *Industry Leaders Magazine*, April 29. Retrieved June 5, 2013 (www.industryleadersmagazine.com/marriage-majestic-william-kate-wedding-to-cost-70-million/).

Mayflower Church. 2013. "Social Justice: Earthwise Congregation." Retrieved June 24, 2013 (www.ucc.org/environmental-ministries/about-us.html).

Mayoux, Linda, ed. 2008. *Sustainable Learning for Women's Empowerment: Ways Forward in Micro-Finance.* Warwickshire, UK: ITDG Publishing.

McAdam, Doug. 1999. *Political Process and the Development of Black Insurgency, 1930–1970,* 2nd ed. Chicago: University of Chicago Press.

McAdam, Doug. 2003. "Beyond Structural Analysis: Toward a More Dynamic Understanding of Social Movements." Pp. 281–98 in *Social Movements and Networks: Relational Approaches to Collective Action,* edited by Mario Diani and Doug McAdam. New York: Oxford University Press.

McCabe, Janice, Emily Fairchild, Liz Grauerholz, Bernice A. Pescosolido, and Daniel Tope. 2011. "Gender in Twentieth-Century Children's Books: Patterns of Disparity in Titles and Central Characters." *Gender and Society* 25(2):197–226.

McCarthy, John D. and Mayer N. Zald. 1977. "Resource Mobilization and Social Movements: A Partial Theory." *American Journal of Sociology* 82(6):1212–41.

McCrone, David. 1998. *The Sociology of Nationalism.* London: Routledge.

McIntosh, Peggy. 2002. "White Privilege: Unpacking the Invisible Knapsack." Pp. 97–101 in *White Privilege: Essential Readings on the Other Side of Racism,* edited by Paula S. Rothenberg. New York: Worth.

McKelvie, Samuel R. 1926. "What the Movies Meant to the Farmer." *Annals of the American Academy of Political and Social Science* 128(November):131.

Mead, Frank, Samuel Hill, and Craig Atwood, eds. 2005. *Handbook of Denominations in the United States,* 12th ed. Nashville, TN: Abingdon Press.

Mead, George Herbert. [1934] 1962. *Mind, Self, and Society.* Chicago: University of Chicago Press.

Mead, Margaret. [1935] 1963. *Sex and Temperament in Three Primitive Societies.* New York: William Morrow.

Mears, Bill. 2014. "Michigan's Ban on Affirmative Action Upheld by Supreme Court." *CNN Justice,* April 23. Retrieved May 11, 2014 (www.cnn.com/2014/04/22/justice/scotus-michigan-affirmative-action/).

Mehan, Hugh. 1992. "Understanding Inequality in Schools: The Contribution of Interpretive Studies." *Sociology of Education* 65(1):1–20.

Mehra, Bharat, Cecelia Merkel, and Ann P. Bishop. 2004. "The Internet for Empowerment of Minority and Marginalized Users." *New Media and Society* 6:781–802.

Mehsud, Saud. 2012. "Pakistani Girl Shot by Taliban Defied Threats for Years." *Reuters,* October 10. Retrieved October 11, 2012 (www.reuters.com/article/2012/10/10/us-pakistan-girl-family-idUSBRE8990T720121010).

Melton, J. Gordon, James Bevereley, Constance Jones, and Pamela S. Nadell. 2009. *Melton's Encyclopedia of American Religions,* 8th ed. Detroit, MI: Gale/Cengage.

Meltzer, Bernard. 1978. "Mead's Social Psychology." Pp. 15–27 in *Symbolic Interactionism: A Reader in Social Psychology,* 3rd ed., edited by J. Manis and B. Meltzer. Boston: Allyn & Bacon.

Meltzer, Bernard N., John W. Petras, and Larry T. Reynolds. 1975. *Symbolic Interactionism: Genesis, Varieties and Criticism.* London: Routledge & Kegan Paul.

Mercola, Dr. 2013. "Want More Tolerant Kids? Keep Them Away From the TV." December 12. Retrieved January 17, 2014 (http://articles.mercola.com/sites/articles/archive/2013/12/12/children-watching-tv.aspx).

Merriam-Webster. 2014. "Black." Retrieved April 9, 2014 (www.merriam-webster.com/dictionary/black).

Merton, Robert K. 1938. "Social Structure and Anomie." *American Sociological Review* 3(October):672–82.

Merton, Robert K. 1948. "The Self Fulfilling Prophecy." *The Antioch Review* 8(2):193–210.

Merton, Robert K. [1942] 1973. *The Sociology of Science: Theoretical and Empirical Investigations.* Chicago: University of Chicago Press.

Merton, Robert K. 1968. *Social Theory and Social Structure,* 2nd ed. New York: Free Press.

Meyer, Elaine. 2012. "Is the Wealth Gap Creating a Health Gap?" 2x2 Project, December 5. Retrieved May 13, 2014 (http://the2x2project.org/health-gap-wealth-gap/).

Michels, Robert. [1911] 1967. *Political Parties.* New York: Free Press.

Mikkelson, Barbara and David P. Mikkelson. 2012. "Urban Legends." Retrieved January 1, 2012 (www.snopes.com/college/college.asp).

Milgram, Stanley. 1967. "The Small World Problem." *Psychology Today* 1:61–67.

Mills, C. Wright. 1956. *The Power Elite.* New York: Oxford University Press.

Mills, C. Wright. 1959. *The Sociological Imagination.* New York: Oxford University Press.

Mills, Theodore M. 1984. *The Sociology of Small Groups,* 2nd ed. Englewood Cliffs, NJ: Prentice Hall.

Milner, Murray. 2006. *Freaks, Geeks, and Cool Kids: American Teenagers, Schools, and the Culture of Consumption.* London: Routledge.

"Misery of the Maquiladoras." 2011. *Socialist Worker,* November 18. Retrieved May 27, 2012 (http://socialistworker.org/2011/11/18/misery-of-the-maquiladoras).

Mishel, Lawrence and Natalie Sabadish. 2012. *CEO Pay and the Top 1%: How Executive Compensation and Financial-Sector Pay Have Fueled Income Inequality.* Economic Policy Institute, May 2. Retrieved June 5, 2013 (www.epi.org/publication/ib331-ceo-pay-top-1-percent/).

Molotch, Harvey. 2003. *Where Stuff Comes From: How Toasters, Toilets, Cars, Computers, and Many Other Things Come to Be as They Are.* London: Routledge.

Morey, Peter and Amina Yaqin. 2011. *Framing Muslims: Stereotyping and Representation After 9/11.* Cambridge, MA: Harvard University Press.

Morris, Joan M. and Michael D. Grimes. 1997. *Caught in the Middle: Contradictions in the Lives of Sociologists From Working Class Backgrounds.* Westport, CT: Praeger.

Morris, Lloyd R. 1949. *Not So Long Ago.* New York: Random House.

Morrison, Maureen. 2010. "New Data Shed Light on Women's Internet Usage." *Ad Age*, August 3. Retrieved May 25, 2012 (http://adage.com/article/adagestat/data-research-women-s-internet-usage/145224/).

Mou, Yi and Wei Peng. 2009. "Gender and Racial Stereotypes in Popular Video Games." IGI Global OnDemand.

Muchhala, Bhumika. 2012. "Students Against Sweat Shops." Pp. 303–12 in *Globalization: The Transformation of Social Worlds*, 3rd ed., edited by D. Stanley Eitzen and Maxine Baca Zinn. Belmont, CA: Wadsworth.

Mydans, Seth. 2002. "In Pakistan, Rape Victims Are the 'Criminals.'" *New York Times*, May 17, p. A3.

Myers, Steven Lee and Nicholas Kulish 2013. "Growing Clamor About Inequities of Climate Crisis." *New York Times*, November 16. Retrieved February 24, 2014 (www.nytimes.com/2013/11/17/world/growing-clamor-about-inequities-of-climate-crisis.html?_r=0).

Myrdal, Gunnar. 1964. *An American Dilemma*. New York: McGraw-Hill.

Nagel, Joane. 1994. "Constructing Ethnicity: Creating and Recreating Ethnic Identity and Culture." *Social Problems* 41(1):152–76.

Nagourney, Adam and Rick Lyman. 2013. "Few Problems With Cannabis for California." *New York Times*, October 26. Retrieved October 27, 2013 (www.nytimes.com/2013/10/27/us/few-problems-with-cannabis-for-california.html?_r=0).

Nakamura, Lisa. 2004. "Interrogating the Digital Divide: The Political Economy of Race and Commerce in the New Media." Pp. 71–83 in *Society On-Line: The Internet in Context*, edited by Philip N. Howard and Steve Jones. Thousand Oaks, CA: Sage.

National Archives and Records Administration. 2008. "What Is the Electoral College?" Retrieved March 21, 2008 (www.archives.gov/federal-register/electoral-college/about.html).

National Center for Education Statistics. 2012. "Fast Facts: Do You Have Information on Postsecondary Enrollment Rates?" Institute of Education Sciences. Retrieved June 16, 2013 (Nces.ed.gov/fastfacts/display.asp?id=98).

National Conference of State Legislatures. 2015. "State Laws Regarding Marriages Between First Cousins." Retrieved January 17, 2015 (www.ncsl.org/issues-research/human-services/state-laws-regarding-marriages-between-first-cousi.aspx).

National Consumers League. 2013. "Parents: Take Control Over Your Child's Viewing, Surfing, and Texting Habits." Retrieved December 6, 2013 (www.ncinet.org/technology/149-parental-controls/537-parental-controls).

National Institutes of Health. 2012. "Stem Cell Information: Stem Cell Basics." February 13. Retrieved March 7, 2012 (http://stemcells.nih.gov/info/basics/basics4.asp).

National Public Radio. 2013. "Closing the 'Word Gap' Between Rich and Poor." Retrieved January 5, 2014 (www.wbur.org/npr/257922222/closing-the-word-gap-between-rich-and-poor).

Nationmaster. 2011. "United States Population Pyramids." Retrieved May 19, 2011 (www.nationmaster.com/country/us/Age_distribution).

Nations Online. 2014. "Countries of the Second World." Retrieved November 17, 2014 (www.nationsonline.org/oneworld/second_world.htm).

Neuman, Michelle J. 2005. "Global Early Care and Education: Challenges, Responses, and Lessons." *Phi Delta Kappan* (November):188–92.

"New Federal Report: Sexual Abuse Plagues U.S. Prisons and Jails." 2010. *Just Detention*, August 26. Retrieved March 8, 2011 (www.businesswire.com/).

New Media Trend Watch. 2013. "Demographics: Percentage of Population Online." Retrieved December 6, 2013 (www.newmediatrendwatch.com/markets-by-country/17-usa/123-demographics).

Newman, David. 2009. *Families: A Sociological Perspective*. New York: McGraw-Hill.

Newman, Matthew L., Carla J. Groom, Lori D. Handelman, and James W. Pennebaker. 2008. "Gender Differences in Language Use: An Analysis of 14,000 Text Samples." *Discourse Process* 45:211–36.

Newport, Frank. 2009. "This Christmas, 78% of Americans Identify as Christian." Gallup, December 24. Retrieved September 26, 2012 (www.gallup.com/poll/124793/This-Christmas-78-Americans-Identify-Christian.aspx).

Newport, Frank. 2010. "American's Church Attendance Inches Up in 2010." Gallup, June 25. Retrieved September 20, 2012 (www.gallup.com/poll/141044/americans-church-attendance-inches-2010.aspx).

Newport, Frank. 2012a. *God Is Alive and Well*. New York: Gallup Books.

Newport, Frank. 2012b. "More Than Nine in Ten Americans Continue to Believe in God." Gallup. Retrieved September 26, 2012 (www.gallup.com/poll/147887/americans-continue-believe-god.aspx).

Newport, Frank. 2013. "In U.S., Four in 10 Report Attending Church in Last Week." Retrieved January 28, 2014 (www.gallup.com/poll/166613/four-report-attending-church-last-week.aspx).

Newport, Frank and Igor Himelfarb. 2013. "In U.S., Record-High Say Gay, Lesbian Relations Morally OK." *Gallup Politics*, May 20. Retrieved January 18, 2014 (www.gallup.com/poll/162689/record-high-say-gay-lesbian-relations-morally.aspx).

News of Future. 2012. "1 Million Hydrogen-Fueled Cars in U.S." Retrieved March 7, 2012 (www.newsoffuture.com/million_hydrogen_fueled_cars_in_us_future_energy.html).

Nichols, Larry A., George A. Mather, and Alvin J. Schmidt. 2006. *Encyclopedic Dictionary of Cults, Sects, and World Religions*, Revised and updated ed. Grand Rapids, MI: Zondervan.

Nixon, Ron. 2012. "New Rules for School Meals Aim at Reducing Obesity." *New York Times*, January 25. Retrieved February 9, 2015 (www.nytimes.com/2012/01/26/us/politics/new-school-lunch-rules-aimed-at-reducing-obesity.tml?_r=0).

Noel, Donald. 1968. "A Theory of the Origin of Ethnic Stratification." *Social Problems* 16(Fall):157–72.

Noguera, Pedro A. 2011. "A Broader and Bolder Approach Uses Education to Break Cycle of Poverty." *Phi Delta Kappan Magazine* 93(3):9–14.

Noguera, Pedro and Robby Cohen. 2006. "Patriotism and Accountability: The Role of Educators in the War on Terrorism." *Phi Delta Kappan* 87(8):573–78.

Nolan, Cathal J. 2002a. "Terrorism." Pp. 1648–49 in *The Greenwood Encyclopedia of International Relations*. London: Greenwood.

Nolan, Cathal J. 2002b. "War." P. 1803 in *The Greenwood Encyclopedia of International Relations*. London: Greenwood.

Nolan, Patrick and Gerhard Lenski. 2014. *Human Societies*, 12th ed. Boulder, CO: Paradigm.

Nolan, Patrick D., Jennifer Triplett, and Shannon McDonough. 2010. "Sociology's Suicide: A Forensic Autopsy." *The American Sociologist* 41:292–305.

Nonhuman Rights Project. 2014. Retrieved March 20, 2014 (www.nonhumanrightsproject.org/).

Nonprofit Vote. 2012. "America Goes to the Polls 2012." Retrieved June 2, 2013 (www.nonprofitvote.org).

Norton, M. and D. Ariely. 2011. "Building a Better America— One Wealth Quintile at a Time." Perspectives in Psychological Science 6(1):9–12.

Nossiter, Adam. 2014. "Wielding Whip and a Hard New Law, Nigeria Tries to 'Sanitize' Itself of Gays." *New York Times*, February 8. Retrieved February 8, 2014 (www.nytimes.com/2014/02/09/world/africa/nigeria-uses-law-and-whip-to-sanitize-gays.html?hp&_r=0).

Oakes, Jeannie, Amy Stuart Wells, Makeba Jones, and Amanda Datnow. 1997. "Detracking: The Social Construction of Ability, Cultural Politics, and Resistance to Reform." *Teacher's College Record* 98(3):482–510.

O'Brien, Denise. 1977. "Female Husbands in Southern Bantu Societies." In *Sexual Stratification: A Cross-Cultural View*, edited by Alice Schlegel. New York: Columbia University Press

O'Brien, Jody. 2011. *The Production of Reality*, 5th ed. Thousand Oaks, CA: Sage.

O'Connor, Liz, Gus Lubin, and Dina Spector. 2013. "The Largest Ancestry Groups in the United States." *Business Insider*, August 13. Retrieved September 5, 2014 (www.businessinsider.com/largest-ethnic-groups-in-america-2013-8).

Ogburn, William F. [1922] 1938. *Social Change, With Respect to Culture and Original Nature*. New York: Viking.

Ogburn, William F. 1933. *Recent Social Trends*. New York: McGraw-Hill.

Ogburn, William F. 1961. "The Hypothesis of Cultural Lag." Pp. 1270–73 in *Theories of Society: Foundations of Modern Sociological Theory*, Vol. 2, edited by Talcott Parsons, Edward Shils, Kaspar D. Naegele, and Jesse R. Pitts. New York: Free Press.

Ogburn, William F. 1964. In *On Culture and Social Change: Selected Papers*, edited by Otis Dudley Duncan. Chicago: University of Chicago Press.

OpenSecrets.org. 2012a. "Overview: Stats at a Glance." Retrieved June 7, 2013 (www.opensecrets.org/overview/index.php?cycle=2012&type=A&display=A).

OpenSecrets.org. 2012b. "2012 Presidential Race." Retrieved June 7, 2013 (www.opensecrets.org/pres12/#out).

Organisation for Economic Co-operation and Development. 2013. "Economic Surveys: China." Retrieved June 23, 2013 (www.oecd.org/eco/surveys/Overview_CHINA.pdf).

Organisation for Economic Co-operation and Development. 2014. "OECD Family Database—Trends in Parental Leave Policies Since 1970." Retrieved February 27, 2014 (www.oecd.org/els/family/PF2.5%20Trends%20in%20leave%20entitlements%20around%20childbirth%20since%201970%20-%2010%20oct%202012%20-%20FINAL.pdf).

Pager, Devah, Bruce Western, and Bart Bonikowski. 2009. "Discrimination in a Low Wage Labor Market: A Field Experiment." *American Sociological Review* 74(October):777–99.

Papalia, Diane E. and Ruth Duskin Feldman. 2011. *A Child's World: Infancy Through Adolescence*, 12th ed. Boston: McGraw-Hill.

Pareto, Vilfredo. [1911] 1955. "Mathematical Economics." In *Encyclopedie des Sciences Mathematique*. New York: Macmillan.

Park, Robert Ezra, Ernest W. Burgess, and Roderick D. McKenzie. [1925] 1967. *The City*. Chicago: University of Chicago Press.

Parker, Kim and Wendy Wang. 2013. "Time in Work and Leisure, Patterns by Gender and Family Structure." *Pew Research Social and Demographic Trends*. Retrieved February 28, 2014 (www.pewsocialtrends.org/2013/03/14/modern-parenthood-roles-of-moms-and-dads-converge-as-they-balance-work-and-family/7/).

Partners in Prepaid. 2012. "Haiti Leads in Mobile Payments." April 23. Retrieved June 8, 2013 (www.partnersinprepaid.com/topics/articles/haiti-leads-in-mobile-payments.html).

Paulson, Amanda. 2013. "Record Number of International Students: Where They're From, Where They Study." *Christian Science Monitor*, November 11. Retrieved January 4, 2014 (www.csmonitor.com/USA/2013/1111/Record-number-of-international-students-where-they-re-from-where-they-study).

Paxton, Pamela and Tess Pearce. 2009. "How Does Social Class Affect Socialization Within The Family?" *Exploring Social Science Research*, April 24. Retrieved March 1, 2011 (http://ibssblog.wordpress.com/2009/04/24/how-dues-social-class-affect-socialisation-within-the-family/).

PBS Newshour. 2013. "Jordan Struggles With Next Door's Chaos and Influx of Syrian Refugees." Retrieved July 3, 2013 (www.pbs.org/newshour/bb/middle_east/jan-june13/jordan_05-31.html).

Peek, Lori. 2011. *Behind the Backlash: Muslim Americans After 9/11*. Philadelphia: Temple University Press.

Pelaez, Vicky. 2013. "The Prison Industry in the United States: Big Business or a New Form of Slavery?" *Global Research*, January 31. Retrieved June 3, 2013 (www.globalresearch.ca/the-prison-industry-in-the-united-states-big-business-or-a-new-form-of-slavery/8289).

Pellow, David Naguib. 2002. *Garbage Wars: The Struggle for Environmental Justice in Chicago*. Cambridge, MA: MIT Press.

People's Daily Online. 2011. March 11. Retrieved May 15, 2012 (http://english.peopledaily.com.cn/90001/98649/7315789.html).

Perez, Marvin G. 2013. "Coffee Consumption Increases in U.S., Association Survey Shows." *Bloomberg News*, March 22. Retrieved February 14, 2014 (www.bloomberg.com/news/2013-03-22/coffee-consumption-increases-in-u-s-association-survey-shows.html).

Perlroth, Nicole and David E. Sanger. 2013. "Cyberattacks Seem Meant to Destroy, Not Just Disrupt." *New York Times*, March 28. Retrieved June 3, 2013 (www.nytimes.com/2013/03/29/technology/corporate-cyberattackers-possibly-state-backed-now-seek-to-destroy-data.html?pagewanted=all).

Persell, Caroline Hodges. 2005. "Race, Education, and Inequality." Pp. 286–24 in *Blackwell Companion to Social Inequalities*, edited by M. Romero and E. Margolis. Oxford, UK: Blackwell.

Persell, Caroline Hodges and Peter W. Cookson, Jr. 1985. "Chartering and Bartering: Elite Education and Social Reproduction." *Social Problems* 33(2):114–29.

Pew Charitable Trusts. 2012. *Pursuing the American Dream: Economic Mobility Across Generations*. Retrieved June 7, 2013 (www.pewstates.org/uploadedFiles/PCS_Assets/2012/Pursuing_American_Dream.pdf).

Pew Forum on Religion and Public Life. 2008. "U.S. Religious Landscape Survey, 2008." Retrieved March 2, 2008 (http://religions.pewforum.org/pdf/report-religious-landscape-study-full.pdf).

Pew Forum on Religion and Public Life. 2009. "Most Latino Evangelicals Pray Every Day." June 11. Retrieved September 26, 2012 (www.pewforum.org/Frequency-of-Prayer/Most-Latino-Evangelicals-Pray-Every-Day.aspx).

Pew Forum on Religion and Public Life. 2012a. "'Nones' on the Rise: One-in-Five Adults Have No Religious Affiliation." Retrieved October 10, 2012 (www.pewforum.org/uploadedFiles/Topics/Religious_Affiliation/Unaffiliated/NonesOnTheRise-full.pdf).

Pew Forum on Religion and Public Life. 2012b. "U.S. Religious Landscape Survey." September 18. Retrieved September 18, 2012 (http://religions.pewforum.org/reports).

Pew Research Center. 2010. "The Decline of Marriage and Rise of New Families." *Pew Social & Demographic Trends*, November 18. Retrieved March 8, 2012 (www.pewsocialtrends.org/2010/11/18/the-decline-of-marriage-and-rise-of-new-families/).

Pew Research Center Internet and American Life Project. 2012. "Teens Fact Sheet." Retrieved August 29, 2014 (http://www.pewinternet.org/fact-sheets/teens-fact-sheet/).

Pew Research Center Internet and American Life Project. 2014a. "Internet User Demographics." Retrieved January 17, 2015 (http://www.pewinternet.org/data-trend/internet-use/latest-stats/).

Pew Research Center Internet and American Life Project. 2014b. "Social Networking Fact Sheet." Retrieved May 11, 2014 (www.pewinternet.org/fact-sheets/social-networking-fact-sheet/).

Pew Research Center on Religion and Public Life. 2014. "Gay Marriage Around the World." February 5. Retrieved February 19, 2014 (www.pewforum.org/2013/12/19/gay-marriage-around-the-world-2013/).

Phillips, Richard. 2013. "Animal Communication" Lecture at *Tuesdays With a Liberal Arts Scholar*, University of Minnesota, May 6.

Phys.org. 2009. "Humans Spread Out of Africa Later." Retrieved October 9, 2012 (http://phys.org/news171286860.html).

Piaget, Jean. 1989. *The Child's Conception of the World*. Savage, MD: Littlefield, Adams Quality Paperbacks.

Pickard, Ruth and Daryl Poole. 2007. "The Study of Society and the Practice of Sociology." Previously unpublished essay.

Picker, Les. 2014. "The Effects of Education on Health." National Bureau of Economic Research, October 28. Retrieved October 28, 2014, (www.nber.org/digest/mar07/w12352.html) .

Pieterse, Jan Nederveen. 2004. *Globalization and Culture*. Lanham, MD: Rowman & Littlefield.

Pinker, Steven. 2002. *The Blank Slate: The Modern Denial of Human Nature.* New York: Viking.

Plato. [ca. 350 BCE] 1960. *The Laws.* New York: Dutton.

Political Geography Now. 2014. "How Many Countries Are There in the World?" Retrieved May 22, 2014 (www.polgeonow.com/2011/04/how-many-countries-are-there-in-the -world.html)

Population Reference Bureau. 2012a. "Fact Sheet: World Population Trends 2012." Retrieved August 25, 2012 (www.prb.org/Publications/Datasheets/2012/world-population-data-sheet/fact-sheet-world-population.aspx).

Population Reference Bureau. 2012b. "World Population Data Sheet." Retrieved August 25, 2012 (www.prb.org/pdf12/2012-population-data-sheet_eng.pdf).

Population Reference Bureau. 2013a. "Rate of Natural Increase." Retrieved March 17, 2014 (www.prb.org/DataFinder/Topic/Rankings.aspx?ind=16).

Population Reference Bureau. 2013b. "Total Fertility Rate, 2012." Retrieved February 7, 2013 (http://www.prb.org/DataFinder/Topic/Rankings.aspx?ind=17).

Potok, Mark. 2013a. "DOJ Study: More Than 250,000 Hate Crimes a Year, Most Unreported." Southern Poverty Law Center, March 26. Retrieved June 1, 2013 (www.splcenter.org/blog/2013/03/26/doj-study-more-than-250000-hate-crimes-a-year-a-third-never-reported/).

Potok, Mark. 2013b. "Editorial: Boston and Beyond." *Intelligence Report* 150. Retrieved June 17, 2013 (www.splcenter.org/get-informed/intelligence-report/browse-all-issues/2013/summer/boston-and-beyond).

Potok, Mark. 2013c. "The Year in Hate and Extremism." *Intelligence Report* 149. Retrieved November 9, 2013 (http://www.splcenter.org/home/2013/spring/the-year-in-hate-and-extremism).

Pramis, Joshua. 2013. "Number of Mobile Phones to Exceed World Population by 2014." February 28. Retrieved January 6, 2014 (www.digitaltrends.com/mobile/mobile-phone-world-population-2014/).

Preston, David L. 1988. *The Social Organization of Zen Practice: Constructing Transcultural Reality.* Cambridge, UK: Cambridge University Press.

"Primary Calendar: Democratic Nominating Contests." 2008. *New York Times.* Retrieved March 30, 2008 (http://politics.nytimes.com/election-guide/2008/primaries/democraticprimaries/index.html).

Project Ploughshares. 2013. "Armed Conflicts Report." Retrieved May 23, 2014 (http://batchgeo.com/map/01f8889add78ece0a88eccffc6d000cb).

Project Vote Smart. 2008. "State Presidential Primary and Caucus Dates." Retrieved April 17, 2010 (www.votesmart.org/election_president_state_primary_dates.php).

Proudman, Charlotte Rachael. 2012. "Sex and Sharia: Muslim Women Punished for Failed Marriages." *The Independent,* April 2. Retrieved May 24, 2012 (http://blogs.independent.co.uk/2012/04/02/sex-and-sharia-muslim-women-punished-for-failed-marriages/).

Pyle, Ralph E. 2006. "Trends in Religious Stratification: Have Religious Group Socioeconomic Distinctions Declined in Recent Decades?" *Sociology of Religion* 67(Spring):61–79.

Quinney, Richard. 2002. *Critique of Legal Order: Crime Control in Capitalist Society.* New Brunswick, NJ: Transaction.

Radcliffe-Brown, A. R. 1935. "On the Concept of Functional in Social Science." *American Anthropologist* 37(3):394–402.

Radelet, Michael L. and Traci L. Lacock. 2009. "Do Executions Lower Homicide Rates? The Views of Leading Criminologists." *The Journal of Criminal Laws and Criminology* 99(2).

Reason. 2011. "In-Depth Study: After Divorce, 44% of Women Fell Into Poverty." *Family Research Council,* May 31. Retrieved June 6, 2012 (http://primacyofreason.blogspot.com/2011/05/in-depth-study-after-divorce-44-of_31.html).

Reid, Scott A. and Sik Hung Ng. 2006. "The Dynamics of Intragroup Differentiation in an Intergroup Social Context." *Human Communication Research* 32:504–25.

Reiman, Jeffrey and Paul Leighton. 2010a. *The Rich Get Richer and the Poor Get Prison: Ideology, Class, and Criminal Justice,* 9th ed. Boston: Pearson.

Reiman, Jeffrey and Paul Leighton. 2010b. *The Rich Get Richer and the Poor Get Prison: A Reader.* Boston: Allyn & Bacon.

Religious Congregations and Membership Study. 2010. "2010 U.S. Religion Census." Retrieved September 25, 2012 (www.rcms2010.org/compare.php).

Religious Tolerance. 2012. "The Status of Women, Currently and Throughout History." Retrieved November 30, 2012 (http://www.religioustolerance.org/women.htm).

Religious Tolerance. 2014. "Stem Cell Research: All Viewpoints." Retrieved March 4, 2014 (www.religioustolerance.org/res_stem.htm).

Renick, Oliver. 2011. "Disconnected: 70 Percent of World Doesn't Have Internet, Despite Rising Phone Usage." *Laptop,* October 31. Retrieved May 18, 2012 (http://blog.laptopmag.com/disconnected-70-percent-of-world-doesn%E2%80%99t-have-internet-despite-rising-phone-usage).

Rice, William. 2013. "Types of Terrorism." Prezi, March 8. Retrieved May 13, 2014 (http://prezi.com/zyhuxjslaame/copy-of-types-of-terrorism/).

Rideout, Victoria J., Ulla G. Foehr, and Donald F. Roberts. 2010. "Generation M2: Media in the Lives of 8- to 18-Year-Olds." A Kaiser Family Foundation Study, January. Retrieved March 2, 2011 (www.kff.org/entmedia/upload/8010.pdf).

Riegle-Crumb, Catherine and Chelsea Moore. 2013. "The Gender Gap in High School Physics: Considering the Context of Local Communities." *Social Science Quarterly,* April 1. Retrieved January. 17, 2014 (http://onlinelibrary.wiley.com/doi/10.1111/ssqu.12022/abstract).

Riley, Robin. 2014. *Journey of Hope: The Mayflower Carbon Neutral Story* [Video]. Retrieved February 16, 2015 (www.youtube.com/watch?v=_Qx1UGTEWMA&list=UUfUaer6k7cf-z6RV2JjAUOA).

Riordan, Cornelius. 2004. *Equality and Achievement: An Introduction to the Sociology of Education.* Upper Saddle River, NJ: Prentice Hall.

Risman, Barbara J. and Pallavi Benerjee. 2013. "Kids Talking About Race: Tween-agers in a Post-Civil Rights Era." *Sociological Forum* 28(2):213–35.

Ritzer, George. 2007. *The Globalization of Nothing,* 2nd ed. Thousand Oaks, CA: Pine Forge.

Ritzer, George. 2011. *Globalization: The Essentials.* Malden, MA: Wiley.

Ritzer, George. 2013. *The McDonaldization of Society,* 20th anniversary edition. Thousand Oaks, CA: Sage.

Ritzer, George and Douglas J. Goodman. 2004. *Sociological Theory*, 6th ed. New York: McGraw-Hill.

Roach, Ronald. 2004. "Survey Reveals 10 Biggest Trends in Internet Use." *Black Issues in Higher Education*, October 21.

Roberts, Christine. 2012. "Most 10-Year-Olds Have Been on a Diet." *Daily News*. Retrieved January 17, 2014 (www.nydailynews.com/news/national/diets-obsess-tweens-study-article-1.1106653).

Roberts, Judith C. and Keith A. Roberts. 2008. "Deep Reading, Cost/Benefit, and the Construction of Meaning: Enhancing Reading Comprehension and Deep Learning in Sociology Courses." *Teaching Sociology* 36(April): 125–40.

Roberts, Keith A. and Karen A. Donahue. 2000. "Professing Professionalism: Bureaucratization and Deprofessionalization in the Academy." *Sociological Focus* 33(4):365–83.

Roberts, Keith A. and David Yamane. 2012. *Religion in Sociological Perspective*, 5th ed. Thousand Oaks, CA: SAGE/Pine Forge Press.

Robertson, Roland. 1992. *Globalization: Social Theory and Global Culture*. London: Sage.

Robertson, Roland. 1997. "Social Theory, Cultural Relativity and the Problem of Globality." Pp. 69–90 in *Culture, Globalization and the World System*, edited by Anthony King. Minneapolis: University of Minnesota Press.

Robertson, Roland and Jan Aart Scholte, eds. 2007. *Encyclopedia of Globalization*. London: Routledge.

Roethlisberger, Fritz J. and William J. Dickson. 1939. *Management and the Worker*. Cambridge, MA: Harvard University Press.

Roof, Wade Clark. 1999. *Spiritual Marketplace: Baby Boomers and the Remaking of American Religion*. Princeton, NJ: Princeton University Press.

Rosenbaum, James E. 1999. "If Tracking Is Bad, Is Detracking Better? A Study of a Detracked High School." *American Schools* (Winter):24–47.

Rosenberg, Matt. 2012. "Maquiladoras in Mexico: Export Assembly Plants for the United States." *About.com Geography*. Retrieved May 28, 2012 (http://geography.about.com/od/urbaneconomicgeography/a/maquiladoras.htm).

Rossi, Alice S. 1984. "Gender and Parenthood." *American Sociological Review* 49(February):1–19.

Rothenberg, Paula S. 2010. *Race, Class, and Gender in the United States: An Integrated Study*, 8th ed. New York: Worth.

Rothenberg, Paula S. 2011. *White Privilege: Essential Readings on the Other Side of Racism*, 3rd ed. New York: Worth Publishers.

Rothkopf, David. 2012. "Two Septembers." Pp. 100–103 in *Globalization: The Transformation of Social Worlds*, 3rd ed., edited by D. Stanley Eitzen and Maxine Baca Zinn. Belmont, CA: Wadsworth.

Rothman, Robert A. 2005. *Inequality and Stratification: Race, Class, and Gender*, 5th ed. Englewood Cliffs, NJ: Prentice Hall.

Royal Society. 2012. *People and the Planet*. April. Retrieved July 31, 2012 (royalsociety.org/uploadedFiles/Royal_Society_Content/policy/projects/people-planet/2012-04-25-PeoplePlanet.pdf).

Rubin, Richard. 2012. "Romney's 47% Comments Distance Him From Bush-Era Republicans." *San Francisco Chronicle*, September 18. Retrieved September 24, 2012 (www.sfgate.com/business/bloomberg/article/Romney-s-47-Comments-Distance-Him-From-3875115.php).

Rumbaut, Ruben G. and Alejandro Portes. 2001. *Ethnicities: Children of Immigrants in America*. Los Angeles: University of California Press.

Rydgren, Jens. 2004. "Mechanisms of Exclusion: Ethnic Discrimination in the Swedish Labour Market." *Journal of Ethnic and Migration Studies* 30(4):687–716.

Saad, Lydia. 2012. "U.S. Confidence in Organized Religion at Low Point." *Gallup Politics*, July 12. Retrieved September 20, 2012 (www.gallup.com/poll/155690/confidence-organized-religion-low-point.aspx).

Saad, Lydia. 2013. "In U.S., 52% Back Law to Legalize Gay Marriage in 50 States." Gallup, July 29, 2013. Retrieved February 8, 2014 (www.gallup.com/poll/163730/back-law-legalize-gay-marriage-states.aspx).

Sachs, Jeffrey. 2011. "With 7 Billion on Earth, a Huge Task Before Us." Retrieved July 10, 2013 (www.cnn.com/2011/10/17/opinion/sachs-global-population).

Sadker, Myra and David Sadker. 2005. *Teachers, Schools, and Society*, 7th ed. New York: McGraw-Hill.

Saez, E. 2012. *Striking It Richer: The Evolution of Top Incomes in the United States* (Updated with 2009 and 2010 estimates). March 2. Retrieved June 18, 2012 (http://elsa.berkeley.edu/~saez/saez-UStopincomes-2010.pdf).

Saha, Lawrence and A. Gary Dworkin. 2006. "Educational Attainment and Job Status: The Role of Status Inconsistency on Occupational Burnout." Paper presented at the International Sociological Association, July 23–29, Durban, South Africa.

Salzman, Michael B. 2008. "Globalization, Religious Fundamentalism and the Need for Meaning." *International Journal of Intercultural Relations* 32(July):318–27.

"Same-Sex Couples Get Wal-Mart Benefits." *Minneapolis Star Tribune*, August 28, 2013, p. D1.

Samovar, Larry A. and Richard E. Porter. 2003. *Intercultural Communication*. Belmont, CA: Wadsworth.

Sandberg, Sheryl. 2013. *Lean In: Women, Work, and the Will to Lead*. New York: Alfred A. Knopf.

Sapir, Edward. 1929. "The Status of Linguistics as a Science." *Language* 5:207–14.

Sapir, Edward. 1949. In *Selected Writings of Edward Sapir in Language, Culture, and Personality*, edited by David G. Mandelbaum. Berkeley: University of California Press.

Sapiro, Virginia. 2003. *Women in American Society: An Introduction to Women's Studies*, 5th ed. Mountain View, CA: Mayfield.

Sapolsky, Robert. 2011. "The Trouble With Testosterone." In *The Kaleidoscope of Gender*, 3rd ed., edited by Joan Z. Spade and Catherine G. Valentine. Thousand Oaks: Pine Forge.

Sauter, Michael B. and Alexander E. M. Hess. 2013. "The States Where the Most People Go Hungry: 24/7 Wall St." September 9. Retrieved January 5, 20142013 (www .huffingtonpost.com/2013/09/08/states-food-insecurity_n_3890209.html=slide=2885737).

Sauter, Michael B., Samuel Weigley, and Alexander E. M. Hess. 2013. "Ten Countries That Hate America Most." March 13. Retrieved October 3, 2013 (http://247wallst.com/ special-report/2013/03/13/ten-countries-that-hate-america-most/2/).

Saxbe, Darby E., Rena L Repetti, and Anthony P. Graesch. 2011. "Time Spent in Housework and Leisure: Links With Parents' Physiological Recovery From Work." *Journal of Family Psychology* 25(April):271–81.

Schaefer, Richard T. 2012. *Racial and Ethnic Groups*, 13th ed. Upper Saddle River, NJ: Prentice Hall.

Schaefer, Richard T. and Jenifer Kunz. 2007. *Racial and Ethnic Groups*. Upper Saddle River, NJ: Pearson/ Prentice Hall.

Schmalleger, Frank. 2006. *Criminology Today: An Integrative Introduction*, 4th ed. Upper Saddle River, NJ: Prentice Hall.

Schmalleger, Frank. 2012. *Criminology Today: An Integrative Introduction*, 6th ed. Upper Saddle River, NJ: Prentice Hall.

School of Philanthropy. 2013. "Giving USA: Charitable Donations Grew in 2012, but Slowly, Like the Economy." Retrieved February 12, 2015 (http://www.philanthropy .iupui.edu/news/article/giving-USA-2013).

Scott-Montagu, John. 1904. "Automobile Legislation: A Criticism and Review." *North American Review* 179(573):168–77.

Scribd. 2011. "Chipko Movement." Retrieved January 1, 2012 (www.scribd.com/doc/27513230/Chipko-Movement).

Selod, Saher. 2016. "Anti-Muslim Sentiments in the United States." Pp. 241–42 in *Our Social World*, 5th ed., edited by Jeanne H. Ballantine, Keith A. Roberts, and Kathleen Odell Korgen. Thousand Oaks: Sage Publications.

Sengupta, Somini. 2014. "U.N. Report Says Progress for Women Is Unequal." *New York Times*. February 12. Retrieved February 20, 2014 (www.nytimes .com/2014/02/13/world/un-report-says-progress-for-women-is-unequal.html?_r=0).

Sentencing Project. 2014. "Facts About Prisons and People in Prison." Retrieved September 4, 2014 (http://www .sentencingproject.org/doc/publications/inc_Facts%20 About%20Prisons.pdf).

Sernau, Scott. 2010. *Social Inequality in a Global Age*. Thousand Oaks, CA: SAGE/Pine Forge Press.

Sharp, Henry S. 1991. "Memory, Meaning, and Imaginary Time: The Construction of Knowledge in White and Chipewayan Cultures." *Ethnohistory* 38(2):149–73.

Sharp, Lauriston. 1990. "Steel Axes for Stone-Age Australians." Pp. 410–24 in *Conformity and Conflict*, 7th ed., edited by James P. Spradley and David W. McCurdy. Glenview, IL: Scott Foresman.

Shaw, Clifford R. and Henry D. McKay. 1929. *Delinquency Areas*. Chicago: University of Chicago Press.

Shaw, Susan M. and Janet Lee. 2005. *Women's Voices, Feminist Visions: Classic and Contemporary Readings*, 3rd ed. Boston: McGraw-Hill.

Sheridan, Mary Beth and William Branigin. 2010. "Senate Ratifies New U.S.-Russia Nuclear Weapons Treaty." *Washington Post*, December 22. Retrieved June 28, 2013 (www.washingtonpost.com/wp-dyn/content/ article/2010/12/21/AR2010122104371.html?sid=ST 2010122205900).

Sherif, Muzafer and Carolyn Sherif. 1953. *Groups in Harmony and Tension*. New York: Harper & Row.

Sherkat, Darren E. and Christopher G. Ellison. 1999. "Recent Developments and Current Controversies in the Sociology of Religion." *Annual Review of Sociology* 25:363–94.

Sherwood, I-Hsien. 2012. "Latest Presidential Election 2012 Map." *Latinos Post*. Retrieved November 12, 2012 (www .latinospost.com/articles/6570/20121107/latest-presi dential-election-2012-map-obama-beats.htm).

Shogren, Elizabeth. 2012. "When This Oil Spills, It's 'A Whole New Monster.'" NPR, August 16. Retrieved March 16, 2014 (www.npr.org/2012/08/16/158025375/when-this-oil-spills-its-a-whole-new-monster).

Short, Katherine. 2009. "Voter Participation Rate, 2008." Retrieved April 17, 2010 (www.askquestions.org/details .php?id=21094).

Siegel, Larry J. 2011. *Criminology: Theories, Patterns, and Typologies*, 11th ed. Belmont, CA: Thomson/Wadsworth.

Simmel, Georg. [1902–1917] 1950. *The Sociology of Georg Simmel*, translated by Kurt Wolff. Glencoe, IL: Free Press.

Simmel, Georg. 1955. *Conflict and the Web of Group Affiliation*, translated by Kurt H. Wolff. New York: Free Press.

Simmons, Rachel. 2002. *Odd Girl Out: The Hidden Culture of Aggression in Girls*. Orlando, FL: Harcourt.

Simon, David R. 2006. *Elite Deviance*, 8th ed. Boston: Allyn & Bacon.

Sizer, Theodore R. 1984. *Horace's Compromise: The Dilemma of the American High School*. Boston: Houghton Mifflin.

Skocpol, Theda. 1979. *States and Social Revolutions: A Comparative Analysis of France, Russia, and China*. Cambridge, UK: Cambridge University Press.

Skocpol, Theda and Vanessa Williamson. 2012. *The Tea Party and the Remaking of Republican Conservatism*. New York: Oxford University Press.

Slaughter, Anne-Marie. 2012. "Why Women Still Can't Have It All." *The Atlantic*, July/August. Retrieved January 17, 2014 (www.theatlantic.com/magazine/archive/2012/07/why-women-still-cant-have-it-all/309020/).

SlideShare. 2014. "Population Pyramids 2014." Retrieved September 16, 2014 (http://www.slideshare.net/sbsgeog/population-pyramids-2014).

Smelser, Neil J. 1963. *Theory of Collective Behavior.* New York: Free Press.

Smelser, Neil J. 1988. "Social Structure." Pp. 103–29 in *Handbook of Sociology,* edited by Neil J. Smelser. Newbury Park, CA: Sage.

Smelser, Neil J. 1992. "The Rational Choice Perspective: A Theoretical Assessment." *Rationality and Society* 4: 381–410.

Smith, Adrian. 2012. "Private vs. Public Facilities, Is It Cost Effective and Safe?" Corrections.com, June 11. Retrieved September 1, 2014 (www.corrections.com/news/article/30903-private-vs-public-facilities-is-it-cost-effective-and-safe).

Smith, Christian and Robert Faris. 2005. "Socioeconomic Inequality in the American Religious System: An Update and Assessment." *Journal for the Scientific Study of Religion* 44(1):95–104.

Smith, Jacquelyn. 2013. "Billionaire CEOs With the Biggest Paychecks." *Forbes,* April 9. Retrieved January 4, 2014 (http://www.forbes.com/sites/jacquelyn-smith/2013/04/09/billionaire-ceos-with-the-biggest-paychecks/).

Smith, Mark K. 2008. "Howard Gardner and Multiple Intelligences." *The Encyclopedia of Informal Education.* Retrieved April 17, 2011 (http://www.infed.org/thinkers/gardner.htm).

Snarr, Michael T. and D. Neil Snarr. 2008. *Introducing Global Issues,* 4th ed. Boulder, CO: Lynne Rienner Publishers.

Snyder, Denson R. 1971. *The Hidden Curriculum.* New York: Alfred A. Knopf.

Sobolewski, Juliana M. and Paul R. Amato. 2007. "Parents' Discord and Divorce, Parent-Child Relationships, and Subjective Well-Being in Early Adulthood: Is Feeling Close to Two Parents Always Better Than Feeling Close to One?" *Social Forces* 85(March):1105–24.

"Sochi 2014: Gay Rights Protests Target Russia's Games." 2014. BBC News, February 5. Retrieved Feb. 24, 2014 (www.bbc.co.uk/news/world-europe-26043872).

Social Security Administration. 2013. "Social Security Basic Facts." Retrieved July 1, 2013 (www.ssa.gov/pressoffice/basicfact.htm).

Sommerville, C. John. 2002. "Stark's Age of Faith Argument and the Secularization of Things: A Commentary." *Review of Religious Research* (Fall):361–72.

Sons of Union Veterans of the Civil War. 2010. "The United States' Flag Code." Retrieved December 21, 2011 (http://suvcw.org/flag.htm).

Southern Poverty Law Center. 2014. "Active U.S. Hate Groups." Retrieved September 1, 2014 (www.splcenter.org/get-informed/hate-map).

Spacey, John. 2012. "Japan's Crime Rate." *Japan Talk,* June 30. Retrieved April 18, 2013 (www.japan-talk.com/jt/new/japans-crime-rate).

Sperling, Gene B. 2006. "What Works in Girls' Education." PBS Wide Angle. Retrieved July 11, 2009 (www.pbs.org/wnet/wideangle/episodes/time-for-school-series/essay-what-works-in-girls-education/274).

Staples, Brent. 2001. "Black Men and Public Space." Pp. 244–46 in *The Production of Reality,* edited by Jodi O'Brien and Peter Kollock. Thousand Oaks, CA: Pine Forge Press.

Stark, Rodney. 2000. "Secularization, R.P.I." Pp. 41–66 in *The Secularization Debate,* edited by William H. Swatos, Jr., and Daniel V. A. Olson. Lanham, MD: Rowman & Littlefield.

Stark, Rodney and Roger Finke. 2000. *Acts of Faith: Explaining the Human Side of Religion.* Berkeley: University of California Press.

State of Alaska. 2006. "Workplace Alaska: How to Apply." Retrieved July 5, 2006 (http://notes3.state.ak.us/WA/MainEntry.nsf/WebData/HTMLHow+to+Apply/?open).

State of Delaware. 2008. "Presidential Primary Election." Retrieved March 21, 2008 (http://elections.delaware.gov/information/elections/presidential_2008.shtml).

Statistica. 2014. "Number of Vehicles Registered in the United States From 1990 to 2011." Retrieved February 23, 2014 (www.statistica.com/statistics/183505/number-of-vehicles-in-the-united-stastes-since-1990/).

Statistical Handbook of Japan. 2010. "Population." Retrieved May 13, 2011 (www.stat.go.jp/english/data/handbook/c02cont.htm#cha2_2).

Steele, Tracey L. 2005. *Sex, Self, and Society: The Social Context of Sexuality.* Belmont, CA: Thomson Wadsworth.

Stephen, Eric M., Jennifer Rose, Lindsay Kenney, Francine Rosselli-Navarra, and Ruth S. Weissman. 2014. "Adolescent Risk Factors for Purging in Young Women: Findings From the National Longitudinal Study of Adolescent Health." *Journal of Eating Disorders* 2(1). Retrieved January 16, 2014 (www.jeatdisord.com/).

Stern, Jessica. 2003. *Terror in the Name of God: Why Religious Militants Kill.* New York: HarperCollins.

Stevenson, Mark. 2013. "At 20 Years, Nafta Didn't Close Mexico Wage Gap." Retrieved January 18, 2014 (http://news.yahoo.com/20-years-nafta-didn-39-t-close-mexico-064658474--financial.html).

Stewart, Susan D. 2007. *Brave New Stepfamilies: Diverse Paths Toward Stepfamily Living.* Thousand Oaks, CA: Sage.

Stiglitz, Joseph E. 2012. "A Real Cure for the Global Economic Crackup." Pp. 104–109 in *Globalization: The Transformation of Social Worlds,* 3rd ed., edited by D. Stanley Eitzen and Maxine Baca Zinn. Belmont, CA: Wadsworth.

Stoessinger, John. 1993. *Why Nations Go to War.* New York: St. Martin's Press.

Stone, Brad and Noam Cohen. 2009. "Social Networks Spread Defiance Online." *New York Times,* June 16. Retrieved June 30, 2009 (www.nytimes.com/2009/06/16/world/middleeast/16media.html?_r=1&ref=world).

Stracansky, Pavol. 2013. "Curbs on Abortion Spread Across East Europe." *Inter Press Service,* July 12. Retrieved March 17, 2014 (www.ipsnews/net/2013/07/curbs-on-abortion-spread-across-east-europe/).

Straus, Murray A., Richard J. Gelles, and Suzanne K. Steinmetz. 2006. *Behind Closed Doors: Violence in the American Family.* New Brunswick, NJ: Transaction.

Stryker, Sheldon. 1980. *Symbolic Interactionism: A Social Structural Version.* Menlo Park, CA: Benjamin Cummings.

Stryker, Sheldon. 2000. "Identity Competition: Key to Differential Social Involvement." Pp. 21–40 in *Identity, Self, and Social Movements,* edited by Sheldon Styker, Timothy Owens, and Robert White. Minneapolis: University of Minnesota Press.

Stryker, Sheldon and Anne Stratham. 1985. "Symbolic Interaction and Role Theory." Pp. 311–78 in *Handbook of Social Psychology,* edited by Gardiner Lindsey and Eliot Aronson. New York: Random House.

Sullivan, Brian. 2013. "HUD Repots Continued Decline in U.S. Homelessness Since 2010." HUD.gov, November 21. Retrieved February 17, 2014 (http://portal.hud.gov/hud portal/HUD?src=/press/press_releases_media_advi sories/2013/HUDNo.13-173).

Sutherland, Anne. 1986. *Gypsies: The Hidden Americans.* Prospect Heights, IL: Waveland.

Sutherland, Anne. 2001. "Complexities of U.S. Law and Gypsy Identity." Pp. 231–42 in *Gypsy Law: Romani Legal Traditions and Culture,* edited by Walter O. Weyrauch. Berkeley: University of California Press.

Sutherland, Edwin H., Donald R. Cressey, and David Luckenbil. 1992. *Criminology.* Dix Hills, NY: General Hall.

Sutton, Joe. 2013. "Maryland Governor Signs Death Penalty Repeal." CNN.com, May 2. Retrieved June 2, 2013 (www.cnn.com/2013/05/02/us/maryland-death-penalty).

Swank, Eric, Breanne Fahs, and David M. Frost. 2013. "Region, Social Identities and Disclosure Practices as Predictors of Heterosexist Discrimination Against Sexual Minorities in the United States." *Sociological Inquiry* 83(2):238–58.

Sway, Marlene. 1988. *Familiar Strangers: Gypsy Life in America.* Urbana: University of Illinois Press.

Tamney, Joseph B. 1992. *The Resilience of Christianity in the Modern World.* Albany: State University of New York Press.

Tanenhaus, Sam. 2012. "History vs. the Tea Party." *New York Times,* January 14. Retrieved July 15, 2012 (www.nytimes.com/2012/01/15/sunday-review/gop-history-vs-the-tea-party.html?pagewanted=all).

Taub, Diane E. and Penelope A. McLorg. 2010. "Influences of Gender Socialization and Athletic Involvement on the Occurrence of Eating Disorders." Pp. 73–82 in *Sociological Footprints: Introductory Readings in Sociology,* 11th ed., edited by Leonard Cargan and Jeanne H. Ballantine. Belmont, CA: Wadsworth Cengage Learning.

Terra Networks. 2013. *Kony 2012 Viral Campaign Sheds Light on Ugandan Violence.* Retrieved March 30, 2012 (http://en.terra.com/latin-in-america/news/kony_2012_viral_campaign_sheds_light_on_ugandan_violence/hof18171/ECID=US_ENGLISH_terrausa_SEMSearch_Kony).

Theroux, David J. 2012. "Secular Theocracy: The Foundations and Folly of Modern Tyranny." *The Independent Institute,* January 11. Retrieved July 13, 2012 (www.independent.org/newsroom/article.asp?id=3206).

Thompson, A. C. 2009. "Katrina's Hidden Race War." *The Nation,* January 5. Retrieved July 7, 2011 (www.thenation.com/article/katrinas-hidden-race-war).

Thorne, Barrie. 1993. *Gender Play: Girls and Boys in School.* New Brunswick, NJ: Rutgers University Press.

Tippett, Rebecca, Avis Jones-Deweever, Maya Rockeymoore, Darrick Hamilton, and William Darity, Jr. 2014. "Beyond Broke: Why Closing the Racial Wealth Gap Is a Priority for National Economic Security." Retrieved September 16, 2014 (http://globalpolicysolutions.org/resources/beyond-broke-report/).

Tipton, Steven M. 1990. "The Social Organization of Zen Practice: Constructing Transcultural Reality." *American Journal of Sociology* 96(2):488–90.

Toffler, Alvin and Heidi Toffler. 1980. *The Third Wave.* New York: Morrow.

Tolbert, Pamela S. and Richard H. Hall. 2008. *Organizations: Structures, Processes, and Outcomes,* 10th ed. Upper Saddle River, NJ: Prentice Hall.

Tollefson, Jeff. 2012. "Heatwaves Blamed on Global Warming." *Nature.* Retrieved September 7, 2012 (www.nature.com/news/heatwaves-blamed-on-global-warming-1.11130).

TransCanada. 2014. "Keystone XL Pipeline Project." Retrieved May 28, 2014 (http://keystone-xl.com/).

"Transnational Crime in the Developing World." 2011. Cited in "The 12 Most Profitable International Crimes." Retrieved April 13, 2012 (http://247wallst.com/2011/02/10/the-12-most-profitable-international-crimes/).

Transparency International. 2012. "Global Corruption Barometer 2010/11." Retrieved October 6, 2012 (http://gcb.transparency.org/gcb201011/infographic/).

Travers, Jeffrey and Stanley Milgram. 1969. "An Experimental Study of the Small World Problem." *Sociometry* 32:425–43.

Trust in Education. 2013. "Life as an Afghan Woman." Retrieved January 16, 2014 (www.trustineducation.org/why-afghanistan/life-as-an-afghan-woman/).

Tull, Matthew. 2012. "The Consequences of Male Gender Role Stress." About.com. Retrieved February 6, 2014 (http://ptsd.about.com/od/relatedconditions/a/MaleGenderRoleStres.htm).

Turnbull, Colin M. 1962. *The Forest People.* New York: Simon & Schuster.

Turner, Bryan S. 1991a. "Politics and Culture in Islamic Globalism." Pp. 161–81 in *Religion and Global Order,* edited by Roland Robertson and William R. Garrett. New York: Paragon.

Turner, Bryan S. 1991b. *Religion and Social Theory.* London: Sage.

Turner, Jonathan H. 2003. *The Structure of Sociological Theory,* 7th ed. Belmont, CA: Wadsworth.

Turner, Ralph H. and Lewis M. Killian. 1993. "The Field of Collective Behavior." Pp. 5–20 in *Collective Behavior and Social Movements,* edited by Russell L. Curtis, Jr. and Benigno E. Aguirre. Boston: Allyn & Bacon.

20-first. 2010. "It's Official at Last: Women Outnumber Men in US Workforce." Retrieved May 25, 2012 (www.20-first .com/1317-0-its-official-at-last-women-outnumber-men-in-us-workforce.html).

UN News Center. 2010. "Senior UN Official Cites Evidence of Growing Support for Abolishing Death Penalty." February 24. Retrieved March 8, 2011 (www.un.org/apps/news/ story.asp?NewsID=33877&Cr=death+penalty&Cr1=).

UN News Center. 2012. "Millions of Children in Cities Face Poverty and Exclusion." *The State of the World's Children 2012,* February 28. Retrieved May 14, 2012 (www/im/prg/apps/news/story.asp?NewsID=41395& Cr=children&Cr1).

UNHCR. 2012. "UNHCR Report Shows Highest Number of Refugees in 15 Years." June 19. Retrieved July 30, 2012 (www.euronews.com/2012/06/19/unhrc-report-shows-highest-number-of-refugees-in-15-yeasrs/).

UNICEF. 2005. "Convention on the Rights of the Child." Retrieved July 23, 2012 (www.unicef.org/crc/ index_30229.html).

UNICEF. 2013. "Progress Towards Millennium Development Goal 4." *Levels and Trends in Child Mortality. Report 2013.* Retrieved February 11, 2015 (www.childinfo.org/ files/Child_Mortality_Report_2013.pdf).

UNICEF. 2014. "Update on Haiti's Children." Retrieved February 23, 2014 (www.unicefusa.org/work/emergen cies/Haiti/?gclid=CJ6zxOK847wCFdE-Mgodt1IANg).

United Nations. 2013. "A Promise Is a Promise." United Nation's Secretary General's Campaign UNiTE to End Violence Against Women. Retrieved June 10, 2013 (www .un.org/en/women/endviolence/pdf/apromiseisap-romise.pdf).

United Nations Framework Convention on Climate Change. 2014. "Status of Ratification of the Kyoto Protocol." *United Nations Framework Convention on Climate Change.* Retrieved February 23, 2014 (http://unfccc.int/kyoto_ protocol/status_of_ratification/items/2613.php).

United Nations Office on Drugs and Crime. 2013. "Global Study on Homicide: Trends, Context, Data." Retrieved October 16, 2014 (http://www.unodc.org/docu ments/gsh/pdfs/2014_GLOBAL_HOMICIDE_BOOK_ web.pdf).

United Nations Office on Drugs and Crime. 2014a. "Human Trafficking FAQs." Retrieved September 5, 2014 (http:// www.unodc.org/unodc/en/human-trafficking/faqs .html#How_widespread_is_human_trafficking).

United Nations Office on Drugs and Crime. 2014b. "Transnational Organized Crime: The Globalized Illegal Economy." Retrieved April 25, 2014 (www.unodc.org/ toc/en/crimes/organized-crime.html).

United Nations Office on Drugs and Crime. 2014c. "UNODC Report on Human Trafficking Exposes Modern Form of Slavery." Retrieved January 3, 2014 (www.unodc .org/unodc/en/human-trafficking/global-report-on-trafficking-in -persons.html)

United Nations Population Division. 2012. "Total, Urban and Rural Populations by Major Area" (Table 7). *World Urbanization Prospects: The 2011 Revision.* Retrieved October 13, 2012 (http://esa.un.org/unup/pdf/ WUP2011_Highlights.pdf).

United Nations Population Division. 2014. "World Urbanization Prospects 2-14." Retrieved September 16, 2014 (http://esa .un.org/unpd/wup/Highlights/WUP2014-Highlights.pdf).

University of Michigan Documents Center. 2003. "Documents in the News—1997/2003: Affirmative Action in College Admissions." Retrieved April 17, 2010 (www.lib.umich .edu/files/libraries/govdocs/pdf/affirm/pdf).

University of Pennsylvania. 2010. "Body Modification." Retrieved November 18, 2010 (penn.museum/sites/ body_modification/bodmodpierce.shtml).

Upbin, Bruce. 2011. "The 147 Companies That Control Everything." *Forbes,* October 22. Retrieved July 13, 2012 (www.forbes.com/sites/bruceupbin/2011/10/22/the-147-companies-that-control-everything/).

UPI. 2014. "OECD: Switzerland Tops 34 Nations for Life Expectancy at 82.8." *Health News UPI.* Retrieved January 2014 (www.upi.com/Health_News/2014/01/07/ OECD/Switzerland-tops-34-nations-for-life-expectancy-at-828/UPI-32701389078243/).

U.S. Census Bureau. 2011. "Income (in Dollars) by Educational Level and Race/Ethnicity" (Table 228). Retrieved April 19, 2011 (http://www.census.gov/compendia/ statab/2011/tables/11s0228.pdf).

U.S. Census Bureau. 2012a. "Educational Attainment by Race and Hispanic Origin 1970–2010 (Table 229)." Retrieved June 17, 2013 (www.census.gov/compendia/ statab/2012/tables/12s0229.pdf).

U.S. Census Bureau. 2012b. "Educational Attainment in the United States: 2010 (Table 2)." Retrieved August 16, 2014 (www.census.gov/hhes/socdemo/education/data/ cps/2010/tables.html).

U.S. Census Bureau. 2012c. "Growth in Urban Population Outpaces Rest of Nation, Census Bureau Reports." Retrieved July 1, 2013 (www.census.gov/newsroom/ releases/archives/2010_census/cb12-50.html).

U.S. Census Bureau. 2012d. "Mean Earnings by Highest Degree Earned: 2009 (Table 232)." Retrieved September 5, 2014 (http://www.census.gov/compendia/ statab/2012/tables/12s0232.pdf).

U.S. Census Bureau. 2013a. "America's Families and Living Arrangements: 2012." Retrieved February 9, 2015 (http:// www.census.gov/hhes/families/data/cps2012.html).

U.S. Census Bureau. 2013b. "Current Population Survey (CPS)—Definitions." Retrieved September 8, 2014 (http://www.census.gov/cps/about/cpsdef.html).

U.S. Census Bureau. 2013c. "Hispanic or Latino Origin." *2007–2011 American Community Survey.* Retrieved November 20, 2014 (http://factfinder2.census.gov/faces/tableservices/jsf/pages/productview.xhtml?pid=ACS_11_5YR_B03001&prodType=table).

U.S. Census Bureau. 2013d. "Same-Sex Couple Households." Retrieved February 19, 2014 (www.census.gov/hhes/samesex/files/SScplfactsheet_final.pdf).

U.S. Census Bureau. 2014. "State & County Quick Facts." Retrieved August 22, 2014 (http://quickfacts.census.gov/qfd/states/00000.html).

U.S. Census Bureau. 2015. "U.S. and World Population Clock." Retrieved February 6, 2015 (www.census.gov/popclock/).

U.S. Department of Commerce. 2011. "Commerce Department's U.S. Census Bureau Reports 55 Percent of Americans Have Married Once in Their Lifetimes." Retrieved February 19, 2014 (www.commerce.gov/blog/2011/05/18/commerce-department%E2%80%99s-us-census-bureau-reports-55-percent-americans-have-married-onc).

U.S. Department of Defense. 2011. *Dictionary of Military and Associated Terms,* January 31. Retrieved January 19, 2013 (http://ra.defense.gov/documents/rtm/jp1_02.pdf).

U.S. Department of Defense. 2012a. "Department of Defense Antiterrorism Program Memo: Instruction No. 2000.12." March 1. Retrieved July 28, 2012 (www.dtic.mil/whs/directives/corres/pdf/200012p.pdf).

U.S. Department of Defense. 2012b. *Sustaining U.S. Global Leadership: Priorities for 21st Century Defense.* Retrieved December 2, 2013 (www.defense.gov/news/defense_strategic_guidance.pdf).

U.S. Department of Education. 2012. *Title VI Enforcement Highlights.* Office for Civil Rights. Retrieved July 8, 2013 (www2.ed.gov/documents/press-releases/title-vi-enforcement.pdf).

U.S. Department of Health and Human Services. 2014. "2014 Poverty Guidelines." Retrieved February 19, 2014 (http://aspe.hhs.gov/poverty/14poverty.cfm).

U.S. Department of Housing and Urban Development. 2013. *The 2013 Annual Homeless Assessment Report (AHAR) to Congress.* Retrieved February 17, 2014 (www.onecpd.info/resources/documents/AHAR-2013-Part1.pdf).

U.S. Department of Interior Office of Education. 1930. *Availability of Public School Education in Rural Communities* (Bulletin No. 34, edited by Walter H. Gaummitz). Washington, DC: Government Printing Office.

U.S. Department of Justice. 2014. "2013 Crime Clock Statistics." Retrieved August 30, 2014 (http://www.fbi.gov/about-us/cjis/ucr/crime-in-the-u.s/2013/crime-in-the-u.s.-2013/offenses-known-to-law-enforcement/crime-clock).

U.S. Department of Labor. 2011. "Highlights of Women's Earnings in 2010." *Report 1031.* Retrieved June 5, 2012 (www.bls.gov/cps/cpswom2010.pdf).

U.S. Department of Labor. 2013a. "Employee Rights and Responsibilities Under the Family and Medical Leave Act." Retrieved February 19, 2014 (www.dol.gov/whd/regs/compliance/posters/fmlean.pdf).

U.S. Department of Labor. 2013b. "Median Weekly Earnings by Age, Sex, Race, and Hispanic or Latino Ethnicity, First Quarter 2013." Retrieved February 19, 2014 (www.bls.gov/opub/ted/2013/ted_20130419.htm).

U.S. Department of Labor. 2014. "Usual Weekly Earnings of Wage and Salary Workers: Fourth Quarter 2014." Retrieved February 1, 2015 (http://www.bls.gov/news.release/pdf/wkyeng.pdf).

"U.S. Elections Map: State by State Guide." 2008. BBC News. Retrieved February 8, 2013 (http://news.bbc.co.uk/2/hi/in_depth/629/629/7223461.stm).

U.S. Elections Project. 2012. "Turnout 1980–2012." Retrieved November 12, 2012 (http://elections.gmu.edu/voter_turnout.htm).

U.S. Flag Code. 2008. "U.S. Flag Code (4 US Code 1)." Retrieved August 28, 2008 (http://suvcw.org/flag.htm).

"U.S. Life Expectancy Ranks 26th in the World, OECD Report Shows." 2013. *Huffington Post,* November 21. Retrieved December 5, 2013 (www.huffingtonpost.com/2013/11/21/us-life-expectancy-oecd_n_4317367.html).

U.S. Trade Representative. 2012. "Joint Stats From 2012 NAFTA Commission Meeting." Retrieved September 8, 2012 (www.ustr.gov/).

Valentine, Simon Ross. 2009. "The Tehrik-i-Taliban Pakistan: Ideology and Beliefs." *Pakistan Security Research Unit.* Retrieved February 24, 2014 (www.eisf.eu/resources/item/?d=1623).

Veblen, Thorstein. 1902. *The Theory of the Leisure Class: An Economic Study of Institutions.* New York: Macmillan.

Verbeek, Stjin and Rinus Penninx. 2009. "Employment Equity Policies in Work Organisations." Pp. 69–94 in *Equal Opportunity and Ethnic Inequality in European Labour Markets: Discrimination, Gender, and Policies of Diversity,* edited by Karen Kraal, Judith Roosblad, and John Wrench. Amsterdam: University of Amsterdam Press.

Vervaeck, Armand and James Daniell. 2011. "Japan Tohoku Tsunami and Earthquake: The Death Toll Is Climbing Again." Earthquake Report, August 15. Retrieved May 13, 2012 (Httlp://earthquake-report.com/2011/08/04/japan-tsunami-following-up-the-aftermath-part-16-june/).

Victor, Barbara. 2003. *Army of Roses: Inside the World of Palestinian Women Suicide Bombers.* Emmaus, PA: Rodale Books.

Voting and Democracy Research Center. 2008. "Primaries: Open and Closed." Retrieved March 21, 2008 (www.fairvote.org/?page=1801).

Wade, Lisa. 2012. "The New Elite: Attributing Privilege and Class vs. Merit." *Sociological Images: Inspiring Sociological Imaginations Everywhere*, June 21. Retrieved September 14, 2012 (http://thesocietypages.org/socimages/2012/06/21/the-new-elite-attributing-privilege-to-class-vs-merit/).

Wade, Lisa. 2013a. "The Number of People in Private Prisons Has Grown by 1,664% in the Last 19 Years." *PolicyMic*, January 25. Retrieved April 26, 2014 (www.policymic.com/articles/24142/the-number-of-people-in-private-prisons-has-grown-by-1-664-in-the-last-19-years).

Wade, Lisa. 2013b. "The Truth About Gender and Math." *Sociological Images*, March 7. Retrieved January 17, 2014 (http://thesocietypages.org/socimages/2013/03/07/the-truth-about-gender-and-math/).

Walk Free Foundation. 2013. "The Global Slavery Index 2013." Retrieved January 2, 2014 (www.globalslaveryindex.org/).

Wallerstein, Immanuel. 1974. *The Modern World System*. New York: Academic Press.

War Child. 2014. "Child Soldier: Some Words Don't Belong Together." Retrieved August 21, 2014 (www.warchild.org.uk/issues/child-soldiers?gclid=CJ_78cL7bYCFSdgMgod11wAmQ).

Ward, Martha C. and Monica Edelstein. 2014. *A World Full of Women*, 6th ed. Boston: Allyn & Bacon.

Warner, R. Stephen. 1993. "Work in Progress Toward a New Paradigm for the Sociological Study of Religion in the United States." *American Journal of Sociology* 98(5):1044–1093.

WaterAid. 2012. "Annual Review 2010/11." Retrieved September 9, 2012 (www.wateraid.org/uk/about_us/annual_report/default.asp).

WaterAid. 2014. "Statistics." Retrieved September 8, 2014 (www.wateraid.org/us/the-water-story/the-crisis/statistics?pageEEF299BDEFB04B4A89206672AC6D5578=2#filterContent).

Waters, Tony. 2012. *Schooling, Childhood, and Bureaucracy: Bureaucratizing the Child*. Basingstoke, England: Palgrave Macmillan.

Watkins, Tom. 2013. "U.S. Woman Killed in Syria Identified by Relatives Via Online Images." CNN.com, May 31. Retrieved May 31, 2013 (www.cnn.com/2013/05/31/world/meast/syria-civil-war/index.html).

Weber, Max. [1904–1905] 1958. *The Protestant Ethic and the Spirit of Capitalism*, translated by Talcott Parsons. New York: Scribner.

Weber, Max. 1946. *From Max Weber: Essays in Sociology*, translated and edited by Hans H. Gerth and C. Wright Mills. New York: Oxford University Press.

Weber, Max. 1947. *The Theory of Social and Economic Organization*, translated and edited by A. M. Henderson and Talcott Parsons. New York: Oxford University Press.

Webster's Unabridged English Dictionary. 1989. New York: Gramercy Books.

Weeks, John R. 2012. *Population: An Introduction to Concepts and Issues*, 11th ed. Belmont, CA: Wadsworth.

Weinberg, George. 1972. *Society and the Healthy Homosexual*. New York: St. Martin's Press.

Wells, Amy Stuart and Jeannie Oakes. 1996. "Potential Pitfalls of Systemic Reform: Early Lessons From Research on Detracking." *Sociology of Education* 69(Extra Issue):135–43.

Wessinger, Catherine. 2000. *How the Millennium Comes Violently: From Jonestown to Heaven's Gate*. New York: Seven Bridges.

West, Candace and Don H. Zimmerman. 1987. "Doing Gender." *Gender and Society* 1(2):125–51.

Wheaton, Sarah. 2014. "Pipeline Fight Lifts Environmental Movement." *New York Times*, January 24. Retrieved March 21, 2014 (www.nytimes.com/2014/01/25/us/keystone-xl-pipeline-fight-lifts-environmental-movement.html?action=click&module=Search&region=searchResults%230&version=&url=http%3A%2F%2Fquery.nytimes.com%2Fsearch%2Fsitesearch%2F%3Faction%3Dclick%26region%3DMasthead%26pgtype%3DHomepage%26module%3DSearchSubmit%26contentCollection%3DHomepage%26t%3Dqry659%23%2Fenvironmental+movement&_r=1).

Whitney, Lance. 2012. "2011 Ends With Almost 6 Billion Mobile Phone Subscriptions." CNET News. Retrieved May 18, 2012 (http://news.cnet.com/8301-1023_3-57352095-93/2011-ends-with-almost-6-billion-mobile-phone-subscriptions/).

Whorf, Benjamin Lee. 1956. *Language, Thought, and Reality*. New York: John Wiley.

Whyte, William H. 1956. *The Organization Man*. New York: Simon and Schuster.

Wilhoit, Sarah. 2014. "Demand That U.S. Coffee Companies Stop Using Child and Slave Labor Overseas." Retrieved February 14, 2014 (http://forcechange.com/62236/demand-that-u-s-coffee-companies-stop-using-child-and-slave-labor-overseas/).

Wilkerson, Isabel. 2010. *The Warmth of Other Suns: The Epic Story of America's Great Migration*. New York: Vintage/Random House.

Williams, Brian K., Stacey C. Sawyer, and Carl M. Wahlstrom. 2013. *Marriages, Families, and Intimate Relationships*, 3rd ed. Boston: Allyn & Bacon.

Williams, Christine L. 2013. "The Glass Escalator, Revisited: Gender Inequality in Neoliberal Times." *Gender and Society* 27(5):609–29.

Williams, Dmitri, Mia Consalvo, Scott Caplan, and Nick Yee. 2009. "Looking for Gender: Gender Roles and Behaviors Among Online Gamers." *Journal of Communication* 59:700–25.

Williams, Robin Murphy, Jr. 1970. *American Society: A Sociological Interpretation*, 3rd ed. New York: Alfred Knopf.

Willis Report. 2014. "The Costs of Raising a Child in 2014." Retrieved May 24, 2014 (www.myfoxla.com/story/24695222/the-costs-of-raising-a-child-in-2014).

Wilson, Edward O. 1980. *Sociobiology.* Cambridge, MA: Belknap.

Wilson, Edward O. 1987. *The Coevolution of Biology and Culture.* Cambridge, MA: Harvard University Press.

Wilson, Edward O., Michael S. Gregory, Anita Silvers, and Diane Sutch. 1978. "What Is Sociobiology?" *Society* 15(6):1–12.

Wilson, Megan. 2012. "Big Business Sides With Obama on Affirmative Action Case Before High Court." *The Hill,* October 28. Retrieved May 31, 2013 (http://thehill.com/homenews/administration/264329-big-business-sides-with-obama-on-affirmative-action-case-before-supreme-court).

Winders, Bill. 2004. "Changing Racial Inequality: The Rise and Fall of Systems of Racial Inequality in the U.S." Paper presented at the Annual Meeting of the American Sociological Association, San Francisco.

Wing, Nick. 2013. "Countries *With the Largest Number of Prisoners per 100,000 of the National Population, as of 2013.*" *Huffington Post,* August 13. Retrieved April 25, 2014 (www.huffingtonpostcom/2013/08/13/incarceration-rate-per-capita_n_3745291.html).

Winkler, Karen J. 1991. "Revisiting the Nature vs. Nurture Debate: Historian Looks Anew at Influence of Biology on Behavior." *Chronicle of Higher Education,* May 22, pp. A5, A8.

Winslow, Robert W. and Sheldon X. Zhang. 2008. *Criminology: A Global Perspective.* Upper Saddle River, NJ: Pearson Prentice Hall.

Witness for Peace. 2012. "Mediation With GM Fails, Workers Re-start Hunger Strike." September 3. Retrieved October 14, 2012 (http://witnessforpeace.org/).

Wolfson, Evan. 2015. "Protections Denied to Same-Sex Couples and Their Kids." From *Why Marriage Matters:* Appendix B. Retrieved February 6, 2015 (http://www.freedomtomarry.org/pages/from-why-marriage-matters-appendix-b-by-evan-wolfson).

Wong, Edward. 2013a. "In China, Breathing Becomes a Childhood Risk." *New York Times.* April 22. Retrieved July 1, 2013 (www.nytimes.com/2013/04/23/world/asia/pollution-is-radically-changing-childhood-in-chinas-cities.html?pagewanted=all).

Wong, Fdward. 2013b. "Urbanites Flee China's Smog for Blue Skies." *New York Times,* November 22. Retrieved March 17, 2014 (www.nytimes.com/2013/11/23/world/asia/urbanites-flee-chinas-smog-for-blue-skies.html?_r=0).

Wood, Julia T. 2008. *Gendered Lives: Communication, Gender, and Culture,* 8th ed. Belmont, CA: Wadsworth.

Wood, Julia T. and Nina M. Reich. 2006. "Gendered Communication Styles." Pp. 177–86 in *Intercultural Communication,* 11th ed., edited by Larry A. Samovar, Richard E. Porter, and Edwin R. McDaniel. Belmont, CA: Wadsworth.

World Almanac. 2014. "World Adherents of Religions by Continental Area 2012." New York: World Almanac Books: 701.

World Bank. 2012. "Girls' Education: Learning for All." Retrieved September 14, 2012 (http://web.worldbank.org/WBSITE/EXTERNAL/TOPICS/EXTEDUCATION/0,,contentMDK:20298916~menuPK:617572~pagePK:148956~piPK:216618~theSitePK:282386,00.html).

World Bank. 2013a. "Featured Conversation: Slums and Service Delivery for the Urban Poor." Striking Poverty. Retrieved July 1, 2013 (www.forbes.com/sites/joelkotkin/2013/03/18/americas-fastest-and-slowest-growing-cities/).

World Bank. 2013b. *Internet Users (per 100 People).* Retrieved December 17, 2013 (http://data.worldbank.org/indicator/IT.NET.USER.P2).

World Bank. 2013c. "Population Density (People per Square KM of Land Area)." Retrieved June 9, 2013 (http://data.worldbank.org/indicator/EN.POP.DNST).

World Bank. 2013d. "Ratio of Female to Male Secondary Enrollment (%)." Retrieved June 15, 2013 (http://data.worldbank.org/).

World Bank. 2014a. "Sub-Saharan Africa (Developing Only)." Retrieved September 16, 2014 (http://data.worldbank.org/region/sub-saharan-africa).

World Bank. 2014b. "Voices and Agency: Empowering Women and Girls for Shared Prosperity." Retrieved September 10, 2014 (www.worldbank.org/en/topic/gender/publication/voice-and-agency-empowering-women-and-girls-for-sharedprosperity).

World Coalition. 2012. "World Database." World Coalition Against the Death Penalty. Retrieved May 29, 2012 (http://www.worldcoalition.org/worldwide-database.html).

World Factbook. 2011. "Field Listing: Suffrage." Retrieved May 6, 2011 (https://www.cia.gov/library/publications/the-world-factbook/fields/2123.html#210).

World Factbook. 2014a. "Afghanistan." Retrieved February 11, 2015 (https://www.cia.gov/library/publications/the-world-factbook/geos/af.html).

World Factbook. 2014b. "Chad." Retrieved September 15, 2014 (https://www.cia.gov/library/publications/the-world-factbook/geos/cd.html).

World Factbook. 2014c. "China." Retrieved September 15, 2014 (https://www.cia.gov/library/publications/the-world-factbook/geos/ch.html).

World Factbook. 2014d. "Congo." Retrieved September 15, 2014 (https://www.cia.gov/library/publications/the-world-factbook/geos/cg.html).

World Factbook. 2014e. "GDP—Per Capita." Retrieved April 18, 2014 (https://www.cia.gov/library/publications/the-world-factbook/rankorder/2004rank.html).

World Factbook. 2014f. "India." Retrieved September 15, 2014 (https://www.cia.gov/library/publications/the-world-factbook/geos/in.html).

World Factbook. 2014g. "Infant Mortality Rate." Retrieved April 18, 2014 (https://www.cia.gov/library/publications/the-world-factbook/rankorder/2091rank.html).

World Factbook. 2014h. "Kenya." Retrieved September 15, 2014 (https://www.cia.gov/library/publications/the-world-factbook/geos/ke.html).

World Factbook. 2014i. "Life Expectancy at Birth." Retrieved April 18, 2014 (https://www.cia.gov/library/publications/the-world-factbook/rankorder/2102rank.html).

World Factbook. 2014j "Niger." Retrieved September 15, 2014 (https://www.cia.gov/library/publications/the-world-factbook/geos/ng.html).

World Factbook. 2014k. "Uganda." Retrieved September 15, 2014 (https://www.cia.gov/library/publications/the-world-factbook/geos/ug.html).

World Factbook. 2014l. "United States." Retrieved September 15, 2014 (https://www.cia.gov/library/publications/the-world-factbook/geos/us.html).

World Famine Timeline. 2014. "Famine." Retrieved May 24, 2014 (www.mapreport.com/subtopics/d/0.html#2013)

World Food Programme. 2013. "10 Things You Need to Know About Hunger in 2013." January 2. Retrieved Jan. 5, 2014 (www.wfp.org/stories/10-things-you-need-to-know-about-hunger-2013).

World Health Organization. 2012a. "Family Planning: Fact Sheet No. 351." July. Retrieved July 29, 2012 (www.who.int/mediacentre/factsheets/fs351/en/index.html).

World Health Organization. 2013b. "Urban Population Growth." Retrieved July 1, 2013 (www.forbes.com/sites/joelkotkin/2013/03/18/americas-fastest-and-slowest-growing-cities/).

World Health Organization. 2014. "Adolescent Pregnancy." *Maternal, Newborn, Child, and Adolescent Health.* Retrieved March 17, 2014 (www.who.int/maternal_child_adolescent/topics/maternal/adolescent_pregnancy/en/).

World Hunger Education Service. 2013. "2013 World Hunger and Poverty Facts and Statistics." Retrieved September 16, 2014 (http://www.worldhunger.org/articles/Learn/world%20hunger%20facts%202002.htm).

Worldatlas. 2014. "Largest Cities in the World." March 16. Retrieved April 15, 2014 (www.worldatlas.com/citypops.htm).

Worldometers. 2014. "Current World Population." Retrieved March 18, 2014 (www.worldometers.info/world-population/).

WorldWideLearn. 2007. "Guide to College Majors in Sociology." Retrieved June 23, 2008 (www.worldwidelearn.com/online-education-guide/social-science/sociology-major.htm).

Yablonski, Lewis. 1959. "The Gang as a Near-Group." *Social Problems* 7(Fall):108–17.

Yamane, David. 1997. "Secularization on Trial: In Defense of a Neosecularization Paradigm." *Journal for the Scientific Study of Religion* 36(1):109–22.

Yamane, David. 2007. "Civil Religion." Pp. 506–507 in *The Blackwell Encyclopedia of Sociology*, Vol. II, edited by George Ritzer. Oxford: Blackwell.

Yinger, J. Milton. 1960. "Contraculture and Subculture." *American Sociological Review* 25(October):625–35.

Yoon, Mi Yung. 2005. "Sub-Saharan Africa." Chapter 7 in *Sharing Power: Women, Parliament, Democracy*, edited by Manon Tremblay and Yvonne Galligan. Aldershot, UK: Ashgate.

Yoon, Mi Yung. 2011a. "More Women in the Tanzanian Legislature: Do Numbers Matter?" *Journal of Contemporary African Studies* 29(January):83–98.

Yoon, Mi Yung. 2011b. "Factors Hindering 'Larger' Representation of Women in Parliament: The Case of Seychelles." *Commonwealth and Comparative Politics* 49(February):98–114.

Yunus, Muhammad and Alan Jolis. 1999. *Banker to the Poor: Micro-Lending and the Battle Against World Poverty.* New York: Public Affairs.

Zeleny, Jeff. 2009. "Obama Vows, 'We Will Rebuild' and 'Recover'." *New York Times*, February 25. Retrieved February 25, 2009 (www.nytimes.com/2009/02/25/us/politics/25obama.html?scp=1&sq=obama%20vows%20we%20will%20rebuild&st=cse).

Ziel, Magda. 2013. "Sati Widow Burning Still Going On." HubPages. Retrieved January 16, 2014 (http://whitemuse.hubpages.com/hub/Sati-Still-Being-Done-in-India).

Zimbardo, Philip C. 2004. "Power Turns Good Soldiers Into 'Bad Apples.'" *Boston Globe* (May 9). Retrieved July 5, 2008 (www.boston.com/news/globe/editorial_opinion/oped/articles/2004/05/09/power_turns_good_soldiers_into_bad_apples).

Zimbardo, Philip C., Craig Haney, Curtis Banks, and David Jaffe. 1973. "The Mind Is a Formidable Jailer: A Pirandellian Prison." *New York Times*, April 8, 38–60.

Zull, James E. 2002. *The Art of Changing the Brain: Enriching the Practice of Teaching by Exploring the Biology of Learning.* Sterling, VA: Stylus.

Index

Note: In page references, f indicates figures and t indicates tables.